Sinews of the Nation

*Dear Rabbi Rosenbaum
Thank you for a very good wedding and everything*

Dan

Sinews of the Nation

Constructing Irish and Zionist Bonds in the United States

Dan Lainer-Vos

polity

Copyright © Dan Lainer-Vos 2013

The right of Dan Lainer-Vos to be identified as Author of this Work has been asserted in accordance with the UK Copyright, Designs and Patents Act 1988.

First published in 2013 by Polity Press

Polity Press
65 Bridge Street
Cambridge CB2 1UR, UK

Polity Press
350 Main Street
Malden, MA 02148, USA

All rights reserved. Except for the quotation of short passages for the purpose of criticism and review, no part of this publication may be reproduced, stored in a retrieval system, or transmitted, in any form or by any means, electronic, mechanical, photocopying, recording or otherwise, without the prior permission of the publisher.

ISBN-13: 978-0-7456-6264-0 (hardback)
ISBN-13: 978-0-7456-6265-7 (paperback)

A catalogue record for this book is available from the British Library.

Typeset in 11 on 13 pt Sabon
by Toppan Best-set Premedia Limited
Printed and bound in Great Britain by the MPG Books Group

The publisher has used its best endeavours to ensure that the URLs for external websites referred to in this book are correct and active at the time of going to press. However, the publisher has no responsibility for the websites and can make no guarantee that a site will remain live or that the content is or will remain appropriate.

Every effort has been made to trace all copyright holders, but if any have been inadvertently overlooked the publisher will be pleased to include any necessary credits in any subsequent reprint or edition.

For further information on Polity, visit our website: www.politybooks.com

Contents

Acknowledgments	vi
Abbreviations	viii
1 The Organization of National Attachments	1
2 Moneymaking and Nation Building	19
3 Gifting the Nation	29
4 National Gift Giving in Crises	56
5 Making National Bonds: Floating the Irish and Israeli Loans in the United States	73
6 Making and Unmaking National Attachments: The Failure of the Irish Bond and the Success of the Israel Bond	98
7 Heterogeneity, Indeterminacy, and the Construction of National Interests	129
Conclusions: Nation Building as an Organizational Accomplishment	154
Notes	171
References	195
Index	207

Acknowledgments

I owe so much to so many, and a few paragraphs can barely express the depth of my gratitude. During my graduate studies at Columbia University, where the idea of this book was first conceived, I had the rare privilege of working under the guidance of unusually gifted and supportive teachers. My greatest gratitude is to my advisor, Professor Gil Eyal. Since my first week at Columbia, Gil has offered me constant intellectual challenges and unending support. Many of the ideas and arguments presented in this book sprang from conversations with Gil. His ability to engage with my undeveloped texts in a critical but productive manner was absolutely invaluable.

While at Columbia, I also benefited from the advice and encouragement of Peter Bearman, David Stark, Allan Silver, Nadia Abu El-Haj, Timothy Mitchell, and Bill McAllister. Coming from very different corners of the social science world, each one of these truly exceptional mentors made a decisive contribution to my thinking as a scholar and to the shaping of this book. Peter Bearman taught me how to think about social mechanisms and challenged me to improve my comparative toolkit. David Stark's insatiable appetite for innovation and creative ideas pushed me to explore the funky transactions that stand as the basis of this book. Allan Silver's and Bill McAllister's endless support and razor-sharp reading of early drafts identified and helped me overcome many faults in the argument. Nadia Abu El-Haj and Timothy

Acknowledgments

Mitchell not only introduced me to the field of Science and Technology Studies but also showed me how to make creative use of it. I also benefited from the comments and suggestions of participants in Columbia's Mellon Graduate Fellows Program and the participants in David Stark's Collaborative Organizational and Digital Ecologies Seminar.

The support of my colleagues, Paul Lichterman, Nina Eliasoph, Bruce Zuckerman, Paolo Parigi, Uri Shwed, Nancy Davenport, Zsuzzsanna Vargha, Yuval Millo, Henry Wassermann, and Robert Zussman has been invaluable. I am also deeply grateful to my father-in-law, Luis Lainer, and to Jesse Lichtenstein for their help in making this manuscript coherent and far more readable. For the many hours you spent with my choppy English – thank you.

Much closer to home, this book would have never been written without Jesse, my wife, and my two children, Noam and Romy. Jesse has been with me from the days I wrote a "statement of purpose" as part of the application for graduate school admission, through the hard process of moving to New York City, adjusting to a new place and language, my writing of far too many half-baked papers, and the writing of this book. Her calm and level-headed advice, her never-ending support, and her love kept me sane through the hard process of writing a dissertation and, later, becoming a professor. Noam and Romy served the same function by distracting me from the work of writing this book in the most adorable and charming manner.

Finally, I am deeply grateful for the helpful staff at the Central Zionist Archive and the Government Archive in Jerusalem, the Ben Gurion Archive in Sede Boker, the National Library, the National Archives, as well as the University College Archive in Dublin, the American Irish Historical Society, the American Jewish Historical Society, and New York's Public Library Manuscript Division.

Abbreviations

Organizations

AARIR	American Association for the Recognition of the Irish Republic
ACII	American Commission on Irish Independence
CJFWF	Council of Jewish Federations and Welfare Funds
FOIF	Friends of Irish Freedom
IRB	Irish Republican Brotherhood
I.I.I.	Israel Investment Incorporated
IVF	Irish Victory Fund
JDC	American Jewish Joint Distribution Committee
NRS	National Refugee Service
UJA	United Jewish Appeal for Refugee and Overseas Needs
UPA	United Palestine Appeal
ZOA	Zionist Organization of America

Archives

AIHS	American Irish Historical Society, New York
AJHS	American Jewish Historical Society, New York
BGA	Ben Gurion Archive, Sede Boker
CZA	Central Zionist Archives, Jerusalem
GA	Government Archives, Jerusalem
NA	National Archives, Dublin
NL	National Library, Dublin
NYPL	New York Public Library, New York
UCDA	University College Dublin Archives

1

The Organization of National Attachments

In early 1920, Ireland was in the throes of a war of independence from England. The *Dáil Éireann* (the self-declared parliament of the Republic of Ireland) sent its fiscal agent, James O'Mara, to the United States as a liaison to the Irish-American community. Upon arrival, O'Mara asked Diarmuid Lynch, the secretary of the powerful Friends of Irish Freedom (FOIF), for an account of collections and expenses of the Irish Victory Fund (IVF) drive. Lynch rejected the request and, in response to further probing, reprimanded O'Mara:

> It is evident from the tone of your letters that you misunderstand the situation ... we [the FOIF] are under no obligation to submit statements to any other organization. In view of the assistance given to the Irish cause by the Friends of Irish Freedom permit me to add that the insinuation of threat contained in your letter ... comes with very bad grace from one in your position.[1]

Almost thirty years later, Arthur Hertzberg, a young Zionist who later became an influential historian, traveled to Israel to witness with his own eyes the wonders taking place in the state that had just emerged from a war of independence. To his surprise, instead of giving him a warm welcome, his hosts nagged him with a barrage of demanding questions:

> "Why don't you stay in Israel? Why didn't more Americans come to fight? Why don't you send us more money? What are you American Jews like anyway?" As soon as the plane landed at Lydda airport [he confided to the readers of *Commentary* magazine] I was in the midst of this argument, and the discussion continued until I walked past the customs barrier on the night of my departure. Mine was not an isolated experience. Every fellow tourist from America had comparable tales to relate. Perhaps we brought much of the discussion upon ourselves. We were all rather pathetically eager to hear a word of commendation for our past efforts and to feel an acceptance of our continued role as partners in the building of Israel. (1950: 1)

Lynch and Hertzberg sacrificed much time and money to support the national struggles in Ireland and Palestine. They now expected the beneficiaries of their support, the Irish Republicans and the Jews in what was now Israel, to recognize their contributions and treat them accordingly. But the Irish Republicans (represented by O'Mara) and Hertzberg's Israeli hosts had an entirely different perspective. From their vantage point, they were entitled to the Irish-American and Jewish-American support, which, in many respects, was thoroughly insufficient, given the needs in the homeland.

The exchanges between O'Mara and Lynch, in the Irish case, and between Hertzberg and his hosts, in the Jewish case, illustrate an important point: nation building is always a process of creating and maintaining relations between disparate groups. To succeed, a small group of visionaries must reach out and recruit other groups, in this case, diaspora communities, who may have different preferences and divergent understandings regarding the rights and obligations associated with national membership. The challenge of nation building, from this perspective, is not merely one of conjuring a representation of the nation as a cultural whole, but fundamentally one of setting up mechanisms that can contain and accommodate heterogeneous interests and preferences so as to allow different groups to cooperate and develop lasting national attachments.

To understand how national movements weave together various groups into the national struggle, this book examines the Irish and Zionist attempts to mobilize their American compatriots in the 1910s–1920s and 1940s–1950s, respectively. The encounters between national entrepreneurs and half-committed diasporas serves as a strategic research site for examining the general problem of how different groups negotiate their position in the nation.[2] Instead of assuming that diasporas in some sense inherently belong to the nation, this book examines the difficulties that arise when national entrepreneurs try to mobilize members of diaspora communities, and it pays close attention to the mechanisms they develop in order to allow different groups to cooperate in making up the nation. Specifically, it examines the mechanisms that the Irish and Zionist movements developed in order to secure a flow of financial resources from the diaspora to the homeland.

Monetary transactions between diaspora communities and national movements may not seem like an obvious place for examining the process of nation building. Sociologists typically treat money as a neutral resource, as something that allows people to do things or accomplish goals. In the context of research on nationalism, scholars often assume that people give money *when* they already identify with the nation. From this perspective, fundraising is secondary and dependent on prior identification. But, as Viviana Zelizer points out, monetary transactions can also be understood as a medium through which social ties are negotiated, stitched together, or dismantled (1994, 1996). Seen from this angle, the tools used to extract funds from diasporas may not be simply ways of maximizing resources, but also organizational mechanisms that, when successful, bind groups and create a sense of belonging.

During the 1910s and 1940s, respectively, the Irish and Zionist national movements teamed up with diasporic organizations to establish large-scale fundraising apparatuses in the United States. The new fundraising organizations, the Irish Victory Fund (IVF) and the United Jewish Appeal (UJA), markedly increased the flow of funds to the respective national movements. Dramatic historical events such as the Easter Rising of 1916 and the Holocaust played important roles in these developments. But the IVF and UJA should not be interpreted as knee-jerk reactions, underpinned by already-existing national sentiments. Rather, the IVF and UJA each played a central role in defining the Irish-American and Jewish-American experiences. It is through participation in IVF and UJA activities that Ireland and Palestine became "homelands" for millions of Irish and Jewish Americans. Close examination of the organization of fundraising events, as well as the interorganizational struggles between the parties involved, allows us to see how the IVF and the UJA turned gift giving into the key mechanism through which Irish Americans and Jewish Americans related to the Irish and Zionist national struggles.

During the late 1910s and late 1940s, the IVF and UJA experienced severe and roughly parallel crises. These crises were related, on the one hand, to the nature of the fundraising mechanisms used to extract diaspora resources, and on the other, to deep-seated disagreements regarding the rights and obligations associated with membership in a nation. Believing that their donations were an act of generosity, the leaders of the Irish-American and Jewish-American diasporas felt entitled to retain part of the money for their communal needs and demanded some control over how the funds were to be used in the motherland. In contrast, the leaders in the homeland saw the donations of their compatriots in the United States as an inadequate contribution to the national cause. That the leaders of the IVF and the UJA dared keep money for their domestic operations and even had the effrontery to demand a voice in determining its use back home was, from their perspective, outrageous.

To overcome these impasses, the Irish and Zionist movements introduced new fundraising mechanisms. The Irish Republicans in 1920 and the Israeli government in 1951 each decided to issue national bonds. On purely financial grounds, these bonds were unattractive investments, but by combining patriotism and pecuniary interests – gift giving and market exchange – Irish and Israeli leaders hoped to obtain more money *and* the freedom to determine its use. The two initiatives were large-scale political and economic projects that demanded sophisticated financial expertise and delicate inter-organizational maneuvering, both in relation to the US government and within the network of homeland and diaspora organizations.

Despite their similarities, the Irish and Israeli bond projects had radically different outcomes. In the Irish case, disagreements stemming from the bond drive led to the termination of the project, and the inter-organizational struggles surrounding the rights and obligations associated with giving money to the nation played havoc with major Irish-American organizations. The Israeli bond initiative, on the other hand, helped to accommodate and smooth over disagreements between Israelis and American Jews and became a key institution linking American Jews to Israel. While the Irish Bond project (hereafter Irish Bond) became an almost forgotten episode in Irish history, the Israel Bond project (hereafter Israel Bond) played a key role in Israel's economic development: over the years, Israel sold more than thirty billion dollars' worth of these bonds. More than a third of Israel's external debt is to Israel Bond subscribers, and the sale of these bonds continues today (Rehavi and Weingarten 2004).

Beyond the loss of money, the collapse of the Irish Bond left Irish Americans with fewer concrete mediums and less motivation to engage in the Irish national project. Furthermore, the struggles surrounding the bond sharpened the boundaries between the Irish in the homeland and Irish Americans. Struggling to legitimize their positions, the Irish leaders and the leaders of the FOIF, the dominant Irish-American organization of the period, invoked the problem of divided loyalty and drew sharp lines separating the "people of Ireland" from Irish Americans. Through this process, the Irish and the Irish Americans came to think of themselves as two distinct and not entirely compatible groups. The collapse of the Irish Bond was not the only factor, but it contributed to the decline of the Irish-American diaspora that took place around 1920 (Miller 1985; Kenny 2000).[3]

In contrast, the ongoing sale of the Israeli bonds provided a new way for Israeli and American Jews to relate to one another. For Israelis, the dollars provided through the American Financial and Development Corporation for Israel (AFDCI), the organization that underwrote the bonds, signaled an end to the humiliating practice of *schnorrerai*.[4] Furthermore, in contrast to the money raised by the UJA, Israel did not have to share the bond dollars with others and could spend these funds as it wished. For Jewish Americans, the Israel Bond offered a new way to participate in the Zionist project without migrating to Israel. Purchasers of $10,000 worth of bonds were given the title "Guardians of Israel", and the AFDCI invited them on special tours of the country. On these tours, subscribers witnessed with their own eyes the fruits of their investment.[5] Not only that, Jewish Americans enjoyed the privilege of making a gift to Israel and then ultimately getting their money back, with interest.

The Israel Bond did not erase the differences between American and Israeli Jews. Rather, it established a convenient division between creditors and the debtor, both with their own distinct legal and (under-specified) moral responsibilities. Instead of replacing the previous method of giving to Israel, the AFDCI complemented the UJA and provided an additional way for American Jews to attach themselves to Israel. By subscribing to the Israeli bond, American Jews became invested not only financially but also emotionally in Israel's future.

The side-by-side analysis of the cases provides a fruitful opportunity to explore the process through which national movements enroll diverse groups in the nation. The goal of the investigation is not so much to identify differences in initial conditions that may be used to explain *why* the Irish national movement failed to regulate its relations with the Irish-American diaspora while the Zionist movement succeeded, but rather to examine the cases in parallel in order to understand *how* national movements weave different groups into the national struggle.[6] Specifically, the examination of the Irish and Zionist cases provides a better grasp of the mechanisms that national movements develop in order to regulate their relationship with the groups that potentially make up the nation. Thus, instead of attributing the outcomes of these bond projects to the spuriousness or authenticity of either national movement, to the religious or class differences among their respective diasporas, or to other possible contextual differences between the movements, my analysis focuses on the difficulties involved in mobilizing diverse groups to take up the national struggle, and on the organizational solutions designed to overcome these difficulties.

In both the Irish and Israeli cases, the bonds' fusion of elements of gift giving and market exchange generated misunderstandings regarding the bonds' true nature. On the one hand, Irish Americans and Jewish Americans, in general, saw the bonds mostly as gifts. The leaders of the Irish Republican movement and the Israeli leaders, on the other hand, discounted the gift-like properties of the bonds and interpreted them mostly as an investment. The results of these misunderstandings, however, differed greatly. In the Irish case, the mismatch in interpretations resulted in conflicting demands and provided grounds for fierce interorganizational struggles. In the Israeli case, in contrast, a very similar misunderstanding was instrumental in smoothing over deep tensions and ideological differences. Close attention to the technical and organizational details of the bond campaigns provides valuable clues to understanding the contrasting outcomes of the Irish and Israeli initiatives.

In the Irish case, certain technical glitches and organizational mistakes led the Irish and the Irish-American leaders into a protracted argument over the rights and obligations associated with contribution to the national cause. These arguments played an important role in the collapse of the bond project and the estrangement of the Irish-American diaspora from Ireland. In contrast, the terms and organization of the Israel Bond – its interest rates, redemption terms, and delivery procedure, as well as the organizational configuration of its sale – allowed Israeli and American Jews not so much to agree on the rights and obligations associated with national membership but rather to suspend the examination of these issues. In more theoretical terms, the organization of the Israel Bond helped create a *zone of indeterminacy* within which Israelis and American Jews could cooperate without agreeing on the meaning of the mutual engagement. As a result, the transatlantic national network that supported the Israel Bond became more robust and allowed these two groups with radically different agendas to imagine that they belonged to the same nation.

By treating the methods and strategies used to funnel diaspora resources to the national struggle as concrete nation-building mechanisms, I am hoping to bring research on nationalism down to earth and to challenge a number of truisms. While researchers now acknowledge that nations are heterogeneous entities whose boundaries are in flux, real or imagined homogeneity is still treated as the hallmark of nationalism. Researchers still attribute national mobilization to some level of unity or consensus, even one as thin as the mere imagination of belonging to the same category or group. This book's emphasis on the mechanisms that allow different groups to cooperate, however, clarifies that nation building is also about the negotiation and orchestration of difference. In the case of the Israel Bond, bringing different fragments of the nation (Chatterjee 1993) into cooperation did not rely on creating consensus. Rather than reaching an agreement, Israeli and American Jews reached temporary and localized settlements.[7] Creating the Israel Bond did not end the disagreements surrounding the rights and obligations entailed in national membership or even the exact nature of the Israel Bond. Despite, or, perhaps better, because of these ambiguities, through the bonds Israeli and American Jews developed their national attachments.

The Irish Bond provides a negative illustration of this point. The collapse of the Irish Bond drive was related not so much to the existence of unbridgeable differences between the homeland Irish and the Irish Americans as to a failure in orchestrating the differences that were present with sensitivity and nuance. Failures in the design and execution of the Bond Certificate drive intensified tensions between the FOIF and the Irish mission in the United States and forced the leaders of the contending sides to make explicit the terms of their relationship. From this perspective, absence of consensus and internal differences do not necessarily constitute a threat to the nation. Instead, internal dissension is the predicament national entrepreneurs inescapably confront, with varying degrees of success.[8] The orchestration of difference, therefore, is the process that allows the different fragments of the nation to cohere.

Rogers Brubaker and Frederick Cooper criticize the contemporary use of the concept of "identity" (2000). Some scholars, they explain, use the concept to denote deep and enduring sameness in a way that effectively reifies the groups under investigation. Other scholars emphasize the unstable, shifting, and a fragmented character of identity. This treatment is not guilty of essentialism but its analytical purchase is questionable. As an alternative, Brubaker and Cooper suggest using terms like "identification," "self-understanding," and "groupness." These concepts provide a nuanced and dynamic means with which to trace nation building and group formation in general.

My analysis concurs with and extends Brubaker and Cooper's critique. Even the more dynamic concept of "identification" suffers from serious shortcomings. Even a dynamic concept like "identification" suggests that the *process* of nation building ultimately rests on the social construction of an inclusive imagined "we" that encompasses all members of the nation.[9] Close examination of the Irish and Jewish mobilization efforts, however, shows that the production of a sense of national belonging does not *necessarily* require members to overlook obvious differences between themselves and others within the nation. National mobilization in the US crucially depended on a continued sense of difference between members of diasporic communities and other members of the nation. Some (members of diaspora communities) imagined themselves to belong to the periphery of the nation, while others (in the homeland) saw themselves as occupying the core of the nation. It was this difference that gave credence to the demand that Irish Americans and Jewish Americans support the national struggle financially (since, allegedly, those in the homeland risked their very lives for the same cause). Thus, the production of a sense of belonging, at least in these cases, required not only the generation of an inclusive "we" encompassing both homeland and diaspora groups but, concomitantly, the drawing of boundaries that emphasize the differences between these groups. Sharing a common marker of nationhood is obviously important, and a widely recognized factor in national mobilization, but the concept of "identity" conceals the productive role that internal differences play in creating national action and a sense of belonging.

A more useful concept to consider while discussing the formation of groups may be "attachment." First, unlike "identity," "attachment" carries no underlying assumptions about the nature of the components that form a given grouping or the process of forming such groupings. Members of the nation are not only different; they also perceive themselves as different from other members, and this sense of difference can sometimes play a constitutive role in generating their sense of belonging. Second, as a verb, "attach" directs attention to dynamic processes rather than fixed states (see Brubaker and Cooper 2000). It foregrounds practices developed to create national attachments rather than the status of particular groups. Third, the antonym of attachment – detachment – suggests that the process is reversible and that it can be studied using the same conceptual tools. It also points to the need to study both successful and failed attempts to mobilize groups in a symmetrical manner. Fourth, while the concept of identity is strongly associated with non-instrumental action (Brubaker and Cooper 2000: 6–7), the concept of attachment is more flexible. It can accommodate both instrumental and non-instrumental action, and it is therefore particularly useful when it comes to exploring how national entrepreneurs weave diverse interests and preferences in the process of creating national associations.

Thinking about nation building using the concept of "attachment" rather than "identity" is more than a minor terminological shift. The concept of identity steers attention to those practices that generate a sense of similarity. The preferred sites for such investigations are novels, museums, maps – i.e. sites where the image of the nation as a cultural whole is conjured. The concept of attachment, in contrast, is more practical. It directs our analysis to a range of sites where different groups who potentially make up the nation meet and do things together (the exchange of objects is merely one example). Examining these encounters allows us to identify the concrete organizational mechanisms that nation builders develop in order to turn the idea of the nation from the fancy of a mere few to a consequential reality.

More specifically, studying the mechanisms used to secure a flow of funds to the nation calls for a renewed appreciation of the relationships between interested action and national membership. Scholars sometimes describe nation building as a process through which patriotic passion overcomes selfish reason. The story goes this way: in early stages, before actors subscribe to national ideology, actors are said to be motivated by their class, gender, and other interests that are related to their concrete social position. National mobilization purportedly pushes these narrow interests aside and instills, instead, a selfless concern for the national common good (it is no coincidence that so many scholars associate willingness to die for others, the quintessential exemplar of altruism, with membership in the nation).[10] In an effort to explain such a fundamental change in the motivation of actors, researchers sometimes portray membership in a nation as a deep emotional reaction.

In the Irish and Zionist cases, however, nation building was not a process of replacing interested orientation with selfless national fervor. Rather, the Irish and Zionist national entrepreneurs worked on how different groups identified their interests and strived to align the particular preferences of the various groups that were assembled to the nation. Success in national mobilization was directly related to eliminating a choice between one's particular preferences and the national interest. Nation building consisted of ongoing negotiations and delicate compromises that gradually transformed the way Irish Americans, the Irish, Jewish Americans, and Israelis defined their respective preferences, interests, and self-conception in relation to one another.

Nation Building and Diaspora Communities

During the 1980s, primordialists and constructivist scholars argued over the historical origins of nations. Anthony Smith and his colleagues asserted that the building blocks of today's nations are kinship ties, religious affiliations, myths of election, common origin, and so on (Smith 1994, 1999, 2003; Hutchinson 1987, 2005). The constructivists, in contrast, argued that nationalism is a relatively recent social construction that emerged in response to industrialization and capitalist development (Gellner 1983; Anderson 1991; Hobsbawm and Ranger 1992). This debate is, for all intents and purposes, over. Today, the constructed nature of nations is a commonplace, and researchers widely acknowledge that nations are heterogeneous entities whose boundaries are historically shifting (Sahlins 1989; Chatterjee 1993; Judson 2006).

Despite significant advances since the early 1980s, Brubaker notes that research on nationalism is still marred by "groupism," i.e., the tendency to think of nations as internally homogeneous and externally bounded groups (2009). Even constructivist scholars tend to slip unwittingly into a language that embodies nationalist assumptions about the boundedness, homogeneity, and historical continuity of "the nation" (Brubaker et al. 2006: 10). The more-or-less accepted remedy to groupist thinking is to treat nationalism as a perspective on the world and examine how groups form and use the *category* of the nation (Verdery 1996; Brubaker 2004; Wimmer 2008). In place of examining the historical emergence of nations, researchers now study the patchwork of practices that somehow holds the *image* of the nation together (Eley and Suny 1996; Goswami 2002). Nation building is now understood as a process of cultural representation, inevitably full of contradictions and ambiguities that somehow, paradoxically, turn the nation into a taken-for-granted entity.

Much of the new research examines the ways in which practices of surveying, mapping, census taking, the issue of various identification documents, and so on, shape how persons identify themselves, construe events, impute interests, and generally make sense of situations as ethnically or nationally meaningful (Anderson 1991; Verdery 1991; Jenkins 1997; Brubaker, Loveman, and

Stamatov 2004; Brubaker 2004, 2009). More than merely describing groups, these practices constitute ethnic and national groupings. This book seeks to contribute to this line of research by highlighting the constitutive importance of the mechanisms that regulate the relationships between the groups that make up the nation.

By closely examining the organizational dynamics and technical details of national mobilization at a level usually below the scrutiny of previous research, this book shows that nation building is not simply a process through which internal differences are imagined away but also, centrally, a process of organizing and regulating relationships to allow groups to maintain their difference and contribute to the national cause. My focus on mechanisms that secure cooperation between the groups that make up the nation complements existing research on the mechanisms involved in representing the nation. Successful choreography of the tensions between different fragments of the nation makes it easier for members to imagine their membership in the same nation. In contrast, failing to regulate the relationships between the groups that can potentially make up the nation renders the imagination of national unity harder to sustain. This approach bridges a gap between second-wave historical comparative researchers who have examined processes of mobilization but have overlooked the process of meaning-making and scholars of nationalism who focus on the representation of the nation (see Spillman and Faeges 2005). Here, belonging and mobilization are inextricably and reciprocally linked.

My analysis starts with the identification of controversies – moments marked by the expression of opposing views and disagreements on questions and events of national importance – and proceeds by examining the strategies and innovations developed in order to overcome them. Such an approach allows me to identify the practical mechanisms that partake in the process of nation building.[11]

Controversies that arise in the encounter between homeland and diaspora communities are particularly interesting (Brah 1996; Lainer-Vos 2010). The analytical value of these controversies stems from the ambiguous status of diaspora communities.[12] Regardless of their subjective orientation, by living abroad, diaspora communities betray ambivalence toward the homeland. It is never entirely clear whether diaspora communities belong to this or that nation (Clifford 1997). The point is not metaphorical but concrete. Each time a national entrepreneur proclaims that this or that group living away from the homeland belongs to the nation, others within the diaspora or in the homeland will step forward and contest the claim. The mechanisms devised by entrepreneurs in order to settle these disputes and enroll "their" diasporas offer an outstanding opportunity to learn about the mechanics of nation building.[13]

Studying the controversies of diasporic belonging can yield more than a detailed understanding of this particular predicament. Even within the nation-state, membership is seldom unambiguous. Some groups are deeply committed to the national project, while other groups (peasants, border communities, various ethnic groups, women) are more hesitant. Thus, even within the nation-state, national movements must find ways to enroll various groups. The point is not to ignore or confuse important differences between diaspora attachments and national attachments within the nation-state but rather to treat the encounter between homeland and diaspora communities as a heuristic model for understanding how national movements regulate their relations to the various groups that make up the nation (see concluding chapter for a fuller exploration of this point).

The Irish and Jewish Homeland–Diaspora Encounters

The Irish and Zionist homeland–diaspora encounters provide an outstanding research opportunity. It is crucial, however, to clarify at the outset what the parallel examination of these cases is designed to achieve. The approach adopted in this book differs from typical variable-based historical–comparative studies. Historical–comparative researchers often seek to identify the causes of particular outcomes by identifying similarities and differences in initial conditions across cases (Ragin 1987; Mahoney and Rueschemeyer 2003; Mahoney, Kimball, and Koivu 2009). In the cases examined here, the different trajectories of the Irish and Zionist cases compel, almost automatically, a search for differences in the initial conditions of the respective projects that can perhaps explain *why* the Irish and Irish Americans failed to stabilize their relationships, whereas the Jews succeeded. But there are serious methodological and substantive reasons to suspend this question, at least for a while, in favor of asking *how* the Irish and Zionist national movements went about mobilizing their diasporas.

However intuitive, variable-based historical–comparative methods suffer from a number of drawbacks. Variable-based comparisons, especially those that include only a small number of cases, hinge on the similarity of cases. But historical processes typically differ in many respects (Ragin 1987). The Irish and Zionist homeland–diaspora encounters are no exception. During the first half of the twentieth century, Irish Americans and Jewish Americans were among the most active and vocal diaspora communities in the United States (Jacobson 1995).[14] But anyone with even superficial familiarity with the Irish-American and Jewish-American diasporas, and the Irish and Zionist national movements, would be quick to note many potentially important differences between them. It may be useful to explore just a few of them.

First, although both the Irish-American and Jewish-American communities were products of emigration, the paths they followed were distinct. Whereas (first-generation) Irish immigrants were born and raised in Ireland, Jewish Americans, by and large, came from Eastern Europe, not from Palestine. This difference had important consequences. Irish migrants carried concrete memories of life in Ireland and many remained in contact with their families back home (Miller 1985). In contrast, most of the Jewish Americans spoke no Hebrew, had no close relatives in Israel, and had never even visited the region. The settlement experiences of these communities were different as well. Both Irish and Jewish immigrants experienced hardships and discrimination upon arrival, but, in comparison, the Jews left the working-class positions they had occupied upon arrival more quickly and, by the time periods examined in this book they occupied higher class positions than the Irish Americans (Fallows 1979; Perlmann 1988; Jacobson 1995).

Second, Irish Americans and American Jews differed in their attitudes toward their putative homelands. In terms of national politics, the Irish and Irish Americans had relatively few disagreements. Irish on both sides often described themselves as "sea-divided Gaels" (Miller 1985), implying that the only difference between them was geographical. The differences between Jewish

Americans and the Jews in Israel were more pronounced. In the first half of the twentieth century, the Israeli polity was dominated by the Labor Zionists, who strongly believed that the duty of every Jew was to migrate to Israel. The choice to live in America was, from their perspective, a sign of moral corruption (Kimmerling 1983). Jewish Americans, on the other hand, took pride in their successful integration and rejected the Zionist description of life in America as exile (Heinze 1990). American and Israeli Jews also differed in their understanding of religion. Israeli Labor Zionists viewed Judaism as a religion *and* a nationality but embraced a secular lifestyle. For many American Jews, in contrast, Judaism was strictly a religion.[15] Even if we discount statements like "sea-divided Gaels" as empty rhetoric, it is clear that in terms of ideology Irish Americans had fewer differences vis-à-vis the Irish Republicans than did the Jewish Americans vis-à-vis the Labor Zionists.

Third, in the periods examined in this book, the Irish and Zionist movements enjoyed very different political and organizational status. During the 1910s and early 1920s, regardless of the *Dáil Éireann* 1918 declaration of independence, the Irish Republican movement was still a small clandestine organization that enjoyed no international recognition. In contrast, the Zionist movement had been developing quasi-state institutions in Palestine since 1918, and by 1948 it had secured an internationally recognized state with effective control over its territory.[16] This difference was matched by a different level of communal institutionalization in the United States. Irish-American organizations (Funchion 1983) were, almost without exception, fraternal associations operating almost entirely on a voluntary basis. American Jews, on the other hand, created a wide array of highly professionalized communal organizations. By 1940, almost four hundred communities around the country had established permanent Jewish Federations and Welfare Funds (Elazar 1995). In terms of capacity to reach individual members of the community and mobilize their resources, the Jewish-American community enjoyed a dramatic advantage in comparison with the Irish-American community.

Fourth, the cultural and political contexts within which the Irish and Zionist national movements operated were separated by a significant gap of thirty years. During and after World War I, engaging in diasporic activities in the United States, especially

Irish diasporic activities, meant that one was subject to accusations of divided loyalty (Ward 1968, 1969; Carroll 1978; Golway 1998; Bhroiméil 2003). In contrast, during and after World War II and the Holocaust, the attitude toward diasporic, and especially Jewish diasporic, activities in the United States was more permissive. Certain displays of allegiance to the motherland, which might have been viewed as un-American in the 1910s and 1920s, were viewed as more permissible in the 1940s and 1950s.

Given these deep differences, and others not mentioned here, it is difficult to assess the adequacy of these potential explanations for why the Irish fundraising project ultimately failed and the Zionist project succeeded.[17] In retrospect, almost any a priori difference can be proposed as the cause of divergent outcomes, but it is hard to distinguish between spurious and genuine causes. More importantly, from the perspective developed here, such a line of inquiry is intellectually frustrating, precisely because focusing on initial conditions identified a priori tends to shift attention away from the nitty-gritty details of the encounters between groups. Accepting these (or other) initial conditions as an explanation for an outcome sidesteps the more interesting question of how divergent groups sometimes manage to cooperate, and how success or failure in accomplishing such cooperation affects their self-understanding and membership in a nation.

To gain a better understanding of the mechanisms involved in orchestrating such cooperation, therefore, the book will examine the controversies that flared up when the Irish and Zionist movements attempted to mobilize their diasporic sympathizers, and it will trace the organizational innovations that the Irish and Jewish nationalists devised in order to overcome them. The basis for the comparison of the Irish and Zionist cases is not their overwhelming similarity, which, as the above section shows, can easily be doubted, but rather a similarity in the problems these two movements confronted in their relationships with their respective diasporas.[18] In both cases, members of diaspora communities – not all but certainly a good number of them – sympathized with the national struggles in Ireland and Palestine, respectively. Yet, translating their sympathy into tangible support was not simple. Over and above the challenge of reaching out to a diverse population scattered all over the United States, members of the Irish and Jewish diasporas differed in their understanding of the obligations and rights associated with national membership from their compatriots in the homeland. Thus, the equivalent challenge for both national movements was not that of conjuring an image of the nation but of actually weaving members of these groups into a robust transnational network so as to generate a flow of resources to the respective homelands. It must be emphasized that the challenges facing the national Irish and Zionist entrepreneurs were not secondary to a more fundamental problem of identification. Since the boundaries of the nation are fluid (Sahlins 1989; Judson 2006), unresolved conflicts or failure to orchestrate the relationships between these groups could result in the exclusion or self-exclusion of certain groups from the nation. Successful regulation of differences, in contrast, might solidify national attachments among groups that were until that point insecurely attached to the nation.

The following chapters examine the Irish and Zionist attempts to mobilize their potential supporters in the United States. Instead of a priori identifying a list of important variables for comparison, the chapters follow national entrepreneurs as they try to overcome various obstacles. The unfolding narratives suggest possible causes for the different outcomes of the Irish and Zionist projects, but more importantly they help us to examine the mechanisms that regulate the relationships between the various groups that make up the nation and turn the nation from a fragile musing into a formidable political force.

A Note About Terminology

Writing about nation building without reifying the subject matter is not easy. Even constructivist scholars tend to unwittingly use language that slips groupist assumptions into the analysis (Brubaker et al. 2006: 10–14). Writing on the relationships between homeland and diaspora groups is surely not exempt from this pitfall (Anthias 1998; Brubaker 2005). In fact, the very conjunction of "homeland" and "diaspora" seems to imply that these two concepts are somehow naturally affiliated. The terms "Irish Americans" and "Jewish Americans" likewise seem to suggest that a category that is actually highly heterogeneous and fluid, constitutes a group with clear boundaries.

It may be proper to craft a terminology that avoids these linguistic pitfalls. One can, for example, use the term "those who identify as Irish Americans" instead of "Irish Americans" in order to make clear that the term does not refer to all those of Irish origin but rather to a self-selected category of people. Alternatively, one can place concepts such as diaspora, homeland, or the relationship between them inside "scare quotes" in order to notify the reader that these concepts are not in any sense natural. Such terminological operations, however, in addition to being cumbersome, bring in a hint of irony and critical distance that I wish to avoid. My aim is not to add the wisdom of hindsight to the events I follow but rather to follow actors and describe the mechanisms they devise in the process of nation building. For that reason, this book refrains from using literary techniques of distancing and entrusts the subjects of the book – national entrepreneurs, leaders of diaspora organizations, and their followers (when they exist) – with the task of questioning the naturalness of the nation.

More technically, throughout this book the labels "Irish Americans" and "American-Irish community,"[19] or "Jewish Americans" and "Jewish-American diaspora," will be used interchangeably to denote those Americans of Irish or Jewish descent who have chosen to participate in Irish or Jewish communal activities. The term "Irish" or "Israelis" will be reserved for Irish from Ireland or Jews from Israel (despite the presence of a very substantial non-Jewish population in Israel (let alone Palestine). Furthermore, to avoid confusion, unless the sentence refers exclusively to the pre-1948 era, I will use the term "Israel" throughout instead of the cumbersome "Palestine (later to become Israel)."

2

Moneymaking and Nation Building

This chapter provides a theoretical framework for following national entrepreneurs as they build the mechanisms needed to attach diaspora groups to the national project and secure a flow of resources to the homeland. The mechanisms we are concerned with here deal with tensions surrounding the entitlements that follow from contribution to the national cause. Our discussion will therefore focus on practices that coordinate the rights and obligations associated with the transfer of objects – that is, with gift giving, market exchange, and transactions that combine elements of these practices.

While the link between capitalism and the emergence of and spread of nationalism is a recurrent theme in the scholarship on nationalism (Hechter 1975; Anderson 1991; Hobsbawm and Ranger 1992), researchers have generally refrained from relating the exchange of objects per se to the making of nations. This avoidance is grounded, I believe, in the highly stylized models of market exchange and gift giving that still animate the sociological imagination of many researchers (Zelizer 2005: 292; Stark 2009: 6–13).

Sociologists often treat the market as the quintessential arena for rational interested action. The market is a place where individual buyers and sellers attempt to maximize their advantages by exchanging alienable goods – that is, commodities. Markets operate as coordination mechanisms in which actor A wants something that actor B possesses. The agreed-upon price renders incommensurable goods relative and allows actors to secure desired resources without resorting to violence (Weber 1978: 72, 635–640). Despite its non-violent character, market exchange does not eliminate conflicting interests. If anything, it forces the parties to be cognizant of their conflicting interests. The buyer wants something that the seller possesses, but he or she is hoping to pay as little as possible. The seller, in contrast, hopes for a high price. Thus, the market is a competitive arena in which the parties involved seek to control opportunities in order to generate profits. For this reason, sociologists often treat market exchange as a cold and alienating practice (Polanyi 1957; Simmel 1990), not exactly the stuff that makes nations.[1]

In contrast with market exchange, gift giving is widely acknowledged as a practice that creates social ties and obligations (Malinowski 1920; Mauss 1967; Lévi-Strauss 1969). Marcel Mauss (1967) formulated an influential account of how the obligation to give, to receive, and to reciprocate with a counter-gift generates social solidarity in "archaic societies." In sharp contrast to the commodities exchanged in the market, Mauss argues that the objects that change hands in gift giving are inalienable. When one gives a gift, she also gives a bit of herself with it, and the ongoing association between the giver and the gift forces the receiver to reciprocate. Importantly, the solidarity created by the exchange of gifts extends beyond the immediate parties involved and engulfs the entire society.

In modern settings, however, researchers often consider gift giving as an interpersonal issue. David Cheal, for example, suggests that, unlike pre-modern gifting, the modern variant is not tightly regulated, and its economic significance is negligible. Ultimately, he argues, modern giving is first and foremost a disinterested and voluntary way of symbolizing closeness between intimates (1988: 19). From this perspective, linking gift giving to the grander political scale of nations is inappropriate. Furthermore, gift giving, especially when the gift is not reciprocated, tends to create dependencies and inequalities (Sahlins 1963; Zelizer 1996). In contrast, nationalism as a type of political organization seems to consecrate independence and equality (regardless of the inequalities that exist within each) (Anderson 1991). For these reasons, linking gift giving to nation building is bound to produce irreconcilable tensions.

Yet, there are good reasons to challenge this avoidance. First, in contrast to Cheal's argument, modern gift giving is decidedly not just an interpersonal thing. The tremendous growth of the philanthropic sector over the past few decades attests to the fact that in modern settings people gift organizations and collective bodies perhaps more than ever before (Titmuss 1971; Barman 2006; Healy 2006). Second, giving plays a tremendously important role in shaping people's identities. People give to organizations and movements with which they identify, often without the expectation of a counter-gift, and they use these acts of giving to shape their self perceptions (Silber 1998). Third, although the ideal typical models of market exchange and gift giving suggest that these forms of transaction are incompatible, a growing body of literature shows that between pure gift giving and pure market exchange lies a whole spectrum of hybrid transactions. Rather than simply enacting innate propensities or strict cultural codes, actors creatively mix and match elements of gift giving and market exchange in order to extract special privileges, advance a cause, or sometimes even gain competitive advantage (Zelizer 1985, 1994, 2005; Davis 1996; Herrmann 1997; Darr 2003; Bird-David and Darr 2009).

Perhaps most crucially, even a cursory observation clarifies that tropes of gift giving and exchange are absolutely central to the way people understand their relationship to the nation. A vast array of national activities are understood in terms of giving: people gift the nation with money, by the bearing of children, with the waving of the flag, and, obviously, through the giving of one's very life to the nation. Selfless giving to the nation is often considered the ultimate patriotic virtue and a testimony to one's national pedigree. The esteem actors derive from giving to the nation is directly associated with the degree to which others perceive their action as disinterested. At the same time, in return for selfless acts of giving, actors often demand and receive special privileges. National membership, in other words, is centrally organized around a more-or-less interested exchange between the nation as a political movement and the people it purports to represent.[2]

Given the centrality of gift and exchange in national rhetoric and the self-understanding of members, it may be useful, following Viviana Zelizer (1985, 1994, 2005) and many others (Davis 1996; Herrmann 1997; Darr 2003; Bird-David and Darr 2009), to put aside the neat analytical models of gift giving and market exchange, and explore how national entrepreneurs tinker and innovate with these forms of exchange in order to mobilize various groups to join the national struggle. From this perspective, the problems identified earlier – the limited scope of modern gift giving and the alienating effect of market exchange – should not steer research away from these practices but rather be used to sensitize our attention to the challenges that confront national entrepreneurs. The empirical investigation should identify the innovations that Irish and Jewish national entrepreneurs introduced in order to overcome the limits of modern gift giving and market exchange in the process of mobilizing Irish Americans and Jewish Americans to their respective national struggles.

Gift Giving, Market Exchange, and Everything in Between

The writings of Pierre Bourdieu (1992, 2000) and Michel Callon (1998; see also Caliskan and Callon 2009) provide a useful analytical framework with which to think about economic transactions that lie somewhere between the pure gift and the pure market exchange. According to Bourdieu, the difference between market exchange and gift giving lies in the organization of these transactions and the type of calculations they make possible.[3] A gift, we all know, should be reciprocated – but the counter-gift must be different from the original gift. Furthermore, proper etiquette requires that the exchange of gifts be delayed. Some time should pass between the presentation of a gift and its reciprocation. Reciprocating with the same gift or reciprocating too quickly is dangerously close to refusing to accept the original gift (Bourdieu 2000).[4] This normative organization, Bourdieu argues, has an important effect. The time lag between gift and counter-gift as well as their dissimilarity makes it harder to compare gifts and creates a never-closing debt of gratitude between the parties (Gouldner 1960; Bourdieu 2000). The organization of gift giving, in other words, creates obstacles to the calculation of the exchanged objects that assure that the debt created by the first gift continues to reverberate between the parties involved, and a sense of gratitude, trust, and solidarity gradually emerge.

Callon (1998) extends Bourdieu's insight by suggesting that, in contrast to the organization of gift giving, where calculation is inhibited, market exchange is constituted by the introduction of devices that facilitate calculation (see also Callon and Muniesa 2005; Muniesa, Millo, and Callon 2007). Placing similar commodities next to one another on a shelf in the supermarket, for example, makes the comparison of various items easier and thus allows actors to behave a bit more like interested economic actors. The simultaneous character of market exchange has the same effect. In short, markets allow fast and easy calculations and thus allow actors to behave in an interested way.[5] The organization of market exchange has important relational consequences. The ability to interact without incurring unclosed debts permits the parties involved to treat each other as strangers despite their sometimes ongoing engagement.[6] Thus, the alienating effect of markets is the result of the calculations that the organization of the marketplace makes possible. The concept of calculability provides a useful framework with which to explore how actors fuse gift giving and market exchange in actual transactions.

Clear appreciation of the blurry boundaries between gift giving and market exchange raises important practical questions. First, if gift giving and market exchange exist along a continuum, there is no guarantee that the parties involved will attribute the same meaning to the objects that change hands (Table 2.1 illustrates this problem). The outcome of a misunderstanding can be dreadful. Treating as a commodity an object intended as a gift (lower left cell of the table) is likely to result in a conflict. The receiver may try to make a payment or, even worse, may begin haggling over the gift's value in an effort to extract a discount.[7] The giver in such a case would probably interpret the response of the beneficiary as a sign of ingratitude or hostility. Treating commodities as gifts (the upper right cell in the table) would be injurious too. This problem is far from a theoretical issue. Since economic transactions often involve elements of both gift giving and market exchange, it is easy to see why an object given as a gift may sometimes be interpreted by the other side as a commodity, or vice versa. When the orientations of the actors involved are heterogeneous, agreement on the meaning of the transaction may be even harder to accomplish.

Table 2.1. Agreement and Disagreement in Economic Transactions.

	Giving a Gift	Selling a Commodity
Accepting a gift	Mutually agreed gift giving	Misplaced gratitude/ misplaced expectation for payment
Buying a commodity	Misplaced expectation for gratitude/ misplaced haggling	Mutually agreed market exchange

Second, and more fundamentally, when economic transactions combine elements of gift giving and market exchange, how can the two sides to the exchange come to an agreement over the value of the exchanged objects and the social relations that exist between them? The stylized model of market exchange suggests that the mechanism of price generates agreed-upon valuation. Similarly, the stylized model of gift giving provides an answer to how actors accomplish such transactions. However, the principles of valuation involved in these two types of transactions are not only different but conflicting. Commodities have a price; gifts are, by definition, priceless. How, then, can the two sides come to an agreement over the value of the exchanged objects and the social relations that exist between them when they engage in transactions that combine elements of these practices?

Clarification practices: Transaction through consensus

Viviana Zelizer is one of the few scholars to consider the practical implications of the blurry boundaries in the practices of gift giving and market exchange (1994, 1996, 2000, 2005). In her work on the social uses of money, Zelizer notes that money can be used as compensation, a gift, or an entitlement. Each type of payment corresponds to and implies different social relations. Using money as compensation, as in typical market exchange, implies equality and independence between the parties. Using money as a gift, in contrast, implies dependence and is usually associated with more durable relations (1996: 482). To avoid harmful misinterpretations, actors "earmark" their exchange medium so as to avoid confusion or to assert their own interpretation of the encounter.

Zelizer's work focuses on monetary transactions that are particularly liable to be interpreted as interested exchange, but actors use clarification practices in other settings as well. Removing a price tag and wrapping an object, for example, increases the likelihood that the receiver will identify the object as a gift. Placing a price tag in a prominent location, in contrast, clarifies that one is dealing with a commodity. More generally, the context within which a transaction takes place typically contains cues that allow actors to agree mutually on whether a particular object should be treated as a gift *or* a commodity. When people smile and sing "happy birthday," you are not expected to pay for the cake. The same cake on the supermarket shelf is a commodity, and failing to pay for it will probably result in a huge embarrassment, or worse. Clearly, in a good number of settings, the context of the interaction contains enough cues to allow the parties involved to treat the transaction as being either gift giving or market exchange and to concur in their interpretations.

Blurring practices: Transaction without consensus

Clarification practices allow actors to treat otherwise ambiguous transactions as either a gift or a commodity and point to agreed-upon principles of valuation. But, as noted before, actors sometimes combine elements of gift giving and market exchange in order to extract special treatment or gain market advantage (Davis 1996).[8] In such instances, reducing the meaning of the transaction to either gift giving or market exchange is likely to be counterproductive. This point is particularly relevant for transactions that combine moral and pecuniary interests. The use of promotional gifts in philanthropic campaigns provides a good illustration. In order to boost giving, fundraisers sometimes give donors discount cards whose benefits have significant economic value. One can probably attach monetary value to these cards but such a clarification would defeat the purpose of this fundraising strategy. The whole point of offering perks whose monetary value is hard to calculate in return for donations is to allow donors to indulge in the thought that they gave a large sum of money *and* enjoy the benefits of the card without discounting the value of the latter from the former. Thus, sometimes – especially when one or both sides of the transaction wish to escape the limitations of or the obligations associated with either gift giving or market exchanges – the actors involved may try to blur the meaning of the exchange in order to complete the transaction on more favorable terms.

Carrying out such hybrid forms of exchange is a tremendous organizational challenge. Attempts to blur the meaning of the exchange are liable to be perceived as sinister or deceitful efforts to avoid the costs associated with more straightforward transactions. Instead of gullibly accepting offers for hybrid transactions as they are presented (that is, as a mixture of gift giving and market exchange), actors often reduce the multivocality of the offer to the dimension most pleasing to themselves. In such a case, if the two sides differ in their interpretations, an argument is likely to ensue.

To prevent actors from reducing the meaning of hybrid transactions to either gift giving or market exchange, it is not enough to rhetorically weave together elements of these practices. Given that actors determine the meaning of transactions with reference to the context within which they take place, an actor may still decide that a particular object is, say, a gift, even if the other side claims that it is a bit of a gift and a bit of a commodity. Thus, accomplishing such an exchange demands the creation of conditions within which the parties involved (or at least one of them) would not reduce the meaning of the exchange either to gift giving or market exchange. In other words, accomplishing hybrid exchanges requires creating a *zone of indeterminacy*, an institutional context within which it is less likely that the bivalent character of the exchange will be reduced or discounted. The challenge of creating a zone of indeterminacy is twofold. On the one hand, the transaction itself should fuse elements of gift giving and market exchange so as to allow different interpretations. On the other hand, the context of the transaction should be arranged in such a way that the two sides would not be motivated to explore its precise meaning. In such a situation, the two sides may be able to attribute different meanings to the exchange without this incongruence becoming immediately a matter of dispute. Successful construction of such a zone of indeterminacy may enable the two parties to transact without agreeing on the meaning of the exchange.

Loans as a Hybrid Type of Transaction

Loans – a type of exchange that is highly relevant for the following chapters – illustrate the complexities of hybrid transactions particularly well. Extending loans entails a temporary provision of resources with the expectation of return (Carruthers 2005: 356). Different loans resemble either gift giving or market exchange (Mauss 1967: 35–37).[9] Loans extended without clear specification of the time and condition of return look and feel like gifts. Their cost is hard to calculate, they are accepted with gratitude, and they are typically extended to close friends or family (Offer 1997). In contrast, loans that include enforceable contracts specifying duration, interest, terms of redemption, and collaterals resemble market exchange and are typically exchanged between strangers.

Regardless of the orientation of actors, loans always include a time lag between initial transfer and the return of principal and interest. This time lag is not different from the time lag that, according to Bourdieu, constitutes gifts. Yet, a loan is not a gift. What distinguishes a loan from a gift is a set of demarcations that enhance the ability to calculate its value. But specification of terms and conditions is only part of the story. In order to increase the calculability of a loan one can, for example, purchase from a third party an insurance against default. This strategy reduces the uncertainty associated with future behavior of the debtor by linking it to the future of the insurance provider. For a loan really to approximate market exchange, however, it needs to be liquid. Liquidity allows, quite literally, the closure of the time lag that separates it from regular market exchange, for a known price.[10] The ability to alter the temporal schedule of a loan – and receive a return prior to the date of maturation – renders the difference between loans and market exchanges meaningless.

Credit transactions are also liable to induce cooperation without consensus. In the period between the extension of credit and the full redemption – both sides to the exchange can tell themselves a story about what the exchange is all about. The lender may believe that the transaction is more a gift than an investment, while the debtor may indulge in the belief that the transaction is an investment, without these differences becoming immediately apparent. The reverse possibility is also not far-fetched. Clear specifications of terms and conditions limit the interpretive flexibility of actors but cannot eliminate it. In other words, prior to maturation, a loan often exists in a zone of indeterminacy wherein both lender and borrower can attribute to it the meanings they are most comfortable with, without having to struggle over an agreed-upon meaning.[11]

Finally, credit also exemplifies how economic transactions can foster or curb social relations. Debtors are obliged to their creditors; this is obvious. But, at least for the duration of the loan, the creditors too acquire deep interest in the success of their debtors (Carruthers 1996). From this perspective, credit is an inherently political instrument because it aligns heretofore disparate interests and creates new allegiances. Thus, the case of credit exemplifies particularly well the relational work that exchange practices perform.

Economic Transactions and the Making of Nations

Gift giving, market exchange, and whatever lies between them, as well as the specific example of loans, are not necessarily or even usually national matters. Actors use economic transactions in the most diverse settings and for many different ends. But the generality of exchange practices does not mean that they have nothing to do with nation building; quite the contrary, the generality of these mechanisms – the fact that economic transactions are used in so many settings – implies that they are extremely effective both for the procurement of resources and for the negotiation of social relations. It would only be surprising if national movements did not use these practices to accomplish the overriding challenge of nation building – stitching together heterogeneous and loosely related groups.

Following this logic, the subsequent chapters trail national entrepreneurs and examine how they exploit these mechanisms, sometimes alone and sometimes in tandem, to create nations. I treat the distinct logics of market exchange and gift giving as both predicaments and opportunities that national entrepreneurs confront when they attempt to enroll diverse groups to the nation. I focus on how national entrepreneurs tinker with these mechanisms in order to generate and maintain national attachments.

3

Gifting the Nation

> A nation is therefore a large-scale solidarity, constituted by the feeling of the sacrifices that one has made in the past and of those that one is prepared to make in the future.
> Ernst Renan, "What is a Nation?"

The idea of gift giving plays a key role in how people understand their relationship to the nation. Members often think of the nation as an entity that commands selfless giving, and respond to national appeals in various ways. The waving of a flag, the singing of the anthem, the bearing of children, and, most notably, the sacrifice of one's life on the battlefield, are often understood as acts of giving to the nation. In diasporic contexts, giving to the nation typically takes monetary form. In all these settings, selfless giving to the nation is considered a patriotic virtue and a testimony to the strength of one's national attachments.

Despite the centrality of the idea of giving in national rhetoric and the self-understanding of members, researchers typically refrain from studying giving to the nation as a constitutive element of the process of nation building and, instead, treat giving to the nation as merely an illustration of the existence of such sentiments (Dillon 2003; Strenski 2003). The paucity of research on gift giving as a nation-building mechanism stems, I believe, from the difficulties involved in transposing to a modern setting a model developed to describe pre-modern societies.

The classical anthropological works on gift giving were developed in small tribal societies. In *The Gift*, for example, Marcel Mauss explains how the ceremonial exchange of gifts constitutes a system of social solidarity (1967). In Mauss's model, reciprocity is absolutely crucial. It is the back-and-forth movement of the gift that gradually generates social ties between the parties. But, in modern philanthropic settings, and also in the context of giving to the nation, giving is typically non-reciprocal. Donors derive moral satisfaction, self-esteem, and sometimes also honor from giving, but they typically do not receive a direct counter-gift from the recipient (Silber 1998). Furthermore, Mauss's model was abstracted from small tribal societies where the imposition of social norms was relatively simple. The imposition of norms in modern settings, and especially at the scale of the nation with its far-flung diaspora, is much harder. Given these differences, trying to apply Mauss's insights to the process of nation building may seem inappropriate.

Trying to impose a strict Maussian perspective on gift giving in a national context is perhaps futile, but treating his work as irrelevant would be hasty. Given the centrality of the idea of giving to the nation in diasporic settings and within the nation-state, it may yet be fruitful to examine how national movements innovate on the practice of gift giving in order to secure desired resources and generate a sense of belonging among members. In such an investigation, the differences outlined above between Mauss's model and the national context serve to sensitize us to the difficulties national entrepreneurs face when they try to create mechanisms of giving to the nation. Thus, the point is not simply to determine whether Mauss's model "explains" national gift giving, but to examine the various practices that national movements develop in order to motivate giving in a context that is drastically different from the one Mauss describes, and to examine how individuals and groups involved in giving to and getting from the nation negotiate the terms of their engagement.[1]

To understand how gift giving is implicated in the making of nations, this chapter explores the Irish and Zionist movements' attempts to secure a flow of money to their respective national struggles from their compatriots in the United States. On the Irish side, this chapter examines the establishment of the Friends of Irish Freedom (FOIF) in 1916 and its fundraising arm – the Irish

Victory Fund (IVF). On the Jewish side, it probes the formation of the United Jewish Appeal (UJA) in 1939 and its growth during the 1940s. The chronological starting points for the analyses are historically and analytically important. The Easter Rising of 1916 signaled the beginning of a violent struggle that led to the creation of the Irish Free State in 1922. In the Jewish case, 1939 marked the beginning of the Holocaust. The Irish-American and Jewish-American communities responded to these events by creating elaborate organizational structures designed to support their fellow compatriots across the ocean. The surge in diaspora activism in the respective communities provides an excellent opportunity to examine the innovations that were introduced in order to engage Irish Americans and Jewish Americans. The investigation seeks to identify and analyze the mechanisms that national entrepreneurs set up in order to allow members of diaspora communities to engage the nation through the giving of gifts.

While the examination reveals deep differences between the Irish and Jewish cases in terms of the level of institutionalization and scale of operation, it also points to important similarities. In order to encourage giving in the absence of direct reciprocity, the Irish and Jewish movements shifted the locus of the giving relationships. Instead of trying to secure a counter-gift from the recipients, the Irish and Jewish philanthropic organizations attempted to spur status competitions among givers. Fundraising depended, to a large extent, on the ability to generate recognition as well as a sense of obligation and satisfaction among a community of givers. The imbalance in the giving of unreciprocated gifts was handled by means of a comparison of the sacrifices demanded from those in the homeland and those in the United States. By highlighting the inconsequential nature of the diaspora contribution, in comparison with giving within the homeland (only money was given by the diaspora, not life itself), the organizers shamed the givers into additional sacrifices. Rather than simply expressing pre-existing sentiments, the construction of these mechanisms allowed Irish Americans and Jewish Americans to contribute to and feel a part of the national community.

Scholars of nationalism often describe nation building as a process through which the differences between members of the nation are rendered somehow irrelevant. Close examination of the Irish and Jewish giftgiving mechanisms, however, reveals an almost opposite trend. Rather than presenting internal differences, that is, differences between members of diaspora communities and other groups in the nation, as extraneous, a key theme in the Irish and Jewish fundraising campaigns was highlighting the differences between the conditions of the Irish and Jews in Ireland and Palestine respectively and in the United States. In comparison with the sacrifices of life, allegedly performed by other groups, the monetary gifts of members of diaspora communities paled. These comparisons tilted the relationships between the two fragments of the nation, created a sense of inadequacy, and served as an effective means to motivate donors to give away more of their resources. Importantly, these comparisons suggest a different model of nation building, one that is based not simply on the marginalization of internal differences but also on a concomitant drawing and erasing of internal differences that generate a sense of unequal commonality.

Gifting Ireland

Prior to the 1920s, many Irish Americans maintained close ties with the Irish national movement. Irish leaders, almost without exception, traveled frequently across the ocean, seeking political and financial support, and their efforts often bore fruit. During the late 1860s, the *Fenian* movement raised almost $730,000 in the United States (McCaffrey 1976: 150). In 1875, O'Donovan Rosa collected some $48,000 for a "Skirmishing Fund" aimed at supporting the bombing of English cities (Brown 1966: 540). Between 1879 and 1882 Irish Americans donated more than $5 million in support of the Irish Land War (Miller 1985). Thus, the Irish national movement relied heavily on contributions from its compatriots in the United States.

Establishing the Friends of Irish Freedom

The late 1910s seemed to be a perfect time for another fundraising campaign in the United States. In Ireland, the Republican party *Sinn Féin* was gathering momentum. The process began with the outbreak of World War I, when John Redmond, the leader of the moderate Irish Parliamentary Party, committed itself to supporting Britain's war efforts. Later, following the Easter Rising of 1916 and the struggle against conscription into the British army, *Sinn Féin* won a landslide victory in the general elections of December 1918.[2] Following their victory, *Sinn Féin* representatives refused to take their seats in the British Parliament and convened, instead, in the Mansion House in Dublin, where they proclaimed they were the lawful Parliament of the Republic of Ireland – the *Dáil Éireann*. Éamon de Valera, the last surviving commander of the Easter Rising, added momentum to this coup when he escaped from a British prison and was anointed by the *Dáil* as the *Príomh Aire*.[3] The Irish Republicans also developed a substantial presence abroad. After the collapse of the Easter Rising, Liam Mellows and Diarmuid Lynch escaped to the United States and became active in Irish-American politics (Greaves 2004). Later, Patrick McCartan and Harry Boland joined them as official envoys of the Republic of Ireland (Fitzpatrick 2003).[4]

In the United States, too, prospects seemed bright. During the late nineteenth and early twentieth centuries, Irish-American nationalists were divided between a minority associated with the *Clan na Gael*, a secretive fraternity that was affiliated with the Irish Republican Brotherhood (IRB) in Ireland, and the popular United Irish League of America (UILA), which supported the Irish Parliamentary Party (Carroll 1978; Golway 1998; Doorley 2005). But if Redmond's support for conscription was contentious in Ireland, in the United States his decision was interpreted as a complete betrayal. Within months the UILA went into a deep crisis. John Devoy, the longtime leader of the *Clan*, and his close associate, Judge Daniel Cohalan,[5] seized the opportunity and organized an "Irish Race Convention" in New York City in March 1916. The convention, attended by more than 2,300 activists and leaders, led to the establishment of the Friends of Irish Freedom, a kind of public front of the *Clan na Gael*, with a mission to "encourage and assist any movement that will tend to bring about the national independence of Ireland."[6] The drama of the Easter Rising, which occurred just six weeks after the first Race Convention, gave the FOIF further opportunity to spread its message (Doorley 2005: 37–46).

Despite the success of the first Race Convention, the FOIF remained partly inactive for several years. This was probably related to the international situation. During World War I, President Wilson increasingly gravitated toward supporting the Allied Forces and in April 1917 the United States joined the war on their side. This development placed Irish Americans in a delicate position. Pursuing an anti-British struggle now ran the risk of seeming unpatriotic. This predicament was not theoretical. At some point, Cohalan himself was accused by the Wilson Administration of collaborating with the Germans (Tansill 1957; Doorley 2005). As a result, during World War I, the FOIF was slow to take off.

When World War I reached an end, Cohalan and his associates hoped to capitalize on the Irish-American contribution to the war effort to press for Ireland's cause. In May 1918, the FOIF convened a second Irish Race Convention. Diarmuid Lynch, the veteran of the Easter Rising, assumed the position of the FOIF's national secretary (Doorley 1995: 135). Instead of trying to supplant existing organizations, the FOIF under Lynch's direction fashioned itself as an umbrella organization, inviting established Irish societies to become affiliates for a nominal annual fee.[7] This federated structure allowed the FOIF to reach sympathetic audiences that heretofore had remained uncoordinated (Lynch and O'Donoghue 1957: 192–198). In addition, Lynch invested huge efforts in creating an updated mailing list not only of branch leaders but of their groups' membership as well. Between late 1917 and early 1919, the FOIF's regular membership grew from less than a thousand to more than thirty thousand members in 204 active branches (Doorley 1995: 310–319).

The third Race Convention in February 1919 marked the emergence of the FOIF as the dominant Irish-American organization of the postwar era. More than 5,000 activists from all over the country gathered in Philadelphia for three days of discussions and celebrations. The FOIF also managed to attract Irish Catholic clergy, who were typically critical of Irish Republicanism due to its support of violence. More than thirty Catholic bishops attended the convention, including the influential Cardinal Gibbons of Baltimore (Doorley 2005). Many former UILA activists, including the former president of the UILA, Michael J. Ryan, attended the conference – this time, as members of the FOIF. For the first time since perhaps the 1880s, the Irish Americans were politically united in an organization that was committed to supporting the Irish national struggle.

Funding the Irish struggle

In order "to carry on the work of pressing Ireland's claim for independence," during the third Race Convention, the FOIF launched the Irish Victory Fund (IVF). The leaders of the FOIF hoped to raise two million dollars, and for that purpose they asked delegates to pledge on behalf of their cities. The *Gaelic American* provided a vivid description of the event:

> The scene during the taking of the pledges was a memorable one. No man or woman who had the privilege of witnessing it will ever forget it. Hurried consultations were held by various delegations and an agreement reached as to the amounts they believed could be collected by an energetic drive. New York, Philadelphia, and Chicago led off with pledges of $150,000 each, and the other cities followed with promises of smaller amounts, but very much larger than had ever been thought of before. As amounts were announced wild cheers shook the building and there was a scene of enthusiasm unparalleled in the history of the National Movement in America. (March 1, 1919)

By the end of the night, the FOIF organizers had collected pledges for more than a million and a half dollars.

Despite the warm-hearted pledges made at the convention, collecting the IVF funds presented a daunting challenge. Lynch explained to IVF volunteers,

> Money does not leap out of purse and pocket. The American public has been called so often in the past two years that a padlock of caution now guards its diminished resources. Not merely the merit of our cause, therefore, but energy combined with well-devised and dignified methods must swell the Fund. (*Gaelic American*, June 14, 1919)

To help set a positive tone for the campaign, the FOIF launched an intensive public relations effort. In millions of leaflets, sticker bumps, and essays, the FOIF emphasized the Irish American contribution to America and the complementary link of American and Irish patriotism (Doorley 1995: 323). A special campaign poster featured a picture of the 69th Regiment, a predominantly Irish-American unit that fought fiercely during World War I (see

Figure 3.1). At the bottom, the poster listed the names and dates of important battles of the Civil War and World War I in which Irish Americans participated. Contribution to the IVF, the poster suggested, was nothing but a repayment of a debt that America owed to Ireland.

Figure 3.1. Irish Victory Drive poster (from an advertisement in the *Gaelic American*, June 28, 1919).

Another key theme in the IVF campaign was the relationships between those who died for Ireland and those still alive. A leaflet distributed in New York, for example, challenged readers:

> In the name of the fathers of American Liberty; in the name of Ireland's martyred dead – Give Now. [Wolfe] Tone died for what we see to-day; [Robert] Emmet's epitaph is ready – shall it be written now? Dublin is hallowed by [Patrick] Pearse's blood. Their spirit lives. Preserve America. Up the Irish Republic. (*Gaelic American*, July 12, 1919)

The grave sacrifice of Ireland's national martyrs served as a foil to challenge Irish Americans to make the more ordinary sacrifice of giving money. The IVF campaign in Philadelphia struck similar chords:

> Easter week should be a heritage of holy memories ... [The Easter Rising] martyrs have passed upward to take their places beside that of dauntless champions of freedom – immortal on earth as they are in heaven. They gave their lives for Ireland's freedom ... Will we raise this amount [$40,000] for democracy, for human happiness, for unfettered knowledge, for lofty civilization, for the life of Ireland? (*Gaelic American*, April 12, 1919)

In both examples, the IVF organizers presented the giving of one's life to the nation as an act that created a personal debt among those still alive. The adequate response to such indebtedness, the ads suggested, was giving money for the same cause. Rather than simply asserting the unity of the "sea-divided Gaels," the IVF campaign actually called attention to the differences between the different fragments of the nation, while in the same breath emphasizing their relatedness.

Given the federated structure of the FOIF, the IVF drive followed different trajectories depending on local constellations. In Philadelphia and Buffalo, IVF committees worked closely with supportive clergy to raise their quotas. Local IVF committees designated Easter Week as a special "Self-Denial" week and canvassing teams organized along parish lines. Each collector carried a card, bearing her or his name, certified as official collector by the signature of the local priest. The close cooperation with clergy helped recruit volunteers and increased public confidence in the drive (*Gaelic American*, July 19, 1919).

In New York City, the existence of Irish Patriotic and Benevolent Associations (P&B Associations) provided other opportunities for fundraising. Since the late nineteenth century, P&B Associations, usually organized on the basis of county of origin in Ireland, sponsored Sunday socials that included athletic competitions as well as dancing and singing (Funchion 1983). In 1919, inspired by the FOIF's appeal, many P&B Associations contributed the proceeds from their events to the IVF and allowed volunteers to solicit donations during the events. The Mayo Men's P&B Association, for example, announced that "[e]very good Irishman and woman is cordially invited to attend the games and while spending a pleasant afternoon in amusement, to aid in raising funds for the benefit of Ireland" (*Irish Advocate*, May 24, 1919). The combination of pleasure and a good cause helped raise money for the IVF and secured attendance at the games.

Collecting money from the public was only half the challenge. Lynch and his associates also had to ensure that the donations would actually be sent to FOIF headquarters. The problem was not only one of preventing dishonest organizers from taking advantage of Irish-American generosity and keeping the money for themselves, but also of finding ways to discipline earnest activists:

> Devoted workers in the cause [Lynch explained], seeing the pressing need for Irish propaganda – are eager to apply a portion of the Fund to good work in their own communities. But no army can win by letting the various regiments fight the enemy immediately in front of them without regard to the situation on the battle-front as a whole . . . Only armies in which co-operation rules gain victories. So it is essential that all collections be made with the sole purpose of increasing the resources in the hands of the National Council of the Friends of the Irish Freedom. (*Gaelic American*, August 23, 1919)

Securing the IVF funds necessitated putting a lid on too enthusiastic activists who wished to use the IVF proceeds for local purposes. To fight fraud, the FOIF instructed the Local Councils of the FOIF, wherever these existed, to select Finance Committees composed of "prominent citizens" that would oversee the collection and handling of the funds.[8] Lynch also urged IVF committees to print special pledge cards, issue receipts to contributors, and clearly identify authorized collectors with a special badge (*Gaelic American*, July 12, 1919; July 19, 1919).

During the months of 1919, donations gradually trickled in and by August, Lynch and his associates secured more than a million

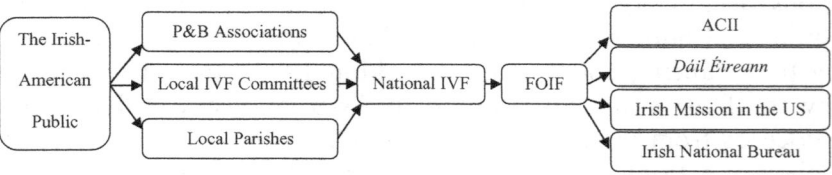

Figure 3.2. The organizational structure of Irish-American fundraising.

dollars in donations.⁹ The success of the IVF allowed the FOIF to expand its operations (Doorley 1995: 159). In March 1919, the FOIF assumed financial and administrative control of the Irish National Bureau in Washington, using it to lobby members of Congress, journalists, and foreign legations. The FOIF also established the American Commission on Irish Independence (ACII) and the three members of the commission, Frank P. Walsh, Eduard F. Dunne, and Michael Ryan,[10] traveled to the Peace Conference in Paris. In addition to pressing for a special hearing regarding Ireland's plight, the ACII provided financial assistance for a small delegation that the *Dáil Éireann* had sent to the conference (Carroll 1985). Thus, by mid-1919, due to the success of the IVF, the FOIF was able to lobby for Ireland not only in New York and Washington but also at the all-important Paris Peace Conference.

Gifting Israel

During the late nineteenth and early twentieth centuries, large numbers of Jews left Eastern Europe in search of a better future. The vast majority of these Jews chose the United States as their destination. Relatively few migrated to Palestine. The Zionists in Palestine were inspired by national and socialist ideologies. They fashioned themselves as productive and self-sufficient Jews, developed unique collectivist lifestyles, and believed that the duty of every Jew was to make *aliya* and help rebuild the homeland (Kimmerling 1983; Liebman and Don-Yihya 1983).[11] Jewish Americans, in contrast, saw the United States as their home and embraced American ideals (Karp 1976; Goren 1982, 1999; Hertzberg 1998). While some Jewish Americans identified with the Zionist movement, they by and large believed that the duty of settlement in Palestine was reserved for Jews from less fortunate countries, not for themselves.[12] Differences aside, after the turn of the twentieth century Jewish Americans had been the main benefactors of Jewish philanthropies and of the Zionist movement. In spite of their ideal of self-sufficiency, the Zionists in Palestine relied on Jewish-American dollars to purchase land and arms and to support institutions of higher education, welfare projects, and various political parties (Halperin 1985; Stock 1987).

Sponsoring the Jewish cause

Between the two World Wars, the major Jewish-American organizations responsible for helping Jews outside the United States were the American Jewish Joint Distribution Committee (JDC) and the United Palestine Appeal (UPA). The JDC catered to the needs of Jewish refugees all over the world, especially in Europe. The UPA, on the other hand, provided support for the Zionists in Palestine.[13] In 1939, in response to a growing concern for Europe's Jewry, the JDC and the UPA – joined by the National Refugee Service (NRS),[14] an organization that helped Jewish refugees in the United States – established the United Jewish Appeal for Refugees and Overseas Needs (UJA). A unified, non-partisan campaign, they hoped, would reduce campaign costs and increase the overall collection (Stock 1987).[15]

To organize the drive in different localities around the country, the UJA teamed up with Jewish Federations and Welfare Funds, confederations of social service and educational agencies. After deducting a portion of the collection to meet local needs, the Federations sent the rest of the money to the UJA, which distributed the funds according to an agreed-upon formula (see Figure 3.3). Arguments about the distribution of funds between the three organizations (JDC, UPA, and NRS) surfaced almost every year (Stock 1987: 110–114).[16] The Zionist members of the UJA Executive Committee demanded that more of the collection be sent to Palestine. The non-Zionist committee members insisted that the JDC must be given priority. Given the conditions in Europe in the early 1940s, the JDC indeed appropriated the lion's share of the collection, but the combined drive was beneficial for the UPA as well. In 1938, the JDC, UPA, and NRS independently raised less than $7 million in the aggregate, but in 1939 the UJA raised

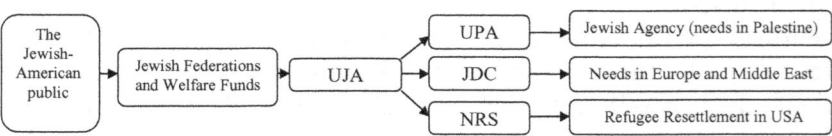

Figure 3.3. The organizational structure of Jewish-American fundraising.[17]

$13,877,477 (Keyserling 1956). Furthermore, through association with the UJA, the UPA reached non-Zionist audiences, including many wealthy philanthropists who formerly had been unmoved by Zionist appeals (Halperin 1985: 201; Stock 1987: 101).

During the 1940s, the UJA developed into a sophisticated, bureaucratic fund-raising machine. The impetus for this transformation was probably the disappointing results of the UJA drive of 1940. Although overseas needs quadrupled, the collection remained almost without change. Isidor Coons and Henry Montor, the executive vice chairmen of the UJA,[18] argued that the problem was one of donor fatigue and despair:

> The wholesale suffering of vast populations, including millions of refugees of faiths other than the Jewish, creates a feeling of futility and resignation in the mind of the average potential contributor.[19]

With proper organization, they suggested, contributions could increase substantially without causing any deprivation to donors.

The dominant figure behind the growth of the UJA was Henry Montor, the executive vice chairman, who also served as the executive director of the UPA.[20] To understand the potential of the campaign, Montor commissioned a study from Eli Ginzberg, a young Columbia University economist. Ginzberg estimated that, collectively, America's Jews enjoyed an annual income of $3.8 billion. Based on this figure, he argued that American Jews contributed "a very small part of their total income to the UJA" (Stock 1987: 120). To improve the organization of drives, Montor created a dense network of salaried field representatives. While the campaign ultimately depended on a massive participation of volunteers, the field representatives helped volunteers to organize effectively, oversaw the collection of pledges, and secured the remittance of funds to the UJA headquarters.[21]

One of the main tasks of field representatives was to create a reliable database of the Jewish community. For each local community, the UJA field representatives prepared a form that contained information regarding its size and socioeconomic makeup, and a breakdown of the donations according to size.[22] Creating this database required hard work and diligence, but the results were extremely useful. Robert Herman, the national coordinator of the field operations, explained that "a simple analysis of this type shows up basic weaknesses in many campaigns and points the way to sound planning for a successful appeal."[23] Perhaps even more importantly, the data helped the UJA in the task of setting challenging quotas. In general, local activists were reluctant to adopt high quotas and relied on the previous year's collection to calculate how much they could raise in the coming year. Detailed community-level data allowed field representatives to spark intercommunal rivalries by comparing one community to similarly composed but better-performing communities around the country. These comparisons persuaded organizers to endorse quotas that were previously considered unrealistic.[24]

To approach donors, the UJA divided the population in each locality into four brackets. The super-wealthy, typically not more than a few hundred donors, were invited to exclusive national events at luxurious resorts. At the local level, big donors were invited to special gala dinners.[25] In national and local big-gift events, the key method was the "card-calling" technique. After dinner, one of the organizers read aloud names from specially prepared cards and announced each person's donation from the previous year. Upon hearing their names, the donors would stand up and announce their donations for the coming year. Essentially, this technique allowed the organizers to generate maximum visibility to the act of giving. At the right moment, all eyes centered upon the donors, discouraging meager giving and providing the donors with an opportunity to display both their wealth and generosity. To set the standard for the donations, the organizers always pre-solicited a few individuals and persuaded them to increase their yearly donation substantially. These donors were the first to be called, and their generosity forced others to follow suit.[26] Donors often complained that the card-calling method was tasteless and coercive, but its effectiveness was unmatched (Goldin 1976: 179). With proper organization, "Big-Gift" events, which typically included less than 10% of the donors, yielded more than 80% of the campaigns' total receipts.[27]

Approaching the intermediary group of donors required a different strategy. The organizers divided these donors along lines of occupation and approached them in small parlor meetings. The goal of the division was to create socially meaningful groups. Thus, owners of retail stores were often subdivided by type of commodity and area of operation so as to create small groups of business owners who shared business ties. The UJA's 1950 campaign in Boston, for example, included more than a hundred different luncheons and dinners – including a special dinner for those in the poultry industry, ladies' underwear, and more (Raphael 1982: 41–42). This grouping prompted donors to prove themselves equal or superior to their peers.

Finally, to approach small donors, which were the vast majority of the population, local UJA committees organized canvassing teams that approached donors in their homes. Although the monetary value of these campaigns was small, Montor insisted that soliciting donations from the entire community was important because it helped generate enthusiasm and a sense of shared communal responsibility.[28]

Montor also experimented with the use of new forms of media. Instead of focusing on Jewish newspapers, the UJA advertised its campaign in venues like *Newsweek* and *Life* magazine. This strategy allowed the UJA to tap the generosity of Jews and perhaps even non-Jews who were not previously affiliated with Jewish organizations. The UJA also produced and distributed voice recordings and short movies to be used in small parlor meetings.[29] The use of sound recordings and movies standardized the UJA's message, ensuring that the work and needs of all three constituent organizations of the UJA would be presented, regardless of the biases of individual organizers.[30]

The catastrophic news from Europe gave the UJA ample material to work with. But this material had to be handled with care. Aware of the despair and resignation that affected many contributors, the UJA crafted emotionally charged appeals while insisting that the donations actually made a difference. For that purpose, the UJA quantified the effect of donations. A letter from the 1939 campaign, for example, explained:

> It costs six cents a day to feed a Jewish child in Poland. If six cents means the preservation of a life, that is surely little enough, but it's six cents for one meal, for one day, for one child. The days of want go on and the ranks of the hungry multiply.... Think of it, your contribution can keep scores, and, perhaps hundreds of children alive until this nightmare of cruelty is brought to an end. We have the responsibility, we have the power of life and death over these tragedy-ridden human beings.

Assigning monetary cost to the saving of a single child allowed donors to take on the role of lifesaver and become a "big man" of the Jewish world (Sahlins 1963). In a flyer for the 1941 campaign, a pair of hands literally lifts two refugees, a mother and a daughter. The caption read: "The Hands That Write The Checks Can Save Them" (see Figure 3.4). Toward the end of the 1940s, the UJA campaigns centered increasingly on Palestine, both as a destination for the refugees and as a place of national renewal (Stock 1987). Yet again, the UJA repeatedly emphasized the responsibility of donors and the effectiveness of generous donations. A leaflet of the 1946 campaign simply read, "Give and they live – Don't and they die."[31]

The US Internal Revenue Service (IRS) provided the UJA with another selling point. "Under the present tax rates," a UJA leaflet explained, "Uncle Sam 'contributes' a very substantial share of the gifts made by individuals to such causes as the United Jewish Appeal . . ." Individuals with a taxable income of $10,000 who contribute $1,500, for example, would receive a tax deduction of $510. Individuals in the highest tax bracket (over $200,000), received a tax deduction for 88% of their donation.[32] On the one

Figure 3.4. A flyer of the 1941 UJA Pledge Collection Campaign (CZA/A371/516).

hand, emphasizing the magnitude of the tax deduction reminded donors of the actual size of their sacrifice, clarifying that big donations effectively cost them less than the actual sum donated. On the other hand, it made the donation seem more worthwhile by suggesting that each dollar given was in effect matched by more dollars from the US government.

Like the Irish IVF, the UJA leaflets repeatedly compared the sacrifices demanded from different groups of Jews while emphasizing the links between them. A special brochure of the UJA of Greater New York, for example, asked readers: "How much does *he* give?" The inside of the brochure explains:

> "He" is an Israeli, any Israeli. Chances are he earns between $100 and $125 a month for himself and his family to live on.
> - He pays the highest taxes in the world, twice as much as we do.
> - He gives his savings, wedding rings, prize possessions to raise extra funds for defense and housing...
> - He risks his life daily, working in the fields under enemy gunsights or guarding a lonely settlement at night.
>
> He can't give much, but he gives **big!**...[33]

Sometimes, these comparisons verged on a shaming campaign. A 1949 letter to volunteers was explicitly critical of the Jewish-American community:

> On the day that the State of Israel introduced its full-scale austerity program so that its citizens could absorb more immigration, the United Jewish Appeal was $24,652,000 behind in its cash collections... The Jews in Israel are giving a model of self-denial on behalf of their fellow-Jews that should be exemplary. At the very least, it would remove any vestige of belief on the part of American Jews that too much is being asked of them.[34]

Reminding Jewish Americans of the relative ease of their situation in comparison with the hardships undergone by other Jews was an effective means of inducing larger donations.[35] Interestingly, instead of simply telling donors "we are one" (Steinberg 1998), the UJA engaged in simultaneous drawing and erasure of the distinctions between those in the homeland, who allegedly were scarified and risked much more, and the Jewish Americans, who were only required to open their purse strings.

As in the Irish case, translating big-hearted pledges into cash was a challenge in its own right. For that purpose, local communities created special pledge-collection committees. These committees were responsible for keeping track of payments and for approaching delinquent donors – first in a letter and then, if that was not enough, by a personal visit. Committees also published lists of donors in the local newspapers. Montor insisted that no new pledges be accepted from those who failed to redeem their previous year's pledge. The combination of punctual reminders and the threat of exclusion from subsequent UJA events was effective. In some cases, the "shrinkage rate," that is, the difference between the pledged amount and the actual cash collected, was as low as 1.5%.[36]

A crucial and particularly challenging part of the field representatives' work was making sure that local organizers actually sent the UJA's allotment to the headquarters in New York.[37] Local Jewish Federations often insisted on keeping a reserve of funds for unanticipated needs and in order to compensate for the "shrinkage" that occurred in the translation of pledges into cash. Herman insisted that field representatives look over the books of the campaign and be firm on sending any such reserves to the UJA headquarters without delay. To embolden field representatives, he reminded them that donors would be the first to resent having their money set aside for the future. If Federation leaders insist on keeping reserves, he maintained, this fact must be made public.[38]

The 1946 "Year of Survival" campaign was, perhaps, Montor's greatest accomplishment in the UJA. Instead of the regular local kickoff functions, big donors from all over the country gathered in Washington, DC. Montor informed the invitees ahead of time that no gift under $10,000 would be accepted (Raphael 1982: 23). The 350 participants met a contingent of Holocaust survivors from the Bergen-Belsen concentration camp. The survivors' testimonies energized the attendees and persuaded them to adopt a campaign goal of $100 million – more than twice the previous year's goal. Reaching this audacious goal forced the UJA to modify its fundraising techniques. "Card-calling" was effective at generating a gradual increase in the size of gifts, but this method, Montor realized, discouraged exceptional generosity. Weary of having to match their donation in 1947, donors would be reluctant to give huge sums, even in times of exceptional emergency. In order to assure unencumbered generosity, therefore, the UJA promised that this year's contributions would not "be used as a wedge for a standard for future giving."[39] The combination of Jewish-American shock in the face of the Holocaust, along with the UJA's techniques, resulted in a collection of $101 million – almost three times more than any annual sum raised by the UJA before.

In 1947, given the conditions in Europe, and notwithstanding its 1946 promise, the UJA adopted the goal of raising $170 million, and once again the community responded with an outpouring, this time of $115 million.[40] Looking for another record, in 1948 Montor persuaded Henry Morgenthau, the former US Secretary of Treasury and probably the most prominent Jewish-American figure of the time, to lead a campaign for $250 million. 1948 was also the first year in which Israel clearly came to occupy the center of the campaign. Key speakers were brought from Israel, and a TWA airplane emblazoned with the UJA's slogan, "Star of Hopes," took key leaders and big donors on a four-week tour of Israel and Europe. The tour helped persuade the leaders of the Jewish Federations to borrow large sums from local banks, using wealthy donors as guarantors, and to advance this money to Israel without delay (Goldin 1976: 195). With the aid of the dramatic events in Israel, the UJA raised $150 million.[41]

Engineering National Giving

Close examination of the IVF and UJA drives provides a textured illustration of the problem of giving to the nation. While the differences between the drives were deep, the predicaments that the FOIF and the UJA dealt with were similar. Unlike the gift exchange that Mauss studied, the decisive characteristic of the IVF and the UJA drives was that they did not provide a venue for a transmission of a counter-gift to donors. In addition, the scale of the operation and the heterogeneity and spread of the respective diaspora communities imposed a daunting challenge. In other words, both the Irish and Zionist movements had to construct large-scale mechanisms of non-reciprocated giving.

However, the similarity between the IVF and UJA should not be overstated. When one examines the circumstances and details of the drives, glaring differences immediately become apparent. First, the historical political circumstances within which these two organizations operated were radically different. Once the United States had sided with Great Britain in World War I, a struggle directed against Britain became illegitimate in the United States (Carroll 1978; Doorley 2005). In contrast, during and after World War II, acting on behalf of Jewish refugees in Europe and on behalf of those in Israel was generally approved of in the United States. This approval had a tangible consequence: the IRS recognized the UJA as a non-profit-making organization for tax-deduction purposes. In addition to providing a huge monetary incentive for donors, this recognition signaled to potential contributors that the US government accepted the UJA as a legitimate cause.

Perhaps even more importantly, the organization of the Irish-American and Jewish-American communities was on an entirely different scale. The Irish community, while fervent in its support for Ireland, relied on loosely coordinated societies that operated almost entirely on a voluntary basis. As a consequence, the IVF was to a large extent a campaign created ad hoc. The point is not that the Irish-American community lacked a permanent organizational basis. Irish-Catholic parishes served as the backbone for many Irish communal activities. However, these parishes, as a general rule, did not support the Irish Republican movement. In contrast, Jewish communities around the country, even prior to the establishment of the UJA, developed a permanent and highly professionalized system of Jewish Federations.[42] This system, and the UJA, it must be emphasized, were not organized around the Jewish national cause, but around a general sense of Jewish humanitarian responsibility (Liebman and Cohen 1990). Regardless of the ideological leanings of the Federations, however, the existence of such infrastructure provided the UJA with a convenient base for operation in local communities.

The difference in organizational structure between the Irish-American and Jewish-American communities was particularly consequential because of the voluntary and non-reciprocal character of the IVF and the UJA. In gift exchange, the size of gifts is largely determined by previous gifts. That is, the first gift contains information that allows the receiver to match the expectations of the giver. The absence of reciprocity, therefore, posed a problem of how to determine or set the bar for an appropriate gift. In such a situation, knowing the potential pool of donors was particularly important, because it allowed fundraisers to set quotas that challenged but did not overwhelm donors. The differences in this respect between the IVF and UJA were glaring. For Lynch and his associates, the "Irish-American community" was for all practical purposes an invisible entity. The leaders of the FOIF regularly claimed to be speaking on behalf of millions of Irish Americans, but they only had a vague understanding of where these Irish Americans lived, what they did for a living, and how much money they could potentially spare on the Irish cause. The magnitude of needs in Ireland was equally unclear. In contrast, the UJA commissioned special studies to estimate Jewish needs worldwide and compiled detailed databases that contained not only information regarding the socioeconomic status of Jewish communities in hundreds of locations around the country but also meticulous lists of important donors, their occupations, and their past donations. No wonder that the UJA leaders were better able to tailor their demands to different groups within the community. They literally knew their clientele better.

A crucial element of the gift systems that Mauss and other researchers describe is the status competition between the parties involved (Malinowski 1920; Sahlins 1963; Mauss 1967). The giving of a gift creates a debt on the side of the recipient. Failing to give back an equal or larger gift dishonors the receiving side. But the IVF and UJA were almost by definition unidirectional.

In order to foster an obligation to give in the absence of direct reciprocity or strong normative regulation, the IVF and the UJA attempted to ignite status competition among givers.[43] In effect, they shifted the loci of the giving relationships. Instead of securing a counter-gift from the receivers, the leaders of the Irish and Jewish organizations used the immediate context of giving to encourage giving (for "donor-side" philanthropic strategies, see Ostrander and Schervish 1991). Diarmuid Lynch, for example, regularly listed in the *Gaelic American* the names of big donors and IVF activists who organized successful campaigns. In addition to increasing confidence in the drive by creating some measure of transparency, the honor of being listed as a contributor, he hoped, would enhance generosity. Montor and his colleagues also magnified the visibility of giving, and the UJA also increased the satisfaction associated with gift giving by providing tangible proofs of the lifesaving effects of the donations. Instead of working on the relationships between givers and receivers, the IVF and the UJA attempted to reshape the interests and preferences of the givers.

Both the IVF and the UJA shifted the loci of the giving relationships and focused on the community of givers, but they did so under different circumstances. In the Irish case, each local community conducted its own campaign with little help or supervision from the headquarters. The IVF remained, therefore, deeply dependent on the acumen of local activists and on existing organizational structures like the church in some places, or different P&B Associations in New York City. The settings provided by these organizations were not always conducive to triggering generosity contests. The UJA, too, relied on existing institutions for approaching the public, but it was able to shape the encounter with the Jewish public and manipulate the visibility of giving so as to ignite generosity competitions at the inter-communal level and between donors. Community-level data allowed field organizers to spark generosity rivalries between communities. The exclusivity of big-gift events motivated donors to give more money so as to purchase the opportunity to become members of and mingle with the communal elite. Big-gift events themselves were meticulously engineered as venues for displaying one's personal economic achievements and generosity. Furthermore, the institutional position of the UJA allowed it to impose sanctions upon the delinquent donors.

The absence of tangible return for handing over the donations also complicated the task of centralizing the collection. The point is not merely that corrupt organizers were tempted to keep donations for themselves. Rather, in both the Irish and Jewish cases, the goals of fundraising campaigns were always broad and underspecified. Slogans like "support the Irish Cause," or helping millions of "Jews in peril of destruction" could cover a huge variety of activities – from local campaigns aimed at particular personalities deemed "anti-Irish," to smuggling weapons. Having a very limited control over the different IVF committees around the country, Lynch regularly listed the sums that were sent from each committee in the *Gaelic American*.[44] This transparency, he hoped, would motivate organizers to cooperate and assure donors of the safe handling of their money; however, up until the very end of the drive, Lynch had no exact list of the organizers across the country, and his ability to impose sanctions on delinquent organizers was obviously limited.[45] The UJA, with its network of paid field representatives, was in a much better position to ensure that the funds collected – not all of them, but a known portion – would actually be sent to the headquarters.

Engineering National Attachments

The differences between the IVF and the UJA were manifested in the amounts raised by these respective fundraising projects. Whereas the IVF of 1919 raised a total of $1,005,080, the UJA, in 1946 alone, raised more than $100 million. Even when one controls for the differences in the value of dollars in 1919 and 1946 and the unequal class positions of these communities, these differences are astonishing.[46] But it would be a grave mistake to focus solely on the financial performance of the IVF and UJA. The transfer of money is also a medium through which actors negotiate and shape their relations (Zelizer 1994). Therefore, it makes sense to examine the UJA and IVF also as mechanisms that reshaped the respective communities and affected their relationships with the recipients of the donations across the ocean.

Numerous scholars have commented on the centrality of philanthropy in Irish-American and Jewish-American communal life (Carroll 1978, 2002; Raphael 1982; Stock 1987; Doorley 1995; 2005; Elazar 1996). Typically, however, scholars depict the outpouring of Irish-American and Jewish-American donations as simply a reaction to dramatic events in their respective homelands. The IVF and UJA, from this perspective, were merely an expression of already existing sentiments that found expression in times of national emergency.[47] Such a perspective, I believe, radically underestimates the productive work of these organizations. First, the IVF and UJA played a major role in construing the Easter Rising and the Holocaust, respectively, as events of unprecedented magnitude and importance. The point, of course, is not to belittle or question the importance of these events but to suggest that even a catastrophe like the Holocaust becomes an efficacious tool of mobilization only within particular organizational contexts. It was the work of the IVF and the UJA, in other words, that turned these events into a call for action.

More importantly, during the late 1910s and the 1940s, respectively, the IVF and the UJA, perhaps more than any other organizations, provided millions of Irish Americans and Jewish Americans, respectively, with an opportunity to engage in meaningful national action. Through their events, Irish-American and Jewish-American organizers and donors were able to visualize the nation as a unity with a history, needs, and destiny. Through the UJA and IVF events, the nation came to life; it became something that Irish Americans and Jewish Americans could take responsibility for and pride in. In other words, the IVF and UJA events provided members of the Irish and Jewish diaspora with an institutional scaffolding within which members could make sense of their position within the nation (Brubaker et al. 2004, 2006).

This point becomes clear once we examine again the way IVF and UJA ads addressed their potential donors: "what will you give to the work of Easter week? Will the Hibernians of Philadelphia contribute $40,000 to make the dream of Easter week come true?" (*Gaelic American*, April 12, 1919). The UJA's publicity manual of 1940 similarly instructed speakers to present the campaign as a test of the Jewish-American community.[48] The IVF and UJA challenged potential donors to prove their belonging by engaging in giving to the nation. To the extent that these challenges were meaningful to donors – and the response thereto, in the number of donors and the amounts given suggests that the challenge was meaningful – giving to the nation served as a proof to oneself and others that the donor was indeed a member of the nation. Using the tangible act of giving, donors could tell themselves a story about their own place in the Irish or Jewish nation. Viewed from this perspective, philanthropic giving is not just an expression of existing ties but a hook on which individuals and groups could clarify their position vis-à-vis the nation to others and for themselves. By giving to the Irish or Jewish nation, donors became more securely attached to their nation.

If gift giving serves to enroll potential members in the nation, it is worthwhile to examine the type of membership that this practice generates. A theme that repeats itself in both the IVF and the UJA campaigns is that of comparative sacrifice. That is, in urging potential donors to make additional sacrifices, the IVF and UJA compared the sacrifices demanded from different members of the nation. In the ad quoted above, for example, the organizers of the IVF campaign in Philadelphia challenged donors:

> In Easter week (1916) a handful of heroes threw their precious lives onto the scale of Irish freedom – remembering that they gave all that God gave them to give – that when the hour was darkest and when the centuries dream of Ireland was melting into gloom, their dauntless spirits shone alone like glorious stars. Then the heart of the race beat high, the ancient spirit was seen to be unbroken, the blood of the people still a blood of warriors... what will you give to the work of Easter week? (*Gaelic American*, April 12, 1919)

The much graver giving in Ireland served to incite the Irish of Philadelphia to give more money. The UJA used similar comparisons to motivate donors:

> [Here in the US,] ... nobody shoots at us. There is no barbed wire coiled and glinting in our streets. We sleep without the abrupt staccato of a Sten gun shattering the night's stillness. Our busses are not armored, and we can travel from Newark to Philly or from 'Frisco to L.A. without death lurking behind every tree... Five, six thousand miles away from the bullets in Jerusalem, in Tel Aviv, from the lonely boy with his rifle under the pale moon... Yes, but we are together... The whole building, fighting, frontline Yishuv[49] is counting on us. Sure, we carry newspapers to work instead of grenades. Sure we never feel the sickening thud of a bullet. But we've got a frontline, and we cannot desert it or go AWOL for a minute for it's the one and the only way we can fight and build side by side with them.[50]

In comparison with the sacrifices of those in the homeland, this ad suggests, members of diaspora communities are required to sacrifice little.

The comparison between the giving of life and the giving of money served the IVF and the UJA as a means to cajole the Irish-American and Jewish-American public into making additional contributions. It is important, however, to note that the gap between these two modes of engaging the nation cannot really be closed. Money is alienable; it can be accumulated and be given away without affecting the giver. Life, in contrast, is radically inalienable. Given this fundamental difference, no matter how much money one gives, monetary donations can never equal the contribution of the national martyr. Therefore, comparing the gift of money and the gift of life generated a permanent gap – the giving of money is always deficient in relation to the giving of life. In comparison with those who died for the nation, all those still alive are condemned to experience a compromised and attenuated membership. Thus, the IVF and UJA served to enroll Irish Americans and Jewish Americanss into a position of attenuated and deeply ambivalent membership in their respective nations.

Our discussion of the difference between monetary gifts and the gift of life points to an interesting paradox. The construction of monetary giving as a mechanism that helps bind disparate communities to the nation rests on the concomitant blurring and drawing of boundaries within the nation. In the ad above, the UJA drew a sharp distinction between two groups of Jews, only in order to immediately fold them together using the metaphor of a (military and economic) frontline. The unbridgeable gap between the giving of money and the giving of life – and the guilt that it can induce among those still alive – creates a tension that national entrepreneurs exploit to press donors to give more money. It is as if the IVF and UJA leaders had told their supporters to "Give and keep giving all you can (time, money, effort, influence) because you are implicated in a struggle for which others like you have given an unmatchable gift: their lives." The mechanism, therefore, is to point out an unbridgeable gap in one instant, but to suggest in the next instant a way to reduce that gap, and to proclaim it as everyone's duty to attempt that reduction.

Scholars of nationalism often describe the process of nation building as one of homogenization, or at least one of generating a sense of belonging to an egalitarian community (Gellner 1983; Anderson 1991). Equipped with a critical perspective, researchers quickly point out that, in practice, the nation is hierarchically differentiated. Not everyone enjoys the same status of membership in the nation (the case of diaspora vs. homeland communities illustrates this hierarchical differentiation well). Typically, however, scholars treat the inequalities that exist within the nation as obstacles that nation builders overcome by representing the nation as an undifferentiated unity. But a close look at how the IVF and the UJA addressed their potential donors reveals something different. The enrollment of Irish Americans and Jewish Americans did not rely only on the presentation of the nation as a unified cultural whole but on a double movement in which differences between homeland and diaspora communities were first articulated and then folded into unity. The IVF and UJA literature repeatedly challenged potential donors to recognize the differences between themselves and other members in the nation, who allegedly gave much more, while stressing the overarching unity of the nation. Instead of stressing the "identicality" of all those lumped under the national banner, the IVF and UJA emphasized the differences between members of the nation and only then subsumed those elements into the nation. A delicate tension between being alike and being different and less of a member was essential for the successful operation of the mechanism of diasporic national giving.

4

National Gift Giving in Crises

Despite the impressive results of the Irish Victory Fund (IVF) in 1919 and the tremendous growth of the United Jewish Appeal (UJA) during the 1940s, toward the end of 1919 and in the late 1940s, respectively, the relations between the Irish and Irish Americans on the one hand, and the Israelis and Jewish Americans, on the other, experienced severe crises. These parallel crises were related, first, to the nature of the fundraising method used to extract diaspora resources – that is, to the mechanism of diaspora gift giving – and, second, to disagreements regarding the rights and obligations associated with membership in the nation. Believing that their donations were essentially an act of generosity, the leaders of the Friends of Irish Freedom (FOIF) and the Jewish Federations and Welfare Funds, the organizations that actually collected the IVF and UJA funds, felt entitled to keep at least some of the money for domestic needs and demanded some control over the use of the funds in the homeland. The homeland leaders, in contrast, saw the donations of their compatriots in the United States as an insufficient contribution to the national common good. Furthermore, the Irish-American and Jewish-American donations, they believed, were given to them, and not to the self-appointed leaders of the FOIF and the UJA. That these leaders dared keep some of the donations and that they demanded a voice in determining the use of the rest in the homeland was, from the perspective of homeland leaders, unacceptable.

Close examination of the parallel crises of the Irish and Zionist fundraising mechanisms provides a fine-grained illustration of the challenge of bringing different groups, in this case, the homeland and diaspora communities, to cooperate and contribute to the national project.

The Crisis of the Irish Victory Fund

Despite near-unanimous support for Irish independence on both sides of "the pond," coming to an agreement between the Irish and Irish Americans on how to carry out the struggle proved difficult. The success of the IVF, which allowed the FOIF to expand its activities, gave rise to disagreements over matters of policy and the control and allocation of the money.

Believing that the United States, especially after World War I, would play a decisive role in determining Ireland's fate, the FOIF leaders geared their struggle toward the American administration and public opinion. John Devoy and Judge Daniel Cohalan, the leaders of the FOIF and the secretive fraternity *Clan na Gael*, lobbied for Ireland's "self-determination."[1] Devoy explained his rationale as follows:

> The term Self-Determination [which Wilson had used to justify the United States involvement in the war] has caught them [the American people], and holding it constantly up to him [Wilson] is the best means of getting him to do something. Recognition of the Irish Republic he could very easily refuse, but making good his oft-repeated words is something of a different kind. He promised Self-Determination to all peoples; why should he deny it to Ireland?[2]

From Devoy's perspective, using the term "self-determination" entailed no substantive compromise. It was simply a clever way of locking Wilson into his pre-peace promises.

The FOIF was also deeply concerned about Wilson's plan to enter the League of Nations. The key problem with the League, from the FOIF's perspective, was hidden in Article X of the Covenant. That article stipulated that "members of the League undertake to respect and preserve as against external aggression the territorial integrity and existing political independence of all

Members of the League." Article X, Cohalan suspected, guaranteed the territorial integrity of England and therefore also the denial of Ireland's freedom. Furthermore, Cohalan feared that Article X could also compel the United States to help England in suppressing the rebellion in Ireland.[3]

The Irish Republican leaders shared the FOIF's assessment regarding the importance of the United States for the Irish struggle. Harry Boland, one of the leaders of the Irish Republican Brotherhood and a member of the *Dáil Éireann*, who later became a "special envoy" of the Republic of Ireland in the United States, explained, "I am not a prophet, but I am a student of international politics, and we know England's power at present has been built upon holding the balance of power in Europe – but now America has the 'strong hand'" (in Fitzpatrick 2003: 113). But members of the Irish mission, along with their close ally, Joseph McGarrity, a *Clan* leader from Philadelphia, were concerned about what they saw as the vagueness of the term "self-determination."[4] The problem, explained Patrick McCartan, who carried the title of a "special emissary" of the Republic, was that every "conservative in Ireland . . . will do his utmost to interpret Self-Determination as a Colonial Home Rule" (1932: 98).[5] They therefore insisted that the FOIF demand from the United States government nothing short of official recognition of the Irish Republic. In addition, the Irish leaders were not disposed against the League of Nations and, in fact, in early 1919 the *Dáil Éireann* expressed interest in joining it as an independent nation.

Thus, despite their mutual commitment to Irish nationalism, the FOIF and the Irish Republican leaders differed on strategy. Many Irish-American historians interpret these disagreements as a sign that by the late 1910s the Irish Americans had already grown apart from their compatriots across the Atlantic (Ward 1969; Cronin 1972; Carroll 1978; Fallows 1979; Miller 1985; Coogan 1995; Fitzpatrick 2003; Greaves 2004; Doorley 2005). It is important, however, not to impose the wisdom of hindsight on the past and not to exaggerate the depths of these disagreements. When Éamon de Valera, the President of the Republic of Ireland, arrived in the United States in June 1919, McCartan and his associates informed him about the outstanding issues. Unimpressed, he and Harry Boland dismissed them as a "tempest in a teapot" (in Fitzpatrick 2003: 122; see also Dwyer 1998: 83). With proper handling, de Valera and Boland assured, these disagreements would soon be overcome. The leaders of the FOIF also did not identify an impending rift, and indeed, in the following months the FOIF adopted McCartan's position and demanded recognition of a "republican form of government" in Ireland (McCartan 1932; Doorley 2005). Later, de Valera also accepted the FOIF's position with regard to the League of Nations.[6]

Far bitterer were the disagreements between the FOIF and the Irish from Ireland over the use of, and entitlement to, the IVF money. Irish leaders in Ireland, and their representatives in the United States, believed that the IVF money belonged to Ireland. On June 3, 1919, Cathal Brugha and Michael Collins, the chairman of the *Dáil Éireann* and the Minister for Finance, respectively, wrote to Diarmuid Lynch, the secretary of the FOIF:

> Since we wrote to you ... the situation has developed a good deal, and the necessity for immediate funds has greatly increased. The expenditure with regard to foreign Propaganda [referring to the *Dáil Éireann*'s mission in Paris] is simply enormous ... In addition there are constructive schemes we want to go in for here. To make any decent start and to secure credit we must first accumulate a considerable reserve ... There are a number of statements being made here by the press that you in America have collected 1,250,000 dollars for the Dáil Eireann. We would like to have some sort of a general idea as to the actual amount. It would very materially affect our calculations.

Brugha and Collins further suggested that Lynch "appoint Trustees for the Dáil Fund in the U.S.A. These names [they explained] would be to guarantee the subscribers out there while the Dáil would in turn be responsible to them [here]" (Lynch and O'Donoghue 1957: 223).

From the perspective of Brugha and Collins, the funds collected by the IVF belonged to the Irish in Ireland (McCartan 1932). As representatives of the governing body of the Republican movement, they saw no difficulty in instructing Lynch about the safe keeping of the money. Echoing this sentiment, McGarrity attended a meeting of the FOIF Executive Council and moved to send 75 percent of the IVF proceeds to Ireland, in addition to providing $50,000 to defray the expenses of the *Dáil Éireann*'s mission to Paris.[7]

The leaders of the FOIF had different plans for the IVF money. Given the centrality of the United States' position, they believed that most of the IVF money should be used for an intensive campaign in the United States. In a letter to members of the FOIF, the National Council explained that the IVF monies would be used to accomplish the following goals:

(a) To urge that the objects for which America entered the war may be fully attained.
(b) To urge and insist upon the recognition of the Republican form of government established in Ireland.
(c) To urge that America shall not enter into any League of Nations which does not safeguard all American rights.
(d) To maintain and preserve the American ideals of government and oppose and offset British propaganda, which is falsifying and misrepresenting the facts of American history.
(e) To maintain for the foregoing purposes a widespread and professional publicity campaign.
(f) To defray the expenses of the Irish American delegation to the Peace Conference. (Doorley 1995: 169)

The FOIF was willing to send money to Ireland and, in response to McGarrity's proposal, agreed to send $250,000 to Ireland and an additional $10,000 to the delegation in Paris.[8] However, instead of directly funding the insurrection in Ireland, the FOIF's leaders believed that the IVF money would be best spent in the United States.

The disagreements over the use of the IVF money were not immediately apparent, but over time they created deep distrust between the FOIF leaders and the members of the Irish mission. Having witnessed the debate in the FOIF's council regarding McGarrity's proposal, Boland reported to Arthur Griffith, the founder of *Sinn Féin*, and de Valera:

> The Judge [Cohalan] held that it is essential that the money be spent here and he has a very comprehensive scheme for linking up the Race so that they may be such a power in American politics that they could be used as one man against England's attempts to *collar* America and to this end, extensive propaganda must be carried out amongst the Irish here.

It took a "very, very stiff fight to get any money for home" he complained (in Doorley 2005: 99).

The struggle over the IVF money was more than an argument about where the money was most necessary or useful. To no small extent, this struggle was also about the way Irish Americans and members of the Irish mission understood their position within the Irish nation. A heated exchange between the parties exemplifies this point nicely. On January 13, 1920, James O'Mara, who joined the mission as the fiscal agent of the Irish Republic, asked Lynch for a detailed accounting of the collections and expenses of the IVF. The national council of the FOIF promptly denied his request, but O'Mara mistakenly believed that Lynch acted without authorization. Therefore, on April 3, 1920 he asked Lynch again for a detailed report. This time he added a threat:

> I am reluctant to take certain steps [such as informing the National Council of FOIF of your position] which will become necessary should you continue to neglect giving me the information which I seek and which it is my duty to seek at once.

Lynch responded to O'Mara's threat immediately:

> It is evident from the tone of your letter [Lynch wrote,] that you misunderstand the situation, and I would therefore point out that the decision of the National Council, Friends of Irish Freedom, on this was voluntary on its part ... we are under no obligation to submit statements to any other organization. In view of the assistance given to the Irish Cause by the Friends of Irish Freedom permit me to add that the insinuation and threat contained in your letter ... come with very bad grace from one in your position.[9]

But O'Mara did not budge. A few days later, the members of the National Council received the following letter from O'Mara:

> There is before me one of the posters issued by your organization asking for public subscriptions. It reads as follows ...
>
> "AMERICA REMEMBER WHAT YOU OWE TO IRELAND
>
> > As you honor the Irish Blood shed for American Liberty, help the cause of Liberty now[.]"[10]
>
> ... Such money [O'Mara continued], morally belongs to Ireland – and it is only reasonable for a representative of the government

of Ireland to ask for a statement of account, both receipts and expenditures [of the IVF].[11]

O'Mara's threat and his decision not to back off were underlain with a deep moral conviction. In his understanding, regardless of the question of legal ownership, the FOIF was nothing more than a subsidiary organization and the legitimate owner of the money was the Irish nation. The decision of the National Council and Lynch's response, in contrast, clarify that they saw the FOIF as an independent organization which was entitled to determine the use of the money.

To some extent, the struggle for control of the Irish money stemmed from the techniques and politics of fundraising. To energize its volunteers and potential donors, the FOIF regularly released rosy assessments with regard to the sums collected for the IVF (collapsing pledges with actual money raised while disregarding campaign expenses). These figures, which were quoted in the press, may have contributed to a false impression in Ireland regarding the amount of money that was actually collected. In addition, when the FOIF launched the IVF in the Race Convention and in the campaign literature, the goals of the fund were not clearly specified. Everyone and anyone who cared about the Irish cause was invited to defray "America's debt" and donate to the IVF, regardless of their specific commitments (the goals of the IVF that appear above were only formulated in May 1919, in response to an intensifying struggle over the funds). The ambiguity regarding the amounts raised and the intended use of the IVF money was probably instrumental in attracting diverse donors, yet it also contributed to the tensions between the Irish leaders and the FOIF.

The conflict regarding the control and use of the IVF money was also related to the status of the IVF donations as gifts. Both the FOIF and the Irish mission treated the IVF money as a gift, but they reached different conclusions based on this interpretation. As gifts, O'Mara believed, it was the intention of the givers that mattered most, and the IVF poster proved that the subscribers wanted to support Ireland, not the FOIF. For this reason, he insisted that the IVF money morally belonged to the *Dáil Éireann*. In contrast, Cohalan and his associates believed that the FOIF, as the organization to which Irish Americans had entrusted their hard-earned money, and as the entity best equipped to handle the intricacies of American politics, had the responsibility to implement the donors' wishes, as expressed in the IVF goals. Furthermore, as chief architects of this massive giving, they expected at least some gratitude from the members of the Irish mission for their tremendous efforts.

Fundamentally, the struggle between the FOIF and the Irish mission unearthed important differences in how these two groups understood their position relative to one another and relative to the Irish nation as a whole. On the one hand, members of the Irish mission sought the support of Irish Americans, but they did not believe all Irish to be equal. The Irish in Ireland, they deemed, enjoyed a privileged position when it came to shaping the national struggle. On the other hand, the leaders of the FOIF, including Devoy and Lynch, who were born in Ireland but forced into exile after participating in Irish rebellions, believed that the long-term contributions of Irish Americans entitled them to determine at least the use of the donations they helped to raise. Devoy and his associates did not aspire to a leading role in the shaping of the struggle, but they rejected the subsidiary role that Brugha, Collins, and O'Mara ascribed to them. Thus, over and above the strictly financial aspects, the crisis of the IVF was related to disagreements with regard to the rights and obligations that each group associated with national membership and with contributions to the national common good.

The Crisis of the United Jewish Appeal

Despite its startling successes, toward the end of the 1940s the UJA experienced a severe political and economic crisis. A number of factors contributed to this crisis. First, after the record-breaking campaign of 1948, contributions to the UJA – and consequently to the United Palestine Appeal (UPA) – dwindled, despite the growing needs in Israel. Second, a temporary loss of the UJA's tax-deductible status during 1948 imposed limits on the use of its funds. Finally, the establishment of the State of Israel in 1948 led to unforeseen developments that threatened Zionist control over the portion of the UJA funds that were designated for Israel.

The creation of the State of Israel in 1948 generated financial needs on an entirely different scale. Almost overnight, the UJA became responsible for a huge number of refugees, this time in Israel. In addition, the UJA became the key source of foreign currency for a state whose economy was in a truly dire condition. With exports at a low of $46 million and imports at $331 million in 1950, the trade deficit ratio exceeded seven to one (Rubner 1960; Ben-Shahar 1965; Barkai 1990). Within two years, the government incurred a short-term debt of more than a quarter of a billion dollars without having a plan for how to pay it back.[12] To make things worse, the UJA collection seemed to be decreasing. In 1948, the UJA raised $150 million; between 1949 and 1951 the sums dropped to $104 million and $76 million, respectively.[13] The gap between the needs of Israel and what the UJA provided grew increasingly wider.

The leadership in Tel Aviv was also upset by the need to share the collections with others. This concern had two aspects. First, the UJA constitutive agreement was such that regardless of the overall sums collected, the National Refugee Service (NRS) received its relatively small share before the Joint Distribution Committee (JDC) and the UPA divided up the rest of the collection. Furthermore, the division of funds between the JDC and the UPA was organized along a sliding scale (Raphael 1982: 136). The larger the collection, the higher the percentage that was allocated to the UPA. As long as collections were on the rise, this situation was comfortable, but once the UJA collections dwindled, the UPA suffered a disproportionately severe decrease in its income.[14]

Second, the Jewish Federations, that actually organized the fundraising drive all over the country, insisted on keeping more of the collections for themselves. Israel Goldstein, chairman of the UPA, explained the situation:

> The communities feel more and more that they have to build hospitals, community centers and all kinds of institutions, having postponed [these projects] heretofore in deference to overseas, European and Palestine needs, and that they can no longer [compromise] their local needs . . . In many communities they will raise the same amount this year as last year, or even more, but they will deduct for their own needs, leaving less for the U.J.A. than a year ago.[15]

Thus, whereas in 1946 the UJA received 79 percent of the overall collections, this percentage gradually declined, and in 1950 it was only 64 percent of what was already a smaller pool.[16]

Henry Montor attempted to curb the gradual diversion of funds to local needs by reversing the order in which the campaign budgeting was done. Prior to 1948, Jewish Federations decided how much money would be handed over to the UJA after the completion of the campaign. Now Montor insisted that the Jewish Federations should come up with allocation formula before the campaign season. Pre-campaign budgeting, he reasoned, would give the UJA an opportunity to contend for its part of the collection by threatening that if an adequate proportion of the proceeds were not reserved for overseas needs the UJA will launch an independent campaign (Stock 1987: 122–126). But Montor's tactic achieved only limited success. Many Federations resisted pre-campaign budgeting on principle, and reaching an agreement with others required painstaking negotiations.[17] By 1950, after pushing the idea of pre-campaign budgeting for two years, only about 10% of the Federations had signed such agreements, and the tendency to keep a larger proportion of the money for local needs continued (American Jewish Committee 1950: 126; Raphael 1982: 42; Stock 1987: 124).

Adding to the financial crisis, beginning in 1948 the use of UJA funds came under increasing restrictions. In 1948, the Internal Revenue Service (IRS) realized that the Jewish Agency, the main beneficiary of the UPA that during the 1940s functioned as a quasi-state formation, spent most of its funds on security-related items.[18] As this was a clear violation of the tax code, the IRS

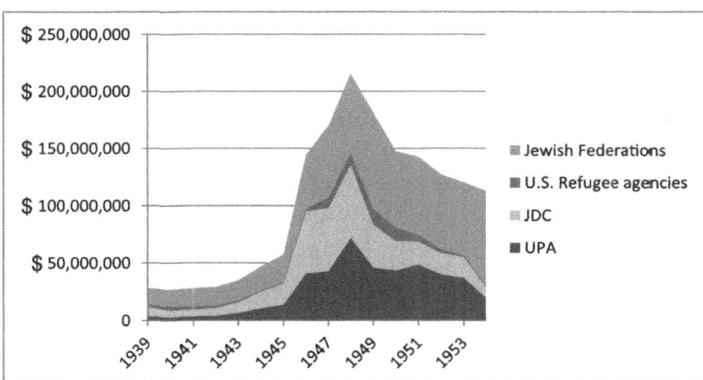

Figure 4.1. Jewish-American philanthropy from 1939 to 1954 (stacked).[19]

revoked the UJA's status as a non-profit organization (Stock 1988: 21). Montor was extremely anxious about this development. In a letter to Eliezer Kaplan, the Israeli Minister of Finance and Treasurer of the Jewish Agency, he explained:

> [T]he moment any public hears of this ruling, it will be disastrous to the campaign. I imagine, the JDC will pull out of the UJA ... it will mean the collapse of the UJA – and perhaps a new kind of campaign without tax-exemption. That will be a terrible kind of campaign to conduct. The proceeds would be minimal.[20]

In addition to dramatically reducing the overall collection, the revocation of the tax-exempt status threatened to disrupt the UJA's coalition and deny the Zionist movement access to the wealthy people who were generally more inclined to sponsor the JDC.

Given the gravity of the matter, Henry Morgenthau, the chairman of the UJA and former US Treasury Secretary, extended all his influence in Washington to try to reverse the IRS's decision. Eventually, the UJA won back its non-profit status, but only after David Ben-Gurion, in his capacity as the chairman of the Jewish Agency, and its secretary, Shlomo Eisenberg, declared that

(a) as from August 1, 1948 no part of the funds of the Jewish Agency would be expended for security, military or political purposes, nor for carrying on propaganda, or otherwise attempting to influence legislation ... ;
(b) no funds would go directly or indirectly to the Government of Israel for any use or purpose whatsoever;
(c) the funds would be used solely for charitable purposes. (In: American Jewish Committee 1950: 180; Stock 1988: 21)

Ben-Gurion and his colleagues in Tel Aviv hoped that these limitations would end the crisis. But they soon discovered that the ordeal had far-reaching consequences. In the months following the affair, the tax-deduction ordeal broadened and eventually threatened Israeli control over the Jewish Agency and, subsequently, of the UPA funds. When Kaplan reported about the crisis to the General Council of the Jewish Agency, the American members of the council argued that the blurry boundaries between the Israeli

Government and the Jewish Agency continued to pose a threat to the tax status of the UJA. To create a clearer separation between these entities, they insisted that Ben-Gurion and Kaplan resign from their posts in the Jewish Agency (Raphael 1989: 174; Ganin 2005: 19).

Ben-Gurion and his friends in *Mapai*, the ruling party, suspected that the real motivation behind these pressures was different. The Americans, they believed – especially Abba Hillel Silver and Emanuel Neumann, the leaders of the Zionist Organization of America (ZOA) – hoped to gain exclusive control over the Jewish Agency. Such control would have allowed the ZOA leaders, who were associated with the liberal General Zionist Party in Israel, a political rival of *Mapai*, to impose laissez-faire economic policies. More alarmingly, a loss of control over the Jewish Agency – which administered the newly constructed refugee camps in Israel (the *ma'abarot*) – would have deprived Ben-Gurion's party of one of its most important political strongholds.[21]

Initially, Silver and his American colleagues appeared to have the upper hand. In late 1948, Ben-Gurion and Kaplan resigned from their posts at the Jewish Agency. However, when Montor and Morgenthau learned about the removal of the Israeli leaders from the Jewish Agency, they were enraged. American Jews, they believed, gave their money to Israel, not to self-appointed Zionist politicians in the United States. To remedy the situation, Montor staged a revolt. On September 10, 1948, he resigned from his positions in the UJA and UPA and accused Silver and Neumann of trying to

> strangle the most decent and progressive forces in the State of Israel and to frustrate the self-determination and the economic freedom of the people of that country.... there have been [he intimated] innumerable instances when frantic appeals from Palestine for needed funds would be questioned as though contributors in this country were giving money to New York corporations instead of to Palestine itself.

Silver and his colleagues, he argued, were not responsible for the funds collected. But by attributing the success of the UJA to themselves, they managed to control every penny of the UPA. In a manner reminiscent of O'Mara's accusations in the Irish case, Montor argued that the leaders of the ZOA "regarded the funds for Palestine as their private treasure chest rather than [a] reservoir of good will of all the Jews of America."[22]

Following Montor, Morgenthau resigned from the UJA, and a new body, the Committee of Contributors and Workers (CCW),[23] prepared to launch an independent campaign the proceeds of which would be sent to Israel without unnecessary deductions (American Jewish Committee 1950: 168).[24] To suspend their plans, the CCW demanded a 50% representation for local communities in the UPA's Executive Committee. Such a change, they argued, would ensure that the UPA would "reflect the interest of the whole Jewish community in America . . ."[25] In addition, the CCW demanded that the UPA's Executive Committee refrain from allocating any funds in America without explicit approval from the Jewish Agency Executive Committee in Israel.[26] Morgenthau further conditioned his return to the UJA on Montor's return.[27] Silver and Neumann denied the accusations, and offered to head the UJA drive themselves.[28] But a special meeting of the Israeli and American executives of the Jewish Agency voted to accept the CCW's and Morgenthau's conditions. Having seen their position thoroughly discredited by their colleagues, Silver and Neumann resigned their posts in the Jewish Agency, the UPA, and the ZOA.[29]

Silver's and Neumann's defeat alleviated, at least temporarily, the threat to Israeli control over the UPA. But during 1949 and early 1950, it became clear that Montor's victory was pyrrhic. His new allies, mostly Jewish Federation activists, proved no more eager to transfer money to Israel than did the ZOA leaders (Jewish Telegraphic Agency 1949; Ganin 2005: 66). In addition, the Council of Jewish Federations and Welfare Funds (CJFWF), the national coordinating body of local Federations, was determined to oversee the use of American funds in Israel. For that purpose, it had established an Institute for Overseas Studies, which recommended, among other things, limiting the power of the *Histadrut* (Israel's powerful trade union), changing Israel's absorption and agricultural resettlement programs, and reforming the allocation of the UPA funds so as to allow more community participation in decision making.[30] Like Silver and his associates in the ZOA, the CJFWF sought to liberalize the Israeli economy. Thus, the essential difficulties associated with the control and allocation of the UJA funds remained almost unaltered.

As in the case of the Irish Victory Fund, the difficulties associated with UJA funds were related to their status as gifts. Accepting the UJA gifts forced the Israeli government to share them with others, restricted their use, and obliged the leadership in Tel Aviv to share power with American Jewish leaders. No matter what strategies Montor adopted, the JDC, the NRS, and especially the Jewish Federations demanded their share of the collection. The ZOA, the Jewish Federations, and even the IRS also insisted on dictating how the UPA money would be spent.

Beyond sheer power politics, the struggle over the UJA money was also an argument about moral entitlement. In the late 1940s, the UJA drive centered on Zionist themes. The leadership in Tel Aviv interpreted this shift as an indication of the motivations that propelled Jewish-American giving and concluded that Israel alone was entitled to the money. Echoing O'Mara's assertion in 1920, Kaplan explained: "The only topic that is dynamic and has needs and has something to say to the public, and what it has to say attracts the public, is Israel . . ."[31] But, he complained, the "theory in America is not that they are trustees that collect money for us but the other way around, that they are the owners of the money and we are their trustees."[32] Jewish-American organizations, in contrast, insisted on playing an active role in distributing the funds entrusted to them (Lehrman 1949, 1950a).

Over and above the difficulties associated with the method of payment, the conflict between the Jewish-American leaders and the Israeli leadership illustrates the ideological tensions discussed in the introduction.[33] The *halutzim*, who now occupied dominant positions in the Israeli polity, believed that American Jews, who proved their moral weakness by failing to migrate to Israel, had absolutely no right to determine policies in Israel (Kimmerling 1983; Liebman and Don-Yihya 1983; Raz-Krakotzkin 1993).[34] On the other side of the ocean, many Jewish Americans admired the *halutzim* but, by and large, also rejected much of their worldview. American Jews, as a whole, saw the United States as their home and aspired to a bourgeois lifestyle (Shapiro 1971; Cohen 1975; Heinze 1990). Thus, given such ideological differences between Jewish Americans and Israeli Jews, it is hardly surprising that these groups disagreed about how to allocate and use the UJA's money.

Nation Building and the Problem of Gift Giving

During the 1910s and 1940s, respectively, the FOIF and the UJA mediated between the Irish and Jewish communities in the United States and their national movements and secured increasingly large sums of money for their respective national movements. The success of the IVF and the UJA, however, may have imperiled the very projects they were designed to bolster. As the members of diaspora communities contributed more money, they also became more deeply interested in how this money would be spent and clashed over this question. Thus, despite their success, during the late 1910s and late 1940s, respectively, the systems of diaspora giving of the FOIF and the UJA experienced severe and roughly parallel crises.

The category of gift giving is absolutely crucial for understanding these crises. In the first place, the actors involved in the drama were informed by the logic of gift giving. When Lynch chided O'Mara for his threat, he opened with "In view of the assistance given to the Irish Cause by the Friends of Irish Freedom..."[35] Thus, the FOIF leaders gifted Ireland and expected a "thank you" rather than an insinuation of dishonesty. O'Mara's lack of trust added insult to injury. On the other hand, O'Mara's behavior was informed by the same logic. Similarly, Montor and later Kaplan relied on an interpretation of the intentionality of the givers when they argued that Israel alone was entitled to more of the UJA's money. The various parties involved in the quandaries had a sense of moral entitlement that stemmed from their interpretation of the diaspora donations as a gift. Unlike market exchange, in which the seller is entirely alienated from the commodity, O'Mara, Montor, and Kaplan believed that the IVF or UJA donors, respectively, enjoyed some ongoing rights over the donations or, at least, their use. Lynch and the Jewish-American leaders held a similar understanding but argued that they, as the representatives of the donors, were entitled to both gratitude and influence. Interestingly, the congruence of perspectives – the fact that the two sides agreed about the nature of the transaction – did not prevent them from disagreeing about the rights and obligations that followed from gifting the nation.

One may suggest that the struggles surrounding Irish and Zionist philanthropy exemplify an inherent tension between the logic of gift giving and the ideals of nationalism. Gift giving implies subordination and dependency on the receiving side (Sahlins 1963; Mauss 1967; Zelizer 1996). In contrast, the national ideal, as Anderson and others have pointed out, is egalitarian, regardless of actual inequalities existing within nations (1991; Gellner 1983). Bringing these two practices together in the IVF and UJA, this line of thought would suggest, was bound to produce tensions and conflicts. But concluding that gift giving and nation building are incompatible would be empirically and conceptually wrong. While it is true that the clashes revolved around the rights associated with gifting the nation, in both cases the warring parties did not harbor an egalitarian conception of nationhood. The leaders across both sides of the ocean did not see themselves and their followers as equal but rather imagined the nation as a hierarchical entity composed of a core (homeland) and a periphery (diaspora). As I showed in Chapter 3, it was precisely this hierarchical understanding of national membership that allowed the Irish and Zionist movements to demand monetary contributions from their diasporic supporters. This understanding also made it possible for those in the homeland to accept diasporic donations without experiencing degradation. Thus, the practice of gift giving in fact complemented the conceptions of nationhood that the Irish and Zionists articulated.

Instead of an expression of an inherent contradiction, the crises of Irish and Jewish philanthropy illustrate the practical implications of each nation's fragmentary complexion. The Irish and Jewish difficulties were not due to lack of national sentiment or a failure to imagine membership in a national community. The Irish and the Jews in the United States – not all, but certainly a good number of them – identified with the national struggles in Ireland and Israel, but they had different priorities and their own ideas about how to best conduct the national struggle. The FOIF's insistence on keeping most of the IVF money in the United States reflected the belief of its leaders that Ireland would be best served through an intensive public relations campaign in Washington. Likewise, the determination of the ZOA and, later, the CJFWF to exert effective control over the use of Jewish-American money in Israel was not just a calculated play for influence. It also reflected a desire to see the Israeli economy flourish and a distrust of the government's policies. Thus, the existence of communities in the United States who identified as Irish or Jewish and who were willing to contribute to the national struggle did not secure a continuous flow of funds to the national movements.

Examining the crises of the IVF and the UJA allows us to restate the equivalent problems that the Irish and the Zionist movements confronted. While the two movements operated under different historical circumstances and the levels of organization of the Irish and Jewish communities in the United States was very different, the challenges they confronted were qualitatively similar. In both cases, the national movements had to find ways to act at a distance on the preferences and interests of a diverse and widely dispersed population so as to enroll it and its resources in the national struggle. Chapter 3 looked at how these movements met this challenge by examining the philanthropic systems they created. In this chapter we explored the difficulties deriving from these mechanisms by tracking the problem of regulating the relationships between the diaspora organizations and the homeland movements. The following chapters will examine the solutions that the Irish and Zionist movements devised in order to overcome this problem.

5

Making National Bonds: Floating the Irish and Israeli Loans in the United States

During the late 1910s and late 1940s, the Irish and Zionist national movements experienced severe and roughly parallel crises in their relations with the Irish and Jewish diasporas in the United States. Regardless of the sympathy and support these movements garnered, the Irish and Jewish nationalists in Dublin and Tel Aviv were unable to persuade their supporters to part with anywhere near as much money as was needed in the homeland. Furthermore, the American leaders believed that they were entitled to retain for domestic use a substantial chunk of the money raised, and to assert the role of the diaspora in determining how the remainder should be spent in the homeland. The leaders in Ireland and Israel saw things differently. The diasporic donations, they believed, were an insufficient contribution. The demands of the diaspora organizations were, from their perspective, simply outrageous. At root, as we have seen, these crises were related both to the methods used to extract these funds and to deep disagreements regarding the rights and obligations associated with national membership and with contribution to the nation's well-being.

Having reached an impasse, leaders of the Irish and Zionist national movements looked for a solution. They had to find a way to extract more money from their American compatriots on better moral and political terms. The solutions that the Irish nationalists and the Zionists devised were remarkably similar. Instead of relying solely on charity, they created new socio-financial mechanisms that combined elements of gift giving and investment. They issued national bonds and sold them to their compatriots as a unique type of moral investment. As a for-profit investment, these bonds were unattractive, but by combining patriotism and pecuniary interests, the Irish and Zionist leaders hoped to overcome the difficulties associated with gift giving. This chapter provides a detailed examination of the launching of these bonds and of the inter-organizational struggles surrounding their sale. Instead of focusing on the monetary aspect of the bonds alone, I will examine these projects as an attempt to reshape the relationship between two fragments of the nation – the homeland and diaspora communities.

Remolding Irish / Irish-American Relations

Shortly after his dramatic escape from a British prison in February 1919, Éamon de Valera, the President of the *Dáil Éireann*, prepared for a visit to the United States. One of de Valera's main tasks in the United States was to raise money quickly for his new government. In addition, de Valera planned to press for the recognition of the Republic of Ireland and to facilitate investment in Ireland by wealthy Irish Americans (see Fanning et al. 1998: 35–36). In his first meeting with his colleagues after his escape from prison, the *Dáil* adopted the following resolution:

> It is obvious that the work of our government cannot be carried out without funds. The Minister of Finance is accordingly preparing a prospectus, which will be shortly published, for the issue of a loan of one million Sterling – £500,000 to be offered to the public for immediate subscription, £250,000 at home and £250,000 abroad, in bonds of such amount as to meet the needs of the small subscribers. (Maher 1998: 81)[1]

In that meeting, the *Dáil Éireann* also nominated de Valera, James O'Mara, and Michael Fogarty, the Bishop of Killaloe, as trustees for the loan (Carroll 2002).[2] When the American Commission on Irish Independence (ACII) visited Dublin on its way back from the Peace Conference in Paris, the idea of a loan was discussed again. The commission's members, Frank Walsh, Edward Dunne, and

Michael Ryan, assured de Valera that the plan for the external loan was feasible (O'Doherty 1957).

When de Valera arrived in New York in May 1919, he met with leading members of FOIF at Judge Cohalan's house. Anxious to advance the loan, de Valera did not waste time in introducing his plan:

> In the initial stages [of the struggle for recognition] ... we need financial help ... as did the colonies here ... The tribute exacted by the foreigner [British Government] prevents us from raising at the moment an adequate tax of our own. An advance loan from countries more happily placed is necessary, and has been sanctioned by the people's parliament – determined that the republic will live and the debt be repaid. Americans can help in the projected work of restoration and reconstruction by subscribing.[3]

De Valera needed the FOIF's support, but the relationships he sought to establish were not those of dependence. The parallel he drew between the condition of the American colonists and the Republic of Ireland clarified that, in his opinion, Ireland's neediness was a temporary matter.

De Valera's suggestions surprised the FOIF at a sensitive moment. During the third Race Convention in February 1919, the FOIF had launched the Irish Victory Fund (IVF) with the goal of raising $2,000,000 (this was the money that Diarmuid Lynch and the members of the Irish mission fought over in the previous chapter). During the first half of 1919, the FOIF had collected pledges of more than a million dollars, but many communities had not even started their IVF drive.[4] Cohalan and his associates planned to continue the IVF drive for another full year. Competition from a second drive led by the President of the Irish Republic could completely frustrate their efforts.

Perhaps as a result of their concern for the IVF, the FOIF's response to the loan plan was dubious. As the Republic of Ireland had yet to be recognized by the United States, Cohalan cautioned, issuing a bond in its name would contravene the Blue Skies laws.[5] The financiers to whom de Valera referred, Cohalan added, had never cooperated in the struggle for the Republic and would surely refuse to underwrite Irish Bonds. Senator Burke Cockran, one of the leading pro-Irish politicians present at the meeting, insisted that "the idea that a[n Irish] loan could be floated on normal financial grounds [is] preposterous ... [Money] might be raised but never as [a] cold financial investment" (Tansill 1957: 348–349; Fitzpatrick 2003: 143). Finally, the FOIF leaders added, no organization could accomplish the task within de Valera's timeframe – and the sums he wished to raise were fantastically high (between the *Dáil*'s decision and this meeting de Valera increased his fundraising goal to $25 million). With their best efforts, they confessed, the IVF had yet to raise $100,000, regardless of the big-hearted pledges made by delegates to the Race Convention in the excitement of the moment.[6] Even Michael Ryan from the ACII, who had supported the idea when he visited Dublin, now advised de Valera against the bonds (McCartan 1932: 141). Cohalan and his associates believed that the proper relationship between the Irish Americans and Ireland was gift giving.

De Valera was disappointed by the FOIF's response, but he was not ready to abandon his plan. To his friends back home he reported:

> He [Cohalan] pooh poohed the idea of bonds in any shape – he called F. P. Walsh [whom de Valera had previously met during the ACII's visit to Dublin] aside when he came here and suggested that I be sent home with ¾ million dollars – 'the biggest sum any Irish leader ever brought to Ireland.'[7]

To the people in the room, he explained that since the loan plan was formally approved by the *Dáil Éireann* he was committed to implementing the resolution to the letter (McCartan 1932). Having reached an impasse in their first private meeting, the FOIF leaders eventually pledged their support for de Valera's plan and established a special committee to advise him on the implementation of the loan.[8]

De Valera's insistence on the sale of bonds stemmed from the added value he attributed to the ability to borrow. From a strictly financial perspective, de Valera thought, a loan could realize more money than could philanthropy; more crucially, he also believed that the ability to borrow was politically significant.[9] A successful loan would allow the *Dáil* actually to assume on-the-ground governmental functions in Ireland. Furthermore, the trust shown by widespread subscription to the bond would, he hoped, demonstrate that the republic was more than a hopeful figment of the imagination.[10] Addressing a crowd of supporters on St Patrick's Day of 1920, de Valera said:

> The Republic of Ireland calls for a loan in the pitiful sum of ten million dollars from all the United States ... An oversubscription would be a notice to the world that the love of Liberty, and particularly of Irish freedom, still burns brightly in America.[11]

A successful loan, de Valera believed, would give credence to the claim that the Republic of Ireland was a fact and improve its bid for recognition.[12]

The struggle between de Valera and the leaders of the FOIF over the Irish Bond was not simply a matter of naked organizational interests. In launching the bond drive, de Valera attempted to remold the Irish-American relationship with Ireland so as to reflect Ireland's new status. From his perspective, since Ireland was now a sovereign nation, its relationship with Irish Americans could no longer be based on philanthropy. Money was necessary, and the method of obtaining it was as important as the fact of obtaining it. The FOIF's resistance, too, was more than a matter of defending their philanthropic turf. Cohalan and his associates insisted that despite hopes there was no such thing as the Republic of Ireland. As proof, they indicated that the *Dáil Éireann* was not recognized by any government. As long as these were the facts, they maintained, the proper form of the relationship between the Irish and the Irish Americans was one of trust and dependency.

Reestablishing the American Commission on Irish Independence

Prior to his arrival in the United States, de Valera planned to issue the bonds using a commercial bank, just like any foreign government or corporation. De Valera and Michael Collins, the *Dáil Éireann*'s Minister of Finance, instructed the Irish mission in the United States to contact "a Bank [that would] ... act as Trustee for the Loan or, failing that, some representative Irishman of high financial standing [should] be secured for the purpose" (in O'Doherty 1957: 41). But de Valera seriously underestimated the difficulties of launching the Irish Bond. American bankers, even those of Irish origin, were reluctant to risk their good names on behalf of the Republic of Ireland and refused to underwrite the loan.[13]

Unable to find a bank that would underwrite the bonds, de Valera decided to entrust the issue of the bonds to the members of the ACII, whom he had met previously in Dublin, but even this proved hard. Frank Walsh, the chairman of the ACII, agreed to take on the challenge, but the other members of the committee were less enthusiastic. Ryan quietly declined the position. Dunne, a former mayor of Chicago and former governor of Illinois, explained his reluctance to engage in the bond project as follows:

> Many a good man or woman with the love for Ireland in his or her heart will buy these Bonds when no misrepresentations are made, will dispose of them to others or die leaving them to relatives. The new holders[,] years from now[,] may come to us with the literature to which our names are attached and say "I am hard up now, my father bought these bonds at your solicitation, I want you to redeem them." Still another class will buy these bonds when they can spare the money, and when they meet with reserves thereafter will go over their papers, find the bonds, and approach us with requests for redemption because we induced them to buy . . . It is one thing to ask *contribution* for a good and holy cause, where the contributor understands what he gives as a *gift*, and another thing to *sell a bond* for money. In the one case there is no room for a claim of misrepresentation, over-reaching and fraud, while in the other case no matter how careful you may be you cannot protect yourself from dishonest charges made against you which may not be legally sustained, but which none the less occasion you worry and annoyance.[14]

The problem Dunne identifies was related to the quasi-philanthropic nature of the bonds and their lifespan. Unlike regular gifts or typical market exchange, the obligations that bonds carry get settled, if at all, only years later. During these years, emotions subside and the subscribers or their heirs may reinterpret the purchase decision according to their current circumstances and forget that it was in part a gift. Weary of accusation of legal or even moral default, Dunne excused himself from the project.

For the bond drive to succeed, de Valera believed that the ACII had to operate without competition. He therefore insisted that the FOIF end the IVF drive. The FOIF leaders were upset by de

Valera's demand. In addition to losing their almost sole source of income, shutting down the IVF, they realized, would cut them off from direct engagement with the Irish-American public. Nevertheless, hoping to avoid an open confrontation, they opted to acquiesce to de Valera's demand and brought the drive to an end by August 1919.[15]

Staffing the executive ranks of the ACII proved no less of a challenge. Harry Boland, who now acted as the secretary of de Valera, was too busy to deal with the loan. De Valera's attempt to recruit Lynch, the able secretary of the FOIF, failed and only intensified the tensions between Cohalan and de Valera.[16] In search of a local organizer, de Valera asked Colonel P. K. Callahan, a former field organizer of the Knights of Columbus, to direct the ACII. Callahan accepted the position but, lacking political finesse, he quickly made damaging mistakes. A circular he distributed suggested that "... the organization [ACII] be extended into a national association on very broad lines, so as to include everyone with Irish sympathies..."[17] The circular confirmed Cohalan and Devoy's fears – de Valera, they were now convinced, intended to supplant the FOIF with the new organization.[18] Worse even, Callahan's contacts proved to be outdated. The majority of the letters he sent out to potential organizers were returned undelivered. It took only a few weeks for de Valera's people to realize that he was not the right man for the position. Abandoning the effort to fill the post with a capable Irish-American figure, de Valera called on James O'Mara of Limerick, Ireland, to take over the drive. O'Mara was a well-known bacon curer, and a member and trustee of the *Dáil Éireann*. His reputation as a successful businessman, de Valera hoped, would inspire Irish-American confidence in the solvency of the Irish bonds (McCartan 1932: 144).

Even with O'Mara at the helm, transforming the ACII from a mere acronym to an effective organization was not simple. O'Mara needed volunteers, thousands of them. Seeking local organizers, he initially approached distinguished Irish-American individuals who were not associated with the FOIF – clergy, university professors, and independent businessmen. But Irish-American professionals, in general, refused to enter the muddy waters of Irish-American politics.[19] In addition, the ACII needed money to cover the initial campaign expenses. The key for both organizers and funds, O'Mara and de Valera reluctantly realized, was in the hands of the FOIF. Therefore, in December 1919, de Valera addressed the National Council of the FOIF and asked for a loan of $100,000 and for a list of potential organizers around the country (in addition to the $26,748 which the FOIF allocated in order to cover de Valera's personal expenses). De Valera and O'Mara also promised that the ACII would not compete with the FOIF. Appeased, the Council approved de Valera's request for the loan, and Lynch urged members of the FOIF to help organize the bond drive in a special circular.[20] Finally, with the FOIF's seal of approval, O'Mara managed to recruit volunteers from the FOIF branches and various independent Irish societies all over the country.

Designing the Irish Bonds

Judge Cohalan's initial concern regarding the legality of issuing Irish bonds in the United States was well founded. Having investigated the matter, in September 1919 de Valera's lawyer, Martin Conboy, advised the ACII that the sale of "the contemplated Bond does not offend federal law, but . . . it offends the Blue Skies laws."[21] Conboy, however, found a creative way to sidestep this obstacle. Instead of issuing regular bonds, the Republic of Ireland would sell bond certificates. Unlike regular bonds, the bond certificates would carry only a conditional obligation to repay. Prior to the recognition of the Republic and the withdrawal of British forces from the island, the bond certificate was a gift, a donation bearing no obligation for repayment. If and when the Irish Republic gained international recognition and British forces withdrew from Ireland, the bond certificates would turn into standard, interest-bearing loans. Thus, unlike regular bonds that could either be redeemed or defaulted upon, the Irish bond certificates could be redeemed, defaulted upon, or simply acknowledged with gratitude, as a gift, depending on future eventualities. This stipulation allowed the ACII to bypass the jurisdiction of the Blue Skies laws.

Determining the interest rate to be paid for the bond certificates posed another dilemma. In Ireland, Collins promised subscribers interest from the day of subscription. De Valera, however, feared that such a condition would make it hard for the young

Republic to meet its obligations.[22] Therefore, de Valera decided that the bond certificates would accrue interest only after the recognition of the Republic and the withdrawal of British forces from the island. Hoping to maintain at least a semblance of a business proposition, de Valera decided that the Republic would pay an annual interest of 5% for the bond certificates.[23] Thus, the Irish bond certificates were:

> ... not negotiable, but exchangeable at par for Gold Bonds of the Republic upon presentation at the Treasury of the Republic one month after the Republic has received international recognition and the British Forces have withdrawn from Ireland. These Gold Bonds will bear interest, payable half-yearly, on 1st January and 1st July, at the rate of Five per cent per annum, calculated from the first day of the seventh month after the freeing of the territory of the Republic of Ireland, and will be redeemable at par within one year thereafter.[24]

The interest rate promised for the bond certificate was slightly higher than the 4.75% offered by American Treasury Certificates of Indebtedness at the time. This interest rate, de Valera believed, was high enough to be considered businesslike but not dangerously expensive. Issuing the bond certificates in denominations of $10, $25, $50, $100, $500, and $10,000, de Valera hoped, would allow Irish Americans of different economic standings to invest in Ireland.

Marketing the bond certificates required the ACII to strike a delicate balance. Perhaps in response to Dunne's reservations, de Valera took pains to clarify that the Irish bond certificate was not a typical investment:

> Our Bond-Certificates cannot be issued on [a] purely financial basis. We must expect subscriptions only from those who seek to serve a good cause, not from those who want immediate pecuniary profit. The appeal is then to Americans who love liberty and desire to see it triumph in Ireland, particularly to Americans of Irish blood who wish to see the Motherland of the race set free and established in its old position of importance amongst the nations.[25]

Thus, the primary returns on investment in the bond certificate, de Valera clarified, were the satisfaction associated with a contribution to a noble cause and the opportunity for Irish Americans to prove the sincerity of their national conviction.[26]

At the same time, members of the Irish mission repeatedly promised subscribers that the bond certificate would be repaid. But rather than providing an economic surety, de Valera and his associates secured the loan by linking it to the honor of the Irish nation. William Maloney, who was closely associated with the mission, explained:

> The loan is authorized by the people of Ireland through their freely chosen and elected representatives; it is secured not upon the fleeting fortunes of tsars and tyrants, but upon the honor and good faith of every individual citizen of the Republic of Ireland. (McCartan 1932: 143)

Similarly, the prospectus of the bond certificates declared that "this advance Loan [would] become the first charge on the Revenues of the Irish Republic" (Carroll 2002: 105). Given the expected revenues of the Republic, de Valera assured potential subscribers, paying this debt would be a trifling task. Thus, the Irish mission emphasized the patriotic value of the bond certificate but, at the same time, reiterated its commitment to repay that loan.

Finally, after months of preparations, the Irish Bond certificate campaign opened in January 1920. Judging from the response of the masses, the Irish Bond drive was a great success. The average Irish American, it seemed, was eager to support the Republic of Ireland and was not too concerned by the mixture of pecuniary and philanthropic motives. Soon after the drive began, organizers all over the country reported widespread subscription to the ACII headquarters in New York, though most of the subscriptions were for small amounts, usually of $10 or $25.[27] During the 10 months of the campaign, more than 300,000 people, most of them Americans of Irish descent, subscribed to the bond certificate, allowing the ACII to gross $5,123,640 – a sum far exceeding any previous Irish collection in the United States (Carroll 2002).[28]

Reshaping Jewish Homeland/Diaspora Relations

In the late 1940s, the fledgling Israeli government faced a complex predicament. It desperately needed funds, but the only available tool for amassing those funds, the United Jewish Appeal (UJA), proved to be increasingly problematic. Some additional and secure source of external capital had to be developed.

The initial idea of issuing Israeli bonds came from within the UJA. Frustrated by the never-ending political struggles between the Jewish Federations and the UJA, and between the beneficiaries of the UJA funds, Henry Morgenthau approached Prime Minister David Ben-Gurion in 1948 and suggested "constituting ... a corporation with three functions: to collect donations for the government – regardless of tax-deduction, to organize private loans, [and] to get governmental loans."[29] As a wartime US Secretary of the Treasury, Morgenthau had raised almost $200 billion in bonds to finance the American military effort. Now, he wanted to repeat this success for Israel. Morgenthau's suggestion was revolutionary. Instead of relying only on Jewish-American generosity, the new corporation would also obtain loans for the new state. Depending on loans and donations, rather than donations alone, he believed, would enable Israel to obtain much larger sums than previously possible.

Morgenthau's suggestion had an unmistakable appeal – expanding the scope of the UJA's activities toward the issuance of loans could dramatically increase the sums Israel received and perhaps also relieve Israel from the need to share income with others. But the suggestion was also risky. What if, instead of doubling their overall contribution, American Jews shifted their money from donation to investment? In such a case, instead of improving its fiscal standing, Israel would receive the same amount of money, but this time it would constitute a crippling debt. Moreover, how could Morgenthau, the figurehead leader of the UJA but otherwise a novice in Jewish-American politics, implement his vision? Ben-Gurion considered Morgenthau's suggestions but decided, for the time being, not to rock the Jewish-American boat, and so the government instead imposed a strict austerity plan in an effort to reduce imports and passed a special law to encourage private investment in Israel (Lehrman 1951).[30]

However hopeful, Isreal at that time, was hardly an attractive place for investment. With low productivity, high wages, excessive economic controls, exorbitant privileges to the public sector, and a disastrously overvalued currency (the official rate of the Israeli pound was $2.80, whereas on the black market it was traded at around $0.80 per pound), the plan to attract foreign investors met with little success (Lehrman 1950a, 1950b, 1951).

Eventually, in 1950 a number of factors forced the government to reconsider the bond plan. In August 1950, Ben-Gurion reported that the Israeli balance of trade had reached a ratio of nine incoming dollars for every dollar exported.[31] If that were not enough, the government had found it increasingly hard to obtain even short-term loans from sympathetic Jewish financiers. Apparently, Eliezer Kaplan, the Minister of Finance, reported, the war in Korea had led many to believe that a third world war was about to erupt and therefore, "requests for deferred redemptions..." on loans "are turned down... because of the fear that the banks in America will be drafted for America's needs."[32] Just when Israel's fiscal difficulties became acute, international conditions conspired to block its access to capital.

Perhaps even more importantly, the decrease in UJA collections and the allocations to Israel convinced Tel Aviv that the current methods of philanthropy had reached their limit. In a government meeting on August 2, 1950, Ben-Gurion explained:

> Following the actions taken so far, there is no solution anticipated to these problems [the foreign currency shortage]. Therefore we must check our ways. The income of the Appeal go[es] down despite inhuman efforts by the organizers, despite the fact that the Appeal uses philanthropic propaganda – and sometimes they say very upsetting things that must be said – but the work is nowhere done by philanthropy... Obviously, the tension has relaxed... Thus, under the present system it must be said – the proceeds will decrease.[33]

Had the UJA been able to provide Israel with adequate income, Ben-Gurion seemed to suggest, Israel would have borne the indignity associated with receiving philanthropic funds. The decline in donations, however, made the struggle to solicit funds no longer worth the debasement.

Thus, facing an increasingly severe financial and political crisis, in the summer of 1950 the government decided to adopt a four-point plan for Israel's economic development: (1) expanded fund-raising using UJA funds for immigration absorption; (2) renewed efforts to obtain inter-governmental loans; (3) enhancement of private investments; and (4) issuance of long-term bonds (Hammer

1985: 103–104). Of the four points, the first three were well underway, with limited degrees of success. The fourth suggestion, however, was yet to be developed.

To advance the four-point plan, in September 1950, Ben-Gurion summoned leaders from every branch of the American-Jewish community to a special economic conference in Jerusalem. Introducing the plan, he explained that

> ... the Jews of America ... and other rich Jewish communities collected in the last ten years hundreds of millions [of dollars] for the support of oppressed and dispossessed Jews. *We chose a different path. We do not engage in gmiluth hasadim,*[34] we built a homeland and are being built in it. And we pave the way for every Jew to build and be built in a homeland. *We believe that every Jew can help himself – and that there is no need to exist from the support of the other* ... We can become a free nation that stands on its own feet and be a moral guide for the entire world.[35]

Nevertheless, he emphasized, in the coming three years Israel would need one and a half billion dollars for immigration absorption and integration.[36] Israel, he declared, would provide a third of that sum. The rest would have to be raised in America.

The Jewish-American delegates supported the first three points unanimously, but, as in the Irish case, the loan plan was highly contentious. Stanley Myers, the president of the Council of Jewish Federations and Welfare Funds (CJFWF), insisted that "philanthropic dollars are priority dollars for Israel and ... nothing should be done in planning for Israel to endanger them."[37] Before Israel launched a risky bond initiative, he argued, it needed to remove the bureaucratic red tape and other obstacles that prevented investors from flocking to Israel. Furthermore, he cautioned, a loan would fail to muster additional funds for Israel. "The very wealthy invest in steel, motors, oil, railways, and the like, not in sentiment – especially not in a region where, in the minds of such investors, there hover the unexorcized specters of socialism and other devils." Small investors, conditioned by years of "misery and crisis propaganda," would also refrain from investing their savings in the bonds (see Lehrman 1950a: 525). Like the leaders of the FOIF 30 years earlier, the leaders of the Jewish Federations cautioned that the bond would fail to meet the expectations of the Israeli leadership.

Critics of the plan were also concerned about how the bonds would affect the Jewish community in the United States. Harold Glaser, the director of the CJFWF's Institute for Overseas Studies, argued that since every dollar invested in the bonds would replace "gift dollars," the UJA collection would be reduced by 50 to 100 million dollars a year. In addition to reducing funds for overseas needs, he believed, local Federations would not be able to support old-age homes, educational programs, and other projects. This danger was made all the more acute by the fact that since 1948 Jewish Federations all over the country had taken out loans in order to provide Israel with fast cash. A cut in the collections now could render them insolvent and force many of them into bankruptcy. Finally, the leaders of the Jewish Federations also feared that the bonds would give rise to accusations of divided loyalty (Lehrman 1950a: 525). The bonds, they therefore argued, threatened the very institutional fabric of Jewish life in the United States.

Supporters of the bonds, primarily Montor and Morgenthau, did not question the importance of the UJA but challenged the assessment and motivations of the "free dollar" camp. Since philanthropy alone failed to provide adequate funds, and private investors refrained from investing in Israel, the loan, they argued, was a solution of last resort. Montor also rejected the grim forecasts of the Federation leaders. A clear understanding of the difference between the Israel Bond and philanthropy, he believed, would guarantee that the loan would not compete with the UJA but rather bring additional funds to Israel:

> Individuals make contributions out of their current income. Contributions [to the UJA] are tax deductible. Contributions are based on emotions alone and are used for relief purposes. Investment funds come from current and accumulated savings. Investment funds must be used wisely and securely. Investment funds can be obtained in part because of an interest in Israel, but there must also be full confidence that such funds will be used for productive purposes, so as to permit the immigrants to become self-supporting and to develop a sound and solid Israel economy, which, in turn, gives a high degree of security to these bonds.[38]

Montor did not deny the fact that American Jews would buy the bonds because of their interest in Israel, but he nevertheless insisted that a clear distinction between the projects, in terms of the motivation for purchase, the sources of its money, and its usage, would allow both the UJA and the bonds to prosper alongside each other and generate more money for Israel.

Montor also questioned the motivation behind the Jewish Federations' opposition. Reluctance to endorse the loan plan, he accused, stemmed from their selfish, vested interests:

> The cry is raised that the "free" dollar is better than the "debt" dollar. But those who raise the cry do not at the same time emphasize that in some communities only 30 to 35% of the gross "free" dollar goes to Israel.[39]

In Montor's interpretation, the Jewish Federations had grown accustomed to taking advantage of money given to the UJA for Israel. Thus, advocates of the "free dollars" were by no means selfless. In reality, he argued, it was Israel that had been giving a gift to the Jewish Federations by allowing them to use its name in appeals. It was the loss of this gift that the Federations dreaded.[40] More fundamentally, the Jewish Federations' attitude, Montor explained, was directed by two principles:

1. [The] UJA must do all that it possibly can do for Israel.
2. Israel must not be permitted to escape from the "clutches" of American Jewish generosity.[41]

Objecting to the Israel Bonds, Montor insisted, was an expression of unwillingness to engage with Israel on an equal footing. On the other hand, he argued, the "moment you give the people of Israel credit for integrity, for capacity to assume and meet obligations," all reservations regarding the Israel Bond vanish.[42]

The exchanges in the conference in Jerusalem and in a follow-up meeting in Washington made clear that a significant segment of the Jewish-American community was against the bond initiative.[43] To lessen the Federations' fears, Ben-Gurion, Kaplan, and Montor emphasized their undying commitment to the UJA. However, as in the Irish case, they were determined to proceed with the bond plan.[44]

Creating the American Financial Development Corporation for Israel

Like Éamon de Valera thirty years before, Montor hoped to persuade Jewish financiers and bankers to underwrite the loan. However, he soon realized that his hopes were unrealistic. Bankers were willing to meet Montor, and share their skepticism about the loan plan, but they refused to underwrite the bonds.[45] Given the bankers' response and the Federations' objections, Ben-Gurion decided to create a new organization that would issue the Israeli bonds. To advance the project, Morgenthau and Montor, the most enthusiastic supporters of the plan, resigned from the UJA, taking with them key executive officers, and established the American Financial Development Corporation for Israel (AFDCI).[46] In the long run, the AFDCI was supposed to support itself by buying bonds from the government at a discount of 3.5% and selling them at par, but in order to jump-start the operation, the Israeli Treasury gave the AFDCI a loan of $100,000.[47] In the following months, Montor, now the chief executive officer, and Morgenthau, the chairman of the AFDCI's board of governors, worked around the clock to prepare the flotation.

As in the Irish case, in order to sell the Israeli bonds, the AFDCI had to create a network of volunteers all across the country virtually from scratch. Although various organizations committed to assist the AFDCI, most of the qualified organizers were busy running the UJA drives. To secure their participation, Montor had to negotiate with the new director of the UJA, Joseph Schwartz, and the leaders of the Jewish Federation. The UJA and Jewish Federations leaders demanded that the UJA and bond campaigns be coordinated so as to avoid direct competition. Montor objected to this demand on principle:

> The Bond Issue is not philanthropy. It is an investment. It does not go to assume the same sources of money from which philanthropy is derived, that is, tax-deductible dollars. Therefore, individuals can give and invest at the very same time.[48]

Montor cautioned that the mere semblance of competition between the UJA and the Israel Bonds would be injurious to both: "We don't want people to think somehow or other that both efforts represent different phases of philanthropy."⁴⁹ Nevertheless, to secure able volunteers, Montor eventually compromised and agreed to limit the period of public solicitations for the bonds to the autumn months.⁵⁰

Passing legislation approving the loan in the Israeli parliament was easy. The AFDCI's legal advisors drafted the "State of Israel Bonds Law."⁵¹ Within weeks, the law passed the three mandatory callings with only negligible opposition.⁵² In the United States things were more complicated. The AFDCI, it turned out, was subject to the Foreign Agents Registration Act of 1938 (FARA) and the regulations of the Securities and Exchange Commission (SEC).⁵³ FARA required people engaged in political, economic, or public relations activities on behalf of a foreign state to register with the Department of Justice. Aside from the burden such registration imposed, it could also deter sympathizers weary of the accusation of divided loyalty.⁵⁴ To get around this obstacle, Montor secured an exemption from FARA by arguing that the AFDCI was an American for-profit corporation having no immediate relationship with Israel.⁵⁵

The SEC regulations, designed to protect the public from fraud, posed additional challenges. First, the SEC required any person engaged in the business of effecting transactions in securities for the account of others to pass a qualifying broker's exam and submit his or her own investments to trade restrictions.⁵⁶ As with FARA, blind compliance with the rule would have rendered the use of volunteers in the AFDCI's activities impractical.⁵⁷ To overcome this obstacle, Montor drew a clear distinction between the activities of paid workers and volunteers in the drive:

> [T]he sale of the bonds ... will be effected through an arrangement by which "volunteers" ... working without profit or compensation, ... will solicit the signing of applications for the purchase of such bonds; that the said applications will contain a provision on the face thereof providing, in substance, that the "volunteers" seeking the application for purchase are not in any manner employed or appointed or authorized to sell such bonds, but that, on the contrary, the application shall be ineffective until countersigned by the duly authorized agent of the corporation.⁵⁸

This division of labor allowed the volunteers to be exempted by the SEC and most of the states' securities commissions.⁵⁹

The Securities and Exchange Act of 1933 also prohibited the use of advertisements for the sale of securities. To surmount this obstacle, Montor requested a special hearing with the SEC commissioners. In the hearing, Montor explained that in the

> ... actual sale [of the bonds], account had to be taken of the nature of this bond issue. It was not designed to enrich individuals, and not even to make a State grow great. Rather, it was animated by the desire to give work to hundreds of thousands of Jews who, otherwise, might have to live forever on the charity of the world ...[60]

A bond with such an appeal, he explained, could only be sold through an intensive public-relations campaign. Having heard the appeal, the commissioners introduced a new rule so as to allow and regulate the publication of newspaper prospectuses.[61] Rule 494 allowed for the publication of prospectuses in a condensed form but instructed that each ad must be submitted to the SEC for prior approval.[62] With these issues cleared, the AFDCI submitted an application, and by March 1951 the SEC approved the Israel Bond prospectus.

Legalizing the sale of Israeli bonds in the United States required a delicate legal minuet. Montor introduced a distinction between paid workers and volunteers in the fine print, which allowed volunteers to be in fact very active in the sale of bonds. To obtain an exemption from FARA, he described the AFDCI as an independent for-profit corporation with little connection to Israel, and then, to the SEC, it was described as an essentially benevolent patriotic endeavor on behalf of Israel. The legal design of the bonds, in other words, required that the AFDCI remained a hybrid entity encompassing profit and non-profit characteristics and maintained an ambiguous association with the Israeli government.

Designing the Israeli Bonds

If it were to have any chance of meeting its goal of selling $500 million worth of bonds in three years, the AFDCI would have to attract as many potential subscribers as possible. To this end, the AFDCI designed a variety of instruments, offering both savings and coupon bonds for 12 and 15 years, respectively. The coupon bonds came with 30 detachable vouchers, payable every six months (yielding a total of 167% of the original investment). In return for the appropriate voucher, local and district banks would pay the subscribers their semi-annual interest. The savings bonds, on the other hand, were to be available at maturity, whereupon subscribers would receive 150% of their initial payment. They were sold in denominations ranging from $25 to $10,000 and the estimated cost of marketing and servicing the bonds was between $5.10 and $6.53 per bond. This rendered small-denomination bonds very expensive (from the ADFCI's standpoint), but Montor decided to offer them in order to maintain the popular appeal of the drive.[63]

The AFDCI considered the option of attracting subscribers by promising a high interest rate. However, in addition to the high cost, Montor was also afraid that such an offer "would . . . deter rather than attract buyers as being a sign of desperate need of the borrower and an almost certain indication of a default."[64] Eventually, the AFDCI offered the Israeli bonds with an annual interest rate of 3.5 percent. As in the Irish case, this rate was higher than the 2.57% interest paid for United States Liberty Bonds (but far below the 6% to 8% which was paid by typical foreign government securities at the time) (see Homer and Sylla 1996: 370–376). The moderately attractive interest rate, Montor hoped, would persuade subscribers that Israel meant business.[65]

While he was still planning the bonds' issue, the skeptical partners of Kuhn Loeb investment bank confronted Montor with a dangerous scenario:

> A man, at a public meeting, enthused by the situation might buy $100,000 worth of bonds and a few days later, in light of financial circumstances or evaporating emotion, might decide to throw the issue back on the market. If there were many of these, it would have the effect of depressing the price . . . and seriously interfering with current sales.[66]

A low market price, the partners explained, would bring sales to a standstill. Potential investors would either be completely deterred or tempted to purchase the bonds on the market. In either case, not only would the flow of dollars to Israel cease, but the depressed price would hurt the government's ability to borrow from other sources. In essence, the possibility of a drop in the price of the Israeli bond was directly related to its hybrid nature. Selling the bond required emotional appeals and social pressuring. While such tactics might generate a large subscription, they were also transient and provided a weak assurance that subscribers would actually hold onto their bonds for a long duration. The AFDCI, therefore, had to find ways not only to sell but also to make sure that subscribers held onto their bonds.

The AFDCI perhaps could have averted the possibility of a drop in the price of the Israeli bonds by "making" a market for the Israeli bonds; that is, by buying off any bonds offered, at a price close to par. This was the typical way in which underwriting firms dealt with price volatility in the days following an initial offering of a bond. However, supporting the market "at all times at about the offering price," Montor realized, "might easily require a substantial portion of the total money that can be raised through sales, and thus diminish the value of the whole operation to Israel."[67]

Dealing with the drop-in-price scenario therefore required an alternative strategy, a strategy that would strike a balance between the pecuniary and benevolent motivations of potential purchasers. Instead of making a market for the Israeli bonds, the AFDCI decided to prevent the market from pricing the bonds altogether. The loan, it was decided, would be sold as a registered and non-transferable bond. Only after three years were subscribers given the opportunity to exchange their registered bonds for bearer bonds of the same value.[68] This stipulation effectively prevented, or at least deferred, the drop-in-price scenario: no trading, no price, and therefore no depressed price.

From the perspective of the subscribers, a non-transferability period, even limited to three years, was very unappealing. As an inalienable and non-fungible asset, the Israeli bond would sit in the pockets of subscribers like a stone for three years. Using the bonds as collateral, already an unlikely eventuality, would become completely impossible. To compensate for this restriction, therefore, the AFDCI designed a number of unusual privileges. First, in case of the death of the registered owner, the AFDCI agreed to purchase the bonds from the inheritors at full price immediately. This clause, which effectively turned the bonds into a type of life insurance policy, was designed to attract elderly subscribers who would otherwise have been deterred from purchasing an illiquid bond. Second, the Israeli government promised to convert the Israeli bonds into Israeli currency at any time – in Israel – provided that the money would be used for tourist expenses, investments, or contributions to a list of authorized organizations.[69] By effectively turning the bond into a kind of limited traveler's check, this stipulation was designed to ease the burden of redemption in foreign currency and encourage tourism. Israel also allowed the UJA and the Jewish Federations to convert bonds in their possession to Israeli currency prior to their maturation.[70] Finally, the AFDCI also allowed purchasers to register the bonds in the name of a third person, thus encouraging the use of the bonds as gifts for weddings, birthdays, *Bar Mizvahs*, anniversaries, academic graduations, and practically every possible life event. The bonds, a special leaflet explained, were a "gift that keeps on giving":

> Your Israel gift Bond to a child will mature in time to contribute to his education, help him on a way to a sound business future or make his adult life richer and more secure. Your Israel gift Bond to a young couple will be their nest-egg, their insurance for a better life in the future. Your gift Bond for a newborn baby will mature in time for his twelfth birthday, to be used for his teen-age education or recreation or saved the next years as the extra security that means so much.[71]

The ability to give the bonds to others in effect doubled the gift value of the bonds: subscribers were now able to gift Israel and "solve their gift problem" with the same purchase.

Taken together, these privileges produced a limited degree of liquidity and use value for the bonds even during the first three years of possession. Under fairly unusual circumstances, like the death of the subscriber, or her visit to Israel, subscribers (or their heirs) could use the bonds immediately. Furthermore, purchasers of coupon bonds realized interest on their investment right away without waiting for maturation. The payment of interest on the coupon bonds and the special privileges did not turn the Israeli bond into a very lucrative investment, but they helped sustain its appeal as a transaction that was distinct from philanthropic gift giving.

To highlight the investment value of the bonds, the AFDCI organized a special "Israel Exposition" in New York. The exposition carried visitors from a new Kaiser-Frazer automobile assembly line through exhibitions of Israel's mineral products, and its ceramics and citrus industries. "The exposition," a promotional booklet explained,

> is intended to present the story of Israel's march toward economic independence . . . [and] to reflect the transition in Israel – from a Land of Promise to a Land of Performance – which is the foundation and objective of the State of Israel Bond Issue.[72]

The theme of economic progress instilled a positive tone in the campaign and suggested that Israel's plans for repaying its debt were realistic. A typical campaign ad presented young men busy over a blueprint, while the captions promised that "They'll pay you back with interest."[73] In a manner similar to the marketing strategy of the Irish bond certificates, the AFDCI reassured potential subscribers by emphasizing the qualities of the borrowers – their integrity, their solemn intentions, and the viability of their plans.

Along with the hopeful depiction of Israel's economy, the AFDCI presented the purchase of bonds as a patriotic act, in relation to both the United States and Israel. Since Israel "represents the one bastion of democracy in the strategic Middle East," helping Israel's economy "strengthens America's defense."[74] Another ad suggested that, "Every time you invest in the State of Israel Bond, you invest in far more than 3½% interest. You also invest in the dignity of man and the future of democracy."[75] To add credibility to this argument, Morgenthau assembled an Advisory Council that included prominent non-Jewish-American figures.[76] In relation to Israel, guilt and pride were woven together to present the purchase of Israeli bonds as a Jewish obligation and an opportunity to participate in the national redemption of the Jewish people. An ad in *Life* magazine boldly declared, "Men died so that these bonds could be born" (October 8, 1951). The purchase of Israeli bonds, another ad suggested, enabled "[y]ou [to] own a share in the future of a great venture . . . Your Israel . . . Bond is a certificate of active participation in the upbuilding of the Jewish State . . . It will *always* be something to be proud of . . ."[77]

The AFDCI used every possible gimmick to get its message across. Every date on the Jewish calendar became a reason to purchase bonds. *Purim*, a holiday commemorating the deliverance from a plot to annihilate the Jews, was transformed into "the festival of Gifts," in which family members gave each other bonds.[78] *Hanukkah*, on the other hand, was transformed into a special Bonds of Israel Government (B.I.G.) Day, dedicated to the collection of unpaid pledges (*B.I.G. Newsletter* 2: 14).

The AFDCI marketed the Israeli bonds as a special kind of moral investment. In an advertisement entitled "A Rich Return for Your Heart . . . A Good Return for Your Purse," the AFDCI suggested:

> You who buy these historic Bonds will be making an investment of your money, calculated to yield a good return. You will also be making an investment that will yield a return of incalculable richness to the heart and spirit.[79]

Thus, the marketing strategy of the Israeli bond aimed at distinguishing it from philanthropy not by presenting it as a regular investment but by rendering the degree to which it was actually different from a gift or an investment incalculable.

Finally, in May of 1951, the AFDCI floated the Israeli bond "Independence Issue." Ben-Gurion himself came to the US for a special tour to promote the sale, accompanied by two Israeli Navy ships and a group of female paratroopers (Stock 1987: 138).[80] The presence of Jewish soldiers on American soil was supposed to illustrate, for the remote American Jews, the magnitude of the events taking place across the ocean. A crowd of thousands greeted Ben-Gurion in Madison Square Garden, and during the following weeks he traveled and spoke on behalf of the AFDCI around the country. During the first three years of the Israel Bond campaign, more than 700,000 subscribers purchased more than $145 million in bonds and in time the AFDCI extended its operations to Canada, Latin America, and Europe (Rehavi and Weingarten 2004).[81] The money flowing from the bond campaign more than doubled the amount of foreign currency Israel received from Jewish sources (Barkai 1990: 57).

Producing National Interests

The previous sections followed Éamon de Valera and Henry Montor as they forged new socio-financial mechanisms to better regulate the relationship between, respectively, the Irish in Ireland and Irish Americans and the Jews in Israel and Jewish Americans. Reshaping these relationships was not simply a matter of rhetoric. While both de Valera and Montor crafted carefully worded slogans and moving images, the crux of their efforts consisted of actually changing the terms of engagement of homeland and diaspora communities. Bringing the fragments of the Irish nation and the fragments of the Jewish nation into cooperation was a matter of developing institutional mechanisms through which homeland and diaspora groups could relate to one another in new ways.

In an effort to alleviate their dependency on diaspora organizations, the Irish and Jewish national leaders attempted to create a more direct link to their potential supporters in the United States. But the point was not simply bypassing the mediation of the diaspora leaders. The Irish and Jewish national movements also sought a different type of link to their compatriots. In place of the degrading method of philanthropy, de Valera and Montor attempted to develop mechanisms that expressed a transition to sovereignty. By combining elements of gift giving and market exchange in their diaspora bonds, they hoped that their American compatriots would become more deeply invested in the future of Ireland and Israel without sacrificing their sense of moral worth and independence.

There is something a bit counterintuitive about these parallel attempts. Sociologists often treat interested exchange as an alienating practice. The common belief is that genuine social relations are essentially disinterested. From this perspective, the entry of material interests into the realm of social relations ultimately depletes their richness (for a powerful critique of this perspective, see Zelizer 2005). Allegedly, interests create social distance, and the absence of interests brings the parties closer together. Echoing this approach, researchers of nationalism often describe national identity as an essentially disinterested social bond. Nation building, from this perspective, is a process of bringing potential members of the nation closer together through the substitution of disinterested for interested ties. The point is not that researchers of nationalism are blind to the existence of interests. On the contrary, scholars of nation building are quite savvy about identifying the interests, usually of the elites, that lurk behind a veneer of disinterested patriotism. Although in most accounts, interested action is treated as the *cause* of nationalism but certainly not its mode of operation (for example, see Hobsbawm and Ranger 1992). However, in the bond projects something entirely different transpired. Here, both the Irish and the Jewish national movements attempted to bind their diasporas more tightly to the national project by *interesting* them in the futures of Ireland and Israel. Interestedness was not a *cause* hiding behind the scenes but quite openly the very means by which the Irish and Jewish leaders attempted to link their compatriots to the national project.

We usually think about nation building as a process aimed at reducing the social distances between groups, or at least generating a perception of the absences of social distance. Nation builders, in this formulation, attempt to bring everyone closer together by rendering internal boundaries irrelevant or invisible. But in the Irish and Israeli cases, it was as if the two national movements wanted to attach their compatriots in the diaspora to the national cause while keeping them conveniently at arm's length. On the one hand, they wished to capitalize on the resources of their American counterparts, and, on the other hand, they wished to keep these supporters outside the inner circles of national decision making. The strategy of nation building reflected in the bond projects was not one of doing away with social distance, in a concrete or imagined sense. Instead, the bond projects were about regulating the social distance between the different groups that made up the nation so that they would remain neither inconveniently close nor impracticably distant.

6

Making and Unmaking National Attachments: The Failure of the Irish Bond and the Success of the Israel Bond

Judged on financial terms alone, the results of the Irish Bond Certificate and the Israel Bond projects were impressive. In the Irish case, more than 300,000 enthusiastic supporters provided Irish Republicans with more than $5 million. This sum was almost five times higher than any previous fundraising campaign had managed to collect. Not only that, unlike the IVF and other philanthropic campaigns, the proceeds of the Irish Bond were under the direct control of the Irish mission, with no limitations whatsoever regarding their use. In the Jewish case, the upwards of $145 million flowing from the bond project dramatically increased the foreign currency available to the government. As in the Irish case, the Israel Bond money – all of it – was subject to the exclusive discretion of the Israeli Government.

But the Irish and Israeli bond projects were more than simply ways of extracting resources from diaspora communities. Fundamentally, the bond projects were attempts to reshape the relationships between the Irish Americans and Jewish Americans and their respective national movements. In this respect, the two projects produced dramatically different results.

In the Irish case, the campaign proved to be a bone of contention between the FOIF and the *Clan na Gael* on the one hand, and the Irish Republican movement on the other. Conflicts arising from the bond campaign spilled over to other areas of activity and eventually led to the organizational collapse of major

Irish-American organizations. More than that, the failure of the Bond Certificate drive changed what it meant to be an Irish American. Disagreements arising from the drive sharpened the boundaries between the Irish in Ireland and the Irish Americans and contributed to the decline of the Irish-American diaspora. The Israel Bond, on the other hand, proved capable of easing, but not eliminating, tensions between Israeli and American Jews, and it provided these fragments of the nation with an additional institutional venue through which to engage one another. Significantly, unlike the institution of philanthropy, which generated sharp tensions along the axis of dependence/independence, the Israel Bond allowed these two communities to engage each other without sacrificing their self-images. Thus, the Israel Bond reinforced the ties between Israeli and American Jews. An examination of the Irish and Israeli attempts to float a second loan in the United States – the Irish in 1921 and the Israelis in 1954 – brings these differences into stark relief.

Irish–Irish American Relations and the Collapse of the Bond Certificate Project

The financial success of the first Bond Certificate campaign provided the Irish Republicans with far more means than they had ever commanded, but the availability of funds did not bring the tensions between the FOIF and the Irish mission in the United States to an end. During 1920, the disagreements between the FOIF and the Irish mission regarding the rights and obligations associated with financial contribution to the Irish cause intensified and spilled over to other issues.

Aside from launching the Bond Certificate campaign, Éamon de Valera sought to obtain international recognition for his Republic. One of the key obstacles to that recognition, he realized, was the claim that Irish independence would threaten Britain's security. In order to counter this allegation, in an interview with the *Westminster Gazette* on February 6, 1920, he presented a moderate position. Specifically, de Valera explained that his government would not allow foreign powers to use its territory as a base for an attack on Britain. As a historical precedent, he mentioned the Platt Amendment, by which in return for the withdrawal of

American troops, the Cuban government agreed not to enter into any treaty with foreign powers that might threaten the United States (in Tansill 1957: 359–360). For the leaders of the FOIF, already aggravated by the Irish mission's activities, de Valera's conciliatory approach seemed like a betrayal of fundamental principles. John Devoy used the front page of the *Gaelic American* to attack de Valera's position. The Platt Amendment, he informed readers, had allowed the United States to invade Cuba legally in 1906. De Valera, he accused, had "lowered the flag" and compromised Ireland's demand for full sovereignty (*Gaelic American*, February 21, 1920).

In the following months, the relationship between the Irish mission and the FOIF deteriorated further. When the Republican Party, a favorite in the coming elections, held its national convention in Chicago in June 1920, the FOIF and de Valera's camp prepared two entirely different campaigns. De Valera opted for an open demonstration of power. He invited his supporters from all over the country to come to Chicago, using the Bond Certificate proceeds to cover their travel expenses. His supporters rented offices across the street from the convention hall, distributed leaflets, and carried out a 5,000-man torchlight parade. The FOIF leaders believed that such a campaign was injurious to the Irish cause and opted, instead, for a low-key lobbying campaign. An attempt to bring the two camps together failed, and on June 9, 1920, Judge Cohalan and de Valera presented the resolutions committee with two competing planks (Tansill 1957; Doorley 2005).

The result of two competing and uncoordinated campaigns was disastrous. De Valera's plank, calling for recognition of the Irish Republic, was defeated 11 to 1. Cohalan's plank, calling for self-determination for Ireland, passed narrowly. This victory, however, was short-lived. Upon learning about de Valera's opposition to Cohalan's plank, the chairman of the resolutions committee withdrew the resolution. Angry and frustrated, Cohalan and his associates returned to New York. De Valera continued with Frank Walsh to the Democratic Party's convention in San Francisco, where he failed to pass a similar plank. The open rift between the two Irish camps in the United States compromised their ability to advocate on behalf of the Republic of Ireland.

The conflict between the FOIF leaders and de Valera and his colleagues was related to their conflicting interpretations of the

Irish Bond campaign and the rights and obligations that followed from it. Devoy addressed this matter directly. In his attack on de Valera's "Cuban interview," he explained that:

> ... every dollar subscribed, either to the Irish Victory Fund, or to the Bond Certificates of the Irish Republic, was given on the distinct understanding that the policy announced in Dublin on January 21, 1919 ... would be firmly adhered to. The Dail Eireann has the power, but not the right, to change the policy and the objectives because its members were elected on a specified mandate to proclaim an independent Irish Republic, entirely separated from England. This aroused the enthusiasm of the Irish in America and loosened their purse-strings ... they would have neither enthusiasm nor money for the so-called free Ireland under an English Monroe doctrine ... (*Gaelic American*, February 21, 1920)

Devoy did not see a difference between the IVF philanthropic money and the money subscribed to the Irish Bond campaign. Both pools of money, he believed, were essentially a gift that entitled Irish Americans to a special consideration. In dealing with the fundamentals, Devoy challenged, even the *Dáil Éireann* could not decide alone but had to consult the Irish in America.

De Valera and his associates harbored a contrasting understanding of the Bond money and the relations it implied. During and after the Republican convention, the leaders of the FOIF repeatedly accused de Valera of misusing Irish national funds. In reply, de Valera released the following statement:

> The moneys that have been subscribed to the Irish Issue Bonds ... is Irish Government money, the property of the Irish nation. It is subscribed for all legitimate governmental purposes ... Some time ago, having noticed the symptoms of a disease of which the present charges are but another symptom, I wrote to my government pointing out the situation. I feared then that an effort would be made to use the power of the purse to make me subservient to the wishes of other than the Irish people. To prevent that policy, I asked for an appropriation from my government giving me and my co-trustees discretionary powers to use governmental funds within specified limits so that I might be free to work untrammeled in Ireland's interest.[1]

Joseph McGarrity, de Valera's close ally from Philadelphia, was more explicit. When the Massachusetts council of the FOIF published a letter in the *New York Times* urging de Valera to send to Ireland without delay the "millions of dollars" he collected in the United States (December 21, 1921), he quickly retorted:

> The people of Ireland, in authorizing through their representatives the floating of a loan, bound themselves to repay the loan at the closest opportunity. These funds are, therefore, their property to be used according to their representatives, the Dail Eireann, shall direct. (*Irish Press*, December 25, 1921)

From de Valera and McGarrity's perspective, the Irish Bond was a loan and it was precisely this character that allowed the Irish Republic to act independently of the FOIF's dictates.

When the ACII launched the Irish Bond drive, the bond's hybrid nature – the fact that it combined elements of gift giving and investment – was an interesting selling point. But now that the parties actually asserted the rights and obligations that followed from the purchase of these bonds, the ambiguous status of the bond certificates became a bone of contention. Believing that the bond certificates had strings attached to them, Devoy demanded special consideration. The same understanding undergirded the FOIF's accusations of misuse of the money. Unlike regular market exchange, wherein buyers lose any right over the money they have parted with, the FOIF leaders believed they still had the right to oversee the use of the bond certificates money. De Valera, on the other hand, based on the difference between philanthropic funds and the Irish Bond proceeds, insisted on his right to use the money free from the whims of Irish-American politicians.

The Irish–Irish American not-so-civil war

After the fiasco in Chicago, Harry Boland met Devoy and the executive of the *Clan na Gael* in an attempt to straighten out the relationship between the Irish mission and the Irish-American leaders. A few days of intensive discussions resulted in a written agreement. On purely American matters, the FOIF leader would preside. In all matters "regarding policy and interests of the Irish

Republic," de Valera would have the last word (August 15, 1920, in Cronin 1972: 12–13). In practice, however, it was not always easy to distinguish between Irish and Irish-American matters. Toward the end of September, Boland reported to Ireland: "things remain much as they were during the Chicago business" (Boland to Collins, September 22, 1920, in Fitzpatrick 2003: 186).

At around the same time, de Valera tried a different approach. Believing that the FOIF's national council acted in a manner that contradicted Irish-American sentiments, de Valera tried to increase the representativeness of the FOIF. He wrote to Bishop Michael Gallagher, the national President of the FOIF, explaining:

> ... if confidence is to be restored it was necessary to democratize the system of control so that when vital differences arose it might always be possible to settle them finally, not by arbitrary suspension and expulsion by the executive, but by the will of the majority of the members.[2]

Specifically, de Valera suggested changing the FOIF's constitution to delegating more power and authority to the state councils of the FOIF. To implement these changes, he asked Gallagher to summon a special Race Convention or, alternatively, to call a national council meeting in Detroit or Chicago, away from Cohalan's stronghold in New York. A more decentralized structure, de Valera hoped, would be more responsive to his demands.

Gallagher refused to call a Race Convention and, instead, convened the national council for a meeting at the Waldorf Astoria hotel in New York on September 17, 1920. The meeting was tense from the outset. In addition to the 162 national council delegates, some 63 observers, mostly de Valera's supporters, were present. De Valera, however, never spoke at the meeting. After being denied the podium for a while, he and his entourage left the room (see Fitzpatrick 2003: 190). Following de Valera's dramatic departure, the conflict between the Irish mission and the FOIF leaders rose to a new level.

In October 22, 1920, Boland decided to cut off the *Clan na Gael* from the Irish Republican Brotherhood:

> We have tried in vain to secure the cooperation which we believe the rank-and-file of the Clan na Gael wishes to give us [he explained]

and having found that the Clan Executive itself is powerless against the veto of Justice Cohalan, we find it our duty to inform the body of the members of that fact and tell them that we have been reluctantly compelled to sever our connection between Clan na Gael and the parent body in Ireland... (*Irish Press*, October 22, 1920)

Several weeks later, de Valera's allies in the *Clan na Gael*'s executive committee, McGarrity and Hugh Montague, announced the establishment of a "reorganized *Clan na Gael*" (Carroll 1978: 159). In the following months, *Clan* members were bombarded with letters from both factions vying for their allegiance (Fitzpatrick 2003: 209).

Not a month had passed before de Valera gathered his supporters in Chicago to announce the establishment of a rival organization to the FOIF, the American Association for the Recognition of the Irish Republic (AARIR). The unpalatable name of the association was not an accident. By choosing what he saw as an unambiguous title, de Valera hoped to clear away any vagueness with regard to the organization's mission. Addressing its members, he envisioned an inclusive and democratic organization, "free from machine politics." At the same time, he insisted, "some provision [must] be made so that any line of action taken ... may not cross that of Ireland's own direct representative" (Lavelle 1961: 184).

For the FOIF, the establishment of the new rival organization meant an intensified struggle for survival. In October 1920, Lynch reported that a number of local councils had implemented de Valera's decentralization initiative without authorization. The disobedient councils also refused to send their membership dues to the national headquarters.[3] In November, de Valera loyalists had crashed FOIF branch meetings all over New York. To deal more effectively with these infiltrations, the national executive committee approved an expedited expulsion process for de Valera's loyalists; but these measures failed to quell the unrest.[4] In terms of membership, the FOIF suffered catastrophic losses. From more than 100,000 in November 1920, membership dropped to 20,000 in mid-1921 (Doorley 2005: 134–135). The "reorganized *Clan*" experienced difficulties as well. Despite Boland's hopes, old *Clan* members did not rush to join the new organization. Only in San Francisco did an entire *Clan* branch transfer its allegiance to the new organization (Fitzpatrick 2003: 209).

The AARIR launch was impressive, but the group soon ran into similar troubles. The AARIR opened national headquarters in Chicago and prepared for a national convention in April 1921 (Carroll 1978).[5] To encourage recruitment, Boland and James O'Mara used Irish Bond money and offered between 25 and 50 cents for every new recruit. At one point, de Valera boasted that the AARIR had more than half a million members (Doorley 2005). But the excitement surrounding the AARIR was short-lived. After the first national convention, Joseph Walsh, the secretary of the AARIR, resigned, accusing Boland and O'Mara of backroom politicking. A few months later, O'Mara reported to Ireland that "the first bloom of enthusiasm has faded from the face of AARIR. Many internal differences have sprung up, and these will grow – especially in idleness. Membership is in standstill."[6]

Launching the second Irish Bond drive

The first Irish bond drive continued for almost a year and ended in December 1920.[7] Less than a year later, the *Dáil Éireann* decided to launch another loan. As with the first loan, de Valera and his associates were not interested in the loan solely for the money it would raise. In July 1921, Lloyd George, the British Prime Minister, and de Valera declared a ceasefire and committed to negotiations over the status of the Irish island. In preparation for the peace talks, the *Dáil Éireann* authorized an external loan of $20 million and an internal loan of £1 million.[8] A successful issue of a loan, Collins and de Valera believed, would demonstrate that the Republic was ready to fight for its life again if needed, and therefore improve their position in the talks.[9] The confidence shown by subscribers, de Valera and his associates believed, would prove the vitality of the Republic of Ireland.

Conditions in the United States in mid-1921, however, were different from the conditions in 1919. Due to the furious conflict, in 1921 the ACII could no longer count on organizational support from the FOIF. The AARIR, which de Valera hoped would shoulder the responsibility of organizing such drives, was not in a position to help either.[10] Whereas in 1919, despite the FOIF's reservations, de Valera received monetary and organizational support, in 1921 no Irish-American organization was in a position to offer such assistance even if it wished to do so.

Despite this difficulty, Stephen O'Mara, who replaced his brother James as the trustee and fiscal agent of the Irish Republic in the United States, believed that with proper adjustments, the second bond drive could be a success. To attract large investors, who on the whole had avoided the first Bond Certificate drive, Stephen O'Mara suggested varying the kind of securities offered.

> All subscriptions of less than $500 [would] be used in the same way as in the old bond drive; subscriptions of $500 and upwards [would] be treated separately and [be] retained in this country for repayment within three years from day of issue[,] interest [would] only be applied for our purposes.[11]

Low- and middle-income subscribers, O'Mara believed, would continue to purchase the bond certificates they already knew. Attracting the more sophisticated high-income crowd, however, required limiting the uncertainty associated with the bond certificates. Instead of giving their money for an unspecified period, big subscribers would give their money for a period of three years only.[12] After three years, investors would be given the choice of either getting their money back without interest, "Or in the event of recognition of the Republic ... exchange [their bond certificates] for Bonds of the Government of Ireland bearing interest *from the date of subscription*." The option of exchanging zero-interest bond certificates for regular interest-bearing bonds, O'Mara argued, would make the offer "more businesslike, [and] consequently more liable to lead to big subscription."[13]

To assure investors that they would be able to get their money back after three years, O'Mara suggested using the funds as an endowment: the principal of the loan would be invested in the United States, and the Irish Republic would enjoy only the interest accruing from these investments. In addition, O'Mara also suggested appointing an Irish American of high standing as trustee for the American funds:

> An agreement will be drawn up between the Irish Representatives and the American Trustees whereby the investment of the funds would require mutual agreement, and whereby the payment

of interest would be made to the discretion of the Irish Representatives.[14]

Careful to avoid a repeat of the struggles with the FOIF over the control and use of the money, Stephen O'Mara suggested a clear division of responsibilities between the American trustee and the Irish mission.

In essence, Stephen O'Mara's plan was to turn the bond certificate into more of an investment than a gift. To compensate for the weakness of the AARIR, he attempted to bank on the pecuniary interests of potential subscribers. O'Mara knew that the monetary appeal of this drive was still limited, but he remained optimistic: "If we could put across such a scheme [he assured Collins] ... the man who under ordinary circumstances would subscribe $25 would, under these circumstances, I believe, be prepared to put up $100 even if he had to go into debt for it."[15] The interest accrued from the endowment, he explained, would easily meet the *Dáil Éireann* needs.

Back in Dublin, Collins and de Valera (who returned from the United States in late 1920) were eager to issue the new loan, but they were skeptical of O'Mara's scheme. The key problem with the endowment plan, from their perspective, was the appointment of an American trustee. "The difficulty about trustees, which you note, also came up," de Valera confided to Collins. "The subscribers would want American trustees and the retention of the money in America. We can never allow Government funds to be controlled by strangers."[16] Having dealt with Irish Americans for over a year, de Valera and Collins were not inclined to deposit Irish money in their hands again, and eventually they instructed Stephen to issue the new loan along the lines of the old scheme.[17]

Given the AARIR's weakness, Stephen O'Mara eventually opted for a state-based campaign rather than a national-scale drive.[18] The drive opened in early December 1921 in Washington, DC and Chicago. Stephen O'Mara and Boland tried to spur excitement about the second Bond Certificate drive by bringing from Ireland Father Michael O'Flanagan, the vice president of *Sinn Féin*, for a tour. But the media, including local Irish weeklies, hardly covered the new drive, and morale remained low. Finally, after failing to expand to other locales, O'Mara terminated the drive in January 1922, having raised only $662,720 of the planned

$20 million (Fitzpatrick 2003: 205; see also *Chicago Daily Tribune*, January 3, 1922).

The Floating of Israel Bonds, Development Issue

As in the Irish case, the floating of the Independence Issue in May 1951 did not bring an end to the struggles surrounding the Israel Bonds. Recall that the SEC, in response to Montor's appeal, created a detailed procedure for certifying ads for securities (Rule 494). The AFDCI followed this procedure but then, on September 25, 1951, Baldwin Bane, the director of the Division of Corporations of the SEC, sent Montor a Comment letter.[19] The AFDCI, Bane argued, failed to submit ads for SEC approval in a timely manner, and as a result a number of misrepresentations had occurred. First, the "advertisement [appearing in the *New York Times*, September 18, 1951] contains a prominent paragraph devoted to the following theme, '... each State of Israel Bond you purchase strengthens American defenses.'" Such a statement, he argued, was misleading. Furthermore, the ad "could easily mislead the layman into thinking that these bonds are of the type ordinarily purchased by fiduciary institutions." Bane concluded with a warning:

> You are advised that if the letter and spirit of the rules are not hereafter complied with, this Division will recommend to the Commission the institution of appropriate injunctive proceedings.[20]

Bane's letter was a serious blow. The SEC, in fact, overturned the AFDCI's main selling points. From Bane's point of view, the bonds could not be considered an investment, and their moral value, at least from an American perspective, was questionable.

Montor was deeply concerned about Bane's letter, but he decided not to back off.[21] In a carefully written response, he contested each of the charges. The AFDCI, he argued, had made an extraordinary effort to comply with Rule 494, and the failure that Bane had noted was a one-time mistake. Furthermore, the "inclusion by Congress of the State of Israel for a substantial amount in the Mutual Security Bill to provide aid and arms to Israel is further testimony..." of Israel's value for America's defense.[22] Montor's detailed and assertive response put the SEC on notice that an injunction against the AFDCI would be met with a team of skilled attorneys, and in the following months the tension with the SEC relaxed.

Montor skillfully staved off the SEC's reservations, but the affair affected the AFDCI's relationship with the Israeli embassy in Washington. Ambassador Abba Eban followed the affair with deep concern. Montor's missteps, he believed, could hurt Israel. Therefore, he informed Montor:

> I... emphatically assert my intention to intervene in the most effective way whenever I see anything done on behalf of the State of Israel in this country.... While it might be technically true that the corporation [AFDCI] is an American institute, and its employees are American citizens, the fact is that the credit and integrity of the Israel Government are directly involved in this operation. Moreover, the money employed in the operation of the Bond issue is the money of Israel taxpayers, whom I represent in this country.[23]

Eban's position clarifies that at least some Israeli officials viewed AFDCI's status as an American institution merely as a technicality.

Montor and Morgenthau, however, insisted that the AFDCI was an independent American corporation. This status, they insisted, was not a formality but the very condition that allowed the AFDCI to operate.[24] To assert their position, Montor and Morgenthau resigned from the AFDCI, conditioning their return on the clarification of the AFDCI's autonomy. Looking for a formula that would bring Montor and Morgenthau back, Ben-Gurion suggested that Montor "should be regarded in effect as a special ambassador of Israel, having authority in a specific field... In any matter which directly affected the official relation between Israel and the United States, Eban had the right to intervene..."[25] This division of labor convinced Montor and Morgenthau to withdraw their resignations.

The AFDCI's position within the Jewish-American communities remained contentious as well. Despite the coordination agreement between the AFDCI and the UJA, in 1951 alone Israel Bonds committees clashed with Jewish Federations in New York, Chicago, Cleveland, Detroit, Los Angeles, Miami,

Newark, Pittsburgh, and Washington, DC. Virtually every major Jewish-American center became a stage for vociferous arguments between "free" and "debt" dollar supporters.[26]

The ongoing conflict prompted the leadership in Jerusalem to intervene. At first, Ben-Gurion tried to reconstitute the coordination agreement.[27] When this strategy failed, he tried a different approach. Instead of dividing the turf between the rivaling organizations, he suggested, the UJA and the AFDCI should lead a joint campaign in New York, home of 40 percent of US Jews. Montor accepted the suggestion immediately. Morris Bernstein, the head of New York's UJA, objected, saying that such a merger would ruin the delicate balance between the UJA constituting bodies and could jeopardize its tax-deductible status.[28] Short of imposing the merger, Ben-Gurion suggested that a coordination committee be formed, to be headed by Abba Eban, the Israeli Ambassador in Washington, but this solution was also rejected. Montor and the UJA leaders were quick to point out that such an arrangement would turn them into agents of a foreign government, and they refused to accept Eban's authority.[29]

In the absence of a solution, it was only a matter of time before further clashes erupted. In 1952, the AFDCI decided to open its drive in Indianapolis in the spring with a tribute dinner for Golda Meyerson, Israel's Minister of Labor.[30] The heads of the Jewish Federation of Indianapolis, especially Julian Freeman, who also served as the vice president of the CJFWF, interpreted the AFDCI's decision as a punishment for his opposition to the bond plan. Attempting to subvert Montor's plan, the Jewish Federation appealed to Eban, offering to host Meyerson's dinner themselves.[31] Eban was working on a compromise when Meyerson declared that she had "fought the Mufti [the defeated Palestinian leader] and Abdullah [the king of Jordan] and would come to Indianapolis [for the AFDCI's event] with or without Freeman's invitation."[32]

The conflict in Indianapolis attracted enormous attention in the Jewish press and was interpreted by both sides as an important trial of strength. Using newspaper ads and telephone solicitations, the local Jewish federation orchestrated a boycott of Meyerson's dinner.[33] A day before Meyerson's arrival, the Federation held a protest meeting that was attended by 600 people who called, again, for the cancellation of Meyerson's visit. Montor exerted extraordinary efforts to make Meyerson's dinner a success. The

AFDCI circulated a leaflet entitled "The Eyes of World Jewry are on Indianapolis – Is it free or is it Throttled?"[34] Opposing the dinner, the leaflet argued, was nothing less than a denial of Israel's right to exist as a sovereign state. To secure attendance, the AFDCI distributed free tickets for the dinner and bussed in supporters from the surrounding cities.

Montor described Meyerson's dinner as a big success. Seven hundred and fifty guests attended the event and purchased over $155,000 worth of bonds.[35] But the costs of the conflict were high: not only had Montor invested a huge amount of work and resources in securing attendance, but leaders around the country also perceived his behavior as bullying. The Israeli Ambassador followed the events and was, again, troubled by Montor's conduct:

> The managers of the welfare funds [he reported to Moshe Sharett, Israel's Minister of Foreign Affairs,] are blocking the way for the loan activity in the spring and early summer and also narrow their action in the fall and winter. There were expressions of lack of confidence in the efficiency of the loan and the capabilities of its managers. Since the welfare funds determine the level of social life in every city, things got to the point that a person that commits himself to the Bonds is excluding himself from the local social elite ... Some of the great and loyal leaders [of the UJA] emphasize in public substantial doubts toward the Bonds and avoid assisting it – in the winter and in the summer.[36]

Instead of creating "strong cemented cells of leadership and activity in every town and city," Eban explained, Montor had created unnecessary conflicts and then appealed to Israel for backing. Without effective supervision, he warned, "the Bonds may [eventually] infect the Government of Israel in its isolation." Prompted by this report, Sharett flew to New York to make another attempt at ending the damaging tensions.[37] But, once again, pacifying the warring sides was hard. Montor welcomed Sharett and scheduled him for a series of speaking engagements on behalf of the AFDCI. Instead of easing the tensions, these events created additional conflicts in new localities.[38] When Sharett attempted to reconstitute the defunct coordination committee, Montor raised countless objections and at some point simply avoided meeting the Israeli Minister. Sharett returned to Israel angry and frustrated, having suffered a painful public humiliation.[39]

During the following months, the disagreements between the Foreign Ministry and the AFDCI regarding the conduct of the campaign widened. Montor, while insisting on the AFDCI's independence, demanded that the Israeli government express unreserved support for the Israel Bonds and urged more ministers to come to the United States for speaking tours. Instead of clarifying that those "who fail to purchase Bonds are . . . acting against the State of Israel," he protested, Israeli leaders convey the message that either contribution to the UJA or the purchase of Israeli bonds is an adequate way of supporting israel.[40] In Israel, Sharett urged Ben-Gurion to replace Montor with an Israeli appointee and enforce the AFDCI's subordination.[41] In November 1952, the situation reached an impasse and Montor and his associates used the weapon of resignation again. In return for withdrawing their resignations, Montor demanded that the Finance Ministry would supervise the AFDCI's work, rather than the Foreign Affairs Ministry.[42] Sharett objected to Montor's demands. Moving the AFDCI to the Finance Ministry, he reasoned, would compromise Israel's already limited ability to supervise Montor.[43] Eventually, Ben-Gurion accepted Montor's demands. The AFDCI was transferred to the jurisdiction of the Finance Ministry, and the government released a strong declaration of support for the AFDCI.[44]

The tensions with the SEC and the conflict in Indianapolis generated deep disagreements between the AFDCI and the Israeli embassy. From Eban's perspective, since Montor collected money on behalf of Israel, and his decisions directly affected it, the AFDCI fell squarely within his jurisdiction as the supreme representative of Israel in the United States. Montor, on the other hand, insisted on maintaining the AFDCI's autonomy. The ambiguous position of the Israel Bond organization became a source of ongoing friction. Interestingly, however, in order to return Montor to the AFDCI, Ben-Gurion came up with a division of labor between Eban and Montor that further blurred rather than clarified the AFDCI's status.

The ambiguous status of the Israeli bonds generated constant arguments between the AFDCI and various organizations. Regardless of the AFDCI's attempt to present the Israeli bond as a sound moral investment, the Jewish Federations saw it mostly as a gift. This interpretation lay at the root of the Jewish Federations' demand that the AFDCI coordinate its activities with the UJA.

Viewing both drives as in competition for the generosity of American Jews, the Federations wanted to defend themselves against a new rival. Montor, on the other hand, insisted that since the Israeli bond was an investment, there was no real competition and so the Federations' demands in effect violated the rights of individual investors to determine the fate of their money. As in the Irish case, the absence of an agreement with regard to the nature of the Israeli bonds proved to be a source of ongoing conflicts.

Launching the Israel Bond Development Issue

Selling the Israeli bonds, sometimes against opposition from local communities, was a costly affair. Unable to rely on the support of Jewish Federations, Montor had to open eighty offices all across the United States and staff them with paid employees.[45] Instead of the estimated weekly budget of $150,000, the AFDCI used more than $200,000, and soon it incurred a debt of $800,000.[46] Given the rate of subscription to the bonds, continued operation on the basis of 3.5% commission was impossible, and the Israeli Government was forced to increase the AFDCI's commission from 3.5 to 6%.[47] Nevertheless, the AFDCI proved to be indispensable. In monetary terms alone, by May 1954, when the Independence Issue ended, the AFDCI had sold $145.5 million worth of bonds (Rehavi and Weingarten 2004). Moreover, on the basis of subscriptions to the bonds, the Israeli government was able to obtain additional loans from commercial banks.[48] Unlike the situation with the UJA money, Israel did not share the proceeds of the Israel Bond campaign with anyone and faced few restrictions when it came to determining how to spend them.

Given the importance of the bonds, toward the end of 1953 the Israeli government approved a "Development Issue" of Israel Bonds for a sum of $350,000,000.[49] As in the Irish case, however, the launch of the first loan created problems that the AFDCI and the Israeli Government had to deal with if they hoped to be successful with a second bond drive. To tackle these issues, in June 1953 Montor traveled to Israel and met with Levi Eshkol, Israel's new Minister of Finance.[50]

Montor was eager to continue with the loan plan, but he insisted that realizing the full potential of the Israel Bonds required a thorough restructuring of the relationship between the AFDCI and the Israeli government. Above all, Montor demanded that the government provide him with unconditional support. Irritated by Israeli attempts to coordinate the AFDCI's activities, Montor demanded complete independence, including the right to decide when and where to sell bonds in the United States. In addition, Montor insisted that "the State be debarred from utilizing its law or permitting any person, institution, or governmental agency from floating in the United States securities which, in the view of the AFDCI, would be competitive with the State of Israel Bonds." Montor's principal aim in this demand was to wean the government off the habit of short-term borrowing from Jewish financiers in the United States. Not only were these loans costly, he reasoned, but the efforts to secure such loans painted a dire picture of Israel's economic condition and negatively affected the AFDCI sales.[51]

Finally, Montor insisted on clarifying the relationships between the State and the AFDCI and reversing the flow of funds between these entities. "Today," he wrote, "the State often gives itself the impression that it is the benefactor of the AFDCI, rather than that AFDCI accumulates money on behalf of the State." To correct this impression, he suggested that "every three months... the *AFDCI* should render an accounting and transmit the proceeds [to the Israeli Government], after deducting costs to it, based on the budget to which the Finance Minister has consented."[52] To continue their efforts on behalf of the AFDCI, Montor and his associates demanded complete autonomy, monopoly over credit operations, and an unequivocal clarification of the AFDCI's special status.

Eshkol and his colleagues were surprised by Montor's demands. David Horowitz, the Governor of the newly created Bank of Israel, argued that if the relationships between the Israeli Treasury and the AFDCI were so poor then the whole project should be cancelled. Eventually, however, Eshkol accepted Montor's reasoning, and the parties signed a new underwriting agreement that reflected his demands.[53]

The Fiscal Agency agreement with the Chase National Bank was modified as well. The terms of the first agreement specified that Israel would provide the bank with money for the payment of interest on coupon bonds every six months. Unredeemed payments, the agreement specified, would remain in the bank for six years, accruing no interest, before the bank returned them to Israel. During the first three years, however, it became clear that a substantial number of interest payments had remained unclaimed. Montor explained that "[m]any people mistakenly believe that they are helping Israel in not presenting their interest coupon for collection."[54] In the new fiscal agreement, Israel insisted that Chase National Bank retain the said money for only a year. Realizing that many American Jews decided to gift Israel again, this time by passing over the collection of interest payments on their bonds, the State amended the contract so as to take advantage of that gift.

With a new Underwriting Agreement and a new Fiscal Agency Agreement in place, the AFDCI launched the new Development Issue on May 1, 1954. Within a few months it became clear that the sales of the Development bond were following the same pattern as that of the Independence Issue. In 1954, the AFDCI sold a total of $40,406,000 worth of new bonds (see Figure 6.1).

Despite the successful launching of the Development Issue bonds, the AFDCI's relations with the UJA and the Jewish Federations remained tenuous. In early 1955, Montor published an article in the AFDCI newsletter entitled "The Nonsense of Coordination" and announced an early kickoff for the bond campaign. The UJA appealed for Eshkol's intervention. Notwithstanding the new underwriting agreement, Eshkol tried to dissuade Montor from conducting a bond drive in the spring and, in response, in late February 1955, Montor and his close associates resigned from the AFDCI again.[55] As on previous occasions, Eshkol hurried to New York to solve the crisis. The leaders of the UJA insisted on the suspension of the AFDCI activities during their spring campaign. They also intimated that they were ready to provide the personnel to run the AFDCI in Montor's stead. Montor, however, was adamant that Eshkol had no right to dictate the AFDCI sales procedures.[56] Having reached an impasse, Eshkol decided to accept the UJA's offer. On March 13, 1955 he accepted the resignations of Montor and his associates and appointed Joseph Schwartz, the former director of the UJA, to lead the Israel Bond (since the AFDCI was registered under Montor's name, Eshkol decided to establish a new corporation, the Development

Corporation for Israel, to continue with the project – American Jewish Committee 1956: 232).

Montor's resignation marked a new era in the relationship between the Israel Bond and the Jewish American community. The UJA and the leaders of the Jewish Federations were grateful for Eshkol's position in the crisis. From their perspective, Israel had finally taken a balanced position on the disagreement between the organizations.[57] Schwartz's close relationships with the leaders of the UJA and his support for the principle of coordination reduced the tensions between the DCI and local Jewish Federations. In the following years, the conflicts surrounding the bonds gradually subsided.

Over the years, the Israel Bonds became a permanent feature of the Jewish-Israeli connection. In 1955, the DCI sold $43,507,000 worth of development bonds, just $3 million more than its sales in 1954, but gradually, the bond sales expanded. Whereas in the 1950s sales averaged $42 million a year, during the 1970s, average annual sales increased to $322 million. In the new millennium, average sales exceed $1 billion each year. Yet in terms of economic importance, the Israel Bond gradually lost centrality. In the early 1950s, Israel Bond dollars served as the government's main source of foreign exchange. During the following decades, however, Israel diversified its foreign currency sources, and today the government also borrows on regular financial markets.[58] Nevertheless, the DCI continues to exist, and the place of the Israel Bond in the national economy remains substantial. The Israel Bond proceeds finance major infrastructure projects such as building power plants, ports, railways, desalinization plants, and so on. About a third of Israel's $30 billion current external debt is owed to Israel Bond subscribers. Altogether over $24 billion worth of bonds were sold, and about $15 billion were redeemed (Rehavi and Weingerten 2004).

Failure and Success in Bond Issuing

The fusion of elements of gift giving and market exchange in the respective bond projects generated contrasting interpretations over the nature of the transaction. The leaders of Irish and Jewish diaspora organizations interpreted the purchase of Irish and Israeli bonds as an act of giving. The leadership in Ireland and Israel, in contrast, emphasized the investment value of the bonds. These divergent interpretations served, in both cases, as a focal point for protracted tensions. However, whereas in the Irish case these disparate readings led to the breakup of the community, in the Israeli case, the different perspectives, while generating serious strain, also served to facilitate the relationship between the parties. Comparing the second issue of Irish and Israeli diaspora bonds gives a dramatic illustration of these differences.

The first issue of Irish and Israeli bonds affected the conditions under which the second loan drives operated in radically different ways. When Stephen O'Mara prepared the second Irish bond drive, neither the FOIF nor the AARIR was in a position to provide the Irish mission with the manpower or funds necessary to launch the campaign. In fact de Valera had to use money from the first bond drive to keep the AARIR alive. The flow of dollars literally reversed. Whereas prior to 1921 American funds had supported the struggle in Ireland, in 1921 the bond money supported struggles between different Irish factions in the United States. Arguments regarding the rights and obligations associated with the purchase of Irish bonds spread to other fields and precipitated the breakup of key Irish-American organizations. In contrast, when the Israeli Ministry of Finance prepared the issue of the Development Bond in 1954, the AFDCI and later DCI were ready to organize the drive. The results of the Development Issue drive indicate that, by and large, the Jewish-American public was ready to renew its investment in Israel's future. Moreover, when in early 1955 Montor resigned from the AFDCI, executives from the UJA were ready to take his place. Clearly, by 1955 the Israel Bonds were institutionalized to such an extent that the project continued without the support of its founder.

The success and failure of the two projects, to be sure, were relative. In spite of the antagonism and conflict that surrounded de Valera's mission, the two Irish bond drives resulted in a collection of more than $6 million from more than 300,000 subscribers.[59] On the Jewish side, the sale of Israeli bonds did not bring an end to the tensions between major Jewish-American organizations, and the project yielded less money than its originators had expected. Yet, despite the fact that failure and success were in neither case absolute, the abrupt termination of the Irish Bond project and the continuation of the Israel Bond drive provides a striking illustration of the different fates of these projects.

The Making and Unmaking of National Attachments

Treating the bond projects merely as attempts to raise more money for the Irish and Jewish national movements, however, would be incorrect. Over and above their monetary goals, the Irish and Israeli bond projects were nation-building projects. Through these bonds, the Irish and Jewish national movements attempted to bridge the differences between homeland and diaspora communities and more securely attach the Irish-American and Jewish-American fragments to the nation. The failure and success of the drives, therefore, meant more than simply reducing or augmenting the flow of dollars to particular national movements.

The Collapse of Irish-American Diaspora Nationalism

The rivalry between the FOIF and the Irish mission had a paralyzing effect on Irish-American activism. During the climax of the Anglo-Irish war, in the first half of 1921, Bishop Gallagher, the President of the FOIF, lamented:

> If ever Ireland needed help from the power of American public opinion, it was during the last six months. During this time, Italy, through her Parliament, voiced a vigorous protest against the British atrocities in Ireland; the French Press stigmatized the outrages on humanity in words burning with indignation; the Belgian Bishops led by Cardinal Mercier denounced in no uncertain terms the British reign of terror in Ireland; in Scandinavia, Holland, Spain and in England itself leading men felt constrained to express their horror at the crimes of England Bashi Bazouks against the Irish people. But America, the champion of freedom . . . where so many millions of Irish blood live, has done practically nothing.[60]

Gallagher's assessment was probably overstated. During 1921, concerned Irish Americans bypassed the FOIF and the Irish mission and collected large sums of money for relief in Ireland (Carroll 1978). Nevertheless, these operations disbanded once the

Anglo-Irish war ended. In concrete terms, therefore, the collapse of the Irish Bond and the infighting between various Irish-American organizations left Irish Americans with fewer venues through which to engage with Ireland.

Perhaps even more importantly, the struggles surrounding the Irish Bond sharpened the differences between the Irish in Ireland and Irish Americans. In early 1920, having been attacked by Devoy, de Valera called Judge Cohalan to order. As the President of the Republic of Ireland, he explained,

> I am answerable to the *Irish people* for the proper execution of the trust with which I have been charged. I am definitely responsible to them and I alone am responsible ... Friends of Irish Freedom is an association of American Citizens founded to assist the Irish people in securing the freedom the Irish people desire ...[61]

De Valera linked himself to the national collective in Ireland and, in the process, he drew sharp lines separating the Irish from Irish-American citizens. In his communication with the *Dáil Éireann*, de Valera was explicit and concise:

> Fundamentally Irish Americans differ from us in this – they being American first would sacrifice Irish interest if need be to American interest ... we, Irish first, would do the reverse. (Fanning et al. 1998: 55)

Struggling to legitimize his position, de Valera explained that the "sea-divided Gaels," as the Irish on both sides of the ocean had been called just a few months before, were actually separated by more than just a body of water.

Judge Cohalan's response to de Valera's letter struck similar chords, but from a different perspective:

> I know no reason why you take the trouble to tell me that you can share your responsibility to the Irish people with no one. I would not let you share it with me if you sought to do so ... What I have done for the cause ... I have done as an American, whose only allegiance is [t]o America, and as one whom the interest and security of my country are ever preferred to those of any and all other lands ... I have no appointment from you or any other spokesperson for another country, nor would I under any circumstances accept one ...

Cohalan, just like de Valera, drew sharp distinctions between Irish Americans and the Irish people in Ireland and clarified the difference in terms of allegiance between the two groups. He ended the letter with a rhetorical question: "Do you think that any self-respecting American will permit himself to be led in such a manner by you?"[62]

De Valera and Cohalan's heated exchange did not remain a private matter. The two sides soon circulated copies of the letters among their supporters, thereby making the differences between the Irish and Irish Americans ever clearer to widening circles. The arguments also traveled across the ocean. De Valera explained the situation to his colleagues in the *Dáil Éireann* as follows:

> A deadly attempt to ruin our chances for the bonds, and everything we came here to accomplish is being made [by Cohalan] . . . The position I have held (I was rapidly driven to assert it or surrender) is the following.
> (1) No American has the right to dictate policy to the Irish people.
> (2) We are here with a definite objective. Americans, banded under the trade name (the word will not be misunderstood), Friends of Irish Freedom, ought to help us to obtain the objective, if they are truly what the name implies.[63]

Hoping to establish an alternative route to the leaders in the homeland, the FOIF leaders also dispatched an emissary to Ireland carrying a message about the need to put "a speedy end to such unwise action . . . by its representatives here. . . ."[64] But in this struggle, de Valera certainly had the upper hand. When the FOIF's emissary was finally allowed to visit Collins's hideout, somewhere in Dublin, he found Boland in the room, exchanging friendly jokes with Collins (Fitzpatrick 2003). Instead of an endorsement, the *Dáil Éireann* issued a strong denunciation of the FOIF's leadership.[65] Faced with such an unequivocal condemnation, Diarmuid Lynch, the secretary of the FOIF who sided with Cohalan and Devoy, was forced to resign from his position in the *Dáil Éireann*.[66]

More than merely describing groups, the exchange between de Valera and Cohalan helped define the boundaries between the Irish and the Irish Americans (Anderson 1991; Verdery 1991; Jenkins 1997). As Fredrik Barth argues, the boundaries between social groups are the contingent outcome of processes of ascription and self-ascription (1998). Actors, engaged in political struggles, try to legitimize their positions by drawing boundaries that include some but exclude others (Gieryn 1983; Sahlins 1989). By marking a sharp distinction between the "people of Ireland," and "Americans banded under the trade name Friends of Irish Freedom," and by stating that Irish Americans are Americans first, the two leaders, in fact, rendered a previously fuzzy boundary sharper. In the process, it became evident that the interests and preferences of the Irish and Irish Americans were not entirely compatible. More than that, in the course of the quarrel, Cohalan and de Valera turned the specter of divided loyalty into an issue. In contrast with what happened to Cohalan during World War I, this time it was an argument between the Irish that clarified that the allegiances of these two groups were, at least potentially, in conflict. A social boundary that had heretofore been blurry became clearer and more meaningful in large part due to the boundary work that the warring parties engaged in.

The collapse of the Irish Bond had long-term repercussions for the Irish-American community. Following the struggles of 1919–1921, Irish-American organizations never again regained the position they held in 1920. The FOIF never even resembled what it once was. Lacking members and funds, it eked out an existence for a while, but after Lynch retired in 1931, the few surviving branches became inactive, and the organization officially disbanded in 1935. Devoy's *Clan na Gael* and McGarrity's reorganized *Clan*, too, ceased to exist after the deaths of Devoy and McGarrity in 1928 and 1940, respectively (Funchion 1983). A few branches of the AARIR continued to support de Valera's tumultuous political career in Ireland, but the organization never recovered from the decline it experienced in 1921. In fact, up until the late 1960s, when sectarian violence engulfed Northern Ireland, the Irish-American community remained largely uninvolved in Irish national politics (Kenny 2000). The strong link between the death of individual leaders (and the retirement of Lynch) and the collapse of major Irish-American organizations is telling. For all practical purposes, after 1921 Irish-American nationalism became a personal matter. Lynch, Devoy, McGarrity, and probably several others remained extremely devoted to the Irish cause, but the movement as a whole was thoroughly de-institutionalized.

Identifying a sharp decline in Irish-American attachments to Ireland is anything but original. Practically every historiography of Irish America marks a break in Irish–Irish American relations in the early 1920s (Ward 1968; McCaffrey 1976; Carroll 1978; Fallows 1979; Miller 1985; Kenny 2000; Doorley 2005). Referring to 1921 as "the last hurrah" of "Irish-America," Kerby Miller, for example, suggests that from that date onward the Irish in America stopped referring to themselves as exiles (1985: 555). It is not, of course, that the Irish in the United States stopped referring to themselves as Irish (Hout and Goldstein 1994). Instead, to a large extent, this self-ascription became a symbolic gesture (e.g., wearing green on St Patrick's Day), devoid of any practical political importance.

Nevertheless, the suggestion that the Irish Bond drive played an important role in this transformation is likely to raise eyebrows. In most accounts, the inactivity of Irish Americans is related to developments in Ireland. Marjorie Fallows, for example, argues that the establishment of the Irish Free State in 1922 allowed "Irish individuals and organizations to wind up the unfinished business, which they were conscious of having left behind them, and permitted them to accept their full Americanization without guilt" (1979: 46). With regard to the civil war that erupted between supporters and opponents of the Anglo-Irish Treaty, Michael Doorley suggests that the "spectacle of Irish fighting Irish disillusioned many erstwhile supporters . . ." in the United States (2005: 153). Allegedly, dramatic events in Ireland, perhaps in combination with creeping assimilation, explain the decline of the Irish-American diaspora.

However intuitively appealing, attributing the decline of the Irish-American diaspora to exogenous events in Ireland is not without difficulties. As the Jewish case makes amply clear, the establishment of a state, especially one as contested as the IFS,[67] does not necessarily spell a decline in national attachments. Likewise, the eruption of the civil war, while obviously disheartening, does not necessarily lead to a decline in activism. Why would Irish Americans, distinguished for decades by their zeal (Brown 1966), respond so passively to the compromise that threw their compatriots in Ireland into a bloody turmoil? One can imagine the Irish Americans wholeheartedly backing the anti-Treaty faction, or (perhaps less likely) supporting the pro-Treaty faction, or even a split opinion – but why inaction?

Perhaps even more importantly, our examination of the second bond campaign reveals that prior to the signing of the Anglo-Irish Treaty and the eruption of the civil war in November 1921 Irish Americans, by and large, were not eager to volunteer their time and money for an endeavor led by the Irish mission. Rather than being a response to dramatic events in Ireland, the decline of Irish-American nationalism was probably an outcome of the struggles between de Valera and the Irish-American leaders. The point is not that the events in Ireland had no effect on the Irish-American community, but that the response of the Irish-American community to these events cannot be understood without taking into account what had occurred in the United States prior to these events. That is, in the two years preceding the signing of the treaty, key Irish-American organizations experienced severe crises, and during this period Irish Americans were involved in a struggle that accentuated the differences between them and the Irish in Ireland. In other words, Irish Americans interpreted the creation of the IFS and the eruption of the civil war in Ireland as a dismissal from duty to no little extent *because* prior events in the United States rendered this interpretation appropriate and attractive. On the one hand, after two years of struggle, they perceived themselves as more American than Irish. On the other hand, due to the exchange of blows between the groups, being active for Ireland became largely unrewarding. The failure in regulating the relationships between the Irish mission and key Irish-American organizations caused the decline of Irish-American nationalism.

The Making of Jewish-American Investment in Israel

As in the Irish case, the ongoing sale of Israeli bonds meant more than simply an increase in the flow of money to Israel. If the termination of the Irish Bond campaign left the Irish Americans with fewer ways to relate to Ireland, the continuation of the Israel Bond provided Jewish Americans with an additional venue through which they could relate to the Zionist project. The prospectuses of the Israeli bonds detailed the different ways in which the loan contributed to Israel.[68] The AFDCI also invited large purchasers to join special tours of the country. On these tours, purchasers were given the opportunity to witness firsthand the fruits of their investments. The AFDCI mission of 1956, for example, visited a *kibbutz* in the Negev desert that relied on fresh water made possible by an irrigation canal that was built with Israel Bond money. On the way to the north, the mission stopped at Elco Transformers, a private industrial venture that used bond money to expand its operation. In addition, the AFDCI dignitaries met the country's political and business leadership, visited key archeological sites, and witnessed the Independence Day military parade from special seats in the grandstand.[69] Through the purchase of the Israeli bonds, Jewish Americans became more intimately involved in Israel.

While many American Jews both purchased bonds and contributed to the UJA, the AFDCI created opportunities for other members of the community to both participate in the building up of Israel and to assume leadership positions. If the UJA, by its emphasis on the size of the donation, was strongly biased in favor of wealthy donors (who enjoyed the ability both to give big gifts and to receive more significant tax deductions), the Israel Bonds attracted mostly middle-income members of the community who served as both subscribers and organizers. These activists and subscribers, often previously unknown in the community, could now take the lead in a key project.[70]

The honorary titles that the AFDCI created to boost sales allowed Jewish-American subscribers to play a special role in Israel's struggle. In the women's division, for example, volunteers who sold more than a $2,500 worth of bonds received a special *CHEN* charm. Miriam Feinman, the director of the women's division, reminded awardees of

> ... the link between CHEN in Israel, where women serve in the physical defense of the country, and members of CHEN in the United States ... who serve Israel on the economic front.[71]

For those who sold or bought $10,000 worth of bonds, the AFDCI created the more exclusive title of "Guardians of Israel." This title was reserved for

> ... [g]roups of devoted American Jews in each community who render service to Israel's economic growth ... [the Guardians] are a counterpart of Israel's "shomrim" or Guardians, and watch over the economic development of Israel.[72]

While the Jewish-American contribution was different in kind from that of the Jews in Israel – Israeli Jews (some of them) served at the military front, while the bond subscribers served on the economic front – the sale and purchase of Israeli bonds allowed Jewish Americans to think of themselves as counterparts in the defense of Israel.

Importantly, the Israel Bond created a new way for Israeli and American Jews to relate to one another. Prior to the issue of the bonds, monetary contributions, while definitely welcome, were also a source of deep apprehension, especially for the Jews in Israel. Each American Jewish dollar served as a reminder of the gap between the Zionist ideal of self-sufficiency and their ongoing dependence. The Israel Bonds changed this state of affairs.

For Jewish Americans, the Israeli bond was primarily a gift. After all, if they were seeking profits, they could have invested in General Motors, not in a semi-socialist economy in the Middle East. This perception, which accounts for the Jewish Federations' reservations vis-à-vis the bonds, can also be gleaned from the long-term trends of sales and redemptions of Israeli bonds (see Figure 6.1). The bonds sales surged, and redemptions declined in wartime. In sharp contrast to typical investors, purchasers of Israeli bonds were not deterred but actually attracted to the risk associated with wars (similar trends can be seen in donations to the UJA, but this is less surprising). However, the Jewish-American subscribers were not unaware of the pecuniary aspects of the Israel Bonds. Over the years, the vast majority (although not all) of the subscribers redeemed the principal and interest owed them (Ketkar and Ratha 2009). Furthermore, subscribers also distinguished between giving to the Israel Bonds and giving to the UJA. Lou Boyar, a leader of the Israel Bonds from Los Angeles, explained his decision to support the Israel Bonds as follows:

> We really believed that the future of the Jewish people in Israel means that they must stand on their own feet. They must earn enough money and they cannot do it without investments. (OHD, 4(128))

Boyar did not necessarily believe that the Israeli bond was a regular investment, but he ascribed to the bond money properties other than those given to the UJA money. Unlike the UJA, he

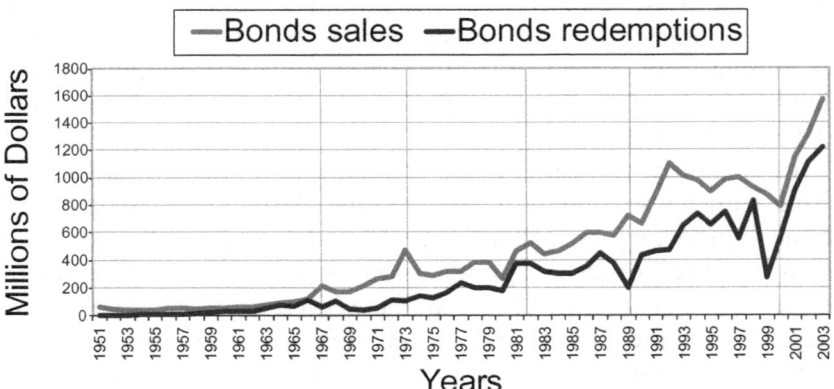

Figure 6.1. Annual sales of the State of Israel Bonds in millions of dollars (the vertical lines represent wars) (adapted from Rehavi and Weingarten 2004).

suggested, the Israel Bond money had the capacity to render the Israeli economy sustainable.[73] If some Jewish Americans began viewing Israel as a bottomless pit, the Israel Bond suggested that Israel's neediness was temporary. By an ironic turn of events, the Israel Bond allowed a reversal of the Zionist ideology – now it was the "unproductive" Jews in the diaspora that provided the Israeli *halutzim* with a fishing rod instead of a fish. Thus, for American Jews, the Israeli bonds were mostly a gift, but with an important added value.

The Israeli interpretation of the Israeli bonds was different. Israeli Jews saw the bonds as mostly an investment and emphasized its pecuniary value. After all, Israel had committed to pay back the loan, with interest. To some extent, playing up the bonds' economic value was part of how the AFDCI marketed the bonds, but this emphasis was extremely important for the Israelis as well. In the *Knesset*, the Israeli Parliament, the Minister of Finance and other leaders extolled the Israel Bond as a long-awaited retreat from the humiliating practice of "schnorrerai" (a Yiddish term for begging) (Israel 1951). Ambassador Eban explained:

> The project [of the Israel Bond] gave the Hebrew nation the vision of Israel's economic independence, and expressed in the field of economic thinking the idea of independence and sovereignty ... A very healthy atmosphere, an atmosphere of equality and mutual respect is emanating from the very idea of the loan.[74]

The definite obligations that the Israeli bonds carried allowed Israelis to attribute to them positive moral properties. To be sure, Israeli Jews, just like their American counterparts, were not oblivious to the gift-like aspects of the bonds. Speaking at AFDCI sales events or hosting missions in Israel, Israeli leaders never failed to thank subscribers for their generosity. Nevertheless, among themselves Israeli leaders played up the aspect of the bonds that pleased them most – that is, their pecuniary value.

The twofold nature of the transaction – that the Israeli bonds was gift-like for American Jews and investment-like for Israeli Jews – served both sides. For Jewish Americans, the AFDCI provided an opportunity to gift Israel, and (perhaps) get their money back, with interest! For Israeli Jews, the Israel Bond proved invaluable too. Unlike previous fundraising methods, the sale of Israel Israeli bonds allowed Israelis to enjoy additional dollars without compromising their independence. That the bonds were purchased for quasi-philanthropic reasons was overlooked as inconsequential. After all, they reasoned, returning this loan was just a matter of time. The independence that the Israel Bonds provided was not merely symbolic. The AFDCI created a direct route through which the Israeli government could reach the Jewish-American public without mediators, and the Israel Bonds' dollars were free from the obligation to share them and from any restrictions over their usage. In a very concrete sense, then, the Israel Bond attenuated the Israeli dependence on the UJA and the Jewish Federations.

By sustaining a strange, willful misunderstanding with regard to the nature of their relations, the Israel Bonds took the edge off encounters between Israeli and American Jews. Previously, meetings between American and Israeli Jews, especially encounters that had to do with money, were threatening to the self-images of the two groups. In the presence of Israelis, Jewish Americans were always susceptible to criticism for their bourgeois lifestyle and for failing to contribute adequately to the Zionist project (that is, by migrating to Israel). In the same settings, Israelis were forced to confront the fact that, ideals aside, they remained deeply dependent on the handouts of successful brethren in the United States. Obviously, the Israel Bond did not eliminate these tensions, but it provided a unique setting in which American and Israeli Jews could engage each other without having to compromise their sense of worth.

The Israel Bond did not replace other ways of relating to Israel. The distinct properties of the Israel Bond allowed it to serve as an additional venue through which Jewish Americans engaged Israel. Alongside the Israel Bonds, the UJA continued to collect philanthropic donations for Israel. Other modes of relating to Israel, through visits, political lobbying, etc., continued as well. Instead of replacing other methods of relating to Israel, the AFDCI provided Jewish Americans with an additional choice in the menu of ways in which they could become involved in the Zionist revival taking place thousands of miles away.

Conclusions

Following the trajectories of the second Irish and Israeli drives clarifies that the bond projects were by no means simply vehicles to procure funds. Rather, the Irish Bonds and the Israel Bonds were also nation-building mechanisms, and the contrasting outcomes of the projects affected the development of Irish-American and Jewish-American ties to Ireland and Israel, respectively. In the Irish case, the conflicts surrounding the bond project left Irish Americans with fewer ways to engage with Ireland. Furthermore, these conflicts contributed to a crystallization of the differences between the Irish and the Irish Americans and to a sense that the interests and preferences of these groups were not always compatible. In contrast, in the Jewish case, the bond program provided American and Israeli Jews with an additional, important venue in which to engage each other and was instrumental in smoothing over differences between them. Through the Israel Bonds, American Jews became invested in Israel's future not only financially but emotionally as well.

7

Heterogeneity, Indeterminacy, and the Construction of National Interests

The previous two chapters presented an interesting puzzle. Chapters 5 and 6 followed Éamon de Valera, the President of the Republic of Ireland, and the Israeli Prime Minister, David Ben-Gurion, along with his ally in the United States, Henry Montor, as they tried to reshape the relationships between the respective diaspora communities and their national movements by introducing new financial mechanisms – the Irish Bond and the Israel Bond. The parallels between the two projects are striking. In both cases, the diaspora bonds were designed to solve intractable difficulties associated with philanthropic giving. Floating the Irish and Israeli bonds in the United States was an enormous practical organizational challenge. Existing organizations in the United States – the Friends of Irish Freedom (FOIF) and the Jewish Federations – were deeply concerned about the new ventures and only reluctantly agreed to support them. In addition, de Valera and Montor had to overcome the skepticism of commercial banks and the political and legal hurdles associated with raising money within the borders of the United States for a foreign sovereignty. The combination of patriotism and pecuniary motivations that characterized the drives gave rise, in both cases, to tensions and misinterpretations regarding the nature of these transactions. The diaspora communities – both the Irish Americans and the Jewish Americans – tended to interpret the exchange as an instance of gift giving, while the leaderships in Ireland and Israel emphasized the bonds' pecuniary value.

Despite these parallels, the outcomes of the Irish and Israeli bond initiatives were markedly different. In the Irish case, disagreements with regard to the nature of the bonds led to conflicting demands and escalating conflict. In the Israeli case, very similar misunderstandings served to facilitate the transaction between the groups and helped them cooperate, despite deep differences and disagreements. Whereas in the Irish case the leaders of the FOIF and the leaders of the Irish mission locked themselves into opposing positions and fought over the rights and obligations associated with contribution to the national common good, in the Israeli case the two sides were able to appreciate the duality of the bonds and overlook, at least for a while, their differing interpretations.

Why is it that in one case, lack of agreement about the nature of the bonds proved destructive, whereas in the other, similar differences facilitated transaction? To answer this question, this chapter delves into seemingly technical details such as the interest rates, redemption procedures, and inter-organizational structures of the drives. Close attention to these often-overlooked details will provide a nuanced appreciation of the dynamics that led misunderstanding to fuel conflict in one case and assuage tensions in the other.

Scholars of nationalism often present nation building as a process through which members of the nation replace class, local, and other types of particularistic interests with patriotic zeal. Allegedly, the process of nation building consists of a switch in orientation – from an interested perspective to a largely disinterested concern for the nation. This depiction, I believe, is too simplistic, and is grounded in a tendency to focus on the effects of nationalism rather than the process of nation building per se. National attachments, of course, can sometimes result in disinterested acts of sacrifice; however, close examination of the nitty-gritty details of nation building clarifies that the process of nation building should not be understood as one of replacing one orientation with another but, instead, of aligning the interests and preferences of the groups that make up the nation. Rather than persuading subjects to abandon their particularistic interests in favor of one uniform, national common good, national mobilization rests on mechanisms that allow different groups to both hold onto their particularistic concerns and contribute to the national struggle.

Organizing National Bonds

At first glance, the Irish and Israeli bond projects seem similar. Rather than relying solely on philanthropic donations, the Irish and the Israeli leaders created financial instruments that combined elements of gift giving and market exchange. Both bond projects were large-scale endeavors that required delicate organizational maneuvering. Yet a close look at the projects reveals deep and consequential differences in the design of the Irish and Israeli bonds, the procedures for their sale and delivery, and the inter-organizational structure of the two projects.

Qualifying the Irish Bonds and the Israeli Bonds

While the Irish and Israeli bonds both combined elements of gift giving and market exchange, they did so very differently. In comparison with the Israeli bond, the Irish bond was a simple, almost primitive financial instrument. Since the Republic of Ireland had yet to be recognized by the US government, the American Commission on Irish Independence (ACII) legalized the loan by selling bond certificates rather than regular bonds (Carroll 2002). If in standard bonds uncertainty is tied to the solvency of the issuer, the uncertainty of the Irish bond was associated not only with the solvency of the Republic of Ireland but also with decisions of third parties: Great Britain, which could withdraw its troops from the island or not, and the international community, which could grant or deny Ireland recognition. Despite this obvious limitation, the Republic of Ireland offered an annual interest rate of 5% for the bonds, as opposed to the 4.75% offered at the time by American Treasury Certificates of Indebtedness. Fundamentally, however, between the time of issue of the bonds and their (uncertain) redemption, there was little to distinguish them from regular philanthropic gifts.

The qualification of the Israeli bond was far more sophisticated. As in the Irish case, the American Financial and Development Corporation for Israel (AFDCI) offered a businesslike interest rate. However, it must be recalled that the AFDCI also offered unusual privileges to the Israel bond subscribers. First, while the Israeli bonds were non-transferable, in case of death the AFDCI agreed to purchase the bonds from the inheritors without delay or penalty. Second, subscribers who traveled to Israel were allowed to convert the Israeli bonds to Israeli pounds at any time. Third, the AFDCI allowed purchasers to register the bonds in the name of another person, thus allowing Jewish Americans to use the Israeli bonds as a gift for various events. Fourth, the AFDCI sold savings and coupon bonds with interest payable in 30 semi-annual installments.[1]

While these measures were, to a large extent, nothing more than clever marketing tricks, the special terms of the Israeli bonds effectively complicated the meaning of the transaction. The payment of interest for coupon bonds together with the special privileges of the Israeli bonds created a limited degree of liquidity and some use value to the Israeli bonds. Rather than sitting in the pocket of subscribers like a stone for 12 or 15 years, under certain circumstances subscribers could cash their bond immediately. These provisions, to be sure, did not convince Jewish Americans that the bond was a regular investment, but they made it harder to claim that the Israeli bond was just a gift in disguise.

Montor and his associates thus built provisions into the Israeli bond that made it difficult to pinpoint the bond's absolute nature. In contrast, the Irish organizers left the bond certificates with practically no qualities that could have been used to distinguish it from a philanthropic gift, other than a doubly conditional promise to repay subscribers.

Safe handling of national money

One of the key challenges confronting the ACII and the AFDCI was to find a way to safeguard the proceeds of the respective campaigns. In conventional philanthropy, loss of donations can damage the public's confidence in a particular drive and reduce the overall collection, but it typically carries no long-term financial ramifications. But what if a local organizer of the bond campaign – in, say, a large American City – decided to pocket the local proceeds? In such a case, not only would the Irish or Jewish nationalists lose out on the support of their compatriots, but years later they would likely be confronted with the demand to redeem both the principal and interest of these bonds – the proceeds of which they had never seen! Unlike the receipts for donations to the Irish Victory Fund or the United Jewish Appeal, the Irish and Israeli bonds potentially held real economic value, so failure to handle them safely could have serious economic implications. The problem of securing campaign proceeds was related to the scale of the projects and of nation building in general. The Irish and Zionist movements reached out to millions of potential supporters and relied on thousands of volunteers all over the country. To the leaders of the ACII and AFDCI, the vast majority of these volunteers were complete strangers, and thus trusting them was hard, and overseeing their work was almost impossible. Furthermore, since the bond drives were designed to show that the Irish and Zionist movements were capable of managing their own affairs, failure to secure the proceeds of the campaigns would have reflected badly on their claims for sovereignty.

In order to secure the campaign proceeds, de Valera and James O'Mara developed special procedures. Hoping to maintain centralized control of the proceeds of the drive, they instructed local committees to open bank accounts under de Valera's name. The proceeds of the campaign, de Valera insisted, should not be used to cover local expenses. "Every cent received for the Bond-Certificates ... [must] be lodged to the account of these funds or remitted [directly] to headquarters. Under no circumstances may anything be retained for local expenses."[2] Local operating costs, they promised, would be paid by the ACII upon the presentation of proper receipts.

To oversee the distribution of the bonds, O'Mara also devised a special subscription procedure. Local Irish Bonds committees received only receipt books. In return for money, organizers issued a receipt to subscribers and sent an application for the bond certificates to the ACII headquarters in New York City. The local committee then deposited the collected funds in the bank and sent the applications for subscription to the ACII headquarters. Upon receiving both applications and money from the local committees, the national headquarters issued the bond certificates and sent them directly to the subscribers via mail. O'Mara considered this procedure a kind of self-correcting mechanism. "By so doing," he explained, "subscribers who did not receive their bond certificate promptly, have in many cases brought pressure to bear on those who attempted to withhold the funds..."³ By withholding the bond certificates, and using the subscribers' pressure, O'Mara hoped to ensure the cooperation of local committees.

Intentions aside, the ACII procedures had destructive consequences. De Valera's insistence that committees not use proceeds of the bond drive to cover campaign expenditures exacerbated the tensions between the Irish Republican leaders and the FOIF. Many local committees had no reserves from which to finance their initial campaign expenses.⁴ Instead of suspending the campaign until the ACII furnished them with funds, local organizers, apparently with the silent approval of O'Mara and Frank Walsh, used the funds of the IVF that were still in their possession to pay for expenses (in many places the bond committees were manned by the same people who organized the IVF drive).⁵ Diarmuid Lynch, the secretary of the FOIF who for months had been urging activists to send the IVF proceeds to headquarters, complained to de Valera:

> At the time of your arrival in America the only city that raised a question about sending the proceeds of the Irish Victory fund to the National Treasurer [of the] F.O.I.F. was Philadelphia. Subsequently, claims arose in other places that the [former IVF] Committees should be allowed to hold portions of the Fund for expenses in connection with your visit and later on similar claims were put forward in the matter of financing the Bond-Certificate campaign in its initial stage...⁶

To their frustration, Lynch and his colleagues in the FOIF discovered that they had been forced to finance the bond drive twice – once through the $100,000 advance loan they gave to the ACII, and again through the deductions from the IVF of proceeds they received from local IVF committees. De Valera addressed local chairmen, asking them not to use the IVF for the bond campaign but, since the difficulties in retrieving the IVF persisted, Lynch was not assuaged.

O'Mara's subscription procedure proved to be problematic as well. Since only the ACII headquarters were allowed to issue bond certificates, the initial success of the drive resulted in a huge bottleneck and great delays in delivery. Over the course of a few months, the few staff members in the ACII headquarters were bombarded with hundreds of thousands of applications for subscription, many of them entirely illegible, and were unable to send bonds to the applicants in a timely manner. Thousands of subscribers, all over the country, waited anxiously for their bonds.[7] Charlotte Dunne, for example, complained:

> Some time ago we subscribed to the Irish Bond Issue... After signing the pledge and making the initial payment, however, we have heard nothing further and can secure no information... It seems as though quite an amount of money has in this way been lost to the [Irish] Cause. The condition seems to hold all over.[8]

In a context of a fierce inter-organizational struggle between the FOIF and the Irish mission, in which accusations of fraud and misuse were frequent, many subscribers interpreted the delays in the delivery of the bond as evidence that their money had been lost or stolen.

The failures in the delivery of the bonds had a particularly devastating effect for local organizers. William Grace from Chicago, for example, wrote to Stephen O'Mara about the following event:

> I spoke at a meeting of the Thomas Jefferson Branch F.O.I.F... During the course of my remarks I answered the question "When are we going to get our bonds?" by telling them that there was a great deal of detailed work necessary in getting out the bonds before they could be mailed to subscribers... Then Father Hannan... said to the people that they should have their Certificates. That if they didn't have them[,] it is because President de Valera did not have the money for their subscriptions. He said that there was a crowd of crooked politicians in Chicago as well as in Brooklyn who were holding back the Bond Certificate money from the President, trying to ruin the Bond certificate drive, to break his heart and send him home [to Ireland] discredited.

Grace went on to describe how he tried to persuade the people that he had sent the monies to the ACII headquarters, but, he bitterly added, against the words of a man of the cloth, my words certainly did not have great weight with the meeting. You can imagine how the news spread in the neighborhood, both among friends and enemies; and you can easily imagine its effect.[9]

Note that Grace, Father Hannan, and all of those present at the meeting stood by de Valera. Father Hannan, in fact, rehearsed de Valera's and Harry Boland's accusations against Judge Cohalan and his associates in the FOIF ("crooked politicians in Chicago as well as in Brooklyn"). Yet, the end result of the argument was that Grace, the dutiful (perhaps) organizer who invested days in promoting the Bond drive, was now suspect. If the event in the Thomas Jefferson Branch meeting was not an isolated instance, and it is not likely to have been, one can see how an entire cohort of activists had been discredited by the failure of the first Irish Bonds.[10] Stephen O'Mara's inability to recruit organizers for the second Irish Bonds was probably related to the disrepute that befell many of the organizers of the first drive.

The AFDCI leaders faced a similar predicament; they, too, had to rely on thousands of volunteers scattered all over the country. But Montor and his associates devised a less centralized and more professionalized system for securing the proceeds of the campaign that proved to be more efficient. Like O'Mara, Montor was careful not to place bonds in the hands of activists. Local activists received only receipt books and application forms. But, instead of working directly with the headquarters, the AFDCI contracted Chase National Bank to act as a fiscal agent, overseeing 18 other district banks and numerous community banks across the country.[11] Local Israel Bond committees handed over the applications for subscriptions along with checks or cash to their designated local bank. The local bank would then deliver the money and the applications to one of the district banks, which issued the bonds and sent them back to the local banks for delivery to individual subscribers.[12] To safeguard the procedure, the AFDCI contacted the Royal Indemnity Company and purchased insurance for lost monies. The close weaving of volunteers, paid fieldworkers, banks, and an insurance company ensured that fewer subscribers and organizers felt cheated or betrayed.[13]

The inter-organizational structure of the homeland–diaspora relations

Our examination reveals important differences in terms of the design of the bonds and their safe handling. It would be premature, however, to conclude that these differences were consequential. While the Irish bonds were probably more gift-like and less ambiguous in comparison with the Israeli bonds, it is not clear why such differences would adversely affect the Irish campaign. Ambiguity is not always a blessing and, as voluminous anthropological literature and the discussion in Chapter 3 of this book show, gift giving is a remarkably reliable mechanism for mobilizing resources and connecting people. Furthermore, the delays in the delivery of the Irish bonds could have been interpreted as a sign of the overwhelming popularity of the drive, rather than a sign of corruption. To understand better what broke down in the Irish case and why the Israel Bond followed a different path, therefore, we have to expand our horizon and examine not only the very objects that changed hands in the transactions between homeland and diaspora communities, but also the organizational context within which these transactions took place.

While both the Irish and the Israeli governments established new organizations to underwrite their bonds – the ACII and the AFDCI – the inter-organizational structure of the homeland–diaspora relations in the two cases was different. De Valera insisted that the Friends of Irish Freedom (FOIF) terminate the Irish Victory Fund (IVF) prior to the issue of the bond certificates. Successful fundraising, he believed, necessitated eliminating potential competitors to the ACII. In structural terms, de Valera replaced one dyadic relationship with another. Before the bond campaign, the relationship between Ireland and Irish America was predominantly mediated by the FOIF and the Irish mission in the United States. During the drive, these relationships were mediated by the ACII and the Irish mission.

In contrast, in the Jewish case, perhaps due to pressures from the Jewish Federations, the United Jewish Appeal (UJA) continued alongside the AFDCI. In structural terms, therefore, the establishment of the Israel Bond created a triad. Before the issue of the Israeli bond, the relationships between Israel and the Jewish-American community were mediated by the UJA (and Jewish Federations at the local level) and the Israeli government. Once the Israel Bond campaign was launched, however, both the UJA and the AFDCI mediated the relationships between the Jewish-American community and Israel.

The dyadic configuration of the Irish–Irish American relationship had damaging consequences. Once de Valera terminated the IVF and handed the task of selling the bonds to the ACII, the FOIF was robbed of its *raison d'être* and its main source of income. Trying to remain at least indirectly involved in the new bond drive, Cohalan suggested that Edward McSweeney, an experienced FOIF organizer from Boston, should serve as Frank Walsh's assistant in the ACII, but de Valera preferred to entrust James O'Mara from Ireland with this task.[14] As a result, the leaders of the Friends of Irish Freedom grew suspicious of de Valera's intentions. John Schell, one of the FOIF's fieldworkers, wrote to John Devoy that

> [de Valera's] persistent attempts to get us to stop the Victory Fund Drive to make way for the Bonds ... was ... for the purpose of depleting our resources for work here, where the real battle is being fought now, and to cripple us.[15]

Many of the FOIF organizers did become involved in organizing the Irish Bonds in different localities, but, as we have seen earlier, this overlap was a source of additional frustration for Lynch and his associates. Thus, the inter-organizational structure of the Irish Bond drive was a source of tension in its own right.

In contradistinction, the triadic configuration of the Israel Bond proved more conducive to cooperation. To be sure, as Chapter 6 illustrates, the concomitant operation of the UJA and the AFDCI created significant tensions, but it also forced the leaders of the Jewish Federations to avoid an out-and-out conflict with the Israeli leadership. Prior to the launching of the AFDCI, if the Israeli government was unsatisfied with the amounts of money allocated by particular Jewish Federations, it could apply various pressures, especially moral denunciations, but it could not risk a complete break in the relations.[16] Such a move could have cut Israel off from Jewish-American dollars completely. Once the AFDCI established a network of local committees, however, the Israeli government could choose not to cooperate with this or that recalcitrant Federation without risking a complete break in its relationship with that community. Thus, the establishment of the AFDCI provided Israel with leverage to discipline unruly Jewish-American leaders.[17]

Perhaps even more importantly, the competition between the UJA and the AFDCI allowed Israel to become distinct from the agencies that collected money on its behalf and to appear as somehow "above" them. It allowed Israel, in other words, to act in a state-like manner, at least in relation to American Jews.[18] Controversial decisions, like the decision to open the Israel Bond campaign in Indianapolis in the spring, for example, could now be attributed to the inflexibility of AFDCI's leadership and not necessarily to Israel's neediness or greediness. Instead of being seen as scrambling for money, Israel could now be seen as an entity that hovered above the petty internecine politics of the Jewish-American community.[19] Reflecting on the transformation of Israel's image in the United States, Ambassador Eban explained that during the early 1950s Israel had become a sort of "Vatican" of American Jewry (Eban 1979).[20] The triadic configuration of the Israeli–Jewish-American relationship, clearly, did not bring about consensus or harmony. If anything, the creation of the AFDCI created new tensions. But effectively, this triadic structure shifted the locus of the conflict from across the ocean to within the United States and helped to make caring for Israel's welfare a matter of consensus among Jewish Americans.

The brittleness of the Irish Bond and the robustness of the Israel Bond were, at least in part, related to the interorganizational structures of the Irish and the Jewish homeland–diaspora relations. In the Irish case, the establishment of the ACII pushed a key organization, the FOIF, to the opposition. In contrast, the creation of the AFDCI resulted in two organizations that remained deeply interested in maintaining cooperation with the Israeli government and forced the leaders of the Jewish Federations to tone down their criticism of the bonds.

Zone of Indeterminacy, Temporality, and the Production of National Associations

The conflicts surrounding the Irish Bond drive were not the outcome of insurmountable differences between the Irish and Irish Americans. Nor were they the result of a fatal flaw in the design of the Irish Bond. During more than half a century prior to the launching of the Irish Bond, Irish Americans donated handsomely to the Irish cause, and these relations, while not always harmonious, were nonetheless quite stable. This willingness to contribute to the Irish cause manifested itself during the first bond campaign, in which hundreds of thousands of Irish Americans purchased the bonds, showing little concern about the terms and conditions of the Irish loan. For scores of Irish Americans, it seems, the likelihood of being paid back mattered less than showing their support to the Republic of Ireland.

This easygoing attitude, however, did not last long. The interorganizational structure of the campaign and de Valera's method of safekeeping the proceeds generated growing friction between the Irish mission and the FOIF. Marginalized and drained of resources, the leaders of the FOIF were almost forced into battle against de Valera. It was at this point that the properties of the Irish bonds became consequential. Specifically, Devoy treated the proceeds of the bond campaign as gifts. That the Irish bonds carried only a conditional obligation to repay allowed Devoy and his colleagues to conveniently ignore the multiple meanings of the bonds, i.e., their being a bit of a gift and a bit of an investment – and treat them as simply gifts. Based on this interpretation, Devoy and his colleagues claimed to be entitled to special considerations.

De Valera and his colleagues' interpretation of the Irish bonds changed over the course of the struggle, too. During the early stages of the first campaign, de Valera explained:

> Our Bond-Certificates cannot be issued on [a] purely financial basis. We must expect subscriptions only from those who seek to serve a good cause, not from those who want immediate pecuniary profit.[21]

In this statement, de Valera acknowledged the gift-like properties of the Irish bonds. However, in the course of the struggle against the FOIF, and in response to Devoy's demand for a voice in determining Irish national policies, de Valera came to interpret the bonds as "Irish Government money" to be used according to the wishes of the Irish people in Ireland and them alone.[22] It was precisely in this context that the obligation to repay the loan came to play a decisive role in his interpretation of the Irish bond certificates as investments (while conveniently disregarding their giftlike properties).

The debacle of the bond certificates subscription procedure displays similar dynamics at a different level. Thousands of Irish Americans volunteered to organize and subscribed to the first Irish bond campaign. Seeing their contributions as an act of generosity, they did not anticipate a high return for their "investment" but expected to be given at least the bond certificates as a token of appreciation for their support. This, after all, was the way the Irish bonds were marketed – a testimony to one's love of Ireland. But in the context of fierce inter-organizational struggle, when accusations of misuse and corruption became rife, the unconcerned attitude toward the Irish bonds gave way to suspicion and to a re-evaluation of the transaction as a whole. The accusations leveled against organizers were not simply a byproduct of the delays in the delivery of the bond. In other circumstances, such delays could have been probably excused as customary in such campaigns. But such interpretations demand a certain amount of goodwill, a state of mind that became particularly uncommon due to the acrimonious struggles between the FOIF and the Irish mission.

The inter-organizational structure of the campaign resulted in the two parties deeply interested in interpreting the Irish bonds as either a gift or an investment. The qualities of the Irish bonds were such that the two parties were able to reduce their meaning to the dimension (gift or investment) that pleased them most and locked them in a bitter struggle. In other words, the struggle between the Irish mission and the FOIF prompted the warring sides to try to clarify the meaning of the bonds and to flesh out an understandings of the rights and obligations that flowed from the transaction. This *forced clarification* rendered the differences between the Irish and the Irish Americans visible and further fueled the dispute.

The Israel Bond campaign almost suffered the same fate. When Ben-Gurion first introduced the bond plan, the leaders of the

Jewish Federations claimed that it was a gift in disguise. As in the Irish case, instead of passively accepting Ben-Gurion's representations of the bonds as a unique type of moral investment, the Jewish-American leaders tried to reduce the multivocality of the Israeli bond and treated it as another form of philanthropy. This was the very basis for their resistance to the plan in the first stages and, later, for their demand to coordinate the Israel Bond and UJA drives. To counter this argument, rhetoric was not enough; the AFDCI had to weave a whole socio-technical network in such a way that any claims that the bond was a simple gift would become less tenable and less advantageous. The terms of the Israeli bonds were just a part of this feat. Of equal importance was the structuring of a whole inter-organizational context within which the parties involved would not be motivated to pin down the meaning of the transaction.

The inter-organizational structure of the campaign together with the qualities built into the bonds themselves combined to create a *zone of indeterminacy* regarding the nature of the Israeli bonds and of the rights and obligations that followed from subscribing to them. The qualification of the bonds themselves made it harder to reduce the ambiguity of the bonds and to claim that they were just gifts. Furthermore, the inter-organizational structure of the relationships reduced the motivation of leaders of the Jewish Federations to clarify both the precise meaning of the Israeli bonds and their own relationship with Israel. Ben-Gurion's commitment to the continuation of the UJA may not have placated the leaders of the Jewish Federations, but their dependence on Israeli speakers and endorsements forced them to tone down their criticism and allowed the two projects to continue in an uneasy alliance.

Side-by-side examination of the bond projects clarifies that the Israel Bond drive's success – its ability to mediate between the two fragments of the Jewish nation – was not the result of an already-existing agreement about the need to support Israel. Likewise, the collapse of the Irish Bond was not simply an outcome of some combative tendency inherent to the Irish nature or some defect in the Irish bonds themselves. Rather, success depended on the creation of a zone of indeterminacy surrounding the bonds – i.e., on the production of an institutional context in which the parties involved would refrain from treating the transaction as either gift giving or a market exchange. In the Israeli case, such a zone of indeterminacy allowed the parties involved to cooperate without agreeing about the meaning of their mutual engagement.

The challenge of creating and maintaining such a zone of indeterminacy thus has two aspects. On the one hand, the zone of indeterminacy must allow the actors to transact without clarifying the precise meaning of their mutual engagement. On the other hand, the zone of indeterminacy must work to reduce the actors' motivation to determine the precise nature of their transaction.

Our discussion of the differences between the Irish and Jewish Bonds points to the crucial importance of temporal framing in creating zones of indeterminacy and in maintaining cooperation between heterogeneous groups. Bourdieu (1992) argues that what distinguishes gift giving from a market exchange is the temporal gap between the gift and the counter-gift. In the case of the bonds, the time lag between subscription and redemption can be seen as a period in which the bond organizations had some flexibility to frame the bonds as either gifts, investments, or something in between. The temporal framing of the Israeli bond allowed it to be always a bit more than just a gift or just an investment. In the short term, prior to redemption, the Israeli bonds were taken to be primarily gifts, but their limited liquidity and the prompt payment of interest for the coupon bonds turned them into something beyond a gift. In the long term, after redemption, the high risk relative to the low return of this security ensured that subscribers could still believe that they were more than a regular investment. The temporal framing of the Israel Bond helped maintain a zone of indeterminacy in which each community could interpret the Israel Bond in a way that was pleasing to it without the two communities clashing.

The ACII did not create a similar temporal duality for the Irish bonds. The struggles between the FOIF and the Irish mission instilled deep distrust throughout the community. In this atmosphere, subscribers interpreted delays in the delivery of the bonds as a sign of ingratitude or an indication of the corrupt nature of the project. It was as if the failure to deliver the bonds punctually brought about a premature ending to the zone of indeterminacy surrounding the Irish Bond. To be sure, subscribers knew that they might not get their money back, but they expected to receive the bonds promptly as a token of appreciation for their support.

Poor temporal management combined with raging inter-organizational conflict forced the Irish Americans and the homeland Irish to clarify what exactly the Irish bonds were and what rights and obligations followed from purchasing them. When they disagreed about these matters, they fought fiercely.

History, Big and Small

Some readers, no doubt, will see my focus on the details of the Irish and Israeli bond campaigns and on the various meanings that were attributed to them as both descriptive and reductionist. In mainstream comparative historical research, contrasting outcomes command – almost automatically – a search for differences in initial conditions that can explain success and failure (Ragin 1987; Mahoney and Rueschemeyer 2003). The general assumption is that macro-sociological variables determine the course of history. The differences between the Irish and Israeli subscription procedures or their inter-organizational structures, from this viewpoint, should be treated as either expressions or effects of consequential structural differences between the Irish and Jews rather than as the causes of success or failure.

Identifying potentially consequential macro-sociological differences between the Irish and Israeli cases is easy. First, anyone with even superficial acquaintance with the two cases will quickly note that the political status of the Irish and Israeli governments and the American political context during the periods examined here were radically different. Regardless of the *Dáil Éireann*'s declaration of independence, the Republic of Ireland had yet to receive international recognition, and British forces effectively controlled the entire Island. In contrast, by 1951, when Israel issued its bonds, the Israeli government had already secured international recognition and effective control of the country. Second, although both projects took place in the United States, they were separated by more than thirty years. The Irish Bond began in 1920, right after World War I, in which the United States had fought together with England, the target of the Irish struggle. This position may have made it harder for Irish-American organizations to cooperate with the Irish mission. In contrast, in the early 1950s, in the aftermath of the Holocaust, Jewish Americans, the general public, and even the American government were likely to be more inclined to cooperate with the Israeli government.[23] Third, Irish Americans were poorer and less educated as a group than American Jews (see Jacobson 1995). Squeezing extra money from the Irish diaspora in the United States was, therefore, probably more difficult. To these differences one might add differences in religion and levels of religious observance, differences in levels of assimilation, and many other things.

Clearly, the conditions under which the Irish and Zionist movements operated were distinct. In retrospect, once the outcomes of the Irish and Israeli bond projects are recognized, almost any difference between the cases seems like a good explanation for the outcomes of the projects. But such an explanatory approach is highly problematic. First, given our limited number of cases, it is easy to identify many potentially consequential differences – including some not mentioned here – as likely explanations, but the limited variability makes it hard to distinguish between genuine and spurious causes.[24]

Second, associating outcomes with differences in initial conditions also trivializes the complexity of historical processes and overlooks the agency of historical actors. While it is easy to identify differences between cases, understanding how such differences influence courses of events is far from simple. For example, at first glance, it seems likely that a dramatic event like the Holocaust would foster Jewish American contributions to Israel and facilitate cooperation with the bond project. But empirical scrutiny reveals that the "effect" of the Nazi atrocities was more complex and variable. Initially, many American Jews responded to the Holocaust with despair and inaction.[25] Only several years later, and in part as a result of the UJA's successful fundraising strategies, did they embrace the goal of supporting overseas Jews on an unprecedented scale. Even then, however, the desperate situation did not lead to automatic cooperation. As Jewish Americans parted with more of their money, they also became more deeply interested in supervising the use of the funds, which led to a sharp dispute with the Zionist leadership in Israel. While *Mapai* (the ruling party) leaders favored state-centered development, American Jews, especially big donors and the organizations that represented them, leaned toward capitalist strategies for development. The point is simple: historical events, even horrendous calamities like the Holocaust, do not force events (cooperation in nation building, in this case) in some mechanical manner. The only way to understand how background conditions shape outcomes is through painstaking exploration of how events and conditions are transformed into a call for action and adapted by various constituencies.

Perhaps most problematically, attributing the failure of the Irish Bond project and the success of the Israel Bond to differences in initial conditions tells us almost nothing about the process of generating cooperation between heterogeneous groups and, more specifically, about the process of nation building. Arguing, for example, that the difference in the political status of the Republic of Ireland and the State of Israel played a decisive role in shaping the outcomes of the bond drives may be accurate, but it reveals little about why, in the Irish case, ambiguity with regard to the nature of the Irish bonds sparked conflict, whereas in the Israeli case, similar ambiguity served to facilitate cooperation between the parties. Such an approach is ineffectual when it comes to exploring the key problem of how national movements orchestrate cooperation among the various groups that are assembled under the banner of a "nation."

Understanding how contexts matter necessitates an alternative comparative strategy that centers on historical processes rather than background conditions. The American suspicion with regard to pro-Irish activities, the Jewish Holocaust, the establishment of the State of Israel, and other factors played an important role in shaping the fates of these respective projects. But like any other force in history, these events and conditions did not act like an invisible hand that mysteriously conducted events toward their expected outcomes (expected, that is, in retrospect). Rather, historical contexts always affect concrete situations, and my focus on the "small" or "technical" details of the Irish and Israeli bond campaigns is designed to allow us to understand how the Irish and Jewish national movements responded to the historical situations that they confronted – and in this way provide a better understanding of the outcomes of the two projects and of the process of nation building.

A useful term to mediate between the small or technical details of the bond projects and the "big" macro-structural differences between the projects is the concept of *expertise*. By expertise, I refer to the complex body of practical know-how accumulated through experience that differentiates between the actions of a novice and those of experienced organizers. Issuing diaspora bonds in the United States posed a tremendous challenge for the Irish and Zionist movements. Notwithstanding the differences in their circumstances, both movements had to confront complex political and legal obstacles in the United States and to navigate the stormy waters of diasporic politics. Yet, the everyday details of the campaigns reveal glaring differences in the level of political and financial expertise of the two movements, on both sides of the ocean. These differences were already quite noticeable in Chapter 3, where we examined the philanthropic drives of the IVF and the UJA; they played an even more consequential role in the course of the respective bond campaigns.

Prior to their arrival in the United States, de Valera, Harry Boland, and their associates had been active in quasi-clandestine organizations – the Irish Volunteers and the Irish Republican Brotherhood – and had spent short terms in prison. They had little experience with party politics or the management of large organizations. Frank Walsh from the ACII Commission and Joseph McGarrity, the two most important American allies of the Irish mission, had some experience with Irish-American politics but had never before run large-scale fundraising campaigns. Finally, James O'Mara and, later, his brother Stephen O'Mara, who were in charge of the day-to-day operations of the Bond drive, were chosen for the position because of their business acumen and family prominence in Ireland. Both of them, however, were foreign to the Irish-American politics of fundraising. The inexperience of the Irish mission was related to the low level of institutionalization of the Irish national movement. To no small extent, the Irish Republican movement of the 1910s and 1920s emerged in response to the events of the Easter Rising of 1916, and this newness was reflected in the composition of its leaders. But the low level of expertise involved in the bond project was also a consequence of de Valera's decision not to entrust the bond campaign to the FOIF, which had considerable expertise and know-how at its disposal. This decision forced the Irish mission to rely on relatively marginal Irish Americans and on inexperienced imports from Ireland.

The contrast with the Israeli case is striking. David Ben-Gurion, Eliezer Kaplan, Golda Meyerson, and Levi Eshkol – the Israeli leaders most deeply involved in the Israel Bond campaign – were experienced party politicians. During the decades prior to the establishment of the State of Israel and issuance of the Israeli bonds, they managed the Jewish Agency, which functioned as a bureaucratic quasi-state apparatus. Reaching agreements, establishing committees to blur and defuse disagreements, and hammering out compromises had been their stock-in-trade for the previous four decades. On the American side, Henry Montor and his staff brought with them from the UJA invaluable experience with fundraising and with the internal workings of the Jewish-American community. Montor and his associates also made extensive use of newly developed survey and marketing techniques that had not existed 30 years earlier. These technologies allowed the AFDCI to gauge more accurately the concerns of the Jewish community and to approach it more effectively.

Thinking about nation building using the concept of expertise should not be interpreted as an attempt to ignore the context within which the two movements operated. Quite the contrary, "expertise" simply provides us with a hands-on and fairly concrete way of linking the macro-structural conditions under which the Irish and Zionists operated to their on-the-ground conduct. These glaring differences in expertise account to no small extent, I believe, for the failure and success of the Irish and Israeli bond drives, respectively.

Interestedness and Disinterestedness in the Production of National Attachments

Weaving national transatlantic networks is a complex practical accomplishment. Tracing the history of the Irish and Israeli bond drives offers a concrete understanding of what the phrase "nation building" actually means in practice. At the beginning of their journeys, de Valera and Ben-Gurion were weak. They had to cross great divides and mediate between communities with diverse and sometimes conflicting orientations. Regardless of the admiration they commanded, they could not persuade commercial banks or supporters to furnish them with either loans or sufficient donations. The way to overcome weakness in both cases was to bind together the different communities using innovative organizational technologies. But these financial technologies were risky. In both market exchange and gift giving, the determination of ownership and entitlement is relatively simple: on one side there is a seller or a gift giver, on the other a purchaser or receiver. Mixing these elements in the bonds made it more difficult to determine who owed money or gratitude to whom. Moreover, when elements of market exchange are added to a gift, the exchange runs the risk of alienating instead of promoting a relationship of trust and affection. When de Valera and Montor issued hybrid bonds, they risked losing the affection of their compatriots.

Aligning the interests and preferences of the different groups that potentially constitute the nation is a fragile organizational achievement. Although the contrast between the cases is clear, at no point did any of the elements in the Irish or Jewish financial networks submit themselves unambiguously to the nation. National attachments were always conditional. When the Irish Bond failed to translate the diverse interests of the Irish and the Irish Americans into mutually reinforcing terms, their transatlantic network disintegrated. The different national fragments detached themselves and drifted apart – the Irish in Ireland to their own dealings, the Irish Americans to theirs.

In the Jewish case, maintaining the attachments of the subscribers to Israel necessitated ongoing work of translation and qualification. A closer look at the floating of the second Israel Bond illuminates this point. When Montor and Levi Eshkol planned the issue of the Development Bonds in mid-1953, they realized that the terms of the Independence Bonds of 1951 created unforeseen obstacles to the issue of the new loan. When the Israeli bonds were sold for the first time, the AFDCI decided that the bonds would be non-transferable for three years but allowed subscribers to convert them to Israeli pounds at any point. At that time, these terms seemed like a stroke of genius, balancing the demand for liquidity while avoiding the need to support the market with a large portion of the proceeds. The few expected conversions, it was thought, would only ease the burden of paying back in dollars.

In 1953, however, when the Independence Bonds were about to become transferable, the convertibility of the Independence Issue bonds posed a serious challenge: as in 1951, Montor and Eshkol suspected that with the coming transferability the market price of the bonds would drop substantially below par. But Israel now could not prevent the pricing of the bonds by fiat. A depressed market price for the bonds, like before, could deter subscribers from extending more credit to Israel. Even worse, a reduced price could tempt speculators to buy bonds on the market and convert them to Israeli pounds at full price.[26] This possibility, which in 1951 seemed unlikely due to the inflated value of the Israeli currency, was, in 1953, especially disturbing.[27] Between 1951 and 1953 the Israeli government successfully devalued its currency. As a result, conversion of dollar-denominated bonds, especially those bought at a steep discount, to Israeli pounds became a potentially lucrative operation. From the government's perspective, wide-scale conversions of Independence Bonds could have disastrous consequences. Faced with the obligation to redeem a large number of bonds immediately, Eshkol feared, the Finance Ministry would be forced to print large amounts of money, which would cause the Israeli economy to face inflation again.[28]

In essence, the convertibility crisis was related to the status of the relationships between Jewish Americans and the Zionist movement. Jewish Americans purchased the Independence Bonds largely out of sympathy for Israel, but their ongoing support was not a given. While now a bit closer to the Zionist project, American Jews, by and large, did not relinquish their other interests; they still needed to build up their retirement savings, and they still needed to pay for the education of their children. If given a choice, Eshkol and Montor realized, at least some of the bondholders would put their personal interests ahead of the national common good, sell their bonds, and turn the above scenario into a reality.

To pre-empt this development, Montor and Eshkol introduced unusual measures designed to reduce the supply of Independence Bonds once they became transferable.[29] First, the AFDCI allowed subscribers to replace their old Independence Bonds with the new Development Bonds. The Development Bonds were non-transferable for five years, giving Israel another temporary shelter from the drop-in-price scenario. To encourage replacements, Israel agreed to pay 4% on the Development Bonds instead of the 3.5% offered on Independence Bonds.[30] Second, the AFDCI created a separate holding company, the Israel Investors Incorporated (I.I.I.), the shares of which could be bought with Israeli bonds. The I.I.I. was supposed to absorb Independence Bonds by allowing subscribers who thoroughly distrusted the government to replace their bonds with indirect holdings in the few lucrative companies that operated in Israel at the time.[31] Third, the AFDCI also created a special Loan Guarantee Fund. The Fund provided purchasers of the new Development Issue Bonds with a loan of up to 75% of their value, which was returned in quarterly installments over two years. This new financing option assured that "holders of Independence Bonds will not sell if they merely want to get cash but will exchange their bonds for the new bond and borrow against them."[32] Finally, for subscribers who demonstrated a need for immediate cash but could not take on a new loan, the AFDCI agreed *ex gratia* to buy their bonds prematurely without penalty.[33] The combination of these measures, Montor hoped, would reduce the availability of Israeli bonds on the market after they became transferable.[34]

More than an anecdote, this interlude illustrates an important point: maintaining Jewish-American attachment to the bonds, and consequently to Israel, required ongoing efforts directed toward aligning the interests of Jewish Americans with the Israeli government's interest. The elaborate privileges of the Development Bonds aimed at bringing the financial and patriotic interests of subscribers into closer alignment. Instead of confronting subscribers with a heroic choice – "support Israel or secure your savings" – the AFDCI revised the terms of engagement with different subscribers so as to prevent this choice from ever materializing. Rather than trying to convince Jewish Americans to place the national interest ahead of their particularistic interests, the bond campaign was an attempt to escape a zero-sum game wherein commitment to the nation required a sacrifice of particularistic interests. The effectiveness of the Israel Bond lies precisely in the fact that the project allowed Jewish Americans to hold onto their particular interests and also contribute to the national cause.

The collapse of the Irish Bond provides a negative illustration of the same principle. Like in the Israel Bond, the hybrid nature of the Irish Bond was designed to diffuse the tension between one's economic interests and the national interest. But, in practice, the design of the project exacerbated tensions between the parties and forced them into a radical choice between their personal and organizational (in the case of the FOIF) interests and their commitment to Ireland's freedom. This choice became strikingly clear at the organizational level. Some scholars attribute the feud between de Valera and the FOIF to the "Americanized" character of the American movements (Carroll 1978, 2002; Doorley 2005). The FOIF leaders were, no doubt, oriented toward the American government and public, but the collapse of the relationships probably was not due to this orientation but rather to a failure to align the interests of the Irish national movement with that of the FOIF. By handing the organization of the bond drive over to the ACII, de Valera presented the Irish-American leaders with an unenviable choice between their organizational interests and the interests of the Republic of Ireland (defined by none other than de Valera).[35] That the Irish-American leaders chose something short of a complete surrender of their own interests is hardly surprising. The crux of the breakdown in the Irish case was not that Irish Americans were not dedicated enough to the Irish cause but that the Irish national movement did not defuse the choice between loyalty to oneself and loyalty to one's nation.

Scholars typically portray nation building as a process through which national interests gradually take precedence over interests related to one's concrete social position. Allegedly, the peasants, for example, stop thinking of themselves as belonging to a particular village and instead identify as members of a nation. The workers, too, abandon their class loyalties in favor of participation in a national struggle (Anderson 1991: 6). Allegedly, narrow, particularistic interests give way to the emergence of a common national (dis)interest.

In our two cases, however, something different transpired. Instead of abandoning their particular interests as Irish Americans or Jewish Americans, members of these communities actually added national attachment to their existing loyalties. To the extent that they were successful, the respective national movements did not cajole Irish Americans and Jewish Americans into selfless sacrifice of their own interests but, instead, assembled together the interests of various groups. The crux of the challenge was to reconcile the different preferences and interests of the various groups that potentially made up the nation. The point is not that membership in the nation should be interpreted as an interested act in some "rational choice" fashion. Obviously, members sometimes sacrifice on behalf of the nation – some of them a great deal. Rather the process of nation building seems to be composed of multiple acts of alignment that gradually lead subjects to perceive national interests as compatible with their own. While national rhetoric and imagery can certainly take part in this process, aligning the interests of the different fragments of the nation is fundamentally a delicate *organizational* accomplishment.

Conclusions: Nation Building as an Organizational Accomplishment

Theoretically and methodologically, this book suggests that nation building should be treated as a practical organizational challenge. To succeed, a small group of visionaries must reach out and enroll others who may be less committed to the national cause. Without reaching out to these potential members, the nation will remain a flimsy musing of a mere few; however, recruiting heterogeneous groups and individuals increases the likelihood of conflicts. As more people enroll in the nation, it becomes harder to reach agreement with regard to "what the nation is", who belongs to the nation, what rights and obligations follow from national membership, and the steps that should be taken to advance the national cause. The challenge of recruiting others is not secondary to a more fundamental challenge of generating a sense of common membership. Successful regulation of internal conflicts may lead members to believe that certain palpable differences between themselves and other members of the nation are inessential. Ongoing conflicts, in contrast, can lead members to identify certain differences between themselves and others as essential and thus render common membership a bit less imaginable. The challenge of nation building, therefore, is one of setting up mechanisms that can contain and accommodate the different understandings of various potential members and sustain the belief in the existence of the nation.

Our examination of the bonds projects provides new answers to important historiographical puzzles. Specifically, the examination helps us to understand the collapse of the Irish-American diaspora as an organized political force and the cementing of the ties between American Jews and Israel.

Scholars unambiguously identify the early 1920s as a major turning point in Irish-American relations with Ireland. Prior to 1920, the Irish-American diaspora was one of the most engaged diasporas in the United States (Brown 1966; Jacobson 1995). After that date, Irish Americans assimilated at an accelerated pace (Ward 1968; McCaffrey 1976; Fallows 1979; Miller 1985; Kenny 2000; Doorley 2005). This break is typically attributed to exogenous events. Allegedly, the establishment of the Irish Free State alone, or in combination with the eruption of the Irish civil war, liberated Irish Americans from their preoccupation with the "old sod" and allowed them to concentrate on their life in the United States (Fallows 1979; Doorley 2005). However, it is not clear why Irish Americans, who until the late 1910s were vehemently opposed to any compromise with England, would respond so passively to events that propelled their compatriots in Ireland to take up arms against each other.

Close attention to the Irish–Irish-American relations provides a nuanced and on-the-ground account of how their ties frayed. In 1920, in the course of the struggle between the FOIF and the Irish mission, John Devoy accused de Valera of betraying Republican principles by expressing willingness to grant England certain concessions, and he identified Michael Collins as the unbending leader of the Irish revolution (*Gaelic American*, February 21, 1920). During the negotiations with Britain, and in the parliamentary debates that preceded the civil war, however, it was Collins who supported compromise and de Valera who led the opposition to the Anglo-Irish Treaty. This turn of events surprised Devoy and other leaders of the FOIF. The principled leader in whom they had placed their trust, Collins, had agreed to take the oath of allegiance to the king, while their sworn enemy, de Valera, suddenly appeared as the stickler. No wonder that the FOIF response to the Anglo-Irish treaty was confusion and ultimately inaction. Initially, when they believed that the Treaty reflected de Valera's opinion, they issued a condemnation of the compromise and only later, when the division between de Valera and Collins became public, did they retract their opposition (Doorley 1995: 235–237). Without taking into account the highly personalized struggle between de Valera and the leadership of the FOIF, it would be hard to understand why Irish Americans reacted with resignation to the heart-wrenching drama that unfolded in Ireland.

This book also improves our understanding of the "Zionization" of Jewish America. Scholars often attribute the increase in Jewish-American support for Zionism during the 1940s and 1950s to the Holocaust and the establishment of Israel in 1948 (see, for example, Urofsky 1978; Hertzberg 1998). While these events were, without doubt, tremendously important, treating them as explanations is an expression of Whig history, that is, of a teleological historiography that presents the past as an inevitable march toward an anticipated present. The initial Jewish American reaction to the Nazi atrocities was despair rather than automatic sympathy for Zionism. Only later, largely in response to the UJA's efforts, did American Jews embrace the role of the saviors of the Jewish world. Importantly, during much of the period discussed here, many Jewish Americans saw the Jewish community in Palestine as part of the Jewish problem, not the solution. Finally, even among those who identified Israel as the solution to the Jewish problem, agreeing on how and how much to support the Zionist struggle was not simple. Support for Zionism, in other words, was not the only or the most obvious conclusion that American Jews could have drawn from the Holocaust.

My aim is not to minimize the importance of the Holocaust, the subsequent plight of Jewish refugees, or the establishment of the State of Israel in generating support for Zionism in the United States, but rather to point out that turning these events into unambiguous historical "lessons" required intense interpretive work. More than any other organization, it was the UJA that, during the mid-1940s, engaged in framing Israel as an answer to the crimes of the Nazis. A close look at the Israel Bond project adds to this analysis by tracing the process by which Jewish-American donors, many of them successful capitalist entrepreneurs, came to accept and support, almost without protest, the centralized economic policies of the Israeli government. Furthermore, our analysis of the bond project helps explain how Israel escaped the role of a perpetual beggar and became a source of pride for American Jews (while continuing to solicit donations).

Conclusions

Beyond Homeland–Diaspora Relations

This book focused on the particular relationships between national movements and diaspora communities. In principle, however, the arguments developed in the preceding chapters are relevant for other settings as well. To support this argument, the following section will show, albeit only in a preliminary and suggestive manner, that the underlying tensions and organizational mechanisms I have outlined in the preceding chapters are relevant beyond the context of homeland–diaspora encounters.

The use of monetary transactions to forge and to maintain social ties is by no means limited to homeland–diaspora relations. For instance, when de Valera prepared to float the Irish bonds in the United States, Collins issued a very similar loan in Ireland (Carroll 2002: 6–9). To lure the public into purchasing these bonds, the Irish Republicans produced a short, silent propaganda film, which presented a parade of national celebrities – almost without exception mothers and widowers of distinguished national martyrs – lining up and purchasing bonds. Collins, in the role of a loan officer, uses as a desk the very block on which the legendary Republican rebel, Robert Emmet, was beheaded in 1803. A letter is shown from Michael Fogarty, the renowned Bishop of Killaloe, urging viewers to subscribe to the loan:

> Now is the time to give proof of the faith that is in us, we must not, in this national enterprise, fall behind our great American friends, it will be a shame to do so... it should be the pride of every Irishman to hold one of these certificates.[1]

While conditions in Ireland during the height of the Anglo-Irish war were very different from conditions in the United States, the rhetoric and underlying message were almost identical with the messages of the Irish-American fundraising drives we examined previously. As in the IVF and UJA campaigns, the graver sacrifices of others – Robert Emmet, the national martyrs, their mothers and widowers, and even the Irish-American donors – served to prompt others to do their part.

In the Zionist context, Uri Ben-Eliezer described how the Israeli public was induced to donate money for the purchase of arms for the military in the early 1950s (1995; 1998). To enhance the public's generosity, the organizers of *Keren HaMagen* (literally "Defender Fund") published the military's shopping list in the newspapers, complete with the price of each item. Donors were allowed to earmark their donations and name their purchases. The city council of Haifa, home to the embryonic Israeli navy, contributed a torpedo boat. The mayor of Ramle, on the other hand, decided to purchase a tank and named it "Ramle 1." Individuals participated in the project as well. Lydia Benlulu, a mother of ten, decided to gift back the hundred pounds she received as a childbearing prize. Yigal Yadin, Israel's chief of staff, took every opportunity to urge parents to "buy a suit of iron, a suit of armor for the defense of your children" (in Ben-Eliezer 1995: 279).

Outside the Irish and Jewish contexts, the most obvious parallel to the bond projects can be found in the American war bond programs of World War I and World War II (which served as an inspiration for the Irish and Israeli Bonds).[2] Facing an unprecedented increase in government spending and inflationary pressures, Henry Morgenthau, then the Treasury Secretary, appealed to the citizens' sense of duty to finance the war. The E series nonnegotiable saving bonds specifically targeted the general population, offering a 4% interest rate for 10 years (Kimble 2006).

To reach every potential subscriber, the US Treasury relied on more than five million volunteers and organized a massive campaign, the themes of which ring familiar. Celebrity speakers urged the American public to "buy our boys back" using a mix of guilt, self-interest, and patriotic duty.[3] Along with frequent comparisons of the sacrifices demanded from frontline soldiers and home-front citizens, the bonds' slogans emphasized the economic value and importance of saving. Polls, however, revealed that, more than anything subscribers understood the purchase of the bond as their way of helping the GIs (tellingly enough, GI is an acronym for "Government Issue") (Sparrow 2008: 269–270). As in the case of the Israel Bonds, the fusion of patriotic and pecuniary interests generated useful ambiguities regarding the nature of the transaction. The results of the campaign were impressive. During the war alone, the Treasury sold more than $185 billion worth of bonds, an average of $314 dollars for every citizen (Sparrow 2008).

Importantly, in addition to generating more funds, the American war bond campaign served to include hitherto excluded groups in the American national community. Laurence Samuel (1997) argues that the bond drive specifically targeted African Americans, Native Americans, and Latinos, and presented the purchase of bonds as a ticket to full participation in US society. James Sparrow forcefully argues that the war bond campaign laid the foundation for the emergence of postwar "fiscal citizenship," whereby citizens' membership in the nation-state was mediated through citizens' financial contributions to the national common good.

Yet it would be a great mistake to limit our discussion to financial contributions alone. Our discussion of the Irish and Israeli drives and the examination of American war bonds demonstrate the deep interrelatedness of various types of sacrifices taken on behalf of the nation. Contributions to the nation come in a dazzling array of forms: such things as waving a flag, donating money, organizing fund drives, volunteering, singing the national anthem, bearing and rearing children, risking one's life, risking the life of a loved one, and, ultimately, sacrificing one's life, are often understood within a framework of giving. The sacrifice of one justifies the demand for sacrifice from others, creating debt obligations that, just as in Bourdieusian gift giving, never close (this dynamic reaches a climax in the case of death, for which the living, in the homeland or without, remain eternally indebted). Each sacrifice, in addition to commanding sacrifices from others, also serves to justify a demand for special status and privileges. As Charles Tilly famously argued, the tension between selfless and interested giving, between contribution of various resources and the privileges that follow from it, plays an absolutely central role in the regulation of relationships among groups that make up the nation within the boundaries of the state (1992: 102; 1996). Clearly, the political utility of mechanisms of exchange is not limited to the context of homeland–diaspora relationships.

My argument regarding the importance of economic transactions in mobilizing and attaching potential members to the nation in a domestic context should not imply that these processes (those within a nation and those in homeland–diaspora contexts) are necessarily similar. The conditions within the nation-state – the existence of tax-extraction mechanisms, public education systems, and, more generally, state bureaucracy empowered with coercive capacities – make an obvious difference in the way national movements approach their potential clientele. But given that even in the homeland the nation is nothing but a collection of fragments (Chatterjee 1993), and given that the tension between selfless and interested giving plays a key role in the rhetoric and self-understanding of members even in the homeland, it is likely that the mechanisms devised to accomplish nation building in a domestic context would similarly deploy elements of gift giving and market exchange.

Beyond Essentialism and Social Constructivism

In an effort to offset the tendency to treat nations as bounded entities, researchers today treat nations as social constructions and emphasize their heterogeneous character. Instead of asking what the nation is, which unavoidably suggests that the nation actually exists, scholars today study the cultural representations and various practices that turn the nation into a taken-for-granted category (Sahlins 1989; Verdery 1991, 1996; Eley and Suny 1996; Brubaker 2004, 2009; Fox and Miller-Idriss 2008). While this new orientation yields important insights, a negative consequence of this shift is that nationalism today is analyzed using increasingly elusive concepts. Researchers today use concepts like narrative (Bhabha 1990), discursive formation (Calhoun 1997), ideology (Handler 1988), master symbol (Verdery 1991), fetish (Ivy 1995), cognition (Brubaker et al. 2004), and perspective (Brubaker 2009) to describe nation building. When these explanations are interpreted to mean that nations are not "real" but only "socially constructed," however, they become enmeshed in contradictions (see Hacking 2000).

My focus on concrete relational mechanisms that bind together heterogeneous groups complements existing research on the practices of nation building and suggests a way forward. The technical details that occupy so many pages in this book help identify additional elements that partake in this process. They clarify that nations are indeed constructed, but that the means used in their construction include much more than what is typically included in the constructivist repertoire.

Concrete organizational work is central to the process of nation building. Mobilizing the Irish and Jews in the United States on behalf of the respective national projects required more than a representation of the nation as a unified whole. To enroll Irish Americans and Jewish Americans, the leaders of the national projects designed organizational mechanisms calculated to create desirable roles for the various groups assembled under the banner of the nation. In addition to moving images and slogans, they developed mechanisms within which people could engage actively and consequently make sense of their position within the nation.

The mechanisms used to create the national attachments examined here – the IVF, the UJA, and the two bond projects – were delicate organizational accomplishments. Each of these mechanisms effectively enrolled Irish and Jewish Americans, but each was also subject to protracted disputes and recurring crises. To some extent, the fragility of these mechanisms reflects a general characteristic of social life: cooperation is a delicate accomplishment (Garfinkel 1967). But more specifically, the delicateness of these projects was related to their national character. National movements strive to generate a sense of intimate comradeship among members (Anderson 1991). Paradoxically, however, members of the nation are strangers to one another. To engineer this paradoxical sense of closeness among strangers, the Irish and Zionist movements first experimented with gift giving and later fused gift giving (a mechanism that typically regulates relationships between intimates) with market exchange (a mechanism that typically assures the alienated character of encounters). This experimentation resulted in weird hybrids, liable to produce effects opposite to those for which they were assembled in the first place. The bureaucratization of gift giving tends to rob the sense of closeness and trust that this type of transaction usually produces. The complexity involved in fusing gift giving and market exchange in the case of the bonds was daunting as well. The mixing of the elements of gift giving and market exchange in the bonds made it exceedingly hard to determine who owed what to whom. The terrible feud between the FOIF and the Irish mission over the Irish bonds arose precisely from these questions. In all cases, translating the interests and preferences of the various entities demanded ongoing work of maintenance and repair. National entrepreneurs constantly had to negotiate and hammer out compromises between the different groups and entities that constituted the nation. Where their efforts were ineffective, the networks connecting homeland and diaspora communities disintegrated quickly.

My focus on organizational processes and concrete practical mechanisms should not be taken to imply that nations are entities with clear boundaries between inside and outside. On the contrary, the organizational efforts of national entrepreneurs were directed precisely toward the unbounded and inhomogeneous character of the nation – toward mobilizing groups whose position vis-à-vis the nation was ambiguous. To weave loosely related groups into the nation, our national entrepreneurs constructed concrete organizational mechanisms which, when they were successful, allowed subjects to tell themselves a story about their own positions within the nation.

Interest and Disinterest in Nation Building

In both popular discourse and scholarly discussions, nation building is often depicted as a process through which particularistic interests are replaced with unitary national concerns. The point is not that scholars fail to identify certain groups, usually elites, that stand to benefit from national mobilization. Sensitive to inequality and domination, critical scholars are obviously aware of that dimension. However, with the exception of a few scholars, genuine national sentiments are typically portrayed as essentially disinterested.[4] The centrality of death in national ceremonies and scholarly writings attests to this generalization. It is not coincidental that this ultimate act of sacrifice receives such honor in the national imagination – death is the one act that cannot be discredited as being somehow instrumental. Allegedly, genuine membership in a nation is more a matter of self-understanding than self-interest. A negative side-effect of this characterization is that it tempts scholars to depict nationalism as a deep emotional response (this tendency is particularly noticeable among primordialist scholars) or emphasize the importance of processes that generate "taken-for-granted" categories, of which subjects are typically not fully aware, in the making of national sentiments.

The analysis presented in this book suggests a different process. Rather than substituting interested action with selfless passion, the IVF, UJA, Irish Bond Certificate, and the Israel Bond overlaid the interests and preferences of the groups that make up the nation. For example, the visibility in the act of giving, which Diarmuid Lynch and Henry Montor labored to produce, effectively aligned the national quest for recognition with the personal search for renown and honor. The success of these mechanisms depended precisely on the continuous production of this overlap. Were the act of donating to the IVF or UJA seen simply as self-aggrandizement, the honor associated with giving would have disappeared, and with it, the donors. Had the IVF or UJA denied recognition from donors (as Jewish tradition recommends), donating would have remained the pursuit of a mere few altruistic souls. In the case of the bonds, the superimposing of personal and national interests became even more explicit.

The principle of overlaying and combining interests can also be gleaned from the general character of the projects examined here. None of the projects discussed in this book were purely national. As de Valera was quick to point out, the FOIF leaders were concerned with American politics no less and perhaps even more than they were in events in Ireland (de Valera may have exaggerated this point, but he was not entirely delusional). Similarly, the UJA was composed of three organizations (JDC, NRS, and UPA), of which only one was "Zionist," and the Jewish Federations, which organized the drive at the local level, were interested in American Jewish communal life above all. The ACII and AFDCI also were not exclusively "nationalist" in their orientation. Each of these projects can be described as "ethnic," "diasporic," or "plainly opportunistic," rather than "national." Furthermore, many of the fundraising practices discussed are used in settings that have nothing to do with nation building. For example, many philharmonic orchestras often rely on some, and perhaps many, of these practices.

However, classifying these organizations as not quite national overlooks a crucially important fact: the existence of "non-national" aspects in these projects was not an accidental or distracting factor but rather their condition of existence. The different fragments of the nation have different preferences and interests. Weaving these fragments into a cohesive national network necessitated bringing together and mixing diverse motivations. That the IVF or UJA events were dedicated to more than a single cause does not take away from their national import. Without offering something to donors, neither of these organizations would have been able to garner support. There is absolutely no reason to believe that in other settings, national projects manifest themselves in "purer" forms or that, when more "purely" nationalist forms of action are identified, they are somehow more consequential or more worthy of study.

My aim is not to reduce nation building to some sort of rational choice model that assumes only interested action. Obviously, many of the actors described in this book – both leaders and lay supporters – were also deeply committed to their national causes and not for selfish reasons alone. Instead, I have tried to trace the delicate process through which actors become more or less interested in the nation and to describe the many translations at the end of which actors conclude (or do not) that the national interest is also their interest (Latour 1988).

National attachments, in our case, were always conditional, and their solidification required intense organizational work. When the Irish Bond failed to align the diverse priorities of the Irish and Irish Americans, their transatlantic ties disintegrated. In the Jewish case as well, maintaining the attachments of bonds subscribers to Israel necessitated ongoing negotiations and an overlaying of interests. The AFDCI continuously labored to align the interests and preferences of the various groups involved. In preparation for the second issue of the Israeli bonds in 1953, Montor and his associates again had to find ways to persuade subscribers to hold onto their old bonds and purchase new ones. Successful nation building did not mean the displacement of particularistic self-interest with a singular concern for the national common good but, rather, ongoing negotiations, compromises, and qualifications that allowed the personal and the national to appear as compatible causes.

Difference and Diversity Within the Nation

While scholars today are careful to emphasize that nations are not homogeneous or unified, consciously articulated differences are still considered an obstacle that national movements must somehow overcome. The cases examined in this book, however, suggest that internal differences and misunderstandings are not necessarily a hindrance but that they can, when properly handled, play a productive role in the making of nations.

The successes of the IVF and the UJA in the 1910s and 1940s were predicated on a simultaneous drawing and blurring of a line separating diaspora and homeland communities. On the one hand, the IVF and UJA organizers emphasized the overarching unity of the Irish and Jewish nations. However, in the same breath, they drew attention to crucial differences between the groups (Americans live safely while those in the homeland, allegedly, risk their lives and sacrifice more). This double movement, and not only the emphasis on unity, played a key role in propelling Irish Americans and Jewish Americans into action.

The case of the Israel Bonds illustrates the productive role of difference from a different angle. As we have seen, Israeli and American Jews attributed different meanings to the Israeli bond. For American Jews, the bond was mostly a gift. Israeli Jews, in contrast, emphasized the pecuniary value of the bond and treated it as a kind of moral investment. While these differences created considerable inter-organizational friction (as when the Jewish Federations demanded coordination between the UJA and the bond campaigns under the assumption that these were campaigns of the same nature), they also allowed the two groups to cooperate. On the one hand, this misunderstanding allowed Israeli leaders to believe that they were (no longer) *schnorrers*, and consequently did not have to resent the Jewish-American generosity. Unlike the UJA funds, the bond dollars did not threaten their self-image as independent, new Jews. On the other hand, the very same misunderstanding allowed American Jews to bolster their own sense of worth by telling themselves that they had gifted Israel once again. Most importantly, through the Israel Bond, American Jews could acquire worth as members of the nation in the eyes of the Israeli *halutzim*, and the *halutzim* could acquire worth in the eyes of Jewish Americans. In other words, the differences in perspectives, the mutual misunderstanding of the nature of the Israel Bond, enabled both American and Israeli Jews to tell themselves compelling stories, albeit different, about their roles within the Jewish nation.

The success of the Israel Bond and the subsequent solidification of the ties between Israelis and Jewish Americans should not be taken as a sign of some deep underlying unity of the Jewish people. During the 1940s and early 1950s, these two communities shared little in common and, as Chapter 4 illustrates, even the dramas of the Holocaust and the establishment of Israel were not enough to keep disagreements at bay for long. Nevertheless, careful handling of these differences allowed these two communities to cooperate without agreeing on fundamental issues and to maintain national attachments. This accomplishment, the orchestration of cooperation between these two groups, allowed the two sides to hold onto the idea that the differences between American and Israeli Jews were not germane to the fundamental question of belonging to a nation.

In contradistinction, the collapse of the Irish Bond in the early 1920s was not a manifestation of unbridgeable differences between the Irish-American community and the Irish in Ireland. Differences between the two communities existed, as one can reasonably expect, but more than anything, the break in the Irish–Irish-American ties was the result of a failure to handle these differences with care and sensitivity. It is tempting to argue that the bond project failed because of pre-existing differences, but close observation clarifies that the conflicts associated with the Irish Bond played an active role in creating differences, in playing up their importance, and ultimately in driving the communities apart. Irish Americans and the Irish in Ireland shared many things in common. However, the deterioration of the relationships between de Valera and the leadership of the FOIF compelled the two sides to explore the differences between them and rendered meaningful a boundary that until that point had been blurry and inconsequential. The eventual estrangement between the communities was, to a large extent, the result of this process rather than its underlying cause.

My emphasis on the productive role of internal differences and misunderstandings in the process of nation building complements existing scholarship on the mechanisms that generate the representation of the nation as a cultural whole. Clearly, the projects examined in this book came into existence due to the existence of some baseline identification as either "Irish" or "Jewish." But given the tremendous heterogeneity of the groups that are assembled under the banner of a "nation," this baseline identification was not enough to generate cooperation when practical political arguments arose. At such a point, the construction of organizational mechanisms to allow cooperation without consensus may prove valuable not only for generating concerted action but also for creating and solidifying a sense of belonging among members. Put simply, successful regulation of the tensions between different groups makes it easier for members to believe that they belong to the same nation. Failure to regulate these tensions, in contrast, makes it harder for members to think of themselves as part of the nation. The crux of the challenge of nation building is orchestrating these differences so as to tame them and turn differences into "internal differences."

From "Identities" to "Attachment"

In a celebrated article, Rogers Brubaker and Frederick Cooper formulate a powerful critique of the concept of "identity" (2000), in which they identify "strong" and "softened" conceptions of the term. The strong conception of identity suggests a deep, enduring, and consequential sameness among members of a group. In contrast, the softened version, which is advocated by constructivist scholars, suggests thinking of identity as a fluctuating, unstable, and fragmentary phenomenon. Both versions are problematic. The strong version confuses nationalist and other identity claims with the actual process of their construction. Instead of examining how essentialist identity claims garner legitimacy, it treats these claims as facts. The softened version of identity is not guilty of essentialism but it is so ambiguous and emptied of content that it carries little analytical value. As an alternative, Brubaker and Cooper suggest using terms like "identification," "categorization," "self-understanding," and "groupness." These concepts provide a more process-oriented and nuanced means with which to approach nation building and identity politics in general.

My focus on difference and on cooperation without consensus suggests that Brubaker and Cooper's critique should be extended even further. Even concepts like "identification," while acknowledging the dynamic nature of group construction, suggest that ultimately the process that generates a sense of membership in a community rests on the relativization or elimination of internal differences – i.e., on the creation of distinct insiders and outsiders. That is, sameness, or the idea of some imagined sameness, still guides the thinking on group formation.

But in our case, the production of a sense of belonging did not simply require Jewish Americans to overlook obvious differences between themselves and the Jews in Israel. Rather than imagining away internal differences, the mobilization of the Irish-American and Jewish American communities rested on a concomitant drawing and blurring of the boundaries between the groups that made up the nation. On the one hand, the IVF and UJA campaigns suggested that the differences between homeland and diaspora communities were insignificant, that the Irish and Irish Americans, and American and Israeli Jews, were, so to speak, in the same boat. On the other hand, the campaigns repeatedly reminded potential donors in the diaspora of the hardships and sacrifices they did not endure, as a means of provoking shame, guilt, and further giving. It was precisely the highlighting of this difference that compelled American Jews to support Israel financially. Some groups (in our case, those in the homeland) were depicted as occupying the core of the nation by virtue of the sacrifices they allegedly embraced, while others (diaspora communities) were imagined at the periphery and were asked to part only with their money. At least in some cases, it seems, the production of a sense of belonging rests not only on the erasure or relativization of boundaries between different constituents of a group but, paradoxically, also on a careful maintenance of internal boundaries – in other words on emphasizing not only the rights and obligations of sameness, but also those that follow from difference. Concepts like "identity" or "identification" do not adequately account for this delicate process.

As an alternative to the concept of "identity," I would suggest the concept of "attachment." Unlike identity, attachment carries no subtle assumptions about the nature of the components that form a given grouping or the processes that create groups. Obviously, the formation of groups sometimes is based on the drawing of commonalities, but there is no reason to assume a priori that this is the only or even the dominant dynamic involved in group formation. Second, as a verb, "attach" directs attention to dynamic processes rather than static states. It invites researchers to identify the agents and mechanisms involved in the formation of groups. Third, the antonym of attachment – detachment – suggests that group formation is a reversible process. It points to the need for studying both successful and failed attempts to mobilize groups or maintain groups in a symmetrical manner.[5] Fourth, "identity" and "identification" are strongly associated with non-instrumental action, with the enactment of one's self-understanding more than (or even in contradiction to) one's self-interest. The concept of attachment, in contrast, is more flexible. It can accommodate both instrumental and non-instrumental action and allows researchers to weave these elements seamlessly while tracing the formation of groups.

Moving from "identity" to "attachment" is more than a superficial shift in terminology. The concept of "identity" directs attention to mechanisms of representation that generate perceived commonalities. The preferred sites for such an examination are such things as a novel, a map of a the museum, etc. – sites where the image of the nation as a unified whole may be conjured up. In contrast, the concept of "attachment" directs attention to the entire range of practices used to generate national associations, of which the exchange of objects is merely one example. One may, for example, examine tours, sport events, and various cultural activities that bring groups into concrete contact with one another. In all of these sites, the concept of "attachment" brings to mind the imagery of a network and directs the researcher to examine the practical challenge of weaving heterogeneous groups into networks of associations within which members can experience belonging to a nation.

Brubaker and his colleagues note that "social construction" has, in recent years, become an empty convention, and they urge scholars to explore the ways in which nations and ethnic groups are constructed (2006: 7). Examining the mechanisms that allow groups to cooperate and consequently make up the nation allows us to accomplish just that. The setting examined here (homeland–diaspora nexus), and the particular mechanisms explored are obviously limited in scope and extent. They flesh out just a segment of what nation building is all about. Examination of the mechanisms involved in the invention of tradition (Hobsbawm and Ranger 1992; Abu El-Haj 2001), the granting or withholding of citizenship (Tilly 1996), the making of geographical and social boundaries (P. Sahlins 1989; Wimmer 2008), and the everyday usages of nations (Brubaker et al. 2006; Fox and Miller-Idriss 2008), helps paint a fuller picture of this delicate accomplishment. In these various contexts, studying nation building in action – that is, following national entrepreneurs as they attempt to create and maintain social relationships between the various groups that they identify as members in the nation – offers a promising way to further develop our understanding of this crucially important process.

Notes

1 The Organization of National Attachments

1 AIHS/FOIF papers/8/6; AIHS/Cohalan papers/1/9.
2 David Stark (2009) associates entrepreneurship with finding new ways of doing and with doing new things. In the same vein, national entrepreneurship consists of finding new ways of bringing the fragments of the nation together.
3 Some readers may argue that the Irish diaspora is still alive and well. My point here is not to argue the opposite but to note, following many historians, that the early 1920s was a turning point in the relationship between the Irish-American community and the Irish national movement (Tansill 1957; Ward 1969; McCaffrey 1976; Fallows 1979; Miller 1985; Kenny 2000). Before that date, many Irish Americans considered their sojourn in the United States as an involuntary and temporary exile. After that date, the community as a whole accepted the US as their home.
4 A Yiddish term for begging.
5 See material on Israel Bond tours to Israel, CZA/A258/208/2.
6 The distinction between "why" and "how" is not analogous to the distinction between causal and descriptive analysis, but rather points to a different emphasis given in comparative analysis. Historical comparative researchers typically explain why more-or-less similar cases result in different outcomes by pointing to contextual variability across cases (Mahoney and Rueschemeyer 2003). Causality, in such cases, is attributed to contextual conditions that enable or prevent an outcome of interest. In the approach suggested

here, in contrast, causality emerges when the contingent empirical cases unfold (Abbott 1984; Mandelbaum 1961; Spillman 2004). In a sense, causality here is an effect of the analysis, not its overriding goal.

7 On the importance of cooperation without consensus in other contexts see Boltanski (1987); Star and Griesemer (1989); Galison (1997); Girard and Stark (2002); Stark (2009: 190–195).

8 That different members attribute different meanings to their national membership and that these differences allow different groups to link themselves to the nation is not a new observation. David Kertzer, among others, claims that the multivocal and symbolic nature of the nation facilitates the tying together of disparate groups (1988; Verdery 1991). Such an assertion, however, does little to clarify how groups negotiate their differences when they surface in the course of practical interaction.

9 To be sure, scholars of nationalism readily note that the national order is highly hierarchical. Typically, however, scholars treat the national pecking order – the fact that some members are considered more than others – as an obstacle in the process of nation building. My analysis unearths the active role of the national pecking order in the creation of national attachments.

10 More precisely, scholars often distinguish between more-or-less interested elites and disinterested masses (Brass 1991; Hobsbawm and Ranger 1992). The force of nationalism, however, is always located in the masses.

11 This approach is deeply influenced by research in the field of science and technology studies, and by actor-network theory (ANT) in particular (Latour and Woolgar 1979; Latour 1988; Law 1992; Callon 1998). ANT scholars typically study how diverse groups come to cooperate in the production of scientific facts, but the approach they have developed is applicable to other fields (Latour 2005).

12 This approach is certainly not new. Elie Kedourie (1960) and Ernest Gellner (1983) used the case of diaspora nationalism, especially the Jewish case, to refute general propositions. Anthony Smith (1995) also takes the Jewish diaspora as a prime example to illustrate the antiquity in the making of nations.

13 An important complicating factor involved in studying nation building through the lens of homeland–diaspora encounter is the existence of a sovereign host state, in the cases examined here, the United States. The relationships we explore, therefore, are nestled within a triadic framework that also includes a host state, and this dimension brings into play important issues pertaining to sovereignty, divided loyalty, and potentially international relations (see Brubaker 1996).

14 Contemporary observers would no doubt note that whereas the organized Jewish-American community today maintains strong ties with Israel, Irish Americans' ties to Ireland are far more attenuated and, especially, less organized. But it is important not to interpret the past in light of the present. As many scholars of Irish America note, up until the early 1920s Irish Americans were more organized and more committed to the Irish Cause than almost any other immigrant group in the United States (Brown 1966; Miller 1985; Kenny 2000).

15 Focusing on a later period, in *Two Worlds of Judaism*, Charles Liebman and Steven Cohen (1990) examine these differences with great detail. Their findings suggest a high degree of continuity – the tensions described here are quite similar to the ones they identify 40 years later between Israeli Jews (not only labor Zionists) and American Jews.

16 Given that the projects we consider here are inextricably linked to state-building processes, these different statuses may be particularly important.

17 On the problems of small N in historical comparative sociology, see Lieberson (1991, 1994).

18 My comparative approach is inspired by Jeffery Haydu's method of "reiterated problem solving" (1998, 2009). Haydu suggests treating historical events as repeated instances of problem solving. This approach has a number of attractive features. First, reiterated problem solving imposes a relatively thin equivalence across cases. The only demand for equivalence is that the actors involved construe the problems they face similarly. Thus, instead of the researcher's imposition of equivalence, reiterated problem solving uses the actors' own interpretations of their situations and behaviors to establish comparability. Second, in Haydu's method, cases are distinguished on the basis of contrasting solutions to recurring problems, not on different macro-sociological units or diverging outcomes (1998: 354). For this reason, reiterated problem solving is markedly open-ended. It does not demand a priori identification of variables or formulation of testable hypotheses, and therefore it can easily accommodate historical switch points and continuities. Third, in contrast to variable-based comparisons, in reiterated problem solving differences in strategies (the fact that actors sometimes pursue different courses of action even when the initial conditions are similar) do not constitute a methodological problem. Instead, such differences help in the identification and analysis the mechanisms developed in response to common problems. Contrasting solutions to a common problem direct attention to the elements of the mechanisms devised to overcome difficulties and to

the creativity of the actors involved in their construction. Thus, reiterated problem solving derives agency directly from the historical process.
19 Most of those who identified themselves as Irish Americans during that period were Catholics. Protestant immigrants from Ireland typically identified themselves as Scotch-Irish and, to the best of my knowledge, excluded themselves from the activities described in this book.

2 Moneymaking and Nation Building

1 Given the belief that market exchange is alienating, researchers link the communal form of the nation to the emergence of markets only as a reaction or as an unintended consequence. In Michael Hechter's work, for example, nationalism appears as a reaction to uneven economic development (1975). Benedict Anderson, on the other hand, treats nationalism as the unintended consequence of the expansion of trade with the American colonies and the development of print capitalism (1991). In both cases, the central function of markets – facilitating exchange through the creation of equivalences – is treated as irrelevant or antithetical to nation building.
2 Without losing sight of the differences between the concepts of "nation" and "state" (but also without ignoring the modern hyphen that links them), it is no accident that theories of membership in a polity, ranging from the heavily normative to the most Machiavellian ones, articulate some kind of reciprocal exchange between members and polity (Marshall 1964; Rousseau 1968; Locke 1988; Hobbes 1991; Tilly 1992, 1996).
3 For a balanced assessment of the importance of the gift in Bourdieu's work, see Silber (2009).
4 Exceptions to this rule are easy to find, but they typically reinforce Bourdieu's point. For example, at Christmas, when the exchange of gifts is contemporaneous, the parties invest extraordinary efforts in personalizing the gift so that it will not be seen as an interested exchange (Burgoyne and Routh 1991).
5 Counter to the assumption of many economists, Callon and Muniesa argue that interested action is not a natural phenomenon but rather a hard-earned social accomplishment. To make an interested choice, actors need to be able to compare potential courses of action and assess the costs and benefits associated with each. This feat is virtually impossible without proper calculative tools (2005: 1231).

6   Economic sociologists have noted that, in real life, market exchange is embedded in social relations (Granovetter 1985; Spillman 1999; Swedberg 2005). Without diminishing the importance of this observation, Callon's analysis allows us to see how, sometimes, the organization of markets allows actors to behave in a way that resembles the economists' calculative model.
7   Barry Schwartz (1967) observes that gift giving is risky because it surrenders delicate information. Givers always reveal something about themselves – their intentions toward the receiver, their taste, their means, etc. In addition, they surrender their own perceptions of the receiver – what they believe the receiver's taste and means are. Therefore, an inappropriate gift can be damaging for both the giver and the receiver. The possibility of a gift mistaken for a commodity multiplies these risks.
8   Zelizer is obviously well aware of this possibility, but she seems to treat this mix-and-match of different mechanisms of exchange as the exception to the rule, requiring no theoretical elaboration (1996: 482–483).
9   In economic sociology, credit is typically discussed as a special type of market exchange, without reference to gift giving (Carruthers 2005). But economic sociologists often distinguish between formal and informal loans. Such a distinction is similar to the one suggested here, but it is under-theorized.
10 Bruce Carruthers argues that negotiability – the ability to transfer a debt to a third party – makes credit closer to money (2005: 370). My point is similar, but whereas Carruthers emphasizes the general character of negotiable loans, I highlight their calculability.
11 Note, however, that even after redemption or default, the meaning of a loan remains open to interpretation. A low return compared with the uncertainty associated with a loan may allow actors to believe that the loan was primarily a gift, even after full redemption. But, after the date of redemption, the conditions for determining what the loan was change significantly.

3   Gifting the Nation

1   Susan Ostrander and Paul Schervish argue forcefully that philanthropy should be studied as a social relation of giving and getting between donors and recipients (1991: 68). Instead of the almost exclusive focus on the motivations of donors, they suggest studying the various strategies adopted by both donors and recipients to give and obtain support. This chapter takes this insight and applies it to the specific case of giving to the nation.

2   *Sinn Féin* won 73 out of the 106 Irish seats in the British Parliament. The previously dominant Irish Parliamentary Party was left with only six seats, and the rest of the votes were concentrated in predominantly Protestant Ulster.
3   The meaning of the term is contentious. Some refer to the title as the head of the *Dáil Éireann*. De Valera translated it as "President of the Republic of Ireland" and was later accused by his opponents of assuming a false title.
4   These individuals were all senior members of the IRB and elected members of the *Dáil Éireann*. The *Dáil Éireann* also sent a delegation to the Paris Peace Conference (see Carroll 1978).
5   Devoy had led the *Clan na Gael* since the 1880s, but his involvement in nationalist politics began much earlier. Born in Ireland in 1842, he acted as a recruiter for the IRB in the British Military. In 1866 he was caught and sentenced to fifteen years in prison. In 1871, however, he was released and exiled. From the United States, Devoy remained involved in Irish politics and also edited the Irish American weekly *Gaelic American*. Cohalan (1865–1946) was one of the most powerful Irish leaders in the United States. A son of Irish immigrants, he served as a Justice in New York's Supreme Court and was closely associated with the Republican Party.
6   See "Constitution of the Friends of Irish Freedom, 1916, AIHS/FOIF papers/6/1.
7   Minutes of the national executive, May 5 and May 20, 1919, AIHS/FOIF papers/6/2; AIHS/FOIF papers/4/1.
8   Lynch to FOIF members, May 1, 1919, AIHS/FOIF papers/4/1.
9   Using the Consumer Price Index calculator, the overall collections of the IVF amounted to $13,168,581 in 2012 dollars (http://www.bls.gov/data/inflation_calculator.htm).
10 Walsh was a known labor lawyer and a former member of the Federal Industrial Commission. Dunne was a former mayor of Chicago and former governor of Illinois. Ryan, in addition to his prior role in UILA, was at one point the city solicitor of Philadelphia.
11 In Zionist parlance, the word *aliya* – which literally means "ascending" – is reserved for Jewish migration to Israel. The term suggests that migration to Israel is not merely a practical choice but an act of moral ascendance.
12 See, for example, the "exchange of views" between David Ben-Gurion and Jacob Blaustein, the president of the American Jewish Committee (American Jewish Committee 1961).
13 The UPA was formed in 1925 as a coalition of Zionist philanthropies, including the Jewish National Fund, the Foundation Fund, Hadassah, and the Hebrew University. In 1951, the UPA changed its name to the United Israel Appeal.

14 In 1946, the NRS merged with the Service for the Foreign Born of the National Council of Jewish Women and changed its name to the United Service for New Americans (USNA). For simplicity, I will use NRS throughout.
15 Many Jewish Americans who grew up during this period remember the *pushke* (Yiddish term for charity box) and tree-planting campaigns of the Jewish National Fund. While these campaigns enjoyed high visibility, they were not where big money was raised. During the late 1940s, for example, when the UJA raised more than $100 million each year, the independent campaign of the Jewish National Fund raised just a bit more than $2 million a year (Keyserling 1956: 9). The JNF continued the *pushke* and tree-planting campaigns for the purpose of keeping the Jewish street engaged and supportive, not for the money.
16 See, for example, Isidor Coons to National Field Representatives, June 11, 1941, CZA/A371/30.
17 An important exception to this structure was New York City, where the Jewish Federations and the UJA ran independent campaigns throughout the period under investigation in this book.
18 Isidor Coons, previously the national director of the JDC's campaign, served as an executive vice chairman of the UJA alongside Henry Montor from the UPA.
19 "Report on the Status of the United Jewish Appeal for Refugees and Overseas Needs," June 26, 1940, CZA/KH7/316.
20 Montor (1905–1982) was active in Zionist affairs for decades. In the 1920s he served as the assistant editor of *New Palestine*, the official organ of the Zionist Organization of America, and later he became the publicity director and executive director of the UPA. During the 1940s and 1950s, he developed close alliances with David Ben-Gurion, Eliezer Kaplan, and Golda Meyerson, key leaders of the Zionist Labor Party in Israel.
21 Robert Herman to National Field Representatives, March 19, 1941, CZA/A371/30.
22 Herman to National Field Representatives, September 10, 1942; September 22, 1942, CZA/A371/24.
23 Herman to National Field Representatives, January 26, 1944, CZA/A371/21.
24 See Herman to National Field Representatives, January 14, 1943; January 15, 1943, CZA/A371/31; February 9, 1944, CZA/A371/21.
25 In the early 1940s, the criterion for inclusion in this group was a $100 donation, but the minimum donations varied across communities and time.
26 See United Jewish Appeal of Greater New York "Handbook for Speakers 1947," CZA/KH7/320; Raphael 1982.

27 Herman to National Field Representatives, December 4, 1941, CZA/A371/30.
28 Herman to National Field Representatives, December 4, 1941, CZA/A371/30.
29 Herman to National Field Representatives, July 12, 1944, CZA/A371/21; "Publicity Manual, 1943," CZA/KH7/305; Herman to National Field Representatives, "Eddie Cantor Recording," March 27, 1942, CZA/A371/24.
30 See "Handbook for Speakers, United Jewish Appeal of Greater New York," CZA/KH7/320.
31 CZA/KH7/320.
32 See "Uncle Sam and Your Gift", CZA/KH7/320; see also Herman to National Field Representatives, May 5, 1941; January 15, 1943, CZA/A371/31.
33 CZA/KH7/319 (bold in the original).
34 CZA/KH7/303.
35 Golda Meir, the star fundraiser of the UJA, turned this delicate play on guilt and pride into a form of art (Burkett 2008).
36 See "Collection Manual, 1939", CZA/KH7/305; "Collection Manual, 1942," CZA/A371/24.
37 Herman to National Field Representatives, January 5, 1942, CZA/A371/24.
38 Herman to National Field Representatives, November 24, 1943, CZA/A371/31; Herman to National Field Representatives, September 11, 1942, CZA/A371/24; October 20, 1942.
39 Edward Warburg, Speech at the Launching of the 1946 campaign, February 24, 1946, CZA/KH7/316.
40 See "Report to Members of the National Campaign Council, United Jewish Appeal," December 6, 1946, CZA/KH7/316.
41 Using the Consumer Price Index inflation calculator, this sum is equivalent to $1,410,778,005 in 2012 dollars (http://www.bls.gov/data/inflation_calculator.htm).
42 On the growth of the Jewish Federations system, see Elazar (1995: 234–276).
43 In a masterful study of gift giving in medieval Europe, Silber (1995) notes that monasteries did not reciprocate. A crucial element that sustained this giftgiving system was the status accorded to big givers within the community at large.
44 See, for example, *Gaelic American*, August 2, 1919; Unnamed document, AIHS/Cohalan papers/7/11.
45 A quick look at donations from major cities supports this argument. Chicago, New York City, Philadelphia, and the State Council of Massachusetts remitted $150,000 each to the headquarters, exactly

the sum they pledged in the Race Convention (August 2, 1919, *Gaelic American*). This too-perfect match between pledge and reported collection suggests that the actual sums collected, in at least some of these places, were higher. But Lynch could not know how much was actually raised and was unable to enforce the remittance of the money.
46 In inflation adjusted 2012 dollars, the IVF raised a bit more than $13 million. In contrast, the UJA raised more than $1 billion in 2012 dollars.
47 Some scholars suggest that Jewish-American philanthropy was an outgrowth of the traditional Jewish practice of giving *tzedakah* (Goldin 1976; Neusner 1983; Steinberg 1998). But the particular way in which American Jews raised and disbursed their money contrasts with the model of *tzedakah*. According to Maimonides, the righteous disbursement of *tzedakah* is a double-blind procedure – givers are not supposed to know to whom they are giving and the receivers should not know their benefactors (Neusner 1999). In contrast, Jewish-American philanthropists insisted on making their donations publicly and on overseeing the use of their money. In form, this way of giving resembles the more rationalized model articulated by Andrew Carnegie in *The Gospel of Wealth* (1901). The responsibilities of philanthropists, Carnegie argued, do not end with giving money. Rather, wealthy philanthropists, endowed with the gift of good management skills, must invest their talents and make sure that their donations are well utilized.
48 See CZA/KH7/305.
49 The *Yishuv*, literally meaning "settlement," is the term used to describe the Zionist community in Palestine during the pre-state era.
50 CZA/KH7/319.

4 National Gift Giving in Crises

1 During World War I, England incurred a huge debt to the American government and was now negotiating the schedule of repayment. The FOIF hoped that the United States would use this leverage to extract concessions vis-à-vis Ireland.
2 Devoy to McCartan, April 21, 1919 (Doorley 1995: 147).
3 NLI/Devoy papers/MS.18007(9).
4 McGarrity, an owner of a liquor store, migrated to the United States in 1892. In addition to being a member of the Executive Committee of the *Clan na Gael* and the National Council of the

FOIF, beginning in 1918 he owned and edited the *Irish Press*, a weekly paper that competed with the *Gaelic American*.
5 McCartan was a member of the IRB and an elected member of the *Dáil Éireann*. In early 1919, he was sent to the United States as the "emissary of the Republic of Ireland."
6 Furthermore, this issue became irrelevant after the defeat of Wilson's proposal to join the League of Nations on November 19, 1919 (Carroll 1978: 147).
7 Minutes of the National Executive of the FOIF, May 7, 1919, AIHS/FOIF papers/8/4.
8 See minutes of the National Executive of the FOIF, May 7, 1919; June 11, 1919, AIHS/FOIF papers/8/4.
9 AIHS/FOIF papers/8/6; AIHS/Cohalan papers/1/19.
10 The poster that O'Mara cites (see Figure 3.1) displayed an image of the Irish-American 69th Regiment in action during World War I.
11 AIHS/Cohalan papers/1/9.
12 See government meeting of August 8, 1950, GA, IBD.
13 The decline was related to the social composition of the donors. The bulk of the UJA's donations during the 1940s came from businessmen who enjoyed the wartime economic boom. With the opening of the war in Korea, these businessmen invested in consumer industries again, but this time their investment did not pay off as well, and as a result they had less money to spare (see "Fund-Raising for Israel in the United States: A Study," CZA/A371/18).
14 Montor to Kaplan, August 26, 1949, CZA/S41/144/23.
15 Minutes of the meeting of the Jewish Agency Executive, July 10, 1949, BGA.
16 See CZA/Montor papers/A371/1.
17 See minutes of the meeting of the UJA's officers with representatives of the Jewish Federation and Welfare Fund of Chicago, January 6, 1950, CZA/KH7/311; interview with Henry Montor, OHD/128/34.
18 The IRS acted on a complaint lodged by the American Council for Judaism, a small but vocal anti-Zionist Reform organization. On face value, the complaint itself was justified. In 1948, 67% of the Jewish Agency's budget was consumed by "security expenses." However, these expenses included medical supplies, tents for refugees, trucks, erection of block houses, and allowances for needy families (Stock 1987: 129). The inflated figure is probably related to Ben-Gurion's expansive definition of the term "security." Rather than limiting "security" to military matters, Ben-Gurion believed that "security" included issues like demography, economic advancement, healthcare, education, etc.

19 Data are compiled from the United Jewish Appeal (1949), Keyserling (1956), and Elazar (1995). The sharp drop in UJA allocations in 1954 reflects the impact of a special loan campaign undertaken in that year and should not be interpreted as a further decline in collections.
20 April 5, 1948, CZA/S53/333.
21 The *ma'abarot* housed hundreds of thousands of immigrants. The *Mapai* amassed electoral support among these immigrants by practicing clientelism through its control of the Jewish Agency.
22 Montor to Israel Goldman, CZA/S57/82. Concomitantly, Morgenthau traveled to Israel and pressed Ben-Gurion to appoint a "Palestinian or an Israelite" to make sure "that the money will flow directly where we [American Jews] wanted it to go and not be redirected in America" (October 24, 1948, BGA).
23 The CCW was closely associated with Silver's opponents in the World Zionist Organization, the Committee for Progressive Zionism (Ganin 2005: 55).
24 See Goldstein to Montor, September 27, 1948, CZA/S57/82; Neumann 1976: 275. To establish a near monopoly, the UJA financed a number of small organizations, including the ZOA. In return, these organizations agreed not to run independent drives. Montor regarded these sums as an unnecessary waste.
25 See "Letter to members of the CCW explaining what was achieved," December 8, 1948, CZA/KH7/309.
26 See minutes of the Jewish Agency meeting in Jerusalem, December 27, 1948, BGA.
27 Minutes of the meeting of the Jewish Agency executive, January 17, 1949, BGA.
28 See transcript of radio broadcast by ZOA, CZA/KH7/309.
29 Minutes of the meeting of the Jewish Agency Executive, March 29, 1949, BGA.
30 See "Proposals presented to plenary session with the Jewish Agency by the Council of Jewish Federations and Welfare Funds," CZA/A371/28; "Our Overseas Responsibilities in 1951," a speech by Philip Bernstein, associate director of CJFWF, October 8, 1950, AJHS/I-69/521; *Jewish Telegraphic Agency*, June 24, 1947; June 5, 1950.
31 Minutes of government meeting, November 16, 1950, BGA.
32 Minutes of the Jewish Agency Executive in Jerusalem, October 24, 1848, BGA.
33 That the problems with the UJA continued after the defeat of Silver and Neumann clarified that the tensions were not simply a matter of personalities or the particular leanings of the ZOA.

34 It was a matter of bitter irony, of which Ben-Gurion and his colleagues were deeply aware, that decades after their initial migration these proud *halutzim* continued to depend on the alms of those who chose another, allegedly inferior path. The contradictory position of the *halutzim* was painful enough; that Jewish Americans sought to cash in on their generosity made things unbearable.

35 AIHS/Cohalan papers/1/19.

5 Making National Bonds: Floating the Irish and Israeli Loans in the United States

1 Michael Collins, the *Dáil* Minister of Finance was in charge of the internal loan. According to Francis Carroll, the internal loan was a big success. By September 1919, £370,165 was raised through 150,000 independent subscriptions (almost 15 percent of the households on the island) (2002: 9).

2 See minutes of the *Dáil Éireann*, April 2, 1919, NA/DE/4/2/2.

3 NYPL/Walsh papers/27; see also de Valera 1980: 31.

4 As late as August 1919, Lynch was still urging organizers in central locations like Portland, Providence, Rochester, Albany, Troy, Baltimore, Columbus, Milwaukee, Minneapolis, St Paul, St Louis, and Kansas City to form IVF committees (*Gaelic American*, August 9, 1919).

5 The Blue Skies laws are state-specific rules governing trade in securities. Prior to the establishment of the Securities and Exchange Commission in 1934, these laws alone regulated the sale of securities in different states.

6 Lynch to members of FOIF, November 20, 1920, AIHS/FOIF/4/1.

7 De Valera to members of the *Dáil*, March 10, 1920, NA/DE/2/245; see also Boland to Collins, January 13, 1920, UCDA/de Valera papers P150/1125.

8 This committee, in fact, never convened. De Valera suspected that it was created only in order to divert him from his original plan and never consulted it.

9 See "Outline of President de Valera" in NL/James O'Mara's papers/MS.21547.

10 Walsh to potential subscribers, April 24, 1920, NYPL/Maloney papers/7/IHP/114.

11 AIHS/Cohalan papers/1/9.

12 Walsh to potential subscribers, April 24, 1920, NYPL/Maloney papers/7/IHP/114.

13 See, for example, American Bank Note Company to McGarrity, December 12, 1919, NL/McGarrity papers/MS.17522 (1).
14 Dunne to Walsh, August 16, 1919, NA/DE/2/245 (emphasis in the original).
15 Lynch to chairs of IVF committees, August 7, 1919, AIHS/FOIF papers/6/1.
16 See Nunan to Collins, September 17, 1919, NA/DE/2/292. Schell to Devoy, February 20, 1920, NL/McGarrity papers/MS.17522 (1).
17 Walsh to unidentified editor, October 1919, NYPL/Walsh papers/28 (Walsh attributed the letter to Callahan).
18 See Devoy to Cohalan, undated, AIHS/Cohalan papers/4/3; NL/McGarrity papers/MS.17522 (1); see also Boland to Lynch, December 10, 1919, UCDA/de Valera's papers/P150/1135.
19 See NL/O'Mara papers/MS.21547.
20 See Lynch to FOIF members, December 27, 1919, AYHS/Cohalan papers/5/4. In addition to the $100,000 loan, the FOIF also provided de Valera with $26,748 for his personal expenses on his tour of the United States.
21 Boland to Cohalan, September 11, 1919, UCDA/de Valera papers/P150/1134.
22 See Nunan to Collins, September 17, 1919, NA/DE 2/292.
23 Interest rates reached a record high level in 1920. In January 1920, high-yield corporate bonds paid an average of 4.95% a year. Government and high-grade municipal bonds paid on average 0.5 percent more (Homer and Sylla 1996: 341–352). The interest rate paid by foreign sovereigns for similar bonds was probably much higher.
24 See Bond Certificate prospectus in Carroll 2002: 105.
25 De Valera to Walsh, September 19, 1919, NYPL/Walsh papers/28.
26 For similar appeals by local organizing committees, see UCDA/de Valera papers/P150/962.
27 In 1920, the average weekly earnings of production workers in the field of manufacturing were $29.39 (see http://hsus.cambridge.org.libproxy.usc.edu/HSUSWeb/toc/tableToc.do?id=Ba4381-4390). Setting aside $10 or $25 was, therefore, not a trivial feat.
28 Using a Consumer Price Index inflation calculator, the income from the first bond drive is worth $58,067,493 in 2012 terms (see http://www.bls.gov/data/inflation_calculator.html).
29 Meeting of October 21, 1948 (Ben-Gurion 1982: 757).
30 Private investment had an obvious appeal for the government. Not only could it curb unemployment and improve the balance of trade but it also imposed no obligations on the government and did not compromise its ability to borrow money and solicit gifts.

31 See minutes from the meeting of the Israeli government, August 8, 1950, GA.
32 See government meeting, August 2, 1950, BGA.
33 Minutes of government meeting, August 2, 1950.
34 A religious term – *gmiluth hasadim* – is often translated as acts of lovingkindness or simply charity.
35 Proceedings of the Jerusalem Economic Conference, September 3, 1950, BGA (emphasis in the original).
36 Ben-Gurion and his associates repeatedly claimed that the American money was needed for the absorption of immigrants, not for themselves. This formulation allowed them both to sustain their self-images as independent and to urge the Jewish Americans to part with more of their money. The "Jews of Iraq and Iran and Morocco [Ben-Gurion explained,] must immigrate to Israel, if you are not willing to take them to the United States" (Proceedings of the Jerusalem Economic Conference, September 3, 1950, BGA).
37 See "Summary of CJFWF Participation in Jerusalem Meetings, September 3–6, 1950," CZA/A371/28.
38 Report on the September 3–6, 1950 Conference, BGA.
39 See "Fund Raising for Israel in the United States: A Study," CZA/A371/18.
40 Ibid.; Montor to Meyerson, August 20, 1950, BGA.
41 Minutes of the Executive Committee of AFDCI, March 4, 1951, CZA/Z6/801.
42 Montor's speech on the eve of Ben-Gurion's visit to the United States, CZA/A371/25.
43 Minutes of the meeting of the Israeli government, December 13, 1950, GA.
44 See Summary of the Resolutions Committee, GA/Foreign Affairs/2420/12.
45 See memorandums, Montor meeting with Kuhn Loeb and Co., December 5, 1950; Montor and Kaplan meeting with Stanley Morgan, November 1, 1950, CZA/A371/2; Montor meeting with Joseph Cherner, December 12, 1950; Montor meeting with Ferdinand Eberstadt, December 13, 1950, CZA/A371/28.
46 Rudolf Sonneborn served as the president of the AFDCI, Julian Venezky became the chairman of the Executive Committee of the AFDCI, and Sidney Green and Joel Gross became the AFDCI's legal advisors.
47 See Underwriting Agreement between the State of Israel and the American Financial and Development Corporation for Israel, GA/State of Israel Independence/GL-47049/1; meeting of the Israeli

government, November 16, 1950, GA. To ensure that no profits would derive from the AFDCI, Montor and his associates created a second organization, the American Committee for the Aid to Israel Immigrants (ACAII). Any profits derived from the sales of Israel Bonds were supposed to be deposited in the ACAII's accounts and be sent back to Israel. In practice, the AFDCI never even came close to generating profit (see Gross to Montor, November 30, 1950, CZA/A371/28).

48 See "'Co-Ordination': The True Story of the Israel Bond", CZA/A371/28.
49 Montor to Joseph Schwartz, June 14, 1951, CZA/S43/79; see also Montor to AFDCI volunteers, January 28, 1952, CZA/S43/79; Montor to Friedman, February 12, 1951, CZA/A371/6.
50 The AFDCI was allowed to sell bonds through Zionist organizations and labor unions throughout the year (Eisenberg to Montor, October 4, 1951, CZA/Z6/521; memorandum of meeting between AFDCI executive and the executive of the UJA of Greater New York, April 5, 1952, CZA/A371/27).
51 See Divery Yemei Haknesset, 1951, State of Israel Bonds (Independence Issue) Law 5711–1951 (Israel 1951).
52 The only opposition to the law came from members of the Communist party who wondered whether the loan would force Israel to ally with the United States (Israel 1951).
53 Since the state-level Blue Skies laws remained in effect, the AFDCI registered with the SEC committees of each state, but the stricter Federal SEC's regulations overshadowed these committees.
54 See minutes of government meeting, November 16, 1950, GA.
55 See Gross to Montor, December 27, 1950, CZA/A371/28.
56 See Securities Exchange Act of 1933 Act section 3(a)(4, codified at 15 USC§ 78c[a](4).
57 See minutes of AFDCI board of directors, March 21, 1951, CZA/A371/20; Montor to Gross, January 2, 1951, CZA/A371/28; memorandum of meeting with William Chesney and Eldon Arnold, November 28, 1950, CZA A371/2; minutes of meeting with Fredrick Warburg, Hugh Knowlton, and Percy Stuart, December 14, 1950, CZA/A371/2.
58 Permutt to Goldberger, March 13, 1951, GA/Gal 47049/2.
59 See AJHS AFDCI I-322/1/10; Bernstein to Goldberger, November 12, 1952, CZA/A371/9.
60 Memorandum of Montor's meeting with Chesney, March 6, 1951, CZA/A371/2.
61 See Bane to Montor, September 25, 1951, CZA/A371/2. The cooperation of the commissioners was secured in a meeting of

Moshe Sharett, Israel's Foreign Minister, with the American Secretary of the Treasury, John W. Snyder (November 28, 1950, CZA/A371/2).

62 See General Rules and Regulations promulgated under the Securities Exchange Act of 1933, Rule 494, August 31, 1951.
63 Report from meeting of the Executive Committee of AFDCI, March 4, 1951, CZA/Z6/801.
64 Notes on the Republic of Israel Loan, October 31, 1950, CZA/A371/2; see also minutes of meeting with Martin, November 28, 1950, CZA/A371/2.
65 See memorandum of meeting with Leon K. Keyserling, October 12, 1950, CZA/A371/2.
66 See memorandum of meeting with Kuhn Loeb partners, December 14, 1950, CZA/A371/2.
67 Notes on Republic of Israel Loan, October 31, 1950, CZA/A371/2; minutes of Montor meeting with Eberstadt, December 13, 1950, CZA/A371/28; memorandum of meeting with Lubin, October 4, 1950, CZA/A371/2.
68 See "Questions and Answers: The Facts About the Israel Bonds," AJHS/AFDCI/I-322/8.
69 See Fiscal Agency Agreement, May 1, 1951, AJHS/AFDCI/I-322/5.
70 Donors routinely paid their pledges with bonds. Typically, the Federations and the UJA sold these bonds and forwarded the cash to its constituent agencies. Since the Israeli bonds were nontransferable, the Federations were afraid of being stuck with bond certificates that would have no exchange value for years. The convertibility privilege allowed these agencies to get cash, albeit Israeli currency, in return for these bonds (see CJFWF to member agencies, June 26, 1951, CZA/S43/79).
71 See "How to Solve Your Gift Problem," CZA/Z6/506.
72 "Israel Exposition," undated booklet, GA/Foreign Affairs/2420/13.
73 See CZA/A371/25.
74 The Facts About the Israel Bonds, CZA/Z6/506.
75 *Life* magazine, October 8, 1951.
76 Eleanor Roosevelt, Governor Thomas Dewey, Secretary of Labor Maurice Tobin, and other prominent figures served on the Council at different times, AJHS/AFDCI/I-322/1/8.
77 "How to Solve Your Gift Problem," CZA/Z6/506.
78 Montor to Bonds Committees, January 28, 1952, CZA/S43/79.
79 GA/Foreign Affairs/2420/12.
80 AFDCI fieldworkers sold bonds aboard the ships (meeting of the Executive Committee of AFDCI, March 4, 1951, CZA/Z6801; Montor to Meyerson, November 24, 1951, CZA/A371/2).

81 Using a Consumer Price Index income calculator, this sum is equivalent to $1,306,062,255 (http://www.bls.gov/data/inflation_calculator.htm).

6 Making and Unmaking National Attachments: The Failure of the Irish Bond and the Success of the Israel Bond

1 AIHS/Cohalan papers/4/3.
2 August 6, 1920, NL/O'Mara papers/MS.21548/3.
3 These councils were by no means peripheral. Lynch mentions Chicago, St Louis, Philadelphia, San Diego, Brooklyn, and several branches from New York (minutes of the meeting of the National Executive, FOIF, October 21, 1920, AIHS/FOIF papers/6/3).
4 See minutes of the National Executive, FOIF, AIHS/FOIF papers/6/3.
5 AARIR to Boland, January 13, 1921, NA/DFA/Prov. Govt/IFS/27/158.
6 S. O'Mara to de Valera, August 12, 1921, NA/DFA/Prov. Govt/IFS/27/170.
7 Walsh to organizers, September 23, 1920, NL/O'Mara Papers/MS.21548/2.
8 Collins to S. O'Mara, May 14, 1921, NA/DE 2/9.
9 See Boland to Collins, April 14, 1921, UCDA/de Valera papers/P150/1125; de Valera to Boland, April 18, 1921, NA/DE 5/57/14; S. O'Mara to de Valera, August 31, 1921, NA/DE 2/359; Collins to de Valera, October 15, 1921, NA/DE 2/450; S. O'Mara to unknown recipient, undated, NA/DE 2/295; S. O'Mara to de Valera, October 14, 1921, NA/DFA Prov. Govt/IFS/27/159.
10 S. O'Mara to Robert O'Brennan, September 14, 1921, NA/DFA Prov. Govt/IFS/27/158.
11 S. O'Mara to Collins, September 8, 1921, NA/DE 5/57/14.
12 See also McGuire to de Valera, June 30, 1920, NA/O'Mara papers/MS.21548/2.
13 S. O'Mara to Collins, September 20, 1921 (emphasis in original) NA/DE 5/57/14.
14 S. O'Mara to Collins, September 20, 1921, NA/DE 5/57/14.
15 S. O'Mara to Collins, September 8, 1921, NA/DE 5/57/14; S. O'Mara to Collins, September 20, 1921, NA/DE 5/57/14.
16 De Valera to Collins, October 13, 1921, NA/DE 2/244.
17 Collins to O'Mara, October 14, 1921, NA/DE 5/57/14; O'Mara to O'Brennon, October 14, 1921, NA/DE 5/57/14.

18 S. O'Mara to O'Brennon, September 2, 1921, NA/DFA Prov. Govt/IFS/27/158.
19 Prior to taking legal action, the SEC issues either "comment" or "no-action" letters. No-action letters usually clarify the SEC's interpretation of the law. Comment letters, on the other hand, are warnings that indicate the SEC's dissatisfaction with the company's conduct.
20 September 25, 1951, CZA/A371/2.
21 To assess the seriousness of the situation, Montor's assistant met Alfred Hill, assistant to the Chairman of the SEC. The letter, Hill clarified, was discussed at the Commission's highest levels; it was not Bane's personal whim (memorandum of Steinglass meeting with Hill, October 8, 1951, CZA/A371/2).
22 Montor to Bane, October 8, 1951, CZA/A371/2.
23 Eban to Montor, December 17, 1951, CZA/A371/2.
24 In Comay to Goitein, January 15, 1952, GA/Foreign Affairs/2420/12; see also Ben-Gurion diary November 25, 1951 (1982).
25 In Comay to Goitein, January 15, 1952, GA/Foreign Affairs/2420/12; Eban to Comay, February 11, 1952, GA/Foreign Affairs/2420/12.
26 See CZA/A371/10; CZA/Z6/582.
27 See Sonneborn to the Board of Directors of CJFWF, June 23, 1952, AJHS/AFDCI/I-322/1/6.
28 Edwin Rosenberg to Ben-Gurion, February 7, 1952, GA/Foreign Affairs/2420/12.
29 Comay to Goitein, January 15, 1952, GA/Foreign Affairs/2420/12.
30 Report of Bronstein to Indianapolis Federation Board, March 19, 1952, AJHS/CJFWF/I-69/194/3.
31 See leaflet "Indianapolis Jewish Welfare Federation," March 27, 1952, GA/Foreign Affairs/2420/12.
32 See report of Bronstein to Indianapolis Federation Board, March 19, 1952, AJHS/CJFWF/I-69/194/3.
33 See "Indianapolis Bond Meeting Story," undated, AJHS/CJFWF/I-69/194/3.
34 AJHS/ CJFWF/I-69/194/3.
35 Montor to City Managers, April 2, 1952, AJHS/CJFWF/I-69/194/2.
36 February 14, 1951, CZA/A371/28; see also Eban to Montor, January 23, 1951; and, from within the AFDCI, see minutes of the Executive Committee Meeting AFDCI, May 13, 1952; Milton Turet to Montor, December 3, 1952, CZA/A371/27.
37 *Haboker,* July 23, 1952; Ben-Gurion to Eban, July 22, 1952, GA/Foreign Affairs/2420/13.
38 See Cramer, Berg, Riche, and Coleman to Eban, May 22, 1952, GA/Foreign Affairs/2420/12.

39 The Israeli dailies followed Sharett's visit to New York and the relations between the AFDCI closely (see reports in *Haboker*, July 23, 1952; *Haaretz*, July 23, 1952; *Yediot Aharonot*, October 22, 1952; Cabinet meeting July 20, 1952, in Sheffer 1996: 628.
40 Eshkol to Venezky, November 23, 1952, GA/Foreign Affairs/2420/13; "Fund-Raising for Israel in the United States: A Study," May 1952, CZA/A371/18.
41 See Sharett to Ben-Gurion, September 23, 1952; October 21, 1952, GA/Foreign Affairs/2420/13.
42 *Haaretz*, December 28, 1952.
43 Sharett to Ben-Gurion, December 30, 1952, GA/Foreign Affairs/2420/13.
44 Attached to a letter from Montor to Goldman, December 29, 1952, CZA/Z6/582.
45 See Julian Venetzky, "Report on Israel Bonds Activities," CZA/A371/27.
46 Martin to Kaplan, April 2, 1952, GA/Foreign Affairs/2420/12.
47 Commission should not be confused with cost. In addition to the commission, the Israeli government picked of the tab for commissions from banks, advertising and mailing costs, and covered the travel expenses of speakers (Eshkol to Montor, October 25, 1954, CZA/A371/10).
48 See Montor to AFDCI activists, January 28, 1952, CZA/S43/79. Montor estimated that in 1951 alone the government borrowed more than $37 million based on the Israel Bonds subscriptions. Eban used these loans as a lever to pressure Jewish community activists to assist the AFDCI (see Eban to Lurie, May 19, 1952, GA/Foreign Affairs/2420/12).
49 See government meeting, September 6, 1953, GA/GL-47049/1.
50 Eliezer Kaplan, Israel's first Minister of Finance and one of Montor's closest allies in the government, passed away in July 1952.
51 See Summary of the Executive Committee Meeting, AFDCI, May 13, 1952, CZA/A371/28; also "Fund-Raising for Israel in the United States: A Study," May 1952, CZA/A371/18.
52 Montor to Gross, June 1, 1953, CZA/A371/4.
53 See memorandums by Goldberger of meetings October 28, 29, and 30, 1953, CZA/A371/9. The Underwriting Agreement was signed on March 1, 1954.
54 See memorandum by Goldberger of meeting October 19, 1953, CZA/A371/9.
55 Statement by Montor, undated, CZA/A371/4.
56 Harman to Sharett, March 14, 1955, GA/Foreign Affairs/2420/14.
57 See Harman to Sharett, March 14, 1955, GA/Foreign Affairs/2420/14.

58 The Reparations Agreement signed by the Israeli Government and the Government of West Germany in late 1952 provided Israel with additional foreign currency. Later, Israel managed to secure more loans from the government of the United States and other institutional sources.
59 This sum is equivalent to $51,300,000 in 2000 terms.
60 April 9, 1921, AIHS/Cohalan papers/5/11.
61 De Valera to Cohalan, February 20, 1920, AIHS/Cohalan papers/4/1.
62 Cohalan to de Valera, February 22, 1920, AIHS/Cohalan papers/4/1.
63 De Valera's report to the cabinet, February 17, 1920, NA/DE/2/245. Boland followed de Valera in a letter to Collins: "Devoy and Cohalan are prepared to knife every man who comes from Ireland if they attempt [in] the slightest way to guide the movement for Irish freedom in this country ... these men cannot be trusted" (Woods to Fields, [cover names]. February 26, 1920, in Fitzpatrick 2003: 153).
64 AIHS/Cohalan papers/5/5.
65 See Devoy to Cohalan, August 7, 1920, AIHS/Cohalan papers/4/4.
66 See NA/DE 2/158.
67 Evidently, substantial segments of Irish society did not see the IFS as the fulfillment of their national aspirations.
68 See, for example, "On the Use and Distribution of the First $50,000,000 of Israel Bonds Receipts," September 12, 1951, CZA/S43/79.
69 CZA/A258/208/2.
70 See "Summary of minutes of Executive Committee, AFDCI" April 15, 1952, CZA/A371/28. Samuel Rothberg, one of the UJA executives that followed Montor to the AFDCI, complained that the card-calling method, which was exceptionally effective in UJA events, was useless in Israel Bonds sales events because so many of the people in the room were new to Jewish affairs (summary of minutes of the Executive Committee, AFDCI, October 21, 1952, CZA/A371/27.
71 In Israel's first decades, CHEN was the acronym of *Chel Nashim*, i.e. the women's corps in the Israeli Defense Forces (see Feinman to city managers, September 16, 1954, CZA/A258/207.
72 See "Suggestions for Speakers for 1954 Israel Bond Campaign," AJHS/AFDCI/I-322/1/6.
73 The difference between giving to the UJA and subscribing to the Israel Bonds was a key theme in discussions among AFDCI volunteers during the ADFCI's annual National Economic Conference for Israel (see CZA/A371/17).

74 Eban to Sharett, June 30, 1952, GA/Foreign Affairs/2420/12. Golda Meyerson went even further. Discussing the problem of unredeemed pledges, Meyerson explained that for the first time in history, Jewish Americans owed money to Israel rather than the other way around. The bond pledges, she insisted, were no different from legally binding obligations to purchase bonds. The delicate question, from her perspective, was how to inform Jewish American debtors that Israel decided to recall their outstanding obligations (see Summary of the Executive Committee Meeting AFDCI, April 5, 1952, CZA/A371/28).

7 Heterogeneity, Indeterminacy, and the Construction of National Interests

1 See Fiscal Agency Agreement, May 1, 1951, AJHS/AFDCI/I-322/5.
2 See "Outline of President de Valera," NL/O'Mara papers/MS.21547.
3 O'Mara to Collins, November 5, 1920, NA/DE 5/57/14.
4 Gallagher to O'Mara, December 12, 1919, ML/O'Mara papers/MS.21547.
5 See Gallagher to O'Mara, December 12, 1919, and Murphy to Walsh, December 29, 1919, NL/O'Mara papers/MS.21547. These incidents were widespread. For example, Leaders of the Ladies Auxiliary of the Ancient Order of Hibernians used the $5,000 they collected during the IVF drive to purchase bond certificates. John A. McGarry and Richard Wolfe from Chicago kept almost $20,000 to finance the bond drive (FOIF national executive minutes, January 9, 1920, AIHS/FOIF papers/6/3). Lynch was forced to threaten these activists with lawsuits unless they promptly remitted the funds, but his success was only partial.
6 Lynch to de Valera, January 15, 1920, NL/O'Mara papers/MS.21548/1; see also Lynch to de Valera, December 27, 1919, NL/O'Mara papers/MS.21547.
7 On December 17, 1921, the *Irish Press* published a list of hundreds of subscribers, from Philadelphia alone, whose Bond Certificates were issued but returned to the ACII headquarters undelivered (see also Nunan to Boland, April 7, 1921, UCDA/de Valera papers/P150/1142; Ward to S. O'Mara, October 14, 1921, NA/DE 5/57/14).
8 Charlotte Dunne to Lynch, April 8, 1920, NYPL/Maloney Collection of Historical Papers/4/5.

9   Grace to O'Mara, October 7, 1921, UCDA/de Valera papers/ P150/1204.
10 Folders 5–9 in box 4 in the collection contain hundreds of letters from angry subscribers. Ironically, complaints were addressed to Lynch, the secretary of the FOIF, who had no control whatsoever over the Bond Certificate campaign.
11 See AJHS/AFDCI/I-322/1/10.
12 Fiscal Agency Agreement, May 1, 1951, GA/GL-47049/1. The Chase National Bank charged 5% commission for its services.
13 In 1951 the Royal Indemnity Company handled 19 complains of lost money (Sanders to Keller, May 15, 1952, CZA/A371/9; Kurash to Montor, May 23, 1952, CZA/A371/9).
14 See McSweeney to Cohalan, undated, AIHS/Cohalan papers/10/13.
15 February 20, 1920, NL/McGarrity papers/MS.17522 (1); see also Devoy to Cohalan, September 5, 1919 (Fitzpatrick 2003: 152).
16 While still heading the UJA, Montor threatened to launch an independent campaign when a particular Federation failed to apportion adequate sums to overseas needs, but he never once acted on this threat (see Eban 1979).
17 Triads, as Georg Simmel (1950) notes, provide for more stable social relations and for the uneven accumulation of power.
18 In contrast to both the pluralist and the state-centered approaches of "bringing the state back in," Timothy Mitchell (1991) urged scholars to treat the distinction between state and society as a matter for investigation and to explore the practices that sometimes allow states to appear as somehow "above" society. Moneymaking practices are probably among the more important practices that can either generate or demolish the "effect of a state."
19 On the process through which states come to be considered as an entity that is somehow detached from society, see Mitchell (1991).
20 This is not to imply that the leadership in Jerusalem orchestrated the tension between the UJA and the AFDCI. On the contrary, Israeli leaders were troubled by these clashes and invested countless hours in preventing them (Ben-Gurion to Eban, July 22, 1952, GA/ Foreign Affairs/2420/13).
21 De Valera to Walsh, September 19, 1919, NYPL/Walsh papers/28.
22 Attached to a letter from Devoy to Cohalan, September 21, 1920, AIHS/Cohalan papers/4/3.
23 This point should not be overstated. During the late 1940s and early 1950s, the American position vis-à-vis Israel was quite ambivalent. The United States voted in favor of the partition plan but, at the same time, imposed an embargo on weapons shipments to the new state and refrained from including it in its ambitious international development plan (Ganin 2005).

24 On the limits of the small-N historical comparative approach, see Lieberson (1991, 1994).
25 See "Report on the Status of the United Jewish Appeal for Refugees and Overseas Needs," June 26, 1940, CZA/KH7/316.
26 Eshkol to Venezky, June 10, 1953, CZA/A371/7.
27 Conversion of bonds at the official rate would have given subscribers only a third of the pounds they could have received on the black market for the same amount of dollars.
28 See "Bond-Conversion," June 7, 1953, CZA/A371/4; Charles Rosenbloom to Venezky, February 3, 1953; Eshkol to Montor, June 22, 1953; Montor to Eshkol, June 30, 1953, CZA/A371/7.
29 Memorandum by Goldberger of meeting October 19, 1953, CZA/A371/9.
30 See memorandum by Goldberger, October 19, 1953, CZA/A371/9.
31 Curiously, the I.I.I. opened the door for the privatization of the Israeli economy in 1954, more than three decades before that process actually started. Ultimately, however, little came of this venture. The vast majority of bondholders kept their bonds, and the I.I.I. did not become a substantial entity (see *Haaretz*, January 21, 1953; May 27, 1953; *Al Hamishmar*, February 20, 1953).
32 This financing scheme is a bit puzzling: Why loan money to those from whom you wish to borrow? Modern corporations often use similar financing schemes to boost consumption. Toyota, for example, regularly offers consumers special financing schemes. In this example, Toyota uses its reserves or a privileged credit line to increase sales. Israel, obviously, did not enjoy extra reserves or a convenient credit line. The costly operation was designed exclusively to prevent the sale of Development Bonds on the market (memorandum by Goldberger of discussion of the 1954 Underwriting Agreement, October 29, 1953, CZA/A371/9).
33 Montor to Sapir, June 15, 1954; Horn to Montor, July 19, 1954, CZA/A371/7.
34 Memorandum by Goldberger of meeting October 19, 1953, CZA/A371/9.
35 See de Valera to Cohalan, February 20, 1920, AIHS/Cohalan papers/4/1.

Conclusions: Nation Building as an Organizational Accomplishment

1 The film is now available online at http://humphrysfamilytree.com/OMara/republican.loan.html.

2. The Irish and Jewish cases of diaspora bonds bear surprising contemporary relevance. During the 1990s, India launched two successful diaspora bonds campaigns, and as in the Irish and Jewish cases, these issues followed acute liquidity crises and involved a similar fusion of patriotic and pecuniary appeal (Chander 2001). Furthermore, in recent years, researchers at the World Bank have promoted the idea of diaspora bonds as a solution to chronic lack of capital in the developing world. Anxious to find nongovernmental sources for economic development, these researchers suggest that diaspora communities can provide an alternative to exorbitantly expensive and risk-averse financial markets on the one hand, and shrinking governmental development funds on the other (Ketkar and Ratha 2009). Responding to this call, countries such as Sri Lanka, Ghana, Armenia, Rwanda, Nepal, and recently also Greece have either launched or are preparing to launch diaspora bond campaigns.
3. One such campaign, a radio marathon hosted by singer and radio star Kate Smith, which raised a record $39 million in a single day, became the subject of Merton et al.'s classic *Mass Persuasion: The Social Psychology of a War Bond Drive* (1946).
4. David Laitin's (2007) work on "identity cascades" and Peter Sahlins' (1989) work on boundaries are among the few to treat the adoption of national identity as an interested act on the level of both the elites and the general population.
5. In the transnational context, the withering of a diaspora's sense of belonging to the homeland is typically treated as a case of "assimilation" to the host nation. This concept assumes a gradual attenuation of ties to the homeland and directs attention to the demographic processes that advance or retard integration in "host" societies. While demographic processes typically studied in the context of assimilation are obviously important, the Irish case suggests that the same phenomenon can sometimes be treated as an outcome of political processes of detachment that is independent of demography.

References

Abbott, Andrew. 1984. "Event sequence and event duration: Colligation and measurement [in medicine]." *Historical Methods* 17(4): 192–204.

Abu El-Haj, Nadia. 2001. *Facts on the Ground: Archaeological Practice and Territorial Self-Fashioning in Israeli Society*. Chicago: University of Chicago Press.

American Jewish Committee. 1950. *American Jewish Year Book*. Philadelphia: American Jewish Committee.

——— 1956. *American Jewish Year Book*. Philadelphia: American Jewish Committee.

——— 1961. *In Vigilant Brotherhood: The American Jewish Committee's Relationship to Palestine and Israel*. New York: American Jewish Committee.

Anderson, Benedict. 1991. *Imagined Communities: Reflections on the Origin and Spread of Nationalism*. London: New York: Verso.

Anthias, Floya. 1998. "Evaluating 'Diaspora': Beyond ethnicity?" *Sociology* 32(3): 557–580.

Barkai, Haim. 1990. *The Beginnings of the Israeli Economy*. Tel Aviv: Bialik Institute.

Barman, Emily. 2006. *Contesting Communities: The Transformation of Workplace Charity*. Stanford: Stanford University Press.

Barth, Fredrik. 1998. *Ethnic Groups and Boundaries: The Social Organization of Culture Difference*. Prospect Heights: Waveland Press.

Ben-Eliezer, Uri. 1995. "A nation-in-arms: State, nation, and militarism in Israel's first years." *Comparative Studies in Society and History* 37(2): 264–285.

——— 1998. *The Making of Israeli Militarism*. Bloomington: Indiana University Press.
Ben-Gurion, David. 1982. *The War of Independence: Ben-Gurion's Diary*. Tel Aviv: Misrad Habitachon.
Ben-Shahar, Haim. 1965. *Interest Rates and the Cost of Capital in Israel, 1950–1962*. Basel: J. C. B. Mohr.
Bhabha, Homi K. 1990. *Nation and Narration*. London: New York: Routledge.
Bhroiméil, Úna Ní. 2003. *Building Irish Identity in America, 1870–1915: The Gaelic Revival*. Dublin: Four Courts.
Bird-David, Nurit, and Asaf Darr. 2009. "Commodity, gift and mass-gift: On gift-commodity hybrids in advanced mass consumption cultures." *Economy and Society* 38(2): 304–325.
Boltanski, Luc. 1987. *The Making of a Class: Cadres in French Society*. New York: Cambridge University Press.
Bourdieu, Pierre. 1992. *The Logic of Practice*. Stanford: Stanford University Press.
——— 2000. *Pascalian Meditations*. Stanford: Stanford University Press.
Brah, Avtar. 1996. *Cartographies of Diaspora: Contesting Identities*. London: New York: Routledge.
Brass, Paul R. 1991. *Ethnicity and Nationalism: Theory and Comparison*. New Delhi: Sage Publications.
Brown, Thomas N. 1966. *Irish-American Nationalism, 1870–1890*. Philadelphia: Lippincott.
Brubaker, Rogers. 1996. *Nationalism Reframed: Nationhood and the National Question in the New Europe*. New York: Cambridge University Press.
——— 2004. *Ethnicity without Groups*. Cambridge, MA: Harvard University Press.
——— 2005. "The 'diaspora' diaspora." *Ethnic and Racial Studies* 28(1): 1–19.
——— 2009. "Ethnicity, race, and nationalism." *Annual Review of Sociology* 35: 21–42.
Brubaker, Rogers, and Frederick Cooper. 2000. "Beyond 'identity'." *Theory and Society* 29(1): 1–47.
Brubaker, Rogers, Margit Feischmidt, John Fox, and Liana Grancea. 2006. *Nationalist Politics and Everyday Ethnicity in a Transylvanian Town*. Princeton: Princeton University Press.
Brubaker, Rogers, Mara Loveman, and Peter Stamatov. 2004. "Ethnicity as cognition." *Theory and Society* 33(1): 31–64.
Burgoyne, Carole B., and David A. Routh. 1991. "Constraints on the use of money as a gift at Christmas: The role of status and intimacy." *Journal of Economic Psychology* 12(1): 47–69.

Burkett, Elinor. 2008. *Golda*. New York: Harper.
Calhoun, Craig J. 1997. *Nationalism*. Minneapolis: University of Minnesota Press.
Caliskan, Koray, and Michel Callon. 2009. "Economization, part 1: Shifting attention from the economy towards processes of economization." *Economy and Society* 38(3): 369–398.
Callon, Michel. 1998. *The Laws of the Markets*. Oxford: Blackwell Publishers/Sociological Review.
—— 1999. "Some elements of a sociology of translation: Domestication of the scallops and the fishermen of St Brieuc Bay." pp. 67–83 in *The Science Studies Reader*, ed. Mario Biagioli. New York: Routledge.
Callon, Michel, and Fabian Muniesa. 2005. "Economic markets as calculative collective devices." *Organization Studies* 26(8): 1229–1250.
Carnegie, Andrew. 1901. *The Gospel of Wealth, and Other Timely Essays*. New York: Century.
Carroll, Francis M. 1978. *American Opinion and the Irish Question, 1910–23: A Study in Opinion and Policy*. Dublin: Gill and Macmillan.
—— 1985. "The American Commission on Irish Independence and the Paris Peace Conference of 1919." *Irish Studies in International Affairs* 2(1): 103–118.
—— 2002. *Money for Ireland: Finance, Diplomacy, Politics, and the First Dáil Éireann Loans, 1919–1936*. Westport: Praeger.
Carruthers, Bruce G. 1996. *City of Capital: Politics and Markets in the English Financial Revolution*. Princeton: Princeton University Press.
—— 2005. "The sociology of money and credit." pp. 355–378 in *The Handbook of Economic Sociology*. 2nd edn, ed. Neil J. Smelser and Richard Swedberg. Princeton: Princeton University Press.
Chander, Anupam. 2001. "Diaspora bonds." *New York University Law Review* 76(4): 1005–1099.
Chatterjee, Partha. 1993. *The Nation and Its Fragments: Colonial and Postcolonial Histories*. Princeton: Princeton University Press.
Cheal, David J. 1988. *The Gift Economy*. New York: Routledge.
Clifford, James. 1997. *Routes: Travel and Translation in the Late Twentieth Century*. Cambridge, MA: Harvard University Press.
Cohen, Naomi Wiener. 1975. *American Jews and the Zionist Idea*. Philadelphia: Ktav Publishing House.
Coogan, Tim Pat. 1995. *Eamon De Valera: The Man Who Was Ireland*. New York: HarperCollins.
Cronin, Sean. 1972. *McGarrity Papers: Revelations of the Irish Revolutionary Movement in Ireland and America, 1900–40*. New York: Anvil Books (Childrens Press).

Darr, Asaf. 2003. "Gifting practices and interorganizational relations: Constructing obligation networks in the electronics sector." *Sociological Forum* 18(1): 31–51.

Davis, John. 1996. "An anthropologist's view of exchange." *Social Anthropology* 4(3): 213–226.

Dillon, Wilton. 2003. *Gifts and Nations*. New Brunswick: Transaction Publishers.

Doorley, Michael. 1995. "The friends of Irish freedom: A study of an Irish-American diaspora nationalism." University of Illinois at Chicago.

—— 2005. *Irish-American Diaspora Nationalism: The Friends of Irish Freedom, 1916–1935*. Dublin: Four Courts.

Dwyer, T. Ryle. 1998. *Big Fellow, Long Fellow: A Joint Biography of Collins and De Valera*. New York: St Martin's Press.

Eban, Abba. 1979. *History of the United Jewish Appeal (128)*. ed. Menachem Kaufman. Jerusalem: Institute for Contemporary Jewry: Oral History Division.

Elazar, Daniel. 1995. *Community and Polity: The Organizational Dynamics of American Jewry*. Philadelphia: Jewish Publication Society.

Eley, Geoff, and Ronald Grigor Suny. 1996. *Becoming National: A Reader*. New York: Oxford University Press.

Fallows, Marjorie R. 1979. *Irish Americans: Identity and Assimilation*. Englewood Cliffs: Prentice-Hall.

Fanning, Ronan, Michael Kennedy, Dermot Keogh, and Eunan O'Halpin, eds. 1998. *Documents on Irish Foreign Policy: 1919–1922*. Dublin: Royal Irish Academy.

Fitzpatrick, David. 2003. *Harry Boland's Irish Revolution*. Cork: Cork University Press.

Fox, John, and Cynthia Miller-Idriss. 2008. "Everyday nationhood." *Ethnicities* 8(4): 536–563.

Funchion, Michael F. 1983. *Irish American Voluntary Organizations*. Westport: Greenwood Press.

Galison, Peter Louis. 1997. *Image and Logic: A Material Culture of Microphysics*. Chicago: University of Chicago Press.

Ganin, Zvi. 2005. *An Uneasy Relationship: American Jewish Leadership and Israel, 1948–1957*. Syracuse: Syracuse University Press.

Garfinkel, Harold. 1967. *Studies in Ethnomethodology*. Englewood Cliffs: Prentice-Hall.

Gellner, Ernest. 1983. *Nations and Nationalism*. Ithaca: Cornell University Press.

Gieryn, Thomas F. 1983. "Boundary-work and the demarcation of science from non-science: Strains and interests in professional ideologies of scientists." *American Sociological Review* 48(6): 781–795.

Girard, Monique, and David Stark. 2002. "Distributing intelligence and organizing diversity in new-media projects." *Environment and Planning A* 34(11): 1927–1949.

Goldin, Milton. 1976. *Why They Give: American Jews and Their Philanthropies*. New York: Macmillan.

Golway, Terry. 1998. *Irish Rebel: John Devoy and America's Fight for Ireland's Freedom*. New York: St Martin's Press.

Goren, Arthur A. 1982. *The American Jews. Dimensions of Ethnicity*. Cambridge, MA: Belknap Press.

——1999. *The Politics and Public Culture of American Jews*. Bloomington: Indiana University Press.

Goswami, Manu. 2002. "Rethinking the modular nation form: Toward a sociohistorical conception of nationalism." *Comparative Studies in Society and History* 44(4): 770–799.

Gouldner, Alvin W. 1960. "The norm of reciprocity: A preliminary statement." *American Sociological Review* 25(2): 161–178.

Granovetter, Mark. 1985. "Economic action and social structure: The problem of embeddedness." *American Journal of Sociology* 91(3): 481–510.

Greaves, C. Desmond. 2004. *Liam Mellows and the Irish Revolution*. London: Lawrence and Wishart.

Hacking, Ian. 2000. *The Social Construction of What?* Cambridge, MA: Harvard University Press.

Halperin, Samuel. 1985. *The Political World of American Zionism*. Detroit: Wayne State University Press.

Handler, Richard. 1988. *Nationalism and the Politics of Culture in Quebec*. Madison: University of Wisconsin Press.

Haydu, Jeffrey. 1998. "Making use of the past: Time periods as cases to compare and as sequences of problem solving." *American Journal of Sociology* 104(2): 339–371.

—— 2009. "Reversals of fortune: Path dependency, problem solving, and temporal cases." *Theory and Society* 39(1): 25–48.

Healy, Kieran Joseph. 2006. *Last Best Gifts: Altruism and the Market for Human Blood and Organs*. Chicago: University of Chicago Press.

Hechter, Michael. 1975. *Internal Colonialism: The Celtic Fringe in British National Development, 1536–1966*. Berkeley: University of California Press.

Heinze, Andrew R. 1990. *Adapting to Abundance: Jewish Immigrants, Mass Consumption, and the Search for American Identity*. New York: Columbia University Press.

Herrmann, Gretchen M. 1997. "Gift or commodity: What changes hands in the U.S. garage sale?" *American Ethnologist* 24(4): 910–930.

Hertzberg, Arthur. 1950. "American Jews through Israeli eyes." *Commentary* 9: 1–7.
—— 1998. *The Jews in America*. New York: Columbia University Press.
Hobbes, Thomas. 1991. *Leviathan*. New York: Cambridge University Press.
Hobsbawm, Eric, and Terence Ranger. 1992. *The Invention of Tradition*. New York: Cambridge University Press.
Homer, Sidney, and Richard Sylla. 1996. *A History of Interest Rates*. 3rd edn Brunswick: Rutgers University Press.
Hout, Michael, and Joshua R. Goldstein. 1994. "How 4.5 million Irish immigrants became 40 million Irish Americans: Demographic and subjective aspects of the ethnic composition of white Americans." *American Sociological Review* 59(1): 64–82.
Hutchinson, John. 1987. *The Dynamics of Cultural Nationalism: The Gaelic Revival and the Creation of the Irish Nation State*. New York: Unwin Hyman.
—— 2005. *Nations as Zones of Conflict*. London: Sage Publications.
Israel, Knesset. 1951. *Divre Ha-Kneset*. Jerusalem: Government Publisher.
Ivy, Marilyn. 1995. *Discourses of the Vanishing: Modernity, Phantasm, Japan*. Chicago: University of Chicago Press.
Jacobson, Matthew Frye. 1995. *Special Sorrows: The Diasporic Imagination of Irish, Polish, and Jewish Immigrants in the United States*. Cambridge, MA: Harvard University Press.
Jenkins, Richard. 1997. *Rethinking Ethnicity: Arguments and Explorations*. Thousand Oaks: Sage Publications.
Jewish Telegraphic Agency. 1949. "Conference of Jewish Federation Leaders Reaffirms Allocation Rights of Communities." *Jewish Telegraphic Agency*, September 20. Retrieved (http://archive.jta.org/article/1949/09/20/3021163/conference-of-jewish-federation-leaders-reaffirms-allocation-rights-of-communities).
Judson, Pieter M. 2006. *Guardians of the Nation: Activists on the Language Frontiers of Imperial Austria*. Cambridge, MA: Harvard University Press.
Karp, Abraham. 1976. *Jewish Perceptions of America: From Melting Pot to Mosaic*. Syracuse: Syracuse University Press.
Kedourie, Elie. 1960. *Nationalism*. London: Hutchinson.
Kenny, Kevin. 2000. *The American Irish: A History*. New York: Longman.
Kertzer, David I. 1988. *Rituals, Politics, and Power*. New Haven: Yale University Press.
Ketkar, Suhas, and Dilip Ratha. 2009. *Innovative Financing for Development*. Washington, DC: World Bank.

Keyserling, Leon H. 1956. "The flow of funds, to date and potential, from the United States to Israel: A study of fund-raising by the American Jewish community."

Kimble, James. J. 2006. *Mobilizing the Home Front: War Bonds and Domestic Propaganda*. College Station: Texas A&M University Press.

Kimmerling, Baruch. 1983. *Zionism and Economy*. Cambridge, MA: Schenkman Publishing.

Lainer-Vos, Dan. 2010. "Diaspora-homeland relations as a framework to examine nation-building processes." *Sociology Compass* 4(10): 894–908.

Laitin, David D. 2007. *Nations, States, and Violence*. New York: Oxford University Press.

Latour, Bruno. 1988. *Science in Action: How to Follow Scientists and Engineers through Society*. Cambridge, MA: Harvard University Press.

Latour, Bruno. 2005. *Reassembling the Social: An Introduction to Actor-Network-Theory*. New York: Oxford University Press.

Latour, Bruno, and Steve Woolgar. 1979. *Laboratory Life: The Construction of Scientific Facts*. Beverly Hills, MA: Princeton University Press.

Lavelle, Patricia. 1961. *James O'Mara: A Staunch Sinn-Feiner, 1873–1948*. Dublin: Clonmore and Reynolds.

Law, John. 1992. "Notes on the theory of the actor-network: Ordering, strategy, and heterogeneity." *Systems Practice* 5(4): 379–393.

Lehrman, Hal. 1949. "The economic test facing Israel." *Commentary* 7: 513–523.

—— 1950a. "A billion dollars for Israel." *Commentary* 10: 518–529.

—— 1950b. "Turning point in Jewish philanthropy?" *Commentary* 10: 201–214.

—— 1951. "Israel and the private investor." *Commentary* 11: 232–244.

Lévi-Strauss, Claude. 1969. *The Elementary Structures of Kinship*. Boston: Beacon Press.

Lieberson, Stanley. 1991. "Small N's and big conclusions: An examination of the reasoning in comparative studies based on a small number of cases." *Social Forces* 70(2): 307–320.

—— 1994. "More on the uneasy case for using Mill-type methods in small-N comparative studies." *Social Forces* 72(4): 1225–1237.

Liebman, Charles S., and Steven M. Cohen. 1990. *Two Worlds of Judaism: The Israeli and American Experiences*. New Haven: Yale University Press.

Liebman, Charles S., and Eliezer Don-Yihya. 1983. *Civil Religion in Israel: Traditional Judaism and Political Culture in the Jewish State*. Berkeley: University of California Press.

Locke, John. 1988. *Two Treatises of Government*. New York: Cambridge University Press.

Lynch, Diarmúid, and Florence O'Donoghue. 1957. *The I.R.B. and the 1916 Insurrection: A Record of the Preparatations for the Rising*. Boulder: Mercier Press.

Maher, Jim. 1998. *Harry Boland*. Boulder: Mercier Press.

Mahoney, James, Erin Kimball, and Kendra L. Koivu. 2009. "The logic of historical explanation in the social sciences." *Comparative Political Studies* 42(1): 114–146.

Mahoney, James, and Dietrich Rueschemeyer. 2003. *Comparative Historical Analysis in the Social Sciences*. New York: Cambridge University Press.

Malinowski, Bronislaw. 1920. "Kula: The circulating exchange of valuables in the archipelagoes of Eastern New Guinea." *Man* 20: 97–105.

Mandelbaum, Maurice. 1961. "Historical explanation: The problem of 'covering laws'." *History and Theory* 1(3): 229–242.

Marshall, Thomas Humphrey. 1964. *Class, Citizenship, and Social Development: Essays*. Garden City: Doubleday.

Mauss, Marcel. 1967. *The Gift: Forms and Functions of Exchange in Archaic Societies*. New York: Norton.

McCaffrey, Lawrence J. 1976. *Irish Nationalism and the American Contribution*. New York: Arno Press.

McCartan, Patrick. 1932. *With De Valera in America*. New York: Brentano.

Merton, Robert K., Marjorie Fiske, and Alberta Curtis. 1946. *Mass Persuasion: The Social Psychology of a War Bond Drive*. New York: Bureau of Applied Social Research.

Miller, Kerby A. 1985. *Emigrants and Exiles: Ireland and the Irish Exodus to North America*. New York: Oxford University Press.

Mitchell, T. 1991. "The limits of the state: Beyond statist approaches and their critics." *American Political Science Review* 85(1): 77–96.

Muniesa, Fabian, Yuval Millo, and Michel Callon. 2007. "An introduction to market devices." *Sociological Review* 55: 1–12.

Neusner, Jacob. 1983. *Tzedakah: Can Jewish Philanthropy Buy Jewish Survival?* Chappaqua: Rossel Books.

—— 1999. "Altruism in Judaism." *The Encyclopedia of Judaism* 1: 46–54.

O'Doherty, Katherine. 1957. *Assignment: America: De Valera's Mission to the United States*. New York: De Tanko Publishers.

Offer, Avner. 1997. "Between the gift and the market: The economy of regard." *Economic History Review* 50(3): 450–476.

Ostrander, Susan A., and Paul G. Schervish. 1991. "Giving and getting: Philanthropy as social relations." pp. 67–98 in *Critical Issues in American Philanthropy: Strengthening Theory and Practice*, ed. Jon Van Til. San Francisco: Jossey-Bass Publishers.

Perlmann, Joel. 1988. *Ethnic Differences: Schooling and Social Structure Among the Irish, Italians, Jews, and Blacks in an American City, 1880–1935*. New York: Cambridge University Press.

Polanyi, Karl. 1957. *The Great Transformation*. Boston: Beacon Press.

Ragin, Charles C. 1987. *The Comparative Method: Moving Beyond Qualitative and Quantitative Strategies*. Berkeley: University of California Press.

Raphael, Marc Lee. 1982. *A History of the United Jewish Appeal, 1939–1982*. Chico: Scholars Press.

—— 1989. *Abba Hillel Silver: A Profile in American Judaism*. New York: Holmes and Meier.

Raz-Krakotzkin, Amnon. 1993. "Galut Be-Toch Ribonut: Le-Bikoret 'Shlilat Ha-Galut Batarbut Ha-Yisraelit'." *Teoria VeBikoret* 5: 113–132.

Rehavi, Yehiel, and Asher Weingarten. 2004. *Fifty Years of External Finance via State of Israel Non-Negotiable Bonds*. Jerusalem: Bank of Israel.

Rousseau, Jean-Jacques. 1968. *The Social Contract*. Harmondsworth: Penguin.

Rubner, Alex. 1960. *The Economy of Israel*. New York: Routledge.

Sahlins, Marshall D. 1963. "Poor man, rich man, big-man, chief: Political types in Melanesia and Polynesia." *Comparative Studies in Society and History* 5(3): 285–303.

Sahlins, Peter. 1989. *Boundaries: The Making of France and Spain in the Pyrenees*. Berkeley: University of California Press.

Samuel, Lawrence R. 1997. *Pledging Allegiance: American Identity and the Bond Drive of World War II*. Washington, DC: Smithsonian Institution Press.

Schwartz, Barry. 1967. "The social psychology of the gift." *American Journal of Sociology* 73(1): 1–11.

Shapiro, Yonathan. 1971. *Leadership of the American Zionist Organization, 1897–1930*. Urbana: University of Illinois Press.

Sheffer, Gabriel. 1996. *Moshe Sharett: Biography of a Political Moderate*. New York: Oxford University Press.

Silber, Ilana F. 1995. "Giftgiving in the great traditions: The case of donations to monasteries in the medieval West." *European Journal of Sociology* 36(02): 209–243.

―― 1998. "Modern philanthropy: Reassessing the viability of a Maussian perspective." pp. 134–150 in *Marcel Mauss: A Centenary Tribute*, ed. Wendy James and N. J. Allen. New York: Berghahn Books.

―― 2009. "Bourdieu's gift to gift theory: An unacknowledged trajectory." *Sociological Theory* 27(2): 173–190.

Simmel, Georg. 1950. *The Sociology of Georg Simmel*. New York: Free Press.

―― 1990. *The Philosophy of Money*. London: Routledge.

Smith, Anthony D. 1994. *The Ethnic Origins of Nations*. Oxford: Blackwell.

―― 1995. "Zionism and diaspora nationalism." *Israel Affairs* 2(2): 1–19.

―― 1999. *Myths and Memories of the Nation*. New York: Oxford University Press.

―― 2003. *Chosen Peoples: Sacred Sources of National Identity*. New York: Oxford University Press.

Sparrow, James. 2008. "'Buying our boys back': The mass foundations of fiscal citizenship in World War II." *Journal of Policy History* 20(2): 263–286.

Spillman, Lyn. 1999. "Enriching exchange: Cultural dimensions of markets." *American Journal of Economics and Sociology* 58(4): 1047–1073.

―― 2004. "Causal reasoning, historical logic, and sociological explanation." pp. 216–233 in *Self, Social Structure, and Beliefs: Explorations in Sociology*, ed. Jeffrey C. Alexander, Gary T. Marx, and Christine L. Williams. Berkeley: University of California Press.

Spillman, Lyn, and Russell Faeges. 2005. "Nations." pp. 409–437 in *Remaking Modernity: Politics, History, and Sociology*, ed. Julia Adams, Elisabeth Clemens, and Ann Shola Orloff. Durham: Duke University Press.

Star, Susan Leigh, and James R. Griesemer. 1989. "Institutional ecology, 'translations' and boundary objects: Amateurs and professionals in Berkeley's Museum of Vertebrate Zoology, 1907–39." *Social Studies of Science* 19(3): 387–420.

Stark, David. 2009. *The Sense of Dissonance: Accounts of Worth in Economic Life*. Princeton: Princeton University Press.

Steinberg, Kerri. P. 1998. "Photography, philanthropy, and the politics of American Jewish identity." Los Angeles: University of California, Los Angeles.

Stock, Ernest. 1987. *Partners and Pursestrings: A History of the United Israel Appeal*. Lanham: University Press of America.

—— 1988. *Chosen Instrument: The Jewish Agency in the First Decade of the State of Israel.* New York: Herzl Press.
Strenski, Ivan. 2003. "Sacrifice, gift and the social logic of Muslim 'human bombers'." *Terrorism and Political Violence* 15(3): 1–34.
Swedberg, Richard. 2005. "Markets in society." pp. 233–253 in *The Handbook of Economic Sociology*, ed. Neil J. Smelser and Richard Swedberg. Princeton: Princeton University Press.
Tansill, Charles Callan. 1957. *America and the Fight for Irish Freedom, 1866–1922: An Old Story Based Upon New Data.* New York: Devin-Adair.
Tilly, Charles. 1992. *Coercion, Capital, and European States, AD 990–1992.* Cambridge, MA: Blackwell.
—— 1996. *Citizenship, Identity and Social History.* New York: Cambridge University Press.
Titmuss, Richard. 1971. "The gift of blood." *Society* 8(3): 18–26.
United Jewish Appeal. 1949. *A Decade of Dedicated Service Through the United Jewish Appeal: 1939–1949.* New York: United Jewish Appeal.
Urofsky, Melvin I. 1978. *We are One! American Jewry and Israel.* Garden City: Anchor Press.
Valera, Eamon de. 1980. *Speeches and Statements by Eamon de Valera, 1917–1973.* ed. Maurice Moynihan. Dublin: Gill and Macmillan.
Verdery, Katherine. 1991. *National Ideology Under Socialism: Identity and Cultural Politics in Ceauşescu's Romania.* Berkeley: University of California Press.
—— 1996. "Whither 'nation' and 'nationalism'?" pp. 235–254 in *Mapping the Nation*, ed. Gopal Blakrishnan. New York: Verso.
Ward, Alan J. 1968. "America and the Irish Problem 1899–1921." *Irish Historical Studies* 16(61): 64–90.
—— 1969. *Ireland and Anglo-American Relations, 1899–1921.* Toronto: University of Toronto Press.
Weber, Max. 1978. *Economy and Society: An Outline of Interpretive Sociology.* Berkeley: University of California Press.
Wimmer, Andreas. 2008. "The making and unmaking of ethnic boundaries: A multilevel process theory." *American Journal of Sociology* 113(4): 970–1022.
Zelizer, Viviana A. 1985. *Pricing the Priceless Child: The Changing Social Value of Children.* New York: Basic Books.
—— 1994. *The Social Meaning of Money.* New York: Basic Books.
—— 1996. "Payments and social ties." *Sociological Forum* 11(3): 481–495.

—— 2000. "How do we know whether a monetary transaction is a gift, an entitlement, or compensation?" pp. 329–333 in *Economics, Values, and Organization*, ed. Avner Ben-Ner and Louis Putterman. Cambridge: Cambridge University Press.

—— 2005. "Circuits within capitalism." pp. 289–321 in *The Economic Sociology of Capitalism*, ed. Victor Nee and Richard Swedberg. Princeton: Princeton University Press.

Index

Actor-Network Theory 12, 172
Anderson, Benedict 7, 11–2, 19, 20, 54, 71, 152, 161, 174
American Association for the Recognition of the Irish Republic (AARIR) 104, 105, 107, 117, 121
American Commission on Irish Independence (ACII) 39, 74–5, 77–80, 81, 82, 131
  subscription procedures and problems 133–6, 141
American Financial and Development Corporation for Israel (AFDCI) 5, 6, 88–95, 108–13, 123–4, 127, 128, 131–2
  development issue 113–14, 115–16, 117
  subscription procedures 136
  Securities and Exchange Commission 89–90, 108–9
  State of Israel 89, 113–6
  Israel's Ministry of Foreign Affairs 109–12

American Jewish Joint Distribution Committee (JDC) 40–1, 64, 66
American War Bonds 158–9
Anglo-Irish Treaty 122, 123, 155–6
"attachment"
  concept of 9–10
  vs "identity" 8–10, 167–70
  interests 10, 96–7, 130
  see also national attachments
assimilation, Irish-American 121–3, 152, 155–6

Bane, Baldwin 108
belonging
  and difference 7–9
  and mobilization 12
Ben-Eliezer, Uri 157
Ben-Gurion, David 66–7
  national bonds 83, 84, 85, 141–2
  inter-organizational rivalry 109–10, 112
  US visit 95
Blue Skies Laws 75, 80, 182, 185

blurring practices 25–7, 125–8, 142–4
Boland, Harry 58–9, 60–1, 79, 102–4, 105, 120, 147
boundary work 8, 17, 119–21, 154
Bourdieu, Pierre 22, 23, 27, 143
Boyar, Lou 125–6
Brubaker, Rogers 11, 17, 52, 169–70
 and Cooper, Frederick 8, 9, 167
Brugha, Cathal 59, 63

Callon, Michel 22, 23
Cheal, David 20–1
Clan na Gael 33, 57, 58, 102–4, 121
clarification practices 24–5, 119–20, 141–4
Cohalan, Judge Daniel 33, 34, 57, 58, 62–3, 75, 77
 conflicts with de Valera 100, 119–21
Collins, Michael 59, 63, 77, 107, 120, 155–6, 157
Committee of Contributors and Workers (CCW) 68
comparative historical research 144–8
 variable-based comparison 13–4, 144–6
 problem-solving 16–7, 146–8
comparing sacrifice 36–7, 45, 52–4, 157–9
constructivism vs. essentialism 11–2, 160–2
controversies, the analytical value of 12–3
convertibility
 Independence Issue 92–3
 Development Issue 149–51
Coons, Isidor 41

cooperation without consensus 4–8, 25–6
Council of Jewish Federations and Welfare Funds (CJFWF) 68, 85–6
 Institute for Overseas Studies 68
crises in homeland diaspora relations 4, 56–7, 70–2
 Irish Victory Fund (IVF) 57–63
 United Jewish Appeal (UJA) 63–9

Dáil Éireann 1, 15, 33, 58, 59, 62, 74, 76, 105, 120
de Valera, Éamon
 Anglo-Irish Treaty 155–6
 appointed *Príomh Aire* 33
 conflicts with Cohalan 100, 119–21
 organizational expertise 147
 FOIF reform and AARIR 103, 104–5, 106
 national bonds 74–5, 76–81, 82, 95–6, 101–2, 133, 134, 137, 138, 140–1
 second Bond Certificate drive 105–6, 107
 recognition of Irish Republic 99–100
 US visit 58–9, 74, 75
Devoy, John 33, 57, 63, 100, 101, 102–3, 121, 140–1, 155
diaspora communities
 homeland relations 13–17, 157–60
 homeland relations as strategic research site 2–3, 12–3
 and nation building 11–13, 54–5
 and national movements 2–3, 8–9

difference and diversity within
    the nation 8–10, 31–2, 45,
    52–55, 164-divided loyalty
    5, 16, 86, 89, 121, 152, 172
Dunne, Charlotte 135
Dunne, Eduard F. 39, 78, 81

Easter Rising (1916) 3, 31, 33,
    37, 51–2
Eban, Abba 109, 110, 111,
    126–7
economic transactions and nation
    building 2–3, 19–22, 28
Eisenberg, Shlomo 66
emigration and settlement
    experiences 14, 144–5
entrepreneurs, national 2–3, 8,
    10, 13, 17, 162, 170
essentialism vs. constructivism
    11–2, 160–2
Eshkol, Levi 113–6, 148–50
Expertise, organizational 146–8

Feinman, Miriam 124
Fogarty, Michael 74, 157
Foreign Agents Registration Act
    1938 (FARA) 89, 90
Friends of Irish Freedom (FOIF)
    1, 5, 8, 30–1
  disagreements over use of IVF
    59–63, 134
  establishment of 32–4
  Irish independence 57–9,
    99–100
  and Irish mission, relationship
    between 99–100, 102–5,
    118–23, 135, 155–6
  national bonds 75–6, 76, 77,
    78–80
  struggle for survival 104,
    118–23
  see also Irish Victory Fund
    (IVF)

Gaelic American 35, 36–7, 38,
    49, 50, 52, 53, 100, 101,
    155
Gallagher, Bishop Michael 103,
    118
gift giving
  engineering 47–51
  Ireland 32–9
  Israel 39–47
  and market exchange 19–26
  and nation building 29–32,
    70–2
  and national attachments 51–5
Goldstein, Israel 64
Grace, William 135–6
"groupism" 11, 17–8
"groupness" 8, 167
"Guardians of Israel" 5, 124

Haydu, Jeffrey 16–7, 173–4
Herman, Robert 41–2, 46
Hertzberg, Arthur 1–2
Holocaust 3, 31, 43–4, 46–7, 48,
    51–2, 156
hybrid transactions 26
  loans as 27–8

"identity"
  vs. "attachment" 8–9, 167–70
  and gift giving 21
  and cultural representations
    10
imagined community, the nation
    as 11–2, 19, 20, 54, 71,
    152, 161, 174
inter-organizational structure of
    homeland-diaspora
    relations 137–139
Ireland: gift giving 32–9
Irish Advocate 37
Irish American community 14–6
  Organizational collapse 5,
    118–23

Irish Bond Certificate 4–5, 7, 8,
    74–80
  collapse 99–108, 118–23,
    140–1
  design and marketing 80–2
  domestic loan 74, 80, 157–8
  second drive 105–8
  see also national bonds
Irish civil war 122–3, 155–6
Irish Catholic Church 34, 48, 50
Irish Free State (1922) 31,
    122–3, 155–6
Irish independence
  Friends of Irish Freedom
    (FOIF) 57–9, 99–100
  see also American Commission
    on Irish Independence
    (ACII)
Irish Patriotic and Benevolent
    (P&B) Associations 37, 50
Irish Press 102, 103–4
Irish Race Conventions 33–4,
    35, 62, 75, 76, 103
Irish Republican Brotherhood
    (IRB) 33, 58, 103–4, 147
Irish self-determination 57, 58,
    100
Irish Victory Fund (IVF) 1, 3–4,
    30–1
  crisis 57–63
  goals 60
  launch 35–9
  and United Jewish Appeal
    (UJA) 47–55
  see also gift giving
Irish—Irish-American relations
    5, 7, 8, 155–6
  see also Irish Bonds
Israel
  economic conditions (1948)
    63–4, 83–4, 149–50
  effect of state 138–9, 192
  gift giving 39–47

Israel Bonds 4–6, 7–8, 82–90,
    141–2
  cost 113
  design and marketing 90–5
  development issue 113–6,
    149–151
  launching 113–16
  making of Jewish American
    investment in Israel 123–8
  see also national bonds
Israeli-American Jews relations
    5–6, 7–8, 137–9
  see also Israel Bonds; Zionist
    movement
Israel Investment Incorporated
    (I.I.I.) 150–1, 203

Jewish Agency 65–7, 68, 148
Jewish American community
    14–15, 39
  organizational structure 40,
    47–9
  attitude toward Israel 5, 14–5,
    40–1, 51–4, 123–8
Jewish Federations 40, 46, 47,
    48, 64–5, 85–7, 93
  conflicts with AFDCI and UJA
    109–11, 112–13, 115–16,
    137–9
Joint Distribution Committee
    (JDC) 40–1, 64, 66
Judaism 15
  and gift giving 179

Kaplan, Eliezer 66–7, 69, 84

League of Nations 57–9
loans as hybrid transactions
    27–8, 75–8, 80–2, 85–7,
    93–5, 100–2, 107, 112–3,
    125–8
loyalty, divided 5, 16, 86, 89,
    121, 152, 172

Lynch, Diarmuid 1, 2
  as FOIF national secretary 34, 59–63, 70, 104
  IVF 35, 38, 49, 50–1, 61, 134
  in US 33, 63
  resignation from the *Dáil Éireann* 120–1

McCartan, Patrick 33, 58, 59
McGarrity, Joseph 58–60, 102–4, 121, 147, 179
Maloney, William 82
market exchange and gift giving 19–26
Mauss, Marcel 20, 27, 30, 49
mechanisms, of nation building 2–4, 6–10, 12–3, 16, 28, 31, 54, 128–30, 154, 160–2, 166–7, 173–4
Meyerson (Meir), Golda 110–11, 190–1
mobilization, belonging and 12
Montor, Henry
  AFDCI and SEC 108–9, 112
  AFDCI and UJA 110, 112
  fundraising activities 41, 43, 46, 47, 49
  Meyerson visit to US 110–11
  national bonds 86–7, 88–9, 90, 91, 92, 95–6
    development issue 113–14, 115–16
    subscription procedures 136
  pre-campaign budgeting 65
  resignations 67, 115–16
  tax code violation 66
  and ZOA 67–8
Morgenthau, Henry 66, 67, 68, 109
  fundraising activities 47
  national bonds 83–4, 158–9

nation building 10
  as work of representation 9–10, 11–12, 160–2, 169
  diaspora communities 11–13, 54–5
  economic transactions 3, 19–22, 28
  gift giving 29–32, 70–2
  interest and disinterest in 96–7, 130, 162–4
  mechanisms 160–2
  as organizational accomplishment 154–70
national attachments
  engineering 51–5
  interested and disinterested in 130, 148–53
  making and unmaking 118
  organization of 1–18
  see also "attachment"
national bonds 4–8, 73–4, 98–9
  failure and success 16–18
  inter-organizational structure 137–9, 141–2
  producing national interests 95–7
  qualifying 131–2
  safe handling of national money 132–6
  see also Irish Bonds; Israel Bonds
national entrepreneurs 2–3, 8, 10, 13, 17, 162, 170
national movements and diaspora communities 2–3, 8–9
Neumann, Emanuel 67–8

O'Mara, James 1, 61–2, 63, 70, 79, 80, 105, 133–4, 147
O'Mara, Stephen 106–8, 117, 135, 136, 147

Palestine 14, 18, 39, 44
Patriotic and Benevolent (P&B) Associations 37, 50
Platt Amendment 99–100
pledge-collection 38, 46
political and cultural contexts 15–16

reciprocity 30
  absence of reciprocity 30–1, 47, 48–51
Redmond, John 32–3
Renan, Ernst 29
Ryan, Michael 39, 78

sacrifice (gift of life *vs* gift of money) 52–4
Schell, John 138
schnorrerai 5, 126–7, 165
Securities and Exchange Commission (SEC) 89–90, 108–9
self-determination, Irish 57, 58, 100
settlement experiences, emigration and 14
Sharett, Moshe 111–2
Silver, Abba Hillel 67–8
Sinn Féin 32–3
social constructivism 11, 169
status competition 49–50, 52–4

tax issues 44–5, 48, 65–7
temporal framing 143–4
terminology 17–18
tzedakah 179

United Irish League of America (UILA) 33, 34
United Jewish Appeal (UJA) 3–4, 5, 6, 31, 40–7, 156
  crisis 63–9
  and Irish Victory Fund (IVF) 47–55
  and national bonds 82–3, 84, 86–7, 93, 125–6, 128
  see also gift giving
United Palestine Appeal (UPA) 40–1, 63, 64, 65, 66–8, 69
United States (US) visits
  Ben-Gurion 95
  de Valera 58–9, 74, 75
  Lynch 33, 63
  Meyerson 110–11

Walsh, Frank P. 39, 78, 147
War bonds, American 83, 158–9
World War I 32–3, 34, 35–6, 48, 158
World War II 158–9
  Holocaust 31, 43–4, 46–7, 48, 51–2, 156

Zelizer, Viviana 3, 20, 24–5
Zionist movement 15, 39, 69, 156–7, 158
Zionist Organization of America (ZOA) 67–8
zone of indeterminacy 7, 26, 28, 142–3
  temporal framing 143–4

Studies in Spanish American Population History

About the Book and Editor

*Studies in
Spanish American Population History*
edited by David J. Robinson

Each of the contributions in this book sheds new light on key elements in the changing size, structure, and distribution of the Spanish American population during the colonial period. Several authors provide new source materials, while others manipulate well-known data in innovative ways to provide new insights into the past. In several of the essays the authors give information on regions and localities that hitherto have lain beyond the frontier of historical knowledge. Particularly important is their search for the broadest significance of their findings, whether investigating an entire region or a specific city, parish, or even family.

David J. Robinson, associate professor of geography at Syracuse University, is the author of several books on Latin America. He has served on the advisory board of the *Journal of Latin American Studies* and is currently general editor of the Dellplain Latin American Studies series.

DELLPLAIN LATIN AMERICAN STUDIES

PUBLISHED IN COOPERATION
WITH THE DEPARTMENT OF GEOGRAPHY
SYRACUSE UNIVERSITY

EDITOR

David J. Robinson
Syracuse University

EDITORIAL ADVISORY COMMITTEE

David A. Brading
University of Cambridge

Daniel Raposo Cordeiro
Syracuse University

William M. Denevan
University of Wisconsin

John H. Galloway
University of Toronto

John Lynch
University of London

William Mangin
Syracuse University

Studies in Spanish American Population History
edited by David J. Robinson

Dellplain Latin American Studies, No. 8

Westview Press / Boulder, Colorado

Dellplain Latin American Studies, No. 8

All rights reserved. No part of this publication may be reproduced or transmitted in any form or by any means, electronic or mechanical, including photocopy, recording, or any information storage and retrieval system, without permission in writing from the publisher.

Copyright © 1981 by the Department of Geography, Syracuse University

Published in 1981 in the United States of America by
    Westview Press, Inc.
    5500 Central Avenue
    Boulder, Colorado 80301
    Frederick A. Praeger, Publisher

Library of Congress Catalog Card Number: 81-68379
ISBN: 0-86531-268-0

Composition for this book was provided by the editor.
Printed and bound in the United States of America.

For

WOODROW BORAH

who for so long
has pointed the way

Contents

List of Tables	xi
List of Figures	xv
Preface	xix
Contributors	xxi
Introduction--DAVID J. ROBINSON	1

1 Population Reporting Systems: An Eighteenth-Century Paradigm of Spanish Imperial Organization   11
   JOHN V. LOMBARDI

2 Census Enumeration in Late Seventeenth-Century Alto Perú: The Numeración General of 1683-1684   25
   BRIAN M. EVANS

3 Colonial Censuses and Tributary Lists of the Sabana de Bogotá Chibcha: Sources and Issues   45
   JUAN VILLAMARIN
        and
   JUDITH VILLAMARIN

4 The Ecology of Race and Class in Late Colonial Oaxaca   93
   JOHN K. CHANCE

5 Marriage Patterns and Regional Interaction in Late Colonial Nueva Galicia   119
   LINDA L. GREENOW

6	Indian Migration in Eighteenth-Century Yucatán: The Open Nature of the Closed Corporate Community DAVID J. ROBINSON	149
7	Population Change in the Quinizilapa Valley, Guatemala, 1530-1770 CHRISTOPHER LUTZ	175
8	The Historical Demography of the Cuchumatán Highlands of Guatemala, 1500-1821 W. GEORGE LOVELL	195
9	Demographic Catastrophe in Sixteenth-Century Honduras LINDA A. NEWSON	217
10	Eighteenth-Century Population Change in Andean Peru: The Parish of Yanque N. DAVID COOK	243
Index		271

Tables

2.1	Distribution of Altiplano and Yungas population, 1683	37
3.1	Tribute deductions in the early seventeenth century	50
3.2	Ausentes in selected communities, Sabana de Bogotá	56
3.3	Officials and others exempted from payment of tribute	58
3.4	Reservados in selected communities, Sabana de Bogotá	59
3.5	Requinteros in selected communities, Sabana de Bogotá	61
3.6	Ratio of total population to tributaries	63
3.7	Tributary numbers in years with complete data	78
4.1	Indexes of segregation for racial groupings, Antequera, 1792 (household heads)	99
4.2	Indexes of segregation for racial groupings, Antequera, 1792 (adult males)	99
4.3	Indexes of dissimilarity for revised racial groupings, Antequera, 1792 (household heads)	100
4.4	Indexes of dissimilarity for revised racial groupings, Antequera, 1792 (adult males)	100

4.5	Indexes of segregation for SEGs and selected occupations, Antequera, 1792	101
4.6	Indexes of dissimilarity for SEGs, Antequera, 1792	101
5.1	Frequency of marriages	122
5.2	Race of marriage partners	125
5.3	Racial distribution of marrying populations	125
5.4	Mean ratios of observed to expected marriages in all parishes	126
5.5	Percent of racially exogamous marriages	128
5.6	Racial exogamy by racial group	128
5.7	Proportion of Inter-parish marriages	131
5.8	Mean migration distances	132
5.9	Racial variation in mean migration distances	132
5.10	Date of arrival of marriage migrants to selected parishes	141
5.11	Spatially exogamous marriages within parishes	143
6.1	Baptisms in Umán parish, 1689-1817	156
6.2	Exogamy rates for selected Yucatecan settlements, 1725-1812	158
7.1	Terrazgos paid by the milpas of the Quinizilapa Valley, ca. 1580	180
7.2	Estimated Indian population of the valley of Santiago de Guatemala, 1548-1581	183
7.3	Comparison of population movements in three Quinizilapa milpas and the valley of the city, 1575-1581	185
7.4	Estimated Crown tributary figures, valley of the city of Santiago de Guatemala, 1570-1581	185
7.5	Coefficients of population change for the Quinizilapa towns	186
7.6	Tributary totals, Quinizilapa towns, 1575-1755	186

7.7	Population data for the Quinizilapa towns, 1768	190
7.8	Comparison of population size of the Quinizilapa towns: 1768, 1880 and 1973	191
8.1	Indian army sizes recorded during the battles of conquest	200
8.2	The population of the Cuchumatán Highlands, 1520-1825	204
8.3	Local outbreaks of disease in the Cuchumatán Highlands, 1548-1819	208
9.1	Population estimates for Honduras, 1571-1582	223
9.2	Population estimates for Honduras, circa 1590	224
9.3	Population estimates for Honduras, 1582-1602	226
10.1	The Yanque parish series, 1684-1800	249
10.2	Averages for numbers of annual births, Yanque village	250
10.3	Average number of annual births in Yanque anansaya	252
10.4	Baptismal sex ratios	253
10.5	Average annual marriages in Yanque	254
10.6	"Normal" monthly patterns of marriage in non-epidemic years	255
10.7	Average annual marriages, Yanque anansaya	255
10.8	General Andean epidemics, 1685-1800, and Yanque	256
10.9	Average annual number of deaths, Yanque community	257
10.10	"Normal" monthly patterns of mortality in non-epidemic years, Yanque community	258
10.11	Average age at death for those twenty and above, Yanque	259
10.12	Baptisms, marriages and deaths, Yanque community	266

Figures

2.1	Location of seventeenth-century provinces in upper Peru	26
2.2	Origins and destinations of selected inter-provincial migrants, upper Peru, 1683	39
2.3	Sample age-sex distribution from the 1683 census	41
3.1	The Sabana de Bogotá, sample communities	46
3.2	Tributary change in Bogotá, and Bosa, 1660-1830	66
3.3	Tributary change in Chocontá, 1660-1810	67
3.4	Tributary change in Cucunubá-Bobota, and Facatativa, 1660-1820	68
3.5	Tributary change in Fontibón, and Fúquene-Nemoga, 1660-1830	69
3.6	Tributary change in Guasca-Siecha, and Guatavita, 1660-1810	70
3.7	Tributary change in Serrezuela, Sequilé-Gachacaca, and Simijaca, 1660-1820	71
3.8	Tributary change in Suacha, and Suba-Tuna, 1660-1830	72
3.9	Tributary change in Suesca, 1660-1820	73
3.10	Tributary change in Susa, 1660-1810	74

3.11	Tributary change in Suta-Tausa, Usaquén, and Usme, 1660-1830	75
3.12	Tributary change in Ubaté, 1660-1820	76
3.13	Sample tributary totals for years with complete data, Sabana de Bogotá, 1660-1810	77
4.1	Streets of Antequera, 1792-1803	95
4.2	Peninsular Spaniards in Antequera by manzana, 1792	103
4.3	Creoles in Antequera, by manzana, 1792	104
4.4	Castizos in Antequera, by manzana, 1792	105
4.5	Mestizos in Antequera, by manzana, 1792	106
4.6	Mulattoes in Antequera by manzana, 1792	107
4.7	The elite of Antequera by manzana, 1792	108
4.8	Preindustrial middle groups of Antequera by manzana, 1792	109
4.9	Preindustrial lower groups of Antequera by manzana, 1792	110
4.10	Percentage of castas in each of Antequera's central manzanas, 1792	112
4.11	Percentage of preindustrial lower groups in each of Antequera's central manzanas, 1792	113
5.1	Settlements in Nueva Galicia	123
5.2	Origins of marriage migrants to Chapala	134
5.3	Origins of marriage migrants to Ameca	135
5.4	Origins of marriage migrants to Tequila	136
5.5	Origins of marriage migrants to Compostela	137
5.6	Origins of marriage migrants to Tepic	139
6.1	Location of Yucatecan study villages	153
6.2	Origins of marriage migrants, San Francisco de Umán, 1689-1812	155

6.3	Origins of migrants, San Francisco de Umán, 1689-1812	157
6.4	Origins of migrants, Sotuta, 1725-1792	159
6.5	Origins of migrants to Sotuta, 1788-1792	161
6.6	Selected migration fields, Yucatán, 1788-1792	162
6.7	Origins of migrants in selected Yucatecan settlements, 1788-1792	163
6.8	Origins of migrants to Tixkokob and its dependent pueblos, 1788-1792	164
6.9	Origins of migrants to Conkal and other intermediate points, 1788-1792	166
6.10	Hypothesized changes in "open/closed" nature of Yucatecan settlements	170
7.1	Settlements of the Quinizilapa Valley, Guatemala	176
7.2	Population change in the Quinizilapa towns, 1575-1755	188
8.1	Location of the Cuchumatán highlands and selected settlements	197
8.2	The population of the Cuchumatán highlands, 1520-1821	205
9.1	Approximate boundaries of jurisdictions and uncolonized areas of Honduras, circa 1600	225
10.1	The Colca River basin, Peru	245
10.2	Yanque and the middle Colca Valley	246
10.3	Births, marriages and deaths, Yanque, Peru, 1685-1800	251

Preface

Six of the ten essays in this collection (Lombardi, Villamarin, Chance, Greenow, Robinson, and Cook) were originally presented at a Special Session during the 43rd International Congress of Americanists, held in Vancouver during August, 1979. Jointly organized by David J. Robinson and Juan Villamarin, the session was designed to bring together a group of individuals who had been working on the changing population of colonial Spanish America from various disciplinary perspectives, to facilitate an exchange of information and ideas, and to promote the further investigation of significant research questions. The paper of Brian Evans was presented at the same Congress, in another session, but given its purpose and content it was thought to provide an ideal complement to several papers in the present collection.

Two other papers (Lovell and Lutz) were initially presented in a "Seminar in the Historical Demography of Highland Guatemala," part of the 27th Meeting of the American Society for Ethnohistory, held in Albany, N.Y., during October, 1979; Linda Newson's essay has been specially prepared for this volume, and is part of a larger forthcoming study of Central American population history. She also participated in the discussions following the presentation of most of the Americanistas papers. It will be clear from a reading of these three papers that the authors are addressing topics that could equally have found a place in the Americanists discussions, and they thus here provide an important Central American dimension to the debate on population change. One of the benefits of hindsight is the possibility of re-assembling a group of persons who should have been together in the first place!

Only those who have ventured beyond the oral presentation stage of conference papers will understand the full significance of my sincere thanks to all of the contributors to this volume for their patience and kind assistance in revising various drafts of their papers.

Multidisciplinary research sounds exciting, but it can too easily founder on a few unanswered letters and missed deadlines.

I owe a personal debt to Juan Villamarin, whose energies and contacts made the task of organizing a special session at the Americanistas much easier than it might otherwise have been.

Almost all of the maps and diagrams were prepared by Valmor Philp of the Syracuse University Cartographic Laboratory, and to him we extend our special thanks. Jane McGraw typed the entire manuscript in its many drafts, as well as all of the inevitable correspondence that such an enterprise involves, with her inimitable speed and good humor, and I am thus even deeper in her debt. Both the typing and cartographics were funded from the Dellplain Latin American Geography Program at Syracuse University, and I would like to thank Robert G. Jensen, Chairman of the Geography Department, for his unfailing support in that regard.

David J. Robinson
Syracuse, New York

Contributors

John K. Chance	Department of Anthropology, University of Denver, Colorado
N. David Cook	Department of History, University of Bridgeport, Connecticut
Brian M. Evans	Department of Geography, University of Winnipeg, Manitoba, Canada
Linda L. Greenow	Department of Geography, Syracuse University, New York
John V. Lombardi	Department of History, Indiana University, Bloomington, Indiana
Christopher H. Lutz	Centro de Investigaciones Regionales de Mesoamérica, Antigua, Guatemala
W. George Lovell	Department of Geography, Queen's University, Kingston, Ontario, Canada
Linda A. Newson	Department of Geography, King's College, University of London
David J. Robinson	Department of Geography, Syracuse University, New York
Juan and Judith Villamarin	Department of Anthropology, University of Delaware, Newark, Delaware

Introduction

David J. Robinson

This brief introduction will serve to place each of the essays within the wider context of Spanish American population history. Limitations of space preclude a detailed bibliographical and historiographical treatment, and in any event, the reader will find in the notes that accompany each of the essays a large number of citations that provide ample evidence of the advancing state of the art. Each of the contributions sheds new light on key elements in the changing size, structure, and distribution of Spanish American population during the colonial period. While some range over centuries to monitor temporal sequences, others adopt a cross-sectional approach to specify the precise conditions at a convenient historical viewpoint. Several authors provide new source materials, while others manipulate well-known data in an innovative manner to provide new insights into the past. In several of the essays information is provided for regions and localities which have hitherto lain beyond the frontier of historical knowledge.

Equally important is the fact that all of the authors share a multidisciplinary approach to their problems, a characteristic that has long enriched the demographic approach to Latin America's past. Without examining the authors' departmental affiliations it might be difficult to separate the historians from the anthropologists and the geographers. And so it should be, for all of the essays address questions that extend beyond the bounds of any one narrow academic focus. The types of evidence, the methods, the techniques, as well as the interpretations, demand a familiarity with a range of often difficult substantive fields.

It is also good to note that even when an individual city, parish, or even family is being investigated, the author is at pains to search for a wider significance for his findings. The typical, the aberrant, the statistically significant, the example, the sample--all the problems that make historical research as exciting as it is

exacting--are to be found throughout this collection.
   While population provides the authors with the means of analyzing Spanish America's past, it is not viewed as an end in itself; the numbing that comes from too many numbers is pleasantly absent. First, the populations studied here are usually large and diverse enough to allow one to approach the mass of socialized individuals that comprised the majority of colonial society. Second, the very mode of counting and classifying such persons allows one to appreciate the cultural perceptions, images and prejudices that were the hallmark of intercultural relations over more than three centuries. Third, the contextual arrangement of people in families, clans, neighborhoods, cities, hinterlands, and the like, permits one to monitor not only demographic trends, but since those same persons were workers and consumers, landlords and peasants, residents and migrants, colonists and conquered, changes in their relative numbers and interrelationships provide one with a singular interpretative opportunity. The populace in this sense was the colonial society. When numbers increased or decreased within significant socio-ethnic groups, the repercussions could be ideological as well as economic. When persons became mobile, political as much as social tensions could be produced. Real people belonged (or were ascribed) to racial groups and social classes, and discerning trends in subtle cultural transformations is no easy task. In this respect the mundane census returns, tribute lists, and parish registers, offer surprising avenues of insight.

THE AFTERMATH OF CONTACT AND CONQUEST

   Our knowledge of the demographic ramifications of the arrival of Europeans in the New World is still imprecise. Some scholars are prepared to utilize the scanty (and mostly Spanish) sources of the sixteenth century to extrapolate a relatively large pre-contact population for some major regions, with densities approaching those of the modern period.[1] Others deny the probabilities of such situations, stressing what they believe to be the ecological limits of the areas under consideration, the socioadministrative capacity of the pre-Hispanic cultures involved, the varied epidemiology of the diseases involved, and the suspect Spanish documentary record.[2] While this debate will doubtless continue, as more regions and records are investigated, it is important to note that in several respects there are major weaknesses in the evidential basis of the debate. We know, for example, very little of the detailed ethnohistory of the contact cultures: how their settlements were spaced, how their subsistence systems operated, how they coordinated the management of diverse ecosystems, how balanced were their diets, how prepared they were to react to a major cultural intrusion.

Similarly, though ecology is often adduced as a key factor affecting population carrying capacity as well as potential rate of change, we know little of the ecotones of the contact and early colonial New World. And where detailed work has been undertaken, the results have been more than a little surprising. In many areas, mid-twentieth century vegetation and soils have been recognized as poor indicators of earlier conditions.[3] In others, the colonial palimpsest has all but obliterated the traces of what might otherwise be susceptible to site catchment analysis and other rigorous techniques of ecological evaluation.[4]

Another geographical factor that finds a place in the agenda of favored explanations is the role of altitude as it allegedly controlled the variable incidence of diseases. Exactly what were the differential probabilities of death in the tropical and sub-tropical lowlands as opposed to the colder climes of the Andean chains and Mesoamerican plateau is still very unclear. Evidence is scant, and climatic controls on disease vectors still undetermined. The crude highland/lowland dichotomy persists only as an epidemiological assumption. Within such large units the contemporary micro-environmental variations are little understood even after a century or more of study.

But beyond the initial and drastic reduction of Indian population (and few would deny it to have been less) in the sixteenth century lie two hundred or more years of continued population fluctuation. Whereas for central Mexico the sixteenth century witnessed the primary shock of demographic change, in other more peripheral regions it was in the seventeenth and eighteenth centuries that god-fearing, gold-hunting and disease-carrying aliens arrived, to disrupt the local economy, to redesign the cultural landscape and to restructure social relations. In the colonial core regions too socio-economic evolution produced an ever-changing balance between births and deaths, between stable and unstable circumstances, and between conquerors and conquered. Within this parabola of episodic decline and recovery several of the present essays contribute new data and opinions.

For two distinctive Guatemalan regions Lutz and Lovell provide evidence to parallel that of central Mexico and Peru: early rapid decline and slow recovery. Both their studies, as well as that of Newson who sheds much new light on the Honduran experience, also demonstrate the problematic nature of the data base, the difficulties of standardizing population segments used to derive totals, the unspecified diseases, the spatial shifts that often compounded the problems and still confound the modern researcher. In a similar vein, but for the seventeenth and eighteenth centuries, Villamarin and Cook examine the potential of tribute lists and parish registers to elucidate changing population patterns. The synchronicity of fluctuations among the Chibcha settlements of the Sabana de Bogotá illustrates the usefulness of the regional approach, though Villamarin is careful to note the difficulties of reconciling changes at the regional level with those operating at the level of individual communities. Multi-level causation is still beyond reach, a fact which Cook implicitly accepts when he sets the Yanque details against the backdrop of Peru in general. How many Yanques make up Collaguas? And for the Andean core how far may we extrapolate? All of the authors demonstrate that a combination of types of documentation is required if the full story is ever to be told, and yet tantalizingly few places have such extant sources.

One solution to the problems confronting the historian of past populations would be an escape to the simplifying assumptions of simulated models of change: the clear counterfactual held up to the blur of historical "reality." If it is possible to examine the probabilities of transpacific contacts,[5] why not a computer simulation of disease diffusion? In that way the settlement net, the density of population (by various types) and the rate of infection could be measured from selected "outbreak" points of specific diseases.[6] Of course bold assumptions would have to be made, but they can always be modified in a controlled manner--and far more easily than in the uncontrolled world of the documentary past. To dismiss recent advances in demographic analysis beyond the context of colonial Spanish America is to ignore a set of powerful investigative tools.[7]

POPULATION ON THE MOVE

Besides appearing (births) and disappearing (deaths) from the scene human populations have another characteristic--that of physically moving, and this aspect of Spanish America's past is highlighted in several of the present essays. Population movement is a characteristic, however, of varying significance, for not all persons behave alike, and the range of factors known, or assumed, to affect the decision to move is immense. Equally important (and here all of the present essays are pertinent) those who did not move are of significance, for in studying their patterns much may be learned of the reasons for immobility.

Within the larger frame of colonial Spanish America it is clear that from an early situation in which mostly sedentary Indians were disrupted by a highly mobile

Spanish minority, the pattern inexorably shifted to one with an increasing number of spatially stable persons of non-Indian origin, with Indians and certain mixed groups becoming increasingly mobile. Indeed one might posit a "mobility transition" in colonial Spanish America that paralleled the shifts from <u>encomienda</u> to <u>hacienda</u>, from Indian to peasant, from urbanite to urbanized, and from <u>patrias chicas</u> to proto nation-states.[8]

As Lombardi argues there was an assumed propriety of place embedded in the Spanish colonial mentality, which may have been either a consequence of cultural development, or an artifice of imperial control. People should be of a place, and attached to that place, and those who were not were suspect. Transients were (as elsewhere) almost always suspect, for a lack of belonging was equated with a lack of caring--either for the law, or for social customs.

The reasons for moving, be it to the next village, the nearby town, or the next province, varied in both time and space. A persistent secular threat to land and livelihood could push Chibchas out of their homelands (Villamarin); an avaricious clergy demanding services in cash or kind could loosen the kin and territorial ties of Yucatecan Mayans (Robinson). With migrants escaping beyond Spanish control from Peru (Cook) to Mexico (Greenow), it is not surprising that new census categories were designed to isolate and calculate the flow which threatened to become a flood (Evans); <u>forasteros</u>, <u>ausentes</u>, <u>vagos</u> and the like needed to be repatriated for the good of all.

To identify the currents of migration in Spanish American colonial populations is no easy task. Just as a migrant could escape tribute or <u>obvención</u> by moving the effective administrative jurisdiction, so too by leaving his parish of birth or marriage he escapes the modern researcher (Greenow, Robinson). Unless one can locate a census that specifies the origins of individuals or family heads (Evans, Cook), one's only recourse is to the interlinkage of birth, marriage and burial records.[9] If individuals did not behave "properly" and be born (i.e. baptized), married (i.e. in a church ceremony) and die (i.e. be buried), then they evidentially did not exist.[10] We must therefore realize that millions of individuals will fall completely outside of our historical knowledge: we can only hope that their more "proper" neighbors offer some clue as to their unrecoverable feelings and behavior. And if one is to become worried about such "non-existent" population, one's anxieties are hardly quieted when one realizes that ethnic and class biases in reporting and recording clearly affect the extant documentation. For every one person who could afford a lawyer or priest, how many do we count who could not? Whether it be the men of Cajamarca,[11] or the nuns of Guadalajara[12] we know that our record is uneven, and suspect.

Yet the fact that much can be gleaned from the records of conscientious parish priests who knew their flock intimately, gives cause for hope. Geobiographies can trace some persons and families through time and space (Robinson), and when aggregated into statistical populations can tell us much of local and regional interaction (Greenow).[13] Extensive multi-stage migration makes nonsense of notions of the closed corporate communities, and those who counterpose a stable past against the mobile present belie the facts as they were so assiduously recorded. It is too easy to assume that Spanish American destabilization of population came, as with Europe and Anglo America, during the nineteenth and twentieth centuries. There was always much in the Spanish American world from which to flee, or to which one could be attracted. Only the complexities of the details of such spatial relocation have yet to be elucidated; these essays contain some clues.

THE COLONIAL CITY AND ITS HINTERLAND

Of the range of institutions that reflected the changing population history of colonial Spanish America, two are of especial significance: the family and the city. While the former provides an opportunity to examine the intrusion of Spanish social organization upon a diverse aboriginal base, the latter allows one to examine the articulation of not only the socio-economic sphere, but also the operation of colonial authority and the developing tensions between those with access to power and those marginalized by the colonial process.[14] The patrilineal nuclear family was promoted as a normative feature of society (Villamarin), and the values of the hierarchical household become evident at every turn of the documentary record. One's place in society was usually reflected at the microcosmic level of the household. In that sense, census becomes symbol, and registration required behavior (Lombardi).

But of the higher level entities which structured social interaction and the relations of production among the larger groupings of ethnic and class divisions, the city was of key significance. As the locus of power and the focus of economic activity it embodied colonial rule. To live beyond the reach of the city extended--outside its hinterland--was to exist outside of the colonial realm.[15]

The urban network provided the Crown with a hierarchical system of population reporting, albeit by the seventeenth century too cumbersome to allow much of the data collected to be efficiently utilized (Lombardi). The urban system, about whose systemic relations so little is known, provided a range of socio-economic opportunities that greatly affected migration patterns (Greenow, Cook). Major changes in population structure may have been directly related to the disruptive effects of the urban economy (Villamarin, Newson, Robinson).

In spite of the quickening pace of research on the internal structure of the Spanish American colonial city, much has yet to be learned. In that respect detailed ecological analysis of social relations in a selected city is to be welcomed (Chance). Though some may express concern over the appropriateness of applying a methodology grounded in twentieth century social relations, when physical distance is a useful proxy for social distance, the fact remains that the patterns produced by such ecological approaches are most useful discriminants of inferred social behavior.[16] As in the nineteenth-century city, one's position in the city was often a reflection of one's position in society.

Of course classificatory problems persist, as they are likely to do so for some time. But the question of how to isolate a lower class group (Chance) is no different from the task of deciphering ethnic and other labels (Evans, Lombardi). One clear signal from recent research is that an approach to population history that uses multiple sources is often very rewarding. Whether it be age data, kin structure, household composition, stage migration, or population decline, the combination of records provides invaluable clues.

If this collection stimulates further research on these and other issues, it will have served its purpose.

NOTES

1. The best introductions to this extensive literature are the three volumes of S. F. Cook and W. Borah, Essays in Population History, Berkeley, 1971-1979. Both the essays and the extensive bibliography in W. M. Denevan, The Native Population of the Americas in 1492, Madison, 1976, provide extremely useful summaries of the various positions.

2. See for example R. A. Zambardino, "Mexico's Population in the Sixteenth Century: Demographic Anomaly or Mathematical Illusion?," Journal of Interdisciplinary History, Vol. XI, 1980, pp. 1-27; also his review of the third volume of Cook and Borah's Essays in Population History, in Annals of Association of American Geographers, 1980, Vol. 70, pp. 583-585. Also D. Henige, "On the Contact Population of Hispaniola: History as Higher Mathematics," Hispanic American Historical Review, Vol. 58, 1978, pp. 217-237.

3. Remote sensing by satellite has recently identified major water-management networks in the Yucatán, which strengthens the views of those who have recently argued for major historic-ecological

changes in that region. For an excellent analysis of soil capacities in the Amazon basin as it relates to historical populations see Nigel J. H. Smith, "Anthrosols and Human Carrying Capacity in Amazonia," Annals, Association of American Geographers, 1980, Vol. 70, pp. 553-566.

4. For a description of the technique, see M. R. Jarman, C. Vita-Finzi and E. S. Higgs, "Site Catchment Analysis in Archaeology," in P. J. Ucko, R. Tringham and G. W. Dimbleby, Man, Settlement and Urbanism, London, 1972, pp. 61-67. For an excellent study of the utility of the archaeological approach to colonial sites see David M. Jones, The Archaeology of Haciendas and Ranchos of Otumba and Apan, Basin of Mexico, Research Report No. 2, Mesoamerican Research Colloquium, University of Iowa, 1980.

5. M. Levison, et al., "A Model of Accidental Drift Voyaging in the Pacific Ocean," Proceedings, International Federation for Information Processing, 1969, pp. 1521-36.

6. Such studies would be much easier if the records are available for a dense network or points. For the available Mexican data see D. J. Robinson, Research Inventory of the Mexican Collection of Colonial Parish Registers, Vol. 5 of Finding Aids to the Microfilmed Collection of the Genealogical Society of Utah, Salt Lake City, 1980.

7. For an excellent account of what may be done with microsimulation see E. A. Hammel et al., The SOCSIM Demographic-Sociological Microsimulation Program, Institute of International Studies, Berkeley, 1976. For an excellent series of case studies see K. W. Wachter, et al., Statistical Studies of Historical Social Structure, New York, 1978. An outline of approaches is provided in B. Dyke and J. W. MacCluer (eds.), Computer Simulation in Human Population Studies, New York, 1974.

8. See the classic article of W. Zelinsky, "The Hypothesis of the Mobility Transition," Geographical Review, Vol. LXI, 1971, pp. 219-249.

9. See for example D. J. Robinson, "Córdoba en 1779: Ciudad y Campaña," in Raul C. Rey Balmaceda (ed.), Homenaje a Federico A. Daus, Buenos Aires, 1979, pp. 279-312. Also L. L. Johnson and S. Migden Socolow, "Population and Space in Eighteenth-Century Buenos Aires," in D. J. Robinson (ed.), Social Fabric and Spatial Structure in Colonial Latin America, Ann Arbor, 1979, pp. 339-368; and M. M. Swann, Tierra Adentro: Society and Settlement in Colonial Durango, Ann Arbor, 1981.

10. A general overview is provided in D. J. Robinson, "The Spanish American Family in the Eighteenth and Nineteenth Centuries," Proceedings of the Third World Conference on Records and Family History, Vol. 5, Salt Lake City, 1980.

11. J. Lockhart, Men of Cajamarca: A Social and Biographical Study of the First Conquerors of Peru, Austin, 1972.

12. A. Lavrín and E. Couturier, "Dowries and Wills: A View of Women's Socioeconomic Role in Colonial Guadalajara and Puebla, 1640-1790," Hispanic American Historical Review, Vol. 59, 1979, pp. 280-304.

13. See for example S. Migden Socolow, "Marriage, Birth and Inheritance: The Merchants of Eighteenth Century Buenos Aires," Hispanic American Historical Review, Vol. 60, 1980, pp. 387-406.

14. Excellent overviews are provided in R. M. Morse, "The Urban Development of Colonial Spanish America," in the Cambridge History of Latin America, Cambridge, 1981; W. Borah, "Latin American Cities in the Eighteenth Century: A Sketch," paper presented at the 43rd Congress of Americanists, Vancouver, 1979.

15. Two excellent recent studies of city-hinterland relations are E. Van Young, Hacienda and Market in Eighteenth-Century Mexico: The Rural Economy of the Guadalajara Region, 1675-1820, Berkeley, 1981; and Linda L. Greenow, Spatial Dimensions of the Credit Market in Nueva Galicia, 1721-1820, unpublished Ph.D. dissertation, Syracuse University, 1980.

16. A good review of the problems is to be found in D. W. G. Timms, The Urban Mosaic: Towards a Theory of Residential Differentiation, Cambridge, 1971. Two useful cautions are sounded in B. S. Morgan, "Social Distance and Spatial Distance: A Research Note," Area, Vol. 6, 1974, pp. 293-297; and R. I. Woods, "Aspects of the Scale Problem in the Calculation of Segregation Indices," Tijdschrift voor Economische en Sociale Geografie, Vol. 67, 1976, pp. 169-174.

1
Population Reporting Systems: An Eighteenth-Century Paradigm of Spanish Imperial Organization

John V. Lombardi

Most historians approach colonial Spanish-American demographic materials with an interest in the number and composition of local and regional populations. We evaluate these documents in terms of their completeness and accuracy of enumeration, we compile elaborate data sets based on this material, and in the end, if our labors are rewarded, we can provide detailed descriptions and analyses of colonial populations which we hope provide insights into the conditions of life throughout the Spanish colonies. Such a sequence of research is admirable, and many important contributions to Spanish-American history have been achieved in this fashion.[1]

But as recent research has shown, these census materials can tell us more than the numbers and composition of populations. Because of their central place in Spanish imperial philosophy, these documents can be made to reveal much about the Spanish colonial self-image, about imperial priorities, about local understanding of social structure, and a host of other non-numerical topics. Although the inferences required to extract these notions may sometimes stretch the historical imagination, the exercise makes us more appreciative of the richness of these documents.[2]

DATA AND POLICY

Even though the census system of Spanish America is relatively well-known to most students of the empire, a review of its major characteristics may be helpful. By defining the term census rather loosely, we can include all those Spanish colonial reports commenting in a more or less systematic fashion on population numbers. These could include such varied sources as missionary accounts of conversions, conquerors' chronicles, baptismal and burial records, lists of merchants, passenger manifests, and the remarkable eighteenth-century annual censuses.

Other documents such as special surveys, <u>relaciones geográficas</u>, plantation accounts, and public registry documents also yield considerable demographic detail. To be sure, the demographer will find much of this data too imprecise and unsystematic to justify detailed technical analysis. But even so, the vision of America provided there is especially valuable.[3]

Because the Spanish empire was organized around highly rational principles, Spain's imperial bureaucrats never doubted the importance of abundant, unbiased data for the elaboration of colonial policy. And their preoccupation with population data was exceeded only by their obsession with financial data. This pragmatic and rationalist Spanish colonial administration operated on two levels simultaneously, supported by an information system requiring two kinds of data corresponding to the management of human resources both as aggregates and as individuals. To plan properly, colonial administrators needed to know what population aggregates could be deployed at various tasks throughout the empire. How many Indians in an <u>encomienda</u>, how many slaves in the colonial trade, how many people resettled to the mines? Similarly, Spain needed to have good data on the individuals who would direct the activities of the aggregates. Thus, the colonial planners wanted to know whether Gómez was married, whether Jiménez had descended from a conqueror, whether Mendoza had been a good viceroy, and whether Tovar had illegitimate grandparents.

To satisfy the demand for aggregate information the Crown ordered surveys, <u>relaciones geográficas</u>, and regular and irregular population counts. To satisfy the need for individual information, the parishes kept baptismal, marriage, and burial records; houselists were prepared; and especially, dossiers or <u>hojas de servicios y méritos</u> were required. This mass of documentation, of which these few examples are but a token, came from a reporting system so prolific it soon overloaded the bureaucracy's ability to assimilate. Nevertheless, in spite of the widely recognized difficulty of processing the data, Spain not only continued to require it, but Crown officials invented more sophisticated data gathering machinery as time went on.[4]

Because this preoccupation with population information so pervades Spanish colonial administration, its origins deserve some comment. Surely the careful attention to numbers and characteristics of the colonial population formed part of the fundamental plan of the colony, responding to a major problem in Spanish colonial administration. Perhaps it may seem elementary, but there is no harm in reviewing the principal dilemma at the outset of Spain's American enterprise. The problem in America in the early years when the basic elements of the reporting system were established was never a lack of natural resources to exploit but the availability of human resources to do it. And because Spain could not provide this human capital, the Amerindian was quickly identified as America's strategic resource. Without Indian labor all the wealth of Potosí and Mexico would have been wasted, locked in the ground awaiting the advent of a technology capable of extraction without a large number of human workers. The principal controversy of the early colonial period involved the <u>encomienda</u> and the treatment of Amerindians because the Spaniards had quickly identified Indian labor as the <u>sine qua non</u> of success in America. And of course, to deal with the controversy the imperial bureaucracy had to develop some information sources.

As often happens in such cases, the Indian problem was well on the way to solution before the bulk of the information could be generated, but the close connection between the numbers and characteristics of population and the production of wealth in America remained a constant theme of colonial administration. Both in surviving instructions and the texts of documents such as <u>relaciones geográficas</u> and special population surveys, this notion emerges. And so it is no wonder that Spain's colonial administrators pursued data on population so relentlessly.[5]

THE URBAN CONNECTION

The above topic could be examined in more depth but that is for another time and place. Instead, let us examine another dimension of the Spanish colonial information system that can be seen through the complex of demographic data included in parish books, houselists, and regular censuses. Within the carefully kept parish registers and equally painstaking houselists and censuses lies the principal Spanish notion about proper social organization. As clearly as in any other source, these documents demonstrate the central function of the urban place, the town in Spanish-American society. It is, of course, a commonplace of Spanish-American history to discuss the urban character of Spain's conquest and settlement of America. But what receives less emphasis is the continuing and pervasive nature of this urban focus. It is not just in the sixteenth-century conquest that towns proved important to the Spanish colonial mission, but right through the Hapsburg and Bourbon periods as well. Eighteenth-century colonials were as eager to register their children's baptisms, marriages, and burials and validate their urban connection as any first-generation conquistador.[6]

Through the population records of the empire emerges a vision of colonial Spanish America that sees the human

landscape through towns. Everyone had to be connected to
a town, and while one could have official residence in
one place and live in another as a visitor or transient,
the distinctions were rather well kept. Moreover, people
not connected to the town network were regarded for the
most part as vagrants, outcasts, or worse.

While this urban-centered social and political arrangement has been much studied, it is important to emphasize the significance of the population accounting
system for its maintenance. Because the token of legitimacy and propriety in Spanish-American society came in
the form of properly registered vital events, contracts,
and legal proceedings in the towns and cities, most
people wanted to be recorded in the parish books and
identified with an urban place. As a result, these documents have a consistency and completeness remarkable for
their time. To be sure, some significant, if difficult
to estimate, number of people existed outside the urban
matrix, or at least unrecorded by the parish registers.
And a fascinating study could be done by comparing court
records, parish books, and houselists for the same place
and time to determine the convergence of these sources
around individual names.[7]

SOCIAL NORMS AND RESIDENTIAL PATTERNS

In evaluating the social context of the population
records, the houselist or _matrícula_ provides considerable
insight. Not only do these remarkably complete inventories of families and individuals permit the location of
people on the town map, they indicate how the clerical
bureaucracy viewed the social composition of households.
While it is not clear how representative this priestly
view of household arrangements might have been, there is
enough consistency among differing list-makers to indicate the presence of a set of norms. For example, the
lists show us households in which every effort is made to
identify a head of household, to place the remaining members of the household in descending order by age and
status and to preserve in the list the subordinate family
organization of slaves, servants, and other dependent individuals.

The houselists are only now beginning to be analyzed,
and the preliminary results so far have been very promising. Although there is still much to be done in this
regard, a paradigm of Spanish-American social and residential structure can be constructed on the evidence contained in these documents plus the data available in the
regularized census reports of the last quarter of the
eighteenth century.[8]

The first principle of this norm of social organization has already been mentioned, the people of the empire should be identified in the first instance through their connections to urban places. This principle permitted the subsequent development of the rest of the norm, for it attempted to guarantee that individuals could be traced and their activities verified through the document trail left in the urban network, thereby increasing the efficiency of scarce colonial managers. From what we can tell from the research completed to date, Spanish Americans moved about the empire frequently. While every town and village had a core of persisting residents, substantial numbers of individuals changed their residence or simply travelled from place to place within the empire. Given the importance of human resources in this imperial design, the urban, parish-based population recording system existed to provide reference points for the identification and location of highly mobile individuals.

Equally obvious, the careful attention paid to the recording of baptisms, marriages, and burials testifies to the social, political, and economic significance of such documents. Were Spanish America a stable, sedentary society with long traditions of land holding and minimal social mobility, these records might not be quite as interesting. But because the Spanish empire was so large, so new, so changeable, and because one generation's landowner and tenants could well be different from the next generation's, the parish books took on increased importance as the touchstones of stability in an everchanging social and economic environment. Furthermore, the combination of short life spans, long communication times, and extended geographic space encouraged even the most unprepossessing members of society to participate in the parish registry system, thereby guaranteeing the greatest possible sense of permanence and continuity within the Spanish world.

From this principle of primal location of vital events in the parish register we can look to the houselists for a more sophisticated vision of the aggregate society of Spanish America. This urban place where Spaniards ought to be located was ideally organized into a clearly defined and delimited space complete with boundaries, jurisdictions, and activities also located and specified according to plan. The Spanish norm in America did not conceive of the city as an environment in which the growth of commerce, industry, and services would define the characteristics of urban space. Instead, this space was to be organized and, in effect, filled with the proper activities. The houselists can be thought of as individualized representations of this ordered sense of the urban landscape. And it is this normative uniformity that permits us to reconstruct the towns and cities, identify the neighborhoods, chart the ethnic arrangements, and calculate household composition, as well as compare these characteristics over time. Other evidence, of course, validates this notion, especially the records of the <u>ayuntamientos</u> where the day-to-day maintenance and administration of the urban norms were carried out.[9]

The houselists also tell us something about the ideal internal arrangements of households. The list-makers expected to find an individual who could be identified as the household head, and except for a few cases they were able to find such a person. Contrary to much popular wisdom about Spanish-American society, there was apparently not much reluctance to identify women as household heads, even where there was a husband present. The rest of the household, according to the norm, appeared to be defined in reference to the household head, not in reference to some standard applicable uniformly across the city. That is, the status of an <u>agregado</u> or servant in one household cannot be construed as lower in socio-economic terms to the status of household head in another residence. For the purpose of the houselists, each household was a social microcosm, a self-contained unit with its own hierarchy and set of relationships not easily compared to those existing outside.

This internal hierarchy is not easy to categorize, for the internal evidence in the household does not seem sufficient to support an unequivocal hypothesis. But for the sake of the argument we can propose a tentative paradigm. These Spanish-American houselists show us a residential unit composed of at least a primary unit and frequently one or more secondary units. The primary unit always included the head of household and was structured to show the relationship of the primary unit's individuals to the head: such as son of, daughter of, wife of, etc. Secondary units were more complex, for a household could have individuals or families as secondary units. Clearly, the norm provided that a family group (husband and wife with or without children) not including the head of household appeared as a secondary unit. Servants also appeared as secondary units, as did slaves. Some people listed in the household had ambiguous status, such as unmarried adults not part of a family unit but nevertheless residing in the household and presumably under the nominal authority of the household head. These individuals could have been single relatives of the household head or of other household members, retainers, or other hangers-on.

These arrangements often became rather complex, but the general principle of organization seems fairly stable. Furthermore, these documents emphasize the hierarchical structure of households, with household head in charge. The primary unit had the highest status, the unmarried slaves the lowest status. The lists carefully arranged the rest of the household in descending order of status by unit and within units: for example, father, mother, older sibling, younger sibling.

Because this is the norm to which the list-makers tried to fit reality, the actual houselists show many exceptions and anomalies, but not enough to seriously compromise the norm. Of course, these documents give little indication of how the households actually managed their affairs. Nevertheless, the consistency and care with which these documents were prepared indicates an effort to apply the norm and a sense that the exercise was important. Especially noteworthy, as has been mentioned before, these lists place careful emphasis on location on the urban map. List-makers followed the same route year after year and took particular notice of empty or abandoned or ruined houses. Such concern indicates the close connection between the notion of personal identity as expressed in the named lists and the identity of place as demonstrated by the parish priests' concern that each house appear in its proper place along the street and that the structures without people also be included so that the urban space described by the houselist be an accurate representation.

RACE, MARRIAGE, AND AGE

Three other characteristics of the population concerned the data collectors of the Spanish empire: race, marriage, and age. These three, of special interest to modern demographers and social historians, give the most difficulty in attempting to apply modern demographic and statistical techniques because the categories themselves seem to have variable meanings and the consistency of reporting leaves much to be desired. But even so, this technical weakness in the data can be helpful in the analysis of social phenomena.

Most population material for the Spanish colonial system includes data on race. And there has been considerable work done on the legal implications and the folklore of racial categorizations in Spanish America. From the earliest days of conquest and settlement, race and the status of racial categories proved to be topics of primary interest to settlers, lawyers, clerics, and social theorists. The earliest classification systems identified the three primary types: white, Indian, and black. These designations helped Spain transpose the peninsular preoccupation with racial-social plurality (Christian, Jew, Moor) into a new key for the new world. And part of the durability of the racial classification can be traced to its theoretical neatness.

Whites (read Christian Spaniards) from the dominant caste functioned as governors and managers of the production of wealth. Indians, that charmingly simplistic consolidation of a wide range of cultural levels, existed to receive the faith and produce the wealth. Blacks, those aliens brought from outside the Spanish sphere, carried a special legal status and lived forever with the color that marked their origin.

Given these simple definitions of the caste society, it proved easy enough to invent tripartite legislation providing for the functions, responsibilities, and rights of the individuals within each group. But the population materials collected over the years of the empire clearly indicate the impracticality of this system. While other sources also show this, especially litigation over the application of racial labels, they have the difficulty that they are almost always particularistic or polemical or both. The population records, however, tend to be broad-gauged efforts by more or less disinterested clerics to apply the ideal types to reality. And the priests' discomfort with the labels is manifest. Whether we see the problem in the parish books where one son of a marriage is classified <u>pardo</u> and the next one <u>negro</u> or where an individual is baptised as pardo and married as white, the sense of inconformity between the ideal and real is palpable. Similarly, if we read the official interpretations of words like pardo and negro we might believe that those classified as negro were simply darker versions of those classified as pardo. But the population records for some regions show too few negros for this to have been so and suggest the hypothesis that in practice, in at least one corner of the empire, negro may have come to mean an ex-slave rather than a darker-than-pardo. Or perhaps the hypothesis itself is too simple, perhaps negros were labelled on the basis of color and distance from slavery. Or perhaps the category was required on the form and the census-taker filled in the blank space relatively arbitrarily.

Some census districts make distinctions between <u>indios</u> and <u>mestizos</u>, some find that subtlety unnecessary. And here too, this disparity, this deviance from colonial uniformity should lead us to continue our reexamination of the empire's practice of racial and social labelling.[10]

The census documents also confirm the difficulty Spanish clerics had with collecting information on marriage. Because marriage only included church-sanctioned unions, the data gatherers were precluded from recording data on consensual unions, although other sources clearly show the widespread existence of such living arrangements. Obviously this informal marriage pattern, of great significance for the analysis of Spanish-American social organization and function cannot be approached through the population data. What is not clear, however, is whether the houselists, with their careful breakdown of living units, list common-law couples as independent singles within the household. A comparison of the sources might yield this useful information. But in any case, it should be evident that as complete records of biological unions and pairing customs, the bulk of population records do not serve.[11]

Finally, there is the demographically critical question of age. Whether looking at those few houselists that include age or the censuses with age-based categories, the Spanish conception of age as a crucial social variable emerges rather clearly. Age apparently had significance only at certain transitional points in an individual's life history. At least insofar as systematic reporting was concerned, Spanish officials thought it important to distinguish the population under and over age seven, the supposed age of reason. And in many surveys there was an understandable interest in the fifteen-year milestone as the age eligible to begin bearing arms in defense of the realm. While there is evidence that bureaucrats in Spain saw some utility in age-based data, the record of collecting such information is poor indeed. Where such data exists, they tend to be unreliable, unbelievable, partial, or some similar combination, rendering the information unusable for most demographic purposes.

But for the student of social paradigms, these incomplete records can be fascinating for they reflect both the individual's perception of his own age and the census-taker's evaluation. Analysis might reveal what ages were _good_ ages and which ones undesirable. And this, in turn, could provide insight into the Spanish colonial perception of youth, maturity, and aging.[12]

DATA, INFORMATION, POLICY

Throughout this discussion Spanish colonial population data has been discussed as if they were designed, collected, and used with a modern preoccupation with demographic techniques. But of course that was not so. Parish registers, houselists, and censuses formed a part of Spain's information system, and as happened with other parts of the imperial design, the population data served individuals and permitted society to insist on its concern with origin and lineage. It is only in retrospect that these materials are being made to yield important demographic information.

The houselists carry the notion of location one step forward by displaying in one place an ordered set of names that form an analogue to the distribution and arrangement of the population. These lists, because they were compiled in a systematic and regular pattern, approximate the procedures of a modern census, but because there was so much attention to social and residential hierarchy instead of age the demographic value of the records is limited. The final step in this evolution brought the aggregate censuses of the last quarter of the eighteenth century. These materials, while clearly and explicitly designed to yield demographic data in a useable way, drew their materials from the same sources using similar procedures as earlier efforts, and the results share some of the same defects. One of the key difficulties in these Spanish imperial population accounting efforts can be traced to the traditional unwillingness of the Spanish bureaucracy to create single-purpose officials, bureaus, or offices. The peculiarly holistic philosophy of government employed by Spain in America provided little comfort for self-contained bureaucratic domains. Not only were officials given multiple functions and responsibilities, but their domains tended to overlap. The benefits of such a system in terms of control and cost, as well as the disadvantages in terms of efficiency and responsiveness, have been extensively studied elsewhere. But from our narrow interest in extracting quality demographic indices from the population materials, the confusion of purposes and goals evident in the records inhibits their usefulness.

This exploration of the context that produced Spanish-American colonial population records could be extended much further, but I would prefer to close with two observations. With the exception of the parish registers, most of the systematic population accounting information was apparently never used for policy purposes. Although there is some indication that gross totals and racial percentages became part of the bureaucratic information pool, the detailed houselists and regular censuses of the eighteenth century languished unexploited until today. The problem, of course, was not that Spanish officials lacked the ability to add, but that the information processing capabilities of the system proved inadequate to cope with the volume and complexity of the population data.[13]

And it is this mismatch between the theory and philosophy of government on one side and the bureaucracy's skills to implement it on the other that symbolizes the decline and collapse of the Spanish empire. Spain's inability to develop a management system equal to the size and complexity of the empire is clearly visible in the history of the colonial population reporting program and can stand as a paradigm of the general failure of Spanish bureaucracy and public management in the late-eighteenth and early-nineteenth centuries.

NOTES

1. For an outstanding review of the recent literature on population and geography with special attention to social and spatial themes see David J. Robinson, "Introduction to Themes and Scales," in Robinson (ed.), Social Fabric and Spatial Structure in Colonial Latin America (Ann Arbor, 1979), pp. 1-24.

2. The collection of essays cited above provides a comprehensive sample of the growing sophistication of research on the social, demographic, and spatial dimensions of Latin American colonial populations. In contrast to other fields of Latin American history, the high quality of monographic work on these themes has led to relatively few overall analyses of the Spanish American or Brazilian social condition. This may be the result of the growing awareness of the complexity and variability of social and demographic conditions throughout the continent. Ironically, while there is considerable variation displayed in the details of microcosmic Latin American conditions, recent research as summarized in Robinson, Social Fabric, tends to support the view that the Latin American phenomenon, including Brazil, is as we expected all along cut from the same cloth according to a remarkably standard pattern.

3. Of course, the standard survey of Spanish American population is Nicolas Sánchez Albornoz, The Population of Latin America: A History (Berkeley, 1974).

4. For a survey of these data types see John V. Lombardi, People and Places in Colonial Venezuela (Bloomington, 1976); and Woodrow W. Borah, "The Historical Demography of Latin America: Sources, Techniques, Controversies, and Yields," in Paul Deprez (ed.), Population and Economics (Winnepeg, 1970).

5. Numerous sources reflect this preoccupation and many scholars have looked at the Indian question. See for an example of recent work on the item by Juan A. Villamarín and Judith E. Villamarín, "Chibcha Settlement under Spanish Rule, 1537-1810," in Robinson (ed.), Social Fabric. The classic controversy over the black legend and the treatment of the Indians exemplified by the works of Lewis Hanke provide a nonquantitative ideological focus on the same imperial complex. For a survey of the demographic interpretations on this subject see William Denevan (ed.), The Native Population of the Americas in 1492 (Madison, 1976).

6. The flowering of Latin American demographic studies in the last decade has produced an extraordinarily rich harvest of specialized studies emphasizing sophisticated techniques. The registry and household data, once relatively neglected, is now being carefully analyzed for insights on social, spatial, and demographic themes. While no comprehensive listing of this literature is possible here, a few examples will indicate the quality of the genre. See especially Stephanie B. Blank, "Patrons, Clients, and Kin in Seventeenth Century Caracas," Hispanic American Historical Review, Vol. 54 (1974), pp. 260-283; Kathy W. Waldron, A Social History of a Primate City: The Case of Caracas, 1750-1810 (Ph.D. dissertation, Indiana University, 1977); Michael M. Swann, "The Spatial Dimensions of a Social Process: Marriage and Mobility in Late Colonial Northern Mexico," in Robinson (ed.), Social Fabric. Also see Elizabeth Anne

Kuznesof, "Clans, the Militia and Territorial Government: The Articulation of Kinship with Polity in Eighteenth-Century São Paulo," and Lyman L. Johnson and Susan Migden Socolow, "Population and Space in Eighteenth-Century Buenos Aires," both from Robinson (ed.), <u>Social Fabric</u>.

7. Because of its methodological difficulty, nominal record linkage between such sources is relatively rare in Spanish-American studies. But some scholars have had success with the technique, although not for precisely the purpose mentioned here. See, for example, the Blank, "Patrons and Clients," and Swann, "The Spatial Dimensions," cited above for their discussion of sources and problems.

8. The Joint Syracuse-Oxford Population Project managed by David J. Robinson is the most ambitious and interesting effort to collect and process the late eighteenth-century houselists and associated documents. That effort has already produced a number of significant studies, some of which are reflected in Robinson (ed.), <u>Social Fabric</u>. See also Kathy Waldron, <u>A Social History</u>.

9. While the Spanish American houselists for various areas of the empire display some obvious differences in compilation techniques, these do not appear to be sufficient evidence of any different conception of what the function of household and urban space should be. Most of this discussion is based on a close examination of the houselists for the Bishopric of Caracas (Archivo Arquidiocesano de Caracas) and a comparison of these documents with the results of the new work currently appearing on other areas of Latin America as cited above.

10. The literature on race and class in Latin America is vast. Some of it focuses on the intellectual perception of racial terminology and the preoccupation with complex mixtures and picturesque nomenclature, especially in the Mexican case. See the classic survey by Magnus Mörner, <u>Race Mixture in the History of Latin America</u> (Boston, 1967). Also very helpful is Swann, "Spatial Dimensions." Other more quantitative studies attempt to analyze the composition and changes in the characteristics of aggregates bearing explicitly racial labels. See Lombardi, <u>People and Places</u>. But all of these works have to deal with the extreme difficulty of knowing what the real life referents for racial designations might have been and whether over any extended period of time these referents were stable. The very complexity of the naming system by the eighteenth century and the wide variations in usage throughout the empire make the utility of many racial categories for comparative purposes less than overwhelming. Slave, of course, being a legally recorded condition, was a much more consistently defined category than, for example, pardo or mestizo. For a discussion of the difficulties in using the category slave for analytical purposes see Lombardi, "Comparative Slave Systems in the Americas: A Critical Review," in Richard Graham and Peter H. Smith (eds.), <u>New Approaches to Latin American History</u> (Austin, 1974).

11. Much very sophisticated demographic work has been done on marriage and the results have given us exceptionally useful insights into Spanish American social and family structure. The technical competence and historical value of these studies should not obscure

their inability to reach a significant portion of the male-female pairs whose lives were married in everything except the parish books. The best of these studies demonstrate an awareness of this difficulty as in Swann, "Spatial Dimensions."

12. Most students of colonial Spanish American populations have treated age-data with great circumspection. Not only do most scholars think detailed age reporting mostly unreliable, but few colonial documents provide really useful data except in isolated cases covering small geographic areas. Furthermore, the best age information, painstakingly derived from the vital events recorded in the parish registers, has only just begun to be evaluated. While it is quite possible to get reliable age profiles for segments of the upper half of the social strata from such sources, estimates for the lower half tend to be rather approximate at best. There is some consensus that the south model life tables are in some cases a fair representation of Spanish colonial reality, but most scholars who use them surround their calculations with such tentative qualifiers that the exercise is mostly proforma. See for example Lombardi, People and Places. Critical demographic indices for infant mortality and the like are almost impossible to come by except for very small selections of the elite.

13. Studies of Spain's imperial bureaucracy abound, and their analyses have shown the incredible complexity of this system as well as emphasizing the inability, in case after case, of the government bureaucracy to manage its information flow. The classic introduction to Spanish American government is Charles Gibson, Spain in America (New York, 1964).

2
Census Enumeration in Late Seventeenth-Century Alto Perú: The Numeración General of 1683–1684

Brian M. Evans

The count of all the Indian population of Alto Perú held in 1683/84 under the auspices of Viceroy La Palata offers the demographic historian a rich mine of information. Yet, with the exception of the works of Sánchez-Albornoz,[1] the materials have been little used or researched, and very many basic questions concerning this "Numeración General" remain unanswered. For example, although there is clear evidence that the census was held in all the provinces of the Viceroyalty of Peru, from Quito to the confines of Tucumán, and while supposedly five copies were made of the returns,[2] those so far discovered cover only part of Alto Perú and are today to be found in Buenos Aires.[3] These surviving returns are in a varied state of preservation, do not follow any fixed format, and are of uneven quality. The most detailed of them cover the provinces of Larecaja, La Paz, Sicasica, and Pacajes (for locations see Figure 2.1). Those for Paria and Carangas are difficult to use because of their extremely bad state of preservation. The returns for Cochabamba, Porco and Chayanta are well preserved but provide in general less detail, while those for Yamparaes, Omasuyu, Chichas, and Tarija are of only limited use for demographic purposes, because of the generalized and unsystematic way in which they were compiled.

The aims of this paper are to give a brief account of the reasons for holding the census, an outline of the ways in which it was organized and carried out, and of the controversies which followed. The paper also presents some preliminary generalizations on the demographic value of the returns, and finally discusses some possible lines of future research.

The original reason for the count was the continuous and drastic fall throughout the seventeenth century in the number of <u>repartimiento</u> Indians available for the <u>mita</u> in the silver mines at Potosí. As originally established by the Viceroy Don Francisco de Toledo in the 1570s, all tributary Indian males from sixteen provinces

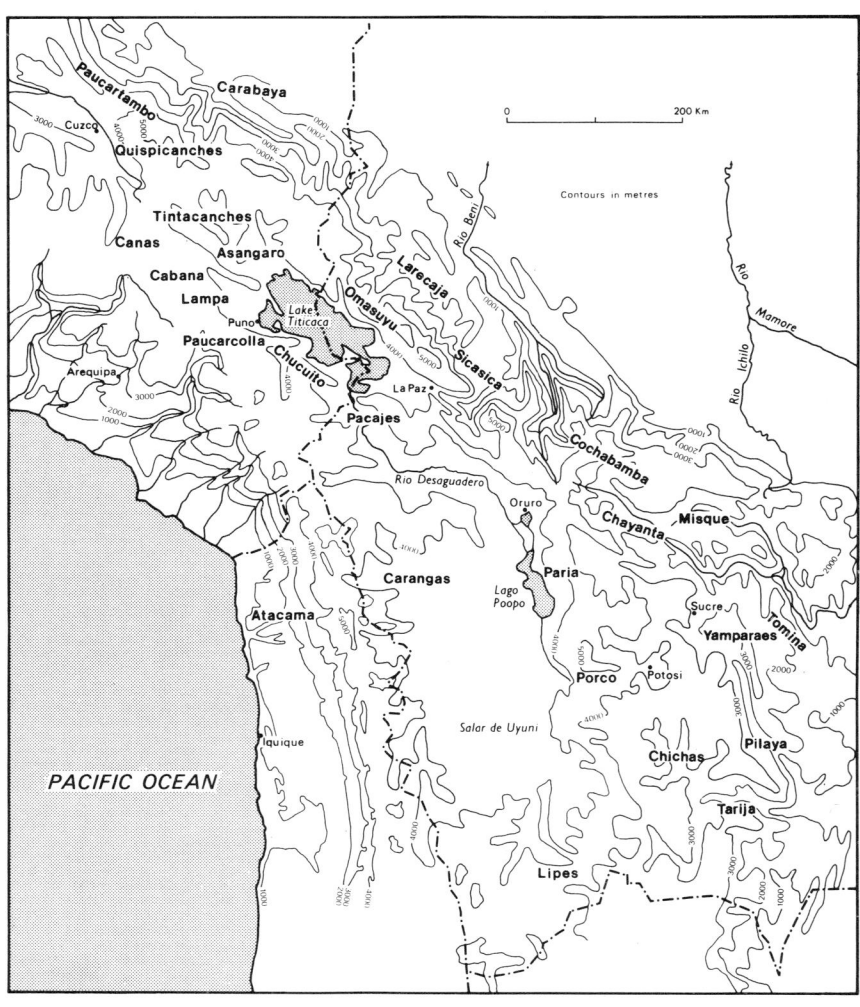

Figure 2.1 Location of Seventeenth-Century Provinces in Upper Peru

or corregimientos were liable to the mita. The "affected provinces" were (1) Quispicanches, (2) Tintacanches, (3) Canas, (4) Cabana y Cabanilla, (5) Asangaro y Asillo, (6) Paucarcolla, (7) Chucuito, (8) Pacajes, (9) Omasuyu, (10) Sicasica, (11) Paria, (12) Carangas, (13) Cochabamba, (14) Chayanta, (15) Porco, and (16) Tarija. In theory in any year one seventh of all tributaries were to be drafted to Potosí, and once there, a third of the group were to present themselves each Monday for their week in the mines, after which they were allowed two weeks for recovery. Until the 1630s the weekly total available fluctuated at around 4,000.

The Indians, with ample justification, regarded the mita with fear and horror. Many died during their terms of labor, others remained in Potosí as mingas or voluntary labor, while still more abandoned their native villages and lands, (and frequently also their wives and children), and fled to those provinces not liable to the mita, there to try and establish themselves as newcomers or forasteros. As such they often ended up as squatters or peones on Spanish owned haciendas.

This process of course, merely served still further to increase the mita burden on the remaining population, who, despite all, had stayed tied to their villages and ayllus of origin. By the middle of the seventeenth century, there were constant complaints that this originario population, had so decreased that tributaries were being forced to mita, not every seventh year, but every fifth, or even third; thus of course causing a still steeper deterioration. By 1660 the weekly total of available laborers had fallen to below 2,000.[4]

Endless contradictory debates and commissions ensued over the next twenty years concerning the correct solutions to be sought; debates which are in themselves an excellent illustration of the paralysis of late Hapsburg colonial policy.[5] Fundamental was the absolute contradiction between the need to maximize silver output and the need to "protect" the Indians. While there was no agreement as to whether the total Indian population was decreasing, there was agreement that (a) many Indians had apparently fled to provinces free of mita, and (b) even within the sixteen provinces many Indians had won exemption through becoming personal servants to Spaniards (yanaconas), or by seeking work on Spanish owned or occupied lands, where they were protected from the draft (yanaconas de chacras). Therefore if any new general census were to be held--and none had been attempted since the Toledo's "Repartimiento General" a century earlier-- it would have to take these changed circumstances into consideration.

By 1680, Madrid had made up its mind, and decided to hold a general census not only of the sixteen affected provinces but of fourteen other provinces which had

hitherto been free of obligation. These comprised
(1) Cuzco (city), (2) Paucartambo, (3) Carabaya,
(4) Condesuyo de Arequipa, (5) Larecaja, (6) La Paz
(city), (7) Atacama, (8) Mizque, (9) Lipes, (10) Tomina,
(11) Oruro, (12) Pilaya y Paspaya, (13) Yamparaes de
Chuquisaca, (14) Potosí (city). The new viceroy designate, Don Melchor de Navarre y Rocafull, Duque de la
Palata, was charged with making this census one of the
main tasks of his administration.[6] The Duke was a forceful character.[7] Almost immediately upon his arrival in
Lima in November 1681, he set the wheels in motion, and
decided after consultations that the census should be
held not merely in the thirty provinces named, but
throughout the Viceroyalty "en todo el reyno desde Quito
hasta Tucumán."[8]

The line of reasoning behind this momentous decision
seems to have been that most of the problems concerning
Indian tribute throughout the Viceroyalty--and not merely
the issue of the Potosí mita--could be explained by the
fact that there had not been a full demographic survey
since Toledo, despite the common knowledge that in the
meantime there had occurred both depopulation and much
internal migration.[9]

Even at this stage arguments and controversy continued as to the necessity, feasibility and even possibility of holding a census of such magnitude. By and
large La Palata's advisors, experienced, as he was not,
in the complexities of Peruvian administration, were far
less sanguine as to the worth of this project than was
the Viceroy.[10]

However, arrangements for the "Numeración General"
proceeded steadily, and in general terms it was agreed
that the count should be organized along lines suggested
by an earlier commission which had reported in 1679, and
had been summarized by Dr. Francisco de Valera in a
Propuesta, copies of which had been dispatched to Spain,
where they had been discussed by La Palata and the Council of the Indies before the Viceroy had departed for
Lima.[11]

By early 1683 the preparations had been completed.
On April 7 the Viceroy sent a letter to all the Bishops
ordering the local priests (curas) to make a list of all
parishioners, men, women, children, originarios, and
forasteros, so that every parish would have an up-to-date
total to remit to the Corregidores. This was followed on
July 24th by a printed proclamation bearing the title
"Instrucción que han de guardar los Corregidores en la
Numeración General que se ha de hazer de los Indios, cada
uno en su jurisdicción."[12]

The content and form of these instructions merit
careful attention, since, had they been fully and conscientiously followed, the Numeración General would have essentially been a comprehensive census of modern type.

The fact that the instructions were frequently misunderstood or ignored however was to be at the root of the criticisms which were to be heaped on the census and which eventually led to the annulment in 1692 of its financial and tributary provisions by Viceroy Monclova, La Palata's successor in office.

It must be admitted that the instructions are verbose, repetitive, over detailed and ambiguous. However, they clearly required that:

1. Everybody was to be enumerated on one chosen day (set as 1st October 1683).
2. All Indians, and not just tributary males, were to be listed with the following information: (a) name, (b) age, (c) civil status, and (d) place of origin, if different from the place of residence on the day of registration.
3. The local lists were to be those compiled by the priests and caciques with the assistance of parochial records of baptisms and funerals.

The prime purpose of the census was stated as the need to count people where they actually resided in order to force the forasteros to assume equal burdens with the originarios. Yet the format recommended almost guaranteed some of the problems which it specifically desired to avoid. Thus, over half of the instructions devote themselves to complex and contradictory statements on just how and where the various types of non-tributary Indians should be listed. The originario population was to be registered by ayllu. But by the 1680s the ayllu system had severely decayed. Population losses had caused many to become extinct; in other cases several small ayllus had merged to form a new unit, whereas in other cases the survivors of small ayllus had joined pre-existing structures. Most important of all, the majority of forasteros and yanaconas no longer remembered or recognized their original ayllu affiliations. The instructions made elaborate provisions for the enumeration of such classes as (a) absentees whose return home was expected, (b) absentees whose whereabouts was known but who were not expected to return, (c) forasteros who still recognized their native pueblos and paid tribute there. These classes were to be registered in their place of origin. Clearly, however, this risked some double counting especially of classes (b) and (c) who might also be counted in their place of actual residence.

The provisions for enumerating the forastero population who no longer paid tribute in their native pueblos, were still more complex. If this group had places of origin within the same province as their actual residence they were to be counted as members of their native villages. This again led to double-counting, since they were frequently also listed in their new locations. If they had moved into other provinces, forasteros who did not wish to return home were to be counted "in situ." Most forasteros, of course, had fled their native villages years, or indeed generations previously, and some no longer knew what their home provinces had been, let alone had any desire to return to them. In addition the forasteros were to be distinguished from such legal classes as <u>yanaconas</u> and <u>mitimaes</u> who were to be counted separately. Originally these two latter groups had been reasonably easy to define, but by the 1680s many forasteros had sought yanacona status in order to avoid tribute. Hence many individuals were registered twice, first as forasteros and separately as yanaconas. If this were not sufficiently confusing, the instructions proposed a distinction between "yanaconas del Rey," and "yanaconas de estancias, de chacras, y de obrajes." Just how the corregidores should make these distinctions was not made clear. If possible all yanaconas too, were to be investigated as to place of origin, the length of time they had been living in their present location, and their claims to be regarded as yanaconas.

Now to have expected the machinery and personnel available to have provided such a mass of detail over so vast an area was a forlorn hope.

The Instructions themselves were subsumed under no less than thirty headings, and called for the returns for each province to be arranged in eight books (<u>cuadernos</u>). In theory they were to be arranged as follows, and contain the following information.

Book 1. Originarios actually present in their pueblos on the day of registration. Men, women, and children were to be arranged by ayllu and family. This book was also to include those temporarily absent for specific reasons and whose prompt return was expected.

Book 2. Originarios absent on day of registration and whose imminent return was not expected, but whose whereabouts was known. They were to be arranged with their families by ayllu. If possible the date and reasons for their departure were to be provided.

Book 3. Originarios who were absent, and whose whereabouts were not known. These too were to be listed by family and ayllu. In some cases, however, the tributaries in this class had fled without their families, while in other cases the whole family had disappeared.

Book 4. Forasteros who "recognized" their pueblos of origin. This book, as has been suggested seems to have given the enumerators their biggest problems. Quite apart from the problems of whether forasteros still recognized or even knew their places of origin, it is obvious that the local authorities had grave problems with this class in obtaining ages and details of family.

Book 5. Yanaconas del Rey. In general the

corregidores seem to have regarded this class as an amalgam of various classes of Indians who had become detached from pueblo and ayllu, and who were indeed in many cases little more than vagabonds. It was the intention to reduce them to a permanent location and status by attaching them to ayllus in those pueblos where they were resident in 1683. This frequently proved impossible.

Book 6. This was to include mitimaes, who after being enumerated were to be added to the appropriate 'padron" and ayllus in their provinces of origin. In theory, this count was to be checked against Book #2. In fact, it proved impossible since most of the mitimae settlements dated back to Inca times and memories by the 1680s were blurred.

Book 7. Yanaconas de estancias, de chacras, y de obrajes. An examination of the actual census returns suggests that to most corregidores this group consisted essentially of forasteros who no longer knew their places of origin and who were therefore quite "irreducible," but who had--unlike the yanaconas del Rey--a specific function. They worked directly for Spaniards or Criollos, on the rapidly developing privately owned haciendas, which, as the seventeenth century advanced had taken over, by one means or another, much Indian land.[13] The yanaconas in general were the source of much anxiety as by one means or another, they had frequently escaped paying tribute altogether--in which they were often aided and abetted by the landowners for whom they worked. The census returns indicate that in Alto Perú, the corregidores frequently had trouble distinguishing yanaconas from forasteros, and that again it was difficult to obtain accurate information on family ties and structure.

Book 8. The last book was to be reserved for the "Yanaconas de iglesias, conventos y comunidades." At first sight this might have appeared as being a straightforward group, but the instructions go on to warn that all these yanaconas claim to be "del Rey." However, they were to be separated from those listed in Book 5, as an accurate check was required of the real needs of the churches and communities. Clearly there was a suspicion that many of the yanaconas de iglesias were surplus to the actual requirement.

So much for the actual instructions. As to the way in which they were actually carried out we have two sources of information. The first is clearly the surviving returns themselves; the other is the correspondence which ensued between the corregidores, and the other officials involved, in Lima, and Spain, as to the progress and accuracy of the undertaking. Let us now examine this second line of evidence.

Presumably the Instructions of 24 July 1683 did not reach many of the corregidores until September. If then they had questions or doubts about the exact procedures

they were instructed to follow, they would not have time
to correspond with Lima before the census date which had,
as we have seen, been set for 1 October 1683. We do not
in fact know how general a count was made on that date,
for there is a peculiar gap in all documents and correspondence relating to the progress of the "Numeración General" until 1685. When the record commences, there is
already a marked dichotomy: on the one hand defending the
progress of the census; whilst on the other hand is a
mounting chorus of doubt, disillusion and dissent. From
all of this one point very clearly emerges; the operation, so to speak, had not "gone to plan" and many--
indeed perhaps most--corregidores had either failed to
follow the "instrucciones" altogether, or had interpreted
them in widely different ways.

First, let us examine the record from the Viceroy's
standpoint. On 10 June 1685 the latter wrote to Spain[14]
announcing that the enumeration was now completed in all
provinces except for some areas especially around Quito.
He added that he had placed extra officials on the work
of examining and ordering the lists (padrones), because
otherwise the work would take years to complete for all
83 provinces.

The year following, on 6 April 1686, La Palata wrote
to the King informing him of the progress of the enumeration and its problems. He claimed that few of the difficulties people had forecasted had actually arisen. He
estimated that the total cost would be in excess of five
thousand pesos, and as a sample, enclosed a list (padrón),
of part of the province of Vilcashuaman which had cost
160 pesos.[15] This particular return is of some interest.
It had been completed on 23 October 1684, and seems to be
the only actual census return which has survived in
Seville. It is quite different in form to the volumes in
Buenos Aires, and is limited to male tributaries only.
Then on 11 October 1687 the Viceroy wrote[16] that the work
had run into no insuperable difficulties, and that the
cost would not be excessive, although he admitted the
work was uneven, yet it was better than one might have
expected:

> esta se ha hecho a muy poco costa, y aunque no se a hecho
> con entera fidelidad, porque no han sido de igual satisfacción ni inteligencia las manos por donde ha pasado que son
> los corregidores, todavía a quedado en mayor estado de lo
> que nunca se pudo esperar.

Lastly, in the file of letters between Viceroy and
Spain on the enumeration is one dated 18 February 1689
praising the work of Don Joseph de Villegas, and Don
Antonio del Castillo "contadores de retasas," for the
census, and asking royal favors for them.[17]

To the very end La Palata defended both his record

and the enumeration. In his "Relación" of 16 August 1689, although admitting that the census finally took six years to complete, rather than the one year initially anticipated (sections #845, 846 & 847), he went on to justify his actions, and his decisions about the work at some length.[18]

Long before he left office, however, it was apparent that the enumeration was giving rise to the most serious problems; problems indeed which were eventually to cause Palata's successor--Viceroy Monclova--to abandon the new taxes and tribute totals which had been based on the 1683 count.

The first major rumbling of discontent emerged in June 1685. On the 12th of that month, Joseph de Villegas drew up a lengthy report (Papel de dudas) of doubts and difficulties which he saw with the enumeration and its progress.[19] As the official concerned was in command at Lima and specifically charged with the collation of the work, none could have been in a better position to make an accurate evaluation.

His report contained eight general points, most of which were individually serious. In order they are:

1. Especially in Upper Peru (las provincias de arriba), there had been innumerable, complex and confusing changes in the names and boundaries of pueblos, and in settlement patterns generally.

2. Despite all attempts at standardization of format, the corregidores had not observed the procedures set forth in the "Instrucciones" of 24 July 1683. Each had gone his own way; the results were very difficult to compare and collate. Few had consulted the parochial books of baptisms and burials.

3. Especially dubious were the statistics in regard to sex and ages. Many corregidores had just given summary statements on the number of women and children, and this was not sufficient to judge whether the population was increasing or decreasing, and for what reasons.

4. Other major problem areas concerned the lists of those absent, and the lower and upper age groups on the lists of tributaries. This was because the lists had not been updated between visitations, and the caciques had been anxious to maximize the number of tributaries. The Indians he states frequently lie about their ages. He quotes examples where fathers aged 20 have sons aged eight or ten.

5. The changes in population numbers and distribution over the last century meant that the relationships between the number of Indians and the size of the doctrina were now much out of line.

6. Regulation #18 of the "Instrucciones" which required that all foresteros should be asked for their home provinces and ayllus had been generally ignored. Usually only the native provinces had been given and this was

insufficient. It had proved impossible to check the list of forasteros in one place with the lists of absentees in their original homes.

7. In need of special attention was the task of checking the absentee lists of each province with those of the Indians residing permanently in Potosí.

8. There was no agreement between provincial, repartimiento, and ecclesiastical boundaries. Some lists used one system, some another. In addition there was a specific difficulty involving boundary problems between Paria, Cochabamba and Chayanta.

The document also details three major problems directly related to the Royal Orders which followed from the holding of the census:

1. It had proved impossible to get Indians to return to or live in their original homes.

2. Many forasteros had been forced to pay tribute twice, and there was enormous confusion over the new tribute totals in general.

3. The decision not to include Indians living in mining settlements within the classes liable for mita had given rise to much dispute.

All in all these criticisms by themselves are so serious that it is difficult to see how the Duque de la Palata could have remained so sanguine about his enterprise.

Worse, however, was to follow. Between 1685 and 1692 there were sufficient difficulties, allegations, charges and counter-charges arising from the enumeration, and more especially its tribute and financial reassessments, that the correspondence today fills three large bundles at Seville.[20]

To deal with these controversies in detail is not the prime purpose of this paper, but before evaluation of the actual returns, some discussion is in order. The major complaints may be summarized as:

1. There had been gross overcounting in the enumeration, especially of the forestero class who frequently had been counted twice or even thrice--usually in their place of origin and where they actually resided.

2. Because of the over-registration the new tribute totals were unrealistically high.

3. Most forasteros and yanaconas were grievously poor and could not meet their tribute payments.

4. Because of the two previous problems (2 and 3), Indians had fled from their homes in unprecedented numbers, thus adding to the difficulty of finding the increased tribute sums demanded. Thus the Numeración General had resulted in an exacerbation of the very problems it had been intended to solve.

The complainants were certainly able to amass a good deal of evidence to support their charges, and they included letters from most corregidores, many local clergy and caciques, through to the Archbishops of Lima, Cuzco, La Paz and Chuquisaca, and into the Real Audiencia itself. Interestingly, nearly all the complaints come from, or deal with, conditions in Alto Perú, both from the sixteen provinces originally affected by the mita, and by the fourteen to which La Palata had extended the obligation. By the end of 1689 official protests had been received from Larecaja, Pacajes, Misque, Pilaya, Tomina, Yamparaes, Porco, Paria, Carangas, Chayanta, Cochabamba, Lampa, Asángaro, Chucuito, Omasuyu, Sicasica, Paucarcolla, Canas y Tintacanches, Quispicanche, and from Potosí itself.

Even La Palata was forced to admit the justice of some of the complaints for, on 29 April 1689, in one of his last acts as Viceroy he issued a <u>consulta</u> reducing the tribute on forasteros by 50%, <u>except for</u> Cochabamba, Porco, Tarija, Tomina, Pilaya, and Sicasica, where, as forasteros were especially numerous, the reduction was to be only 25%. However, he defended the charge that the Numeración had grossly overstated numbers by claiming that "possible" overcounting in one province was matched by undercounting in others.[21]

His successor, Viceroy Monclova, had no vested interest in his predecessor's work, and no great faith in the desireability or necessity of the mita, his previous experiences in Mexico having predisposed him to the system of voluntary mine labor which had there proved successful. On 16 December 1690 he established a <u>junta</u> of seven experts to collate the complaints and investigate their seriousness.[22] This first junta held 32 meetings, and its successor set up on 19 May 1691 held a further 51, during which time they do indeed seem to have conducted quite detailed investigations, primarily however in regard to the new tribute totals, and only secondarily upon the demographic accuracy of the returns, although the junta did accept the charges of frequent double counting as having validity.

Their final decisions called for a return to the system which had preceded La Palata's reassessment. Monclova accepted their judgement and issued two proclamations which officially brought most of La Palata's innovations to an end.[23]

So the Numeración General was officially annulled, apparently discredited, and was quickly forgotten. It had cost the Real Hacienda over 15,000 pesos,[24] which at first sight appears a modest sum for so large an undertaking, but the main time, trouble and effort had of course been borne by the curas, caciques and corregidores at the local level and without special renumeration.[25]

It is my belief however that a study of the surviving returns of Alto Perú would seem to indicate that the sweeping condemnations of the Numeración General, had frequently been motivated by special pleadings, and that at least some of the provincial corregidores had made very conscientious efforts to gather as full and accurate information as possible.

The remainder of this study is therefore devoted to an examination of, and commentary upon, the surviving returns.

THE SIZE OF THE TOTAL INDIAN POPULATION OF ALTO PERU IN 1683

For the provinces of Omasuyu, Larecaja, Sicasica, Pacajes, Cochabamba, Yamparaes, Paria, Carangas, Porco, Chayanta, Tarija, and the cities of La Paz, Potosí, and Oruru, the Numeración General recorded a total of 55,946 tributaries.[26] Tributaries were defined as all liable Indian males from 18 to 50 years old. The "tributary index" (or tributaries as a percent of the total population), cannot be calculated for all provinces and pueblos, but for those where it can, it averages 23.7%. Thus one may assume that the total recorded Indian population of the above listed provinces and towns was about 236,000 or say between 220,000 and 250,000.

This clearly represented a considerable decline since the Repartimiento General of Toledo especially in the Altiplano provinces. Nor did the new census "find" the allegedly high numbers in those provinces which had been reported as having over 20,000 tributaries, and Yamparaes over 4,000.[27] However, the real totals were revealed as 7,133 and 1,415 respectively.

Indeed time after time in the legajos of complaints, there are admissions that, whatever its shortcomings, the enumeration had clearly revealed that the supposedly large numbers of Indians who had managed to avoid tribute and mita obligations, simply did not exist. Potosí had been alleged to have been harboring at least 25,000 potential tributaries, the census recorded but 5,557; Cuzco's supposed 30,000 tributaries, were in reality only 3,320.[28]

If indeed the Numeración had tended to inflate the real numbers then depopulation had been very marked not only on the Altiplano, but equally in provinces hitherto unaffected by mita obligations. Thus, the widespread belief that the depopulation of the Altiplano had been caused by flight to the Yungas, and that growth had therefore occurred in the receiving provinces, was not supported by the evidence. Direct comparison is difficult but since Toledan times the population overall had decreased at least 30%. It would seem, however, as though the bulk of the decline had occurred prior to the 1630s, since Chinchon's repartimiento in 1633 generally listed numbers of tributaries very comparable to those found by La Palata.[29]

THE DISTRIBUTION OF THE INDIAN POPULATION IN 1683

The provinces for which returns have survived fall into two basic groups in terms of natural environment (Table 2.1).

TABLE 2.1
Distribution of Altiplano and Yungas population, 1683

Provinces of the Altiplano:			Provinces of the Yungas:		
	Number of Tributaries	Percent Originario		Number of Tributaries	Percent Originario
Omasuyu	4,903	26.41	Larecaja	7,113	11.00
Pacajes	3,615	68.24	Sicasica	4,494	24.18
Paria	2,748	80.20	Cochabamba	6,466	6.18
Carangas	2,579	90.61	Yamparaes	1,415	24.94
Porco	5,775	54.85	Chayanta	7,732	63.89
			Tarija	1,325	54.11
(plus cities of: La Paz, 353; Potosí, 5,557; Oruru, 1,851)					
Total Number of Tributaries:			Total Number of Tributaries:		
	27,381	48.94%		28,565	51.06%

In the 1680s, therefore, over half of the recorded Indian population was to be found in the Yungas, a situation not very different from that recorded in the time of Toledo. However, the status of the population in the two regions was in contrast. With the exception of Omasuyu, the majority of the Altiplano population was "originario," whereas in most of the Yungas, originarios formed a minority, especially in Larecaja and Cochabamba. The first named province, it will be recalled, was not liable to mita, and neither in fact were most of the pueblos of Cochabamba, which had been freed of obligation in order to encourage agricultural production.[30] Clearly then, migration had been of major importance, even though the influx into the receiving provinces had in general not caused an actual population increase. By implication therefore, originario population losses must have been greater in the Yungas than on the Altiplano.

ORIGINS AND DESTINATIONS OF MIGRANTS

Studies were made of the following:

1. The provinces of origin of the 3,306 forasteros resident in Larecaja.
2. The provinces of origin of the 2,950 forasteros resident in Chayanta.
3. The origins of the 1,288 forasteros resident in the town of Oruro.
4. The origins of the 886 forasteros resident in Pacajes.
5. The place of residence of 575 people absent from their homes in Pacajes but whose whereabouts were known.

Of the Larecaja sample, the largest groups had originated in Omasuyu (23.2%), Chucuito (14.6%), Lampa (14.6%), Paucarcolla (12.7%) and Asángaro (11.2%) (see Figure 2.2). Between them these accounted for 76.3% of the total. Another 6.2% claimed origins in La Paz and 3.6% in Cuzco. However, individuals had also come from as far away as Lima and Quito. The bulk though were clearly from the neighboring provinces of the Altiplano.

Chayanta reveals a similar pattern although here there was less concentration and more evidence of longer distance migration. The most frequent provinces of origin were Pacajes (14.3%), Paria (14%), Carangas (12.6%), and Canas (12.5%). Other provinces which accounted for more than 5% were Lampa (8.5%), Chucuito (6.9%), and Omasuyu (6.7%).

In Oruro the majority had come from the neighboring provinces, notably from Paria (20.4%), Pacajes (17.4%), Carangas (15.6%), and Chucuito (12.1%), whilst immigrants from the Yungas were conspicuous by their infrequence.

The Pacajes samples are especially revealing, as the population of this province seems to have been unusually mobile. As we have seen, emigrants from Pacajes were very numerous in Chayanta and Oruro. They also formed one of the largest of the forastero groups in Cochabamba. Yet Pacajes paradoxically was also an area of inmigration, whose percentage of originarios (68.24%), was lower than that of most comparable Altiplano regions. Of the 886 forasteros recorded, the single largest group (22.8%), were natives of Chucuito, the second (17.6%), people who had moved within the province but who had severed ties with their native villages, and the third (15.5%), had moved from Omasuyu. Other sizable cohorts had origins in Sicasica (8.7%), La Paz (7.5%), and Larecaja (4.4%).

Of the out-migrants the major destinations were Sicasica (20.1%), Cochabamba (14.4%), Potosí (12.5%), and La Paz (6.8%). Groups of individuals had, however, moved to places as far away as Tucumán, Cuzco, and Lima.

Clearly migration was a major feature throughout Alto Perú in the late seventeenth century. All told over one third of the population recorded in the Numeración

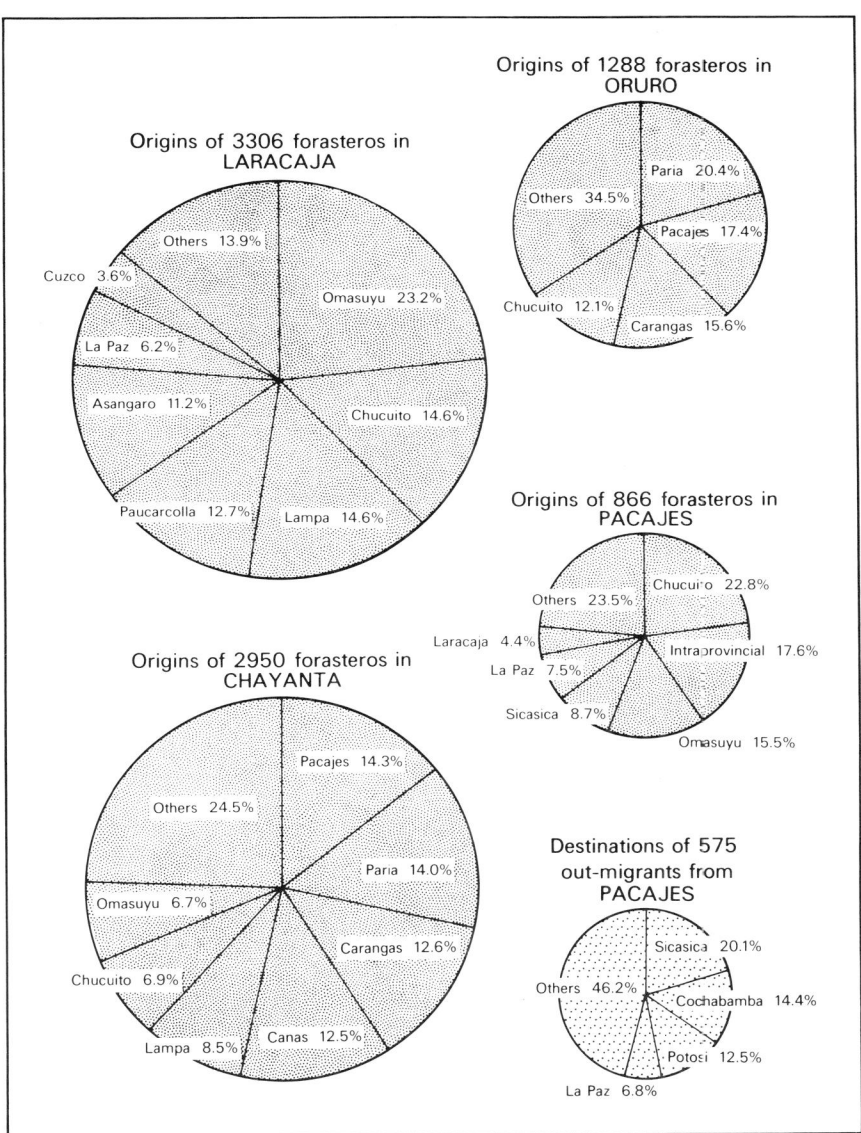

Figure 2.2 Origins and destinations of selected inter-provincial migrants, Upper Peru, 1683

were no longer living in their provinces of origin.

THE SALIENT DEMOGRAPHIC FEATURES OF THE POPULATION

The statistical accuracy of early censuses and methods of correction are topics of considerable complexity and debate, a discussion of which is beyond the scope of this paper.[31]

The population pyramid for some 23,000 individuals recorded in the 1683 count is shown in Figure 2.3. It is in fact a composite based on the age-counts of fifteen pueblos from the provinces of Pacajes, Sicasica, Larecaja, and Chayanta, whose returns are exceptionally full and well organized, and which in total comprised about 10% of the recorded Indian population of Alto Perú. The sample is thus large enough to smooth out any extreme local variations, and enable one to make some generalizations on the accuracy of age recording and degree of under-registration of the census as a whole.

First--and this is even clearer at the individual level of the pueblos, and in the actual raw returns--the ages are usually approximate at best. Clearly, the "Instrucciones" to the contrary notwithstanding, ages were not in general checked against the books of baptism. There is marked "bunching" at the five and ten year digits, and little attempt or trouble taken over the correct ages of the elderly. The greatest oddity however is the under-representation of both males and females from age ten to twenty. One would have expected this group (especially the boys) to have been of major interest and concern to the Spanish, as the males after eighteen years entered tributary status, and hence under-registration appears at first sight unlikely. There is always the possibility, of course, that the Indians and their caciques might have been especially anxious to have concealed the existence of as many teenagers as possible, but in all the detailed criticisms heaped upon the census, this point is never raised. De Villegas indeed suggested the opposite in his "Papel de Dudas." Another possible explanation is that especially virulent epidemics may have decimated the infant population around 1670, but again the written sources fail to provide confirmation.

For children under ten there is some evidence as a whole of a tendency to under-register females, although in this respect the individual pueblos vary.

Taking the sample as a whole, 40.43% of the population (or 9,419 out of a total of 23,297), were under fifteen. Allowing for the possible under-registration of the children, this indicates that the fertility of the population was extremely high. Yet so was mortality, especially infant mortality. Family size, when it can be

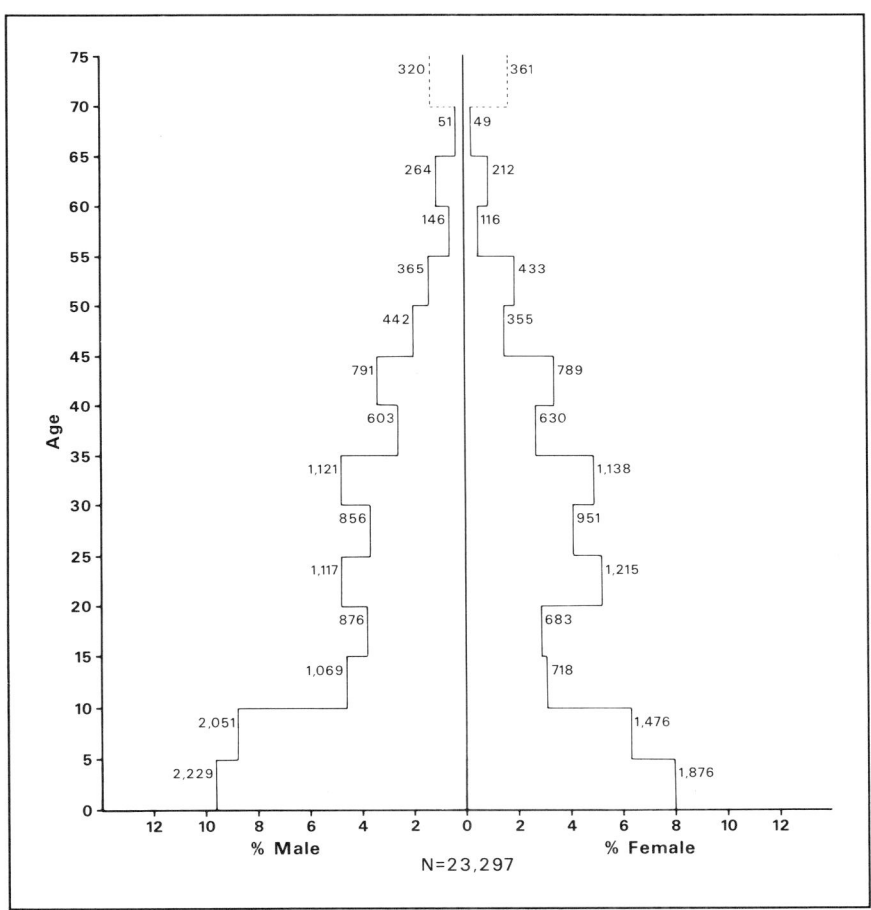

Figure 2.3 Sample age-sex distribution from the 1683 census

reconstructed, was usually small. While the occasional large family with six or more children did exist, it was far more common to have only two or three children living--the irregular spacing of whose ages strongly suggests that many of their siblings had died in infancy. Yet there is also evidence that, despite all hardships and recurrent epidemics, the population had stabilized. The childless families and broken structures, which Cook describes as typical for the period 1570-1620[32] were not frequently encountered. Marriage after age 20 was well nigh universal, and there is clear evidence for the rapid remarriage of the widowed, at least until they reached old age.

Just over 5% of the sample survived to age 60. Evidence from seventeenth century parish registers from Alto Perú which record age at death[33] again tell the same story: nearly half of those born did not survive infancy and childhood, and had died before their tenth year. However the registers record about 15% of deaths at over age 60.

The life expectancy judged from both the "Numeración" and the parish registers was about 25 years or less. With a figure as low as this there could have been little natural increases in population, despite the high fertility.

The adult population shows a fairly normal sex ratio. In the age group 15-50, our sample provides a total of 5,806 males and 5,761 females or 99.2 females per 100 males. This finding is at variance with the usual sixteenth century figures which indicate a far higher survival rate among the Indian female population of both Peru and Mexico, and it too indicates that by the 1680s a new demographic balance had been reached.

CONCLUSION

The holding of the Numeración General was not only as La Palata claimed the greatest single act of his viceregal tenure, but it has claims to be regarded as the major--indeed virtually the only--attempt to hold a general demographic survey in the seventeenth century Spanish colonial empire. One can indeed but hope that investigators will begin to discover some of the missing returns in the local archives of Bolivia, Peru and Ecuador.

The returns from Alto Perú indicate that in many provinces the returns are sufficiently well-compiled to merit serious and detailed demographic research. Quite apart from some of the topics discussed in this paper, the materials can be used to illustrate various aspects of the social and economic history of Alto Perú, such as the growth and composition of the labor force on the rapidly expanding Spanish owned haciendas, and the considerable changes that this had involved in the settlement patterns.

The census was a vast and ambitious project. Full elucidation of its resources will also prove a major task. It is to be hoped that these remarks may encourage other scholars to study this particular census, and indeed the generally neglected demography of the late Hapsburg Empire.

NOTES

1. Nicolas Sánchez-Albornoz, "El indio en el Alto Perú a fines del siglo XVII," *Seminario de historia rural andina*, Lima 1973. See also his *Indios y tributos en el Alto Perú*, Lima 1978. I.E.P., and the review of this work by Nathan Wachtel in *Annales, Economies, Sociétiés, Civilisations*, Vol. 33, 1978, pp. 1206-1209.

2. "Relación del estado del Peru en los ocho años de su gobierno que haze el Duque de la Palata," Biblioteca Nacional, Madrid [hereafter cited as BNM] Ms. #3004.

3. Buenos Aires, Archivo de la Nación, Sala XII, Legajos 17.2.3, 17.2.4, 17.3.1, 17.3.2, 17.3.3, 18.1.1, 18.1.2, 18.1.3, 18.4.2, 18.4.3, 18.4.4, 18.6.5, 18.7.4 & 19.7.3.

4. Archivo General de Indias, Sevilla [hereafter cited as AGI] Charcas 270, ff. 3-67 for a full discussion.

5. AGI, Charcas 268.

6. BNM, Ms. #3004.

7. For a general account, see Margaret E. Graha, "The Administration of Don Melchor de Navarra y Rocafull," *The Americas*, Vol. 27, 1971, pp. 389-412.

8. AGI, Charcas 272, ff. 194-226. BNM, Ms. #3004, Section 825.

9. "Relación del estado del Peru," BNM, Ms. #3004, Sections 822-830.

10. AGI, Charcas 268.

11. AGI, Charcas 268. "Propuesta del Dr. D. Francisco Valera al Don Melchor de Liñan," 28 ff., dated 30 January 1680.

12. Several copies of this document are extant in the archives at Madrid, Seville, Buenos Aires and elsewhere; e.g. AGI, Charcas 270.

13. See for example AGI, Indiferente General 1660, for a detailed survey of this problem in Alto Perú.

14. AGI, Charcas 270, "Expedientes y cartas sobre la Mita de Potosí 1682-1690."

15. AGI, Charcas 270.

16. *Ibid*.

17. *Ibid*.

18. "Relación del estado del Peru," BNM, Ms. #3004.

19. AGI, Charcas 270.

20. AGI, Charcas: much of legajo 270, all of 271 and 272, and some of 273.

21. AGI, Charcas 271.

22. Ibid.
23. AGI, Charcas 273.
24. AGI, Contaduría 1759 B, "Gastos extra-ordinarios de Hacienda."
25. This point is made specifically in points #833-837 of La Palata's "Relación," BNM, Ms. #3004, and in various items of Viceregal Correspondence.
26. AGI, Charcas 271.
27. AGI, Charcas 272, ff. 127-129.
28. AGI, Charcas 272 especially.
29. Figures for Chinchón's repartimiento are supplied in AGI, Charcas 270.
30. AGI, Charcas 271.
31. See for example the discussion and bibliography in S. F. Cook and W. Borah's Essays in Population History, Vol. 1, Los Angeles, University of California Press, 1971, especially pp. 201-299, which deals with the problem of Mexican eighteenth-century censuses.
32. N. David Cook, The Indian Population of Peru, 1570-1620 (Unpublished Ph.D. dissertation, University of Texas, 1973).
33. I have studied those for Puna and Aymaya (both in Chayanta), and Tomahave (in Porco). They are to be found with the Numeración General material in the Archivo de la Nación in Buenos Aires.

3
Colonial Censuses and Tributary Lists of the Sabana de Bogotá Chibcha: Sources and Issues

Juan Villamarin
Judith Villamarin

INTRODUCTION

Although a good deal of demographic work has been done on Indian populations of New Granada, little has been published regarding the Chibcha in the Sabana de Bogotá, one of the colony's most important regions in terms of socio-cultural complexity, population development and colonial organization. The present work will deal with the major sources for study of the area, discussing the available documents on Sabana Chibcha population as a whole, and on tributaries, adult males assessed tribute and labor quotas.[1]

Our approach to the material is primarily socio-cultural; however, we hope that the information presented will be of use to demographers and others interested in population studies. Here as in our other work on the Chibcha, the unit of study is the region and not the province. This insures that we are dealing throughout with a relatively homogeneous ecological background, a matter of importance since the province of Santa Fe in 1592-1595 encompassed a substantial range of altitudes with corresponding differences in climate, soils and other natural resources. The Sabana de Bogotá and Valley of Ubaté, whose communities made up fifty-nine percent of those in the province at that time, are highland basins with elevations of 2,550 m. to 2,650 m., and are surrounded by mountains that ascend to 3,000 m. (Figure 3.1). Almost all other communities in the Province were situated at elevations of 1,000 m. to 2,000 m. in warmer lands (<u>tierra templada</u>) with very different resource

---

We wish to thank the University of Delaware, whose Faculty-Grants-in-Aid to Juan A. Villamarin provided support for travel and collection of data for this paper. We also thank Professor Peter M. Weil, University of Delaware, for his comments and suggestions on the paper.

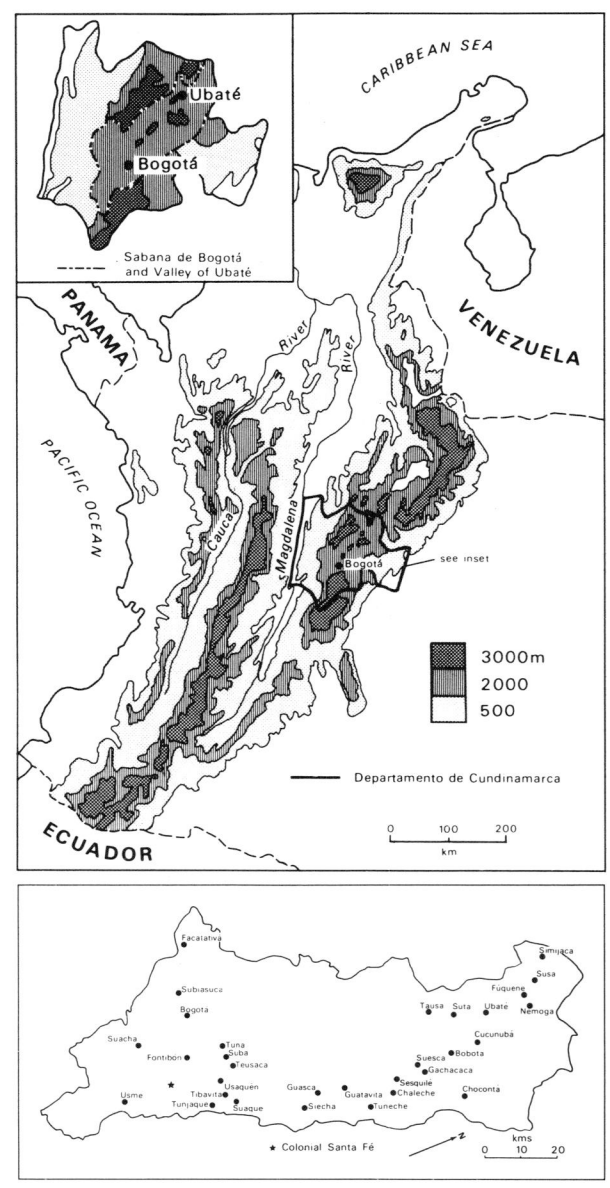

Figure 3.1 The Sabana de Bogotá, sample communities

potential.²

The Chibcha were a sedentary agricultural people with local, ranked political hierarchies, and incipient state formation at the regional level when the Spanish conquerors arrived in 1537. The Spaniards immediately drew on the Indians for labor, goods and services after conquest, but did not make a complete and reliable count of them in the Sabana region until over half a century later, by which time there had been great population loss.³ The first full, well-documented census of the Sabana natives was carried out in the years 1592-1595, when the crown was beginning to consolidate its authority over Chibcha and Spaniards alike.⁴ Altogether, throughout the colonial period there were three major censuses including the one of the 1590s. The second was taken between 1636 and 1640, and the third in 1758-1759, but reported in 1761.⁵ The seventeenth century census, which was probably terminated for lack of funds before its completion, does not have population figures for all the communities in the region.⁶

Between the second and third major censuses, the most abundant archival information on population is in tributary accounts. In the Archivo General de Indias there are lists of tributary Indians in the Sabana which, with some gaps, cover the period from the middle of the seventeenth century to the middle of the eighteenth century. Supplementary data for the years between 1740 and the early 1800s are found in unclassified documents in the Colombian National Archives in Bogotá.⁷

In the following sections we will discuss the documents available on population, their uses and limitations. The meaning of the term, tributary, and its relation to male and total population will be explored; and finally the tributary accounts will be discussed with regard to the other data and their contribution to our understanding of population trends.

CENSUS MATERIAL

The Sixteenth Century

One of the earliest documents containing data on population is a partial estimate that appears to refer to tributary Indians in some Sabana communities in 1556.*
It includes Indian pueblos within a six league radius of Santa Fe, and was part of the information submitted by clergy to the crown as the basis for their petition for aid in building monasteries.⁸ Jiménez de Quesada,

---

*The classification and changing responsibilities of tributaries are discussed in the next section, "Tributaries."

reporting in the 1560s on the conquistadores who came with him and who had encomiendas, also gave estimates of Indian tributaries.[9] Although there are scattered reports on tributaries and censuses for a few communities,[10] during this period a systematic and general census of all the communities was not made in the region, despite the crown's repeated orders that such information be sent to Spain. The region's powerful encomenderos resisted having the Indians under their control counted, most likely to prevent curtailment of their extraction of goods and services from the natives. Officials cautiously avoided open confrontation with the encomenderos since the crown had not yet established a strong presence in the colony.[11] Although there were two visitas during this period, one in 1560 and another in 1563, neither included a census even though the visitador told the Indians in 1563 that he was coming, among other things, to count them.[12]

Indirect sources of information, such as tribute assessments, which have been useful elsewhere for reconstructing population, cannot be used here with ease, for although there is a fairly complete list of them for 1564 (recopied in 1575) they lack the consistency necessary to make the link between them and tribute-paying men.[13] This is not so of the assessments for Tunja, where it has been possible to derive tributary numbers.[14] Through the early seventeenth century the tasa was levied on communities as wholes; to date documents indicating what it was assumed individuals should have to contribute have not been found. A tribute system based on individual responsibility for payment, with specified taxes per tributary, was instituted in the Sabana in 1625.[15]

From 1592 to 1595 Visitador Oidor Miguel de Ibarra supervised the only complete census of the sixteenth century. He reported it in detail to the crown in 1595, stating that he was accounting for:

> . . . los indios que cada pueblo y encomendero tiene, poniendo el número de caciques, capitanes e indios útiles para pagar demora y los reservados de ella y no se ponen los huidos ni los que se han llevado a la población de las minas de la plata por solo poner los presentes, y asimismo de todas las indias y muchachos poniendo los indios de por si y las indias y chusma de por si . . . .[16]

Ibarra recorded the number of males, females and children (chusma), but did not give the number of tributaries per se. Instead they were included along with Indian officers and reservados, men who did not pay tribute because they were too old. As a result the exact number of tributary Indians is known only for a very few communities. The census does have each community's total population, which can be used for general comparison with figures available for later in the colonial period. In our opinion any calculation of sixteenth century Sabana population must be based on this census, and not on earlier figures which were, essentially, estimates that sometimes were based on secondary and impressionistic information.[17]

The Seventeenth and Eighteenth Centuries

There were two visitas carried out in the early seventeenth century, from which population figures on a few communities are available. One was done in 1600, and has very little on population as such aside from the infrequent mention of numbers of indios útiles (tributaries).[18] The other was carried out in 1603-1604, and has a breakdown of population, distinguishing tributaries from other categories of natives, but covering a very limited number of communities.[19]

In 1593, as the crown asserted greater control over the colony, the office of corregidor was established in the Sabana. Incumbents were ordered to keep updated lists of tributary Indians, each year adding on those who had reached seventeen years, the age of tribute payment, and subtracting those who had passed fifty-four or had died.[20] Each community was responsible for paying the tribute, which was calculated on the basis of ninety percent of its tributaries. The ten percent allowance for the community was most likely initiated with the Visita of 1603-1604, and was given in order to take into account absentee Indians and emigrees.[21] In reality ten percent appears to have been a maximum figure; the number of tributaries in each community's deduction was arbitrary, as one can see in Table 3.1, which is based on figures from the few communities for which numbers of both the total tributary population and the assessed population are available in the early seventeenth century.

The real audiencia revoked the ten percent discount on 6 March 1625, ordered that the corregidores make censuses of the tributary Indians (indios útiles) and that tribute be collected from each one.[22] The head tax system, based on the idea of payment by individuals rather than by communities as wholes, remained in effect for the rest of the colonial period. From 1625 on males categorized and listed as tributaries were only those who actually paid (or were supposed to pay) tribute. As we will discuss below there were other able-bodied men who stayed in the communities but were exempt from payment.

There were two more visitas during the seventeenth century, the one of 1636-1640 and a very limited one in 1670. On the basis of the first, population was reported in a document which, in spite of physical deterioration, gives a fairly comprehensive account of the numbers of

TABLE 3.1
Tribute Deductions in the Early Seventeenth Century

	Tributaries Resident in Community	Number of Assessed Tributaries	Deduction	
			Number of Tributaries	Percentage of Total
Chocontá	571	514	57	9.98
Fúquene-Nemoga	276	270	6	2.17
Guasca	300	300	0	0
Nemocón-Tasgata	133	122	11	8.27
Sesquilé-Gachacaca	200	190	10	5.00

Sources: AHNC, Miscelanea: Vol. 8: fol. 555r (Chocontá); Visitas de Cundinamarca: Vol. 6: fol. 812r (Fúquene-Nemoga); Vol. 7: fol. 751r (Guasca); Vol. 12: fols. 762r-762v (Nemocón-Tasgata); Vol. 10: fol. 365r (Sesquilé-Gachacaca).

tributaries in the Sabana and New Granada.[23] Total population figures are available for about half the Sabana communities in visita documents and in later references to it based on parts no longer in existence.[24] In the visita of 1670 the Indian population was reported in several different categories (útiles, reservados, officials, etc.); however, the number of communities covered was very small.[25]

The next large scale, comprehensive census was carried out in 1758-1759 by Oidor Joaquin Aróstegui y Escoto. In his general report of 1761 Aróstegui y Escoto gives an account of tributaries and total population. In the individual visitas (of which only a small number are extant) a more detailed breakdown (útiles, officers, ausentes, etc.) is provided.[26] This is the last complete set of figures for the colonial period. There is some population information in a partial visita of 1778-1779, and reports on some communities' tributaries and/or total populations in the early nineteenth century, containing data that can be compared with earlier figures and which are utilized in the graphs in this paper.[27]

Finally, there is the series of accounts of tributary Indians in the Archivo General de Indias, extending from 1660 to the 1740s. The series is unique for the area in being the single longest-run set of figures for a given segment of the population. With some qualifications the accounts provide information on trends of the Indian population during that time. The data for these lists was supposed to be compiled by corregidores on the basis of head counts carried out with the aid of local priests.[28] Some records suggest that the lists may not always have been done this way. Corregidores may have made one or two lists (descripciones) during their tenure by actual counts, and then used them as bases for their subsequent reports, taking into account changes in the number of Indians paying tribute each time.[29] The series is fairly complete. From the seventeenth century on, tribute was paid in two installments, one in June (tercio de San Juan) and the other in December (tercio de Navidad). Both sets of figures are found in the documents. For the graphs in this essay we have used the tercio de San Juan accounts because they appear to be more complete. We will return to a discussion of the graphs after exploring the effects on census taking of Indian post-conquest social organization, the use of the term, tributary, and the relationship of tributary counts to other population figures in the Sabana.

TRIBUTARIES

"Tributary" (tributario, indio útil, indio de demora) was a Spanish administrative concept employed for the

collection of money and goods from the Indians and allocation of their labor. The Chibcha had a broadly based system of labor and goods allocation with respect to native political hierarchies, which the Spaniards drew on but modified according to their own concepts and needs.[30]
From 1539 to the end of the sixteenth century, a period of encomendero dominance, Spaniards considered tributaries to be adult males, and their estimates of them in official documents included only men. During this time, however, women also may have served in providing encomenderos with gold, goods and services.[31] Tributary classification was formalized toward the end of the sixteenth century and beginning of the seventeenth by a much strengthened colonial government. From then until 1740 in the Sabana, it included married and unmarried adult males between the ages of seventeen and fifty-four, who had to pay tribute in money and goods, and who were also liable to serve in labor quotas (forced labor--repartimiento).[32] Tribute and labor assessments were determined and managed by crown officials. The establishment of repartimiento made the Indians accessible to other Spaniards in addition to the encomenderos. Change from a community-assessed tribute to a head-tax type in 1625 did not change the form of tributary classification established in the early 1600s, nor did it alleviate the Indians' work load.[33] Between 1740 and 1810 tributaries continued to be classified as described above, and to pay tribute, but labor quotas were abolished.[34]
How the tributary category is to be viewed within the context of total Chibcha population is influenced by data on native organization on the one hand and Spanish classification on the other. We shall discuss first Indian factors--kinship, territoriality and emigration--that may have affected the accuracy of tributary and general census counts, and second the Spanish systems of categorization of adult males.[35]

Chibcha Kinship and Territoriality

Implicit in the Spanish use of the term, tributary, was that such men were heads (or potentially heads) of individual nuclear families who traced descent patrilineally and were patrilocal in mode of residence.[36] In fact the Indians had matrilineal descent with patrilocal residence during the father's lifetime, and eventual preferential residence in the mother's brother's territory (avunculocal residence). Along these lines natives moved from one community to another, especially in the sixteenth century. Crown officials were aware of the situation and utilized the concept of matrilineal descent in solving problems of conflicting claims for Indians by encomenderos and caciques.[37] Baptismal documents sometimes recorded the mother's community or section of it.[38] None of this, however, was reflected in the censuses, despite the continued importance of matrilineal ties among the Chibcha in the sixteenth and seventeenth centuries. The counts specify individuals present at the time, but not their final community affiliation. Sixteenth century parish records are scarce, but those that remain might provide some indication of the extent of movement based on matrilineal bonds in selected areas.

Although the Spanish model implied the idea of monogamous nuclear families, it appears that polygyny, which had been mainly the pre-conquest nobles' prerogative, was also practiced by individuals of lesser rank after the conquest. In the visita of 1563 the visitador ordered that in the Sabana:

> . . . que agora e de aqui adelante cada uno de ellos no tengan mas de una mujer propia y no se casen con las hermanas de las mujeres que hubieren tenido y se les hayan muerto.[39]

Other documents suggest the existence of polygyny after the conquest, but its extent is difficult to assess.[40] The Indians seem to have been aware of Spanish prejudice against the practice and may have attempted to conceal some of the women and children from census takers. Generally the size and composition of Indian households is not known and does not appear to have been of great importance to Spanish officials. This may have had an effect on the accuracy of censuses, and makes it difficult for modern investigators to formulate ratios of total population to tributaries.

By the early seventeenth century Spanish clergy were established permanently in rural communities to oversee native life and enforce church rules. Polygyny may have declined partly as a result of active intervention by them and crown officials, and partly of other effects of conquest such as diminished economic capability of adult males to take more than one wife, population upsets caused by disease, emigration and forced labor, as well as other factors that disrupted traditional organization.

Toward the end of the sixteenth century permanent records based on baptism, death and marriage began to be kept by priests. Individuals could turn to these in order to make claims of community membership, and conversely, communities could use such records on which to base their cases for the return of natives who had left. Priests, who soon became important members of rural society, also influenced Indian inheritance patterns by writing wills for them with a patrilineal bias. Patrilineality and patrilocality became more widely practiced by the Chibcha in the late colonial period, but did not completely replace matrilineal inheritance of land, making it possible for an individual to claim membership in one community on the basis of land he might have inherited via the Spanish patrilineal model, or in that which he had rights to by the Chibcha matrilineal system.[41] The overlapping of Spanish and native systems probably enhanced opportunities for mobility, contributing to the movement of Indians in and out of Sabana pueblos.

Emigration

Men, women and children moved from their communities to others in the region as well as to Santa Fe de Bogotá and areas outside the Sabana during the entire colonial period. Although emigration from Sabana pueblos did not occur on as large a scale as in the early years of colonial rule, it was a constant process, and was important over the long term. From the middle of the sixteenth century individuals who took up residence in communities other than their own became clients or dependents of other Indians, especially of members of the local political hierarchies.[42] Probably in return they obtained access to land and other resources. Male Indian immigrants, forasteros, were not reported in census counts until 1670, and they were not required by the Spanish authorities to pay tribute on a regular basis until the late seventeenth century.[43] They may, however, have been paying some form of tribute all along to Indian authorities in return for the privilege of living in their communities. This practice provided the grounds for conflicts among community heads, caciques, who made claims and counterclaims for disputed subjects. A cacique could make a demand for individuals who had left his community, basing his argument on custom, yet resist returning immigrants who were requested by their native caciques in order to keep enough manpower to meet Spanish demands for goods and services.[44]

Probably some of those who left their native communities were lost to Spanish counts entirely, while others showed up in the lists of absentees (ausentes) that the Spaniards made in conjunction with the censuses. Loss of population through emigration is clear. However, the gains that at least some communities must have had as a result of the Indians' movement are much more clouded, for newcomers were probably not reported if it could be helped, to avoid taxation. The movement of individuals points to the fact that there were differences in economic and political conditions in different communities, drawing (or driving) Indians from one pueblo to another, a matter we will discuss further in the last section of this paper. In some cases the Indians left the area entirely, moving to other regions or towns.

Spanish Classification, and Tributaries in Relation to Total Male Population

The tributary category did not cover all adult males. In addition there were reported for each community ausentes (absentee tributaries), Indian officials exempted from tribute payment, and reservados (men exempted because of illness, old age or special jobs). Most of the material that follows is from the seventeenth and eighteenth century documents; there is very little on these categories in the 1592-1595 census.

Ausentes. The absentee adult males discussed in the preceding section were considered by the Spaniards to be potential tributaries. A specific ratio of absentees cannot be established, since the numbers vary so much among communities and even within particular communities over a span of time (Table 3.2). For example in the 1636-1640 census of Chocontá ausentes were 6.8 percent of the total number of potential tributaries for the pueblo; in 1778-1779, 14.1 percent and in 1804/1806, 10.8 percent. In Fúquene-Nemoga in the census of 1636-1640 they made up 8.1 percent; in 1778-1779, 37.7 percent. The percentages in Sesquilé-Gachacaca went from 1.5 in 1636-1640, to 39.0 in 1778-1779, to 11.6 in 1804/1806.

The highest proportion of ausentes is found in the visita of 1778-1779, and can probably be correlated with the land problems that the Indians were facing at the time, along with the difficulties caused by massive immigration of non-Indians into their reservations.[45]

Ausentes were not included in the census tallies of 1592-1595. Visitador Oidor Ibarra gave some information on them, but his figures are very difficult to use, since he did not report them by communities, but gave the total number of absentees per encomendero, many of whom had more than one community as a single encomienda during the period.[46] In the censuses of 1636-1640 and 1758-1759 ausentes were included in total population counts. In the individual visitas, however, they were listed separately from tributaries, and their numbers are known for those communities whose documents have survived.[47] The number of extant visitas for 1758-1759, with more than two thirds of the particular accounts lost, is smaller than for 1636-1640. Fortunately total population of each of the pueblos was recorded in the general report.

Ausentes are usually not mentioned in the Archivo General tributary series. In the nineteenth century documents in Bogotá, some reports give an account of them as well as of the tributaries.

Indian Officials and Others Exempted from Tributary Status. A number of able-bodied adult males were exempted from paying tribute. Through most of the seventeenth

TABLE 3.2
Ausentes

	A Number of Resident Tributaries	B Ausentes	A + B	Ausentes-- Percentage of A + B
		From Visita of 1636-1640		
Bogotá	292	15	307	4.9
Chocontá	345	25	370	6.8
Fontibón	193	8	201	4.0
Fúquene-Nemoga	160	14	174	8.1
Guasca	216	6	222	2.7
Sesquilé-Gachacaca	128	2	130	1.5
		From Visita of 1778-1779		
Chocontá	220	36	256	14.1
Fúquene-Nemoga	104	63	167	37.7
Guasca	102	10	112	8.9
Sesquilé-Gachacaca	89	57	146	39.0
		From Tribute Lists of 1804/1806		
Bogotá	117	12	129	9.3
Chocontá	166	20	186	10.8
Fontibón	46	6	52	11.5
Guasca	67	6	73	8.2
Sesquilé-Gachacaca	76	10	86	11.6

Sources: For 1636-1640--AHNC, Visitas de Cundinamarca: Vol. 8: fol. 205v (Bogotá); Miscelanea: Vol. 8: fol. 597r (Chocontá); Visitas de Cundinamarca: Vol. 12: fol. 938v (Fontibón); Vol. 6: fol. 833r (Fúquene-Nemoga); Vol. 7: fol. 779r (Guasca); Vol. 10: fol. 380r (Sesquilé). For 1778-1779--AHNC, Visitas de Cundinamarca: Vol. 7: fol. 442r (Chocontá); Vol. 10: fol. 924v (Fúquene); Vol. 7: fol. 485r (Guasca); Vol. 7: fol. 461v (Sesquilé). For 1804/1806--AHNC, Tributos: NC #32 (Bogotá, Fontibón 1806; Chocontá, Guasca, Sesquilé 1804/1805).

century these were the native political officials--the traditional chief of the community, cacique (<u>sijipcua</u>), and heads of subdivisions, capitanes (<u>sivintiva</u>). The census of 1592-1595 indicates that they did not pay tribute, but there is very little information on their numbers. In the census of 1636-1640 they made up 2.3 percent to 4.6 percent of able resident men (Table 3.3). The number of men exempted greatly increased in the eighteenth and nineteenth centuries as people holding specific church and government related jobs came to be excused from the tribute lists. The proportions of these together with Indian officers rose to between 8.9 and 14.4 percent in 1778-1779, and up to 30.3 percent in 1804/1806 in the communities in our sample. During that time span they probably outnumbered exemptions for age and illness (Table 3.4). A great diversity of job-holders had come to be included --<u>fiscales</u>, <u>alcaldes</u>, <u>sacristanes</u>, church singers and deputies of the corregidor.

In 1636-1640 capitanes and caciques were reported separately from tributaries in the visita, while the sacristan and fiscal were included in the category of reservados. In the eighteenth century all officers and church/government job-holders were included in the new category, <u>reservados por oficio</u>. During the later part of the colonial period it appears that such jobs were sought by the Indians purposefully in attempts to gain exempt status.

<u>Reservados</u>. In most communities there were a number of adult males who did not pay tribute because they had passed their fifty-fourth birthday or were sick (Table 3.4). Priests kept Indians' baptismal records, that could be checked for the purpose of exemption due to age. One could be classified as reservado for a temporary illness or permanent disability. Individuals had to submit proofs, and in the latter case were erased permanently from the lists of contributors. Information regarding the nature or degree of disability was seldom given.[48] As has been pointed out, sacristanes and fiscales were included in the reservados category in the seventeenth century.

Individuals on this list, whether because of illness or as a way to escape payment, appear to have been few in number in the eighteenth and nineteenth centuries, offsetting the tributary rolls least of any of the non-paying categories at that time. The proportion of men considered reservados because of age, in contrast to illness, is difficult to determine, since the two classes were usually not reported separately. There is some information on this for 1804/1806. In Bogotá, Fontibón and Guasca, all the men on the reservado list were over fifty-four years old. In Chocontá fourteen out of sixteen (87.5 percent) were reservados because of age. In

TABLE 3.3
Officials and others exempted from payment of tribute

	A Number of Resident Tributaries	B Number of Officials and Others Exempted[1]	A + B	Officials and Others Exempted-- Percentage of A + B
		From Visita of 1636-1640		
Bogotá	292	14	306	4.6
Chocontá	345	8	353	2.3
Fontibón	193	9	202	4.5
Fúquene-Nemoga	160	4	164	2.4
Guasca	216	9	225	4.0
Sesquilé-Gachacaca	128	4	132	3.0
		From Visita of 1778-1779		
Chocontá	220	26	246	10.6
Fúquene-Nemoga	104	14	118	11.9
Guasca	102	10	112	8.9
Sesquilé-Gachacaca	89	15	104	14.4
		From Tribute Lists of 1804/1806		
Bogotá	117	19	136	14.0
Chocontá	166	25	191	13.1
Fontibón	46	20	66	30.3
Guasca	67	9	76	11.8
Sesquilé-Gachacaca	76	12	88	13.6

Sources: For 1636-1640--AHNC, Visitas de Cundinamarca: Vol. 8: fol. 205v (Bogotá); Miscelanea: Vol. 8: fol. 597r (Chocontá); Visitas de Cundinamarca: Vol. 12: fol. 938v (Fontibón); Vol. 6: fol. 833r (Fúquene-Nemoga); Vol. 7: fol. 779r (Guasca); Vol. 10: fol. 380r (Sesquilé). For 1778-1779--AHNC, Visitas de Cundinamarca: Vol. 7: fol. 442r (Chocontá); Vol. 10: fol. 924v (Fúquene); Vol. 7: fol. 485r (Guasca); Vol. 7: fol. 461v (Sesquilé). For 1804/1806--AHNC, Tributos: NC #32 (Bogotá, Fontibón 1806; Chocontá, Guasca, Sesquilé 1804/1805).

[1] In the Visita of 1636-1640 only caciques and capitanes were included in this category. In the eighteenth and nineteenth centuries, members of the traditional political hierarchy and church/government job-holders were included.

TABLE 3.4
Reservados

	A Number of Resident Tributaries	B Number of Reservados	A + B	Reservados-- Percentage of A + B
		From Visita of 1636-1640		
Bogotá	292	16	308	5.2
Chocontá	345	26	371	7.0
Fontibón	193	40	233	17.2
Fúquene-Nemoga	160	17	177	9.6
Guasca	216	19	235	8.1
Sesquilé-Gachacaca	128	2	130	1.5
		From Tribute Lists of 1804/1806		
Bogotá	117	4	121	3.3
Chocontá	166	16	182	8.8
Fontibón	46	0	46	0
Guasca	67	1	68	1.5
Sesquilé-Gachacaca	76	16	92	17.4

Sources: For Visita of 1636-1640--AHNC, Visitas de Cundinamarca: Vol. 8: fol. 205v (Bogotá); Miscelanea: Vol. 8: fol. 597r (Chocontá); Visitas de Cundinamarca: Vol. 12: fol. 938v (Fontibón); Vol. 6: fol. 833r (Fúquene-Nemoga); Vol. 7: fol. 779r (Guasca). For 1804/1806-- AHNC, Tributos: NC #32 (Bogotá, Fontibón 1806; Chocontá, Guasca, Sesquilé-Gachacaca 1804/1805).

Sesquilé, however, seven out of sixteen on the list (43.7 percent) were reported to be ill at the time.

Requinteros. As discussed earlier, there were other adult male Indians, classified as forasteros. They were infrequently reported, and not included in the lists of tributaries. These were men who had married into a community other than their own or had immigrated, sometimes alone and sometimes with their families. By late seventeenth century they had to pay a tribute to the crown. The assessment was uniform for them but, in most cases, lower than the amounts paid by natives of the communities in which they lived. The tribute-paying forasteros were called requinteros, and were reported as a separate category. Most likely, for local administrative reasons discussed above, there were many more forasteros than those few reported as requinteros (Table 3.5).

Indian Manipulation of Spanish Classification

Eligible adult males were faced, until the 1740s, with meeting forced labor demands, and throughout the entire colonial period with tribute payments. It appears that some were successful in managing their situation so as to escape classification as tributaries. Exemption due to illness, as would be indicated on the reservado lists, appears to have been difficult to obtain, but may have served as an outlet, however limited, in the seventeenth century. By the nineteenth century it seems to have become the least opted way for exemption. Instead classification as holder of a designated non-tributary job was more common. In the eighteenth and nineteenth centuries the number of men holding such positions in the Indian communities greatly increased, indicating that much greater opportunity was allowed with respect to this work for legitimately avoiding tribute payment while remaining in the pueblo. A certain way of escaping tribute and labor demands was emigration, which was partially reflected in the ausentes figures, and was carried out by Indians during all periods of the colonial era. Some remained in the Sabana as forasteros, and later requinteros, while others were lost completely to the local native population.

Spanish Classification of Tributaries in Relation to Total Indian Population

Given the Spanish classification of tributaries and the Indians' manipulation of the system, one expects that the ratio of total population to tributaries would increase through time. This was indeed the case in the

TABLE 3.5
Requinteros: From Tribute Lists of 1804/1806

	A Number of Resident Tributaries	B Number of Requinteros	A + B	Requinteros-- Percentage of A + B
Bogotá	117	8	125	6.4
Chocontá	166	2	168	1.2
Fontibón	46	3	49	6.1
Guasca	67	2	69	2.9
Sesquilé-Gachacaca	76	6	82	7.3

Source: AHNC, NC: Tributos No. 32 (Bogotá, Fontibón 1806; Chocontá, Guasca, Sesquilé 1804/1805).

seventeenth and eighteenth centuries (Table 3.6). The increments are partly a function of decrease in individuals classified as tributaries, and not of increase in family size, fertility or improvement of the resource base.[49] Unfortunately we do not have the exact numbers of tributaries for the end of the sixteenth century, but must use the total number of adult males as given in the census of 1592-1595. Using these figures we find that at the end of the sixteenth century the ratio of total population to adult males was between 2.2 and 3.8. The data suggest that during this period tributary classification of adult males was offset least by the exemptions discussed above, an interpretation supported by specific information on tributaries in three communities from our sample in the 1590s. In Chocontá the ratio of total population to adult males was 3.4, in Guasca 3.7 and in Suesca 3.0. The ratio of total population to tributaries was 3.6 in Chocontá, 4.5 in Guasca and 3.1 in Suesca.[50]

Ratios of total population to tributaries in 1636-1640 ranged between 3.6 and 5.8. By the census of 1758-1759 the ratios had risen to between 4.4 and 11.3, probably reaching their highest levels at this point. It should be noted that in 1758-1759 absentee tributaries were counted in among the population totals, and that therefore the ratios we have obtained are somewhat high. For example in Guasca, one of the few communities with specific data, the ratio corrected for ausentes would be 7.0 instead of 8.0.

In the early nineteenth century the ratios for seven communities were between 4.3 and 8.9. Four of the six pueblos show increase while two dropped below the 1758-1759 values.

Accounts of tributary Indians have been important for analyzing and calculating total populations and their long term trends in New Granada. In some cases only counts of tributaries have been available and have served as bases on which to reconstruct population curves for whole Indian communities.[51] Calculation of the Sabana communities' population between 1660 and the early 1800s on the basis of the tributary series may be possible, but would pose many difficulties. One would have to interpolate the likely rates of population change relative to men classified as tributaries, while keeping track of changing rates in exemptions as well. Other shortcomings in the data, already discussed, would also have to be taken into account.[52] More precision can be gained by using parish records, which so far have not been utilized extensively in the area. This would be a worthwhile, if painstaking task for an investigator with an interest in demographic studies, and would help us to use what census and tributary material we have with greater accuracy. In the meantime the series, which we will discuss in the following section, can tell us a great deal about the

TABLE 3.6
Ratios of total population to tributaries

Communities	1592-1595*			1636-1640			1758-1759**			1805		
	Total Population	Adult Males	Ratio	Total Population	Tribu- taries	Ratio	Total Population	Tribu- taries	Ratio	Total Population	Tribu- taries	Ratio
Bogotá	2,263	673	3.4	1,262	292	4.3	646	110	5.9			
Bosa-Suacha	2,928	1,005	2.9		466		831	117	7.1			
Chocontá	2,570	765	3.4	1,715	345	5.0	1,345	234	5.8	1,176	166	7.1
Cucunubá-Bobota	737	217	3.4				563	81	7.0			
Facatativá	872	233	3.7		160							
Facatativá-Chueca	1,139	307	3.7		202		659	91	7.2	570	95	6.0
Fontibón	1,831	507	3.6	1,084	193	5.6						
Fontibón-Techo	1,927	540	3.6	1,152	218	5.3	827	136	6.1	328	46	7.1
Fúquene-Nemoga	816	282	2.9	920	160	5.8	742	91	8.2			
Guasca-Siecha	1,489	402	3.7	1,037	216	4.8	622	78	8.0	375	67	5.6
Guatavita-Chaleche-Tuneche	1,400***	404	3.5				1,264	221	5.7	1,352	210	6.4
Serrezuela (Subiasuca)	294	82	3.6		65		327	29	11.3	127	30	4.3
Sesquilé-Gachacaca	682	229	3.0	466	128	3.6	708	131	5.4	675	76	8.9
Simijaca	758	235	3.2		176		427	43	9.9			
Suba-Tuna	1,332	428	3.1		172		298	46	6.5			
Suesca	905	306	3.0		241		942	129	7.3			
Susa	756	342	2.2		246		801	83	9.7			
Suta-Tausa	750	199	3.8		122							
Ubaté	2,769	938	3.0		440		1,890	324	5.8			
Usaquén-Tibavita-Teusaca-Tunjaque-Suaque	1,787	505	3.5		166		180	41	4.4			
Usme	800	237	3.4				255	42	6.1			

Sources: For 1592-1595--Ruiz Rivera, Fuentes Para la Demografía Histórica, pp. 23-33. For 1636-1640--AHNC, Visitas de Cundinamarca: Vol. 8: fol. 205v. Miscelanea: Vol. 8: fol. 59r; Visitas de Cundinamarca: Vol. 12: fol. 938v; Vol. 6: fol. 833r; Vol. 7: fol. 779r; Vol. 10: fol. 380r; Gobierno: Vol. 1: fols. 34r-45v. For 1758-1759--AHNC, Visitas de Cundinamarca: Vol. 8: fol. 794v-829r. Rojas, Corregidores y Justicias, p. 523. For 1805--AHNC, Tributos: NC #32.

*Only figures for total adult male population are available in the 1592-1595 documents. See Text.
**Ausentes are included in total population figures in the 1758-1759 column.
***Tuneche is not included in the 1592-1595 figures.

tributary population itself, and also, with qualifications, about the general course that the rest of the Indian population followed. Consideration of the series in light of other kinds of data can give us insights into factors affecting both tributaries and the native population as a whole.

TRIBUTARY ACCOUNTS: 1660-1800s AND POPULATION TRENDS

This discussion is based on the Archivo General de Indias tributary series that extends from 1660 to the 1740s, on data in eighteenth century censuses and on unclassified documents in the Archivo Histórico Nacional in Bogotá, which cover the early nineteenth century. The communities represented in our sample cover most sections of the Sabana, and at the end of the sixteenth century made up forty-four percent of the region's seventy-seven native communities. We selected them for discussion because of the completeness of their data through the entire period dealt with here. All indications are that data for other communities existed but were lost, or, for the nineteenth century are as yet unavailable to the public.

Our treatment of the thirty-four communities in twenty graphs reflects the Spaniards' reporting and their resettlement of many native communities together in nucleated zones in the early seventeenth century. Although in many cases the Indians maintained their traditional identities and did not remain in the nucleated areas, the Spaniards consistently treated them in terms of the units given here for administrative purposes.

Thirty-six of the seventy-seven Indian communities mentioned above survived through the late eighteenth century; among these were nineteen of our sample. Nine of the surviving communities (six of those in our sample) were then made parishes (_parroquias_), and although retaining their Indian names, became very strongly identified with non-Indian populations. The rest of the communities (including fifteen of those in our sample) disappeared completely or were incorporated as parts of the remaining ones.[53]

Tributary Counts and Total Population--The Overall View

Tributary population declined in the seventeenth century and early eighteenth century far more than would be indicative of the attrition discussed in the previous section, suggesting processes that had a bearing on the population as a whole. The drop was especially marked in the years between the 1680s and the early 1700s after a short upswing in many communities, such as Bogotá, Bosa,

Chocontá, Fontibón, Fúquene-Nemoga, Guatavita and annexes, Guasca-Siecha, Simijaca, Suacha, Suesca, Susa and Ubaté, from 1660 to the 1680s (Figures 3.2 to 3.12). A mid-eighteenth century increase can be noted in several communities (Bogotá, Chocontá, Cucunubá-Bobota, Facatativá, Fontibón, Guatavita and annexes, Simijaca, Suba-Tuna, Suesca and Ubaté). At the end of the 1700s and beginning of the 1800s the tributaries dropped to levels far below those reached in the early seventeenth century (for example: Chocontá, Cucunubá-Bobota, Fúquene-Nemoga, Guasca-Siecha, Sesquilé-Gachacaca, Suesca, Suta-Tausa, Susa, Ubaté and Usaquén). Over the long run population also declined, showing no indications of sustained recovery such as occurred in Mexico. We do not have the data that would tell us whether it followed the more specific trends of the tributary population; however, there is some information to suggest that there was a slight growth within at least some communities for a short period in the mid-eighteenth century after which, as with tributaries, decrease again ensued.[54]

The similarities among the graphs of several of the communities in our sample suggest the operation of region-wide processes. With the exception of Guatavita and its annexes (Figure 3.6) all show an absolute decrease in numbers by the early nineteenth century. We have calculated percentage drops for those years in which the data on all the communities are complete (Table 3.7 and Figure 3.13), and found that between 1673 and 1803 the number of tributaries decreased by 51.4 percent. The decline was broken by the two periods of growth mentioned above. During the first, 1660-1680s, there was an increase in tributary numbers in about half of our sample communities, followed by a drop which was especially steep through the 1690s and early part of the 1700s. Again, basing computation only on figures for which there are years with complete data (Table 3.7), we find that after a period of fourteen years of rather slow decline (1673-1687, with a drop of 6.83 percent) a period of rapid decline followed, particularly in the eight years between 1687 and 1695, when the number of tributaries decreased by about a third (33.63 percent). In several communities in the mid-eighteenth century another less sharply defined period of growth took place. Though figures for the eighteenth century are not complete enough to allow one to compute annual percentage losses and gains, it is evident that between 1706 and 1761 there was a growth in total numbers of 13.6 percent, followed from 1761 to 1803 by a drop once again, of some 18.5 percent. We shall return to a discussion of these trends, looking into possible interpretations of the losses and gains after an overview of important differences among the graphs.

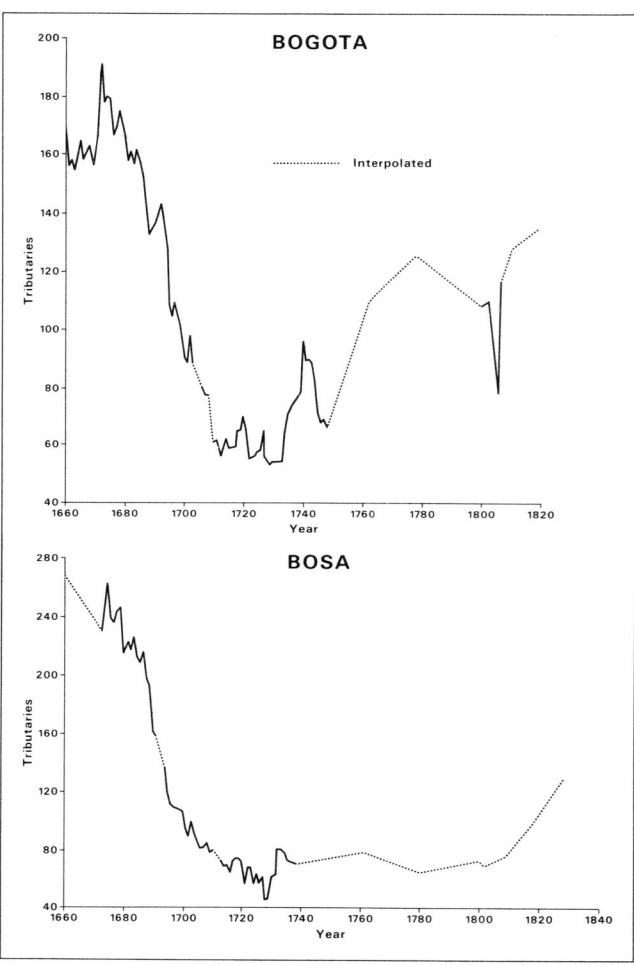

Figure 3.2   Tributary change in Bogotá and Bosa, 1660-1830

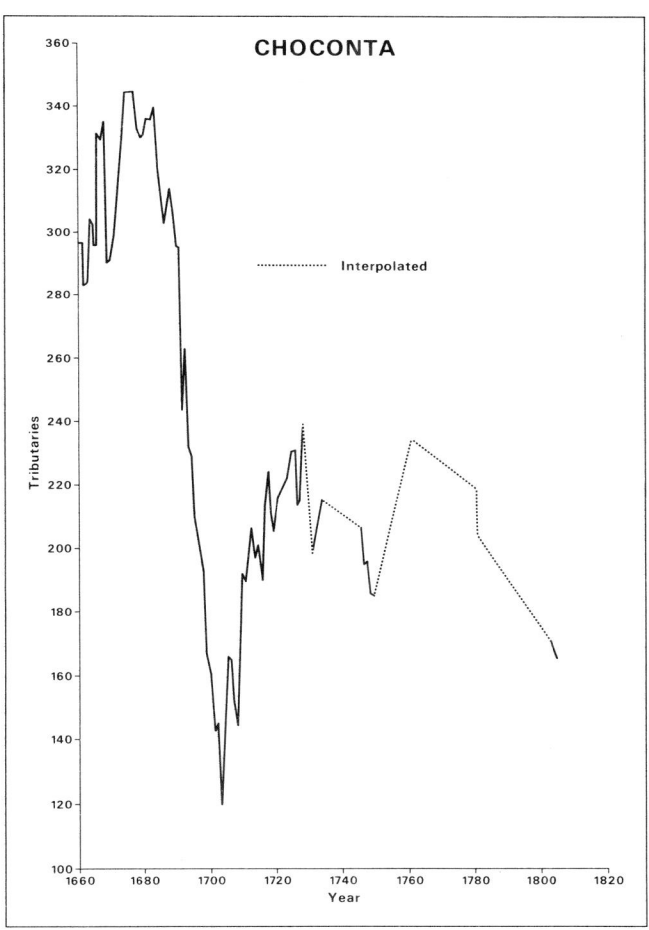

Figure 3.3 Tributary change in Chocontá, 1660-1810

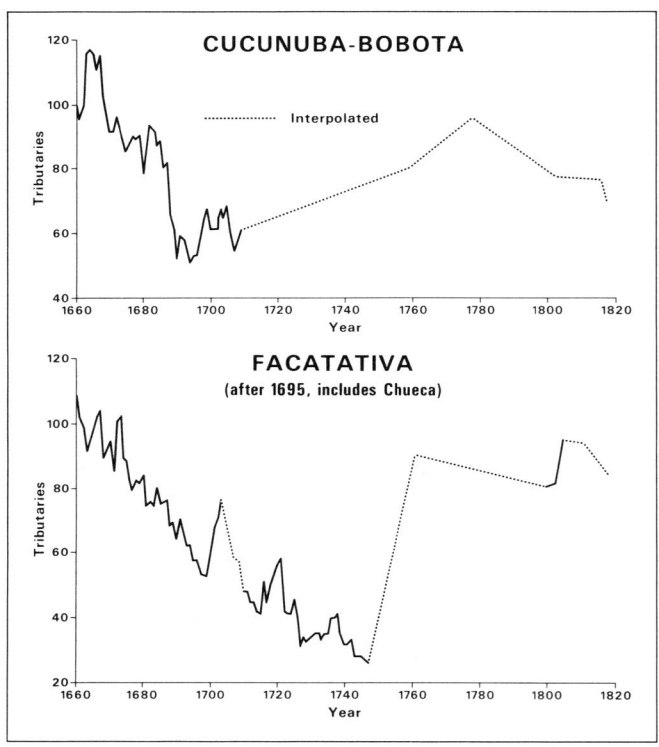

Figure 3.4 Tributary change in Cucunubá-Bobota and Facatativá, 1660-1820

69

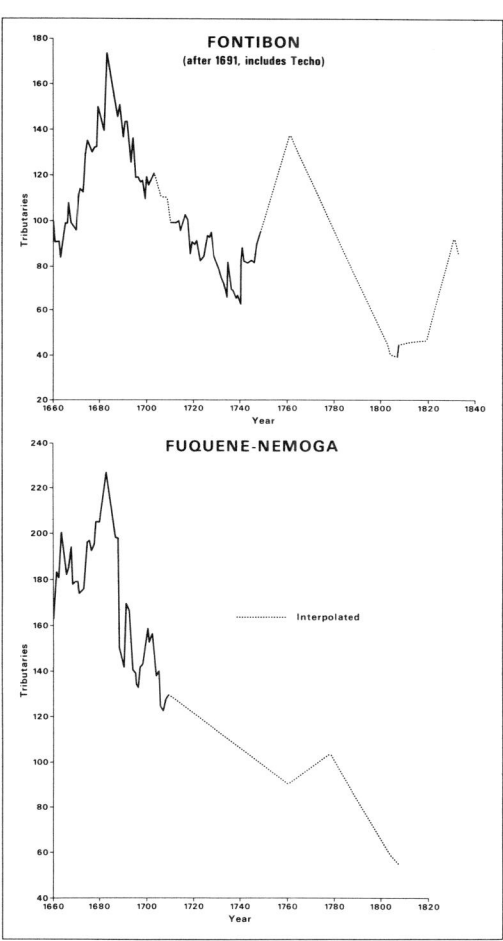

Figure 3.5 Tributary change in Fontibón and
Fúquene-Nemoga, 1660-1830

70

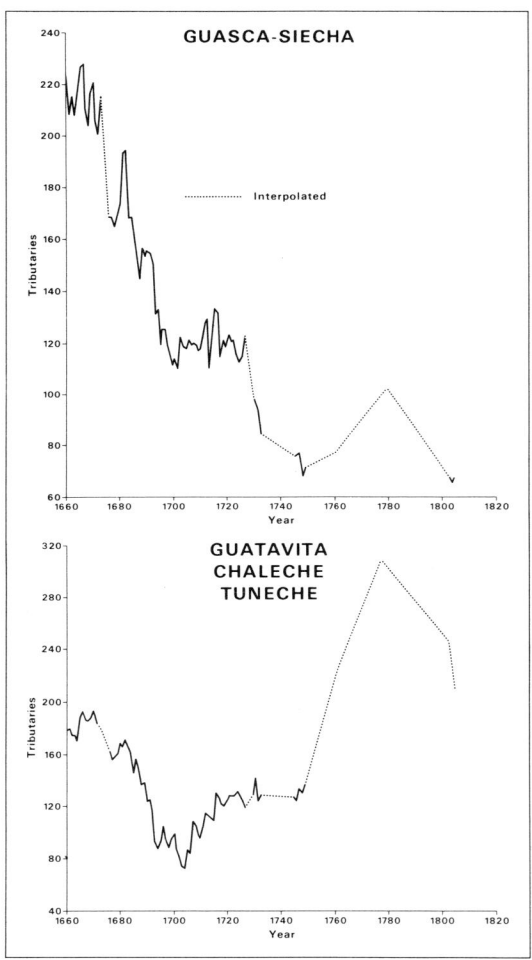

Figure 3.6 Tributary change in Guasca-Siecha and Guatavita, 1660-1810

71

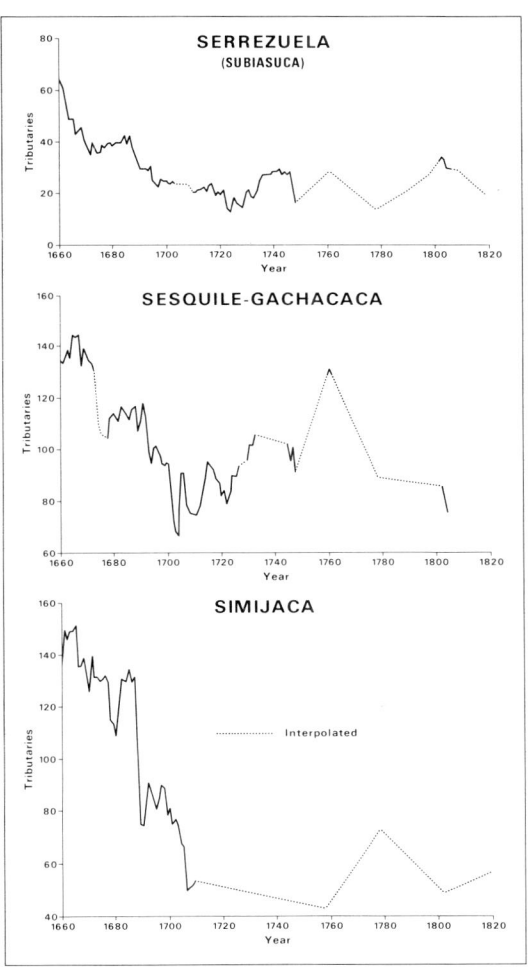

Figure 3.7 Tributary change in Serrezuela, Sesquilé-Gachacaca, and Simijaca, 1660-1820

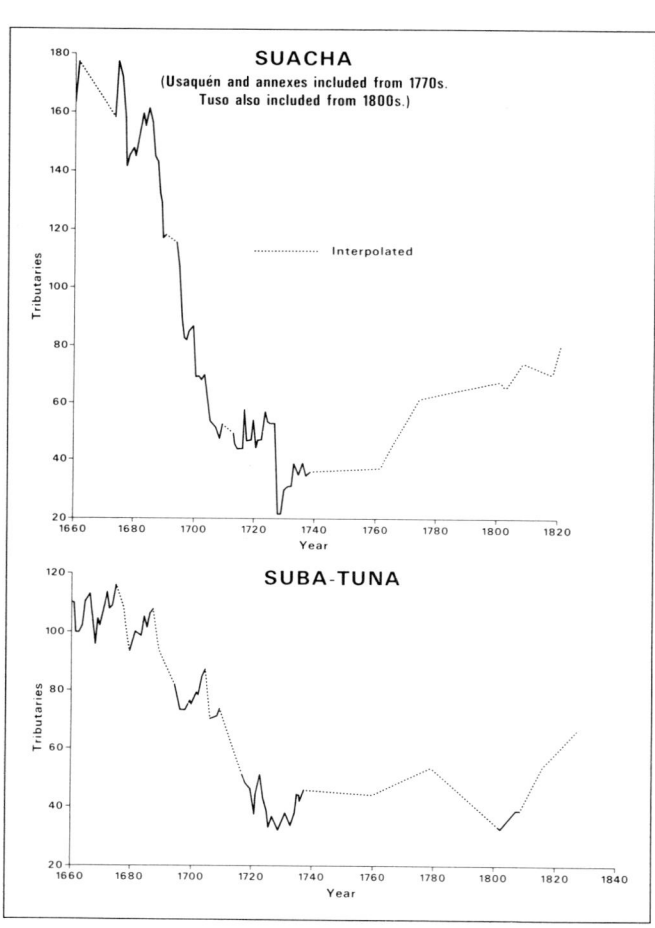

Figure 3.8 Tributary change in Suacha and Suba-Tuna, 1660-1830

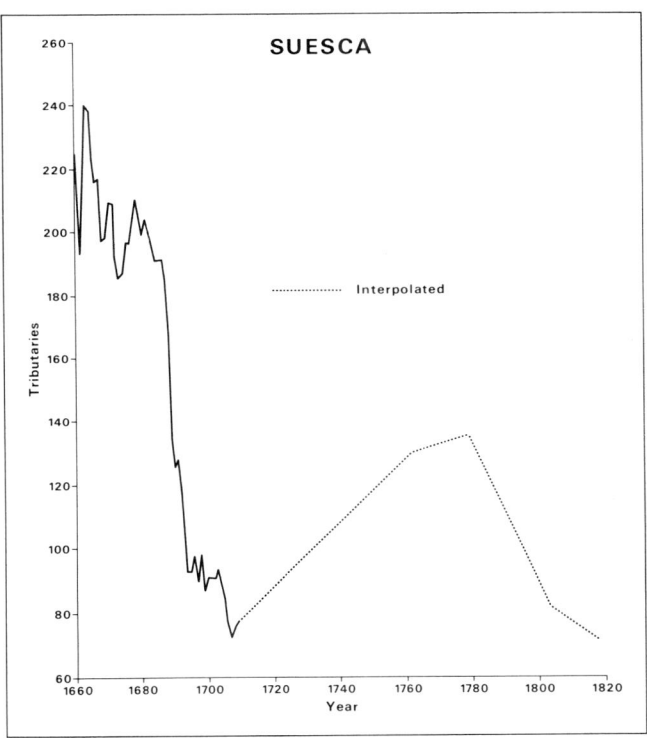

Figure 3.9 Tributary change in Suesca, 1660-1820

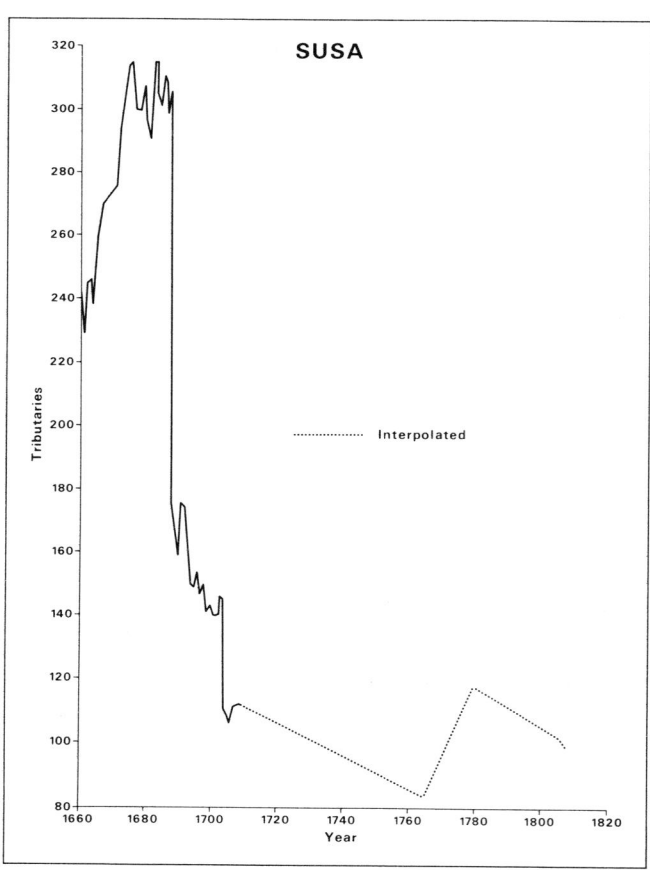

Figure 3.10 Tributary change in Susa, 1660-1810

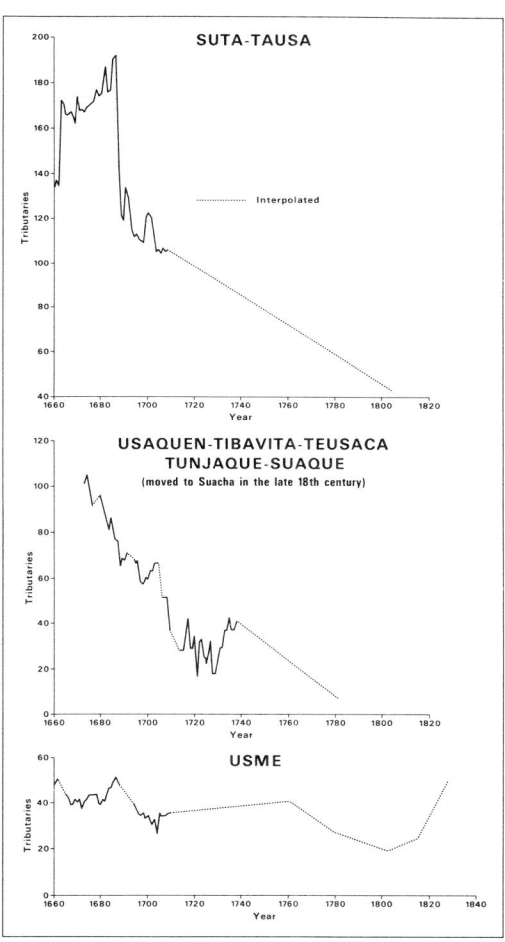

Figure 3.11 Tributary change in Suta-Tausa, Usaquén, and Usme, 1660-1830

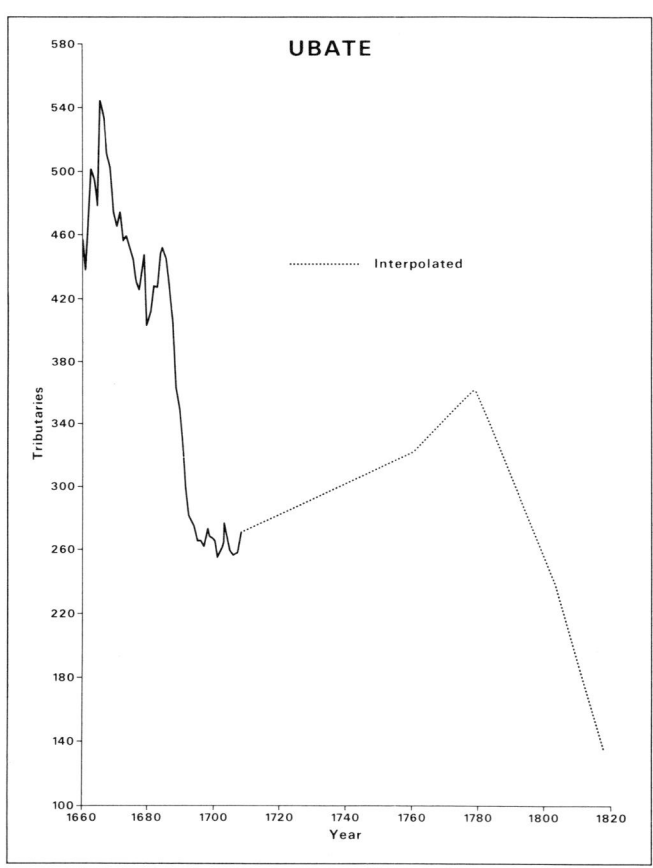

Figure 3.12 Tributary change in Ubaté, 1660-1820

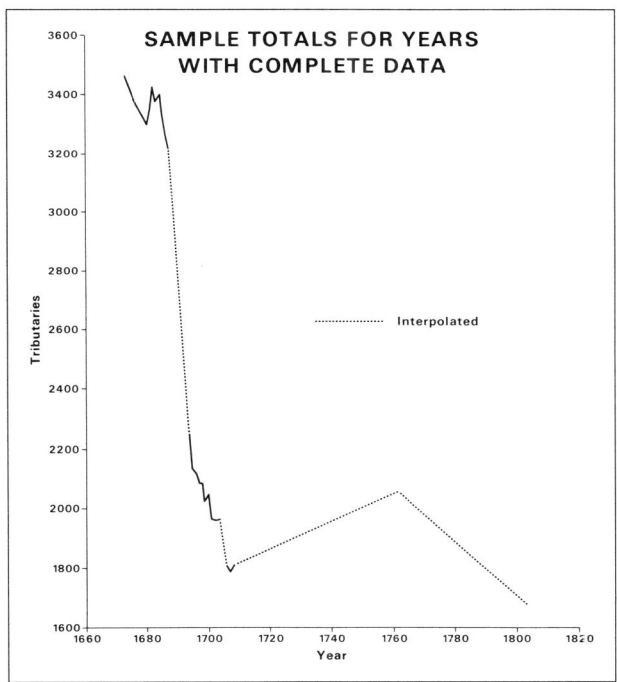

Figure 3.13 Sample tributary totals for years with complete data, Sabana de Bogotá, 1660-1810

TABLE 3.7
Tributary numbers in years with complete data

Year	Tributary Totals	Percentage Change
1673	3,453	
1676	3,376	-2.2
1679	3,326	-1.4
1680	3,299	- .8
1681	3,349	+1.5
1682	3,421	+2.1
1683	3,373	-1.4
1684	3,397	+ .7
1685	3,336	-1.8
1686	3,269	-2.0
1687	3,217	-1.6
1694	2,255	-29.9
1695	2,135	-5.3
1696	2,122	- .6
1697	2,086	-1.7
1698	2,085	-.05
1699	2,028	-2.7
1700	2,048	+1.0
1701	1,966	-4.0
1702	1,965	-.05
1703	1,967	+ .1
1706	1,811	-7.9
1707	1,799	- .7
1708	1,816	+ .9
1761	2,058	+13.3
1802-1803	1,678	-18.5

Sources: See Notes 27 and 28.

Tributary Counts and Individual Communities

Inspected community by community, the tributary counts indicate that there were also variations in patterns. Some are minor, probably reflecting differences in timing of reaction to similar conditions. Bogotá's tributaries began to increase between 1672 and 1675, Fontibón's in 1684, Suesca's in 1663 and Ubaté's in 1665 (see Figures). Other patterns, however, are clearly unique. For example Guatavita and annexes (Figure 3.6) are unlike any other community in our sample in that their peak in tributary numbers for the time span in question, occurred in the late eighteenth century, rather than in the seventeenth. Usaquén, whose annexes had been incorporated into it, was an extreme case in its termination as an independent pueblo in 1770 (Figure 3.11). The smallest communities--Serrezuela and Usme--have profiles that are different from most of the others, not indicating distinct long-term periods of rise or fall. Chocontá and Susa, which are both among the larger communities have fairly similar patterns through the early 1700s, and then diverge, with Chocontá regaining numbers through the middle of the century and Susa losing them until a short upswing around 1780.

An examination of the data demonstrates that the more detailed the census information, the more precision is called for in the qualitative data that is associated with it. Uncovering overall trends still leaves open questions regarding how particular stresses or opportunities affected particular communities, and points out the differences in focus between regional and community approaches to population change. One mode of analysis does not replace the other, but rather each provides a complementary clarification of the issues. Collection of information at the community level beyond that which is found in the National Archives in Bogotá and those in Seville is time-consuming and may be limited in content and extent. But some significant information about communities may be buried in local documents, especially in parish records. Records of pastoral visits may prove to be another source of information. Although most were burned in 1948 during the uprising in Bogotá, some records may remain in the Vatican archives and might have valuable information.

What sort of problems would we be looking to solve in searching for more data in both the local and general archives? Differential effects of three major factors in population decline--disease, labor extraction and limitations on native land use would be among the most important to approach. We know that all of these had negative impact on the population as a whole, but the tributary data in the series suggest some degree of variation in different areas. We shall briefly explore these three

Epidemics

Measles and smallpox continued to be the two most serious diseases among the Indians in the seventeenth and eighteenth centuries. Since an epidemiological study of the colonial period has yet to be done, the information is very incomplete. We do know, however, that there were measles epidemics in 1692 and 1729, epidemics of smallpox in 1693, 1756, 1781-1783 and 1801-1803, and sporadic outbreaks of smallpox in Santa Fe and the Sabana in other years as well. There were also other epidemics of unclearly identified diseases. One was supposed to have come from Japan in 1760; "peste" occurred in 1739, 1793-1794, and "pasa-diez" in 1808. Toward the end of the eighteenth century there are specific references to crop failures and hunger occurring both before and after periods of disease.[55]

Of all the epidemics, that of measles in 1692 and smallpox in 1693 appear to have contributed most to population decline. The number of tributaries in all the communities in our sample fell from 3,217 in 1687 to 2,255 in 1694, a decline of thirty percent. Inspection of the year to year tributary figures suggests that the epidemics intensified a decline that had already begun in the 1680s. They may also have had a delayed effect on tributary numbers, indicating that fatalities occurred primarily among the very young, and pregnant women, eliminating the potential tributaries of the next twelve to fifteen years. Tributary numbers reached the lowest point of the era in 1707. Furthermore the epidemics may have struck earlier in some areas. In Susa, Fúquene, Simijaca and Ubaté, communities that are close to each other, tributary population dropped precipitously between 1687 and 1688; in Susa from 306 to 175, in Simijaca from 131 to 111, and the next year to 75, in Fúquene from 198 to 151, and in Ubaté from 410 to 364 (see relevant Figures). Decline occurred but was less pronounced in the epidemic year of 1692, and the years thereafter. Whether measles or another catastrophic disease occurred first in Susa, Simijaca, Fúquene and Ubaté, remains unknown.

Data on epidemics can be gained through inspection of the yearly differences in burials in parish records. Persistence as well as access to supplementary documentary material will be necessary, however. Sometimes priests made notations in the records regarding disease, but other times not, even when the figures suggest that an epidemic may have been occurring.[56]

Labor

The Indians lost manpower to the Spaniards through personal services during the early years of colonization and through the forced labor systems (repartimiento) that were established by the crown in the early seventeenth century.⁵⁷ In 1657 legislation was implemented to reduce demands on the Chibcha for labor in the city, rural and mining areas. The rise in tributary population in many of the communities between the 1660s and the 1680s may have developed partially in response to the decreased labor demands, with adult males possibly less resistant to being counted. Nevertheless each tributary was still expected to spend one month every second year in forced labor in the city, at least one year in every three to ten years in the mines, between six months and a year every three years in agricultural work (concertaje) and at least two months a year in seasonal agricultural work. Women and children were also called on to do some of the seasonal work. Wages, set by crown officials for Indians engaged in forced labor, served mainly to help meet tribute payments and not for purchases.⁵⁸

The phase of increasing numbers of tributaries that we find in most of the communities in mid-eighteenth century roughly corresponds to an easing of labor demands in urban areas, the abolition first in the mines and later in agriculture of forced labor, and the permanent establishment of free labor by 1740.⁵⁹ As we have suggested above, Indian population rose in the eighteenth century, reaching a peak in the 1760s and 1780s, and then went into another decline thereafter.

We suspect that some of the Indians' movement within the Sabana was attributable to variations in labor demands as well as to those in tribute. Information is available regarding differences in tribute assessments, but labor needs to be explored further in the general and local archival records. Both should be looked at in terms of tributary population data available for the individual communities. Land tenure probably is a factor to be considered concurrently, since large Spanish estates had access to forced native labor, while farms of small and medium size did not. There may also have been variations in labor requirements for work in the mines. Officials' protection of the tributaries may have varied from pueblo to pueblo, and finally, varying degrees of skill in evading tributary classification, and consequently labor drafts, may have contributed to the differences in extant figures.⁶⁰

Land

As a result of the assignment of reservations in the

late sixteenth century, the Sabana Chibcha were left with access to a maximum of five percent of the land, parts of it in zones of low productivity. Resettlement programs also contributed to limitations on the Chibcha's resource base. Techniques or tools to improve productivity were not introduced for the cultivation of native staples, nor were the new sources of protein such as beef or mutton accessible to them, because of their lack of lands for pasture and the animals' costs. Even chickens and fish were destined for the tables of the encomendero, corregidor and priest or for marketing rather than for the Indians' consumption.[61]

Throughout the Sabana native crops were in constant danger of destruction by livestock that the Spaniards allowed to graze freely. The Chibcha's use of land was therefore further reduced by the need to maintain some distance from non-Indian estates where herds were kept. The accumulation of foodstuffs or animals appears to have been difficult for the Indians and perhaps not very attractive, since such goods could be confiscated for payment of tribute and taxes, and later in the eighteenth century for the supply of Santa Fe. Taxes, resettlement, land and property appropriations no doubt affected the Sabana Chibcha's nutrition and fertility as well as material wealth. Toward the end of the eighteenth century their continued existence in their own pueblos was threatened by the pronounced growth of non-Indian populations. Poor mestizos, mulattos and whites settled on Indian lands as renters at first, particularly in the nucleated zones which the Indians had been forced to build. The mixed population, that came to form the most important component of nineteenth and twentieth century rural population, began to take over Indian land, in some cases, such as in Usaquén and annexes, completely, and in others at least partially.[62]

Some of the tributary and general population losses among the Indians in this period no doubt were due to *mestizaje* through marriage and/or acculturation, attractive routes since mestizos were not subject to tribute. Many other natives opted to leave their pueblos and go to others where conditions were less onerous, or to the city or even other regions. In the late eighteenth century priests, crown officials and others remarked on the apparent ease with which the Indians moved.[63]

The increase of non-Indians on Indian land at the end of the eighteenth century corresponds to a decline in both tributary and total Indian population numbers in most communities in our sample, and in the Sabana in general. More detailed research might indicate whether proximity to Spanish estates was correlated with greater loss of tributary population, because of increased demands for labor and chances of crop damage. It would also be useful to investigate what impact resettlement attempts by the Spaniards had on both the tributary and general population, the effects of different rates of influx of non-Indians, and the relation between distance from the capital and native decline. Our findings on the last point indicate that the greater proportion of communities that declined by over fifty percent between 1592-1595 and the middle of the eighteenth century were within a radius of twenty kilometers of Santa Fe (Usaquén, Teusaca, Suba, Tuna, Bosa, Fontibón, Bogotá among others); but communities at great distances also lost substantial numbers, Chocontá, Guasca-Siecha, Simijaca and Suta-Tausa among them declining by between a third and a half.

SUMMARY

We have discussed the population material available for the Sabana and pointed out that there are three major reliable censuses of total population--1592-1595, 1636-1640 and 1758-1759--of which only the first and last are fairly complete. For some indication of trends between these dates and afterward, tributary counts can be used, particularly the long series found in the Archivo General de Indias, with supplementary data from the Archivo Histórico Nacional in Bogotá.

We have explored the meaning of "tributary" in relation to male and total populations, and have shown that the increase in population:tributary ratios in the eighteenth and nineteenth centuries had to do with Spanish classification and Indian avoidance of tributary classification rather than with increasing family size, change in fertility or improvement in the resource base. Finally we have inspected the tributary series with regard to population as a whole, population trends in the late seventeenth and eighteenth centuries and differing patterns among the communities. Some of the problems regarding epidemiology, labor and land have been suggested that might be profitably addressed using the tributary series and more detailed local research.

NOTES

1. Archival material for this paper comes from the Archivo Histórico Nacional de Colombia (Bogotá), cited as AHNC; the Biblioteca Nacional--Libros Raros (Bogotá), referred to as BNLR; parish records of Sabana communities; and the Archivo General de Indias (Seville), cited as AGI. María Angeles Eugenio Martínez, <u>Tributo y Trabajo del Indio en Nueva Granada</u> (Seville, Escuela de Estudios Hispano-Americanos, 1977), p. 204, has recently commented on the lack of demographic work for the Sabana.

2. Even within the highland basins there were variations in rainfall, frost and other factors, but these differences were less pronounced than those between areas at different altitudes. S. F. Cook and Woodrow Borah have pointed out the importance of taking altitude (as a determinant of differing natural zones) into consideration in population data analysis. See S. F. Cook and Woodrow Borah, Essays in Population History. Mexico and the Caribbean (2 vols., Berkeley, University of California Press, 1971-1974) Vol. 1, pp. xiii, 79ff., 411-429; and The Indian Population of Central Mexico 1531-1610 (Berkeley, University of California Press, Ibero-Americana 44, 1960), pp. 33-56.

3. Juan A. Villamarin, Encomenderos and Indians in the Formation of Colonial Society in the Sabana de Bogotá, Colombia: 1537-1740 (Ph.D. dissertation, Brandeis University, 1972), pp. 94-108; Villamarin and Judith E. Villamarin, Indian Labor in Mainland Colonial Spanish America (Newark, University of Delaware Latin American Studies Program, Occasional Papers and Monographs No. 1, 1975), pp. 85-89; Villamarin and Villamarin, "Chibcha Settlement Under Spanish Rule: 1537-1810," in David J. Robinson (ed.), Social Fabric and Spatial Structure in Colonial Latin America (Ann Arbor, University Microfilms International, 1979), pp. 29-33.

4. Villamarin, Encomenderos and Indians, pp. 141-161; Eugenio Martínez, Tributo y Trabajo, pp. 204-212; Julian Ruíz Rivera, Encomienda y Mita en Nueva Granada (Seville, Escuela de Estudios Hispano-Americanos, 1975), pp. 27-35.

5. Ruíz Rivera, Encomienda y Mita, pp. 48-57, 351-354 (1636-1640). The visita of the Sabana was done primarily in 1638-1639. A few Sabana communities (such as Guachetá and Lenguazaque) were included in the Province of Tunja, and were visited in 1636. AHNC, Visitas de Cundinamarca: Vol. 8: fols. 779r-836v (1761); this document has information on most of the communities in the Sabana. The 1755-1756 visita of Tunja has population figures for the following Sabana pueblos: Guachetá, Lenguazaque, Simijaca, Susa, Tausa, Zipaquirá and Usaquén. See Ulises Rojas, Corregidores y Justicias Mayores de Tunja (Tunja, Imprenta Departamental de Boyacá, 1963), pp. 522-523.

6. A final, overall report has not been found. There are population figures on a number of communities for which individual visitas have been located in the AHNC. The most complete set of figures are those of tributary Indians, included in a general report on New Granada's tributaries in AHNC, Gobierno: Vol. 1: fols. 4r-78r. This document has also been published in the Anuario Colombiano de Historia Social y de La Cultura, No. 2 (1964), pp. 410-530 (462-485, Province of Santa Fe), transcribed by Alvaro González under the supervision of Jaime Jaramillo Uribe.

7. See notes 27 and 28 below. The communities in our sample are Bogotá,* Bosa,* Chocontá,* Cucunubá,* Bobota, Facatativá,* Chueca, Fontibón,* Techo, Fúquene,* Nemoga, Guatavita,* Chaleche, Tuneche, Guasca,* Siecha, Serrezuela,* Sesquilé,* Gachacaca, Simijaca,* Suba,* Tuna, Suacha,* Suesca,* Suta,* Tausa, Susa,* Ubate,* Usaquén, Tibavita, Teusaca, Tunjaque, Suaque, Usme.* Those marked with an asterisk survived through the early nineteenth century. The others were associated with them administratively, and

ultimately became sections of them, or disappeared entirely. This process and the grouping together of some of the communities in the graphs are discussed in the last section of this study. Examples cited here are taken from the above sample, and are not necessarily exhaustive of the information.

    8. AGI, Santa Fe 233, r 1, num. 11. For the communities in our sample we have the following: Bogotá 900 tributaries, Bosa 500, Facatativá 250, Fontibón 800, Serrezuela 130, Suba-Tuna 800, Usme 300. Eugenio Martínez, Tributo y Trabajo, pp. 583-586, also has these figures.

    9. Juan Friede (ed.), Fuentes Documentales Para la Historia del Nuevo Reino de Granada. Desde la Instalación de la Real Audiencia en Santa Fe (8 vols., Bogotá, Biblioteca Banco Popular, 1975-1976), Vol. 5, pp. 129-135. According to the estimates Bogotá had 800-1,000 tributaries, Suba-Tuna had 900-1,000, and Usme 200-300.

    10. AHNC, Visitas de Cundinamarca: Vol. 1: fols. 813r-838v, 844r-871v; population figures on Cucunubá-Bobota and Simijaca in 1586 when they were being resettled by the Spaniards.

    11. Villamarin, Encomenderos and Indians, pp. 31-70. Juan Friede (ed.), Documentos Inéditos Para la Historia de Colombia. Coleccionados en el Archivo General de Indias, de Sevilla (10 vols., Bogotá, Academia Colombiana de Historia, 1955-1960), Vols. 5-10; Fuentes Documentales, Vols. 1-8. Esperanza Galvez Piñal, La Visita de Monzon y Prieto de Orellana al Nuevo Reino de Granada (Seville, Escuela de Estudios Hispano-Americanos, 1974). Ulises Rojas, El Cacique de Turmequé y su Epoca (Tunja, Imprenta Departamental, 1965).

    12. AHNC, Encomiendas: Vol. 26: fols. 870r-909v (Bogotá 1560); Vol. 9: fols. 310r-330v (Subiasuca, later called Serrezuela, 1563). It is not known how many pueblos were covered in the two visitas.

    13. AHNC, Reales Cedulas: Vol. 1: fols. 192r-195v.

    14. See German Colmenares, La Provincia de Tunja en el Nuevo Reino de Granada (Bogotá, Multilith, Universidad de los Andes, 1970), pp. 115ff. Hermes Tovar Pinzón, "Estado Actual de los Estudios de Demografía Histórica en Colombia," Anuario Colombiano de Historia Social y de la Cultura, No. 5, pp. 65-140; Tovar Pinzón has found the following information for the provinces of Tunja and Velez (pp. 121-125):

Tribute

Community	Pesos de Medio Oro	Mantas	Tributaries
Duitama	750	750	750
Sasa	300	300	300
Sutamanga	200	200	200

The correspondence of number of tributaries to tribute, as illustrated above, is found to exist in 93.3 percent (104) of the communities that have information on both factors. In seven communities there are differences as in the following:

Community	Pesos de Medio Oro	Mantas	Tributaries
Tibaquirá	150	150	50
Sora	500	500	450
Pisba	650	650	700

Our data for Sabana communities (see Villamarin, Encomenderos and Indians, p. 60) does not have the internal conformity of the Tunja and Velez material. Tribute assessments on some of the communities in our sample in 1564 were as follows:

Tribute

Community	Pesos de Buen Oro	Mantas
Bogotá	660	330
Chocontá	--	950
Cucunubá-Bobota	--	200
Guasca	400	150
Simijaca	158	100
Suta-Tausa	200	120
Ubaté	--	1,000
Usme	200	120

Eugenio Martínez (Tributo y Trabajo, pp. 251-259) has data showing that in Nemocón-Tasgata (in the Sabana), tribute assessment was 230 pesos and 100 mantas for 201 tributaries.

15. Villamarin, Encomenderos and Indians, pp. 55-63, 218.

16. Julian Ruíz Rivera, Fuentes Para la Demografía Histórica de Nueva Granada (Seville, Escuela de Estudios Hispano-Americanos, 1972), p. 23; see pages 23-33 for census of 1592-1595.

17. Juan López de Velasco, Geografía y Descripción Universal de las Indias (1574, Madrid, Ediciones Atlas. Biblioteca de Autores Españoles, 1971), p. 181; López de Velasco's figures of 40,000-50,000 tributaries for the Province of Santa Fe in the early 1570s have no basis in an actual count, and may have been based on a report on New Granada, now found in the Archivo General de Indias (see Friede, [ed.], Fuentes Documentales, Vol. 5, p. 264). Fiscal Valverde, in a letter of 4 February 1572, says that there were a total of 17,000 tributaries at the time (see Eugenio Martínez, Tributo y Trabajo, p. 207). Neither Eugenio Martínez's search in Seville, nor ours in Bogotá found indications of any extensive count prior to the 1590s.

18. Ruíz Rivera, Fuentes Para la Demografía Histórica, pp. 37, 42-51; Encomienda y Mita, pp. 37-38.

19. AHNC, Visitas de Cundinamarca: Vol. 6: fols. 1r-247v (Tenjo and annexes); fols. 399r-530v (Cajica, Tabio and annexes).

20. AHNC, Caciques e Indios: Vol. 42: fols. 81r-93v.

21. AHNC, Visitas de Cundinamarca: Vol. 7: fol. 145r; Vol. 1: fol. 410r; Caciques e Indios: Vol. 72: fols. 166r-168v.

22. AHNC, Caciques e Indios: Vol. 72: fol. 168v.
23. AHNC, Gobierno: Vol. 1: fols. 4r-78r.
24. On the tributary population also see Ruíz Rivera, Encomienda y Mita, pp. 351-354. For the Visitas of 1636-1640 see AHNC, Visitas de Cundinamarca: Vol. 8: fols. 167r-205v (Bogotá); Vol. 12: fols. 643r-656v (Cajica); Miscelanea: Vol. 8: fols. 559r-597r (Chocontá); Visitas de Cundinamarca: Vol. 1: fols. 235r-241r (Engativá); Vol. 12: fols. 913r-938v (Fontibón); Vol. 6: fols. 815r-833r (Fúquene-Nemoga); Vol. 7: fols. 157r-166r (Gachancipá); Vol. 7: fols. 758r-779r (Guasca-Siecha); Vol. 12: fols. 750r-761r (Nemocón-Tasgata); Vol. 10: fols. 369r-380r (Sesquilé-Gachacaca); Vol. 1: fols. 414r-425v (Sopó-Meusa-Queca); Vol. 13: fols. 606r-610v (Subachoque); Vol. 13: fols. 592r-603r (Tabio-Gines-Chibiasuca); Vol. 2: fols. 576r-583v (Tenjo-Gongotá); Vol. 5: fols. 32r-40r (Usaquén); Vol. 2: fols. 192r-208v (Zipaquirá-Gotaque-Tenemequirá-Suativa).
25. AHNC, Visitas de Cundinamarca: Vol. 11: fols. 535r-554r (Cajicá); Vol. 11: fols. 369r-383r (Cota); Vol. 11: fols. 446r-460v (Gachancipá); Vol. 13: fols. 465r-486r (Sopó-Meusa-Queca); Vol. 13: fols. 361r-381r (Tabio-Chibiasuca-Gines-Subachoque); Vol. 13: fols. 258v-289r (Zipaquirá and annexes).
26. AHNC, Visitas de Cundinamarca: Vol. 8: fols. 779r-836v (1761); Vol. 7: fol. 521r (Guasca).
27. For visitas of 1778-1779 see AHNC, Visitas de Cundinamarca: Vol. 7: fol. 1086r (Bogotá); Vol. 8: fols. 843r-847v (Bojacá-Bobase-Cubiasuca); Vol. 7: fols. 842r (Bosa); Vol. 7: fol. 442r (Chocontá); Vol. 10: fol. 964r (Cucunubá-Bobota); Vol. 10: fol. 924v (Fúquene-Nemoga); Vol. 7: fol. 428r (Guatavita-Chaleche-Tuneche); Vol. 7: fol. 485r (Guasca-Siecha); Vol. 7: fol. 1086r (Serrezuela); Vol. 7: fol. 461v (Sesquilé-Gachacaca); Vol. 10: fol. 945r (Simijaca); Vol. 7: fol. 495v (Sopo-Meusa-Queca); Vol. 7: fol. 842r (Suacha); Vol. 7: fol. 842r (Suba-Tuna); Vol. 10: fols. 973r-973v (Suesca); Vol. 10: fol. 940r (Susa); Vol. 10: fol. 958v (Sutatausa); Vol. 10: fol. 952r (Tausa); Vol. 10: fol. 913v (Ubaté).

For reports on early nineteenth century figures see AHNC, Tributos: NC (Not Classified) #1 (Bogotá, Bojacá, Engativá, Facatativá, Fontibón, Serrezuela, Tenjo--1800); #11 (Bosa, Suacha, Suba 1800-1801; Usme 1817-1818); #13 (Suacha, Suba 1801-1802); #14 (Bosa, Suacha, Suba 1808); #21 (Chocontá, Guasca, Guatavita, Sesquilé 1804-1805; Bogotá, Fontibón, Serrezuela, Tenjo and annexes 1805; Bosa-Suacha, Suba 1809; Bosa 1830); #25 (Cucunubá, Simijaca, Suesca, Suta, Ubaté 1817); #26 (Bogotá, Bojacá, Engativá, Facatativá, Fontibón, Serrezuela, Tenjo 1803); #28 (Usme 1803); #29 (Chocontá, Guasca, Guatavita, Sesquilé 1803-1804; Cucunubá, Fúquene, Simijaca, Suesca, Susa, Suta, Ubaté 1803-1804); #32 (Chocontá, Guasca, Guatavita, Sesquilé 1804-1805; Bogotá, Bojacá, Engativá, Facatativá, Fontibón, Serrezuela, Tenjo 1806-1810, 1818; Bosa, Fontibón, Suba 1828; Fontibón, Usme 1830); #33 (Fúquene, Susa 1817; Bosa, Suacha, Suba 1817; Chocontá, Guasca, Guatavita, Sesquilé 1816-1819--For this period in these communities the figures of 1804-1805 were used by the Spaniards because of their lack of control during the Independence struggle; Cucunubá, Suesca, Simijaca, Suta, Ubaté 1818-1819; Bogotá, Bojacá, Engativá, Facatativá, Fontibón, Serrezuela, Tenjo 1816-1818); #37 (Bogotá, Bojacá, Engativá, Facatativá, Fontibón,

Serrezuela, Tenjo 1802-1804); #40 (Bosa, Suacha, Suba 1806-1807); #41 (Bogotá, Bojacá, Facatativá, Tenjo 1804); #43 (Bogotá, Bojacá, Engativá, Facatativá, Fontibón, Serrezuela, Tenjo 1801). AHNC, Resguardos de Cundinamarca: Vol. 1: fol. 465v (Tausa 1804).

    28. AGI, Contaduría, 1341, 1344, 1344A, 1344B, 1345, 1346, 1346A, 1346B, 1347, 1544, 1546, 1554, 1591, 1595, 1596. Sabana communities covered were Bogotá, Bojacá-Bobase, Chinga, Chise, Chitasuga, Chueca, Churuaco, Ciénaga, Cubia, Engativá, Facatativá, Fontibón, Guangata, Serrezuela, Sisativa, Tenjo, Tibaguya--from San Juan 1658 to San Juan 1670; from Navidad 1671 to Navidad 1703; San Juan 1706 to San Juan 1708; and Navidad 1710 to San Juan 1748. Cucunubá-Bobota, Fúquene-Nemoga, Simijaca, Susa, Suesca, Ubaté--from Navidad 1657 to San Juan 1692; Navidad 1694 to San Juan 1709. Chocontá, Guasca, Guatavita, Sesquilé--from Navidad 1659 to Navidad 1673; San Juan 1676 to San Juan 1727; San Juan 1730 to San Juan 1733; San Juan 1745 to Navidad 1749. Cajicá, Chia, Cogua, Gachancipa, Gotaque, Nemocón-Tasgatá, Suativa, Subachoque, Sopo, Tabio, Tenemequirá, Tibito, Tocancipa, Zipaquirá--from San Juan 1658 to Navidad 1681; Navidad 1689 to Navidad 1691. Guachetá, Lenguazaque--from Navidad 1669 to Navidad 1674; Navidad 1677 to San Juan 1731; Navidad 1733 to Navidad 1739. Usme--from San Juan 1665 to San Juan 1688; Navidad 1694 to Navidad 1710. Bosa-Suacha, Teusaca, Tibavita, Tunjaque--from Navidad 1673 to San Juan 1691; San Juan 1694 to San Juan 1704; Navidad 1706 to San Juan 1710; Navidad 1713 to Navidad 1738; for Bosa and Suacha also Navidad 1659 to Navidad 1661. Cota-- from Navidad 1673 to Navidad 1678. Suba-Tuna--from Navidad 1660 to San Juan 1691; San Juan 1694 to San Juan 1704; Navidad 1706 to San Juan 1710; Navidad 1717 to Navidad 1738.

    29. AHNC, Residencias de Cundinamarca: Vol. 4: fol. 692v (1727); Vol. 5: fol. 90v (1753); Vol. 5: fol. 799r (1641); Vol. 6: fol. 1018r (1655); Vol. 9: fol. 312r (1645).

    30. Villamarin and Villamarin, Indian Labor, pp. 82-89.

    31. Villamarin, Encomenderos and Indians, pp. 13-93. Eugenio Martínez, Tributo y Trabajo, pp. 185-187, 204-212.

    32. Villamarin, Encomenderos and Indians, pp. 141-210; Villamarin and Villamarin, Indian Labor, pp. 2, 18, 85-89. Ruíz Rivera, Encomienda y Mita, pp. 242-244. AHNC, Caciques e Indios: Vol. 55: fol. 634v; both married and single men had to pay full tribute. The ages formally delimiting tributary status differed slightly from province to province. In Tunja they were seventeen to sixty years (Colmenares, La Provincia de Tunja, p. 63); and in Cartago fourteen to fifty years in 1559, fourteen to forty-five in 1568, and seventeen to fifty-four in 1627 (Tovar Pinzón, "Estado Actual de los Estudios," pp. 83-84).

    33. Under this system tribute differed among communities but in most cases was uniform for all native males within a given community. Villamarin, Encomenderos and Indians, pp. 153-161, 218-228. Ruíz Rivera, Encomienda y Mita, pp. 224-235.

    34. Villamarin and Villamarin, Indian Labor, pp. 85, 88-89.

    35. Cook and Borah (Essays in Population History, Vol. 1, p. 17) have pointed out the importance of defining terms, stating: "Use of Indian tribute material for demographic information must be based upon detailed understanding of the tribute system and changes in

classification of tributary." We find in analyzing the Sabana material that it is essential to explore changes in classification, exemptions and other factors affecting tributary and general population counts.

36. In the censuses nuclear families were used as the basic units. First the male head of the family was listed, then his wife and children. Single individuals were reported separately. See AHNC, Visitas de Cundinamarca: Vol. 6: fols. 412r-440v (1603); Vol. 7: fols. 758r-779v (1639); Vol. 8: fols. 843r-847v (1778).

37. Juan A. Villamarin and Judith Villamarin, "Kinship Organization and Inheritance Among the Sabana de Bogotá Chibcha at the Time of Spanish Conquest," Ethnology, Vol. 14 (1975), pp. 173-179. AHNC, Caciques e Indios: Vol. 57: fols. 685r-720v.

38. Sylvia M. Broadbent, Los Chibchas. Organización Sociopolítica (Bogotá, Universidad Nacional de Colombia-Facultad de Sociologia, 1964), pp. 32-33. Chia, Libro de Bautismos 1 (1720-1744).

39. AHNC, Encomiendas: Vol. 9: fols. 312v-313r (Subiasuca, later called Serrezuela, 1563). Also see AHNC, Visitas de Cundinamarca: Vol. 4: fol. 977v (Suta, Tausa, Simijaca) and Encomiendas: Vol. 12: fols. 222r-222v (Cota 1563):
> que agora y de aqui adelante cada uno de ellos no tengan mas de una mujer propia y no se casen con las mujeres de sus hermanos aunque esten vivos o esten muertos, ni tampoco con las hermanas que ovieren tenido y se les hayan muerto.

40. AHNC, Visitas de Cundinamarca: Vol. 5: fols. 211v-212r (Ubaté 1592). In the interrogation of the Indians a question dealt with this matter. One of the caciques of Ubaté stated that all the Indians were Christians, ". . . bautizados e casados segun orden de la Santa Madre iglesia," and that they didn't have, ". . . parientas con quien use de las cosas que dice la pregunta (concerning sexual relations) ni que sean parientas unas de otras, ni otras de otras, que si algunos (indios) tuvieran se vera por la lista que se hiciera por el señor visitador." In Teusacá, Visitas de Cundinamarca: Vol. 5: fol. 558v (1593), the cacique made a similar statement, but declared that he had six females in his service, "y que con algunas de ellas, de cuando en cuando tiene parte con ellas carnalmente, y que esto es de tarde en tarde." Polygyny in the Sabana needs to be further explored, as do other factors affecting marriage patterns and access to women after the conquest. See also Vernon Dorjahn, "The Factor of Polygyny in African Demography," in William R. Bascom and Melville J. Herskovits (eds.), Continuity and Change in African Cultures (Chicago, University of Chicago Press, 1959), pp. 87-112. Dorjahn discusses some of the census problems associated with polygyny and the socio-cultural, fertility and general demographic ramifications.

41. Villamarin, Encomenderos and Indians, pp. 121-122, 270-271. Villamarin and Villamarin, "Kinship Organization."

42. Villamarin, Encomenderos and Indians, pp. 243-249, 254-258. Although it is clear that women and children emigrated during all periods of the colonial era, quantitative data on their emigration is usually not available, because the documents are geared mainly

toward reporting tribute-paying men.

43. AHNC, Visitas de Cundinamarca: Vol. 11: fols. 446r-460v (Gachancipá 1670). Crown officials were trying to collect a tax of four pesos from each forastero. AGI, Contaduría, 1596 (1671-1673). AHNC, Visitas de Cundinamarca: Vol. 8: fols. 783r-783v (1761). Visitador Aróstegui y Escoto stated that there were many ausentes, and that the forastero tribute of 4 p 4 r a year favored Indian movement, because it was lower than what men had to pay in their native communities. He proposed, and apparently ordered, that forasteros pay the same tribute as that of the community in which they were living, but this was not carried out. See AHNC, Tributos: NC #1 (1800).

44. AHNC, Caciques e Indios: Vol. 21: fols. 12r-19v (1585). BNLR, Manuscrito #181 (1597) Oidor Visitador Ibarra ordered that caciques and capitanes "no recojan, tengan y escondan en sus pueblos a ningunos indios que no fueren del naturales, y los forasteros los embien, y restituyan a su pueblo y natural." There were few disputes among caciques for Indians on the boundaries of their territories. The number of such cases was small probably because the Europeans did not break up communities, but followed Chibcha sociopolitical and geographical divisions fairly regularly in allocating encomiendas.

45. Villamarin and Villamarin, "Chibcha Settlement," pp. 67-77.

46. Ernesto Restrepo Tirado, "Lista de los Encomenderos del Partido de Santa Fe en 1595 (Documentos del Archivo de Indias)," Boletín de Historia y Antiguedades, Vol. 23 (1936), pp. 116-127. Ruíz Rivera, Fuentes Para la Demografía Histórica, pp. 23-33.

47. The total figures including ausentes were generally used in documents. For example Visitador Aróstegui y Escoto referred to some of the 1636-1640 census in his 1761 report, and when giving totals used figures that included ausentes. Guasca's total 1639 population is cited as being 1,049 (AHNC, Visitas de Cundinamarca: Vol. 8: fol. 794v); we know from its visita that there were six ausentes included in the 1,049 figure (Visitas de Cundinamarca: Vol. 7: fol. 779r). Figures also remain for Chocontá, that had a total of 1,335 including twenty-five ausentes (Visitas de Cundinamarca: Vol. 8: fol. 801r; Miscelanea: Vol. 8: fol. 597r); Fúquene-Nemoga with a total of 934 including fourteen ausentes (Visitas de Cundinamarca: Vol. 8: fol. 803r; Vol. 6: fol. 833r); and Nemocón-Tasgata, with a 452 total including four ausentes (Vol. 8: fol. 806r; Vol. 12: fol. 761r). In 1758 Guasca's total population was given as 622, including seventy-six ausentes (Visitas de Cundinamarca: Vol. 7: fol. 521r); Bosa's was 499 including twenty-eight ausentes (Vol. 8: fol. 823r; Vol. 7: fol. 633r), and Tocancipá's was 776 including thirty-six ausentes (Vol. 8: fol. 812v; Vol. 4: fol. 713r). It should be noted that in visitas there are sometimes small arithmetical discrepancies between the actual enumeration of people, and the summing of categories and totals. Usually only totals were referred to in other documents.

For our Table 3.6 we have been able to delete ausentes from total population figures of 1636-1640. There is insufficient data to do so for 1758-1759.

48. AHNC, Miscelanea: Vol. 78: fols. 940r-940v (1669); Vol. 113:

fols. 444r-444v (1672).

49. Juan Friede, "Algunas Consideraciones Sobre la Evolución Demográfica en la Provincia de Tunja," Anuario Colombiano de Historia Social y de la Cultura, No. 3 (1965), pp. 5-19. Friede establishes a ratio of 4.82 for the visita of 1636 in Tunja, and states (p. 12):

> Tan alto coeficiente, indicio de familias numerosas, se debe indudablemente al benigno clima de la altiplanicie andina, a su fértil suelo apto para la agricultura y a la carencia de una intensiva explotación minera.

50. Villamarin, Encomenderos and Indians, pp. 245-246. AHNC, Visitas de Cundinamarca: Vol. 8: fols. 794v, 801r.

51. Colmenares, La Provincia de Tunja, pp. 58-69; Historia Económica y Social de Colombia 1537-1719 (Cali, Universidad del Valle, 1973), pp. 60-71. Eugenio Martínez, Tributo y Trabajo, pp. 212-223. Ruíz Rivera, Encomienda y Mita, pp. 94-100.

52. The matter of appropriate ratios for different segments of the colonial era has been addressed by several investigators. Jaime Jaramillo Uribe ("La Población Indígena de Colombia en el Momento de la Conquista y sus Posteriores Transformaciones," Anuario Colombiano de Historia Social y de la Cultura, No. 2, 1964, pp. 239-293) suggests (pp. 244-246) using a coefficient of 3 for the sixteenth century, 4 for the seventeenth century and 5 for the eighteenth century, in contrast to using 4 as a multiplier to calculate Colombian Indian population in all three centuries, as had been done previously. Ruíz Rivera (Encomienda y Mita, p. 98) has established the ratios of 3.12 for 1595 and 3.06 for 1602-1604 in the Province of Tunja. Eugenio Martínez (Tributo y Trabajo, p. 216) is in agreement. Ruíz Rivera also offers the following values for the Province of Santa Fe: 1595:5.53; 1600-1604:4.31; 1635-1640:4.78; 1670-1671:5.53; 1687:7.26; 1690:6.03. It is not always clear how he derives the figures. Also see Colmenares, La Provincia de Tunja, p. 66; and Note 51 above.

There already exist works calculating the population of the Province of Santa Fe. See Eugenio Martínez (Tributo y Trabajo, pp. 204-223) for the sixteenth century; Ruíz Rivera (Encomienda y Mita, pp. 27-61, 89-110) for the seventeenth century. These authors are clear about the shortcomings of the data. Professor Hermes Tovar Pinzón is preparing a detailed population study of the Chibcha area.

53. See Villamarin and Villamarin, "Chibcha Settlement" for more detailed information on the Sabana communities' settlement patterns during the colonial period. The nineteen communities in our sample that remained in existence through the late eighteenth century were Bogotá, Bosa, Cucunubá, Chocontá, Facatativá, Fontibón, Fúquene, Guasca, Guatavita, Serrezuela, Sesquilé, Simijaca, Suacha, Suba, Suesca, Susa, Suta, Ubaté and Usme. The fifteen that did not were Bobota, Chaleche, Chueca, Gachacaca, Nemoga, Siecha, Suaque, Tausa, Techo, Teusaca, Tivavita, Tuna, Tuneche, Tunjaque and Usaquén (Usaquén remained in name but its Indians had been moved to Suacha).

54. Villamarin, Encomenderos and Indians, pp. 247, 250-251.

55. Villamarin, Encomenderos and Indians, pp. 135, 252-253. Major epidemics in the sixteenth and seventeenth century were smallpox (1558, 1588, 1621, 1651), measles (1618) and tobardillo

(exanthematic typhus?) (1630-1633). There were other serious diseases of unknown nature (1568-1569). As stated, smallpox and measles continued to be the most devastating epidemics afterward. On the late seventeenth century through the early nineteenth century, see J. A. Vargas Jurado, "Tiempos Coloniales," in J. A. Vargas Jurado, J. M. Caballero and J. A. deTorres y Peña (eds.), La Patria Boba (Bogotá, Biblioteca de Historia Nacional, Vol. I, Imprenta Nacional, 1902), pp. 13, 45, 52; and in the same volume, J. M. Caballero, "En La Independencia," pp. 93, 99, 102, 108. Also, AHNC, Tributos: Vol. 20: fol. 571r (1782); Miscelanea: Vol. 2: fols. 809v-810r (1782); Caciques e Indios: Vol. 25: fol. 879r (1783); Resguardos de Cundinamarca: Vol. 2: fol. 884r (1783); Caciques e Indios: Vol. 25: fols. 608v-620r (1793-1794); Miscelanea: Vol. 22: fols. 266r-389v (1801); Vol. 33: fols. 379r-398v (1801); Vol. 44: fols. 495r-524v (1801); Vol. 2: fols. 817r-868v; 909r-919v, 930r-1003r (1802-1803); Vol. 3: fols. 269r-280v; 316r-326v (1802-1803).

On the epidemics' coincidence with crop failure and hunger, see AHNC, Tributos: NC #18 (Chia 1780-1781); Tributos: Vol. 20: fol. 571r (Bogotá, Bojacá, Facatativá, Fontibón, Tenjo 1782-1783); Caciques e Indios: Vol. 25: fol. 879r (Cucunubá 1783); Vol. 25: fols. 608v-620r (Bojacá, Engativá, Facatativá, Fontibón, Tenjo, Serrezuela 1793-1794); Tributos: Vol. 22: fols. 738r-764v (Guatavita 1803); fols. 149r-161v (Chocontá 1803). Further work is needed to establish the relations among these factors.

56. Bogotá, Libro de Bautizmos, Vol. 2 (1782, 1783). In 1782 thirty-six deaths were registered, and in 1783, 137; almost all of the latter were cited as having resulted from smallpox.

57. Villamarin, Encomenderos and Indians, pp. 211-214, 228-233, 253-254. Villamarin and Villamarin, Indian Labor, pp. 86-88.

58. Villamarin, Encomenderos and Indians, pp. 212-228. AHNC, Tierras de Boyacá: Vol. 17: fols. 517v-519v.

59. Villamarin and Villamarin, Indian Labor, pp. 88-89.

60. Villamarin, Encomenderos and Indians, pp. 218-228. Juan A. Villamarin, "Haciendas en la Sabana de Bogotá, Colombia, en la Epoca Colonial (1539-1810)" in Enrique Florescano (ed.), Haciendas, Latifundios y Plantaciones en América Latina (Mexico, Siglo Veintiuno Editores, 1975), pp. 335-337. Julian Ruíz Rivera, "La Plata de Mariquita en el Siglo XVII: Mita y Producción," Anuario de Estudios Americanos, Vol. 29 (1972), pp. 121-169.

61. Villamarin, Encomenderos and Indians, pp. 148-151, 263-266, 272-276. Juan A. Villamarin, "Factores Que Afectaron la Producción Agropecuaria en la Sabana de Bogotá en la Epoca Colonial" (Tunja, Ediciones Pato Marino, 1975). Villamarin and Villamarin, "Chibcha Settlement."

62. Villamarin and Villamarin, "Chibcha Settlement," pp. 67-84.

63. AHNC, Visitas de Cundinamarca: Vol. 8: fol. 783v; Tributos: NC #6.

4
The Ecology of Race and Class in Late Colonial Oaxaca

John K. Chance

The use of quantitative sources in studies of colonial Latin American societies has become increasingly sophisticated in recent years. Analyses of census data in particular have provided new insights into social structure and social change, especially in urban areas. A number of recent studies have extended our knowledge of the ecology of the eighteenth-century Latin American city by matching census counts with city plans to plot the spatial distribution of households and individuals.[1] The present paper provides new data on the residential patterns of racial and occupational groups in a late colonial Mexican city, applying to them some statistical indexes of segregation developed by North American sociologists for United States cities.[2] These measures have previously been applied mainly to blacks and whites, though some studies have dealt with a variety of ethnic and socioeconomic groupings.[3] In recent years, some of these measures of segregation have also been applied successfully by social historians to nineteenth-century American cities.[4] It is time, I think, that we try them out in the Latin American context to see if they can bring more clarity and precision to our understanding of colonial urban social structure.

In this paper I am concerned with the case of Oaxaca, Mexico (or Antequera as it was known in colonial times) in 1792. Though it had a population of only 18,000 in that year, Antequera was typical of the highland towns of Spanish America in that it had significant numbers of Spaniards, Indians, and <u>castas</u> (people of mixed racial ancestry), surrounded by a dense and highly developed Indian peasant population. Mining was of minimal significance in the Oaxaca region, and the economy revolved around agriculture, trade (especially in the cochineal dyestuff), and textile manufacture.

The data used in this paper come from the 1792 Revillagigedo military census, which gives a complete house-to-house count of the city's 12,600 non-Indian and non-slave inhabitants in that year.⁵ While this source has the disadvantage of excluding all Indians and most blacks, it is fairly consistent in its listing of racial affiliations and occupations of the rest of the adult males. But of course, reliable census data are not enough for the study of social segregation; a map which permits the placement of particular individuals in households on the grid of city streets is also required. Fortunately, there exists such a map for Antequera: it was drawn in 1803 and carries the same street names as those employed in the 1792 census.⁶ A sketch of the city with the street names then in use (all are different today) appears in Figure 4.1.

By matching up street addresses in the census with the 1803 map, it is possible to locate each household in a specific "linear block" consisting of the facing sides of a block-long street segment. In 1792, Antequera had 303 of these. There is no doubt about the actual street on which each household in the census was located, though in some cases where the addresses were unclear I have had to resort to estimates in order to place households within particular facing blocks. This did not prove to be very difficult, since the city was laid out in a uniform fashion and the streets for which complete information is available contained on the average 10 houses per block, increasing to 15-20 in the area immediately surrounding the Plaza de Armas. Breaks between blocks were also fairly easy to identify in the census because of the frequent presence of corner stores and familiar landmarks such as churches and government buildings. In any case, it is doubtful that any errors in placement would be off by more than a block, and I feel confident that the matching of the census with the map provides a fairly accurate model of Antequera's urban ecology at the close of the eighteenth century. While the segregation statistics discussed below are based on the 303 linear or facing block units, for the sake of clarity these entities have been aggregated into manzanas ("island blocks") in Figures 4.2 to 4.11.

The physical plan of the city shows that Antequera came close to meeting the ideal of the grid-pattern town that was applied so often throughout Spanish America.⁷ Much as it does today, life revolved around the central square, the Plaza de Armas, which was bordered on the north by the Cathedral and on the south by the Casas Consistoriales and the residence of the Intendente of Oaxaca. Close by to the southwest of the Plaza de Armas was the focal point of the city's market, the Plaza de San Juan de Dios. Excluded from all the Figures (and necessarily from the analysis in this paper) are the outlying suburban communities where much of the urban Indian population resided: Santo Tomás Xochimilco to the north, San Matías Jalatlaco to the northeast, Trinidad de las

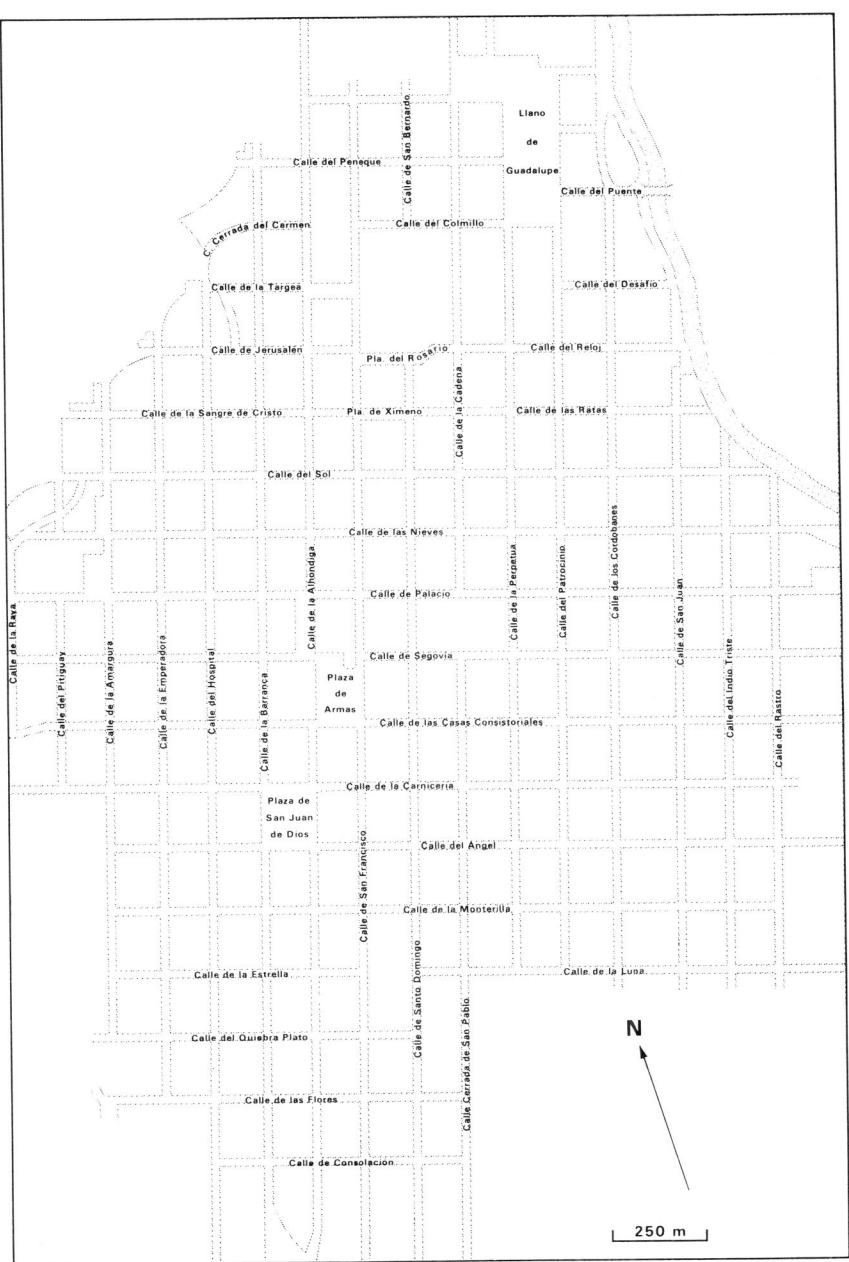

Figure 4.1 Streets of Antequera, 1792-1803

Huertas to the southeast, San Martín Mexicapan and San
Juan Chapultepec to the southwest, and the Villa de
Oaxaca (today part of the city and known as El Marquesado)
to the northwest.[8]

My central concern is the relationship between social distance and geographical space of the major racial
groupings of peninsular Spaniards, creoles, castizos,
mestizos, and mulattoes, and three occupational clusterings which I call Socioeconomic Groups (SEGs): the elite,
preindustrial middle groups, and lower groups. The elite
consisted of the city's leading merchants, high royal
officials, and large landowners (the clergy is excluded
from this analysis because of its atypical residence pattern). The middle groups included the professionals,
high-status artisans, small landholders, and traders,
while among the lower groups were the low-status artisans,
male servants, and those listed as unemployed.[9] I will
refer to these groupings interchangeably as SEGs or
classes.

The analysis of segregation is based on a total of
4,550 household heads for race and 3,246 adult males for
class. For comparative purposes, the indexes for race
have also been computed for the adult males. The basic
hypothesis of this paper derives from the ecological
branch of urban sociology: that the greater the degree of
difference between the spatial distributions of groups
within an urban area, the greater their social distance
from one another. In other words, I am hypothesizing a
general fit between the residential distribution of race
and class on the one hand, and the place of these dimensions within the overall urban social structure on the
other.

In previous work on colonial Oaxaca which relied to
a great extent on the same census material, William B.
Taylor and I have emphasized the utility of a multidimensional approach to social stratification which minimally distinguishes between racial and socioeconomic determinants of social status. We maintain that by 1792,
urban population growth, an expanding capitalist economy,
and a high rate of interracial marriage and "passing" had
considerably weakened the estate-based racial hierarchy--
the sistema de castas--devised by the elite and the official bureaucracy.

> . . . by the end of the colonial period the complexity
> and range of variation within the economic class structure were as great as those of the status hierarchy embodied in the sistema de castas, if indeed the latter
> had not been overtaken in this respect. The city's
> dramatic growth and increased opportunities for trade
> after the Bourbon reforms rendered the sistema de castas
> all but obsolete as a mechanism of status definition.
> More than ever, social honor came to be dependent on

economic considerations as the number of claimants to white status multiplied.

Only at the top and perhaps at the bottom of the socioeconomic scale did racial affiliation correspond to ethnic identity and class-like behavior.[10]

The basic argument, then, is that caste and racial estate models are inadequate for the analysis of stratification in eighteenth-century Mexico, at least in Antequera. I find it preferable to posit at least two analytically separate hierarchies of racial status ("social honor" in Weber's terms) and economic class, recognizing that these determinants were frequently working at cross purposes with each other. If this interpretation is valid, one would expect the city's residence pattern to be mixed, with a relative absence of clearly segregated neighborhoods based on either race or class (with the exceptions of the peninsular-dominated elite and the urban Indian proletariat). This is the specific hypothesis that I wish to test in this paper.[11] It should be kept in mind, however, that Indians, slaves, and blacks are omitted from the analysis because they were not included in the census. We know from other sources that many of Antequera's urban Indians did in fact live in highly segregated barrios on the fringes of the city.[12]

II

I have applied two measures of segregation to the data. Both were introduced by Otis Dudley Duncan and Beverly Duncan in 1955 and have become widely used among North American sociologists.[13] The first measure is the _index of dissimilarity_. Given the distribution of two racial or occupational groups over all the areal units of the city (in this case, facing blocks), this index measures on a scale of 0 to 100 the degree of spatial dissimilarity between the two groups. To compute this index, it is necessary to calculate the percentage of all members of each group that reside in each block. The index of dissimilarity between the two groups is then one-half the sum of the absolute values of the differences between the respective distributions. This statistic yields a measure of displacement. A score of 80, for example, would tell us that 80 percent of the people in group A would have to move to a different area in order to make their distribution identical with that of group B. The index of dissimilarity therefore measures the extent to which the observed degree of segregation differs from a hypothetical state of _total_ segregation. The second statistic, the _index of segregation_, is computed in much the same way, except that in this case dissimilarity is measured between a given group and all other groups in the city combined. This is a broader, more general purpose index that measures the place of a particular group in the city as a whole.

Once the statistics are calculated (and with 303 blocks, a computer is indispensable), the question of course arises as to how to interpret the values. How do we decide what figures represent high and low segregation scores? In theory there is no answer to this problem, but there is a practical solution. Following Nathan Kantrowitz, it seems reasonable to consider indexes upward of 70 as high, indexes of 30 or less as low, and variations in level of less than 5 points as unimportant.[14] These thresholds are, of course, arbitrary, but they have found some acceptance among researchers, and until comparative data become available for other Latin American cities, they may serve as a point of departure.[15]

One final word of caution: the indexes of segregation and dissimilarity, like the concept of residential segregation itself, are sensitive to differences in size of the groups being measured. Thus, a group numbering in the hundreds is likely to exhibit a higher index of segregation, other things being equal, than a group numbering in the thousands. This "distortion" occurs because the index is partially dependent on the relationship between the size of the total population, the number and population size of the areal units (blocks), and the number and proportion of group members. This is inevitable, however, for the whole notion of residential segregation is dependent on these same variables, and any statistical measure must have some dependence on them.[16] Given these limitations, it is highly desirable to supplement these statistical indexes with maps which plot the actual distribution of different groups within the city. This has been done in Figures 4.2 through 4.9, which show the distribution of the principal racial and class groupings by manzana.

III

The indexes calculated for Antequera in 1792 are presented in Tables 4.1 to 4.6. It should be noted that the indexes for racial groupings have been calculated twice with two different data bases. The population of 4,550 household heads in Tables 4.1 and 4.3 is the most comprehensive and permits comparison of the corresponding indexes with studies done in North America and elsewhere. But it is equally desirable to have indexes for both race and class in Antequera based on the same population, so in Tables 4.2 and 4.4 the "class" population of 3,246 adult males has been used. Thus by comparing Tables 4.2 and 4.4 with Tables 4.5 and 4.6, we can more accurately compare segregation by race versus class.

TABLE 4.1
Indexes of segregation for racial groupings, Antequera 1792
(household heads)

Peninsulars (263)	65.7
Creoles (2,417)	29.4
Castizos (107)	64.7
Mestizos (1,015)	34.9
Mulattoes (748)	39.6
Castizos Mestizos Mulattoes (1,870)	30.4
Mestizos Mulattoes (1,763)	30.3

TABLE 4.2
Indexes of segregation for racial groupings, Antequera 1792
(adult males)

Peninsulars (236)	70.0
Creoles (1,572)	33.9
Castizos (132)	60.6
Mestizos (702)	30.3
Mulattoes (589)	43.5
Castizos Mestizos Mulattoes (1,423)	37.3
Mestizos Mulattoes (1,291)	38.5

TABLE 4.3
Indexes of dissimilarity for revised racial groupings, Antequera 1792 (household heads)

	1	2	3	4
1. Peninsulars	-	64.7	70.7	73.1
2. Creoles	-	-	35.2	39.7
3. Castizos and Mestizos	-	-	-	45.6
4. Mulattoes	-	-	-	-

TABLE 4.4
Indexes of dissimilarity for revised racial groupings, Antequera 1792 (adult males)

	1	2	3	4
1. Peninsulars	-	68.0	76.5	76.6
2. Creoles	-	-	40.5	45.5
3. Castizos and Mestizos	-	-	-	47.7
4. Mulattoes	-	-	-	-

TABLE 4.5
Indexes of segregation for SEGs and selected occupations, Antequera 1792 (adult males only; Indians, Negroes, and clergy excluded)

Elite: Total (328)		64.6
Merchants (217)	76.2	
High royal officials (72)	77.1	
Large estate owners (42)	86.3	
Preindustrial Middle Groups: Total (803)		35.1
Professionals (210)	59.5	
High-status artisans (277)	48.5	
Small landholders, sharecroppers, and farm laborers (156)	67.5	
Traders (127)	64.5	
Lower Groups: Total (2,112)		40.9
Low-status artisans: total (1,900)	41.7	
Blacksmiths and farriers (128)	75.4	
Carpenters (133)	72.5	
Hatters (94)	74.2	
Shoemakers (217)	55.4	
Tailors (349)	43.8	
Weavers (284)	55.6	
Male servants (93)	78.7	
Unemployed (102)	65.7	

TABLE 4.6
Indexes of dissimilarity for SEGs, Antequera 1792 (adult males only; Indians, Negroes, and clergy excluded)

	1	2	3
1. Elite	–	60.0	68.2
2. Preindustrial Middle Groups	–	–	37.2
3. Lower Groups	–	–	–

As an inspection of the maps (Figures 4.2 to 4.6) would suggest, among the racial groups in Table 4.1 we find a fairly high index of segregation for peninsular Spaniards (65.7), and fairly low ones for the creoles (29.4), mestizos (34.9), and mulattoes (39.6). The corresponding values in Table 4.2 are slightly higher because the population represented in that Table is smaller, but the differences are of the magnitude of only about 4.5 points and hence not significant. The one anomalous case (in both Tables) is that of the castizos (offspring of Spaniards and mestizos), who have an unexpectedly high index. The map of their actual distribution in Figure 4.4, however, makes it clear that this high score is due more to their small numbers than to their residential concentration per se. Lumping all of the castas (castizos, mestizos, and mulattoes) together, we get an index of segregation for non-whites of 30.4 (Table 4.1) or 37.3 (Table 4.2). As the maps confirm, there were no discernible "all white" areas of the city. To be sure, there was a clustering of whites in the manzanas around the Plaza de Armas, but even here the castas were well represented (Figure 4.10).

While peninsulars (many of whom were merchants) clustered in the central city, there seems to have been no obvious pattern for the other groups. For example, of the total of 303 facing blocks, 77 percent had three or more white (peninsular or creole) household heads, while 75 percent had three or more castas. Allowing for five or more per block, the respective proportions are 65 percent and 56 percent. Nor were there any particular areas of the city which uniformly contained fewer than five casta household heads per block. Indeed, only one principal street—Calle de Segovia—can be so characterized. It seems, then, that there was a very low degree of racial segregation among the mestizo and mulatto populations of Antequera. The indexes of dissimilarity in Tables 4.3 and 4.4 support this conclusion. While the peninsulars remain spatially distinct no matter who they are compared with, dissimilarity among the rest is noticeably lower. Especially noteworthy is the spatial heterogeneity of the large white creole group, a pattern which fits with their socioeconomic heterogeneity which I have discussed elsewhere.[17]

Turning now to the classes or SEGs in Table 4.5 and Figures 4.7 to 4.9, we find a similar pattern. The elite was highly centralized, with a segregation index of 64.6. Elite residence was densest on the east-west streets of Casas Consistoriales, Segovia, and Palacio, and the north-south street of San Francisco (also the most densely inhabited street in the city). These streets, together with the Plaza de Armas, contained 63 percent of the entire elite group (clergy excepted). Much more dispersed were the middle groups with a segregation index of

103

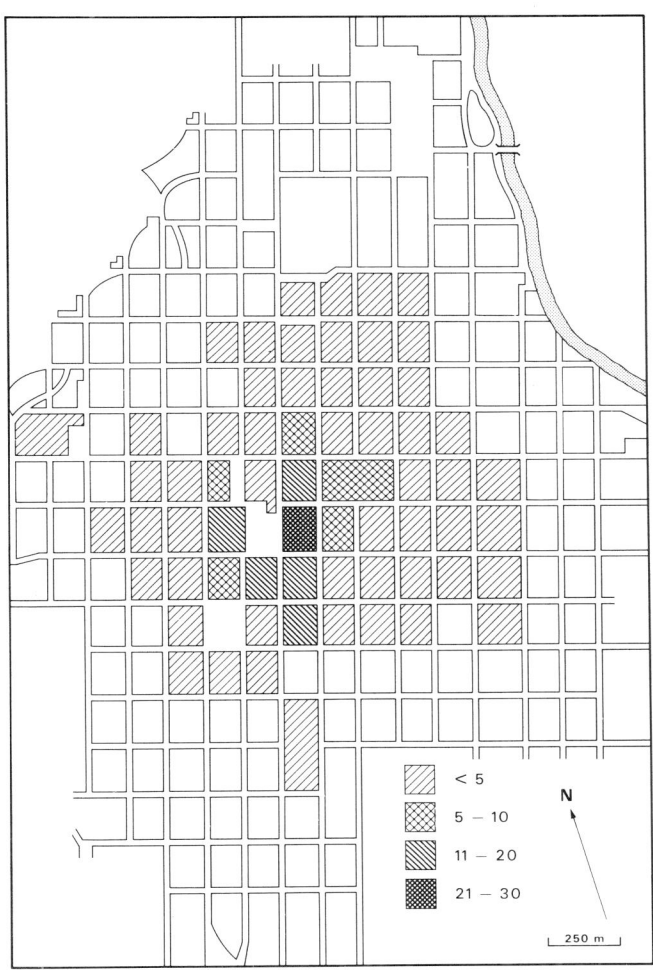

Figure 4.2 Peninsular Spaniards in Antequera by manzana, 1792
(N = 263 household heads)

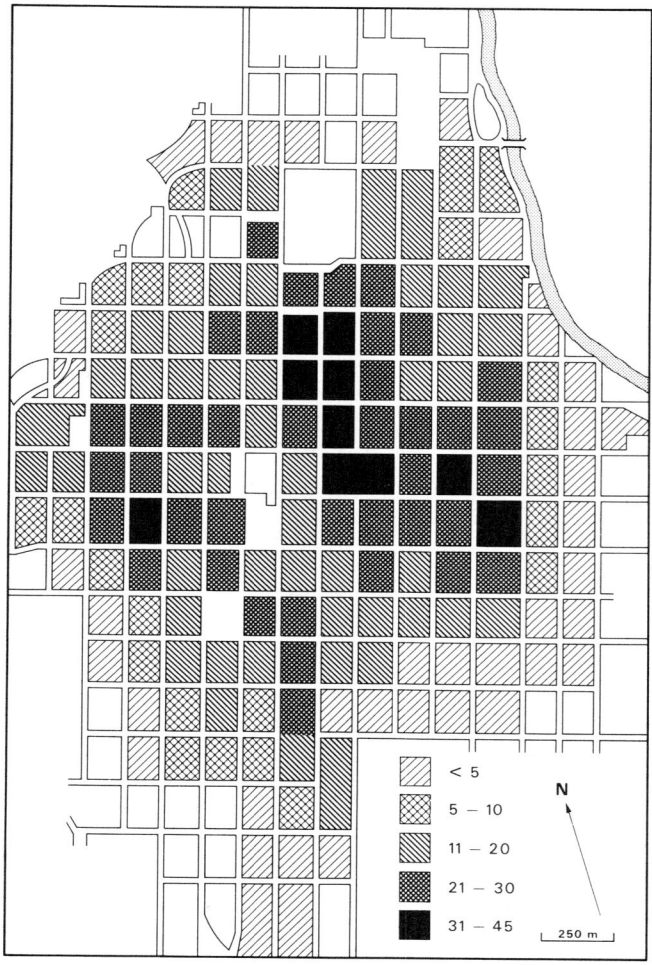

Figure 4.3 Creoles in Antequera by manzana, 1792
(N = 2,417 household heads)

105

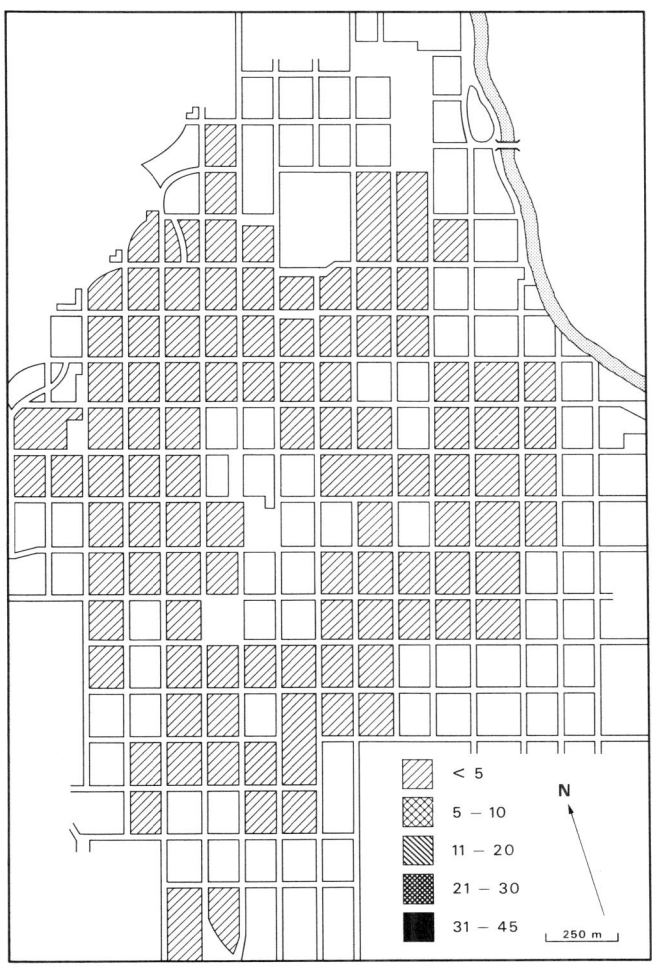

Figure 4.4 Castizos in Antequera by manzana, 1792
            (N = 107 household heads)

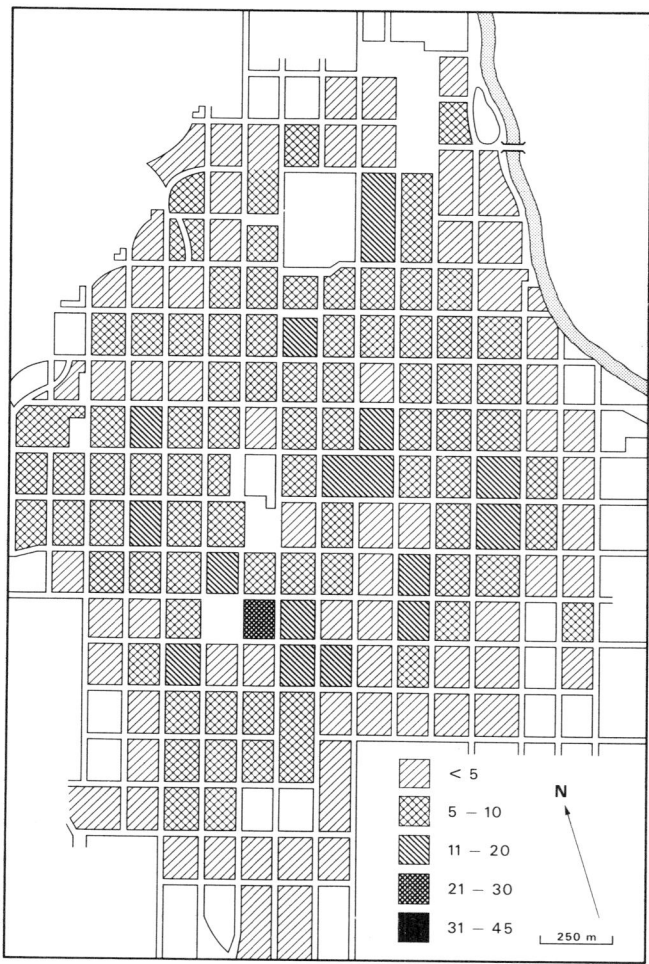

Figure 4.5 Mestizos in Antequera by manzana, 1792
(N = 1,015 household heads)

107

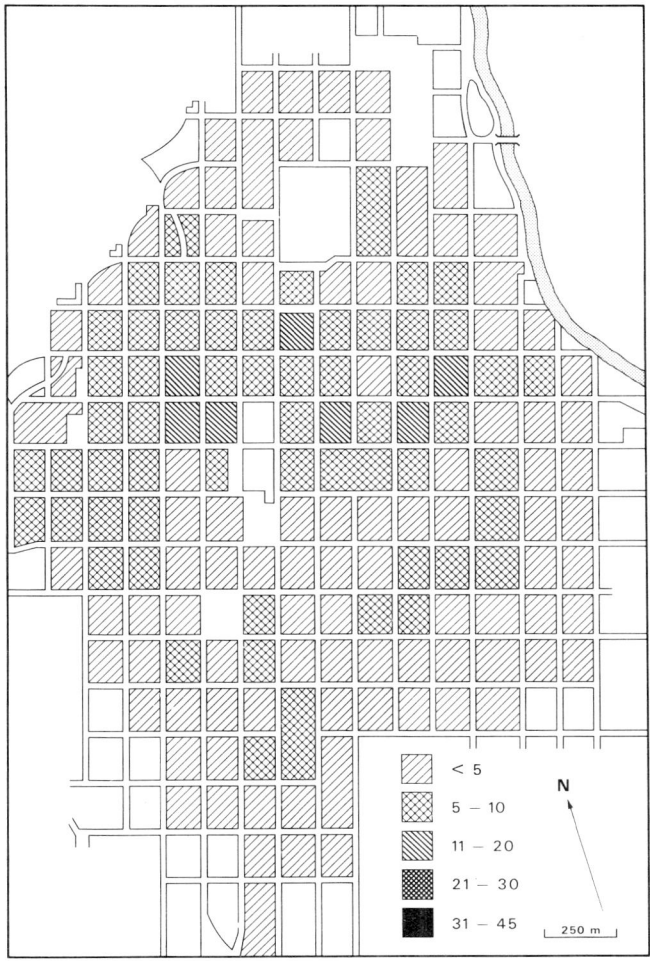

Figure 4.6 Mulattoes in Antequera by manzana, 1792
(N = 748 household heads)

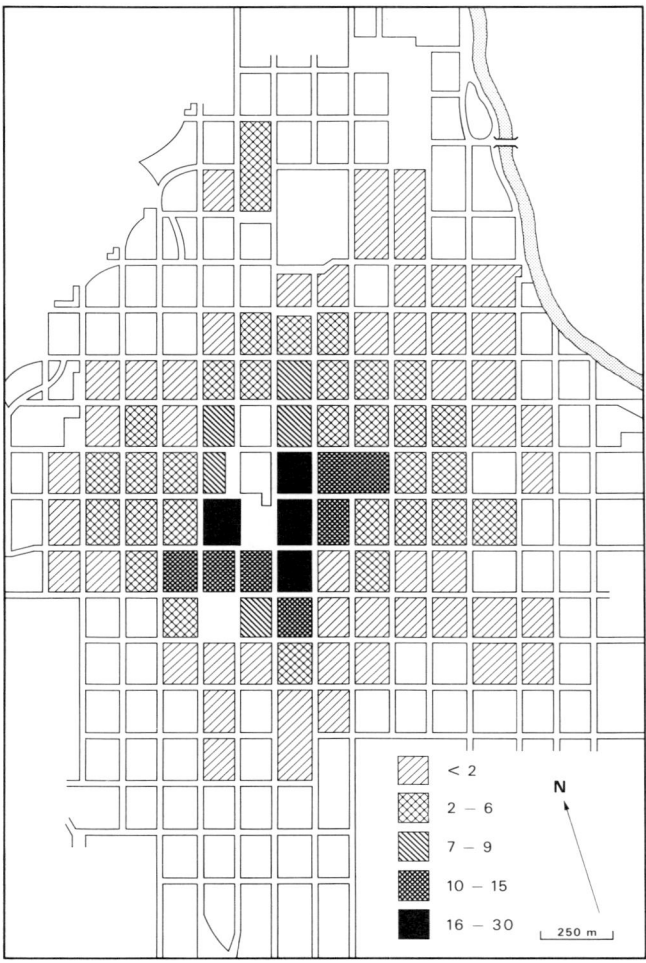

Figure 4.7 The elite of Antequera by manzana, 1792
(N = 331 adult males)

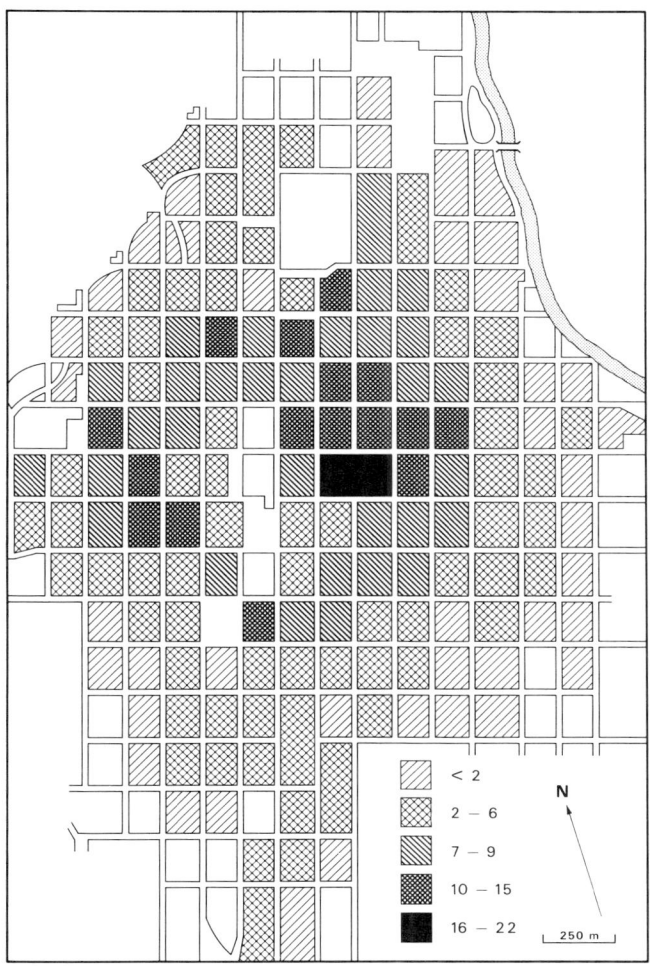

Figure 4.8 Preindustrial middle groups of Antequera by manzana, 1792 (N = 803 adult males)

110

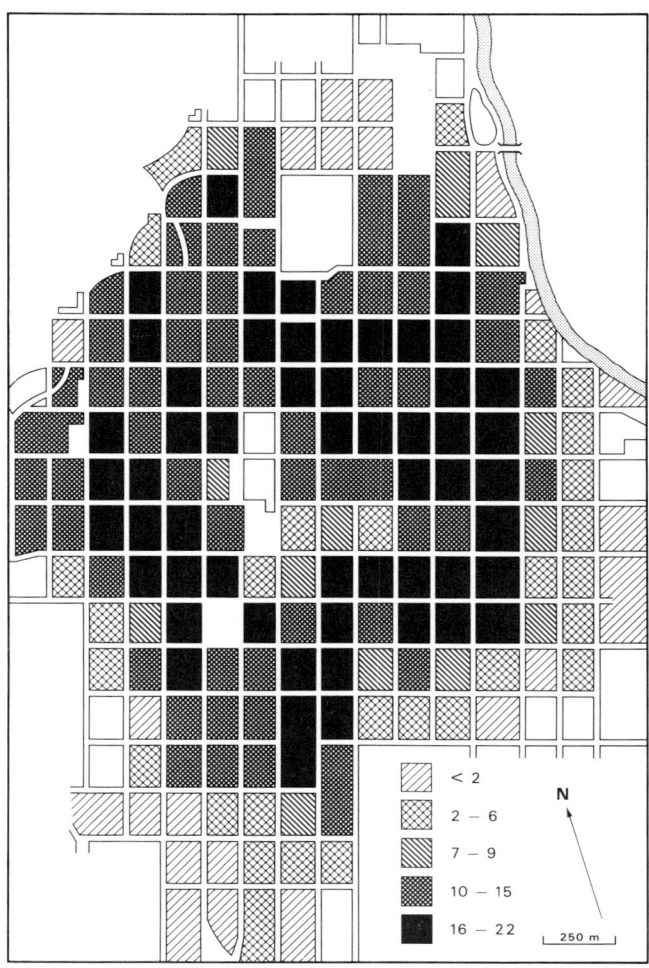

Figure 4.9 Preindustrial lower groups of Antequera by manzana, 1792 (N = 2,112 adult males)

35.1 and the lower groups with an index of 40.9.

The indexes for the various occupational subgroupings are higher, reflecting in part the smaller size of these groups. Maps of these occupations (not included here) reveal some significant patterns, however. By far the most segregated segment of the elite was the merchant group, which clustered around the Plaza de Armas. High royal officials were somewhat more dispersed, and the large estate owners extremely (and surprisingly) so. Among the middle groups, the professionals showed a marked tendency to congregate on a few central streets, whereas the high-status artisans (including barber-surgeons, druggists, gilders, and silversmiths, among others) did not and were much more evenly distributed. Small landholders and traders (tratantes) were drawn more toward the periphery than the center. The low-status artisans were scattered throughout the city, though they were notably absent from the central core surrounding the Plaza de Armas. Some broad residential concentrations can be discerned for particular occupations: the majority of the blacksmiths lived on the east side of town; there was a concentration of carpenters in the southeast; hatmakers gravitated toward the periphery on the east, south, and west sides; shoemakers preferred the west and north-central locations; and weavers inhabited the northwest and southeast corners. The more numerous tailors were found in virtually all parts of town outside the central core. While a precise understanding of the factors responsible for these spatial clusterings of crafts remains elusive, surely considerations of kinship and compadrazgo, space needs, access to delivered raw materials, and proximity to labor in the Indian barrios were relevant variables.[18]

When particular occupations are combined into the broader class groups, however, much of the distinctiveness disappears. There was at least one representative of the middle groups in 77 percent of the city's facing blocks, and only 6 percent of the blocks did not contain at least one employed member of the lower groups. That the middle groups comprised the least spatially distinct category is not surprising in this preindustrial setting where class consciousness was only in its infancy. Table 4.6 shows that the dissimilarity between the middle and lower groups was correspondingly low.

A final comparison of the ecology of race and class can be made by contrasting Figures 4.10 and 4.11, which show the percentage of castas and lower groups residing in the city's 46 central manzanas. Despite the high prestige placed on center-city residence in colonial Latin American cities, we see that low-status people in both the racial and socioeconomic hierarchies had effectively penetrated the center of Antequera. While the Plaza de Armas was dominated by whites, who accounted for

112

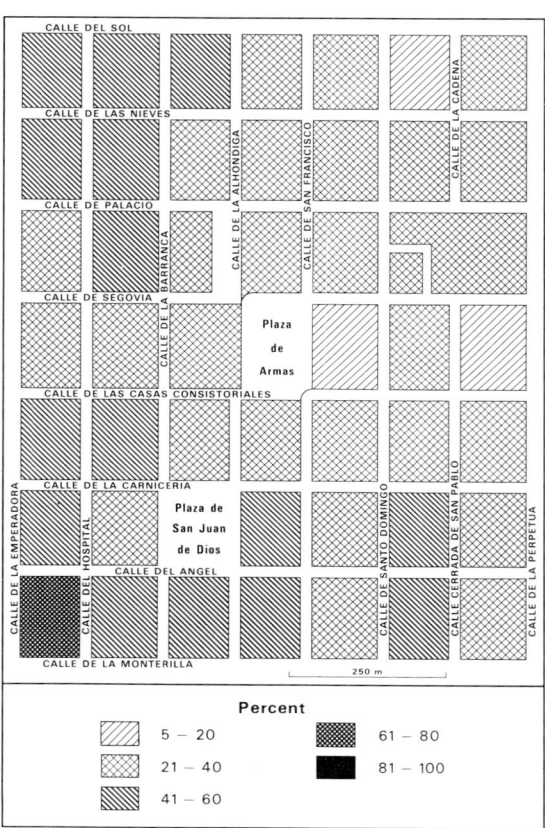

Figure 4.10 Percentage of castas in each of Antequera's central manzanas, 1792 (household heads)

113

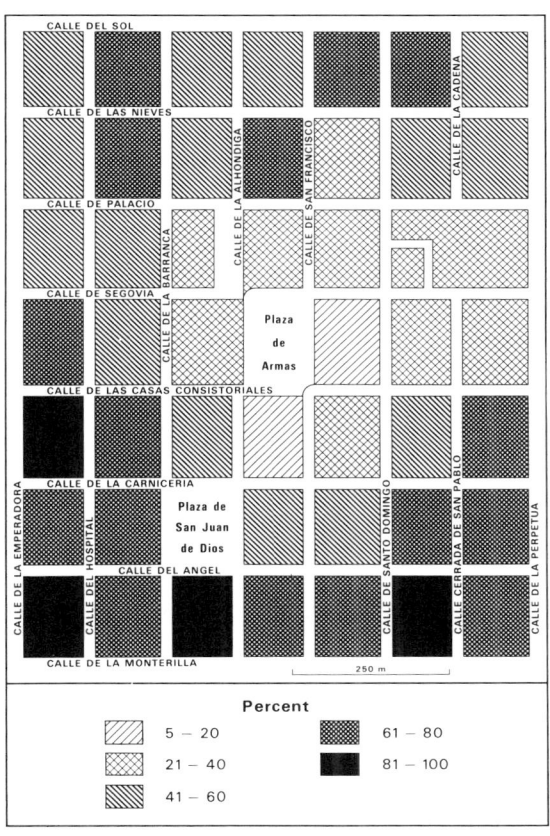

Figure 4.11 Percentage of preindustrial lower groups in each of Antequera's central manzanas, 1792 (adult males)

47 of its 52 household heads, the Plaza de San Juan de Dios--the city's principal market area--was home to 37 white and 38 casta households. Only two of the 39 adult males living in the Plaza de Armas belonged to the lower groups, but in the Plaza de San Juan de Dios, 36 were from the lower groups and 23 from the elite and middle groups. Taken as a whole, the area mapped in Figures 4.10 and 4.11 shows a slightly higher degree of segregation by class than by race. Although both the castas and the lower groups were underrepresented in the prestigious central city, the former were slightly <u>less</u> underrepresented than the latter. Compared to their average numbers per manzana in the city as a whole, adult males of the lower groups were underrepresented in the central area by 11 percent, whereas casta household heads were underrepresented by only 5 percent. The difference is small, but it suggests that segregation by class was at least as significant (if not more so) as segregation by race in Antequera in 1792.

IV

Further research on other colonial Latin American cities is needed in order to determine the broader significance of the case dealt with in this paper. Despite its importance in New Spain, Antequera was still a small, provincial city in the eighteenth century, and it may well be that patterns of segregation were significantly different in major capitals such as Mexico City or Lima. For the case at hand, however, the following conclusions may be drawn:

1. In 1792, Antequera had no "all white" or all Spanish areas apart from a few manzanas in the central core.
2. Except for the center and the outlying Indian barrios not included in this study, all neighborhoods and most blocks were racially mixed.
3. While the peninsular Spaniards and the elite (especially the merchants) were markedly segregated, the other racial groups and SEGs were not.
4. The socioeconomic diversity of the large creole group is underscored by its diversity of residence. Membership in the white, Spanish category was no guarantee of a high position in the socioeconomic hierarchy nor a prestigious, centrally-located residence.
5. Taken as a whole the residential analysis provides support for the proposition that in 1792, there was no longer a viable system of racially defined estates in Antequera. By this time, class had become just as important as race as a

determinant of social status in the stratification system.

NOTES

1. See David J. Robinson, "Córdoba en 1779: la Ciudad y la Campaña," in Raul C. Rey Balmaceda (ed.), Homenaje a Federico A. Daus (Buenos Aires, Sociedad Argentina de Estudios Geográficos, 1979), pp. 279-312; David J. Robinson and Michael M. Swann, "Geographical Interpretations of the Hispanic American Colonial City: A Case Study of Caracas in the Late Eighteenth Century," in R. J. Tata (ed.), Latin America: Search for Geographic Explanations (Boca Raton, 1975), pp. 1-15; Lyman L. Johnson and Susan Migden Socolow, "Population and Space in Eighteenth-Century Buenos Aires," in David J. Robinson (ed.), Social Fabric and Spatial Structure in Colonial Latin America (Ann Arbor, 1979), pp. 339-368. For a good discussion of methodology and mapping techniques see David J. Robinson, "The Analysis of Eighteenth Century Spanish American Cities: Some Problems and Alternative Solutions," Discussion Paper Series No. 4, Department of Geography, Syracuse University, 1975.

2. I want to thank William T. Markham for his criticisms of an earlier draft of this paper and for his help with computer programming. Thanks are also due to David M. Cook for assistance with the computing. For the preparation and drawing of the maps I am deeply indebted to Julia H. Chance, Lancha A. Chance, and especially David J. Robinson and Valmor Philp. All interpretations in this paper are my own, however, as are any shortcomings of the analysis.

3. See especially Otis Dudley Duncan and Beverly Duncan, "A Methodological Analysis of Segregation Indexes," American Sociological Review 20 (1955), pp. 210-217; Duncan and Duncan, "Residential Distribution and Occupational Stratification," American Journal of Sociology 60 (1955), pp. 493-503; Reynolds Farley, "Residential Segregation in Urbanized Areas of the United States in 1970: An Analysis of Social Class and Racial Differences," Demography 14 (1977), pp. 497-518; Ceri Peach (ed.), Urban Social Segregation (London and New York, 1975); Karl E. Taeuber and Alma F. Taeuber, Negroes in Cities (Chicago, 1965). For comparative studies done outside the United States see Peach, op. cit.; Kent P. Schwirian and Jesús Rico-Velasco, "The Residential Distribution of Status Groups in Puerto Rico's Metropolitan Areas," Demography 8 (1971), pp. 81-90; Surinder K. Mehta, "Patterns of Residence in Poona, India, by Caste and Religion: 1822-1965," Demography 6 (1969), pp. 473-491.

4. For examples, see Kathleen Neils Conzen, "Patterns of Residence in Early Milwaukee," in Leo F. Schnore (ed.), The New Urban History: Quantitative Explorations by American Historians (Princeton, 1975), pp. 145-183; Theodore Hershberg, et. al., "A Tale of Three Cities: Blacks and Immigrants in Philadelphia: 1850-1900, 1930 and 1970," Annals of the American Academy of Politics and Social Sciences 441 (1979), pp. 55-81; Nathan Kantrowitz, "Racial and Ethnic Residential Segregation: Boston, 1830-1970," Ibid., pp. 41-54;

Zane L. Miller, "Urban Blacks in the South, 1865-1920: An Analysis of Some Quantitative Data on Richmond, Savannah, New Orleans, Louisville, and Birmingham," in The New Urban History, pp. 184-204; Leo F. Schnore and Peter R. Knights, "Residence and Social Structure: Boston in the ante-Bellum Period," in Stephan Thernstrom and Richard Sennett (eds.), Nineteenth-Century Cities: Essays in the New Urban History (New Haven, 1969), pp. 247-257; Paul B. Worthman, "Working Class Mobility in Birmingham, Alabama, 1880-1914," in Tamara K. Hareven (ed.), Anonymous Americans: Explorations in Nineteenth-Century Social History (Englewood Cliffs, 1971), pp. 172-213.

    5. The census is located in the Archivo General de la Nación (Mexico City), Ramo de Padrones, 13.

    6. The map is included in an unpublished manuscript by José María Murguía y Galardi entitled Extracto general que abraza la estadística toda en su primera y segunda parte del estado de Guaxaca y ha reunido de orden del Supremo Gobierno y yntendente de provincia en clase de los cesantes José María Murguía y Galardi (1827). It is located in the Benson Latin American Collection of the University of Texas-Austin.

    7. In addition to works cited in note 1 above, contributions to the study of Latin American urban ecology include S. D. Markman, "The Gridiron Town Plan and the Caste System in Colonial Central America," in Richard P. Schaedel, Jorge E. Hardoy, and Nora Scott Kinzer (eds.), Urbanization in the Americas from its Beginnings to the Present (The Hague, 1978), pp. 471-490; Theodore Caplow, "The Social Ecology of Guatemala City," Social Forces 28 (1949), pp. 113-133; F. Dotson and L. O. Dotson, "Ecological Trends in the City of Guadalajara, Mexico," Social Forces 32 (1954), pp. 367-374; A. T. Hansen, "The Ecology of a Latin American City," in E. B. Reuter (ed.), Race and Culture Contacts (New York, 1934), pp. 124-142; H. B. Hawthorn and A. B. Hawthorn, "The Shape of a City," Sociology and Social Research 33 (1948), pp. 87-91; N. S. Hayner, "Mexico City: Its Growth and Configuration," American Journal of Sociology 50 (1945), pp. 295-304; Leo F. Schnore, "On the Spatial Structure of Cities in the Two Americas," in Philip M. Hauser and Leo F. Schnore (eds.), The Study of Urbanization (New York, 1965), pp. 347-398.

    8. A more extensive plan of Antequera and its environs which shows these places as well as the location of churches and government offices can be found in John K. Chance, Race and Class in Colonial Oaxaca (Stanford, 1978), p. 35.

    9. For further details see John K. Chance and William B. Taylor, "Estate and Class in a Colonial City: Oaxaca in 1792," Comparative Studies in Society and History 19 (1977), pp. 454-487; or Chance, Race and Class, Chapter 6.

    10. Chance, Race and Class, pp. 194, 181.

    11. Our interpretation of Antequera's stratification system has recently been subjected to a detailed critique by Robert McCaa, Stuart B. Schwartz, and Arturo Grubessich in "Race and Class in Colonial Latin America: A Critique," Comparative Studies in Society and History 21 (1979), pp. 421-433. Taylor and I respond in detail to these criticisms in "Estate and Class: A Reply," Comparative Studies in Society and History 21 (1979), pp. 434-442. The findings in the present paper are germane to this debate and provide, I believe,

further support for our position that both racial <u>and</u> class factors were at work.

12. For more on Antequera's urban Indians see John K. Chance, "The Urban Indian in Colonial Oaxaca," <u>American Ethnologist</u> 3 (1976), pp. 603-632.

13. Duncan and Duncan, "Residential Distribution and Occupational Stratification."

14. Nathan Kantrowitz, <u>Ethnic and Racial Segregation in the New York Metropolis</u> (New York, 1973), p. 15.

15. In their comprehensive study of non-white residential segregation in 207 U.S. cities in 1960, Taeuber and Taeuber (<u>op. cit</u>., pp. 34, 36) obtained a range of values from 60.4 to 98.1. Half the cities had values above 87.8; the mean value was 86.2. On the whole, they found no significant differences among them:

> In the urban United States, there is a very high degree of segregation of the residences of whites and Negroes. This is true for cities in all regions of the country and for all types of cities--large and small, industrial and commercial, metropolitan and suburban. It is true whether there are hundreds of thousands of Negro residents, or only a few thousand. Residential segregation prevails regardless of the relative economic status of the white and Negro residents. It occurs regardless of the character of local laws and policies, and regardless of the extent of other forms of segregation or discrimination (<u>ibid</u>., pp. 35-36).

16. Taeuber and Taeuber, <u>Negroes in Cities</u>, p. 215.

17. Chance, <u>Race and Class</u>.

18. I am indebted to J. Douglas Uzzell for this observation.

5
Marriage Patterns and Regional Interaction in Late Colonial Nueva Galicia

Linda L. Greenow

INTRODUCTION

    Colonial Mexican marriage records provide a useful measure of social interaction between racial groups, and spatial interaction between a wide range of settlements.[1] Here, marriage registers of eight parishes in late colonial Nueva Galicia, an area which has attracted the attention of almost no historical demographers in the past, provided the data base for such an analysis.[2] All the records were legible, and complete for the periods chosen for study, and contained both racial and place of origin information for the great majority of the marriage partners. Three five-year sample periods were chosen for study representing developmental phases of the mid- and late-eighteenth century and early nineteenth-century. These periods were chosen on the basis of completeness and comparability of records for all eight parishes, and on the basis of other events which shed light on critical developments in the area, such as the "año de hambre" of 1786, the opening of the port of San Blas in 1772, and the population enumeration of 1791.

    It is important to remember that, for the most part, the marriage registers studied here reveal only the places of "origin" and residence of marriage partners. A person who came to a parish center from some other <u>pueblo</u> or <u>hacienda</u>, either inside or outside the parish, was said to be an "<u>originario</u>" of that place. This term was undoubtedly used to distinguish a person's birthplace or previous place of residence from his residence within a parish at the time of marriage, and the priests usually wrote that a bride or groom was, for example, "originario de Agualulco y residente en este pueblo desde ocho años." But the term "originario" cannot be defined any more precisely than that. For some people it probably referred to birthplace, since they were described as having arrived in the parish center when they were infants. Others were "originarios" of a town they had once lived in, but from which they had since moved (possibly several times) and had only been a "residente" for a short time in the parish where they were married. It is therefore not clear whether a person's place of "origin" was his birthplace, any previous place or residence, or his most recent place of residence for some period.

It is also difficult to determine the limits of the term "residente," which referred to both long-term residents and recent arrivals. (In several parishes, the length of time of residence was not indicated at all.) Two people in Tepic married outsiders who had been "residentes" for only one week, and in several other cases, the priest identified "residentes" who had been in Tepic "muy poco tiempo." Whether or not these recent arrivals had established a permanent home and became a part of the community before marriage is not at all clear.

Where the marriage partners took up residence after marriage is simply not known. Out-migration cannot be measured through the marriage documents unless an entire region is considered a closed unit so that the individuals leaving a given parish and marrying in another together make up the out-migrating population from that location.[3]

One of several possible migration scenarios could therefore have taken place in each marriage: first, both partners could have been "originarios" of the parish center where they were married and either remained there or moved away; second, one or both partners could have moved to the parish during childhood, where they lived for a long period of time, and either remained there permanently after marrying or moved away; and third, one partner could have arrived in the parish and married a resident there, planning either to return home after the ceremony or remain there as a resident.

Not knowing which of these situations was the case in a given marriage places temporal and geographic limitations on the use of marriage registers for measuring migration flows within the general population. The registers capture a pattern of migration of individuals at only one critical period in the life-cycle, which happened to be recorded by the Church, and the information on previous places of residence is ambiguous. For this reason, the populations referred to in marriage migration analysis are better distinguished as "marrying populations," since the conclusions drawn about them should not be assumed to be characteristic of the general population. The term "migration" should be qualified as "marriage migration" since the population movements that can be studied through marriage registers of a given parish are movements of people who married in that parish center after their arrival there.

The interaction represented by marriage migrants had both social and economic implications, since much of the population movement of all kinds that occurred in colonial Mexico was a function of economic opportunity, and since settlement patterns, miscegenation, population concentration and economic growth were all affected by population movement. These economic and social consequences, however, were functions of casual, transitory population movement as well as permanent residential changes, and care must be taken not to assume that it is only the latter which is indicated in the marriage registers.

THE STUDY AREA

A total of approximately 5200 marriages were analyzed from eight parishes in late colonial Nueva Galicia: Tonalá, Tlaquepaque, Zapopan, Chapala, Tequila, Ameca, Compostela and Tepic (Table 5.1 and Figure 5.1). The parish boundaries were not determined, but since pueblos and haciendas within the parishes' jurisdictions were indicated in the registers it was possible to interpolate such boundaries and locate them on base maps.[4] These parishes were not the largest in Nueva Galicia, but they played important roles in the region's economic development at various points in time.[5]

Zapopan, Tlaquepaque and Tonalá were Indian parishes on the outskirts of the capital city of Guadalajara. Today, Zapopan and Tlaquepaque have been absorbed within the city limits and both Tlaquepaque and Tonalá are regional artisan centers for the production of pottery and glassware. The development of the relationship between the capital city and Tlaquepaque is unclear before the late nineteenth century, when city residents began constructing summer homes in the pueblo. The surrounding agricultural lands of Zapopan and Tonalá were the source of wealth of some of the city's powerful landowning families.

Tequila, Chapala and Ameca were centers of a prosperous agricultural region based on the production of maize, wheat and livestock. Many of the wealthiest and most powerful _hacendados_ of the _audiencia_ derived their wealth from family-based agglomerations of haciendas and _ranchos_ in this region. These landowners consolidated commercial interests with city-based merchants, or owned tanneries, mills and shops of their own. They also served often in the municipal government of Guadalajara and therefore held both financial and political power.

Compostela and Tepic represent a commercial and livestock sector of Nueva Galicia's economy which played a critical role in late eighteenth-century economic growth. When the port of San Blas opened in 1772, merchants in Tepic emerged not only as traders but as financiers for the development of western ranching and mining. Whether Compostela accompanied Tepic's rise to power has

TABLE 5.1
Frequency of Marriages

Parish	1759-1763	1790-1794	1805-1810	Total	%
Tlaquepaque	111	93	124	328	6.2
Tonalá	219	212	187	618	11.7
Zapopan	225	429	300	954	18.1
Chapala	151	160	184	495	9.4
Ameca	147	436	453	1036	19.7
Tequila	153	157	170	480	9.1
Compostela	197	251	100	548	10.4
Tepic	248*	273	286	807	15.3
Total	1,451	2,011	1,804	5,266	100.0

*Figures for Tepic are for 1779-1783.

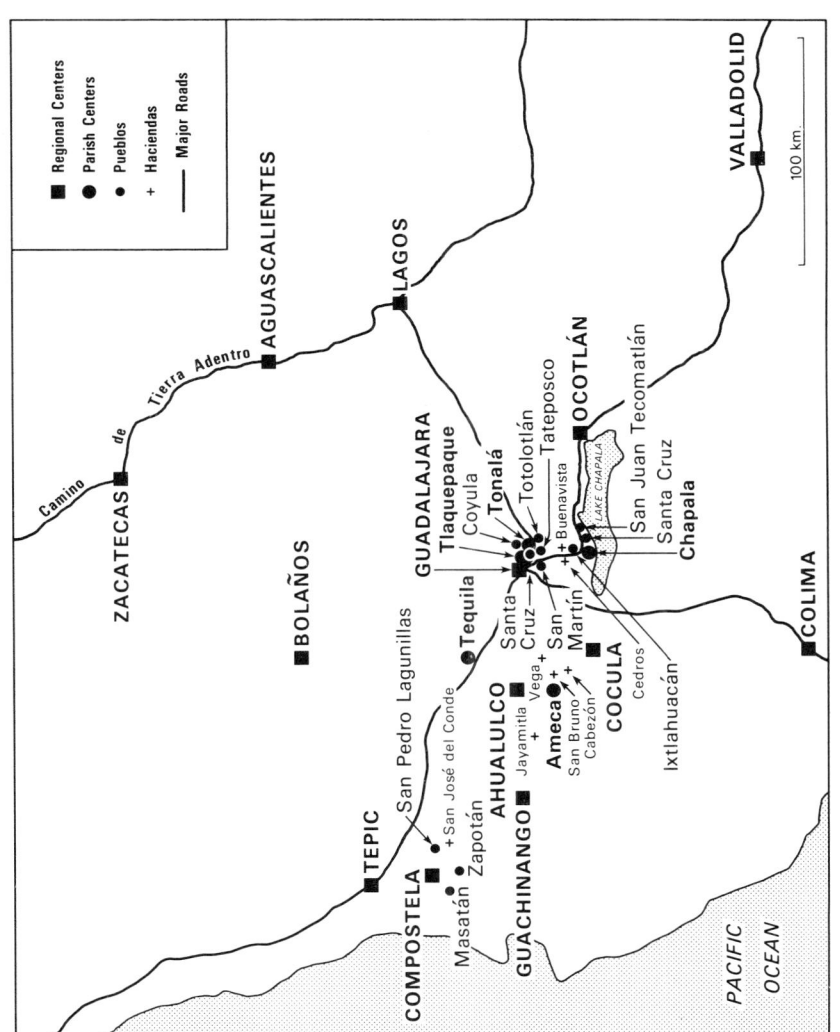

Figure 5.1 Settlements in Nueva Galicia

yet to be established.

PATTERNS OF INTERRACIAL MARRIAGE

Because marriage was a function of the availability of appropriate partners, any variable affecting the probability of marriage for various segments of the population also affected the set of marriages which resulted, which in turn forms the base of data for marriage migration analysis. Race in particular is a critical variable to examine, since it is one of the few descriptors consistently indicated in the marriage registers. Age, occupation, and previous marital status of marriage partners are sometimes indicated, but only inconsistently through time and for different places.

The eight parishes represent a cross-section of marrying populations of a variety of racial mixtures (Tables 5.2 and 5.3). Zapopan's, Tonalá's and Tlaquepaque's marrying populations were the most homogeneous, almost entirely Indian. Tequila's and Chapala's marrying populations were principally composed of Indians as well, with large proportions of Spaniards, mulatos and mestizos. Ameca's, Compostela's and Tepic's marrying populations were fairly balanced mixtures of Indians, Spaniards and mulatos.

The populations of Zapopan, Tonalá, and Tlaquepaque seldom married outside their racial groups (Table 5.4). Interracial marriages never accounted for more than eleven percent of all parish marriages. This is not surprising since there were few non-Indians in the marrying population. Interracial marriage is therefore best considered by studying Chapala, Tequila, Ameca, Compostela and Tepic. The general trends for racial intermarriage in these parishes are shown in Table 5.4, in which the Cook and Borah method of describing racial marriage mixing is utilized.[6] The index is the ratio between the observed number of marriages taking place, and the number of such marriages that would be expected to take place if marriages between the races was a random process, dependent only on the relative proportions of partners of each racial group. When the ratio is greater than one, more marriages than expected have taken place between the two races involved, and when the ratio falls below one, then the converse is the case.

In general, Spaniards tended increasingly to marry members of other socio-racial groups, a fact not noted elsewhere in eighteenth-century Mexico; they became as a group more exogamous as time passed. On the other hand, Indians and mulatos became increasingly endogamous. It is clear, as elsewhere, that the patterns of intermarriage between other racial groups changed inconsistently throughout the period, but with two exceptions: marriages

TABLE 5.2
Race of marriage partners

	Percent of marrying population						
Parish	Spanish	Mulatos	Indians	Mestizos	Coyotes	Other	Not in-dicated
Tlaquepaque	1.8	0	97.6	0.3	--	--	0.3
Tonalá	4.2	0.6	92.7	1.3	--	--	0.1
Zapopan	5.5	1.1	90.5	1.8	0.8	0.2	--
Chapala	12.9	10.4	63.1	5.0	5.1	0.9	2.6
Ameca	29.9	28.4	23.1	11.0	4.7	1.2	1.6
Tequila	32.2	(7.9)**	44.1	11.5	2.5	0.5	1.3
Compostela	21.0	31.4	23.4	2.4	7.6	0.5	13.9
Tepic	23.2	29.6	19.7	9.5	5.1	0.8	12.1

**Mestizos

TABLE 5.3
Racial distribution of marrying populations

	Percent of marrying population		
	1759-1763	1790-1794	1805-1810
Chapala			
Spanish	8.3	12.6	15.5
Mulato	10.6	12.3	9.5
Indian	61.9	67.9	64.7
Ameca			
Spanish	46.3	24.9	29.5
Mulato	1.0	28.7	37.1
Indian	43.2	23.2	16.6
Tequila			
Spanish	22.2	30.9	42.7
Mestizo	16.3	11.1	7.3
Indian	42.5	46.8	43.0
Compostela			
Spanish	21.8	19.1	24.0
Mulato	31.9	30.3	33.0
Indian	22.6	24.7	22.5
Tepic			
Spanish	17.7*	21.6	29.4
Mulato	30.8	20.9	36.7
Indian	11.9	28.2	18.4

*Figures for Tepic are for 1779-1784.

TABLE 5.4
Mean ratios of observed to expected marriages in all parishes

1759-1763

		Males		
		Spanish	Indian	Mixed
Females	Spanish	4.33	0.01	0.91
	Indian	0.03	2.13	0.49
	Mixed	1.61	0.52	1.49

1790-1794

		Males		
		Spanish	Indian	Mixed
Females	Spanish	2.66	0.46	0.38
	Indian	0.30	2.17	0.60
	Mixed	0.90	0.46	1.96

1805-1810

		Males		
		Spanish	Indian	Mixed
Females	Spanish	2.75	0.22	0.54
	Indian	0.25	2.54	0.76
	Mixed	0.64	0.53	1.90

of casta women to Indian men became more common, while the marriages between Spanish females and Indian men became quite common later, especially among non-Indians (Table 5.5). The most noticeable feature of interracial marriage in Chapala was that Indians, which formed a large part of the population, never married into any other single racial group at a significant rate.

In Ameca, racial barriers to marriage became less important through time among Indians as their proportion of the population decreased. By the turn of the century, only 16.6 percent of marriage partners were Indian; clearly they could not expect to marry other Indians, and nearly two-thirds of them married exogamously (Tables 5.3 and 5.5). The large increase in marriages between Indians and non-Indians between 1759-1763 and 1790-1794 deserves further examination. The appearance in the second period of a large mulato population with highly exogamous tendencies suggests that it was the Indian-mulato marriage that increased the rate of exogamous marriage for Indians. An examination of the rates of marriage between Indians and each of the other races shows that it was the collective increase in numbers of mulatos, mestizos, coyotes and other racial groups which gave Indians opportunities to marry outside their race. The possibility of marriage to a Spaniard remained minimal.

In Tequila, the general trend for increasing racial exogamy was reversed (Table 5.5). Mestizos, which always formed the smallest proportion of the marrying population, consistently married into other races (Tables 5.3 and 5.6). However, by the end of the century, mestizos and other mixed racial groups formed a relatively insignificant portion of the marrying population; over 85 percent of the marriage partners were either Spaniards or Indians, the two racial groups which were least likely to intermarry. This strengthening of racial boundaries in marriage can be seen in the pattern of specific interracial pairings; the only significant interracial marriages by the final period took place between mulato males and mestiza females. Intermarriage between Indians and Spaniards, the largest part of the marrying population, was almost nonexistent.

A similar pattern occurred in Compostela, where the 1790s witnessed an overall dip in interracial marriage which was present in all three major racial groups (Tables 5.5 and 5.6). The mestizo and coyote groups were always the most exogamous races. In the 1790s, they formed a very low percentage of the marrying population and the consequences were illustrated in lower exogamous rates among Spaniards, Indians and mulatos, the racial groups with whom they normally intermarried.

In Tepic, interracial marriage was a function of the links between the mulato and Indian populations. In the second period, the proportion of mulatos in the marrying

TABLE 5.5
Percent of racially exogamous marriages

	1759-1763	1790-1794	1805-1809
Tlaquepaque	0	3.2	3.2
Tonalá	5.5	3.8	1.1
Zapopan	1.8	8.2	10.7
Chapala	3.3	21.2	29.5
Ameca	14.9	31.2	32.2
Tequila	43.8	38.2	30.9
Compostela	24.1	9.2	26.0
Tepic	16.3*	37.7	26.1

*Figures for Tepic are for 1779-1783.

TABLE 5.6
Racial exogamy by racial group

	Percent of marriages in each period		
	1759-1763	1790-1794	1805-1809
Chapala			
Spanish	43.8	41.7	64.3
Mulatos	23.6	60.0	75.0
Indians	13.0	17.1	24.4
Ameca			
Spanish	31.6	22.1	26.2
Mulatos	**	52.9	41.0
Indians	1.6	50.4	59.8
Tequila			
Spanish	38.1	43.5	32.1
Mestizos	86.4	75.0	90.9
Indians	44.7	41.9	38.6
Compostela			
Spanish	40.7	25.5	45.2
Mulatos	47.6	21.2	50.0
Indians	43.9	22.9	56.7
Tepic			
Spanish	26.3*	24.6	27.4
Mulatos	33.8	71.6	33.3
Indians	16.3	37.7	26.1

*Figures for Tepic are for 1779-1783.
**Insufficient cases.

population was the lowest of the three periods (Table 5.3). With few of their own racial group to marry, mulatos married mestizos and Indians. The effect on the Indian marrying population was clear; at that same time, the Indian proportion of the marrying population reached a peak, along with its overall tendency to marry into other racial groups.

What were the essential principles of interracial marriage in eighteenth-century Nueva Galicia? First, a significant change in exogamy rates of any one segment of the population had widespread consequences. The set of potential marriage partners at one point in time was theoretically a zero-sum population. If, as in Ameca, Spanish females tended to marry men of other races, then the chances for other females to marry outside their racial group were increased. If, as in the cases of Tequila and Compostela, the only racial groups with exoganous tendencies formed a small part of the population, then everyone's chances to marry outside their race were reduced, and Indians were the least likely to find partners of other racial groups.

Second, in parishes with large Indian populations such as Zapopan, Tonalá, Chapala and Tlaquepaque, relatively little interaction took place between Indians and non-Indians. The non-Indian may have been highly exogamous with respect to marriage, but little of that interaction took place with Indians. This occurred even in the pueblos of Tonalá, Tlaquepaque and Zapopan, which were on the outskirts of the city of Guadalajara and its large population of many racial types.[7] The city's population, however close to those parishes, apparently did not send potential marriage partners to these parishes. Whether or not Indians left these parishes to move into Guadalajara and marry there cannot be determined from these data. It is clear, however, that an Indian had a better chance for upward social mobility by moving out of these parishes to a small town where the Indian population was only part of a heterogeneous society.

Finally, in a racially mixed population such as Tepic's, in which the Indian population did marry across racial lines, demographic changes which shifted the balance of racial groups in the marrying population led to variable rates of racial exogamy. In parishes with a fluctuating mixture of racial groups, there was insufficient evidence of a direct correlation between the changes in a racial group's proportion of the total marrying population and its rate of exogamy. Rather, racial exogamy in marriage depended on the balance of all racial groups and their tendency to interact. If Spaniards and Indians composed the majority of the population, racial exogamy was less likely than if the Spaniards had been mestizos or mulatos. Brading and Wu demonstrate a long-term trend in the integration of mulato and Indian populations through intermarriage in León.[8] This also occurred in areas of Nueva Galicia where the distinctions between Indians and non-Indians were not as strong as in Tonalá and Tlaquepaque. In those areas, when demographic conditions raised the exogamous marriage rate of Indians, the increase came from marriage to mulatos and, to a lesser extent, mestizos and coyotes. This seems to have been a widespread phenomenon; preferences of Indians for these racial groups have also been noted in Parral, Guanajuato and San Luis Potosí.[9] To compare rates of exogamy for racial groups of different places and times does not necessarily indicate cultural biases or similarities; the differences in rates may simply reflect variation in the population bases which generated the set of marriage partners.

INTER-PARISH MARRIAGE

The same parishes with nearly homogeneous Indian populations and low rates of racial exogamy also had relatively closed populations with respect to spatial exogamy (Table 5.7). Few people from outside the parishes of Tonalá and Tlaquepaque married into the local populations. The case of Zapopan is somewhat more complex. A higher proportion of marriages involved spatial exogamy than in Tonalá and Tlaquepaque; however, almost all the marriage partners resided in the parish at the time of marriage and had lived there all their lives.

Five of the parishes had significant levels of interaction with other parishes in western Mexico (Table 5.7). Chapala's residents married outsiders the least frequently of the five; Tequila's were the most exogamous. However, frequency of exogamous marriage, while it indicates the level of interaction between a parish's population and those of other parishes, does not indicate the degree of localization of that interaction. Mean marriage migration distances for the five parishes show that Compostela and Tepic, on the western fringes of colonial settlements, drew marriage partners from a much wider field than the parishes closer to the administrative, agricultural and population center of Nueva Galicia (Table 5.8). Disaggregating the mean distances by race shows that it was principally Spaniards migrating from the far north and the Bajío to Tepic and Compostela who extended their marriage fields far beyond those of the more central parishes (Table 5.9). What is surprising, however, is the distances covered by Indians coming into these areas. In every case except Chapala, Indians migrated further than the mixed racial groups. In some cases, Indians migrated as far as Spaniards.

Mapping the marriage fields illustrates some of the complexities of marriage migration. Except for an

TABLE 5.7
Proportion of inter-parish marriages

Parish	1759-1763	1790-1794	1805-1809
Tlaquepaque	1.8	9.7	8.9
Tonalá	9.8	7.2	6.9
Zapopan	10.4	14.6	18.1
Chapala	13.5	17.6	18.8
Ameca	22.5	25.5	16.0
Tequila	45.2	42.1	46.0
Compostela	21.8	4.4	18.0
Tepic	47.7*	27.9	39.7

*Figures for Tepic are for 1779-1783.

TABLE 5.8
Mean migration distances (kilometers)

Parish	1759-1763	1790-1794	1805-1809
Chapala	61.7	66.5	51.5
Ameca	75.9	69.2	58.9
Tequila	78.2	88.5	62.5
Compostela	115.9	86.7	91.9
Tepic	144.1*	134.1	113.0

*Figures for Tepic are for 1779-1783.

TABLE 5.9
Racial variation in mean migration distances (kilometers)

	1759-1763	1790-1794	1805-1809	Total
Chapala				
Spanish	60.5	52.8	64.3	60.0
Castas	66.5	78.8	42.3	63.9
Indians	47.0	65.9	37.3	50.3
Ameca				
Spanish	77.9	70.6	76.6	74.2
Castas	48.0	64.7	49.9	59.5
Indians	76.0	75.6	35.5	62.8
Tequila				
Spanish	93.1	103.1	63.0	79.7
Castas	69.7	53.5	32.8	60.9
Indians	75.5	100.2	62.5	77.7
Compostela				
Spanish	126.5	70.9	142.2	154.5
Castas	104.0	88.6	82.4	109.6
Indians	138.6	104.9	60.3	142.6
Tepic				
Spanish	154.1*	151.2	164.9	154.5
Castas	113.2	118.5	91.5	109.6
Indians	164.3	134.1	113.0	133.2

*Figures for Tepic are for 1779-1783.

occasional newcomer from the north or from Valladolid, Chapala's marriage field was quite localized. Significant numbers of Chapala's residents married people from Ocotlán, Guadalajara and the area immediately surrounding Lake Chapala. The area's economy, based on the export of fish to Guadalajara and an agricultural base of grain and livestock, probably did not generate as much general population movement as mining towns or trade centers, and it seems to have served to supply the populations of Ocotlán and Guadalajara with foodstuffs (Figure 5.2).

Marriages between originarios of Ameca and individuals from places quite far away from their parish were common (Figure 5.3). By the 1790s, interaction with northern mining areas had been particularly heavy. Guadalajara, Cocula and Guachinango were always well-represented among marriage migrants to Ameca. Except for Guachinango, however, Ameca's marriage field extended furthest to the east, north and south, over-reaching Chapala's marriage field and including many of the towns which were Chapala's major sources of extra-parish interaction. The economic base of Ameca was agricultural; large, prosperous haciendas owned by wealthy families dominated the local economy and probably gave this area economic stability which was attractive to unlucky miners, prospective farmers and ranchers, and merchants interested in steady trade. A large proportion of marriage partners from outside Ameca were Spaniards, who were typically active in these occupations.

Tequila's marriage field was remarkably stable throughout all three periods. Its economic base was similar to Ameca's, but a larger proportion of its marriage partners came from outside the parish, particularly from small towns near Tequila, such as Cocula, Atemanica and Hostotipaquillo. Many of the migrants were Indians and probably worked as laborers in the maguey fields (Figure 5.4).

Compostela was another setting entirely. Isolated, and far from the prosperity and sophistication of Guadalajara and the large towns of the Lagos area, Compostela was originally founded as the administrative center of western Mexico. The seat of government was quickly moved to Guadalajara when it became clear that distance to Mexico City was a major disadvantage. It was, however, on the edge of the mining areas of Hostotipaquillo and Bolaños, and had the advantage of proximity to the port of San Blas without the uncomfortable coastal climate. Many of the outsiders who married into Compostela's population were Spaniards or mulatos who came from mining centers both nearby and farther to the northeast (Figure 5.5). A substantial number also came from towns between Compostela and Ameca, apparently an area with stronger functional links to Compostela than to Ameca or Tequila. Certainly the highway linking Compostela to Guadalajara

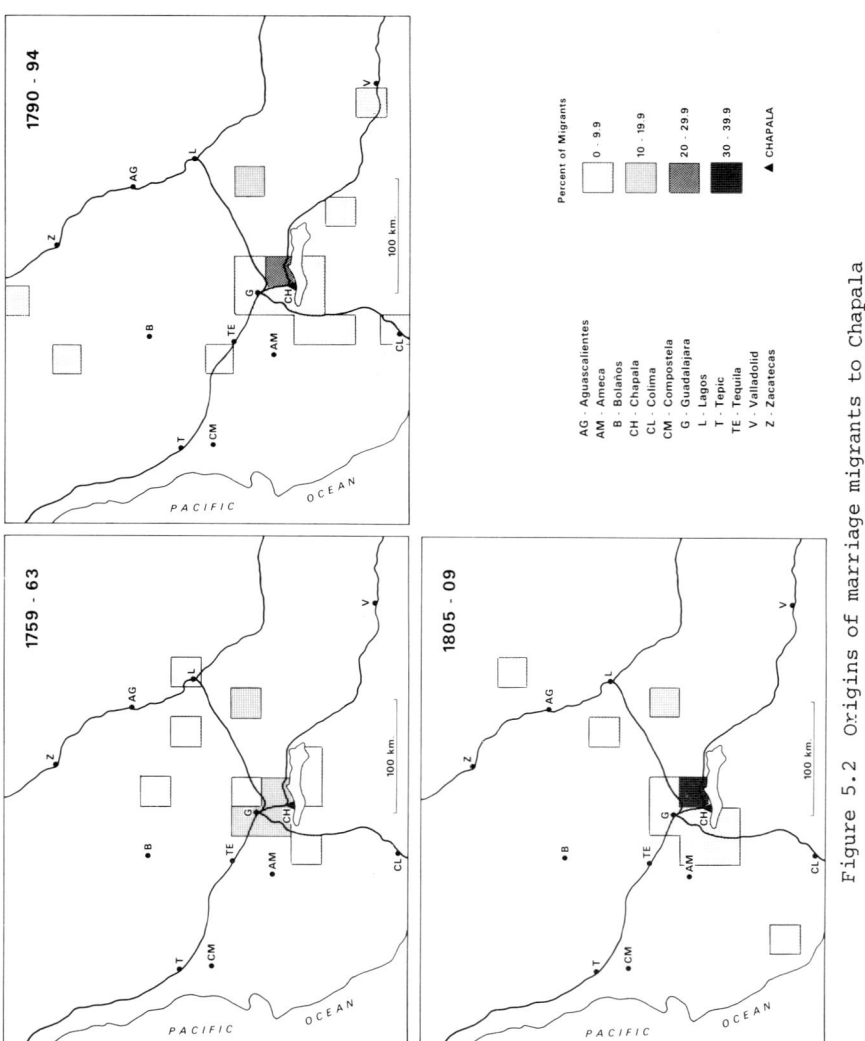

Figure 5.2 Origins of marriage migrants to Chapala

135

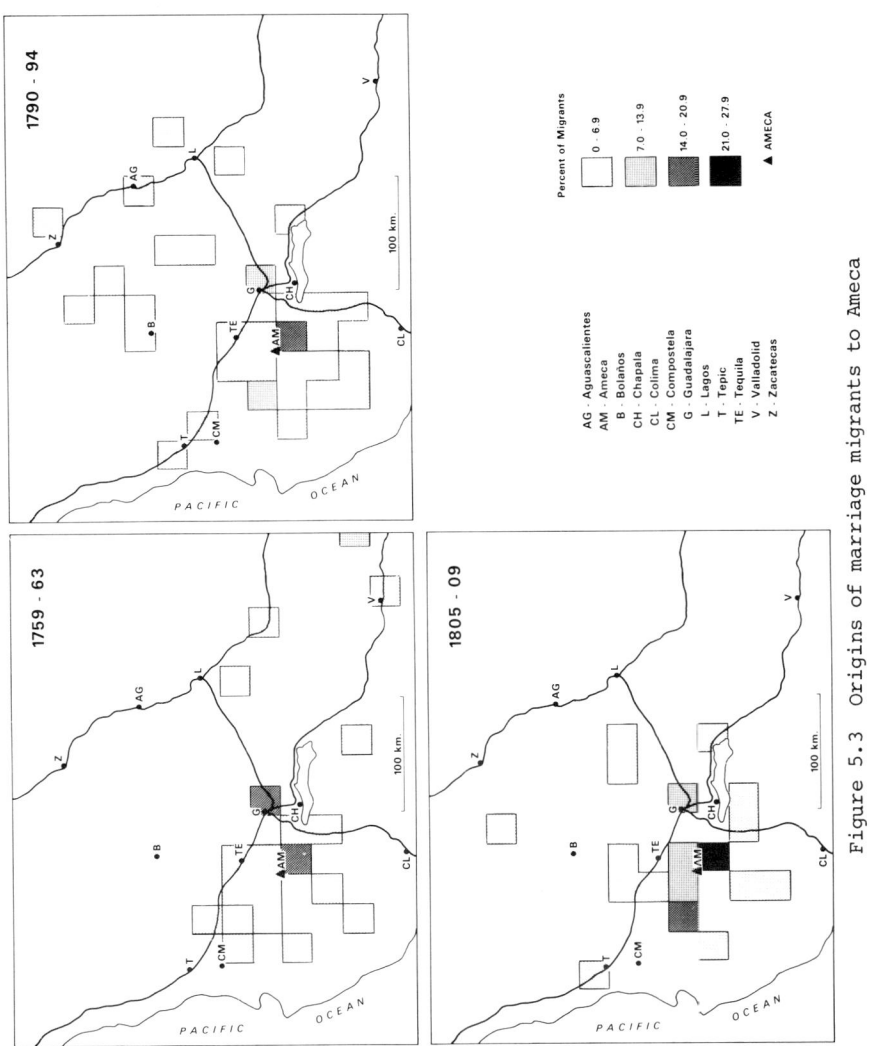

Figure 5.3 Origins of marriage migrants to Ameca

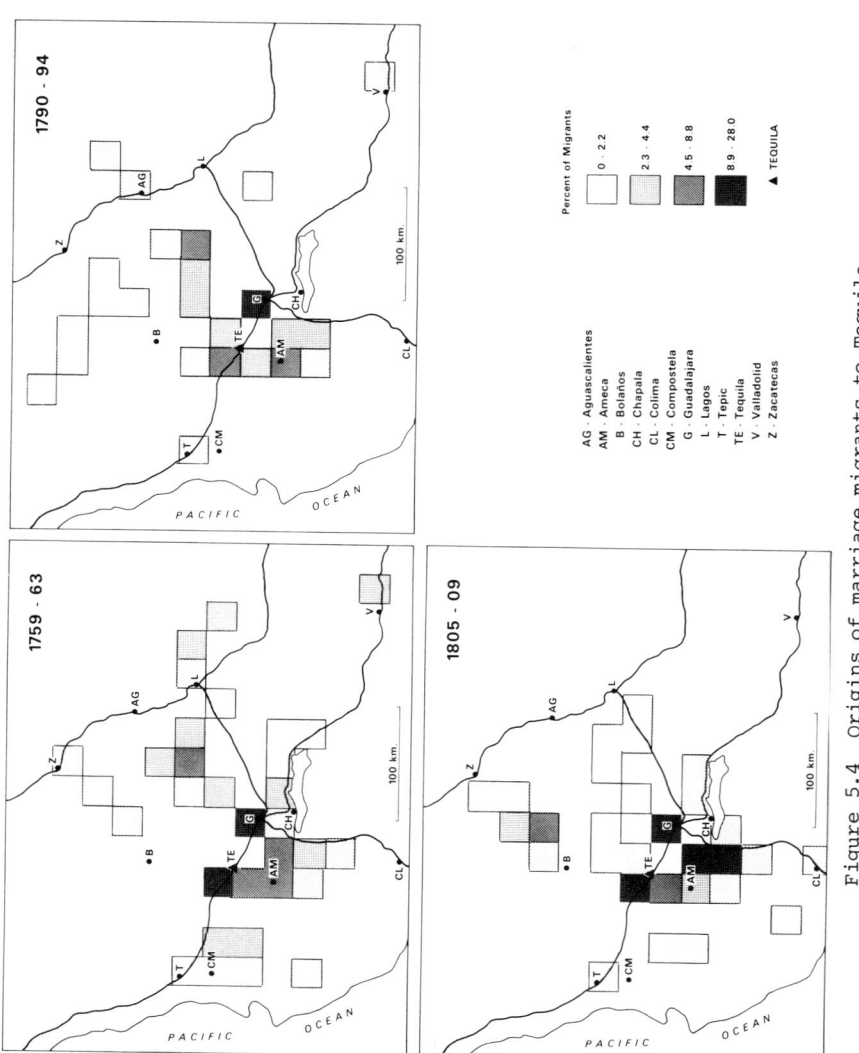

Figure 5.4 Origins of marriage migrants to Tequila

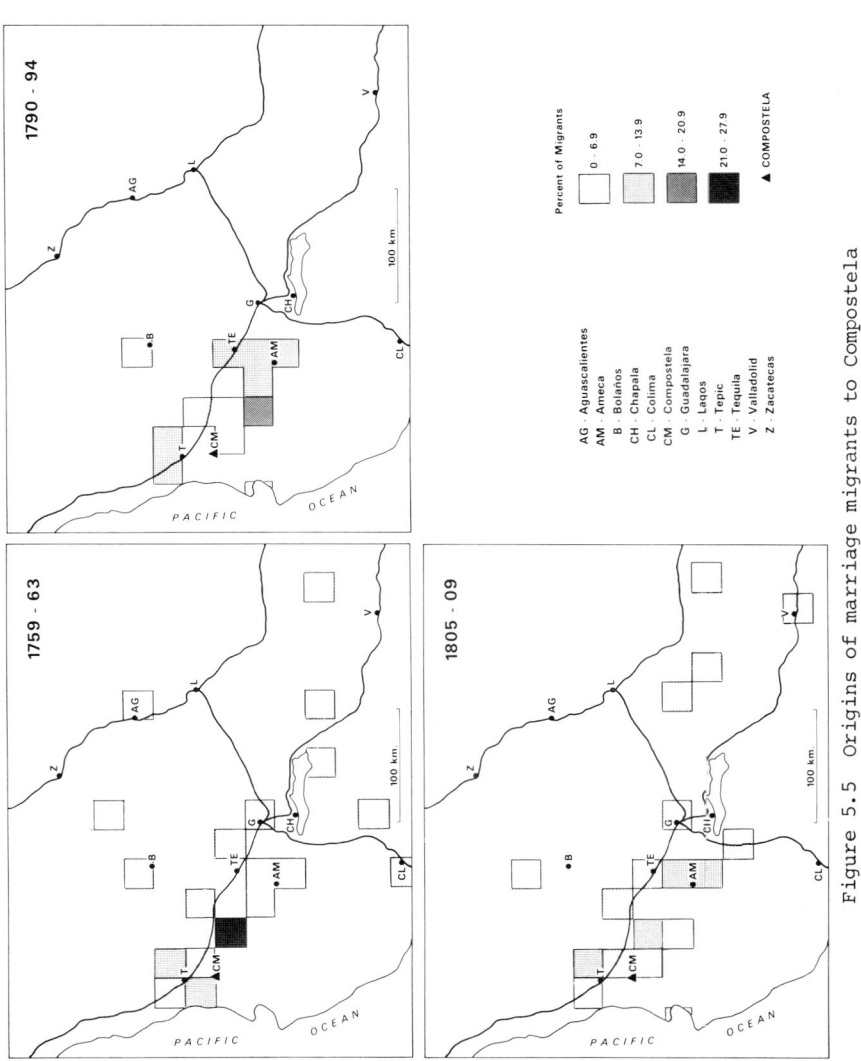

Figure 5.5 Origins of marriage migrants to Compostela

was a factor in the origins of newcomers; many of the towns along that road were well-represented among Compostela's marriage partners. In addition to transportation links, the races of migrants also clearly affected the shape and size of marriage fields. In the 1790s, Compostela's marriage field shrank when its racial exogamy rate declined dramatically. By that time, the proportion of Indians among migrants reached a peak; they came primarily from pueblos and parishes near Compostela.

Of all the eight parishes, Tepic's population must have been the most cosmopolitan. Its marriage field overreached those of the other parishes and extended beyond, to Spain, Mexico City, Chihuahua, California and Manila (Figure 5.6). Its dynamic economy and demographic profile was based on its prominence as a major supplier of livestock to many parts of Mexico, and the trading community which grew as a result of that economic base as well as activity generated by the port of San Blas. Many naval officers stationed in San Blas had their permanent residences or vacation homes in Tepic, and it probably served as well to supply miners further north along the coast and in the east around Hostotipaquillo and Magdalena, providing both equipment and capital from the accounts of wealthy merchants. In particular, however, Tepic's residents married migrants from the area immediately around the parish (San Blas, Iscuintla, Sentispac and Santa María del Oro), and from the region around Ameca, including Cocula, San Martín de la Cal, Tala, Ahualulco, Etzatlán and other towns within approximately a 20-kilometer radius of Ameca. No single racial group consistently dominated the incoming marrying population; both the Spanish and Indian populations married across racial lines at a significant rate when their racial group dominated the incoming population (1790-1794 for Indians and 1805-1809 for Spaniards).

The question of timing of the migrants' arrival at the parish plays havoc with any attempt to fit marriage migration patterns into a temporal context. Unless the priest consistently recorded the length of time in years that outsiders had spent in his parish, the marriage field derived from his records can only represent cumulative population movement for an undefined period of time for that segment of the population which eventually married in that parish. (Most disappointing of all is to find that a priest meticulously recorded the arrival of each migrant in terms such as "residente desde su infancia" or "desde su tierna edad," without indicating the migrant's age.) The marriage fields compiled here therefore represent the cumulative movements of potential marriage partners for a period of at least 25 years before each study period.

This 25-year period can be examined in five-year intervals for the three parishes whose priests did

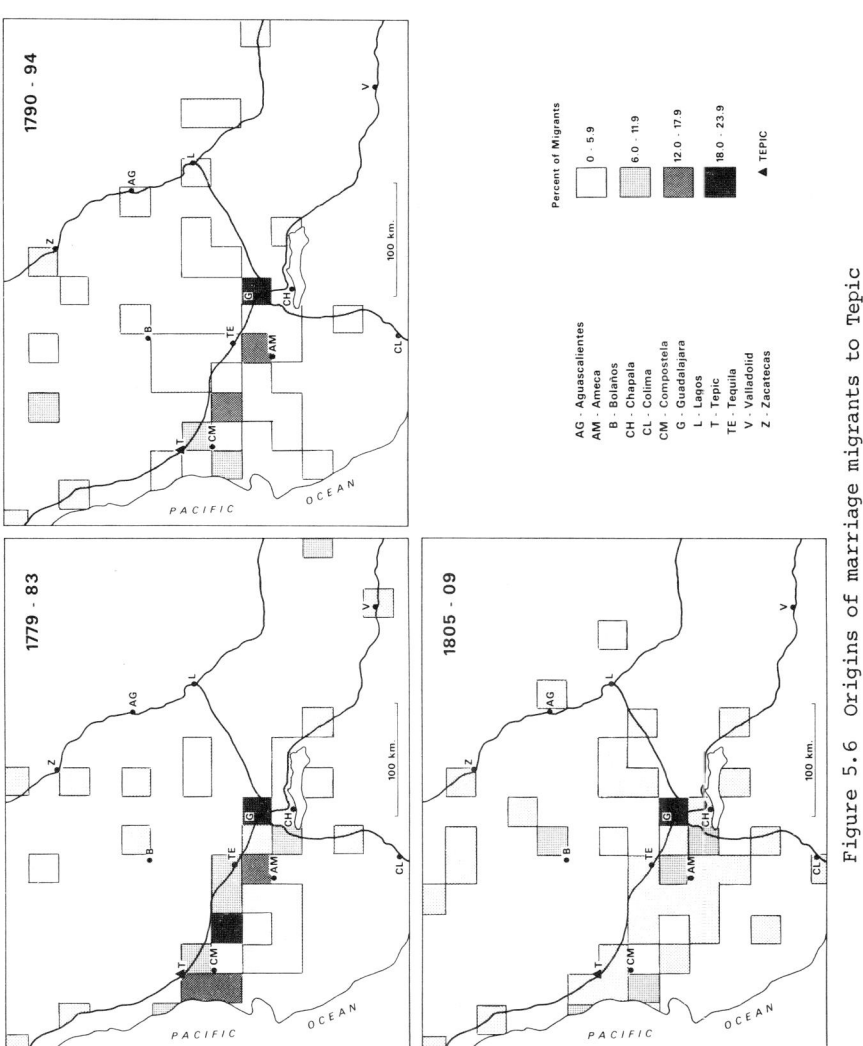

Figure 5.6 Origins of marriage migrants to Tepic

consistently record the length of residence of migrants (Table 5.10). In the period 1759-1763, most marriage partners who were born outside the parish had migrated there within ten years of marriage. Those who had lived in the parish for longer than that had either been brought in as infants, or were older widows or single people who had migrated when they were younger. This pattern held throughout the century.

The one outstanding feature of this temporal dimension of migration is the great increase in movement following the epidemic of 1785. In every parish, no matter how inconsistent the priests' records, more marriage partners had migrated in 1786 than in any other year. Furthermore, many of them married in the period 1790-1794; by 1805, nearly all the migrants who would marry had done so. The effect of this massive population movement was to expand marriage fields somewhat, although mean marriage migration distances did not necessarily increase. The region to the east of the line connecting Zacatecas and Guadalajara seemed to be the origin of many of the disaster migrants. For example, migrants who arrived in Tepic in 1784 and 1785 came primarily from its immediate local area, from communities around Ameca--Guachinango, Cocula and Ahualulco--and from the north (Teul, Guejuquilla and Valparaiso). By 1786, migrants arrived from Silao and Guanajuato. The effect in Compostela and Tequila was less dramatic; in 1786, migrants began arriving from Jalpa, Juchipila, Nochistlán, and Teocaltiche, not traditional sources of marriage partners for Tequila's and Compostela's residents.

This event clearly demonstrates the complexities of race, regional economic development, demographic change and the "openness" of communities. The differential impacts of economic activity and demographic crises on specific racial groups was reflected in their tendency to migrate, their patterns of physical movement, and their social mobility through interracial marriage. This is evidenced not only in Nueva Galicia, but in northern New Spain, where Swann has examined variation in spatial exogamy in mining and agricultural centers, and in urban and rural settings, and in Michoacán, where Yacher has noted the correlation between migration and racial endogamy.[10]

SPATIAL EXOGAMY WITHIN PARISHES

Because parish priests identified the pueblos and haciendas of which their own parishioners were originarios, it is possible to examine regional interaction at another scale: marriage between people from different haciendas and pueblos of the same parish.

For this analysis, three parishes will be excluded.

TABLE 5.10
Date of arrival of marriage migrants to selected parishes

	Percent of migrants with known arrival dates		
Date	Ameca	Tequila	Tepic
1759-63	14.3	28.1	
1754-58	39.3	31.3	
1749-53	7.1	28.1	
1744-48	3.6	1.6	
Before 1744	35.7	10.9	
Total	100.0	100.0	
1779-83			21.5
1774-78			31.6
1769-73			26.5
1764-68			8.5
Before 1764			11.9
Total			100.0
1790-94	17.3	16.9	20.4
1785-89	39.7	52.5	28.7
1780-84	21.5	10.2	21.5
1775-79	6.6	9.9	6.8
Before 1775	14.9	19.3	13.6
Total	100.0	100.0	100.0
1805-09	29.2	21.8	19.8
1800-04	22.9	31.8	24.2
1795-99	2.1	24.5	28.6
1790-94	12.5	6.4	16.5
Before 1790	33.3	15.5	10.9
Total	100.0	100.0	100.0

Tlaquepaque, a vice-parish of San José de Analco, apparently consisted of only the pueblo itself; no other place is mentioned as being within its jurisdiction. In Tequila, only one pueblo in addition to the parish center appeared frequently enough in the marriage records to be appropriate for study.[11] In Tepic, marriage partners from within the parish came from a number of haciendas and ranchos in the parish, none of them alone supplying a significant proportion of marriage partners.[12]

Clearly the proportion of inter-pueblo and inter-hacienda marriages varied through time (Table 5.11). In most cases, only one or two pueblos within a parish tended to interact with other parish communities, and therefore affected the overall rate of spatial exogamy. In Zapopan, for example, it was principally residents of the parish center who married someone from outside their pueblo. The decline of this phenomenon over time was reflected in the overall level of spatial exogamy. Marriages between originarios of the parish center and other pueblos declined to almost negligible proportions by the turn of the century.

A similar situation existed in Compostela in the first period, when originarios of the Hacienda San José del Conde and the pueblo of Masatán were the only parishioners who married into other communities, both within and outside the parish. When they tended to interact less frequently with others outside their communities, as in the second period, the overall rate of inter-pueblo marriage declined until originarios of Compostela, San Pedro Lagunillas and Guichichila began marrying into other pueblos in the third period. In Tonalá, spatial exogamy at the sub-parish level was not only minimal, but was restricted primarily to the parish center and the haciendas and ranchos surrounding it. In Chapala, it was marriage partners from the Haciendas Cedros and Buenavista who were most likely to marry originarios from other places in the parish. In Ameca, where all the significant sub-parish units were haciendas, no single place was more "open" than the others; indeed, at one time or another, originarios of all of the haciendas married into other communities at a significant rate.

The general pattern of interaction that seems to have been characteristic among pueblos and haciendas in a given parish is fairly clear. First, the official parish center seemed to be more "open" than other pueblos; migrants from other parishes usually married natives of the parish center, perhaps because it was the most populated or most important place within the parish and therefore attracted newcomers on their arrival. Second, members of secondary parish settlements usually married within their own communities; if they did not, they were most likely to marry someone from the parish center, rather than a resident of another secondary pueblo. Third, the

TABLE 5.11
Spatially exogamous marriages within parishes

	Percent of all marriages in parish in each period		
Parish	1759-1763	1790-1794	1805-1809
Zapopan	12.4	8.9	8.0
Tonalá	6.8	6.6	11.8
Chapala	19.9	15.0	15.2
Ameca	9.5	27.8	22.7
Compostela	7.6	1.6	14.0

haciendas of Chapala, Tonalá and Ameca were more "open" than the pueblos of any of the parishes, which suggests that the economic and social life of the agricultural unit led to more interaction and population movement than life in a pueblo.

The spatial relationships that result from this pattern of interaction are similar to those of the hierarchy of cities within Latin American countries today; a parish center, like a national capital, had as its satellites outlying pueblos and haciendas, with which it interacted but which did not interact much among themselves. This provides at least one clue to the nature of the parish as a socio-economic unit: parish boundaries seem to have included communities with functional relationships to a common parish center, but did not necessarily represent the limits of a cohesive, well-integrated set of communities and agricultural units.

CONCLUSION

How does marriage migration analysis help to describe regional patterns of interaction among communities in colonial western Mexico? How do these patterns compare with those of other areas of colonial Mexico?

First, it is clear that there were fundamental differences between Indian parishes and those of mixed populations. Obviously, rates of interracial marriage would be low in communities with relatively homogeneous populations. Less self-evident is the almost negligible level of interaction between Indian parishes and a nearby regional center such as Guadalajara, or any other center for that matter. There were, of course, administrative ecclesiastical ties and probably functional economic links through the tithe system. Essentially, however, these Indian parishes were isolated from the mainstream of social interaction, regardless of how closely it passed by (Tonalá and Tlaquepaque were located along the major highway connecting Guadalajara with the large population centers of the Lagos commercial and agricultural district; Zapopan was on the road to the Pacific coast and the port of San Blas). Even more surprising is the isolation of pueblos within Indian parishes. It was not the case that Indians as a racial group simply did not move. In Tequila and Tepic they accounted for up to one-third of all marriage partners who originated from outside the parish; in Ameca, Chapala, and Compostela they accounted for roughly 30 percent less than that. It is important to remember, however, that western Mexico did not offer a large indigenous population even at the time of Conquest. Cook and Borah have estimated general population growth throughout west-central Mexico in the colonial period and illustrate an early decline in indigenous population.[13] Total population figures for later periods indicate a relatively well-balanced ethnic mixture which was generally reflected at the pueblo level. Patterns and principles of interracial marriage in Nueva Galicia may therefore not be comparable to areas with Negro populations or with high concentrations of any of the other three racial groups, and the relative isolation of Indian communities may not be typical of the Indian population as a whole.

Second, if a hierarchy of parishes were to be conceptualized, with isolated Indian parishes on the first level, the second level might be parishes of mixed populations with a localized field of economic and social relationships. The absence of integrated pueblos and haciendas within the parish is also characteristic. Certainly Chapala is an excellent example of this configuration, with an economic base that tied it to the nearby regional capital of Guadalajara, and social links primarily with Guadalajara, Ocotlán and local parishes. In the cases of Ameca, Tequila and Compostela, their marriage fields complemented each other, and probably their economic hinterlands as well. Ameca and Tequila seemed to face eastward to their marriage fields; most of those living further west, except for the parish of Guachaningo, appeared in the marriage registers of Compostela and Tepic. In the 1790s, Ameca's marriage field expanded to the north and northwest, and Compostela's contracted, with nearby Indian pueblos forming the core of the marriage field. A region of locally-oriented parishes can be imagined whose patterns of social and economic development were interdependent. In particular, recalling the impact of racial variations in marriage migration on the "openness" of racial groups, it is clear that economic changes in one parish must have affected the shapes and characteristics of social and economic regions of surrounding parishes.

Third, in the case of an important regional center such as Tepic, the field of social interaction overreached those of less significant parishes for quite a distance, just as the field of economic links extended to the trading communities of Spain. In Tepic, local haciendas provided such a small number of marriage partners that spatial endogamy below the parish level is impossible to measure. It is unclear whether this was a function of a physical environment incapable of sustaining densely-populated agricultural units or whether the parish priest simply did not always distinguish the various haciendas by name.

Given the economic bases of a set of communities, then, and a general characterization of their demographic bases, the measurement of marriage migration fields and the analysis of the impact of change in the racial composition of the marrying population provide a set of general regional boundaries within which those communities functioned. It is difficult to determine with certainty the temporal and spatial dimensions of general migration flows from marriage records, but regions of social and economic links can be determined and gross changes in their shapes and sizes can be identified.

NOTES

1. Carmagnani analyzes the effect of economic change on interracial marriage for San Luis Potosí and Charcas in Marcelo Carmagnani, "Demografía y sociedad: La estructura social de los centros mineros del norte de México, 1600-1720," Historia Mexicana, Vol. 2 (1972), pp. 419-459. The relationship between race, occupation and intermarriage is discussed in: David A. Brading, "Grupos étnicos, clases y estructura ocupacional en Guanajuato (1792)," Historia Mexicana, Vol. 21 (1972), pp. 460-480. A classic study of racial patterns of marriage is found in Sherburne F. Cook and Woodrow Borah, "Racial Groups in the Mexican Population since 1519," in Essays in Population History: Mexico and the Caribbean, 2 vols. (Berkeley, 1971 and 1974), Vol. 2, pp. 180-269. Brading and Wu analyze marriage preferences and social interaction in David A. Brading and Celia Wu, "Population Growth and Crisis: León, 1720-1860," Journal of Latin American Studies, Vol. 5 (1973), pp. 1-36. A geographical perspective on marriage is more difficult to come by. Both racial aspects of marriage and spatial dimensions of marriage migration are analyzed in: David J. Robinson, "Population Patterns in an Old Mining Region: Parral in the Late Eighteenth Century," Geoscience and Man, Vol. XXI (1979), pp. 83-96; Michael M. Swann, "The Spatial Dimensions of a Social Process: Marriage Migration in Late Eighteenth-Century Nueva Vizcaya," in David J. Robinson (ed.), Social Fabric and Spatial Structure (Ann Arbor, 1979), pp. 117-181; and Leon Yacher, Marriage, Migration and Racial Mixing in Colonial Tlazazalca (Michoacán), 1750-1810 (Syracuse University, Department of Geography, Discussion Paper No. 37, 1977).

2. The marriage registers were available through the kind assistance of the Genealogical Society of Utah.

3. For just such studies, see Robinson in this volume; and also D. J. Robinson, "Population Patterns," op. cit.; Swann, op. cit.; and Yacher, op. cit.

4. Because the relative locations of settlements within parishes did not affect the analysis, the base maps are not included here.

5. For further discussion of economic regions in late colonial Nueva Galicia and the importance of the places discussed here, see Linda L. Greenow, Spatial Dimensions of the Credit Market in Late Colonial Nueva Galicia, dissertation, Syracuse University, 1980; and Eric Van Young, "Urban Market and Hinterland: Guadalajara and Its Region in the Eighteenth Century," Hispanic American Historical Review, Vol. 59 (1979), pp. 593-635. According to the population

count of 1791 by subdelegación, the parishes studied here were of a moderate size: Etzatlán (including Ameca): 10,714; Tonalá (including Tlaquepaque): 5,447; Tepic (including Compostela): 5,015; Tlajomulco (including Chapala): 5,938; Tala (including Zapopan): 3,497. These figures are available in José María Serrera, Guadalajara Ganadera (Sevilla, 1976), p. 21.

6. Sherburne F. Cook and Woodrow Borah, "Racial Groups in the Mexican Population," op. cit.

7. The racial distribution of the capital of Guadalajara in 1791 was as follows: Europeos, 186; Españoles, 9,386; Indios, 4,241; Mulatos, 6,538; Otras castas, 3,898; Población total, 24,249. "Censo de la Intendencia de Guadalajara (años 1791-1793), elaborado por el visitador Dr. Menéndez Valdés durante la visita que practicó al territorio," Archivo General de las Indias (Sevilla), Guadalajara 250. Cited in Serrera, op. cit., p. 21.

8. Brading and Wu, op. cit.

9. Robinson, op. cit.; Brading, op. cit.; and Carmagnani, op. cit.

10. Swann, op. cit.; Yacher, op. cit.

11. The pueblo was Amatitlan, which accounted for by far the largest single share of marriage partners who were originarios or residentes de pueblos outside the town of Tequila but within its parish. In the period 1759-63, 45% of such marriage partners came from Amatitlan; from 1790-94, 43%; and from 1805-09, 51%. The remainder came from a number of haciendas and pueblos scattered throughout the parish.

12. Marriage partners in the parish of Tepic but outside the parish center were originarios or residentes of fourteen haciendas and ranchos. These units supplied the following percentages of marriage partners: 1779-83: 5.6%; 1790-94: 3.1%; 1805-09: 3.5%.

13. Sherburne F. Cook and Woodrow Borah, "The Population of West-Central Mexico (Nueva Galicia and Adjacent New Spain), 1548-1960," in Essays in Population History: Mexico and the Caribbean (Berkeley, 1971), Vol. 1, pp. 300-375.

6
Indian Migration in Eighteenth-Century Yucatán: The Open Nature of the Closed Corporate Community

David J. Robinson

INTRODUCTION

Colonial developments within the Yucatán peninsula have received increasing attention during recent years. Gerhard[1] has provided a superb guide to the changes in administrative structures and a mine of information on encomienda developments. Other authors have outlined the process of agricultural extension and diversification,[2] or the changing population structure of the region.[3] Such works can be added to a distinguished list of earlier studies that have stood the test of time.[4] Though few of the above studies relate specifically to Indian population change, it is clear that for each and every one of them, that topic is of vital significance. Whether it be the encroachment of Hispanic culture on native practices, the changing structure of the urban market, the evolution of the encomienda system, developments in kinship and compadrazgo relationships--all these and more require a detailed knowledge of the state of, and changes in, the Indian population. It may also be suggested that the many more modern analyses that probe the Yucatán process of modernization[5] also have relied to a considerable extent upon assumed patterns of socio-economic development during earlier periods.

One of the most significant features to have surfaced as a result of recent historical investigations is the extent of spatial movement within and between the Indian communities. Farriss[6] has identified three types of population redistribution: "flight," which is the escape of Indians from Spanish rule into the unpacified frontier margin; "drift," which is the movement to other towns within the Spanish colonial domain; and "dispersal," which represents the hiving-off of new settlements from parent townships. Such a migration typology is very similar to that outlined by Hunt,[7] who stresses that the actual migration pattern was structured in a hierarchical fashion, with Indians moving first to nearby larger settlements, and then eventually onwards and upwards to Mérida:

> Mérida was the largest beacon of them all, and Indians came from far and wide, though often the advance was a gradual one from a far-away district, to a closer one, until the barrios of the city were reached. The jump might be made by an individual, or it could take generations.[8]

While the push and pull factors that may have operated are outlined below, it is important to note that Farriss and Hunt, as well as others who have noted Indian migration, see such patterns as reflecting the impact of Hispanic culture upon an acculturating native population. Thus, when agricultural developments lead to pressure on Indian lands, migration might be initiated. Similarly, as Patch has argued, when population growth at the central place of the region, Mérida, reached certain levels, this triggered a stimulation of agricultural development that also had a dislocating effect upon the Indian population. Embedded in all of such arguments, of course, lies the Indian community. To Wolf it possessed all the hallmarks of his "closed corporate" model--with restricted membership, communal jurisdiction over land, a religious system of notable endurance, and mechanisms which ensured the redistribution of surplus wealth, and maintained barriers against the entry of goods and ideas from outside.[9] And for Redfield[10] the ethnographic present was used as a direct window on the Yucatecan past; the most remote, and usually the smallest, communities of the 1940s were said to reflect a past condition of much of the peninsular Indian world, a realm of "closed" communities, in the words of Wolf[11] "socially and culturally isolated from the larger society in which they exist."

Yet such a view of the past condition of Indian Yucatán hardly matches the mounting number of clues regarding mobile Indians. This paper thus addresses various aspects of the central question--what was the rate, extent, and direction of Indian migration in the colonial period. It confines itself to the eighteenth century since that period provides both the best set of data, and the changing economic circumstances that allow one to monitor the relations between population change and the development process in the widest sense. Some might argue that such a study is unnecessary given the work of authors quoted above. However, it may be noted that in none of those works is it possible to assess population movement in any quantitative manner. With the census data of Cook and Borah, and Gerhard, it is possible to infer a shifting population base, if one could assume that the distinctive regions each had a stable population, but a study of one parish has shown that to be a most unwise assumption.[12]

Another feature of many of the studies quoted above is their lack of precision regarding the spatial dimensions of population distribution and change. In spite of the elegance of Farriss' typology, and the comprehensiveness with which Hunt examines the local records, there still remains much that is unstated. Which were the towns that served as way-stations en route to Mérida? And where did the frontier lie at specific dates? Without such specific information it is more than a little difficult to adequately test such notions as "dispersal" and "drift." And the crude sketch maps of Hunt[13] may suggest the expansion and crosscurrents of relationships of settlements in the Mérida area, but they do little more than that. Like many other regions in colonial Mexico, we know remarkably little of the geography of the eighteenth century.

THE DATA SOURCES

Instead of attempting to utilize the fragmentary data base provided by nominative censuses of the Yucatán, here, use is made of data pertaining to individuals, which can be gained from the parish registers. Two data sets can be generated for the eighteenth century. First, population migration can be ascertained from the origins of both spouses given in the marriage certificates, and recorded in the libros de matrimonios. Since such data has now been used for the analysis of several other colonial Mexican communities[14] it is possible to compare patterns, rates, and types of migration concerned with marriage. Normally, outside of the Yucatán the phrase "natural de" has been assumed to refer to "native of" in the sense of place of birth or nurture. However, it is clear from references in the Yucatán registers that here we are dealing not with place of birth (known by the stated place of baptism), but rather with their pueblo of tribute and encomienda affiliation.[15] For bride, groom, and often their parents and the testigos to the ceremony, is given their place of origin in this manner. A peculiarity in the data is the fact that many fathers were recorded as natives of communities other than those of their children, which might mean that affiliations were altered by means of residential rules, or that in some cases the tribute and baptism pueblos are intermingled? There appears to be no easy solution to this problem, other than a detailed tracing of sample individuals from their baptismal registration, through their appearance on tribute lists, to their marriage, and thence to the baptism of their children. Such work was not possible for the present study.

Since it might be argued that records that allow one

to only monitor the moves of those who got married in the legal sense could provide a biased sample, it is fortunate that in the Yucatán--and quite unlike any other area yet studied in Mexico--a second source permits one to monitor shifts in residence of a larger population. In the registers of Indian baptisms (and only Indian baptisms it should be noted) each parent is specified as "natural de," again allowing one to trace the movement of persons from one settlement to another. Many of the entries include phrases such as "Martín Pech, natural de Tixkokob, originario de Santiago . . . ," or ". . . tributario de Tekax, originario de Yaxa, y vecino de la estancia . . . ." As with marriage records, it appears that the phrase "natural de" refers to the pueblo of tribute, rather than the pueblo of birth. However, for the purposes of tracing population movements such data as exists is extremely valuable, for it permits one to calculate at the level of large numbers of individuals the relative proportions leaving certain pueblos and entering others. This paper utilizes data on some 2000 individuals getting married, and 10,000 parents of children being baptised.

Four settlements were selected for analysis, Umán, Tixkokob, Conkal, and Sotuta (Figure 6.1). They were chosen for the following reasons: Umán had been analyzed earlier with regard to its demographic evolution from the late seventeenth century, and it had extremely good marriage and baptismal records (it may be noted that "good" has to be construed within the relatively "poor" condition of most of the Yucatán parish records which have been very badly damaged by water, worms and neglect). Since it was located some ten miles southwest of Mérida, it was decided that a community to the east, at approximately the same distance would provide a comparable location to examine intra-regional movements. So that it would be possible to identify any southward, frontier movement, it was decided to select a community with good records in what had been designated the "borderlands" by Cline,[16] and which lay towards the frontier margin on the maps of Cook and Borah[17] and Gerhard.[18] Sotuta appeared to be the best documented settlement. Since the <u>costa</u> region appeared to be of great significance in patterns of population movement, a second settlement was chosen from that zone, Conkal, as a means of controlling for any variation between settlements in the same general proximity to Mérida. Mérida and Valladolid were not selected for this analysis, principally because of the much larger numbers of calculations that would have to be performed. They are, however, presently being studied in the hope of presenting a range of settlements from the largest to some of the smallest, and from close by the socioeconomic core to the margins of Spanish control.

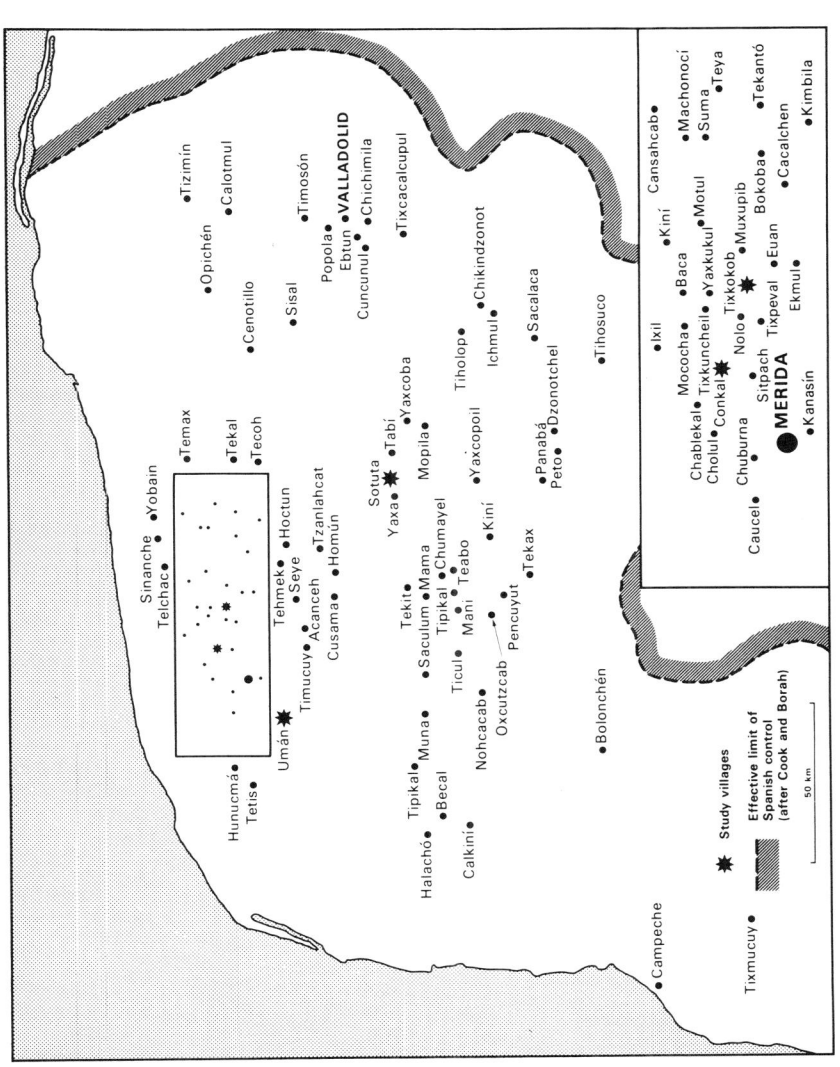

Figure 6.1 Location of Yucatecan study villages

ANALYSIS OF RESULTS

Longitudinal Profiles of Migration

One of the principal difficulties in presenting the results of an analysis of migration in Yucatán, as elsewhere, is that of reducing the units of analysis to a level that facilitates comprehension, but does not remove the complexity of the patterns and processes which existed in reality. Here, most of the data is presented at the partido level, rather than at the level of individual pueblos.

The origins of marriage partners in Umán (Figure 6.2) reflect a high and sustained level of exogamy throughout the eighteenth century. While the usual figures for exogamous marriages in colonial Mexico range between 15-20 percent, the evidence from Umán is quite distinctive. From 38.5 percent exogamous in the period 1689-1693, the percentage steadily increases to climax at mid-century and decrease slightly to 50 in the late 1760s. By the end of the eighteenth century it had again increased to over 65 percent. This meant that of those marrying in Umán's church (or the dependent chapels at Samahil, Bolonpoyche, and Dzibikal), over two thirds had previously been attached to other Indian settlements. One is clearly dealing with a century-long process of regional population movement. The costa region is the principal source area for the migrants in all periods save that of 1808-1812, when the Mérida barrios of Santiago, Santa Ana, and San Cristóbal combine to equal the stream of persons from the east. Another notable feature is the fact that although Umán is located west of the provincial capital, its main source regions lie to the east. There is little evidence in these maps to show that Mérida was the primary goal of migrants; indeed, many moved from their communities across the urban center to settle in Umán. Again, with so many moving to a settlement without a great deal of open land, one wonders just what the attraction of Umán was?

If one examines the data for origins of parents whose children were baptised in Umán parish, a very similar pattern emerges. It is important to note that the intervals between the sample five year periods have been maintained at about 25 years to ensure that very few parents are included in subsequent sample periods. The data demonstrate that from some 25 percent of non-local individuals at the close of the seventeenth century, the proportion increases to over seventy percent by the beginning of the nineteenth century (Table 6.1).

The location of the migrant origins is remarkably similar to that of marriage partner origins (Figure 6.3). More migrants enter Umán from the Campeche region in the 1720s, but the predominant trend is for migrants to have

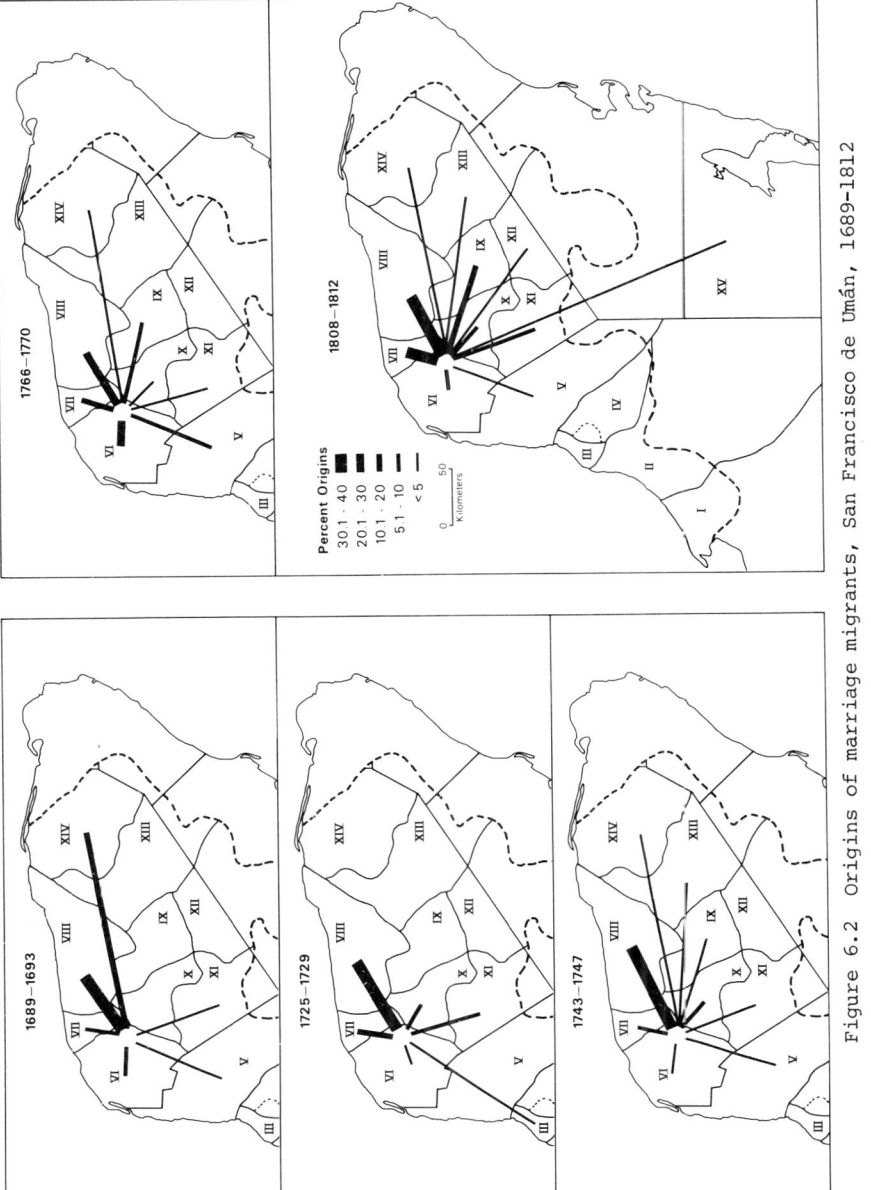

Figure 6.2 Origins of marriage migrants, San Francisco de Umán, 1689–1812

TABLE 6.1
Baptisms in Umán parish, Yucatán, 1689-1817

ORIGINS	1689-1694 N	%	1725-1729 N	%	1743-1747 N	%	1766-1770 N	%	1788-1792 N	%	1808-1812 N	%
Within parish												
Bolonpoyche	63	28.6	25	3.1	30	2.5	35	2.9	63	3.8	50	2.5
Umán	23	10.4	55	6.7	49	4.1	59	5.0	219	13.3	266	13.5
Samahil	60	27.2	56	6.8	94	7.9	2	0.2	34	2.0	32	1.6
Dzibikal	--	--	64	7.8	89	7.4	121	10.2	148	8.9	110	5.6
Unspecified	20	9.1	260	31.9	150	12.6	200	16.9	28	1.7	--	--
Total	166	75.4	460	56.5	412	34.6	417	35.3	492	29.8	458	23.3
Outside parish	54	24.5	355	43.5	778	65.3	762	64.6	1154	70.1	1500	76.6
Total Indios	220	100.0	815	100.0	1190	100.0	1179	100.0	1646	100.0	1958	100.0
Non-Indios	25		196		222		326		252		114	
Total baptisms	245		1011		1412		1505		1898		2072	

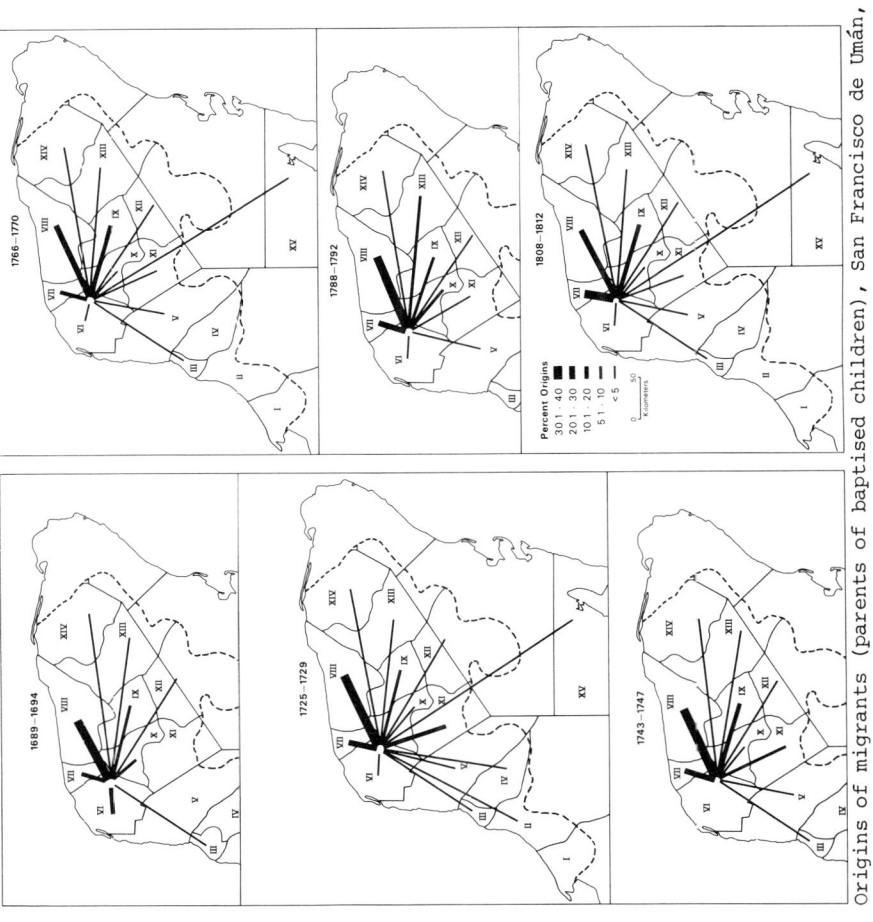

Figure 6.3 Origins of migrants (parents of baptised children), San Francisco de Umán, 1689-1812

originated in the east and north, from settlements in the densely populated coastal and Mérida zone, as well as from afar as Tizimín and Bacalar.

If one now examines the same series of data for Sotuta, a more peripheral settlement in the Beneficios Bajos district, it is evident that a lower rate of exogamy prevails (Table 6.2). Nevertheless, marked and nonrandom patterns are clear (Figure 6.4). In the early part of the century the Mérida barrios provided most of the migrants who moved to Sotuta, but by the middle of the century the costa region was increasing its share of the total flow, and in the 1770s exceeded that of Mérida. In the latter part of the century a three-pronged movement can be observed from Mérida, the costa, and also along the frontier line from the Sierra Alta district. Less than 30 percent of the total number of migrants ever originate from within the Beneficios Bajos region itself, a feature which is paralleled in the case of Umán. It appears that if one moved at all, then one moved usually to a destination outside one's own local region.

TABLE 6.2
Exogamy rates for selected Yucatán settlements

Period	Conkal %	Umán %	Tixkokob %	Sotuta %
1725-1729	33.3	43.5	69.1	22.1
1743-1747	34.9	65.3	43.9	34.7
1766-1770	50.2*	64.6	NA	52.5
1788-1792	62.0	70.1	56.2	67.2
1808-1812	NA	76.6	31.7	NA

NA = Not available due to records in illegible condition or missing.
*Figures for Conkal refer to years 1772-1776, since all others missing.

Cross-sectional Analysis of Migration

Since the diachronic mode of analysis makes it difficult to accurately compare the situations of different settlements, it is advantageous to examine the synchronic patterns at selected temporal cross-sections. If, for example, one changes the scale of analysis from the regional shifts of population to that at the individual

159

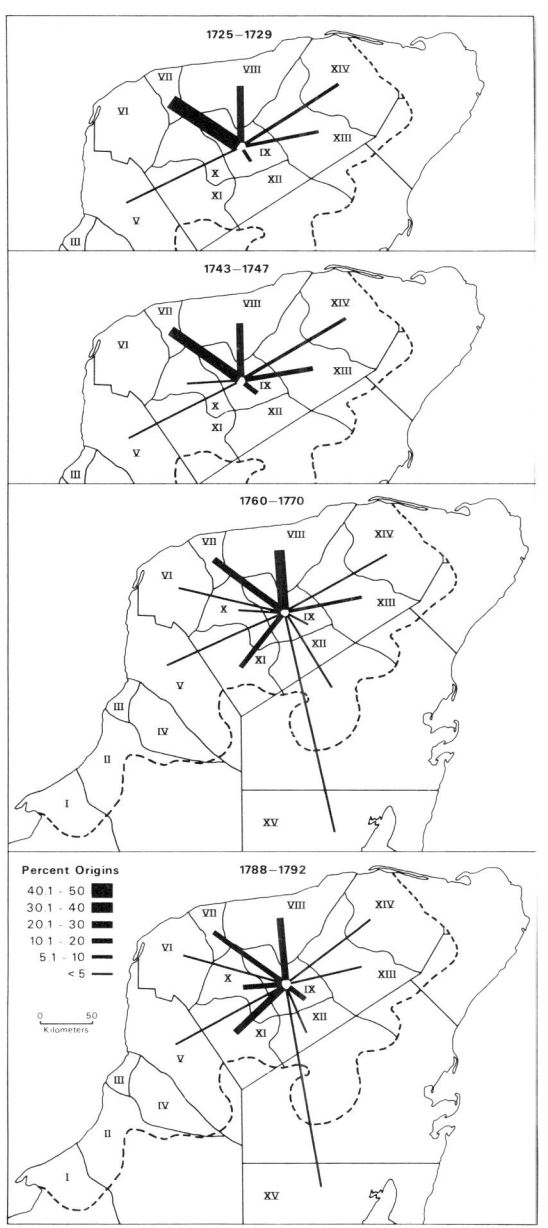

Figure 6.4 Origins of migrants (parents of children baptised), Sotuta, 1725-1792

pueblo level, then the complexity of migrant origins becomes clear. The 1788-1792 origins for Sotuta now disintegrate from the three-pronged regional flows to a mass (some might say mess) of distinctive sources. Only Maní and Mérida account for more than ten percent of the total migrant population, others coming from as far north as Yobain, from the Valladolid region to the east, and a scatter from the southern borderlands of Peto, Tihosuco, Sacalaca and Tecax (Figure 6.5).

If, instead of plotting the origins of migrants one examines the geometry of the several migration fields, some quite interesting contrasts emerge (Figure 6.6). First, it is clear that the total extent of the Tixkokob/ Umán/Sotuta fields are not significantly different, some 22,000 square kilometers for the total area of each. However, the areas from which fifty percent of all migrants originate show considerable variation. Tixkokob's smaller field includes only some 280 square kms., mostly including the important settlements of the nearby Mérida area, and a scatter in the Costa district. Umán, on the other hand, though the same distance away from Mérida, has a much more extensive fifty-percent field extending into the Sierra Alta. Sotuta's smaller field, almost circular in shape, accurately reflects the balanced distribution of settlements sending migrants to it.

A comparison of the patterns of migration to Conkal, Tixkokob, Umán, and Sotuta in the period 1788-1792 shows just how regionalized the flows were (Figure 6.7). Both Tixkokob and Conkal reflect their location to the east of Mérida, collecting most of their migrants from the Costa (some 55%) and the Mérida district. It is of interest to note that while 28 percent of Sotuta migrants originated from the Costa, only 18 percent left the Beneficios Bajos for Tixkokob. Clearly one of the next tasks will be to calculate net migration rates for sets of regions.

Another aspect of migration within Yucatán which is evident from the detailed records of the parish registers is the extent to which individual pueblos within the same parish have relatively distinctive migration fields. Since in all cases the records of individual chapels and churches have to be aggregated to the parish level before they are tabulated and mapped, it is possible to isolate the specific migration fields of pueblos. The results for Tixkokob parish in the period 1788-1792 are seen in Figure 6.8. While the cabecera of Tixkokob had a fairly extensive field, with most migrants coming from a zone of settlements in the southwest (including Halachó, Becal, Calkiní, and Maní) and the southeast (from Sotuta, Chikindzonot and Popola), if one examines the field of the dependent pueblos of Ekmul and Euan it is clear that they had distinctively restricted fields of migrants. Euan attracted most of its migrants from the north, west and east--mostly from within a radius of 20 kms.; only

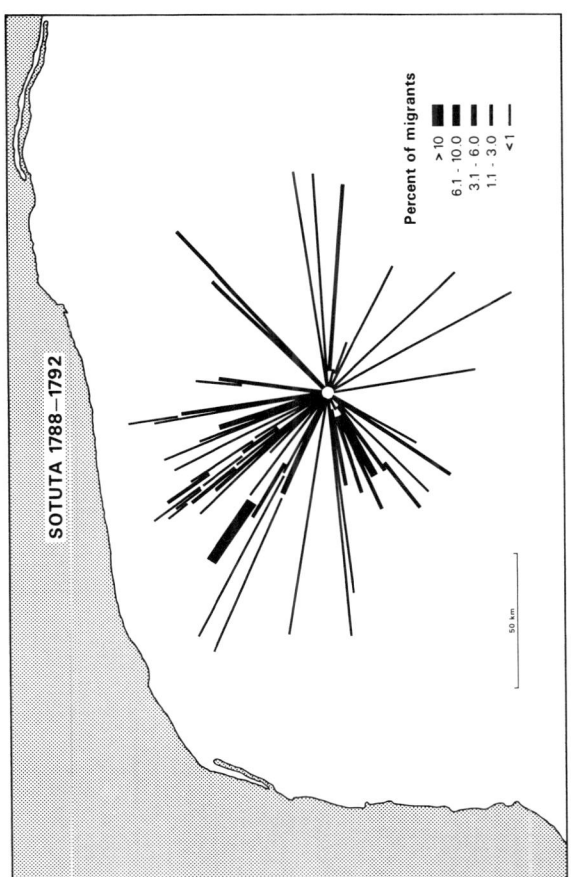

Figure 6.5 Origins of migrants to Sotuta, 1788-1792

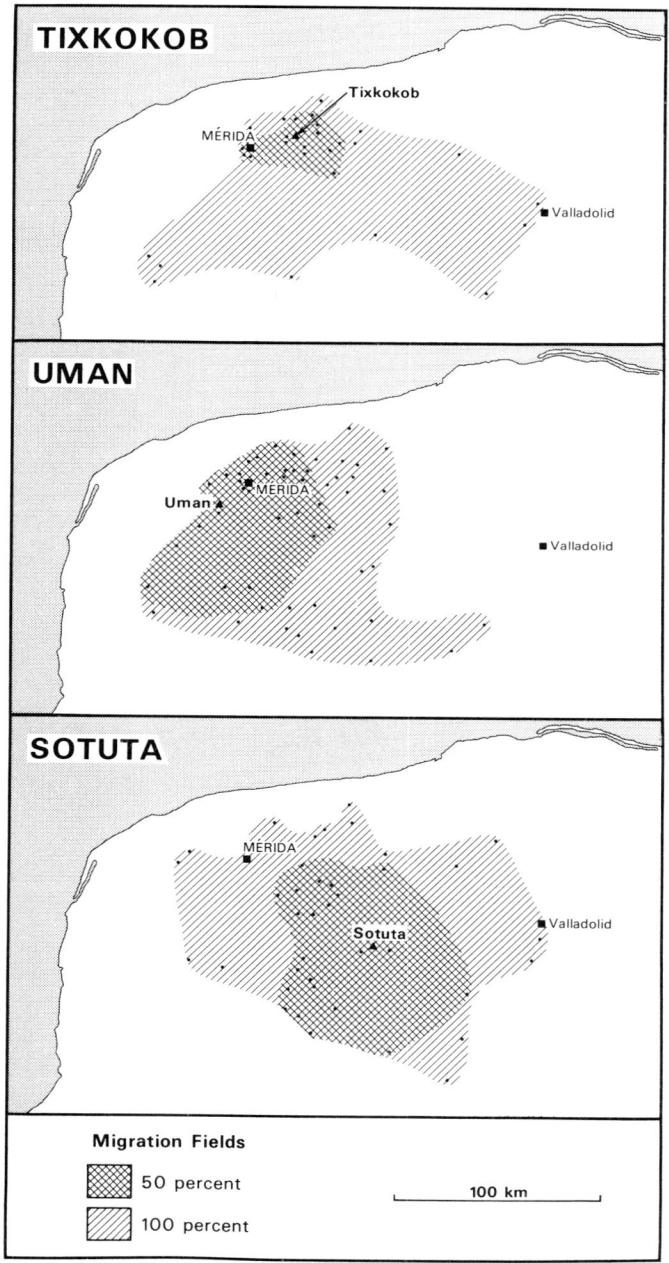

Figure 6.6 Selected migration fields, Yucatán, 1788-1792

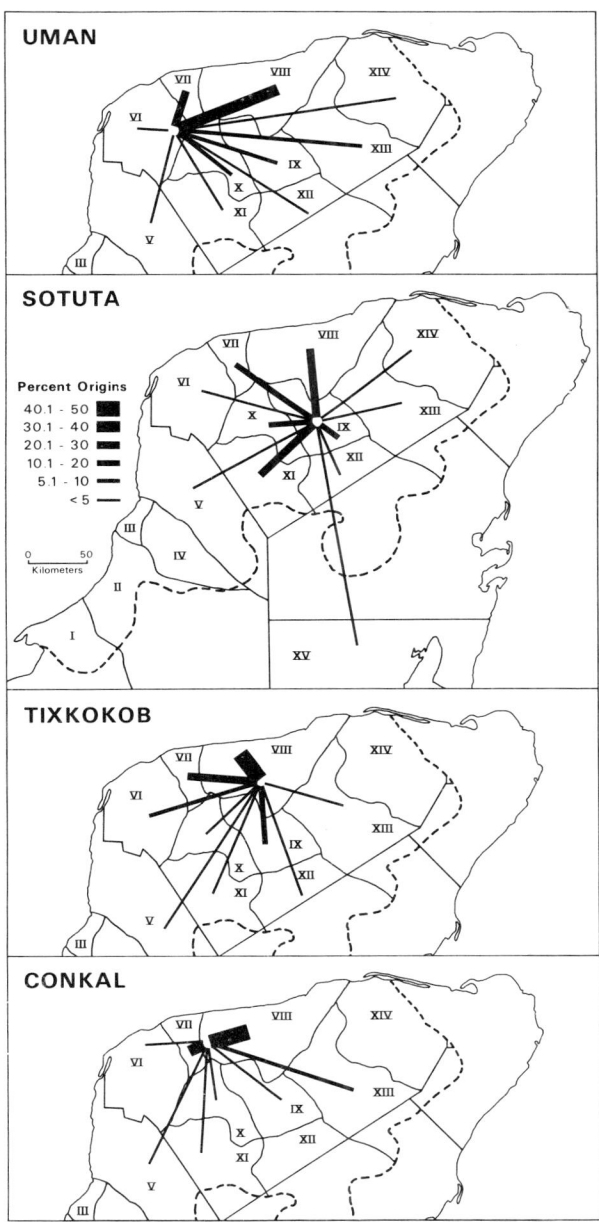

Figure 6.7 Origins of migrants (parents of children baptised), in selected Yucatecan settlements, 1788-1792

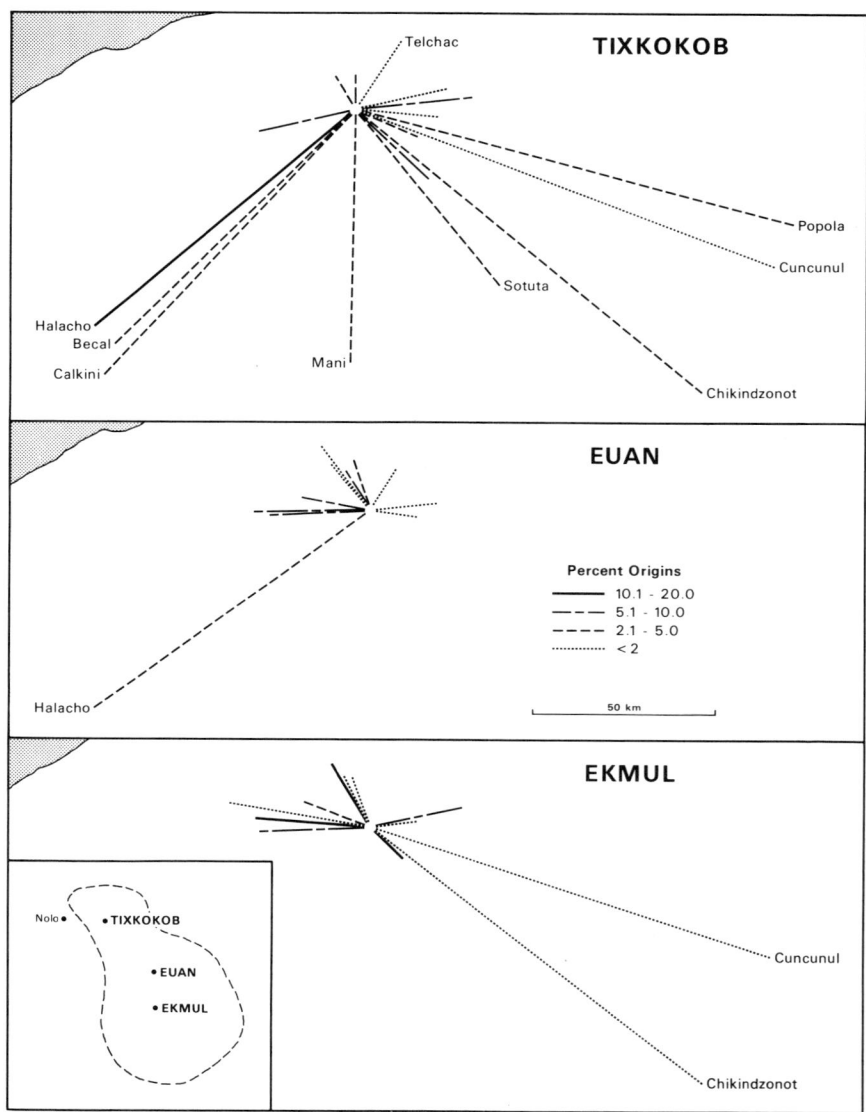

Figure 6.8 Origins of migrants to Tixkokob and its dependent pueblos, 1788-1792

the stream from Halachó in the southwest disturbed this
general pattern. Similarly Ekmul's links out to Chikindzonot and Cuncunul were the only ones extending further
than a broad zone of origins within 35 kms. of that
pueblo. Other settlements demonstrate similar differentiation at the sub-parish level, which suggests that migration streams may not have been moving from cabecera to
cabecera, as is suggested by the hierarchical model of
Hunt, but rather in a much more complex pattern. Some
moved from pueblo to pueblo; others moved from pueblo to
cabecera; yet others moved from cabecera to pueblo. What
is certain is that the largest proportion of migrants
within each parish normally migrated to the central cabecera (e.g. Tixkokob in Figure 6.8). Depending upon the
total number of dependent sub-settlements, and these did
vary considerably within the Yucatán, then the cabecera's
percentage of the total migration might be relatively
high (e.g. 75% in Sotuta) or quite low (34.5% in Conkal).
    Another means of measuring migration flows is also
available. Since for each parent their place of origin
is identified, it is possible to calculate the range of
settlements involved in the marriage selection process
(Figure 6.9). Conkal is here used as an example. The
top diagram in Figure 6.9 identifies those places from
which spouses migrated to marry a partner from Conkal itself. It can be seen that some fifty percent of all such
partners came from the band of settlements including
Chicxulub, Cholul, Motul, and further afield Ebtún, and
Calkiní. The remaining diagrams identify for separate
settlements the origins of marriage partners who had arrived in Conkal and baptised a child there in the period
1788-1792. Thus the Mérida figures show how important
the urban barrios were as an origin for many later Conkal
residents; equally important is the fact that those marrying into the Mérida population came from a wide area--
from again Ebtún, Calkiní, and also Izamal, Ixil and
Sinanche. This demonstrates that stages in the migration
process may be identified. Before all of these persons
had arrived in Conkal they had passed through the Mérida
jurisdiction.
    The origins of marriage partners for Cholul, Motul,
and Ekmul are also well differentiated (Figure 6.9).
Cholul received most of its migrants from persons who had
come from Motul, Ebtún and Sitpach; Motul marriage partners came principally from Ixil, Ebtún, Temax, Kiní, and
Mama. Ekmul's field included Ixil, Yobain, and Acanseh.
Ebtún, on the other hand, was firmly linked to Santiago
barrio of Mérida, and to Tixkokob and Sitpach. Mococha
partners found most of their spouses in Santiago and
Yobain. Ixil too was linked to Santiago, Izamal, and
Tixkokob. These diagrams show that the patterns of movement between Yucatán settlements were complex and multi-
staged.

166

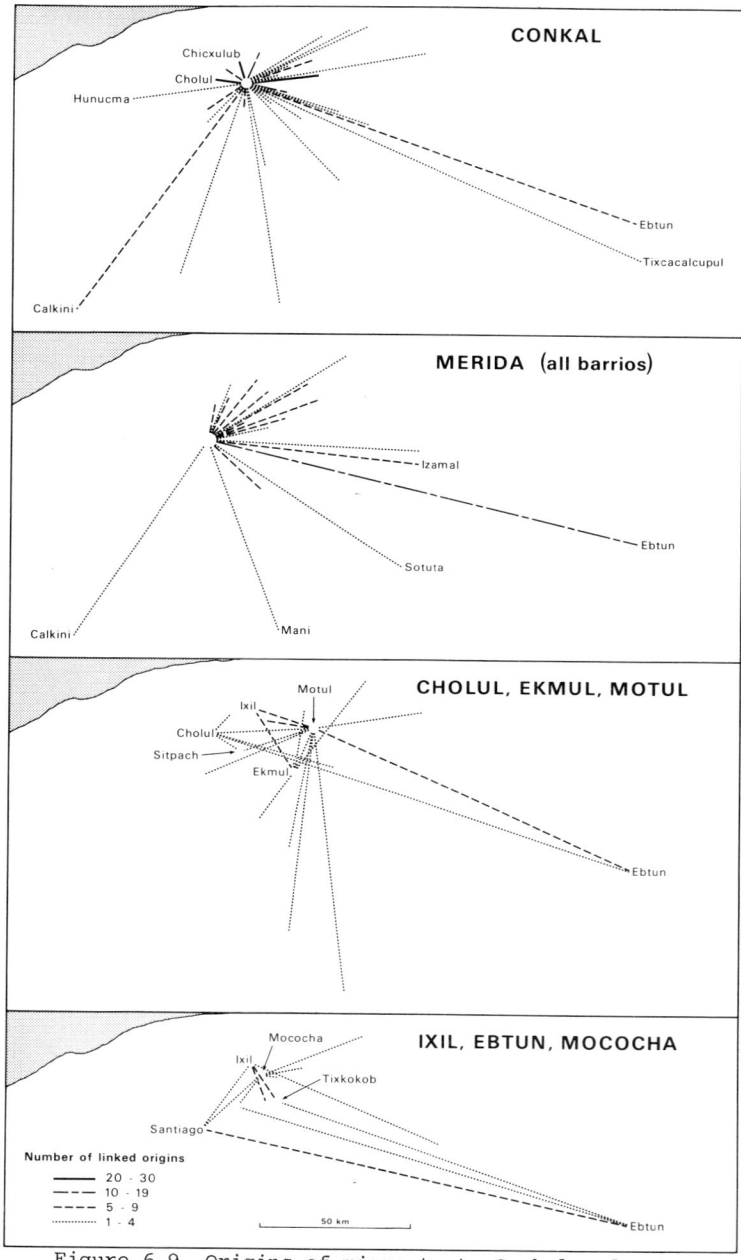

Figure 6.9 Origins of migrants to Conkal and other intermediate points, 1788-1792

The complexity of the migration process is only fully revealed when sets of individuals are traced through time and space. As an example one may cite cases involving the settlement of Tixkokob. In almost all of the eighteenth century baptisms not only are the parents of the child given, but in many cases so too are the names of its maternal and paternal grandparents, together with their pueblos of origin (of tribute?). This means that it is possible to identify three generations of individuals, and in many cases to identify what was happening to an individual family as its members migrated from their original pueblo.

On 9 November 1796, in Tixkokob a son of Ignacio Chi and Francisca Yuit was baptised. Chi himself had come from Becal, and his father was Marcos Chi, his mother Antonia Chucab. They too were from Becal. The next year Mauricio Chi, Ignacio's brother, baptised his child. Mauricio's wife, Rosa Yuit came from Bokoba, the same pueblo as Ignacio's wife Francisca. Two brothers had married two sisters from the same pueblo. That same year Damaso Pat, from Maní baptised his child at Tixkokob. His wife was Estebana Chi from Becal, and her father was Marcos Chi. She was the sister of Ignacio and Mauricio, and had married a man from Maní before both of them had moved to Tixkokob.

Space precludes any further exemplification of the manner in which it is possible to trace the fortunes of the common Indian families of the Yucatán in the eighteenth century. It should be clear, however, that for a sample of cases it would be possible to recover the migration paths of individuals from a sample of settlements. In that way it might be possible to ascertain whether there were any persistent streams of migrants from settlement to settlement over several generations. That this was the case is suggested by the incidence of very distinctive name groupings in the parish registers. A Poot, a Pat, a Chi, or a Chan can readily be identified with specific settlement areas, a feature that appears to be of some antiquity in the peninsula.[19]

SOME ALTERNATIVE EXPLANATIONS FOR MIGRATION

That a relatively high rate of migration characterized the Yucatán peninsula in the eighteenth century can no longer be denied. More difficult is the task of identifying reasons for such a rate. Some of the migration may well be associated with the moves of Indians to and from the frontier of Spanish control and settlement. Certainly the data for Sotuta would tend to support such an idea. However, until we have Farriss' detailed monograph, which should identify with more precision the specific location of that frontier margin, it is

difficult to be certain of the amount of migration that
may be explained by such a changing set of circumstances.
Since such moves to the open lands of the frontier would
presumably have been in search of land, such a process of
migration should be in direct relationship to population
pressure on land resources in the northern portion of the
Yucatán. Patch's study of the changing density of Spanish estates and commercial agriculture also provides valuable data. It may be noted that the parishes selected
here for analysis fall neatly into Patch's range of categories of Indian involvement in Spanish estate agriculture,[20] but the differences in the rate of Indian migration does not appear to be related in any way to such
agricultural development. It is encouraging to note that
in the 1720s large numbers of forasteros are reported in
several communities outside those studied here,[21] suggesting that non-local population was a common feature
throughout the region.

Another potential explanation is that most of the
migrants had to search out mates from outside their own
communities owing to the lack of suitable eligibles from
within the local marriage pool. While this can be seen
to have been an important cause of migration elsewhere in
colonial Mexico, there is little reason to believe that
exogamy rules, or shortages of potential partners was the
reason for such significant migration. Even if those who
shared the same patronym were excluded from marriage, it
seems unlikely that the relatively large settlements
could not have provided sufficient eligibles. However,
it will only be possible to estimate the field of eligibles when more work has been completed on baptismal and
marriage rates in selected regions of the area.

A much more reasonable explanation of the high rate
of migration may be that most Indians who moved did so to
avoid the burdens of tribute, servicio personal, the repartimiento sales, and limosnas and obvenciones. Clearly,
as Gosner has pointed out,[22] it was in the interests of
the encomendero, the priest and the pueblo caciques to
ensure that the Indians did not withdraw from the taxation system, but from an Indian point of view the reverse
was the case. If by moving from one's village one could
escape the burden of Spanish authority then that would
have been a strong incentive indeed. Since those who remained in the villages had to pay more to make up for
those who left, the situation could only have got steadily worse. The chief complaint of the Juzgado de Indios
by the 1720s was the fact that so many Indians were
leaving their settlements.

> en razón de su poco afán por el trabajo, y de su deseo
> de verse libres de las presiones de que eran objeto por
> parte de sus caciques, justicias y fiscales, no solo
> para que trabajasen los tequios y milpas de su comunidad,

> sino también para que participasen de los repartimientos
> y servicios a españoles . . . Este era, pues, el motivo
> de que prefirieran las estancias, ranchos y milperías--
> estos dos últimos sobre todo, por su mayor aislamiento.[23]

By this means the estate owners procured labor, and the Indians escaped all the pressures of social obligations. Of course, this escape cost the Indians much in terms of breaking up family and community ties, but if, as was suggested above, it turns out that whole families, or indeed groups of families engaged in the practice, then such costs may not have been so onerous. It is clear that the Spanish could not halt the process of migration, for the lack of attention paid to cédulas of the 1740s which ordered the reduction of all forasteros, necessitated the creation of the position of cobrador de indios dispersos.[24]

RESEARCH FOR THE FUTURE

The present study has done no more than expose the rate and range of migration in the Yucatán during the eighteenth century. Much more work will need to be done to fill in the details of the complex process. First, more communities will need to be examined to see whether the migration patterns vary significantly by size of settlement, or by distance from the center of economic activity. Second, since the notion of "closed corporate communities" is seriously eroded by the Yucatán colonial data, the means of controlling access to land resources by Indians, the rate of incorporation of non-locals into the new settlements' compadrinazgo structure, and the openness of communities all need to be studied in depth. One may now hypothesize a long-term secular change in the spatial "openness" of the Yucatecan Indian village (Figure 6.10) that may be more closely calibrated by empirical data. It is of interest to note that criticisms of the "closed corporate community" model are now appearing in widely dispersed contexts.[25]

Only when such questions as these have been addressed will it be possible to fully estimate the significance of the Indian migrations within colonial Yucatán. For the moment, however, such migration appears to be yet another characteristic quite unique to the Yucatán, setting it off from other Indian regions of colonial Mexico.

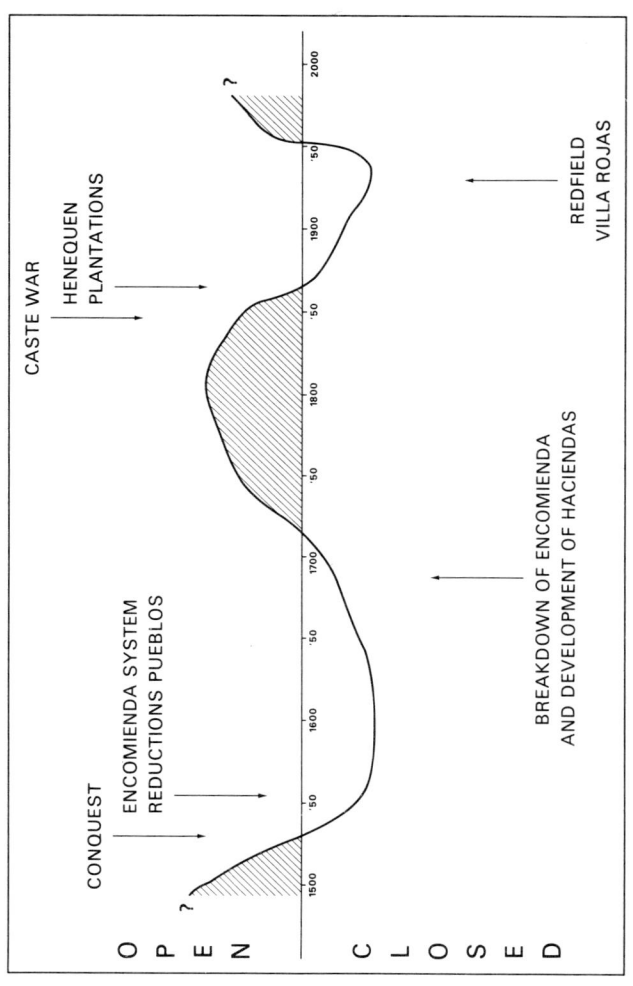

Figure 6.10 Hypothesized changes in "open/closed" nature of Yucatecan settlements

NOTES

1. P. Gerhard, The Southeastern Frontier of New Spain (Princeton: Princeton University Press, 1979).
2. M. Espejo-Ponce Hunt, Colonial Yucatán: Town and Region in the Seventeenth Century, Ph.D. dissertation, University of California, Los Angeles, 1974; M. Espejo-Ponce Hunt, "The Process of Development of Yucatán, 1600-1700," in I. Altman and J. Lockhart (eds.), Provinces of Early Mexico (Los Angeles: University of California Press, 1976); R. Patch, "La formación de estancias y haciendas en Yucatán durante la colonia," Revista de la Universidad de Yucatán, Vol. 18, No. 106 (1976), pp. 95-132; R. Patch, "El mercado urbano y la economía compesina en Yucatán durante el siglo XVIII," Revista de la Universidad de Yucatán, Vol. 20, Nos. 117-118 (1978), pp. 83-96; A. Strickon, "Hacienda and Plantation in Yucatán: An Historical-Ecological Consideration of the Folk Urban Continuum in Yucatán," América Indígena, Vol. XXV (1965), pp. 35-63.
3. S. F. Cook and W. Borah, Essays in Population History (Berkeley: University of California Press, 1971-1974), "The Population of Yucatán, 1517-1960," Vol. II, pp. 1-179; N. M. Farriss, "Nucleation versus Dispersal: The Dynamics of Population Movement in Colonial Yucatán," The Hispanic American Historical Review, Vol. 58 (1978), pp. 187-216; M. C. García Bernal, La Sociedad de Yucatán, 1700-1750 (Sevilla: Estudios Hispano-Americanos de Sevilla, CCVII, 1972); K. Gosner, "Umán Parish: Open, Corporate Communities in Eighteenth Century Yucatán," Paper presented at 75th Annual Meeting of Association of American Geographers, Philadelphia, 1979; D. J. Robinson and C. McGovern, "Population Change in the Yucatán, 1700-1820: Umán Parish in its Regional Context," Paper presented at 75th Annual Meeting of Association of American Geographers, Philadelphia, 1979; J. Ryder, "Internal Migration in Yucatán: Interpretation of Historical Demography and Current Patterns," in Grant Jones (ed.), Anthropology and History of Yucatán (1977), pp. 191-231; F. de Solano y Pérez-Lila, "La población indígena de Yucatán durante la primera mitad del siglo xvii," Anuario de Estudios Americanos, Vol. 28 (1971), pp. 165-200; F. de Solano y Pérez-Lila, "Estudio socio-antropológico de la población rural no indígena de Yucatán, 1700," Revista de la Universidad de Yucatán, Vol. 17, No. 98 (1975), pp. 73-149; P. Thompson, Tekanto in the Eighteenth Century, unpublished Ph.D. dissertation, Tulane University, 1978.
4. H. F. Cline, Regionalism and Society in Yucatán, 1825-1847: A Study of Progressivism and the Origins of the Caste War, Ph.D. dissertation, Harvard University, 1947, available in "Related Studies in Early 19th Century Yucatán Social History," Microfilm Collection of Manuscripts on Middle American Cultural Anthropology, 6th Series, University of Chicago, 1950; J. F. Molina Solis, Historia de Yucatán durante la época española (Mérida, 1921-1927); R. L. Roys, Personal Names of the Maya of Yucatán, (Washington: Carnegie Institution of Washington, Publication 523, 1940); R. L. Roys, The Indian Background of Colonial Yucatán (Washington: Carnegie Institution of Washington, Publication 548, 1943); R. L. Roys, Political Geography of the Yucatán Maya (Washington: Carnegie Institution of Washington, Publication 613, 1957); J. I. Rubio Mañé, Archivo de la Historia de

Yucatán, Campeche, y Tabasco (1539-1795) (México: Imprenta Aldina, 3 vols., 1935); F. V. Scholes, C. R. Menendez, J. I. Rubio Mañé and E. B. Adams (eds.), Documentos para la historia de Yucatán (Mérida, 1938).

    5. V. Inge Buisson, "Gewalt und Gegengewalt im 'Guerra de Castas' in Yukatan, 1847-1853," Jahrbuch für Geschichte, Vol. 15 (1978), pp. 17-27; R. Redfield and A. Villa Rojas, Chan Kom: A Maya Village (Stanford: Stanford University Press, 1962); N. Reed, The Caste War of Yucatán (Stanford: Stanford University Press, 1964); B. Riese, "Kulturelle Aspekte Indianischer Gewalt im Kastenkrieg in Yukatan," Jahrbuch für Geschichte, Vol. 15 (1978), pp. 29-40; R. A. Thompson, "Structural Statistics and Structural Mechanics: The Analysis of Compadrazgo," Southwestern Journal of Anthropology, Vol. 27 (1971), pp. 381-403; E. Wolf, "Closed, Corporate Peasant Communities in Meso-America and Central Java," Southwestern Journal of Anthropology, Vol. 13 (1957), pp. 1-18.

    6. N. M. Farriss, "Nucleation versus Dispersal," p. 204.

    7. M. Espejo-Ponce Hunt, Colonial Yucatán, pp. 226-230.

    8. M. Espejo-Ponce Hunt, Colonial Yucatán, p. 227.

    9. E. Wolf, "Closed, Corporate Peasant Communities," p. 6.

    10. R. Redfield, Folk Culture of Yucatán (Chicago: University of Chicago Press, 1941), p. 341.

    11. E. Wolf, "Closed, Corporate Peasant Communities," p. 5.

    12. D. J. Robinson and C. McGovern, "La migración regional Yucateca en la época colonial--el caso de San Francisco de Umán," Historia Mexicana, Vol. 30 (1980), pp. 99-125.

    13. M. Espejo-Ponce Hunt, Colonial Yucatán, p. 243.

    14. L. L. Greenow, in this volume; and D. J. Robinson, "Population Patterns in a Northern Mexican Mining Region: Parral in the Late Eighteenth Century," in J. J. Parsons (ed.), Geoscience and Man, Essays in Honor of Robert C. West (Louisiana State University, 1979), Vol. XXI, pp. 83-96; M. M. Swann, "The Spatial Dimensions of a Social Process: Marriage and Mobility in Late Colonial Northern Mexico," in D. J. Robinson (ed.), Social Fabric and Spatial Structure in Colonial Latin America (Ann Arbor: University Microfilms International, 1979), pp. 117-180; L. Yacher, Marriage Migration and Racial Mixing in Colonial Tlazazalca (Michoacán), 1750-1800, Syracuse University Department of Geography Discussion Paper Series, No. 32, 1977.

    15. K. Gosner, "Umán Parish," p. 4.

    16. H. F. Cline, Regionalism and Society in Yucatán, p. 165.

    17. S. F. Cook and W. Borah, Essays in Population History, pp. 140-141.

    18. P. Gerhard, The Southeastern Frontier, p. 19.

    19. R. L. Roys, Personal Names of the Maya, p. 35.

    20. R. Patch, "La formación de estancias," map 2.

    21. M. C. García Bernal, La Sociedad de Yucatán, pp. 14-15.

    22. K. Gosner, "Umán Parish," p. 12.

    23. M. C. García Bernal, La Sociedad de Yucatán, p. 95.

    24. K. Gosner, "Umán Parish," p. 13.

    25. E. B. Keatinge, "Latin American Peasant Corporate Communities: Potentials for Mobilization and Political Integration," Journal of Anthropological Research, Vol. 29 (1973), pp. 37-58;

A. T. Rambo, "Closed Corporate and Open Peasant Communities: Reopening a Hastily Shut Case," *Comparative Studies in Society and History*, Vol. 19 (1977), pp. 179-188.

7
Population Change in the Quinizilapa Valley, Guatemala, 1530-1770

Christopher Lutz

The parish of San Miguel Dueñas is situated in a valley southwest of Antigua Guatemala and Ciudad Vieja (Figure 7.1) in the Department of Sacatepequez. Today this parish comprises the municipios of San Miguel Dueñas, Santa Catarina Barahona and San Antonio Aguas Calientes with its aldeas of San Andrés Ceballos and Santiago Zamora. From around the mid-sixteenth century until about 1750 these five pueblos (i.e. the three municipio cabeceras and the two aldeas mentioned) plus the contiguous pueblo of San Lorenzo el Cubo (today part of the municipio of Ciudad Vieja), known as San Lorenzo Monroy in the colonial period, were administered by the Franciscan convent in Almolonga or Ciudad Vieja. With the secularization of the jurisdictions of the religious orders in the mid-eighteenth century came the creation of the separate parish of San Miguel Dueñas. Today this parish is slightly reduced in size as San Lorenzo forms a part of both the parish and the municipio of Ciudad Vieja.[1]

The valley in which these six pueblos are located undoubtedly displayed a greater natural beauty and geographical unity prior to the draining of Lake Quinizilapa in the late 1920s than it does today.[2] Up until that time all of the Quinizilapa Valley's pueblos, with the exception of the more elevated San Lorenzo, sat near or on the shores of the lake. Due to the lower altitude of this valley than that of Antigua (Panchoy) and its more coastal climate (a transitional climate between the tierra templada and the tierra caliente zones) Lake Quinizilapa appears to have been a long-term health hazard for the surrounding pueblos. The lake was partially drained in the 1920s out of concern for the apparently high incidence of yellow fever and malaria in the region.

Even without the lake the towns which make up the parish of Dueñas (plus San Lorenzo) have a geographical unity forming a micro-region apart from the surrounding area. The Quinizilapa Valley lies between the volcanos of Agua to the east and Acatenango and Fuego to the west.

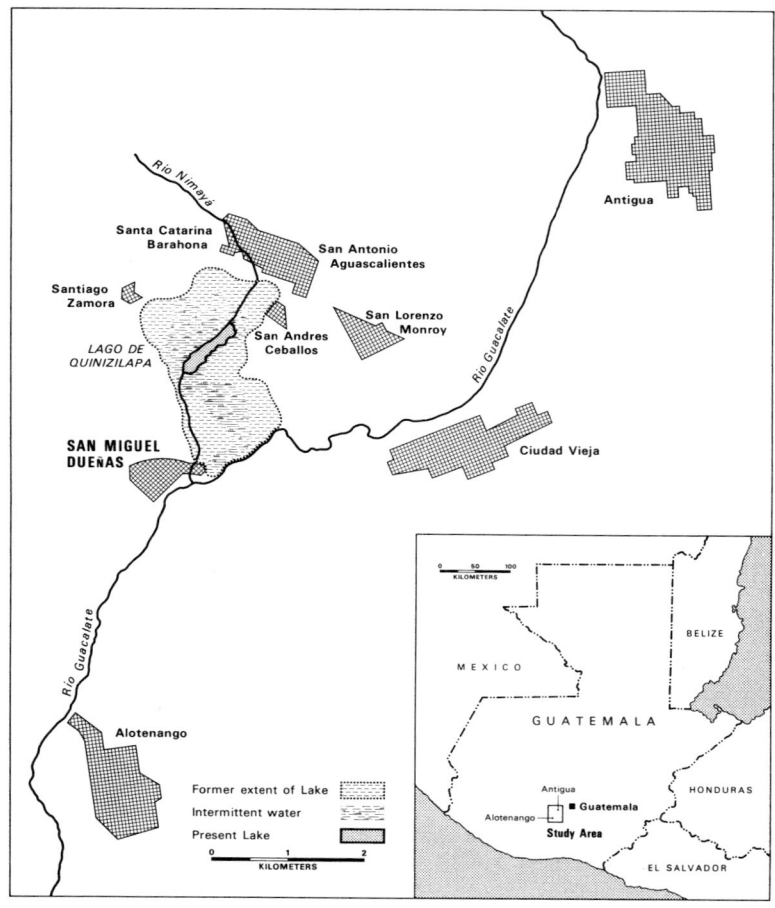

Figure 7.1 Settlements of the Quinizilapa Valley

The explosions and smoking of Fuego have been a constant part of the lives of the inhabitants of these pueblos since their founding over 450 years ago.

These pueblos, and almost all the towns in the immediate hinterland of the two early, permanent capitals of Spanish Central America, Santiago en Almolonga (1527-1541) and Santiago de Guatemala (1541-1773--today La Antigua Guatemala), were established around 1530 (probably in the late 1520s) by Spanish conquistadores-vecinos of the earlier of the two cities. Most Guatemalan Indian pueblos originated in preconquest settlements or were formed by the forced aggregation of a number of scattered settlements in close proximity to their present sites by Spanish civil and ecclesiastical authorities in the first decades after the conquest.[3] But this was not the case in this region. When the Spanish under Pedro de Alvarado founded Santiago en Almolonga (approximately three kilometers east of Lake Quinizilapa) in 1527 the Cakchiqueles had already been in revolt for three years. Cakchiquel resistance was not crushed until 1530.[4] The unrest of the times, however, did not reduce the Spanish vecinos' desires and needs for lands to provide for their families, servants and slaves.

Little is known about the late post-classic and Spanish contact period settlement patterns of the region where the Spanish established their early capitals. Archaeological surveys up to now reveal little or no evidence of late Mayan occupations with the exception of the Cakchiquel encampment Bulbuxyá (gushing water), established to protect nearby milpas. Under Spanish rule this settlement came to be called in corrupted Nahuatl Almolonga and, later, Ciudad Vieja.[5]

Whatever the indigenous settlement patterns which existed at Spanish contact by the late 1520s the Cakchiqueles were in revolt and had withdrawn from the valleys to more inaccessible refuges. The Spanish vecinos were obliged to acquire by capture or purchase Indian slaves and settle them on their lands, including those which the Quinizilapa pueblos occupy today.[6]

The lands on which the valley's Indian settlements were established dated from the distribution of lands made to the first generation of Spanish conquistadores soon after the foundation of Santiago en Almolonga in 1527. It appears that most Spaniards received lands on the same day that they were accepted as vecinos of the city and were formally ceded already designated urban lots (solares) by the Cabildo. Each Spaniard who sought citizenship in the city presented a written petition to the Cabildo formally requesting that he be accepted as a vecino and that he be ceded the solar he had been designated sometime earlier. On the reverse side of these written petitions each prospective vecino described the agricultural lands that he wished to be granted. It appears that the requests were usually acceded to, providing that a particular grant did not prejudice the rights of vecinos who had already received lands nearby. The distribution of agricultural lands in the valleys and surrounding mountains was especially heavy in 1528 and 1529.[7]

The settlement of these slaves created a series of milpas or pueblos in the region representing diverse linguistic groups from widespread regions of present-day Guatemala and beyond. Santa Catarina Barahona, one of the pueblos under study, according to the vecinos' own testimony, was founded with Indian slaves from Chamelco (probably San Juan Chamelco in Alta Verapaz), Utlatecas (Utatlán, capital of the Quiché state), Atitlán (Santiago Atitlán, capital of the Tzutujil state), Chontales (Tabasco or Oaxca in modern, southern Mexico) and Pipiles (Pacific coast of Guatemala, possibly Esquintepeque or today, Escuintla). The precise origins of the slaves settled on the other lands or milpas in the Quinizilapa Valley are unknown but the pattern found in Santa Catarina Barahona appears to have been typical of both that valley and the rest of the immediate hinterland of the Spanish capital.[8] While a large number, probably a majority, of the slaves were settled on the milpas as agricultural laborers, some Spanish vecinos used their slaves in the mining of precious metals nearby, as in the case of the inhabitants of Santiago Zamora, and probably more distant regions (Honduras?) in the case of the slaves of Diego de Monroy, the señor of the milpa of San Lorenzo Monroy. In 1575 the vecinos and, by then, former slaves and descendents of slaves of the milpa of San Lorenzo Monroy stated:

> . . . and then they sent us to the mines with bateas [for gold panning] to work and then came President Alonso Cerrato [Alonso López de Cerrato], may he be in Heaven, who in the name of His Majesty ended our work in the mines . . .[9]

Our knowledge of the daily lives of the slave inhabitants of the milpas of the Quinizilapa Valley in the second quarter of the sixteenth century is vague at best. In 1549-50, a landmark date for the inhabitants of the valley, the slaves of this valley and of the entire adjoining valley of the Spanish capital (Panchoy) were emancipated when Licenciado Alonso López de Cerrato, the President of the Audiencia of the Cofines, arrived and sought to enforce the New Laws. The Indian inhabitants of Santa Catarina Barahona claimed López de Cerrato had ordered that they be liberated and return to their homelands but that God decided to ". . . settle us [here] with woman and children and grandchildren . . . ."[10] López de Cerrato's attempts to enforce the New Laws on behalf of the Indians of the city's hinterland did not, however, change their lives for the better to the degree that the term "emancipation" suggests.[11] For all too soon the former slaves were burdened with the payment of land rents (terrazgos; see Table 7.1) on the lands where they lived as they still belonged to their former Spanish masters or their heirs. San Antonio was an exception to this pattern; the former slaves of Juan de Chavez said that they were ceded the lands on which they were settled and that when other Spaniards sought to take away their lands President López de Cerrato defended their rights.[12]

While the terrazgos came almost simultaneously with emancipation more onerous forced labor obligations soon followed along with the imposition of tribute payment to the Crown beginning in the early 1560s. Forced labor or mandamiento labor and tribute were burdens which the former slaves suffered in common with many highland Guatemalan Indian pueblos which could be conveniently exploited by the Spanish authorities and individual vecinos. The close proximity of the former slave settlements to the center of Spanish power and population in the city of Santiago de Guatemala served to increase the pressures placed on them.

The male inhabitants of the Quinizilapa pueblos and other Indian pueblos and barrios surrounding the Spanish capital were regularly called upon to supply the city with products not available elsewhere and labor services. Due to their lacustrine setting most of the Quinizilapa pueblos were obliged to supply the Spaniards of the city with fodder (sacate) for their horses at a fixed price of one real per load (carga). The cutting, bundling and hauling on their backs with the aid of a tumpline to the assigned location in the city and the return trip must have cost one Indian vecino from the Quinizilapa towns the better part of an entire day's labor.[13] In addition to these obligations, at least in the late sixteenth century, the tributaries of the Quinizilapa pueblos were obliged to send large numbers of men (apparently a number in proportion to their total populations) to plant, weed and harvest Spanish wheat fields near the capital. On other occasions the vecinos of these towns and others surrounding the Spanish city complained of having to sweep the city's streets and the Casas Reales without any compensation. Another unpleasant task that regularly befell the male vecinos of these pueblos was the cleaning of drainage canals and the river bed of the Río Pensativo just prior to the rainy season so as to reduce the chances of flooding in the Spanish city.[14]

An accurate estimate of the number of slaves settled in the six milpas of the Quinizilapa Valley around 1530 is difficult to derive. We do know the number of slaves owned by certain vecinos of the Spanish capital at various times during the 1530s and 1540s, but the use made of

TABLE 7.1
Terrazgos paid by the milpas of the Quinizilapa Valley, c. 1580

Name of Milpa	Name of Founder c. 1530	Recipient of Terrazgo c. 1580	Annual Payment
San Andrés Ceballos	Pedro de Ceballos	heirs of Ceballos	20 fanegas maize 20 chickens 20 tostones
San Lorenzo Monroy	Diego de Monroy	María de Monroy (1576)	20 fanegas maize
Juan de Chaves llamada San Antonio de Padua (Aguas Calientes)	Juan de Chaves	no terrazgo paid; lands ceded c. 1550 by Chaves to the vecinos of the milpa	
Santa Catarina Barahona	Sancho de Barahona	Sancho de Barahona "El Mozo"	60 fanegas maize 40 chickens
Santiago de Zamora	Alonso de Zamora	Juan de León (1575) "señor de las tierras"	20 fanegas maize 15 tostones
San Miguel Dueñas	Miguel de Dueñas	"Dueñas, señor de las tierras"	40 fanegas maize 20 chickens

Source: Lutz, Santiago de Guatemala, Tables 6 and 9, pp. 130 and 159-161, respectively.

these slaves, whether they worked on agricultural lands near the Spanish capital or were mostly used in mining operations in distant Honduras, is usually unclear. It is also possible that slaves settled on the milpas around the Spanish capital were used seasonally or for a few years at a time panning or mining precious metals in say, Honduras, and then returned. The hardships of long marches combined with mine-related labor (especially at lower altitudes where the risk of death from epidemic diseases increased) must have taken a heavier toll on their numbers.[15] But then we cannot be certain that mine labor necessarily took a heavier toll than the demands placed on the slaves who resided in or near the capital. Aside from agricultural labor the 1530s and 1540s were decades of intense construction activity. One has only to remember that one city, Santiago en Almolonga, was founded in 1527 only to be destroyed by massive mud slides in September, 1541; and another, Santiago de Guatemala, was laid out and under construction a few months later.[16] Building construction must have been continuous throughout the period.

Another unknown concerns the frequency with which the Spanish vecinos acquired new slaves to replace those who died. Without the information (which is the equivalent of data on inward migration) it is nearly impossible to reconstruct the early population history of the milpas settled by slaves surrounding the early Spanish capital and its successor, Santiago de Guatemala. While slaves might have spent seasons or years engaged in mining in Honduras and periodically returned to Guatemala, there is also some evidence that other slaves, upon their emancipation by President López de Cerrato in 1548-1549, were settled on their former masters' milpas near Santiago de Guatemala. The precedent for settling former Indian mine slaves near the city was established by Bishop Francisco Marroquín in 1543 when the recently deceased Pedro de Alvarado's mining slaves (men, women and children) were freed and settled in the parcialidad of Jocotenango, known as Santiago Utatleca, located on the northern periphery of the then newly-established capital of Santiago de Guatemala.[17] As has already been mentioned, under López de Cerrato the former mine slaves of Diego de Monroy, the señor of the milpa of San Lorenzo Monroy, were returned and settled on that milpa around 1549; and this may not have been the only settlement among the Quinizilapa milpas to have experienced this process. It can be safely assumed, however, that while former mine slaves were added to one or more of these six milpas during emancipation (1548-49), after that period Spanish-directed immigration halted.

The coincidence of emancipation from slavery with the mid-sixteenth century would serve as a useful bench mark from which to begin an analysis of population changes in the six milpas of the Quinizilapa Valley. Unfortunately, however, anything resembling reliable population data does not begin until around 1575. One explanation for the lack of specific population data for the Quinizilapa pueblos until the mid-1570s is that none of the former slave settlements even began to pay tribute to the Crown until the mid-1560s.

Population estimates for the valley of the city of Guatemala, which includes the Quinizilapa milpas, exist from 1548-1550 through 1582. One estimate (Table 7.2) refers to freed slaves, another to married Indians who were not paying any tribute and the remaining figures are contradictory and probably incomplete tributary counts.

By removing the most inconsistent data from consideration it is possible to demonstrate that the valley's Indian population was in sharp decline between 1550 and 1581. The decline in population totals is corroborated by reports of flight and high Indian mortality resulting from hunger, sickness and epidemics.[18] It would be close to pure speculation to even attempt an estimate of the Quinizilapa milpas' population around 1550, but it would be surprising if they all did not lose a large percentage of their inhabitants in the course of the quarter century that followed.

The impact of the great pandemics of the late 1540s and 1570s upon the native populations of New Spain and Spanish Guatemala is by now well established. But aside from these two destructive waves of pestilence there are documented reports of serious outbreaks of disease of epidemic proportions during every decade (except the 1580s) between 1560 and 1770 in the immediate hinterland of the Spanish urban center which includes the Quinizilapa micro-region.[19] The direct impact of these epidemics on the Quinizilapa pueblos is unknown in almost all cases until the mid-eighteenth century when parish burial registers provide direct information on epidemics and the resulting mortality.[20]

RECONSTRUCTION OF THE POPULATION OF THE QUINIZILAPA PUEBLOS

Reconstruction of population movements in the six Quinizilapa pueblos will be based on a reduced series of tribute and tributary totals. Unfortunately, there are only four dates between 1575 and 1754-55 for which we have population data for all six pueblos. These data are expressed in every instance as numbers of tributaries. Padrones would be useful to determine the ratio of tributaries to population for these towns but they are only extant from the mid-eighteenth century for the Quinizilapa towns. While padrones are extant for a number of highland Indian towns from the sixteenth and

TABLE 7.2
Estimated Indian population of the valley of Santiago de Guatemala, 1548-1581

Date	Population size (Males)	Remarks	Source
1548-50	Est. 3000-5000 freed slaves	Number of slaves freed in the city and surrounding valley; naboríos apparently not included	William L. Sherman, personal communication, 7 January 1972
1560	Est. 5000-6000 married Indians	Number of married Indians in and around Spanish capital who did not pay tribute to anyone	Audiencia to the King, AGI, Guatemala 9 (Santiago: 30 June 1560)
1567	1669-1654 tributaries	Tributaries in the jurisdiction of the Corregidor of the valley; lower figure due to correction for 15 reserved, deceased or absent	Accounts of 1567 and 1572, AGI, Contaduría 967
1571-72	4025 tributaries	Many persons reported counted who were lawfully exempt from tributary status	Accounts of 1567 and 1572, AGI, Contaduría 967
1574	2663 tributaries	Probably an accurate count	Audiencia to the King, AGI, Guatemala 10 (Santiago: 13 September 1574)
1581	2271 tributaries	Married Indian tributaries	AGI, Patronato 183, Ramo 1°.

seventeenth centuries it would be unwise to apply their tributary to total population (T/P) ratios to the Quinizilapa towns because of the differences in their origins.[21] Towns with preconquest roots often survived the conquest period and the sixteenth century population decline with at least remnants of their prehispanic socioeconomic structures intact. Hereditary rulers and their families often continued to rule their towns and maintained a degree of special status and privilege vis-à-vis their subject populations. All of this resulted in a more complex social structure in the sixteenth century prehispanic towns than in the settlements populated by slaves and, after 1550, their descendents. These basic differences would appear to have resulted in two different pueblo types with distinctive population structures. Given these differences it seems unlikely that a T/P ratio for a preconquest town could be safely applied to the towns of slave origins without seriously distorting upward the population size of the latter towns. For this reason population changes will be discussed here only in terms of tributaries until census-type data becomes available beginning in the mid-eighteenth century.

The tributary data for the Quinizilapa towns begins for all six pueblos around 1575, or just prior to the devastating pandemic of the late 1570s. For three of the pueblos (Santiago Zamora, San Andrés Ceballos and San Lorenzo Monroy) tributary totals also exist for 1581. While Santiago Zamora actually grew between 1575 and 1581, San Andrés Ceballos and San Lorenzo Monroy sharply declined (Table 7.3) during the same short period. In order to make comparisons of population change between individual towns or between different periods we have adopted the <u>coefficient of population movement</u> (ω) developed by Cook and Borah.[22] When the tributary totals for the three towns for each year (1575 and 1581) are combined and the coefficient of population movement value is compared with that for the valley of the city of Guatemala (for the period 1574-1581) we see that the values are very similar.[23] Table 7.4 shows in more detail the extent of population decline (as measured by tributaries) for the entire valley of the city of Santiago de Guatemala between 1570 and 1581.

For the period 1575-1638 comparative data exist for all six Quinizilapa pueblos. The ω values for four of the towns demonstrate a small population decline between 1575 and 1638. The data in Tables 7.5 and 7.6 and other less comparative and more scattered data for intermediate dates suggest that the nadirs of population decline for three of these pueblos (San Lorenzo Monroy, San Miguel Dueñas and Santa Catarina Barahona) probably occurred sometime between 1600 and 1630.[24] The same pattern also appears to apply to San Antonio Aguas Calientes except that this town recovered more vigorously and slightly

TABLE 7.3
Comparison of population movements in three Quinizilapa milpas and the valley of the city between 1575 and 1581

Jurisdiction	Tributaries circa 1575	Tributaries circa 1581	Coefficient of Population Movement (ω)
Santiago Zamora	37	44	+2.89
San Andrés Ceballos	30	20	-6.80
San Lorenzo Monroy	64	49	-4.46
Total of the three milpas	131	113	-2.46
Valley of the city	2,663*	2,271	-2.27

Sources: Audiencia to the King (Santiago: 13 September 1574), AGI, Guatemala 10; "Los indios que eran esclavos . . . [1576]," AGI, Guatemala 54; Accounts of 1576, AGI, Contaduría 968; "Razón de las tasaciones . . . [1582]," AGI, Guatemala 966; and AGI, Patronato 183, Ramo 1°.

*Tributary total for 1574.

TABLE 7.4
Estimated Crown tributary figures, valley of the city of Santiago de Guatemala, 1570 to 1581

Year	Number of Tributaries	Total tributary decline from previous count
1570	3,093	--
1571	3,022	-71
1574	2,663	-359
1579	2,531	-132
1581	2,271	-260

Sources: AGI, Contaduría 967 and 968; and Audiencia to the King (Santiago: 13 September 1574), AGI, Guatemala 10.

186

TABLE 7.5
Coefficients of population change (ω) for the Quinizilapa towns

Period	Santiago Zamora	S. Andrés Ceballos	S. Lorenzo Monroy	S. Antonio A. C.	S. Miguel Dueñas	Sta. Catarina
1575-1581	+2.89%	-6.80%	-4.46%	--	--	--
1575-1638	+0.51%	-0.50%	-0.71%	+0.02%	-0.27%	-0.62%
1581-1638	+0.26%	+0.17%	-0.31%	--	--	--
1638-1684	+2.12%	+0.32%	+2.18%	+0.75%	+2.84%	+2.25%
1684-1755	+0.71%	+0.41%	+0.42%	+0.22%	-0.29%	+0.62%

TABLE 7.6
Tributary totals (tributarios enteros): Quinizilapa towns, 1575-1755

Year	Santiago Zamora	S. Andrés Ceballos	S. Lorenzo Monroy	S. Antonio A. C.	S. Miguel Dueñas	Sta. Catarina
1575	37	30	64	~102	~45	~57
1581	44	20	49	--	--	--
1638	51	22	41	103	38	39
1684	131	25½	108	145	130	105½
1755*	216	34	145	169	106	162

Sources: "Los indios que eran esclavos . . . [1576]," AGI, Guatemala 54; "Razón de las tasaciónes . . . [1582]," AGI, Guatemala 966; "Relación del Proceso . . . [1638]," AGI, Guatemala 70; AGCA, A3 824 15.207 ("Liquidación . . . [1684]"); AGCA, A3 1616 26.578 ("Razón de los Tributarios . . . [1754]"); AGCA, A3 948 17.706 (1755).

*Tributary counts for San Antonio Aguas Calientes, San Miguel Dueñas and Santa Catarina Barahona are from 1754 not 1755. All of the 1754-55 tributary totals are adjusted upward to compensate for the elimination of women from the tributary rolls so that these totals are comparable to those for the earlier dates, all of which include women in the tributary counts.

earlier than the four which showed negative ω values for the period 1575-1638. As in the period 1575-1581 of the six Quinizilapa towns only Santiago Zamora demonstrated sustained growth during this period of transition. Nevertheless, it appears as though a majority of the Quinizilapa pueblos began their demographic recovery during the 1620s and 1630s. As has been pointed out previously by other researchers, population studies based on tributary counts must always take into account the lapse that occurs between the time when a given population begins to increase (more annual births than deaths) and the time when that growth results (when the new born have reached their majorities) in increased numbers of tributaries.

In the period 1638-1684 all six pueblos (Figure 7.2) of the Quinizilapa Valley experienced population growth. The towns of Santiago Zamora, San Lorenzo Monroy, San Miguel Dueñas and Santa Catarina Barahona grew at faster rates than either San Antonio Aguas Calientes or San Andrés Ceballos, the smallest of the towns. Explanations as to the reason why San Antonio, the largest of the pueblos in 1638, should have grown more slowly than all the other Quinizilapa towns, with the exception of San Andrés, are not apparent. The slower population growth of San Andrés Ceballos could have been the result of near stagnation due to the small size of that pueblo, at least from the late sixteenth century. A reduced pool from which to select prospective spouses might have pushed younger vecinos, especially men, outside the village in search of marriage partners. In 1755 out of a total married male population of twenty-five, thirteen men from San Andrés Ceballos were married to Indian women from other pueblos. This total was higher than that for Santa Catarina (9) and slightly lower than that for Santiago Zamora (16) even though both these latter pueblos were five to six times more populous than San Andrés.[25]

The pattern of population increase which began in the mid-seventeenth century (1638-1684) in the Quinizilapa towns continued during the period 1684-1755. The only exception to this pattern was the pueblo of San Miguel Dueñas which, from the early sixteenth century, had experienced an historical development quite distinctive from the other five pueblos. The divergent history of Dueñas derived from the introduction of sugar cultivation combined with the settlement of an unknown but apparently reduced number of African slaves on Spanish-owned lands which lay near the shores of Lake Quinizilapa and the pueblo of Dueñas in the early post-conquest decades. At present little is known about the success or failure of sugar cultivation in this region during the colonial period. But in the late 1760s only Dueñas of the region's pueblos contained an agricultural estate deserving of mention by Archbishop Cortés y Larraz—the Hacienda de Batres with nine resident mozos and a

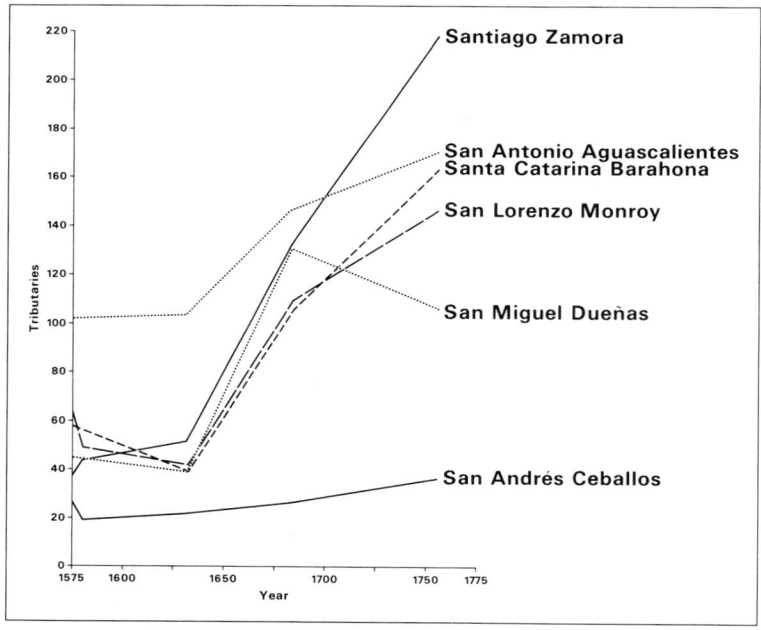

Figure 7.2 Population change in the Quinizilapa towns, 1575-1755

mayordomo.²⁶ The earliest parish registers from Dueñas reveal the impact of the African slaves introduced more than two centuries earlier. Free mulattoes and ladinos are frequently mentioned as vecinos of Dueñas. By the mid-eighteenth century San Miguel Dueñas was well along in the process of ladinization. Ladinization in Santiago de Guatemala and, by extension, in certain towns which for reasons of commerce and/or sugar cultivation had concentrations of persons, both slave and free, of African descent was strongly influenced by this element and not just by mestizos as has so often been claimed in the traditional historical and anthropological literature on Guatemala.²⁷

Tributary counts for the Quinizilapa pueblos for the late eighteenth and early nineteenth centuries have yet to be located. However, for the late 1760s the first apparently reliable population counts or censuses by categories of civil status are available. This information consists of the responses to questionnaires sent out under the direction of Archbishop Pedro Cortés y Larraz. These responses are not uniformly complete but the one by the parish priest of the six pueblos provides the total numbers by pueblo (Table 7.7) of the following: number of families; married males and couples; widows and widowers; adults (unmarried); and children (párvulos, probably including everyone from 0 to 12 years of age). Later research will have to determine the accuracy of these data by checking them against parish register totals and new tributary lists. Likewise, the relative accuracy of the modern, published Guatemalan national censuses (beginning with that of 1880) in terms of completeness of data and the changing ratios of Indian and ladino populations needs to be considered.²⁸ Taking into account the possible problems with the data, Table 7.8 demonstrates the magnitude of the growth of the Quinizilapa pueblos over the last two centuries (1768-1973) by comparing census totals from 1768, 1880 and 1973. All of the pueblos have consistently grown over this period with the exception of Santiago Zamora which, curiously, was by far the most populous of the six towns in 1768. The low percentage of children (10%) in Santiago Zamora's 1768 population compared with a total of 35 percent children in the five other towns (combined) suggests that perhaps it had suffered from some localized epidemic(s) which struck infants and children.²⁹ The combined Indian and ladino populations for the six towns shows almost a four-fold increase in the course of 200 years which is a far smaller increase than that experienced for the Republic of Guatemala as a whole.³⁰

Subsequent population studies on the Quinizilapa towns must come to terms with the possible impact of the formerly more extensive lake on the health conditions of the pueblos. The introduction of coffee culture and

TABLE 7.7
Population data for the Quinizilapa towns, 1768

	S. Miguel Dueñas		S. Antonio A. C.		S. Andres Ceballos		Sta. Catarina Barahona		Santiago Zamora		S. Lorenzo Monroy		Total		Total less Zamora	
	(N)	(%)	(N)	(%)	(N)	(%)	(N)	(%)	(N)	(%)	(N)	(%)	(N)	(%)	(N)	(%)
Indians:																
Families	98		81		20		83		131		57		470		339	
Married persons	124	(42)	260	(47)	62	(53)	254	(43)	504	(62)	176	(59)	1380	(52)	876	(47)
Widows/Widowers	22	(8)	25	(4.5)	8	(7)	17	(3)	36	(4)	13	(4)	121	(4.5)	85	(4.6)
Adults (unmarried)	63	(21)	75	(13.5)	14	(12)	81	(14)	193	(24)	14	(5)	440	(16.5)	247	(13.4)
Sub-total	209		360		84		352		733		203		1941		1208	
Children (párvulos)	86	(29)	194	(35)	32	(28)	232	(40)	79	(10)	97	(32)	720	(27)	641	(35)
Total	295		554		116		584		812		300		2661		1849	
Persons per family	3.0		6.8		5.8		7.0		6.3		5.3		5.7		5.5	
Persons per married man(casado)	4.7		4.3		3.7		4.6		3.3		3.4		3.9		4.2	
Children per married couple	1.4		1.5		1.0		1.8		0.3		1.1		1.0		1.5	
Children per family	0.9		2.4		1.6		2.8		1.7		1.7		1.5		1.9	
Ladinos:																
Families	36															
Married persons	56	(36)														
Widows/Widowers	8	(5)														
Adults (unmarried)	50	(33)														
Sub-total	114															
Children (párvulos)	40	(26)														
Total: Indian & Ladino	449															
Men*	224		196		62		308		423		146					
Women*	225		258		54		276		389		154					

Source: AGI, Guatemala, 948, Vol. 30, "Testimonio de las respuestas . . . [1768]."

*Sum of Men and Women for all towns except Dueñas to be found above as total of Indian population.

TABLE 7.8
Comparison of population size of the Quinizilapa towns: 1768, 1880 and 1973

Town	1768			1880			1973		
	Indian	Ladino	Total	Indian	Ladino	Total	Indian	Ladino	Total
San Miguel Dueñas	295	154	449	383	2734	3117	1425	2790	4215
San Lorenzo Monroy	300	--	300	375	--	375	464	790	1254
Sta. Catarina Barahona	584	--	584	926	9	935	1064	82	1146
San Antonio A. C.	554	--	554	1508	12	1520	3024	150	3174
San Andrés Ceballos	116	--	116	200	--	200	377	5	382
Santiago Zamora	812	--	812	392	6	398	307	3	310
Total--6 towns	2661	154	2815	3784	2761	6545	6661	3820	10,481

Sources: "Testimonio de las respuestas . . . [1768]," AGI, Guatemala 948, Vol. 30; Guatemala, Censo General de 1880; Guatemala, Dirección General de Estadística, VIII Censo de la Población, 1973. Data from the 1880 and 1973 censuses were kindly provided by Sheldon Annis, (University of Chicago).

other forms of commercial agriculture since the middle of
the last century and the resulting loss of lands due to
these intrusions also have to be studied and considered
in terms of their impact on population change, especially
seasonal and permanent migration patterns. As in so many
other fields of study in Guatemala, the changing land
tenure patterns may be the key variable in the study of
the Quinizilapa Valley's population history.

NOTES

1. Mateo Morales Urrutía, La división política y administrativa de la República de Guatemala con sus datos históricos y de legislación (Guatemala: Editorial Iberia-Gutenburg, 1961), Tomo II, pp. 341-346, 357-359, 363-365, and 377-379.

2. Quinizilapa is often spelled Quilizinapa but the first spelling appears to make more sense linguistically, meaning in Nahuatl "place of intermittent waters." See Alonso de Molina, Vocabulario en Lengua Castellana y Mexicana y Mexicana y Castellana, Edición Facsimilie (México: Editorial Porrua, 1970), p. 90.

3. See, for example, mention of the founding of Sololá in 1547 in the Cakchiquel chronicle, The Annals of the Cakchiquels. Title of the Lords of Totonicapán, Adrian Recinos, Delia Goetz and Dionisio José Chonay, editors and translators (Norman: University of Oklahoma Press, 1974), p. 136; and the establishment of Alotenango, at its first site, about 1540 with Indians collected from Pacific coastal towns. Francisco Vázquez, Crónica de la provincia del Santísimo Nombre de Jesús de Guatemala (Guatemala: Sociedad de Geografía e Historia de Guatemala, 1937-44, Biblioteca "Goathemala," Vols. XIV-XVII) I, p. 87.

4. One recent study that covers this period is Francis Polo Sifontes, Los Cakchiqueles en la conquista de Guatemala (Guatemala: Editorial "José de Pineda Ibarra," 1977), pp. 79-88.

5. For a more complete discussion see Christopher H. Lutz, Santiago de Guatemala, 1541-1773: The Sociodemographic History of a Spanish American Colonial City (Ph.D. Dissertation, University of Wisconsin-Madison, 1976). Also see: Stephen F. de Borhegyi, "Estudio arqueológico en la falda norte del volcán de Agua," Revista de Antropología e Historia de Guatemala, Vol. II, No. 1 (January, 1950), pp. 3-22; and Edwin M. Shook, "Lugares arqueológicos del altiplano meridional central de Guatemala," Revista de Antropología e Historia de Guatemala, Vol. IV, No. 2 (June, 1952), pp. 3-40.

6. See William L. Sherman, Forced Native Labor in Sixteenth-Century Central America (Lincoln: University of Nebraska Press, 1979), esp. pp. 20-82, for a detailed discussion of Spanish slaving practices; and Lutz, Santiago de Guatemala, pp. 122-127.

7. This paragraph is taken from Lutz, Santiago de Guatemala, pp. 123-124. The primary source is the Libro viejo de la fundación de Guatemala y papeles relativos a Don Pedro de Alvarado (Guatemala: Sociedad de Geografía e Historia de Guatemala, 1934, Biblioteca

"Goathemala," Vol. XII), pp. 33-34 and passim.

8. See Lutz, Santiago de Guatemala, pp. 125-127 and William L. Sherman, Indian Slavery in Spanish Guatemala, 1524-1550 (Ph.D. Dissertation, University of New Mexico, 1967), pp. 120-121 for list of the names and places of origin of Cristobal Lobo's slaves in 1549. Lobo was a vecino of Santiago de Guatemala.

9. See: "Los indios que eran esclavos . . . [1576]", Archivo General de Indias [hereafter cited as AGI], Guatemala 54; Lutz, Santiago de Guatemala, pp. 139-143 for a discussion of mining labor provided by Indian slaves who were later settled in and around Santiago de Guatemala; and Sherman, Forced Native Labor, passim.

10. "Los indios que eran esclavos . . . [1576]", AGI, Guatemala 54, f. 29.

11. See William L. Sherman, "Indian Slavery and the Cerrato Reforms," Hispanic American Historical Review, Vol. 51 (1971), pp. 25-50 and the contrasting view of Murdo J. MacLeod, Spanish Central America: A Socioeconomic History, 1520-1720 (Berkeley, University of California Press, 1973), pp. 109-119.

12. "Los indios que eran esclavos . . . [1576]", AGI, Guatemala 54, f. 28. This would have occurred in the early 1550s.

13. Without exception all of the Quinizilapa towns complained of this burden. "Los indios que eran esclavos . . . [1576]", AGI, Guatemala 54, ff. 28 v. -32.

14. "Los indios que eran esclavos . . . [1576]", AGI, Guatemala 54; and Archivo General de Centroamerica [hereafter cited as AGCA], Al 2824 25.071 (1706). In the seventeenth and eighteenth centuries these towns are rarely mentioned in the repartimiento de indios to the wheat farms (labores) as wheat came to be cultivated more intensely in the valleys north, northeast and east of the immediate valley of the capital city, the valley of Panchoy. See, for example, Lutz, Santiago de Guatemala, pp. 555-556 and 585, n. 12.

15. Sherburne F. Cook and Woodrow Borah, Essays in Population History, 2 vols. (Berkeley: University of California Press, 1971-1974), I, pp. 79-82 discuss differential population decline in coastal and highland ecological zones in sixteenth-century Mexico.

16. For Santiago en Almolonga see: Janos de Szecsy, Santiago de los Caballeros de Guatemala en Almolonga (Guatemala: IAHG, 1953); and for Santiago de Guatemala see: Sidney David Markman, The Colonial Architecture of Antigua Guatemala (Philadelphia: American Philosophical Society, 1966); and Verle L. Annis, The Architecture of Antigua Guatemala, 1543-1773 (Guatemala: Universidad de San Carlos de Guatemala, 1968, Bilingual edition).

17. See Lutz, Santiago de Guatemala, pp. 139 and 171, n. 32. Alvarado, who had many more slaves than other vecinos, had 330 gold-mining slaves from Totonicapán, Tecpanatitlán and Atitlán in 1538. See William L. Sherman, "A Conqueror's Wealth: Notes on the Estate of Don Pedro de Alvarado," The Americas, Vol. XXVI, No. 2 (October, 1969), p. 209.

18. See Lutz, Santiago de Guatemala, pp. 251-253 and 286.

19. The dates of documented epidemics are: 1560-61; 1563-65; 1592-93; 1600-01; 1607-08; 1614; 1623; 1631-32; 1647; 1650; 1665-66; 1669; 1676; 1686-87; 1693-94; 1696; 1699; 1704-05; 1707; 1708; 1709; 1716; 1723; 1724; 1725; 1728; 1733; 1741; 1746 (food shortage too);

1748; 1749; 1752; 1761 and 1769. See Lutz, Santiago de Guatemala, Appendix VI, pp. 743-752 and MacLeod, Spanish Central America, pp. 98-100.

20. The parish archive of San Miguel Dueñas has recently been microfilmed by the Genealogical Society of Utah.

21. Excellent padrones and tasaciones exist for the Cakchiquel speaking pueblos of Chimaltenango, Comalapa, Sumpango, San Juan Sacatepéquez, and San Pedro Sacatepéquez, in the AGI, Guatemala 45, for the late 1560s. For a detailed discussion of the T/P ratio see Cook and Borah, Essays in Population History, I, pp. 280-286.

22. Cook and Borah, Essays in Population History, I, pp. 89-91.

23. We must keep in mind that the decline in tributary numbers between 1578 and 1581 is not totally due to Indian deaths caused by hunger and epidemics but was also caused by flight. See, for example, the complaints of the Cabildo members and principales of San Antonio Aguas Calientes (called the Milpa de Juan de Cháves) and other Quinizilapa towns in "Los indios que eran esclavos . . . [1576]", AGI, Guatemala 54, f. 28 and ff.

24. See Accounts of 1622 and 1623, in AGI, Guatemala 15. But data on San Andrés Ceballos suggests that that pueblo might have reached a peak ca. 1600 and then gradually declined until some point in the mid to late 1660s. See AGCA, A3 258 5763 (1603); AGCA, A3 477 9960; and the Bishop to His Majesty (Santiago, 18 September 1661), AGI, Guatemala 157.

25. While San Andrés had a disproportionate number of its males married to women from other pueblos for its size Santiago Zamora (with 12) and Santa Catarina (with 13) each had a number of women married with men from other pueblos and with absent men (ausentes). On the other hand San Andrés had a total of only three women married to men from other pueblos or absent. See AGCA, A3 948 17.706.

26. See Pedro Cortés y Larraz, Descripción geográfico-moral de la diócesis de Goathemala, 2 vols. (Guatemala: Sociedad de Geografía e Historia de Guatemala, 1958, Biblioteca "Goathemala," Vol. XX), I, p. 37. The Luis Diez de Navarro map of the valley of the city of Santiago de Guatemala drawn soon after the earthquake of July 29, 1773 includes the Hacienda de Urias in Dueñas but apparently not that of Batres. See this map in the AGI map collection or in that of the AGCA Mapoteca.

27. For more detailed discussion of this point see: Lutz, Santiago de Guatemala, pp. 28-29 and 411-418.

28. John D. Early has demonstrated the problems in ethnic reporting resulting in inflated ladino totals and lower Maya Indian totals in the Guatemalan censuses of 1950 and 1964. See John D. Early, "Revision of Ladino and Maya Census Populations of Guatemala, 1950 and 1964," Demography, Vol. 11, 1974, pp. 105-116.

29. Santiago Zamora did suffer a "Peste de fríos calenturas" during 1764 and 1765 but not one párvulo is listed among the 46 deaths recorded in those two years. Archivo de la Parroquia de San Miguel Dueñas, "Libro no. 1°.--Defunciones del pueblo de Santiago Zamora desde el año 1764 hasta el de 1790," ff. 2v.-3.

30. See Nicolás Sánchez-Albornoz, The Population of Latin America: A History (Berkeley: University of California Press, 1974), Tables 5.11 and 6.1, pp. 169 and 184, respectively.

8
The Historical Demography of the Cuchumatán Highlands of Guatemala, 1500-1821

W. George Lovell

INTRODUCTION

    In many colonial societies there exists a close relationship between population size and economic well-being. Spanish Central America illustrates this relationship clearly. The economic prospects of the colony were intimately linked to its historical demography. Thus with a large population from which to draw labor, the initial economic outlook seemed promising. As population declined during the sixteenth and seventeenth centuries, a severe economic depression set in. When population began to increase towards the end of the seventeenth and throughout the eighteenth century, the economy revived.[1]

    The operation of this crude, causal connection between population size and economic well-being permeates a number of developments in Spanish Central America. Indian depopulation was a major factor behind the demise of the encomienda system. It also contributed towards the formation of the great estate, or hacienda, and the emergence of debt peonage.[2] Such important developments can therefore be fully understood only when viewed in relation to population trends and fluctuations. It is to the establishment of a demographic profile for the Cuchumatán highlands of Guatemala during the three centuries of Spanish domination in Central America that this paper is directed.

THE REGIONAL SETTING

    The Cuchumatán highlands of Guatemala are the most

The author wishes to thank the Izaak Walton Killam Memorial Fund for Advanced Studies for the financial support during the years in which the archival investigations central to this paper were conducted.

massive and spectacular non-volcanic region of all Central America. Lying to the north of the Río Cuilco, and to the north and west of the Río Negro or Chixoy, the Cuchumatanes form a fairly well-defined physical unit bordered on the north by the sparsely settled tropical lowlands of the Usumacinta basin and to the west by the Mexican state of Chiapas. The Cuchumatanes, with elevations ranging from 500 to more than 3600 meters, are contained within the Guatemalan departments of Huehuetenango and Quiché, and comprise some 15 percent (approximately 16,350 square kilometers) of the national territory of the Central American republic (Figure 8.1).

During the first two centuries of Spanish rule in Guatemala the Cuchumatán country was part of the administrative division known as the corregimiento or alcaldía mayor of Totonicapán and Huehuetenango. This unit included all of the present day department of Totonicapán, most of Huehuetenango, the northern half of Quiché, the easternmost portion of Quezaltenango, and the Motozintla area of the Mexican state of Chiapas. Towards the end of the colonial period the corregimiento or alcaldía mayor of Totonicapán and Huehuetenango was made a provincia composed of two jurisdictions: the partido of Totonicapán and the partido of Huehuetenango. The jurisdiction referred to as the partido of Huehuetenango corresponds in approximate territorial extent to the area here designated the Cuchumatán highlands. Today about one-half million people inhabit the region, of whom roughly three out of four are Indian. The native peoples of the Cuchumatanes are of Mayan descent and speak several closely related languages belonging to Mayan stock, the most important of which are Aguacateca, Chuj, Ixil, Jacalteca, Kanjobal, Mam, Quiché, and Uspanteca.

DEMOGRAPHIC PROFILE OF THE CUCHUMATAN HIGHLANDS (1520-1821)

Any attempt to reconstruct the population history of the Cuchumatán highlands is beset by a lack of consistent, representative data. The paucity of source materials containing demographic information is particularly notable for the sixteenth and early seventeenth centuries. The late seventeenth and eighteenth centuries, by comparison, are reasonably well-documented. Perhaps the safest procedure is to regard early estimates of population size as necessarily tentative and to scrutinize with caution later calculations before reaching any final conclusions.

The earliest surviving record known to contain population data for every significant settlement in the Cuchumatán highlands is a list of tributarios (Indian tribute payers) for the years 1664 to 1678.[3] Prior to this

197

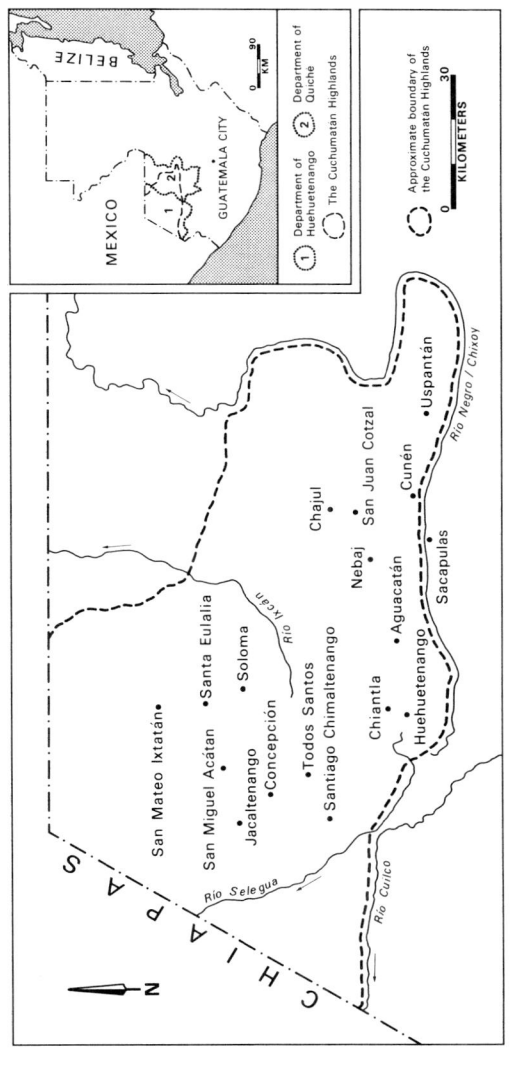

Figure 8.1 Location of the Cuchumatán highlands and selected settlements

late seventeenth century tribute count few reliable figures exist. The data upon which estimates of the magnitude of the sixteenth century population can be made are appallingly scarce. Among these data are reports of the size of Indian armies encountered during the battles of conquest, as recorded by the seventeenth-century chronicler Francisco Antonio de Fuentes y Gúzman in his monumental Recordación Florida;[4] the number of tributarios in certain Cuchumatán towns assessed by the President of the Audiencia of Guatemala, Alonso López de Cerrato, between 1548 and 1551;[5] and the number of tributarios in the town of Huehuetenango, assessed by President García de Valverde between 1578 and 1582.[6]

Employing as a demographic source estimates of the size of the Indian armies which confronted the Spaniards in the course of conquest is obviously not undertaken without considerable risk. It has been alleged, for example, that Spanish conquistadores, in order to glorify their military feats, were guilty of grossly exaggerating the size of the Indian forces defeated in battle. This argument, however, fails to take into account the fact that successful conquerors often later became influential administrators and would therefore frequently be charged with tribute assessment for both the Spanish Crown and Spanish colonists. Since population size directly determined the levy of tribute, any conquistador with prospects of one day being responsible for assessing Indian tribute capacity would tend to count with at least some measure of discretion.

Consistent with a view which favors taking contemporary testimony and subjecting it to scholarly scrutiny, a study by Thomas Veblen has shown that Spanish estimates of Indian army sizes recorded for the Totonicapán area correspond reasonably well with data derived from other historical sources.[7] Perhaps most significantly, Veblen claims that the work of Fuentes y Gúzman, long considered an unreliable source for pre-Hispanic population data, in fact contains highly plausible figures for Indian army sizes. Veblen explicitly states that "the data available on the size of the pre-Hispanic population of Totonicapán provide no basis for rejecting the demographic information contained in Fuentes y Gúzman."[8] This appraisal is of crucial importance because reports of Indian army sizes are among the few extant historical data which can be used to derive an estimate of the population of the Cuchumatán highlands on the eve of Spanish conquest.

Spanish estimates of the size of Indian armies encountered during the conquest of the Cuchumatanes have been recorded by Fuentes y Gúzman in the Recordación Florida. Fuentes y Gúzman's source for the conquest of the Mam was a document, now unfortunately lost, written by the conquistador Gonzalo de Alvarado after the successful subjugation of the Mam in 1525. In his account the chronicler gives no indication of the size of the Indian army which defended Mazatenango (San Lorenzo), but does state that the town "in those days was well-populated."[9] Fuentes y Gúzman's chief sources for the conquest of the Ixil and the Quichean people of Uspantán included the first <u>Libro de Cabildo</u>, records of the municipal council of Guatemala, and a collection of documents entitled the <u>Manuscrito Quiché</u>. Estimates of the size of the Indian armies which confronted the Spaniards during the <u>entradas</u> into the Cuchumatanes, along with the names of towns supplying warriors, are shown in Table 8.1.

The total number of Indian warriors the Spaniards faced in battle in the Cuchumatanes between 1525 and 1530 was recorded by Fuentes y Gúzman as 34,000. For Totonicapán, Veblen uses a one to four ratio in correlating army size to total population; for the Tlaxcala region of central Mexico, Gibson uses a warriors to total population ratio of one to five.[10] A ratio of one to four, which Veblen considers "conservative," indicates a population of 136,000; a ratio of one to five gives a total of 170,000. An average of these two figures produces a rough estimate of the population of the Cuchumatán highlands between 1525 and 1530 of around 150,000.

In the years immediately prior to the Spanish conquest, however, it is likely that Cuchumatán communities were struck by the same lethal epidemic which, in 1520, swept over much of highland Guatemala. This epidemic, possibly a combination of smallpox and pulmonary plague, entered the highlands of Guatemala from Mexico and had a devastating impact on the Indian peoples of the region. Old World in origin and consequently unknown in the Americas until the arrival of the Spaniards, the epidemic decimated the immunologically defenseless native population and thus reduced both Indian numbers and resistance to military conquest.[11] The ravage of the disease is described in a poignant passage from the Annals of the Cakchiquels:

> It happened that during the twenty-fifth year [1520] the plague began, oh, my sons! First they became ill of a cough, they suffered from nosebleeds and illness of the bladder. It was truly terrible, the number of dead there were in that period . . . . Little by little heavy shadows and black night enveloped our fathers and grandfathers and us also, oh, my sons! When the plague raged . . . , when the plague began to spread . . . . It was in truth terrible, the number of dead among the people. The people could not in any way control the sickness . . . . Great was the stench of the dead. After our fathers and grandfathers succumbed, half of the people fled to the fields. The dogs and the vultures devoured the bodies. The mortality was terrible. Your grandfathers died, and with them died the son of the king and his brothers and

TABLE 8.1
Indian army sizes recorded during the battles of conquest

Date and Place of Battle	Estimated Indian Army Size	Towns Supplying Warriors
1525: Mazatenango (San Lorenzo)	--	Mazatenango
1525: near Mazatenango	5,000	Malacatán
1525: Zaculeu	6,000	Huehuetenango, Zaculeu, Ixtahuacan and Cuilco
1525: Zaculeu	8,000	Various Cuchumatán communities affiliated with the Mam of Zaculeu
1530: Nebaj	5,000	Nebaj and other towns
1530: Uspantán	10,000	Uspantán, Verapaz towns, Cunén, Cotzal, Sacapulas

Source: F. A. Fuentes y Gúzman, Recordación Florida.

kinsmen. So it was that we became orphans, oh, my sons! So we became when we were young. All of us were thus. We were born to die!¹²

In terms of numerical decline, MacLeod claims that one-third to one-half of the Indian population of highland Guatemala must have perished as a consequence of the epidemic:

> Given present day knowledge of the impact of smallpox or plague on people without previous immunities, it is safe, indeed conservative, to say that a third of the Guatemalan highland populations died during this holocaust.¹³

A Cuchumatán population which between 1525 and 1530 numbered around 150,000 could, therefore, some five to ten years earlier have numbered as much as 225,000 to 300,000. An average of these two figures produces a population estimate for 1520 of around 260,000. In order to place this estimate into some kind of perspective, it is worth noting that the population of the Cuchumatanes in 1950 was around 265,000.¹⁴ This means that the population of the Cuchumatán highlands on the eve of Spanish conquest may have been approximately the same size as the mid-twentieth century population of the region. Although this calculation is no more than a tentative estimate based on meager historical documentation, its credibility is supported by Veblen's estimate of the contact population of Totonicapán as being of roughly the same magnitude as that region's mid-twentieth century population.¹⁵

Of the two other sources which contain demographic information relating to Cuchumatán towns in the sixteenth century, the tribute count made by President Valverde between 1578 and 1582 is somewhat more reliable than the one compiled 30 years earlier by President Cerrato because the latter relied partly on reports submitted by local Indian leaders (caciques) rather than on personal town inspections conducted by officials of the Crown. In order to reduce the amount of tribute demanded by the Spaniards, and thus perhaps secure more for themselves, it is possible that caciques under-reported the number of eligible tributarios each town supported.¹⁶ The Valverde count, undertaken personally by the President and his designated officials, is particularly useful because it contains two figures; the first is apparently a revised version of the Cerrato assessment dating back to the mid-sixteenth century while the second is the new Valverde assessment.¹⁷

The town of Huehuetenango, formerly assessed at 570 tributarios, was adjusted downwards by Valverde to 367 tributarios.¹⁸ A tributario at this time was a married male Indian between the ages of 18 and 50; roughly one out of every five persons would have fallen into this category.¹⁹ The Valverde statistics therefore suggest a total population for Huehuetenango in the middle years of the sixteenth century of around 2800, a figure which by 1580 had fallen to around 1800. In the tribute list for 1664-1678, the earliest extant document with comprehensive tributary data for every significant Indian community in the Cuchumatán highlands, Huehuetenango accounts for 3.9 percent of the total number of tributarios.²⁰ Assuming that Huehuetenango represented this same proportion in the sixteenth century, then the total number of Cuchumatán tributarios in 1550 was around 14,600 and in 1580 was around 9400. Using a population to tributario ratio of five to one, these figures indicate that the population of the Cuchumatán highlands in 1550 may have numbered about 73,000 and in 1580 may have numbered about 47,000.

These estimates alone are highly tentative, but it is possible to provide some independent frame of reference by which they can assume greater credibility. According to both MacLeod and Veblen, the mid-sixteenth century population of highland Guatemala probably numbered approximately half the size of the contact population owing to the devastating impact of the gucumatz plague of 1545-1548. Similarly, the number of Indians alive in the year 1580 was about half that of the mid-sixteenth century because of the equally devastating impact of the matlazahuatl pandemic of 1576-1581.²¹ Acceptance of this thesis means that a contact population of 150,000, the estimate for the Cuchumatanes obtained from the size of Indian armies confronting the Spaniards during the battles of conquest, would by 1550 have fallen to about 75,000. This figure compares exceptionally well with the estimate of 73,000 derived from the Valverde count. A mid-sixteenth century population of 73,000 would by 1580 have numbered around 37,000. This figure compares reasonably well with the estimate of 47,000 also derived from the Valverde assessment.

For close to 100 years after the Valverde count there is almost no documentation which contains demographic information relating to Cuchumatán communities.²² The one exception is an ecclesiastical census for the year 1604 which lists the number of towns and vecinos (householders) under the charge of the Dominican monastery at Sacapulas. Unfortunately, this census includes only those settlements under the jurisdiction of the Dominican and Franciscan orders. Since the majority of Indian towns in the Cuchumatanes were under the administration of the Mercedarian order, and consequently were not recorded, the utility of this otherwise important source is minimal.²³

The tribute count of 1664-1678 is the next document after the Valverde assessment which contains detailed demographic data on the Cuchumatán highlands. This extremely valuable document gives a complete breakdown, by town and occasionally by small social components (parcialidades) comprising certain towns, of the entire tribute paying population of the region. The total number of tributarios at this time was 4040.[24] Fuentes y Gúzman, during the second half of the seventeenth century, reckoned on a population to tributario ratio of four to one.[25] Using this same ratio, 4040 tribute payers would be indicative of a total Cuchumatán population of 16,162 between the years 1664 and 1678.

For the remainder of the colonial period there is no shortage of reliable and comprehensive sources, chiefly in the form of unpublished documents in the Archivo General de Centroamérica, upon which to reconstruct the population history of the Cuchumatán highlands. The abundant eighteenth- and early nineteenth-century documents from which demographic data can be gleaned include tribute lists, reports of officials of the Crown, ecclesiastical records, and meticulous censuses which enumerate the Cuchumatán population in great detail by age, sex, class, and race. This information is synthesized in Table 8.2 and is represented graphically in Figure 8.2.

The overwhelming feature of the historical demography of the Cuchumatán highlands is the catastrophic decline in population following the Spanish conquest. Massive demographic collapse probably began in the years immediately preceding the battles of conquest and continued throughout the sixteenth and for most of the seventeenth century. Reaching its nadir about 1670, population began to recover and grow throughout the eighteenth century, although there were still occasional fluctuations. By the end of the colonial period population was on a steady, if slight, upward trend. Some explanations of this overall pattern of decline, recovery, and growth may be offered.

CAUSES OF DEMOGRAPHIC COLLAPSE AND READJUSTMENT

Amidst an almost perennial controversy, recent research by a number of scholars has convincingly demonstrated that several parts of the New World were densely populated on the eve of its "discovery" by the Old World and that native American populations declined drastically in size following contact with the European invaders.[26] The traditional interpretation of the catastrophic decline of the indigenous population in Spanish America, between 80 and 90 percent in some regions, is the infamous Leyenda Negra. The Black Legend attributes the post-contact decrease in Indian numbers to the unmitigated slaughter, ruthless enslavement, and harsh exploitation of the native population by Spanish conquerors and colonists.[27] It is not difficult to find references in

TABLE 8.2
The population of the Cuchumatán highlands, 1520-1825

Year	Population	Source
1520	260,000	Extrapolation of size of Indian armies recorded by Fuentes y Gúzman
1525-1530	150,000	Estimate based on size of Indian armies recorded by Fuentes y Gúzman
1550	73,000	AGI:AG 966. P/T ratio of 5:1. Huehuetenango as 3.9% of Cuchumatán tributarios
1580	47,000	AGI:AG 966. P/T ratio of 5:1. Huehuetenango as 3.9% of Cuchumatán tributarios
1664-1678	16,162	AGCA:A3.16, leg. 1601, exp. 26391. P/T ratio of 4:1
1690	19,824	Fuentes y Gúzman, Recordación Florida. P/T ratio 4:1
1760	21,176	AGCA:A3.16, leg. 950, exp. 17715. P/T ratio of 4:1
1768-1770	23,418	Cortés y Larraz, Descripción Geográfico-Moral de la Diocesis de Goathemala
1778	27,505	AGCA:A1.44, leg. 6097, exp. 55507
1779	28,047	AGCA:A1.44, leg. 6097, exp. 55507
1782	23,021	AGCA:A1.44, leg. 6097, exp. 55507
1783	25,027	AGCA:A1.44, leg. 6097, exp. 55507
1784	24,828	AGCA:A1.44, leg. 6097, exp. 55507
1788	24,678	AGCA:A3.16, leg. 246, exp. 4912. P/T ratio of 4.82:1
1790	23,623	AGCA:A3.16, leg. 237, exp. 4706. P/T ratio of 4.82:1
1797-1798	24,129	Hidalgo, Gaceta de Guatemala
1801	27,477	AGCA:A3.16, leg. 243, exp. 4853. P/T ratio of 4.82:1
1811	29,571	AGCA:A3.16, leg. 953, exp. 17773. P/T ratio of 4.82:1
1825	34,691	AGCA:B.84.3, leg. 1135, exp. 26030-26034

P/T = Population to Tributario ratio.

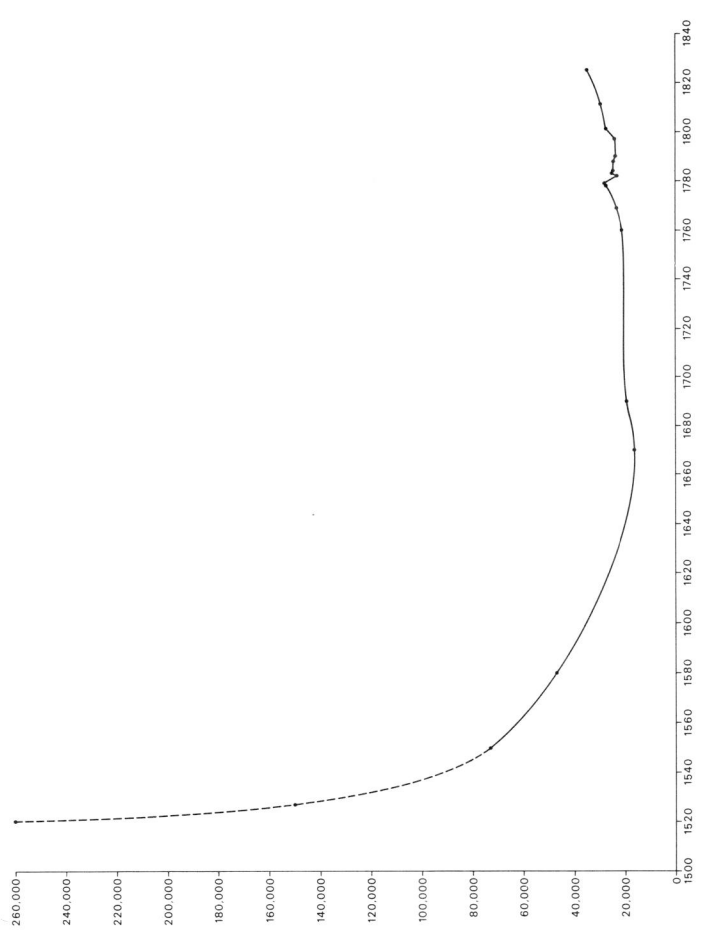

Figure 8.2 The population of the Cuchumatán highlands, 1520-1821

the literature which support the thesis of the Black Legend. According to Bartolomé de las Casas, for example, five million Indian lives were lost in Guatemala alone because of the excesses of the conquistador Pedro de Alvarado and his henchmen. In las Casas' own words:

> And this I dare affirm, that the enormities committed by . . . him especially that was sent to Guatemala . . . are enough to fill a particular volume, so many were the slaughters, violences, injuries, butcheries, and beastly desolations [committed by that abominable] tyrant [Pedro de Alvarado]; how many tears, how many sighs did he provoke, upon how many did he bring desolation in his worldly pilgrimage and endanger their damnation in the world to come?[28]

It is now quite certain, however, that the principal cause of aboriginal depopulation was not massacre and mistreatment at the hands of the conquering Spaniards but the introduction by the invaders of Old World diseases to which the Indians of the New World had no natural, physiological immunity.[29]

Until the arrival of the Europeans, the inhabitants of the New World lived in virtual isolation from those of the Old World. This long period of isolation weakened considerably the resistance of American Indians to most of the major diseases of mankind. Possibly because of the harsh climate characteristic of the Bering region, many diseases were never carried over from the Old World to the New World by the first migrants; the Arctic cold simply killed off both the disease organisms and those humans suffering from chronic sickness or contamination.[30] Alternative explanations may be that the migrations across the Bering Strait occurred so long ago that many diseases had not yet evolved in the Old World before the departure of the Amerindian ancestors; or the original group of migrants was so small that the loss of immunity factors was due to genetic drift.[31] Whatever the reason, the inhabitants of the New World developed tolerances only for a limited number of indigenous American diseases. During pre-Columbian times, the Indians of America appear to have been subjected primarily to gastro-intestinal disturbances and respiratory disorders.[32] Prior to the arrival of the Spaniards, therefore, the Indians enjoyed an existence relatively free of infectious diseases. Maladies such as smallpox, measles, mumps, typhus, influenza, and diptheria--all of which were endemic to the Old World--were completely unknown. When these diseases were inadvertently brought to America by Spanish conquerors and colonists, their devastating impact on hitherto isolated human communities may well have caused, in the words of one scholar, "the greatest destruction of lives in history."[33]

The first Old World disease to arrive in America was smallpox.[34] The impact of smallpox on the native population of the New World was at least as cataclysmic as the impact of the Black Death of 1346 to 1350 on European society; that is, one-third to one-half of the Indians who came in contact with the disease must have perished.[35]

Soon after sweeping through Central Mexico, smallpox spread southwards to the highlands of Guatemala, accompanied perhaps by pulmonary plague or typhus.[36] By the end of 1520, four years before the entrada of Pedro de Alvarado, the Indians of highland Guatemala were reeling from their initial encounter with what MacLeod has appropriately called "the shock troops of the conquest."[37] The chroniclers of the Cakchiquel lament that it "was in truth terrible, the number of dead among the people . . . in that period . . . when the plague raged."[38] This first bout of pestilence was followed about 12 years later by a pandemic of measles. Thereafter, major outbreaks of Old World diseases were a common feature of Indian life in colonial Guatemala and consistently resulted in high mortality among the immunologically defenseless native population.

It is unlikely that the Indian peoples of the Cuchumatán highlands escaped these deadly visitations. The testimony of Thomas Gage, in connection with an outbreak of typhus in 1631, indicates that the impact of disease tended to be widespread:

> The year following [1631], all that country [highland Guatemala] was generally infected with a kind of contagious sickness, almost as infectious as the plague, which they call tabardillo [typhus]. This fever in the very inward parts and bowels scarce continued to the seventh day but commonly took its victims away from the world to a grave the third or fifth day. The filthy smell and stench which came from those who lay sick of this disease was enough to infect the rest of the house, and all that came to see them. It rotted their very mouths and tongues, and made them as black as coal before they died. Very few Spaniards were infected with this contagion, but the Indians generally were taken with it.[39]

In addition to being affected by diseases of pandemic proportion, such as the one described above, the Indian people of the Cuchumatán highlands were also exposed throughout the colonial period to more localized outbreaks of disease (Table 8.3).

The recurrent outbreak of diseases to which the native population was immunologically defenseless is the chief factor behind the demographic collapse of the Indian peoples of the Cuchumatanes following the Spanish conquest. From 1520 until the end of Spanish colonial

TABLE 8.3
Local outbreaks of disease in the Cuchumatán highlands, 1548-1819

Year	Disease	Towns Affected	Source	Comments
c1548-c1615	"Pestes" (unspecified)	Towns of the "sierras de Cuchumatlán"	Remesal, Vol. II, p. 259	"Ahora con las pestes han venido los pueblos en diminución."
1666-1670	Tabardillo (typhus)	Huehuetenango	A3.16, leg. 1600, exp. 26390	Indian tribute lowered after epidemic carried off 45 adults.
1733-1773	Viruela (smallpox)	Sacapulas and Cunén	A3.16, leg. 2819, exp. 40918	Many tribute-payers perished. Indians unable to pay tribute and ask for exemption.
1774	"Peste" (unspecified)	Various towns	A3.16, leg. 943, exp. 17608	Alcalde mayor informs treasury that certain towns will not be able to pay tribute.
1780-1781	Viruela (smallpox)	All forty towns of the Partido de Huehuetenango	A1.44, leg. 6097, exp. 55507	Over 4000 deaths. Alcalde mayor authorized to use community funds to help fight the disease.
1786	Tabardillo	Concepción and Petatán	A1.4, leg. 6101, exp. 55666	
1795-1799	Tabardillo and viruela, tabardillo was particularly	Numerous towns, including Nebaj, Chajul, Todos Santos and San Martín	A1.24, leg. 6101, exp. 55666-669; A1.47, leg. 385 exp. 80121; A3.16, leg. 255, exp. 5719; A3.16, leg. 244, exp. 4869;	Over 500 deaths in Jacaltenango alone and an equal number in Concepción; visit to stricken towns by the alcalde mayor and a doctor, the former to adjust

	widespread	Cuchumatán, Jacaltenango, Concepción	A1.49, leg. 192, exp. 3911; A3.1, leg. 2894, exp. 42846	tribute payment, the latter to fight the spread of disease.
1802–1807	Tabardillo, viruela, and sarampión (measles)	Numerous towns including San Juan Ixcoy, Santa Eulalia, Nebaj, San Pedro Soloma, San Mateo Ixtatán	A1.1, leg. 6105, exp. 55795; A1.24, leg. 6091, exp. 55306; A3.16, leg. 245, exp. 4909; A1.4, leg. 6107, exp. 55836; A1.4, leg. 6091, exp. 55307; A1.47, leg. 2162, exp. 1558; A3.16, leg. 2899, exp. 43063	Alcalde mayor requests that tribute should not be collected from certain towns. Locust invasion exacerbates situation. Food shortages and much human suffering.
1809–1812	Tabardillo, viruela, and fiebre putrida (type of fever)	San Miguel Acatán, San Mateo Ixtatán, San Juan Cotzal	A1.1, leg. 6093, exp. 55337; A1.49 leg. 386, exp. 8055; A1.4, leg. 6113, exp. 56214; A1, leg. 394, exp. 8238	Indians in stricken communities given a reprieve in the payment of tribute.
1814–1819	Tabardillo	Chiantla and Jacaltenango	A1.49, leg. 387, exp. 8072; A1.49, leg. 388, exp. 8099	Measures taken to halt spread of disease.

All archival citations refer to unpublished documents housed in the Archivo General de Centroamérica, Guatemala City.

rule in 1821, the Indians were subjected to unrelenting waves of pestilence. Mortality was high. Between 1520 and 1670 population declined by more than 90 percent, falling from perhaps 260,000 to a little over 16,000. By the end of the seventeenth century the collapse had abated and there were signs of a slight but significant demographic recovery. Several fluctuations towards the end of the eighteenth century, however, suggest that the Indians had still not built up effective immunities to diseases such as smallpox and typhus. Only at the very end of the colonial period are there positive indications of a general increase in Indian numbers (see Table 8.2 and Figure 8.2).

The impact of disease on Indian life in the Cuchumatán highlands was profound. Guatemalan archives contain thousands of documents which describe, in lugubrious detail, the disruptions wrought by outbreaks of disease on scores of Indian communities. These dislocations included: substantial loss of life; the inability of certain towns to meet the semi-annual tribute requirement demanded by the Crown; the abandonment of disease-ridden towns for the safety of uninfected or less infected rural areas; and the failure on the part of Indians to work their land, resulting in widespread hardship and deprivation. The plight of the Indians under such desperate circumstances is nowhere more tragically conveyed than in a letter addressed to the <u>alcalde mayor</u> of Huehuetenango by the <u>ladino comisionado</u> of the parish of Soloma, Marcos Casteñeda. His observations may be considered representative of a substantive body of archival documentation and have an applicability far beyond the time and place of which he writes:

> For four years now [1803-1807] in the towns of [the parish of] Soloma there has been great distress owing to the high mortality caused by the epidemic of typhus which kills [the Indians] without relief or remedy, leaving them only in dire hardship. Through fear of death we [the ladino residents Marcos and Santiago Casteñeda] fled with our families to the solitude of the mountains and barren wastes of Chemal, suffering there the extremity of its climate, abandoning our houses and possessions in Soloma. But God having saw fit to end this terrible affliction, we are returning once again to our homes. To our horror we find that the majority of the Indians of Santa Eulalia have perished, and are lying unburied all over the place, their decaying corpses eaten by the animals which roam the countryside . . . . It is even more painful, however, to see the great number of orphaned children crying for the laps of their parents, asking for bread without having anyone to receive it from . . . . After so much hard work, these unfortunate Indians have been

> reduced to a life of misery. Having returned to their
> town [the Indians who survived] are without homes,
> without resources to pay their expenses and tribute,
> and without corn to feed themselves and their families.
> If no measures are taken to assist these wretched peo-
> ple, they will without doubt starve to death, because
> they did not plant corn in the places where they sought
> refuge [from the epidemic], and so they have nothing to
> live on, both for this year and for the next, since it
> is now too late to plant their crops. It is very com-
> mon in this parish to find large numbers of Indians,
> old and young alike, walking from town to town, from
> house to house, begging and searching for food . . . .
> Señor Alcalde Mayor, inform the President that help
> should be extended to the towns of this parish of
> Soloma; at the very least [the Indians] of Santa Eulalia
> and San Miguel Acatán could be exempted from paying
> tribute for the years during which they have suffered
> great misfortunes.[40]

Casteñeda, in another communication, reckoned that the outbreak of typhus had killed "three-quarters of the Indian population of San Miguel Acatán and Santa Eulalia" and stated that most of the survivors of the epidemic were rendered "destitute and homeless because their houses were burned to rid them of the contagion."[41]

In response to a plea by the Indian alcaldes and <u>principales</u> of Santa Eulalia to exempt the town from pay-ing tribute during the disruptive years of the typhus epidemic, the alcalde mayor was able only to obtain a royal order granting a temporary respite from the obliga-tion.[42] The refusal of the Spanish authorities to grant the Indians a total tribute exemption prompted the parish priest of Soloma, Fray Juan José Juarez, to write the following rebuke to the alcalde mayor:

> It strikes me that what is most important to you is
> that the Indians pay their tribute so that you receive
> your salary, but I think the Indians will be unable to
> pay, either this year or later, [because] they have
> lost their crops and consequently have nothing to pay
> with.[43]

The tone of this address imparts some sense of the numbed resignation with which servants of the Crown in outlying rural districts would respond, during times of crisis, to the apathy, ineptitude, and lack of responsi-bility of men in distant seats of authority. Apparently even during an epidemic involving considerable loss of life and appalling human suffering, an appropriate course of remedial action was beyond the workings of government bureaucracy.

CONCLUSION

By introducing Old World diseases to an immunologically defenseless native population, the Spanish conquest of America precipitated a demographic collapse that was probably the most catastrophic in the history of mankind. The magnitude and rapidity of Indian depopulation in the Cuchumatán highlands following conquest by Spain conforms to a pattern already well-established for a number of other long settled parts of Latin America.[44] A population of perhaps 260,000 on the eve of conquest, roughly the same size as the mid-twentieth century population of the Cuchumatanes, had by 1670 declined to around 16,000, a fall of slightly more than 90 percent over a period of 150 years. The demographic recovery which began in the last quarter of the seventeenth century continued throughout the eighteenth and nineteenth centuries. For most of this time population increase was slow and sporatic because of the persistent outbreak of diseases to which the Indians only gradually acquired immunities. It was not until the third decade of the present century that population began to increase sharply, due chiefly to the impact of modern medical technology in substantially reducing rates of human mortality. By 1950, after a process of decline, recovery, and growth lasting over 400 years, the population of the Cuchumatán highlands reached a level equivalent to that which it may have numbered prior to the arrival of the Spaniards and their pestilential allies.

NOTES

1. M. J. MacLeod, Spanish Central America: A Socioeconomic History, 1520-1720, (Berkeley and Los Angeles: University of California Press, 1973), p. 374.
2. MacLeod, op. cit., pp. 130 and 224.
3. Archivo General de Centroamérica (hereafter AGCA), A3.16, leg. 1601, exp. 26391.
4. F. A. de Fuentes y Gúzman, Recordación Florida: Historia Natural, Material, Militar y Política del Reino de Goathemala, (Madrid: Biblioteca de Autores Españoles, Tomo CCLIX, 1972), pp. 18-22 and 51-71.
5. Archivo General de Indias: Audiencia de Guatemala (hereafter AGI:AG), 128. Although at least 11 Cuchumatán towns may be identified in the Cerrato census, only nine have a record of how many tributarios they contained. The breakdown is as follows:

Name of Town	No. of Tributarios	Name of Encomendero
Ixtatán	65	Diego Sánchez Santiago
Jacaltenango	500	"Menor hijo de Gonzalo de

Name of Town	No. of Tributarios	Name of Encomendero
		Covalle"
Aguacatán	100	Juan de Celada
Chalchitán	60	Hernán Pérez Penale and Alvaro de Pulgar
Soloma	40	Diego de Alvarado and Juan de Castrogui
Uspantán	--	Ignatio de Bobadilla and Santos Figueroa
Huehuetenango	500	Juan de Espinar
Sacapulas	160	Juan Paez and Cristobal Salvatierra
Malacatán	80	Ignatio de Bobadilla
Motozintla	138	Hernán Gutierrez de Cibaji and Hernán Mendez de Sotomayor
Cuchumatán (Todos Santos)	--	"Menores hijos de Marcos Ruíz" and García de Aguilar

A partial version of the Cerrato census may be found in published form in F. de Solano, Los Mayas del Siglo XVIII: Pervivencia y Transformación de la Sociedad Indígena Guatemalteca durante la Administración Borbónica, (Madrid: Ediciones Cultura Hispanica, 1974), pp. 80-82.

    6. AGI:AG, 966. A brief analysis of the Valverde census may be found in R. M. Carmack, Quichean Civilization: The Ethnohistoric, Ethnographic, and Archaeological Sources, (Berkeley and Los Angeles: University of California Press, 1973), p. 143.

    7. T. T. Veblen, "Native Population Decline in Totonicapán, Guatemala," Annals of the Association of American Geographers, Vol. 67, No. 4, December 1977, pp. 496-497.

    8. Ibid., p. 497.

    9. Fuentes y Gúzman, op. cit., p. 57.

    10. Veblen, op. cit., p. 487; and C. Gibson, Tlaxcala in the Sixteenth Century, (New Haven: Yale University Press, 1952), p. 139.

    11. MacLeod, op. cit., pp. 39-40.

    12. A Recinos and D. Goetz (translators), The Annals of the Cakchiquels, (Norman: University of Oklahoma Press, 1953), pp. 115-116.

    13. MacLeod, op. cit., p. 41.

    14. M. M. Urrutia, La División Política y Administrativa de Guatemala, (Guatemala: Editorial Iberia, 1961), Tomo I, pp. 432 and 644.

    15. Veblen, op. cit., p. 499.

    16. Carmack, op. cit., pp. 138-140; and Veblen, op. cit., p. 495. Cerrato was strongly criticized by Bishop Marroquín for relying on tribute counts provided by caciques. This practice, together with the freeing of Indian slaves and the lowering of the amount of tribute required of each Indian tributario, made Cerrato extremely unpopular among the Spanish residents of Quatemala.

    17. Carmack, op. cit., p. 143.

    18. AGI:AG 966.

19. Veblen, op. cit., p. 495.

20. AGCA, A3.16, leg. 1601, exp. 26391. The total number of tributarios in the Cuchumatanes was 4040½. Huehuetenango was assessed at 156½.

21. MacLeod, op. cit., p. 19; and Veblen, op. cit., p. 496. Gucumatz, cocoliztli, is an undetermined type of plague; MacLeod believes the descriptions of the disease resemble the symptoms of pulmonary plague. Matlazáhuatl is a disease of disputed origin which some scholars believe to be typhus; cf. S. S. Cook, "The Incidence and Significance of Disease Among the Aztecs and Related Tribes," Hispanic American Historical Review 26 (1946), p. 321, and P. Gerhard, A Guide to the Historical Geography of New Spain (Cambridge: Cambridge University Press, 1972), p. 23.

22. The fact that almost no documentation exists for the period 1580-1664 may be due to any number of survival hazards, such as flood, fire, earthquake, theft or negligence. The lack of documentation, however, may also be simply a reflection of how relatively neglected were the Indian peoples of the Cuchumatanes during the seventeenth century.

23. The 1604 ecclesiastical census, entitled Memoria de los frailes menores que hay en la provincia de Guatemala, is housed in the Biblioteca del Real Palacio, Madrid. It appears in published form in Solano, op. cit., pp. 106-108.

24. AGCA, A3.16, leg. 1601, exp. 26391.

25. Fuentes y Gúzman, op. cit., pp. 15-18 and 22-44.

26. W. M. Denevan (ed.), The Native Population of the Americas in 1492 (Madison: University of Wisconsin Press, 1976), pp. 1-12. S. F. Cook and W. Borah, Essays in Population History: Mexico and California, Vol. 3, (Berkeley and Los Angeles: University of California Press, 1979), p. 102, summarize their decades of collaborative research on the historical demography of central Mexico in one succinct sentence: "We conclude, then, that the Indian population of central Mexico, under the impact of factors unleashed by the coming of the Europeans, fell by 1620-1625 to a low of approximately 3% of its size at the time that the Europeans first landed on the shore of Veracruz."

27. Gibson, Spain in America (New York: Harper and Row, 1966), pp. 43-47 and 136-137.

28. B. de las Casas (trans. J. Phillips), The Tears of the Indians: Being an Historical and True Account of the Cruel Massacres and Slaughters of Above Twenty Millions of Innocent People; Committed by the Spaniards in the Islands of Hispaniola, Cuba, Jamaica, etc. As also in the Continent of Mexico, Peru, and Other Places to the West Indies, to the Total Destruction of These Countries (London, 1656), pp. 43-53.

29. A. W. Crosby, Jr., The Columbian Exchange: Biological and Cultural Consequences of 1492 (Connecticut: Greenwood Press, 1972), pp. 35-58 and "Virgin Soil Epidemics as a Factor in the Aboriginal Depopulation in America," William and Mary Quarterly, Third Series, Vol. 33, 1976, pp. 289-299; Gerhard, op. cit., p. 23; MacLeod, op. cit., pp. 19-20 and 38-40; and W. H. McNeill, Plagues and Peoples (New York: Anchor and Doubleday Press, 1976), pp. 176-207.

30. Crosby, op. cit., pp. 30-31.

31. R. Gruhn (personal communication).
32. Cook, op. cit., p. 324. Some scholars think that syphilis is a New World disease introduced to Europe after the Spanish conquest. For a review of the early history of the disease, see Crosby, Columbian Exchange, op. cit., pp. 122-164.
33. MacLeod, op. cit., p. 20.
34. Crosby, Columbian Exchange, op. cit., pp. 42-58, examines the impact that the first pandemic of smallpox had on the native peoples of America.
35. MacLeod, op. cit., pp. 6-19. For a review of the effect of the Black Death on European society in the mid-fourteenth century see McNeill, op. cit., pp. 132-175, and P. Ziegler, The Black Death (Harmondsworth: Pelican Books, 1976), especially pp. 232-259.
36. MacLeod, op. cit., pp. 19 and 98.
37. MacLeod, op. cit., p. 40.
38. Recinos and Goetz, op. cit., p. 115.
39. T. Gage (ed. J. E. S. Thompson), Thomas Gage's Travels in the New World (Norman: University of Oklahoma Press, 1958), p. 263.
40. AGCA, A3.16, leg. 249, exp. 5036.
41. AGCA, A1.14, leg. 386, exp. 8037.
42. AGCA, A3.16, leg. 249, exp. 5036.
43. AGCA, A3.16, leg. 2899, exp. 43049.
44. The monumental work of Sherburne F. Cook and Woodrow Borah has been of primary significance in establishing a model of large Indian populations at Spanish contact experiencing a rapid and precipitous post-contact decline. The Preface to Volume One of their magnificent three-volume Essays in Population History (Berkeley and Los Angeles: University of California Press, 1971, 1974 and 1979), pp. V-XIV, serves as a succinct bibliographical and chronological survey of their painstaking years of research. Other works which establish the existence of large pre-Columbian populations and which support the Cook and Borah thesis of massive post-contact collapse include the following: C. Sauer, Colima of New Spain in the Sixteenth Century, Ibero-Americana No. 29 (Berkeley and Los Angeles: University of California Press, 1948), pp. 59-63 and 93-96; W. M. Denevan, The Upland Pine Forests of Nicaragua: A Study in Cultural Plant Geography, University of California Publications in Geography, Vol. 12 (Berkeley and Los Angeles: University of California Press, 1961), pp. 289-291; C. L. Johanessen, Savannas of Interior Honduras, Ibero-Americana No. 46 (Berkeley and Los Angeles: University of California Press, 1963), pp. 27-47; H. F. Dobyns, "Estimating Aboriginal American Populations: An Appraisal of Techniques with a New Hemispheric Estimate," Current Anthropology, Vol. 7 (1966), pp. 395-416 and 425-435; C. O. Sauer, The Early Spanish Main (Berkeley and Los Angeles: University of California Press, 1966), pp. 65-69, 155-156, 178-181, 200-204, and 283-289; A. W. Crosby, Jr., "Conquistador y Pestilencia: The First New World Pandemic and the Fall of the Great Indian Empires," Hispanic American Historical Review, Vol. 47 (1967), pp. 321-337; C. T. Smith, "Depopulation of the Central Andes in the 16th Century," Current Anthropology, Vol. 11 (1970), pp. 1-12; Gerhard, op. cit., pp. 22-28; MacLeod, op. cit., pp. 37-45; C. H. Lutz, Santiago de Guatemala, 1541-1773: The Socio-Demographic History of a Spanish American Colonial City (University of Wisconsin-

Madison, unpublished Ph.D. dissertation, 1976), pp. 249-317 and 743-752; D. Madigan, *Santiago Atitlan, Guatemala: A Socioeconomic and Demographic History* (University of Pittsburgh, unpublished Ph.D. dissertation, 1976), pp. 176-206; Veblen, *op. cit*., pp. 486-494; P. Gerhard, *The Southwest Frontier of New Spain* (Princeton: Princeton University Press, 1979), pp. 23-30; and W. L. Sherman, *Forced Native Labor in Sixteenth-Century Central America* (Lincoln: University of Nebraska Press, 1979), pp. 4-6 and 347-355.

9
Demographic Catastrophe in Sixteenth-Century Honduras

Linda A. Newson

In terms of the historical demography of Latin America, Central America is probably the least well-known area, and within that region there is no doubt that the least-researched country is Honduras. This is a reflection of the country's marginal location in the Spanish Empire and of the fragmentary nature of the documentary record for the area. Although there have been a number of estimates of the aboriginal population of the area, they have relied heavily on a small number of published documents and on comparisons with other Central American countries for which more evidence is available. Research on the historical demography of the sixteenth century is also lacking. Although MacLeod and Sherman have published tables of figures for the Indian population in the sixteenth century taken from the documentary record,[1] they have not analyzed the figures or examined the causes of the demographic decline, as this paper will attempt to do.

ESTIMATES OF THE ABORIGINAL POPULATION

The controversy that exists over estimates of the native population in the New World is more difficult to resolve in Central America because of the relative lack of documentary evidence and the speed with which the population declined. Estimates of the size of the Indian population on the eve of discovery range from Kroeber's calculation of 100,000 for Honduras and Nicaragua together

---

This paper forms part of a more extensive study of the colonial experience of the Indian in Honduras and Nicaragua for which financial support was received from the Social Science Research Council, the Central Research Fund of the University of London, and the Sir Ernest Cassel Educational Trust to all of whom the author wishes to express her thanks.

to Dobyns's estimate of between 10,800,000 and 13,500,000 for Central America.² Kroeber maintains that the estimates of early observers were exaggerated, a conclusion which he arrived at after an examination of the demographic history of Indian groups in the United States, particularly California. He assumed that the Indian population had grown at a regular rate since the time of conquest and derived his estimates by projecting the growth rate backwards from figures provided by Humboldt for the end of the eighteenth century. He thus disregarded the devastating impact of newly-introduced diseases and the disruptive effect of conquest and colonization on the economic and social life of the Indians. Steward accepts Kroeber's conclusion that the estimates of contemporary observers were exaggerated and, on the basis of evidence provided by the contributors to the Handbook of South American Indians, he suggests that the population of Central America, excluding Guatemala, was 736,500 of which 392,500 were in Honduras, Nicaragua and El Salvador together.³ This estimate is somewhat lower than that of Rosenblat, who on the basis of readily available documentary evidence has estimated that the native population of Central America was 800,000.⁴ Alternative approaches have suggested that these estimates may be too low. Sapper, who had an intimate knowledge of Mexico and Central America, estimated that on the basis of the climate, resources and Indian technology the native population of Central America was between five and six million.⁵ More recently Dobyns has reviewed the literature available for the demographic history of the hemisphere and concluded that insufficient account has been taken of the devastating impact of disease and suggests that the Indian population was between twenty to twenty-five times greater than that recorded at its nadir, which for many Indian groups in Latin America was in the middle of the seventeenth century. For Central America he estimates that the Indian population was 540,000 in 1650 thus giving between 10,800,000 and 13,500,000 Indians at the time of conquest.⁶

These estimates have been proposed on the basis of only a limited reading of the documentary evidence and only recently has archival research by Radell, MacLeod and Sherman begun to provide more detailed information about the size of the Indian population at the time of conquest and its decline during the sixteenth century. These authors are not, however, in complete agreement over the interpretation of the documentary evidence, particularly that relating to the Indian slave trade. Radell has suggested that the population of Nicaragua was over one million at the time of discovery, given that up to 1548 between 450,000 and 500,000 were removed from the country as a result of the slave trade, 400,000 to 600,000 probably died of disease, in war or fled the province, whilst 200,000 to 250,000 were probably residing in the Central Highlands to be decimated during the ensuing twenty to thirty years.[7] Denevan adopts this estimate in his calculation of the aboriginal population of Central America and suggests on the basis of incomplete comparative evidence that the population of Honduras and Belize was 750,000.[8] He proposes that the Indian population of Central America in 1492 was 5,650,000. Radell's estimate of the number of Indians exported as a result of the slave trade is comparable to the 500,000 and 400,000 Indians enslaved reported by Las Casas and Oviedo respectively,[9] but despite the convergence of estimates Sherman considers these figures too high.[10] He maintains that the capacity of the ships was small and that only a small number of ships were involved in the early years of the trade, whilst in later years heavy cargo demands for space reduced that available for slaves. He suggests that a more realistic figure for the whole period from 1524 to 1549 would be 50,000 and this figure includes Indian slaves exported from the whole of Central America not just Nicaragua. He estimates that the aboriginal population of Central America was about 2.5 million. Although MacLeod does not provide an estimate of the Indian population of Central America, he does suggest with respect to the slave trade that a figure of 10,000 per year for the decade 1532 to 1542 would appear to be too low and 200,000 for the duration of the slave trade a conservative estimate.[11] It seems possible therefore that about half a million Indian slaves were exported from Nicaragua, although a proportion of those would have come from Honduras. In addition, some Indian slaves were shipped from northern Honduras and the Bay Islands to the Caribbean Islands but the flow was undoubtedly much smaller than that which passed through the ports of Nicaragua. It will be suggested that between 100,000 and 150,000 Indians were exported from Honduras during the same period. Unfortunately none of the three authors proposes an estimate for the aboriginal population of Honduras and before doing so it is necessary to examine in detail the evidence available.

THE DOCUMENTARY EVIDENCE

Although numerous archaeological sites have been uncovered in Honduras, the majority have not been investigated scientifically and it is not possible to estimate the aboriginal population on the basis of archaeological evidence, so that the basic source of information is the documentary record.

Contemporary observers were impressed by the size of the Indian population in Honduras, although few gave precise estimates. In 1539 the Bishop of Honduras, Cristóbal de Pedraza, wrote that at the time Gil González Dávila and Hernan Cortés came to Honduras it had possessed almost as many people as Mexico, and in a later letter he described the country as having been as highly populated as Mexico and Peru.[12] In 1541 Benzoni recorded that the population of Honduras on the eve of conquest had been 400,000.[13] Unfortunately this is the only precise estimate made by a contemporary chronicler. It seems likely, however, that Benzoni's figure is an underestimate and this may be due to the late date of the account occurring after Pedro de Alvarado's brutal conquest of western Honduras and after the Indian slave trade had taken its heaviest toll. Prior to that time the country had been highly populated. In 1535 Andrés de Cerezeda reported that around the town of Naco alone there were 200,000 Indians, who could be of service,[14] whilst further south the legendary leader Lempira was able to muster a fighting force of 30,000 Indians to resist Spanish conquest.[15] There were a large number of settlements in Honduras, although the majority did not exceed several thousand households. Cerezeda reported that all the way from Naco to the sea were villages with 300 to 2,000 houses,[16] whilst Stone believes that the abundance of archaeological remains in the Comayagua valley indicates that, "in pre-Conquest times the Comayagua region must have been a mass of villages with the population running well into the thousands."[17] Similarly Gracias a Dios was founded in "a good area of many villages"[18] and some of them such as Taloa, Guarcha, Cerquin and Telulocelo possessed 2,000 and 3,000 houses.[19] It is also clear that eastern Honduras had a large population, but little was known about this unconquered and colonized area at that time, so that their numbers could not have been included in the early population estimates. In 1548 when the Indian slaves were liberated there were said to be 27,000 pans working gold in the Río Guayape and by the end of the century it had been revealed that 4,000 to 5,000 Indians were living between Trujillo and Cabo de Camarón.[20] There were thus dense populations in Honduras, for although the majority of settlements were small, what they lacked in size they made up for in numbers. Benzoni's estimate thus seems too low especially when the devastating impact of disease and the Indian slave trade are also taken into account. An aboriginal population of about 800,000, of which 200,000 were living in the uncolonized areas, seems not unreasonable and could easily have been supported given the natural resources and the nature of the Indian economies.[21] This estimate is the highest so far proposed for Honduras.

By 1539 according to Bishop Pedraza the Indian population of Honduras had been reduced to 15,000, whilst in 1541 Benzoni maintained there were only 8,000.[22] It is unlikely that either of these accounts took into consideration the Indian population living in the east of the country. Unfortunately there are no more detailed accounts of the Indian population until the 1540s when lists were drawn up for the purpose of tribute assessment.[23] Although the Crown ordered that official assessments or <u>tasaciones</u> should be made in the 1530s and it is possible that some were conducted, the earliest evidence of assessments for Honduras is for 1544.[24] These tasaciones were made by the <u>oidores</u> Rogel, Herrera and Ramírez and although it appears that they covered a large part of the country only the tasaciones for the jurisdiction of Gracias a Dios have been found. These assessments are contained in the <u>residencia</u> of the first <u>Audiencia</u> undertaken by the President of the Audiencia, Alonso López de Cerrato, from 1548 to 1550.[25] Although the assessments do not indicate the number of Indians in each of the sixty-four villages, they do list the number of Indian carriers or <u>tamemes</u> each was to supply, as well as the number who were required to provide "<u>servicio ordinario</u>" (to work as household servants) and render other services such as tending livestock, supplying fish on Fridays and holy days and making pans for washing alluvial gold. Together the sixty-four villages supplied 4,354 tamemes and 373 Indians for other kinds of service. It is assumed that the tamemes were adult males, whether married or single, as were probably the majority of other Indians who provided services. This number thus represents only a proportion of the total Indian population to be found in the area. In addition not all villages were required to provide tamemes or services. As such it is impossible to estimate accurately the total Indian population from these figures, but it seems likely that it would not have been below 15,000.[26] This suggests that the figures for the Indian population given by Bishop Pedraza and Benzoni for 1539 and 1541 respectively were underestimates. When Alonso López de Cerrato became President of the Audiencia in 1548 he reported that the Indians could not pay half of what was due even if they were doubled in number.[27] He thus set about moderating the amount of tribute and personal service which the Indians were required to pay. His reassessments constitute one of the best sources of information about the Indian population in Central America in the sixteenth century.[28] Unfortunately for Honduras the <u>libro de tasaciones</u> only includes the assessments for Comayagua and even then the population of only 38 of the 48 villages listed is included. These villages had a total of 2,745 tributary Indians. Given that the tasaciones regulated the amount of maize to be sown at one <u>fanega</u> per ten tributary Indians, it is estimated that the tributary population for those villages where the population is not stated but where the amount of tribute is indicated was about 485, giving a total for the jurisdiction of 3,230.[29] The term *tributario* referred to married male Indians only, for it was not until 1578 that other able-bodied males such as widowers and single men were made liable for tribute payment.[30]

There is very little evidence for the size of the Indian population in the following two decades. Although general reassessments of tribute were made by the oidores Alonso Zorita and Tomás López in 1554 and by the oidores Dr. Mexía and Jufre de Loaysa in 1562, there is no evidence of the number of tributary Indians, only the amount of tribute they paid. Since the amount of tribute assessed by Mexía and Loaysa was considered to be much heavier than that of their predecessors it is impossible to use the tasaciones as indicators of demographic change.[31] According to Batres Jáuregui, in 1561 the bishopric of Comayagua contained 145 villages with a population of 10,000 Indians.[32] Unfortunately he does not cite the source of his information but it may have been one of these reassessments.

López de Velasco's *Geografía y descripción universal de las Indias* is often used by historians to obtain an overview of the social and economic conditions in Latin America in the early 1570s, but the population figures he gives for Central America should be used with caution. It is almost certain that the figures he gives for individual villages in the jurisdiction of Comayagua were taken from the tributary lists drawn up in 1549. Only summary figures are given for other jurisdictions and their origin is unknown. It is possible that they were based on other tributary lists which were drawn up at the same time but which have since been lost, but more likely they were based on later tasaciones or general estimates. The figure of 10,000 tributary Indians is the same as that recorded in an unsigned and undated document in the Biblioteca Nacional in Madrid and it is clearly a mistake.[33]

There is no evidence of other general assessments until the end of the 1570s, when Lic. García de Valverde took office as President of the Audiencia and in 1578 ordered a general survey of the conditions of the Indians.[34] Unfortunately there are no detailed accounts of the numbers of Indians counted during the *visita*, although one report from Francisco Cisneros encharged with part of the visita of Honduras said that in the jurisdiction of Gracias a Dios there were only 2,400 Indians, whereas at the time they had been counted by Loaysa there had been 5,000, and that the Indian population of the jurisdiction of San Pedro had been reduced by two-thirds.[35] Probably in connection with the visita ordered by Valverde, the Governor of Honduras, Alonso de Contreras visited the region in the late 1570s and early 1580s. His account written in 1582 lists the number of tributary Indians in each village and they sum to 5,106.[36] Another letter

TABLE 9.1
Population estimates for Honduras, 1571-1582

Jurisdictions	1571-74[a] Velasco's account tributarios	1582[b] Governor's account tributarios	1582[c] Bishop's account vecinos naturales	
			(indiv. figs.)	(summary figs.)
Comayagua	2,600	1,723	1,640	1,800
Gracias a Dios	3,000	1,769	2,160	2,100
San Pedro	700	415	330	330
Puerto de Caballos		60	120	120
Trujillo	600	413	590	590
Olancho	10,000	726	460	460
Total		5,106	5,300	5,400

[a] Velasco, op. cit., pp. 307-313.
[b] BAGGG vol. 11, pp. 5-19, Contreras to Crown 20.4.1582.
[c] AGI,AG 164 Bishop to Crown 10.5.1582 and 12.5.1582.

from the Bishop of Honduras written in the same year lists 5,400 vecinos naturales but it is more general giving only the total figures for the jurisdictions.[37] In both accounts many of the figures are fives or tens suggesting rounding or estimation rather than accurate counting.[38]

In 1590 the President of the Audiencia Francisco de Valverde drew up an account of the tributary population of Honduras as part of a proposal to establish a road from Trujillo to the Bay of Fonseca to carry trade to and from Peru. Two accounts exist of the Indian population, one of which includes the number of tributary Indians for each village.[39] With the exception of the jurisdiction of Olancho the coverage is complete and includes Choluteca. In the detailed account there are errors in addition and the more general account, which was probably based on the former, possesses several errors in transcription. The summary figures give a total tributary population of 5,965 with a further 663 in Choluteca.

The most detailed and comprehensive accounts of the Indian population for the end of the sixteenth century is contained in the treasury accounts for that period. In 1591 the Crown introduced a capitation tax known as the servicio del tostón to help pay the costs of defence.[40]

TABLE 9.2
Population estimates for Honduras circa 1590

Jurisdictions	Relación of 1590[a] Indios	Memorial[b] Indios	casados tributarios
		(indiv. figs.)	(summary figs.)
Comayagua	1,061	1,666	2,061
Gracias a Dios	2,188	1,888	2,188
San Pedro	376	376	363
Puerto de Caballos	104	104	104
Trujillo	not given	510	510
Olancho	470	464	469
Total	4,199	5,008	5,695
Choluteca	663	663	663

[a] RAHM 9/4663 No. 15, Relación geográfica, Francisco Valverde, 24.8.1590.
[b] AGI,MEX 257 Memorial de todos los pueblos . . . Francisco de Valverde, no date.

Each tributary Indian was required to pay one tostón a year in two installments of two reales. The treasury accounts list the number of tostones paid by each Indian village and thus they may be used as a rough guide to the size of the tributary population. The figures are an imperfect guide because some Indians only paid for half of the year because they either ceased to pay tribute or became tributary during the year, whilst others avoided payment completely. As such, the figures if anything slightly underestimate the size of the tributary population and it is possible that part of the decline could be attributed to tax evasion. Accounts of the income from the servicio del tostón for Honduras are more or less complete for 1592 to 1602, and are available for the jurisdiction of Comayagua until 1614.[41] Although the income from the servicio del tostón is an imperfect guide to the size of the tributary population, the figures are consistent with other reports of the size of the Indian population already discussed and with a report from the oficiales reales in 1626 in which they complained about the lack of Indian labor for the mines indicating that there were not 3,000 Indians in the country.[42]

With the exception of the figures provided by Valverde, the Indian population in all jurisdictions

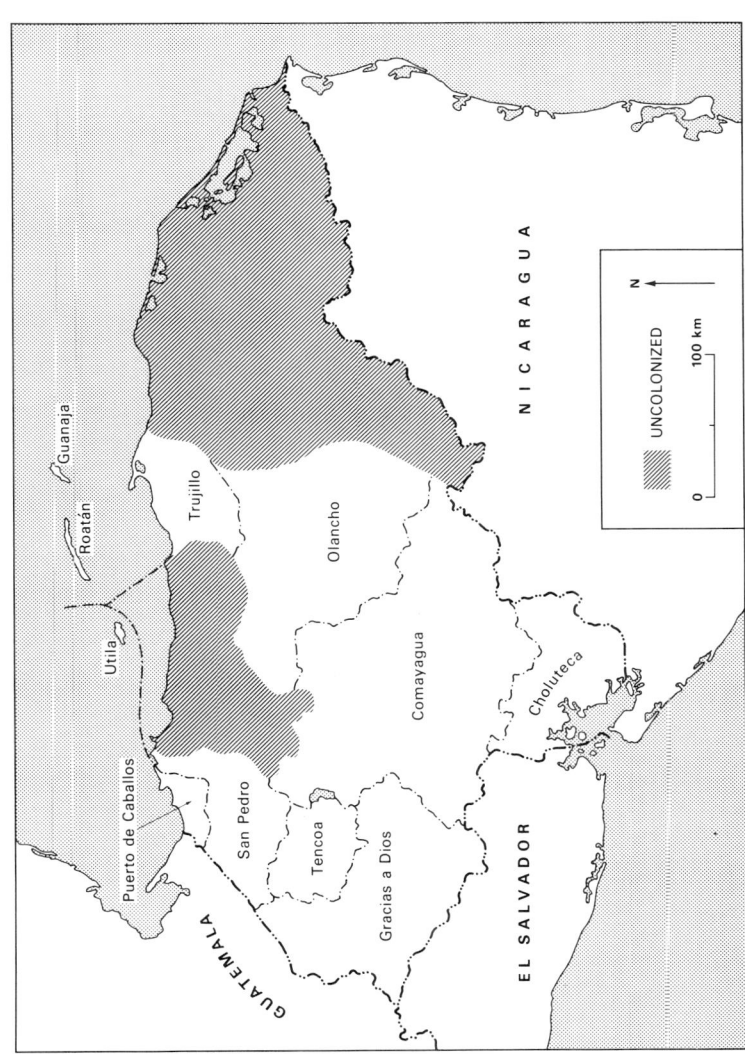

Figure 9.1 Approximate boundaries of jurisdictions and uncolonized areas of Honduras, circa 1600

TABLE 9.3
Population estimates for Honduras, 1582-1602

Jurisdictions	1582[a] Governor's account tributarios	ca. 1590[b] Memorial indios casados tributarios	1592[c] Servicio del tostones	1602[d] tostón
Comayagua	1,723	2,061	1,893	1,325
Gracias a Dios	1,369	1,618	1,088	639
San Pedro	444	620	532½	309½
Tencoa	249	301	205	124
Puerto de Caballos	80	116	88	66
Trujillo	337	436	301	209
Olancho	904	543	627	363
Total	5,106	5,695	4,734½	3,035½

[a] BAGGG vol. 11, pp. 5-19, Contreras to Crown 20.4.1582.

[b] AGI,MEX 257, Memorial de todos los pueblos . . . Francisco de Valverde, no date.

[c] AGI,CO 989, Treasury accounts 1592.

[d] AGI,CO 991A, Treasury accounts 1602.

NOTE: The figures for 1582 and ca. 1590 have been transformed to conform with the jurisdictions delineated in 1592 and 1602 and thus do not correspond with those contained in Tables 9.1 and 9.2.

shows a fairly consistent decline through the last quarter of the sixteenth century (1582 to 1602) at the average rate of decline (ω) of about 2.6% per year and a loss of about 40% of the tributary population. There were considerable variations in the percentage loss of the Indian population between jurisdictions ranging from -17% to -59% but they do not form any clearly identifiable spatial pattern.[43] Taking the jurisdiction of Comayagua for which data are available for a longer period from 1549 to 1612 it would appear that from the third quarter of the sixteenth century the rate of decline slowed down. The rates of decline for these periods are: 1549-1582 = -46.7% at the average rate of decline (ω) of -1.9% per year; 1582-1602 = -23.1% at the average rate of decline (ω) of -1.3% per year; 1602-1614 = -14.1% at the average rate of decline (ω) of -1.3% per year. It should be noted, however, that the decline for the period 1549 to 1582 would have been greater than that recorded, for in the former year only married male Indians were regarded as tributary Indians, whereas after 1578 other ablebodied males were also included in this category. It is also clear that the jurisdiction of Comayagua experienced a slower decline than most other jurisdictions in the country.

It has been shown that at the turn of the century there were about 3,500 tributary Indians in Honduras, taking into account some slight underestimation of the number of Indians as indicated in the records of the servicio del tostón, but they represented only a small proportion of the total Indian population of the country. There were in addition a large number of Indians who by virtue of their age, marital status, official status or physical disability were exempt from tribute payment. Men paid tribute from between the ages of 18 and 55, whereas women only paid until the age of 50. The age at which women began to pay tribute varied considerably. Initially only married female Indians were required to pay with the result that many postponed marriage. Later single women were legally required to pay tribute from 18, but in practice the age at which they commenced payment was extremely variable. Caciques and their eldest sons were exempt from tribute payment as were those who held secular and ecclesiastical offices in their communities. Individual Indians could also petition the Audiencia for exemption on the grounds of ill health or disablement. They could also avoid enumeration by being absent from their villages at the time the tribute lists were drawn up. The proportion of Indians who were absent from their villages often living in towns, on estates or in the mining areas was substantial towards the end of the seventeenth century, but in the sixteenth century did not account for a significant number. Some Indians who lived in these areas paid a reduced amount of tribute as naborías or lavoríos. These were originally Indians who worked and lived permanently in Spanish households and they did not account for more than a very small proportion of Indians who were living within the Spanish settled area.[44] It seems reasonable, therefore, to suggest that there were about 25,000 Indians in the colonized area at the end of the sixteenth century, thereby giving a ratio of tributary to non-tributary Indians of about 1:7. If it is accepted that the aboriginal population of this area was 600,000 then the depopulation ratio for the sixteenth century was about 24:1. There were, however, a large number of Indians who remained outside Spanish control. As has been noted, at the end of the sixteenth century there were said to be about 4,000 to 5,000 Indians between Trujillo and Cabo de Camarón,[45] and between 1622 and 1623 missionaries working amongst the Paya Indians inland from the north coast managed to settle 700 Indians in 7 villages and to baptise another 5,000.[46]

Although these Indians did not come under Spanish control during the sixteenth century they had intermittent contact with Spaniards and were thus affected to some degree by conquest, slavery, disease, and economic and social disruption. It is possible that the population in these uncolonized regions was reduced by a half or two-thirds during the sixteenth century leaving about 65,000 and 100,000 Indians in 1600.

CAUSES OF THE DECLINE

The causes of the decline in the Indian population were manifold, complex and interwoven. Contemporary observers identified three major factors--the Indian slave trade, conquest and disease--but the overwork and ill treatment of the Indians and the severe disruption to Indian economies and societies brought about by conquest and colonization contributed significantly to the decline in the Indian population and later miscegenation also began to take its toll. The Indian slave trade and conquest were only significant factors in the first half of the sixteenth century, whilst the other factors were operative throughout the period.

THE INDIAN SLAVE TRADE

The largest and easiest profits to be made in Central America in the first half of the sixteenth century were in the Indian slave trade. The Crown's attitude towards the enslavement of Indians vacillated throughout the first half of the sixteenth century as it tried to reconcile its humanitarian views towards the Indians with the practical needs of Empire. Finally in 1542 the New Laws abolished Indian slavery, although the order was not put into effect in Central America until 1548 when Alonso López de Cerrato became President of the Audiencia.[47] By that time, however, there were few Indians left to be enslaved and the trade in Indian slaves had long passed its peak. Comments have already been made concerning estimates of the numbers of Indians involved in the slave trade, particularly in Nicaragua, and here it is only necessary to emphasize its importance in contributing to the decline in the Indian population in Honduras and to note that it did not affect all areas equally. The worst affected areas were the hinterlands of the ports, notably Trujillo, whilst it was noted that those Indians living in inland areas were protected by their remoteness from the coast.[48] When Cortés arrived in Honduras in 1525 the Bay Islands had already been depopulated as a result of enslaving raids from Cuba, Española and Jamaica[49] and in 1527, 2,000 Indians from the neighboring coast of Trujillo and from Olancho were enslaved by the Governor, López de Salcedo, and taken to Nicaragua for export.[50] In 1530 Andrés de Cerezeda complained that Vasco de Herrera had made war on Indians in the vicinity of Trujillo and had enslaved so many Indians that in villages which had possessed 1,000 souls only 30 were left.[51] Thus in 1547 Bishop Pedraza reported that villages of 3,000, 2,000, 1,000, 800 and 600 houses which had existed in the vicinity of Trujillo had been reduced to 150 and 180 people, whilst one village located five leagues from the town which had possessed 900 houses had been completely depopulated such that the only survivor was the daughter of the cacique who had hidden under a boat.[52] The area around Naco was also badly affected. Bishop Pedraza maintained that when Andrés de Cerezeda entered the valley of Naco there had been between 8,000 and 10,000 men but by 1539 there were only 250 left.[53] This was confirmed by the Governor, Francisco de Montejo, who reported that Cerezeda had destroyed 27 to 28 villages in the valley of Naco carrying off the Indians in chains.[54] By 1586 the "great province of Naco" had been reduced to less than ten Indians.[55] Given this scale of depopulation it is reasonable to suggest that about 100,000 to 150,000 Indians were enslaved and exported from Honduras, both to the Caribbean islands and Guatemala, as well as south through Nicaragua to Panama and Peru.

CONQUEST

The conquest of Honduras was a protracted affair during which innumerable battles were fought and many Indians killed. Conquest was difficult because of the presence of a large number of Indian groups, which were not integrated by any political structure through which the Spanish could achieve control. The whole area thus had to be conquered piecemeal. No sooner had one group been pacified than it revolted, often with increased resistance, against the harsh treatment meted out to it by the Spanish with the result that the whole process of pacification had to begin again. Meanwhile the rebellious nature of the Indian groups provided justification for their enslavement. In addition <u>conquistadores</u> moving south from Mexico and Guatemala and north from Panama met in Honduras and the country became a battleground for rival Spanish forces. Efforts to pacify the area were thus accompanied by battles between the Spaniards themselves and even between rival elements of the same faction, generally using Indians as fighting forces. Altogether it took the Spanish nearly twenty years to achieve political control of the area.[56] Conquest and enslavement went hand in hand so that it is difficult to estimate the numbers that were killed in battle as opposed to those who were enslaved; the impression given is that conquest was a more significant factor in the decline of the Indian population in Honduras than it was in the neighboring countries of Guatemala and Nicaragua, where political control was more easily achieved using the existing native political organization.[57] Particularly disruptive was the conquest of western Honduras in 1536 by Pedro de Alvarado with the help of 3,000 Indian auxiliaries from Guatemala known as Achies (or Aches), who were notorious for looting Indian villages and roasting people alive. In 1539 Governor Montejo reported that Taloa only possessed 40 houses whereas when Alvarado arrived there had been 400 and other villages had been depopulated as follows: Carcamo from 500 houses to 20; Araxagua from 250 to 40; Yopoa from 270 to 30 and Lepaera from 400 to 70 or 80.[58] As a result of this conquest Bishop Pedraza maintained that altogether 6,000 Indians had been killed, enslaved or sacrificed, of which 3,000 had been shipped to Guatemala or sold in the Caribbean islands.[59] This was only one of the many campaigns that were conducted in Honduras and as such it seems reasonable to suggest that between 30,000 and 50,000 Indians were killed as a result of conquest.

DISEASE

Diseases were undoubtedly a major factor in the decline of the Indian population of Honduras. Epidemic diseases attracted most attention from contemporary observers but there were other unrecorded diseases, particularly intestinal ones such as typhoid, paratyphoid, bacillary and amoebic dysentery, hookworm and other helminthic diseases, which took their toll and increased the susceptibility of the Indians to other diseases. The first recorded epidemic disease in Middle America was smallpox, which was introduced into Mexico in 1520.[60] In 1520 and 1521 Guatemala was ravaged by disease but it is uncertain whether it was smallpox; it has been suggested that it was influenza.[61] The only reference to disease spreading further south at this time comes from an account written in 1527, which stated that it was necessary to introduce slaves to "Panama City, Nata and the port of Honduras" because smallpox had killed off the Indians there.[62] In 1531 Guatemala and Nicaragua appear to have been ravaged by a disease, probably some form of plague[63] but the only reference to its presence in Honduras comes from Herrera, who said that two years before the major outbreak of measles, which was in 1533, "there was a general epidemic of pains in the side and stomach, which also carried away many Indians." The measles epidemic appears to have hit Honduras badly. Herrera describes the epidemic as follows:

> At this time there was such a great epidemic of measles
> in the province of Honduras spreading from house to
> house and village to village, that many people died;
> and although the disease also affected the Spaniards . . .
> none of them died . . . . This same disease of measles
> and dysentery passed to Nicaragua where also many Indians died.[64]

In Honduras Oviedo maintained that the measles epidemic and other diseases had killed half of the population and the most susceptible were those who were servants in Spanish households or workers on Spanish estates.[65] Since diseases do not act uniformly but are affected by environmental factors such as population density, the degree of interpersonal contact, sanitation, dietary habits and immunity, it seems likely that there would have been great spatial variations in the proportion of Indians killed by the disease and the estimate of one half of the population is likely to have been a local maximum. Nevertheless it is clear that a substantial proportion of the decline in the Indian population can be attributed to successive waves of disease.

Over a decade later in 1545 an epidemic of either pneumonic plague or typhus struck Mexico and Guatemala, but it does not appear to have spread further south at that time.[66] In fact there is little evidence of either of these diseases in Honduras throughout the colonial period and it seems likely that, with the exception of the west of the country, they were unable to survive in the warmer climatic conditions. In 1578 there was an outbreak of <u>romadizo</u> in Nicaragua, generally translated as catarrh or hay fever, which affected the Spaniards as well as the Indians.[67] It is possible that the disease was a mild form of pneumonic plague unable to become more virulent in the unfavorable climatic conditions.

There is some controversy over the origins of the tropical diseases yellow fever and malaria, and whether either was present in Central America in the sixteenth century. Yellow fever is generally considered to be an introduction from the Old World. The first agreed epidemic of yellow fever occurred in Yucatán and Cuba in 1648; Ashburn effectively argues that skin coloration recorded in the sixteenth century was the result of starvation rather than yellow fever.[68] Recent zoological and historical evidence, however, suggests that sylvan yellow fever may have been present in Latin America in pre-Columbian times.[69] If this was the case then outbreaks of the disease in the tropical coastal lowlands of Central America in the sixteenth century cannot be ruled out. Nevertheless it was only at a later date that these coasts, and particularly Panama, earned the reputation of being unhealthy.[70] Similar comments may be made with respect to malaria. It now seems certain that malaria was introduced from the Old World. This is based on the fact that Indian populations in Latin America do not produce polymorphisms resistant to malaria, whereas those in Africa do, and the fact that the malarial parasites are relatively unspecialized and have a restricted number of hosts thus suggesting their recent appearance in the New World.[71]

ILL TREATMENT AND OVERWORK

As long as the Indian population could be seen to provide an inexhaustible supply of labor, little attention was paid to its preservation with the result that Indians were subject to ill treatment and forced to work long hours in poor conditions on inadequate diets and under threat of punishment for shortcomings. Many of the tasks in which Indians were employed were strenuous and contributed directly to illness and death; particularly important in Honduras were the transportation of goods, mining, and the manufacture of indigo. Indians were forced to travel with heavy loads over long distances, which often traversed climatic zones with the result that they fell ill and died.[72] In 1547 Bishop Pedraza reported 500 Indians, which had been hired out by the Governor, Francisco de Montejo, had died and he recorded that generally on the journey from Comayagua to San Pedro and Puerto de Caballos one half of the Indian carriers did not return, one third dying or becoming ill on the journey.[73] Despite a ban on the employment of Indians as carriers in 1541, the lack of paved roads and the difficult communications made the implementation of the order impossible.[74] Indian bearers were used primarily for moving goods between the ports, major cities and mining areas, but in the early years of conquest they were also used on expeditions to carry supplies. In 1527 López de Salcedo on an expedition to Nicaragua took with him 4,000 Indian bearers of which no more than 6 returned.[75] Conditions in the mines were sufficiently bad to stimulate Indian revolts[76] and persuade the Crown to ban the employment of Indians in the mines in 1546.[77] Similarly Indians were banned from working in the unhealthy task of manufacturing indigo. The process of indigo manufacture often required Indians to stand for several hours in vats of warm water which gave off unhealthy vapors and resulted in them catching colds and other respiratory infections. In addition the rotting leaves which were left after the manufacture of the dye attracted insects, which encouraged the spread of disease and earned the obrajes the reputation of being unhealthy places of work.[78] As a result, after 1581 repartimiento Indians could not be employed in this work, although they could work there voluntarily until 1601 when their employment in indigo obrajes was banned completely.[79] Other tasks in which Indians were employed, whilst not contributing directly to the death rate, were exhausting and with the poor diets that prevailed contributed to the susceptibility of the Indians to illness and disease. The burden of work which fell on the Indians was also increased directly and indirectly by demands made for tribute, the repartimiento, and other goods and services by <u>encomenderos</u>, royal officials--particularly <u>corregidores</u>, <u>alcaldes mayores</u> and <u>jueces de milpas</u>--and priests. Whilst each demand or exaction may have been small, together they combined to keep the Indians in continual labor like "frightened deer" leaving them little time to attend to their own subsistence needs.[80]

ECONOMIC AND SOCIAL DISRUPTION

Although very few contemporary observers attributed the decline in the Indian population to the economic, social, political, and ideological changes brought about by Spanish conquest and colonization, it is clear that their effects were considerable. Disruption to the Indian economy led indirectly to food shortages and famines and hence to a decline in the Indian population. Many Indians fearing attack and enslavement, or later excessive tribute and labor demands, abandoned their lands and fled to the hills, where they attempted to survive on wild fruits, vegetables, fish and game. Unaccustomed to such a form of livelihood many of them suffered from malnutrition and some died.[81] Meanwhile those Indians who remained on their lands experienced a decline in food production as a result of a reduction of their land holdings and a decline in labor inputs, particularly at the time of sowing and harvest, resulting from heavy demands for labor services, tribute, and other goods.[82]

There is some evidence to suggest that the breakdown in the social organization of Indian communities and the psychological impact of conquest also contributed to the decline in the Indian population. Whilst diseases and famines took their toll on the youngest and oldest sections of the community, enslavement, ill treatment and overwork largely effected the adult male population probably resulting in an imbalance in the sex ratio. It is uncertain, however, whether this imbalance effected the birth rate, but it seems likely that the endless tiring work which the Indians were forced to carry out would have dampened their desires to procreate, particularly since additional children would have placed an increased burden on already inadequate food resources. In addition Indians did not wish to bear children that would be born into slavery. These factors resulted in Indians practicing birth control by abstaining from sexual intercourse and inducing miscarriages, as well as practicing infanticide.[83] In 1584 the Bishop of Honduras reported that as a result of the overwork of the Indians "mothers kill their children at birth because they say that they wish to free them from the misery they suffer."[84] Apart from infanticide, the infant mortality rate would have increased as a result of malnutrition increasing their susceptibility to the newly-introduced diseases. Unfortunately there are no early accounts of the age and sex structure of Indian communities that could give insights into the effects of a decreased birth rate and an increased infant mortality rate.

MISCEGENATION

Although miscegenation occurred during the sixteenth century it did not make a significant contribution to the decline in the Indian population as it did in succeeding centuries. The degree of miscegenation was dependent on the intensity of contact between the races and was stimulated by the predominance of men amongst the white and Negro elements of the population. Miscegenation was most common in the towns, where Indians were ordered to work and where a substantial number of Indians lived as servants in Spanish households. It was also common in the mining areas of Olancho and later Tegucigalpa to which Negro slaves were imported. In 1543 it was estimated that there had been 1,500 Negroes working gold in the Guayape valley and about 2,000 were employed in mining in the whole country.[85] Although repartimiento Indians could not be employed in the mines, Indians were allowed to work there on a voluntary basis, such that in 1590 there were 200 Negro and Indian peons working in the Guacucarán mines and a further 90 in the mines of Tegucigalpa.[86] Later with the development of agriculture, Negroes and people of mixed race were often employed as domestic servants and overseers on estates where they came into contact with Indians, who worked as free laborers or under the repartimiento, and thus the rural estates also emerged as racial melting pots.

CONCLUSION

It is thus argued that the aboriginal population of Honduras was about 800,000, with 600,000 living in the area which was settled during the sixteenth century and 200,000 in the uncolonized east. This represents the highest estimate for the whole area to have been proposed to date. It has also been demonstrated that during the sixteenth century the Indian population suffered a decline that was more severe than in many other parts of Latin America. The depopulation ratio for the settled area during the sixteenth century was about 24:1, whilst the population in the uncolonized areas may have been reduced to one half or one third. Whilst the impact of disease and the general disruption to Indian life probably accounted for the greatest proportion of the decline, in Honduras several other factors contributed significantly to the mortality rate, which were to a certain degree peculiar to that country. First, the slave trade took a heavy toll on the Indian population because the area was discovered, conquered and colonized from an early date before the New Laws were introduced, which gave a measure of protection to the Indian population. Also, and more importantly, there were insufficient Indians in Honduras to form large <u>encomiendas</u> and there were no other economic incentives in the area to encourage colonists to remain there and preserve the labor supply. As such the country was raided for the only wealth it possessed--its Indian population. Conquest was also particularly destructive in Honduras, partly due to the nature of the native societies, which made political control difficult to achieve, and partly due to the country's location on the boundary of conflicting jurisdictions. As such the Indian slave trade and conquest together probably resulted in the loss of 130,000 to 200,000 Indians. It was a loss from which the Indians did not recover until the eighteenth century.

NOTES

1. M. J. MacLeod, <u>Spanish Central America: a Socioeconomic History, 1520-1720</u> (University of California Press: Berkeley and Los Angeles, 1973), p. 59; W. L. Sherman, <u>Forced Native Labor in Sixteenth-Century Central America</u> (University of Nebraska: Lincoln and London, 1979), pp. 350-352.

2. A. L. Kroeber, "Cultural and Natural Areas of Native North America," <u>University of California Publications in Archaeology and Ethnology</u>, Vol. 38 (1939), p. 166; H. F. Dobyns, "Estimating Aboriginal American Populations: An Appraisal of Techniques with a New Hemispheric Estimate," <u>Current Anthropology</u>, Vol. 7 (1966), p. 415.

3. J. H. Steward, "The Native Population of South America," in J. H. Steward (ed.), <u>The Handbook of South American Indians</u>, Bulletin of the Bureau of American Ethnology, 143, Vol. 5 (1949), p. 664.

4. A. Rosenblat, <u>La población indígena y el mestizaje en América</u> (Editorial Nova: Buenos Aires, 1954), Vol. 1, p. 102.

5. K. Sapper, "Die Zahl und die Volksdichte der Indianischen Bevölkerung in Amerika vor der Conquista und in der Gegenwart," <u>Proceedings of the International Congress of Americanists</u> (The Hague, 1924,), Vol. 1, p. 100.

6. Dobyns, op. cit., p. 415.

7. D. Radell, "The Indian Slave Trade and the Population of Nicaragua in the Sixteenth Century," in W. M. Denevan (ed.), The Native Population of the Americas in 1492 (University of Wisconsin: Madison, 1976), pp. 67 and 75.

8. Denevan, op. cit., 291. Denevan's estimates for the Central American countries are: Guatemala 2,000,000; Honduras and Belize 750,000; El Salvador 500,000; Nicaragua 1,000,000; Costa Rica 400,000; and Panama 1,000,000.

9. Bartolomé de las Casas, Breve Relación de la Destrucción de las Indias Occidentales (London, 1812), pp. 43-45; G. Fernández de Oviedo y Valdés, Historia Natural y Moral de las Indias (Biblioteca de Autores Españoles, Vols. 117-121, Ediciones Atlas: Madrid, 1959), Vol. 4, p. 385.

10. Sherman, op. cit., pp. 4-5. For a full discussion of estimates of the volume of the Indian slave trade see pp. 74-82.

11. MacLeod, op. cit., p. 52.

12. Archivo General de las Indias, Seville (hereafter AGI), Audiencia de Guatemala (AG) 9; and Real Academia de la Historia, Madrid (hereafter RAHM), Colección Muñoz (CM) A/108 4843 ff. 285-8, Pedraza to Crown 18.5.1539; AGI,AG 164, Pedraza to Crown 1.5.1547.

13. G. Benzoni, La Historia del Mundo Nuevo (Biblioteca de la Academia Nacional de la Historia, Vol. 86: Caracas, 1967), p. 163; Johannessen believes that Benzoni was referring to tributary Indians and thus multiplies the figure of 400,000 by three to give a total population of 1,200,000 (C. L. Johannessen, "Savannas of Interior Honduras," Ibero-Americana 46 [University of California Press: Berkeley and Los Angeles, 1963], pp. 29-31).

14. AGI,AG 39; and RAHM,CM A/107 4842 ff. 160-191, Cerezeda to Crown 31.8.1535.

15. F. A. Fuentes y Guzmán, Recordación Florida (Tip. Nacional: Guatemala, 1933), Vol. 2, p. 145.

16. AGI,AG 39; and RAHM,CM A/107 4842 ff. 160-191, Cerezeda to Crown 31.8.1535.

17. D. Z. Stone, "The Archaeology of Central and Southern Honduras," Papers of the Peabody Museum, Vol. 43, No. 2 (1957), p. 9.

18. AGI,AG 39, Cerezeda to Crown 14.8.1536.

19. AGI,AG 49, Celis to Crown 10.3.1535.

20. RAHM, 9/4663 No. 15, Valverde to Crown, no date.

21. Clark and Haswell have estimated that groups practicing shifting cultivation can achieve a population density of 20 persons per sq. km., whilst simple agriculture can only support 10 persons per sq. km. and those dependent on wild food resources only .1 per sq. km. (G. Clark and M. Haswell, The Economics of Subsistence Agriculture [Macmillan: London, 1966], p. 37). Indians in western and central Honduras practiced a form of shifting cultivation, though in some areas agriculture was more permanent in nature and thus may have supported higher densities. In eastern Honduras the Indians practiced agriculture to some degree, but they were also dependent on hunting, fishing and gathering; agriculture appears to have been most poorly developed amongst the Jicaque Indians. Nevertheless there were no Indian groups that were entirely dependent on wild food resources. It is suggested that the population density of the

Jicaque was 1 per sq. km., whilst other Indian groups in eastern Honduras, the Paya and Sumu, could have achieved densities of 10 per sq. km. The population supported by different Indians' economies could thus have been as high as 1,396,858 or even higher for if anything the population density estimates err on the low side, particularly for western and central Honduras.

	sq. kms.	estimated density	estimated population
Western and central Honduras[a]	42,563	20	851,260
Eastern Honduras[b]	52,897	10	528,970
Area occupied by the Jicaque[c]	16,628	1	16,628
TOTAL			1,396,858

[a] Departments of Cortés, Santa Barbara, Copán, Ocotepeque, Lempira, Intibucá, Comayagua, La Paz, Francisco Morazan, Valle and Choluteca.

[b] Departments of El Paraíso, Olancho, Gracias a Dios, Islas de la Bahia and half of Colón.

[c] Departments of Atlántida, Yoro and half of Colón.

22. AGI,AG 9; and RAHM,CM A/108 4843 ff. 285-8, Pedraza to Crown 18.5.1539; Benzoni, op. cit., p. 167.

23. Until the middle of the 1530s the amount of tribute that could be exacted from the Indians was at the discretion of encomenderos but, due to their excessive demands, the Crown ordered that official assessments should be made in New Spain and Guatemala in 1533 and 1534. Officials in Central America presented objections to implementing the order arguing that the income from encomiendas would decline and as a result encomenderos would leave the area. Nevertheless, in view of the benefits that had been derived from the implementation of the order in New Spain, the Crown repeated it in 1536. An order requiring official assessments to be made in Honduras was issued in 1538 but it was not carried out until the 1540s due to continued warfare, political instability and the reluctance of royal officials to implement it. (Archivo General de Centroamerica, Guatemala [hereafter AGCA] Al.23 4575 f. 28v. real cédula 28.2.1536; Fuentes y Guzmán, op. cit., Vol. 2, pp. 256-258; R. S. Chamberlain, The Conquest and Colonization of Honduras, 1502-1520 [Carnegie Institution of Washington Publication 598: Washington, 1953], p. 241; S. Rodríguez Becerra, Encomienda y conquista: Los inicios de la colonización en Guatemala [Universidad de Sevilla: Sevilla, 1977], pp. 115-117.)

24. It would appear that tasaciones of parts of Guatemala, San Miguel, San Salvador and Chiapas were made by the visitador Lic. Maldonado and the Bishop of Guatemala, Francisco Marroquín, in the late 1530s but there is no evidence that tasaciones of Honduras were made at that time (AGI,AG 156, Marroquín to Crown 20.1.1539; Rodríguez Becerra, op. cit., p. 117).

25. AGI, Justicia (JU) 299, residencia of the first Audiencia 1548 to 1550. It appears that tasaciones were also made of villages

in the jurisdictions of San Pedro and Comayagua (AGI,AG 9, Herrera to Crown 10.7.1545) but there is no detailed evidence of them.

26. The service of tamemes had been banned in 1541 (AGCA, A1.23 4575 f. 50 reales cédulas 28.1.1541, 31.5.1541). Following a reprimand from the Crown in 1546 (AGCA, A1.23 1511 f. 40 real cédula 5.7.1546) in 1547 the service of tamemes was removed from the tribute assessments for villages in the jurisdiction of Gracias a Dios (AGI,JU 299, residencia of the first Audiencia 1548 to 1550).

27. AGI,AG 9, Cerrato to Crown 28.9.1548.

28. AGI,AG 128, libro de tasaciones 1548 to 1551.

29. This excludes the village of Ynquibiteca for which no tribute assessment is indicated.

30. Recopilación de las Leyes de los Reynos de las Indias (Madrid, 1943), Vol. 2, lib. 6, tit. 5, ley 7, pp. 226-227, 5.7.1578.

31. AGI,AG 9, Audiencia to Crown 25.5.1555. For evidence of the tasaciones see the amount of tribute paid in succeeding years in AGI Contaduría (CO) 987 and 988, 1554 and 1562. For comments on the tasaciones of Zorita and López see L. B. Simpson, The Encomienda in New Spain: The Beginning of Spanish Mexico (University of California Press: Berkeley and Los Angeles, 1950), p. 152; A. de Zorita, The Lords of New Spain (Phoenix House: London, 1965), p. 36.

32. Batres Jáuregui, La América Central ante la Historia (Sánchez y de Guise: Paris, 1920), Vol. 2, p. 367.

33. A. López de Velasco, Geografía y descripción universal de las Indias (Real Academia de la Historia: Madrid, 1894), pp. 307-313. The source of his information for jurisdictions other than Comayagua is likely to have been different from the tasaciones made in 1548 to 1551, since all of those recorded in the libro de tasaciones are included in detail by Velasco; he only gives summary figures for other jurisdictions. His summary figure of 2,600 for the jurisdiction of Comayagua does not correspond to the total for the individual villages, which is 1,955. The latter figure is somewhat smaller than the total of 2,745 found in the tasaciones for 1549, but this is because the population of about one fifth of the villages is not included by Velasco. Where the population of the villages is recorded in both accounts, it is the same. The document in the Biblioteca Nacional, Madrid is reproduced in Colección de documentos inéditos relativos al descubrimiento, conquista, organización de las antiguas posesiones españoles de América y Oceanía (hereafter CDI) (Madrid, 1864-1884), Vol. 15, pp. 409-572, no author, no date.

34. Simpson, op. cit., pp. 154-155; MacLeod, op. cit., pp. 130-131.

35. AGI,AG 56, Cisneros to Crown 20.4.1582.

36. Boletín del Archivo General del Gobierno, Guatemala (BAGGG), Vol. 11 (1946), pp. 5-19, Contreras to Crown 20.4.1582.

37. AGI,AG 164, Bishop of Honduras to Crown. There are two copies of the same letter with different dates: 10.5.1582 and 12.5.1582.

38. Using the Bishop's account MacLeod, op. cit., p. 59, calculates the total number of vecinos naturales at 4,840. This is clearly a miscalculation although it is not possible to identify the source of the error. Sherman, op. cit., p. 351, gives the total as 5,840. He appears to have erred in transcribing the figure for

Olancho, which he gives as 400 and which is clearly 460 in the document and to have counted Agalteca and Tegucigalpa as separate jurisdictions instead of as parts of the jurisdiction of Comayagua, so that those areas have been double-counted.

39. RAHM, 9/4663 No. 15, Relación geográfica of Valverde 24.8.1590; and AGI, Mexico (MEX) 257, Memorial de todos los pueblos . . . Valverde, no date.

40. AGCA, A1.23 1513 f. 719, real cédula 1.1.1591.

41. AGI,CO 989, 990, 991A and 992, Treasury accounts 1592 to 1614. The accounts for the whole country from 1592 to 1602 show a steady decline in income as follows:

1592	4,734½ tostones	1598	3,302
1593	incomplete	1599	--
1594	4,055½	1600	3,094½
1595	--	1601	2,924½
1596	3,619	1602	3,035½
1597	--		

42. AGI,AG 49, oficiales reales to Crown 23.7.1626.

43. The average rate of decline is calculated using Cook and Borah's coefficient of population movement ω (See S. F. Cook and W. Borah, Essays in Population History: Mexico and the Caribbean [University of California Press: Berkeley and Los Angeles, 1971], Vol. 1, pp. 89-91). The regional rates of decline for 1582 to 1602 are:

Comayagua	-23.1% at a rate of decline ω of	-1.3% per year.
Gracias a Dios	-53.3%	-3.9%
Tenoca	-30.3%	-1.8%
San Pedro	-50.2%	-3.5%
Puerto de Caballos	-17.5%	-1.0%
Trujillo	-38.0%	-2.4%
Olancho	-40.6%	-2.6%

44. There are no comprehensive accounts of the number of lavoríos in Honduras in the sixteenth century. However, a detailed account of the inhabitants of the parish of Tatumbla in 1689 reveals that they accounted for 3.3 percent of the total population of 2,658 which included men, women, children, Indians and ladinos (Archivo Nacional, Honduras [ANH], Paquete 4, Legajo 135, padrón 1689).

45. See footnote 15.

46. AGI,AG 371, Fray Joseph Ximénez to Crown 9.9.1748.

47. For a detailed discussion of Indian slavery in Central America see Sherman, op. cit., pp. 20-82.

48. Colección de documentos inéditos relativos al descubrimiento, conquista y organización de las antiguas posesiones españoles de Ultramar (CDIU) (Madrid, 1885-1929), Vol. 11, p. 400, Pedraza to Crown, 1544.

49. E. de Vedia, Historiadores primitivos de Indias (Madrid, 1918), Vol. 1, p. 147, Cortés to Crown 3.9.1526.

50. Colección Somoza: Documentos para la Historia de Nicaragua (CS) (Madrid, 1954-1957), Vol. 1, pp. 293-299, Treasurer of Honduras to Crown, no date but probably 1527. Of the 2,000 enslaved only 100 arrived in Nicaragua alive.

51. AGI,AG 49, Cerezeda to Crown 31.3.1530.

52. AGI,AG 164, Pedraza to Crown 1.5.1547.
53. Sherman, op. cit., pp. 49 and 380 reference to AGI, Patronato 170-145.
54. AGI,AG 39, and RAHM,CM A/108 4843 ff. 239-257; also CDI 24, pp. 250-297, Montejo to Crown 1.6.1539.
55. Fray Alonso Ponce, Relación breve y verdadera de algunas cosas que sucedieron al padre Alonso Ponce en las provincias de Nueva España (Viuda de Calero: Madrid, 1873), Vol. 1, p. 349.
56. The best account of the difficult conquest and colonization of Honduras is Chamberlain, op. cit.
57. For a comparison of the conquests of Honduras and Guatemala see S. Rodríguez Becerra, "Variables en la conquista: los casos de Honduras y Guatemala," in A. Jiménez (ed.), Primera Reunión de Antropologos Españoles (Universidad de Sevilla: Sevilla, 1975), pp. 127-133.
58. AGI,AG 39; and RAHM,CM A/108 4843 ff. 239-257; and CDI 24, pp. 250-297, Montejo to Crown 1.6.1539.
59. AGI,AG 9; and RAHM,CM A/108 4843 ff. 285-288, Pedraza to Crown 18.5.1539.
60. A. W. Crosby, The Columbian Exchange: biological and cultural consequences of 1492 (Greenwood: Westport, Conn., 1972), p. 47.
61. F. W. McBryde, "Influenza in America during the sixteenth century (Guatemala: 1523, 1559-1562, 1576)," Bulletin of the History of Medicine, Vol. 8 (1940), pp. 296-302; J. E. S. Thompson, "The Maya Central Area at the Spanish Conquest and Later: A Problem in Demography," Proceedings of the Royal Anthropological Institute of Great Britain and Northern Ireland for 1966 (1967), p. 24; Crosby, op. cit., p. 51; MacLeod, op. cit., p. 98; T. T. Veblen, "Native population decline in Totonicapán, Guatemala," Annals of the Association of American Geographers, Vol. 67 (1977), p. 490.
62. Colección de documentos inéditos para la historia de Costa Rica (CDHCR) (Imprenta Pablo Dupont: Paris, 1881-1907), Vol. 4, pp. 7-11, Instrucciones a los procuradores de la ciudad de Granada 10.7.1527; Crosby, op. cit., p. 51.
63. MacLeod, op. cit., p. 98 identifies the disease as pneumonic plague but the symptoms of the disease, especially as described for Nicaragua where the Indians developed swollen glands (AGI,AG 9; and CS 3, pp. 68-78, Castaneda to Crown 30.5.1531), suggest that it was bubonic plague.
64. A. de Herrera y Tordesillas, Historia general de los hechos de los castellanos en las islas y tierra firme del mar oceano (Real Academia de la Historia: Madrid, 1934), Vol. 10, dec. 5, lib.1, cap. 10, p. 72; Ashburn, The Ranks of Death: A Medical History of the Conquest of America (Coward-McCann: New York, 1947), p. 91 translates "cámaras de sangre" as dysentery.
65. Fernández de Oviedo y Valdés, op. cit., Vol. 3, lib. 31, cap. 6, p. 388.
66. AGI,AG 9; and CDI 24, pp. 442-447, Maldonado to Crown 31.12.1545; H. Zinsser, Rats, lice and history (Bantam: New York, 1965), pp. 194-195; Thompson, op. cit., p. 24; MacLeod, op. cit., p. 98; W. H. MacNeill, Plagues and Peoples (Blackwell: Oxford, 1977), p. 209.
67. AGI,AG 55, Moreno to Crown 8.1.1578.

68. Ashburn, op. cit., pp. 130-134; J. Duffy, Epidemics in colonial America (University of Louisiana: Baton Rouge, 1953), p. 140; MacNeill, op. cit., p. 213.
69. Denevan, op. cit., p. 5.
70. C. O. Sauer, The Early Spanish Main (University of California Press: Berkeley and Los Angeles, 1966), p. 279.
71. F. L. Dunn, "On the antiquity of malaria in the western hemisphere," Human Biology, Vol. 37 (1965), pp. 385-393; C. S. Wood, "New evidence for a late introduction of malaria into the New World," Current Anthropology, Vol. 16 (1975), pp. 93-104.
72. AGI,AG 9; and CDI 24:343-351, Maldonado to Crown 15.1.1545; AGI,AG 164, Pedraza to Crown 1.5.1547; AGI,AG 968B, Pedraza to Crown no date; AGI,AG 44, Cabildo of Gracias a Dios to Crown 16.2.1548.
73. AGI,AG 164, Pedraza to Crown 1.5.1547.
74. See footnote 26.
75. A. J. Saco, Historia de la esclavitud de los indios en el Nuevo Mundo (Cultural: Havana, 1932), Vol. 1, p. 173.
76. For example: CDI 24, pp. 352-381, García to Crown 1.2.1539; AGI,AG 9, Anon 21.2.1546.
77. AGCA, A1.23 1511 f. 40, real cédula 5.7.1546.
78. AGI,AG 10, Audiencia to Crown 4.4.1580; R. S. Smith, "Indigo production and trade in colonial Guatemala," Hispanic American Historical Review, Vol. 39 (1959), pp. 185-186.
79. AGCA, A1.23 1512 f. 594, real cédula 15.5.1581 and AGCA, A1.23 4756 f. 46, Ordinances 24.11.1601.
80. AGI,AG 164, Pedraza to Crown 1.5.1547.
81. AGI,AG 164, Pedraza to Crown 1.5.1547; AGI,AG 968B, Pedraza to Crown, no date; AGI,AG 44, Cabildo of Gracias a Dios 16.2.1548; AGI,AG 56, Contreras to Crown 20.4.1582; AGI,AG 39, Albardez to Crown 29.4.1598.
82. AGI,AG 39, and CDI 24, pp. 250-297; RAHM,CM A/108 4843 ff. 239-257, Montejo to Crown, 1.6.1539; AGI,AG 164, Pedraza to Crown, 1.5.1547.
83. Although there is little documentary evidence for such practices in Honduras, they are well-documented for neighboring Nicaragua and the experience of the two countries, particularly when the Indian slave trade was at its height, is likely to have been similar (AGI,JU 293, and CS 7, pp. 151-224, Petition against the conduct of Castañeda 16.11.1541; CDHCR 6, pp. 199-211, Rodríguez to Crown 9.7.1545; Saco, op. cit., Vol. 2, p. 168).
84. AGI,AG 164, Bishop of Honduras to Crown 20.4.1584.
85. AGI,AG 9, and RAHM,CM A/110 4845 f. 108v; and CDI 24, pp. 343-351, Maldonado to Crown 15.1.1543; RAHM,CM A/110 4845, oficiales reales to Crown 20.2.1543.
86. AGI, Patronato 183-1-16, Antonelli and López de Quintanillas to Crown 7.10.1590.

10
Eighteenth-Century Population Change in Andean Peru: The Parish of Yanque

N. David Cook

Eighteenth century parish registers in Latin America allow the historical demographer to reconstruct the population history of specific locales, and, as the results of regional studies become available, provide the material to develop a more global view of the evolution of population, and the relationship between population and social, economic and political history. In contrast to the limited number of sixteenth and seventeenth century parish registers remaining in parts of Middle and South America, records of the eighteenth century are abundant, and should furnish ample documentary evidence for comparative analysis.[1]

Local parish studies are particularly well-advanced in Mexico. There are to date several investigations of parishes which chronologically span more than a century.[2]

The study of eighteenth century Peruvian population history is, by comparison with Mexico, still in its infancy. General reviews of the subject have been published. Vollmer's compilation of eighteenth century censuses in Spain; Kubler's research in Peruvian archives on the late colonial and national period Indian population; and Robinson and Browning's critical review of the deficiencies of eighteenth century Peruvian censuses introduce the field.[3] Macera has published several volumes of population data for eighteenth and nineteenth century Peru, but Mazet's thorough investigation of the parish of San Sebastián of Lima from 1562 to 1689 is the first modern study of a Peruvian parish series.[4] Unfortunately for our purposes, Mazet's work does not continue into the eighteenth century, although the author is planning on extending the research chronologically. Coleman's study

---

Investigation in Peru for this project (1977) was funded by the Wenner Gren Foundation for Anthropological Research. My wife, Alexandra Parma Cook, collaborated in all aspects of the study, from the collection of data to the final revisions of the manuscript.

of Trujillo, 1600-1784, which includes population analysis, is based primarily on a series of colonial censuses rather than parish registers.[5] The same is true of Mörner's survey of Cuzco's population.[6] Cushner uses parish registers with great success in his investigation of slave mortality and reproduction on coastal Jesuit haciendas for the period from 1714 to 1767.[7] Population change during a single decade, 1738-1747, in the parish of Yanahuara, the Indian suburb of Arequipa, has been examined by Cook.[8]

Much is to be gleaned from research in parish archives. Although the investigation can at times be tedious, the results enhance our understanding of not only local demographic developments, but also social and economic history at a broader level. The purpose of the present article is to analyze parish data from the Andean highland Indian community of Yanque from 1685 to 1800, in the hope that the study will stimulate others to probe the rich historical data in Peruvian parish archives.

THE SETTING

The community of Yanque, the Spanish colonial administrative center for the control of the Collaguas Indians, is located in the south Peruvian Andes about one-third the distance from Arequipa to Cuzco (Figure 10.1). In the pre-modern era the trip by mule or horse required a journey of several days, although the air distance from Arequipa to Yanque is only about 85 kilometers. Yanque lies on the south side of the Colca River, whose valley provides water and agricultural lands for a series of settlements. The Colca rises on the edges of the snow-capped peaks and windswept puna at elevations from 4000 to 5000 meters, in the direction of Lake Titicaca. It then descends through a break in the mountains as it flows towards the Pacific Ocean. The downward plunge moderates as the Colca enters an elongated intermontane basin at the village of Tuti (3800 m.) until it enters a precipitous canyon west of Cabanaconde (c. 3200 m.) and empties into the Majes River for its brief journey to the sea. The inhabitants of the valley live in a series of villages, more than 50 kilometers in distance east to west (Figure 10.2). The aerial photographs of the Johnson mission provide one of the first twentieth century views of the valley. The viewer is immediately struck by the spectacular terraced hillsides and irrigation canals, and well planned villages in the valley. Until recently, however, access from the outside to the valley has been difficult. The Greater Majes Irrigation project has been responsible, in the last decade, for the construction of a reasonably good all-season road into the region. Relatively reliable bus transportation is now available for

245

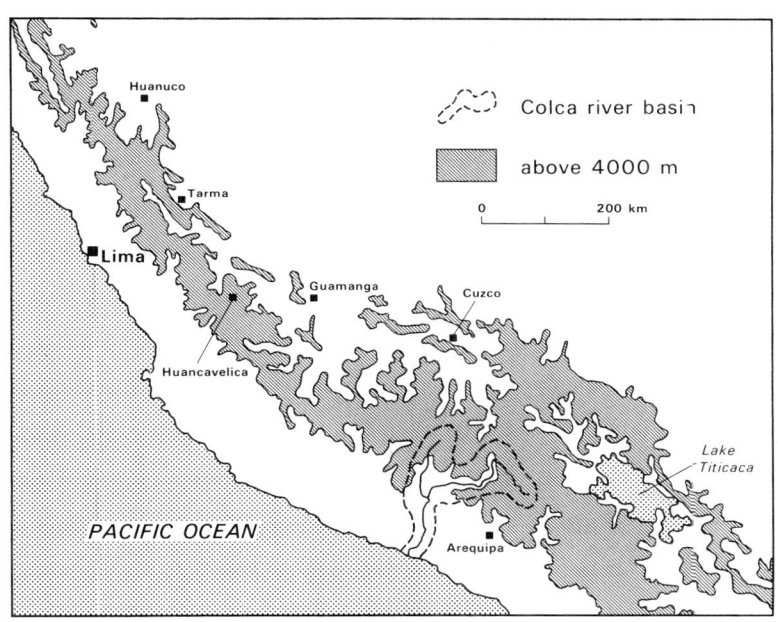

Figure 10.1   The Colca River basin, Peru

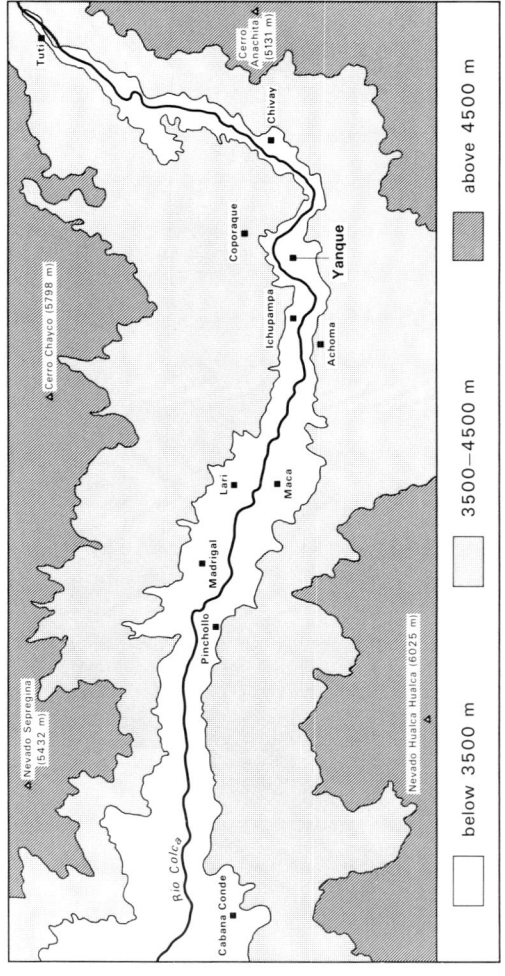

Figure 10.2 Yanque and the middle Colca Valley

villagers who need to make the eight to ten hour trip to the departmental capital of Arequipa. Change in the valley has consequently rapidly accelerated.[9]

A late colonial description of the villages and their agricultural products remains as valid now as it was when it was written in 1804. The "Memoria de la Santa Iglesia de Arequipa" was authored by Xavier Echeverría (1748-1826). His description of the parishes in the Colca valley is especially complete. Tisco, the major settlement at the upper end of the valley, is at too high an elevation for permanent farming. Livestock production, however, was a major activity from pre-conquest times. Copper veins were at one period worked extensively. Mercury was discovered nearby at Chununi (between Tisco and Sivayo), but was unexploited when Echeverría composed his report. Callalli also was dependent primarily on livestock, although it was warm enough there for the inhabitants to cultivate potatoes, oca and cebada (a type of barley). The village of Chivay (3693 m.), although cold, provided potatoes, barley, quinoa and some beans. Coporaque was the first village in the valley in which corn could be cultivated. Potatoes and livestock were also produced. The fact that Coporaque was at the upper limit of corn cultivation and that it was the major center of preColumbian settlement and political control, suggests a possible correlation which should be examined in the context of other valley systems.

Yanque (3417 m.), on the south side of the valley, and with more land under cultivation, produced corn, potatoes, beans, oca and barley on the surrounding terraced fields. Inhabitants of Yanque, more numerous than the villages higher in the valley, transported agricultural produce to Arequipa, and worked in Spanish vineyards of the Vitor valley to provide cash to pay tribute and debts. Just below Yanque a bridge was built across the Colca in 1801, using labor from Yanque and Maca. Maca (3267 m.), down the valley across the river and around a sharp bend, produced corn, wheat, potatoes, and alfalfa. Products of the nearby anexo of Ichupampa appear to have been similar. Across the valley from Ichupampa, and also below Yanque lies Achoma, at an elevation similar to that of Yanque, but situated on the edge of a mountain spur, which was noted as a cold and disagreeable place. The lack of land resulted in a population more closely linked to livestock grazing than Yanque or Coporaque.

Lari, lower in the valley appeared to be a very poor village by the end of the eighteenth century. Madrigal (3252 m.), with its anexo Tapay, produced fruits and vegetables and had an extensive trade based on these items. Cabanaconde produced wheat, corn and potatoes and in a valley toward the Majes river, some fruit. Two smaller villages were nearby--Huambo and Pinchollo. The pasturelands above Cabanaconde were inhabited by runaway burros, that were captured and used for transportation in the valley. Even today, however, man and not animal or machine, is the most important carrier for the trade which takes place in the small plazas of the villages of the valley.[10]

THE SOURCES

The parish registers of Yanque are not complete. Franciscan friars, who Christianized the Collaguas region in the mid-sixteenth century, established their headquarters for the entire province at Yanque, rather than across the Colca River at the Inca capital of Coporaque. Yanque is closer to the Spanish colonial administrative center of Arequipa, than it is to Cuzco. Hence, for most of the colonial era Arequipa, and not Cuzco, was the primary link with the world of the Coast and the European invaders. By the end of the sixteenth century the Franciscans, and the secular clergy who administered to residents further down the valley, were following the Church injunctions for the careful keeping of parish registers. But the first full century's records for the village of Yanque appear to have been lost. The earliest remaining books for Yanque begin early in 1684, just about a century and a half after the Spaniards entered the Andean area.

In the early years separate registers were kept for the moieties of Yanque. The first baptismal record for the lower sector (urinsaya) is 10 March 1684, while the upper moiety (anansaya) entry is for 20 May of the same year. The moiety structure of Yanque has survived to the present. There was (and continues to be) little intermarriage between the residents of the two units. One might think of them as two distinct communities, sharing the same general living space, but occupying separate sectors. The Church in the center of the plaza acts as a focal point for the entire village, yet even the church is divided, with the residents of anansaya worshipping at one side, and urinsaya at the other. And the parish registers were kept separately, until at least 1754. That year the entries for baptisms and deaths begin to be kept in a single book, with the appropriate moiety, however, still designated. The ayllu affiliation is recorded on the respective series, again until the middle of the eighteenth century when it begins to be dropped from the registers. Even in the 1680s ayllu connections in the community of Yanque appear to be in process of decay, and therefore generalizations concerning the structure and function of the ayllu cannot be extended to the sixteenth century on the basis of the community's historical experience in the mid-colonial era.

The Yanque parish series (Table 10.1) is frustratingly

TABLE 10.1
The Yanque parish series, 1684-1800

	1680	1690	1700	1710	1720	1730	1740	1750	1760	1770	1780	1790	1800
Baptisms													
Anansaya		——————————————————————————————————											
Urinsaya		————————————————————					———————————————————————						
Marriages													
Anansaya		————————————————————————————————						—	————————————				
Urinsaya		————————————————————					———		————————————				
Deaths													
Anansaya		————————————————————————————					——————		————————				
Urinsaya		————————————————————					————		————————				

incomplete. Between 1684 and 1800 a complete set of the registers for both moieties runs only for 1684-1722, and 1783 to 1793. Only some forty percent of the full time period is complete. The largest gap is for urinsaya marriages between 1722 and 1780. A series for Yanque anansaya is only slightly better, with data from 1684 to 1722, 1728 to 1744, and 1780 to 1787. In the anansaya sector we have a total of 61 of 116 years with a complete set of marriages, births, and deaths. Thus the question arises, "What can be extracted from such incomplete data?" The answer, as will be demonstrated below, is only partly satisfactory.[11]

THE FLUCTUATION OF BIRTHS

The rise in births in the community of Yanque, as calculated using baptismal records, is minor in the period from 1685 to 1720. A slight upward movement is visible in the averages in Table 10.2 but by the mid-eighteenth century, a major transformation seems to have taken place. The average number of annual births nearly doubles by the 1760s, and becomes even higher between 1771 and 1776. But the rapid increase in births appears to have been sustained only to the end of the 1780s (Figure 10.3). The total births of the last decade of the century parallels the figures at mid-century. Several questions arise. Why did the pattern in births appear to change so sharply between 1720 and 1754? When did the change take place? Was it rapid, or were there gradual

TABLE 10.2
Averages for numbers of annual births, Yanque village

Years	Number
1685-1690	29.7
1691-1700	30.6
1701-1710	31.1
1711-1720	32.5
1754-1760	59.9
1761-1770	60.8
1771-1776	74.7
1784-1790	72.3
1791-1800	56.5

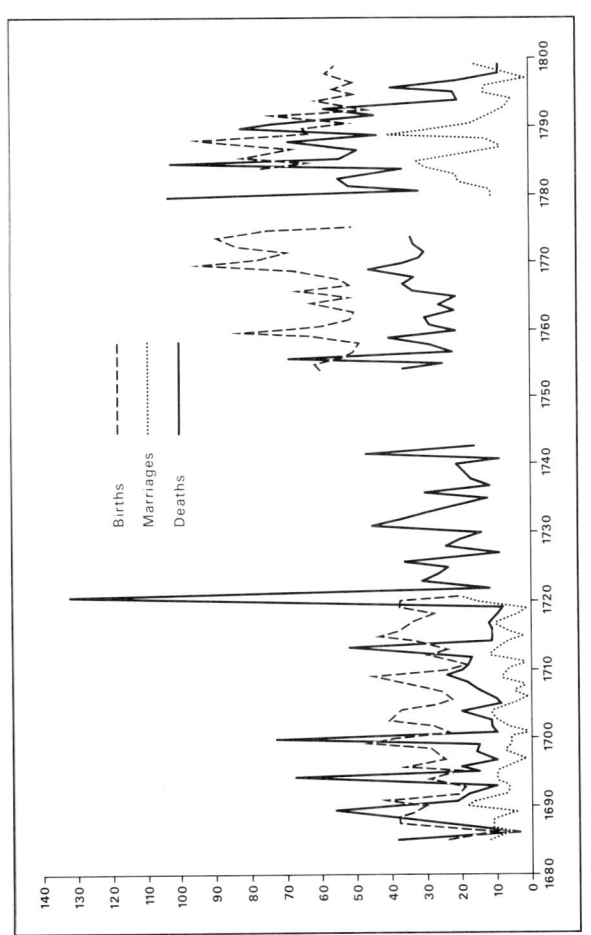

Figure 10.3 Births, marriages and deaths, Yanque, Peru, 1685-1800

transformations during the 45 year period? Also, why were the periods 1771-1776 and 1784-1790 characterized by such a large number of births? And what accounts for the slowdown by the last part of the century? Unfortunately, the extant information cannot provide answers to all such questions. However, it is at least possible to develop a tentative understanding of the changes of the 1720 to 1754 period by looking at one segment of the data which is extant: Yanque anansaya for 1728 to 1753. In the anansaya the gap in the data is far smaller than that of the urinsaya. The anansaya series is listed in Table 10.3. The anansaya information on births suggests that

TABLE 10.3
Average number of annual births in Yanque anansaya

Years	Average
1685-1690	14.8
1691-1700	16.5
1701-1710	18.7
1711-1720	18.6
1731-1740	21.1
1741-1750	21.0
1751-1760	29.1
1761-1770	31.9

the transformation to a higher number of births has been a gradual one, at least until 1750. There is no sharp increase in births, only a slow upward tendency until the 1750s. Then, in a single decade, the break is more abrupt. On average, the number of births each year between 1751-1760 exceeded the previous ten year period's annual totals by eight. During the next decade the upward movement continued but less sharply.

In a small rural Indian parish such as Yanque underregistration of births might be expected. How can one check on potential poor record-keeping and the significance of the problem? One possibility is via the sex ratio at the time of baptism. If large numbers of births were for some reason omitted, a sexual bias, on the part of the priest might be suspected. Is this the case with regard to Yanque? The average sex ratio in the period from 1685 to 1776, for which data are available, is 97.5

TABLE 10.4
Baptismal sex ratios

Years	Male	Female	Ratio
1685-1690	85	94	90.4
1691-1700	143	152	94.1
1701-1710	166	144	115.3
1711-1720	155	170	91.2
1754-1760	209	208	100.5
1761-1770	290	325	89.2
1771-1776	233	221	105.4
Total	1281	1314	97.5

(Table 10.4). The slight excess of females is not enough to lead to a conclusion that one sex went under-reported. A higher male than female infant mortality is clear. The figures suggest that the priests were fairly diligent in their collection of vital data for the parish. Perhaps the fact that Yanque was the religious administrative headquarters for the upper Colca valley explains a relatively complete annual record. Since age at baptism was recorded by the priests, it is possible to note that most infants were baptised within a week of birth, many on the first day itself. We do not, of course, have a record of stillbirths, nor do we have a count of infants who died within the first few hours of life. Nor, by the end of the eighteenth century, are we sure of the true yearly number who died in the puna before the priest made his periodic rounds of the chapels to perform his religious duties. It is evident that not all births were reported, but even though the total number omitted from the registers is impossible to ascertain, the Yanque series indicate that at least there was little bias between the recording of males and females on the part of the church record keepers.

THE TREND OF MARRIAGES

The marriage registers are the least complete of the three series. Combined data for the Yanque moieties are not available from 1723 until late 1780. In spite of this long break, it is useful at least to compare the early series with the latter. For the purposes of analysis, as with births and deaths, the same chronological

TABLE 10.5
Average annual marriages in Yanque

Years	Average
1685-1690	10.2
1691-1700	7.9
1701-1710	6.0
1711-1720	7.3
1781-1790*	22.2
1791-1800	10.1

*Forastero marriages are included, but not Spanish-Indian or Mestizo-Indian unions.

divisions will be made.

At first glance, it is evident that the average number of marriages in the first two decades of the eighteenth century did not match the number in the last part of the previous century (Table 10.5). But most striking is the very large average of the 1780s, then a decline in the 1790s to a level very similar to the decade of the 1680s. Variations in the annual number of marriages (Table 10.6) are greater than the variations in the births. Once again, the more complete series for the anansaya permits a closer view of changing marriage patterns.

In Yanque anansaya we see a marked increase in the number of marriages in the decade of the 1720s (Table 10.7). This level is roughly maintained until 1749. Then, if we carry the average for the three years 1751 to 1753, the number for anansaya slightly exceeds 10 per year. In the birth series for Yanque anansaya we also noted a sharp increase in the 1750s.

THE DEATH SERIES

The most complete sets of data, for both anansaya and urinsaya, relate to deaths. The only gaps which exist are between 1743-1754 and 1774-1780. The mortality statistics demonstrate vividly both general trends and the periodic devastation wrought during epidemic years. For analysis of the death patterns the results of both the moieties have been combined. In the last decade of the seventeenth century and first two decades of the eighteenth century, the average yearly number of deaths ranged in the low to mid-twenties. Then, in the period

TABLE 10.6
"Normal" monthly patterns of marriage in non-epidemic years*

Month	Average number
January	0.7
February	1.6
March	0.3
April	1.0
May	0.6
June	1.8
July	1.4
August	1.1
September	0.8
October	1.6
November	1.5
December	0.8

*Based on the experience of 1701, 1702, 1704, 1706, 1708, 1781, 1784, 1791, and 1792.

TABLE 10.7
Average annual marriages, Yanque anansaya

Years	Number
1685-1690	4.7
1690-1700	2.9
1701-1710	3.0
1711-1720	4.3
1721-1730	5.9
1731-1740	5.4
1741-1750*	6.0

*No marriages listed for 1745 and 1746.

from 1720-1729 the figure nearly doubled. This large increase was predominantly the consequence of the 1720-1721 epidemic period. The number of deaths of the following decade, the 1730s, is more similar to the earlier years of the century. Between 1754-1774 the average number of annual deaths in Yanque seems to have risen to the low thirties. Then, by the last two decades of the eighteenth century the numbers increase. Part of the reason for the elevated figure for the 1780s lies in the fact that there were several years of high mortality: 1780, 1785, and 1788. In both 1780 and 1785, 102 Yanqueños died.

In the years between 1685-1800 for which data are available, we can pinpoint the years of exceptional mortality: 1689-1690, 1694, 1700, 1713, 1720-1721, 1731, 1742, 1756, 1769, 1780, 1785, 1788, and 1790-1791 (Figure 10.3 and Table 10.8). The surge in deaths can often best be seen when the epidemic year is compared with the year

TABLE 10.8
General Andean epidemics, 1685-1800, and Yanque*

Year	Epidemic
1687	Various, plus general contagion
1689	Yanque
1692-1694	Measles, (Cuzco, 1693), Yanque, 1694
1700	Yanque
1708	Lima, perhaps smallpox
1713	Yanque
1719-1720	Various: Smallpox, influenza, yellow fever, exanthematic typhus, pneumonic plague, Yanque 1720-21
1731	Yanque
1742	Influenza, Yanque
1746	Tabardillo, Lima
1749	Smallpox, Lima
1756	Smallpox, Mainas, Yanque
1764	Smallpox, Lima
1769	Yanque
1779	"Bone-Breaker" (influenza?)
1780	Yanque
1781	Typhus (yellow fever?) Callao
1784	Measles, Lima
1785	Yanque
1786	Measles and croup
1788	Yanque
1789	Measles--to Peru from Bogotá
1790	Croup and measles, smallpox, Lima
1790-1791	Yanque
1795	Measles, Lima, or scarlet fever
1796	"Tabardillos," Andaguaylas

*The major periods of mortality at Yanque are noted, but no symptoms are given in the parish registers. Based on Dobyns and Lastres (see notes).

preceding and following. For example, ten died in 1693, fifteen in 1695, and 68 in 1694. The figures for the 1700 epidemic are similar: 73 that year, opposed to fifteen the preceding year and ten the following. The most devastating epidemic occurred in 1720-1721, with 62 and 132 deaths respectively, but only eight in 1719 and twelve in 1722.[12]

In the epidemic period of 1720 we find one of the few mentions of disease symptoms. On 11 December, 26-year old Miguel Trujiano died, "without receiving the sacraments, having fallen dead from the peste." On 3 February 1721, a 60 year-old female passed away, also without sacraments because the peste did not allow time. On 9 June of the same year the priest noted that during the epidemic death came very quickly. In this case the victim was a thirty year old male.

Parish registers of the seventeenth and eighteenth centuries rarely record the cause of death. However, some unusual circumstances of death are listed. Often, the victims of lightning are noted by the parish priest. For example, on 20 February 1721, a sixteen year old boy, Sebastián, was hit and killed by a lightning bolt while on the road to Arequipa. On 20 October 1717 a ten year old boy died after being dragged by a horse. One of the worst accidents befell the community on 24 March 1715, when four men working on the bridge across the Colca canyon connecting urinsaya agricultural areas, fell into the

TABLE 10.9
Average annual number of deaths, Yanque Community

Years	Number
1685-1690	33.7
1691-1700	26.7
1701-1710	15.0
1711-1720	21.2
1721-1730	31.9
1731-1740	24.5
1754-1760	34.4
1761-1770	31.2
1771-1774	32.3
1781-1790	57.1
1791-1800*	31.5

*Separate book added in 1791, includes the puna surrounding Yanque, then apparently the sole book after 1793. Figures for this decade are questionable.

river and drowned.

Some other causes of death are occasionally noted. For example, on 5 August 1782, a 35 year old woman of anansaya died during childbirth; on 3 November of the same year, one Manuel Arequipa, a twenty year old from Vincocaya, was discovered with his throat slit in a ravine of one of the nearby hills.

In order to calculate the monthly cycle of mortality to distinguish seasonal fluctuations among the annual averages (Table 10.9), the experience of several non-epidemic years has been utilized. I believe this provides as close to a "normal" pattern for Yanque as is possible, given the nature of the evidence (Table 10.10). The small numbers involved provide an inadequate base for definitive generalizations. But there are, clearly, sharp variations from month to month in the series. March, April and May appear to be the months of lowest mortality. These months follow the heavy rains, and are the period of highest agricultural productivity, when food is most abundant. December, January and February are months of normally high rainfall, and certain diseases associated with warmer weather and higher precipitation might be expected. The reason for the high number of average deaths in June and September is less clear from the historical record.

The average age of death for adult members of the community (aged twenty or more) has been calculated for

TABLE 10.10
"Normal" monthly patterns of mortality in non-epidemic years, Yanque community*

Month	Average Number
January	1.8
February	2.5
March	1.4
April	1.4
May	1.4
June	2.9
July	1.6
August	1.7
September	3.1
October	1.5
November	2.2
December	2.8

*Based on the following years: 1701, 1702, 1704, 1706, 1708, 1781, 1784, 1789, 1791 and 1792.

TABLE 10.11
Average age at death for those twenty and above, Yanque*

Period	Males	Females
1691-1700	51.1	42.1
1781-1790	49.4	55.1

*For 1691-1700 there are a total of 36 males, 56 females, and for 1781-1790, 130 male deaths opposed to 118 female.

two periods: 1691-1700 and 1781-1790 (Table 10.11). These two decades were chosen so as to see if significant changes take place in the century-long span. The parish registers are usually inexact in their report of age at death. In most cases the age is listed as within the decades ninety, seventy, sixty or forty and so on. Such approximations appear with much greater frequency than an exact numeric age, such as 57 or 63. This is a similar pattern to that found in the colonial visitas, or padrones. Exactitude is impossible, but comparative generalizations, if carefully made, do shed light on major developments. The results are here analyzed by sex, so that at least the outlines of differential mortality can be seen. Most striking is the large number of deaths of women who were in their twenties and thirties in the 1690s. It is much rarer to find male deaths in these age categories. The obvious cause is a relatively high rate of mortality associated with childbirth. In the 1690s the average age of death for males is 51.1, for the females it is 41.2. In the 1780s a major difference occurs. The average age of death for men is slightly lower than before: 49.4, yet for women it is 55.1, which is significantly higher than the previous century. Why did this change take place? Was it true only for the single decade? Unfortunately the answers are not to be found in the data.

YEARS OF CRISIS

Periods of demographic crisis occur with some regularity during the eighteenth century. By far the worst was the period 1720-1721. Review of such crisis periods presents common patterns which help illuminate the demographic experience of the Yanque region. Some crises may be of solely local importance, others may extend to wider areas.

The crisis of 1685 began in late March, and continued

through July. All deaths were of children, under the age of seven. In 1689 an epidemic began in March, but lasted only until the end of May. Most victims were the old people of Yanque. In 1694 an epidemic commenced in August and ended in November. Most who died were under ten years of age, plus a handful of young adults. The disease could have been measles, which was recorded for Cuzco in 1693. The 1700 crisis extended from June through August and affected children under seven. In 1713 another epidemic peaked in October and November, with most of those who succumbed being children, with a few elders. The crises of 1695, 1689, 1700 and 1713 are not noted in the standard epidemic references for Peru as being years of exceptional mortality, yet it is evident that these were disastrous for the residents of Yanque.

The years 1719-1720 are critical for Peru's population growth. George Kubler's generalization that the first major epidemic to affect the aboriginal population of the Andean region occurred then is obviously incorrect, nonetheless 1720 was a year of major crisis. Dobyns suggests the disease was multiple, which my research tends to confirm. A general epidemic was reported in Huánuco from 1714 to 1718. Smallpox was noted in Socabaya in 1718 and Argentina in 1720. Influenza afflicted Andean residents simultaneously. It is also possible as Lastres posits, that a major component of the 1720 series is typhus. Dobyns suggests pneumonic plague or severe influenza but discounts the likelihood of typhus.[13] On the basis of the parish evidence of Yanque, two epidemics struck the community. The first occurred in January of 1720, in which almost all the victims were children. Perhaps this was an epidemic of smallpox. The next epidemic began in November 1720, and continued through June of 1721. This disease affected all elements of the population, but especially the older members of society. Large numbers between the ages of fifty and ninety succumbed. Only those in their twenties appear less likely to fall victim to the devastating epidemic.

The 1731 crisis was brief, and relatively insignificant reaching a peak in November and December. There was a stronger shock which hit Yanque in June and July of 1742, with 17 residents dying in the former month. Here most deaths were of children under six, but a few adults also died. Influenza was noted elsewhere in Peru that year. In November and December of 1756 a short but severe epidemic passed through. A total of 28 recorded deaths were listed in November. The vast majority of these were children. Perhaps the epidemic was of smallpox, recorded for Mainas in 1756 in Peruvian epidemiological research.

The single month with the highest number of deaths in Yanque was July of 1780, when 51 members of the community died. An epidemic began in May and continued at

least through July, and almost all who died were children
under six. Might this be influenza, which was recorded
elsewhere in 1779? Next, a crisis took place from August
through December of 1785. In the month of August, adults
were the victims, but from September to the end of the
period children predominated. November was especially
bad, with 29 people dying. Measles is noted in Lima for
the preceding year. In December of 1787 and January of
1788 another crisis took place. In these two months all
age sectors of Yanque's population were afflicted. Measles and croup are recorded elsewhere in Peru the previous year. The 1790 crisis was prolonged, from June to
the close of November. At peak mortality, children were
the primary victims. Measles, croup and smallpox are
noted in Lima the same year.

What monthly patterns are visible in the figures?
October, November and December are bad months for years
of demographic crisis in Yanque. During the normal years
high mortality commences in September, with a lull in
October. These are the last of the dry months of the local agricultural cycle. The rains which provide the
moisture for the planting season begin in earnest, normally late in December. Daily rains continue until April
to May. This is Yanque's main growing season, and beginning in March it is also the period of generally lowest
mortality. There are exceptions to the pattern: the
1720-1721 epidemic clearly breaks the normal pattern.
Table 10.10, based on average monthly deaths of ten non-
epidemic years of the century, gives a general, if not
exact illustration of this pattern.

What else do we learn from the Yanque death registers? First, the standard works on Peruvian epidemic
history are incomplete, at least insofar as local histories are taken into consideration. To have a more comprehensive picture of eighteenth century epidemics, several
local studies should be undertaken, in diverse geographical regions of the Andes, which are composed of different
ecological systems. It would be useful to compare these
results, not only with each other, but with local studies
of other regions of eighteenth-century Hispanic America.

Further, it is quite clear from the death registers
that in reality we know little of the true causes of
death of the residents. On rare occasions the parish
priest did note the cause of death, but eighteenth century notations in Yanque are unusual. The diagnosis of
measles in Lima in 1784 does not necessarily mean that
Yanqueños suffered the disease the following year. Furthermore, one must be extremely cautious of any of the
eighteenth century diagnoses in even a major city of
Spanish South America.

MIGRATION AND MISCEGENATION

Yanque parish registers provide information on the geographical and social background of individuals. While data are included within the three record groups, the marriage registers give us the best picture of the origin of adult, working aged inhabitants. The marriage series provides some tentative views of migration to the community during the years from 1685 to the end of the following century.

Of the slightly more than forty marriages which take place from 1685-1689, six local males married females from outside the village. Three were from nearby Achoma, two from Chivay, and one from Yauri in Cavanas. In only three cases did outside men marry local women. Here the origins were more dispersed: Arequipa (San Lázaro), Cayma, and Quiquixana. And in three marriages, both parties were from outside Yanque: one couple from Pucara in Lampas, a man from Cibayo and a woman from Andaray, and a male of the neighboring Coporaque who married a woman from Arequipa (San Lázaro). There were apparently no mixes between anansaya and urinsaya during the five years.

During the decade of the 1690s approximately ninety weddings occurred in Yanque. Of these only two were outside the moiety: one anansaya male with an urinsaya female, and another case in reverse. In several cases male immigrants took local brides: one male from nearby Tisco, another from Cibayo, one from Coporaque. Females who married into the community were from Tisco, Ichupampa, Guasacache, Coporaque, and Lari. The outsider who had come from the most distant region was a male from Copacavana, on the shores of Lake Titicaca. He claimed to be of the _parcialidad_ of the Incas. In one case a Spaniard married an Indian: on 23 August 1696 Francisco de Lastarría married Teresa Casqui, an Indian from the village of Chachas.

In the following decade a remarkable change in the number of marriages outside the moiety takes place. In ten cases out of sixty, marriage was moiety exogamous. The anansaya females married outside more than males (six cases opposed to four). Three females were from Achoma, one from Ichupampa, another from Coporaque, one from Arequipa, and another from Tiquillaca. Two male immigrants married within the community. One of the immigrants was from Tuti, and the other originated in the village of Yacamaque.

The ten years beginning in 1710 saw about sixty-five marriages celebrated. Of this group of unions, six were outside the moiety. Two were of anansaya males with urinsaya women, but four were the reverse. Females from Monopata, Lari, and Pichigua married local men while Yanque males married women from Achoma, Viuñas, and

Chivay. In one marriage both were outsiders; a male from urinsaya of Caylloma married a female of anansaya Chivay. Then, on 17 September 1715, a Spaniard from Potosí, a widower named Sebastián Vasconcelos married a widow of anansaya, Rosa Cuadra. She had been married to Pedro Suri, and the marriage was included in the urinsaya register.

By the last part of the century, in the 1780s, marriage patterns indicate a relatively similar pattern of migration. About 210 couples united during the decade, of these only two marriages were between members of the opposite moieties. If anything, the moiety structure seems tighter in the later part of the century than it was before. Numerically more outsiders enter the community. Four males from Caylloma married into the village; there were two from Arequipa; two from Tisco; two from Juliaca; the same number from Cabinilla and Tuti; and one each from Coporaque, Langui in Cuzco, Cibayo, and Yauri. Fewer outside females entered; one each from Lari, Cibayo, Chivay, Sicuani, and Cabinilla. A large number of marriages were also celebrated in the puna. During the decade eleven marriages took place between residents of upland Ranran, nine from Casca and nine from Chuca, eight from Pulpería, six from Chalguanca, four from Coito, three from Rayo, two from Tocra, and one from Vincocaya. There were also several marriages between partners of different puna districts. The marriage records suggest dispersal of the residents of Yanque to the surrounding upland region during the final part of the century. Four cases of Spaniards marrying Indian women also occurred during the decade. In all but one instance the female was from urinsaya.

About 115 marriages took place during the closing decade of the century. Of these, five were moiety exogamous; in four of the cases the males were of urinsaya. Three men entered the community via marriage from neighboring Coporaque; two were from Tuti, with one each from Cibayo, Caylloma, Umachiri and Hacarí. Female migrants were from Umachiri, Tuti, and Pichigua. Several marriages were celebrated in the punas: six at Casca, three at Ranran, and one at Coito. One union was between a male of Ranran and a female from the punas above Lari. An indication of the complexity of late eighteenth century Yanque society can be seen in some of the combinations which took place. On 17 September 1795 a Spanish couple was united in Yanque, with don Jacinto Sánchez, from downstream Cabana marrying doña Paula Adrian from nearby Coporaque. Then, on 8 February 1796, Diego Caseres, a Spaniard living in Yanque anansaya, married María Perales, an illegitimate española of urinsaya. On 25 November 1795, a Spanish orphan of Yanque, named Domingo Bernedo, married Rosa Checa. Then on 27 January 1796, one Felipe Visa married a widow, Jacoba Suico.

This marriage is unusual for two reasons. In the first place, there is cause to suspect Felipe was a <u>mestizo</u>. As the priest states, there is some question as to whether Visa "is Indian as implied, or mestizo as he appears by the aspect, and for other reasons . . . ." The marriage took place with the bishop's dispensation which was allowed to Indians within the third degree of consanguinity. Perhaps the most interesting marriage of the decade, and an indication of the growing social complexity of even rural areas by the end of the century, was the marriage on 14 April 1795, of Alexo Corrales and Melchora Olmedo. The groom's mother was Ignacia Otanula, and the bride's parents were Antonio Felejo and María Carmen Gonzalez. Alexo was an illegitimate from Ichupampa but residing in Yanque. Melchora had come to the valley from Lima two years earlier. Both were slaves of the subdelegate of the <u>partido</u>, Don Joachím Miguel de Arnaco.

For the decades with data on the origin of marriage couples, the percentage of outsiders marrying within the community remains relatively constant. In about ten percent of the marriages, at least one of the partners is from another community. The periods 1685-1690 and 1710-1719 have averages which are higher, at about twenty-five percent for the earlier of the two, and fifteen percent for the latter. Male immigrants generally outnumbered female. Most migrants were from the nearby villages of the Colca valley: Coporaque, Cibayo, Chivay, Achoma, Pichigua, and Ichupampa. The number of migrants from beyond was relatively small. There are not even many who come to Yanque from the Spanish administrative center of Arequipa. Data are extant which suggest the eighteenth century flow of Indian migrants to the Arequipa region from the Colca valley was relatively strong, but obviously the information on the extent of this flow will be found in the Arequipa parish books, and the registers of suburban Indian communities such as Yanahuara and Cayma.[14] One factor stands out clearly and persistently in the Yanque registers: moiety endogamy. With the exception of the period from 1700 to 1719, when the number of moiety exogamous marriages roughly equals the number of unions outside the community, marriages between members of anansaya and urinsaya were quite unusual. Marriages between Spaniards and Indians were also rare. Only seven such marriages took place in the years 1685-1719 and 1780-1799, with four of the seven celebrated in the 1780-1789 decade.

In the last decade two marriages were recorded between Spaniards, a Spanish-Indian and Mestizo-Indian match, and a case of negro slaves uniting in matrimony in the Yanque church. What is most striking from such local evidence is the apparent stability of the community for the period from 1685 to 1800. Both moiety and racial exogamy are quite rare. The village remains essentially Indian in spite of the occasional influx of outsiders at various times during the period.

Yet the situation is not that simple. There is a remaining register for Spanish baptisms which covers the period 1685 through 1722. About 112 baptisms are recorded for the period, of these 51 occur in 1694, 1695, and 1713. From the data most of the entries appear to be Indians, not Spaniards. But some intermixture was noted. Permanent Spanish residents of Yanque were rare. A few examples provide an illuminating glimpse of the complexity of late seventeenth century society, as well as the specific experience of individuals. One case is that of Juan Gonzalez de Huelva and his wife María Veronica, who had one daughter in 1685, and a second in 1688. In 1685, two women, one definitely an Indian, had illegitimate daughters. The fathers were probably Spanish. In the following year, Pedro Cid, a Yanque resident (vecino) had an illegitimate daughter with one Tomasina Córdova, from Chincheros. Nicolás Martínez de Montoya and his wife had a son in 1687, but Nicolás had an illegitimate daughter by an urinsaya widow the next year. Miguel Pérez Romero had an illegitimate daughter by Juliana Angulo in 1688, and a son by an anansaya female, María Ana de Saavendra in 1689. Martín Pérez Romero appears to have had a stable union with his wife María Vasconcelos with children in 1688, 1689, 1690, 1691, and 1693, and 1696. In 1704 Don Alfonso Tinco and his wife Doña Bernardina Mendiguren y Buytrón had a daughter. In June of the same year Sebastián Joseph Romero and Gregoria Gonzalez, mulato slaves of the corregidor's wife, Doña Francisca Zaraya y Zarate, also had a daughter. Though legal unions between racial groups did take place, interracial liaisons outside marriage were much more typical; many illegitimate children appear in the baptismal lists, and abandoned infants are frequently reported.

THE TRENDS

The three series, side by side, illustrate if not the total population of the community of Yanque at a given point in time, then the gradual evolution of its population over a number of decades. The series of births, marriages and deaths elucidate the evolution of one moderate-sized, and relatively isolated south Andean village through the eighteenth century. The trends are important because they may have broader applicability. What are these trends?

During the last decades of the seventeenth century and the early years of the eighteenth century community growth was in all likelihood minimal. The difference between births and deaths was marginal. In fact, in the 1685-1690 period, deaths exceeded births. During the first decade of the eighteenth century the excess of births increases, but the epidemic period of 1720-1721 probably wiped out the gains of the previous decade. The twenty year period between 1754-1774 shows a very wide divergence in the excess of births over deaths. Yet the 1780s brings a narrowing of that margin, with a surplus of births similar to the early part of the eighteenth century. The 1780s was a period of exceptional mortality; though the number of births was high, the number of deaths that decade was much higher than earlier or later.

The community of Yanque was probably larger in 1799 than it was at the start of the century. Yet, demographic growth within the region was not continuous. Negative growth in the 1685-1690 period gave way to a gradually enlarging population. Growth accelerated in the 1710s, but the gains were subtracted by the impact of the 1720-1721 epidemic period. The years 1754-1774 are ones of continuous and accelerated population expansion for Yanque, but the epidemics of the 1780s, with several years of large numbers of deaths, again deplete the ranks of the village. The situation improves only slightly, if at all, in the last decade of the century (Table 10.12).

The eighteenth century was the world of Malthus. The era of improved medicine did not reach isolated communities of the Andean area until the introduction of smallpox vaccination. The campaign against smallpox began in Lima late in 1805, with the arrival of nine

TABLE 10.12
Baptisms, marriages and deaths, Yanque community

Period	Marriages	Baptisms	Deaths	B - D
1685-1690	10.2	29.7	33.7	-4.0
1691-1700	7.9	30.6	26.7	3.9
1701-1710	6.0	31.1	15.0	16.1
1711-1720	7.3	32.5	21.2	11.3
1721-1730	--	--	31.9	
1731-1740	--	--	24.5	
1754-1760	--	59.9	34.4	25.5
1761-1770	--	60.8	31.2	29.6
1771-1774	--	74.7[a]	32.3	42.4
1781-1790	22.2	72.3[b]	57.1	15.2
1791-1800	10.1	56.5	31.5	25.0

[a] 1771-1776 average

[b] 1784-1790 average

containers of vaccine from Buenos Aires. Vaccination reached Lambayeque, Huamanga, Piura and probably Cuzco, Ica and Arequipa in 1806. But the eradication of smallpox from Peru was not completed until the twentieth century.[15] Other diseases, such as measles, influenza, typhus, took their toll each time the susceptible population became large enough.

Unfortunately, we lack a series of eighteenth century censuses for the community of Yanque. The tribute records, with <u>repartimiento</u> data for the whole of the repartimiento of Yanque anansaya and urinsaya obviously include the other communities which made up the administrative unit: Callalli, Chivay, Coporaque, Maca, Achoma, and Ichupampa. There is, however, one count of Yanque which dates from the early nineteenth century, probably 1804. That year 885 residents were recorded in Yanque itself, with 1194 residing nearby, but counted within the administrative unit. Crude birth, marriage and death rates, using a three-year average for 1803, 1804, and 1805, give the following figures: births, 22.5 per thousand; marriages, 4.7 per thousand; and deaths, 10.7 per thousand. The resulting annual growth rate (obviously excluding migration) is 1.2 percent for the early years of the nineteenth century. By twentieth century standards, these figures are quite low, and there is clearly underregistration of vital data. But the growth of Yanque's population was destined to be limited. The community's urban and rural sectors (the puna surrounding the village) included a total of 2,079 in 1804, fell to 1,876 in 1843, then 1,578 at the time of Peru's first national census (1876), rose to 2,530 in 1940, then 2,545 for the third census of 1961, then declined to 2,170 for the most recent (1972) national count.[16] What is the meaning of these figures? Did the low point of the population curve of Yanque occur in the late nineteenth century? Why has there not been a very rapid increase in Yanque's population in the most recent half-century? Further research is required to shed light on the answers to such questions. It is evident that external and internal economic factors were influencing the community's growth during the eighteenth century and beyond. There was an obvious shift of population away from Yanque's "urban" core in the eighteenth century. Increasingly economic surplus became associated with the puna livestock grazing. An earlier era of forced Spanish urban concentration gave way to a more traditional Andean pattern of dispersed settlement. The precise dates for this transformation are not yet clear, but it should be possible to place the movement in its chronological context. In the nineteenth century, economic control of the puna resources was challenged, and it appears community Indians waged a losing battle as they faced the encroachments of private landholders. The outlines of the conflict are well established by the mid-nineteenth century. Then, the concentration of economic power shifted away from Yanque. The mining center of Caylloma drew both outside capital and talents. Even nearby Chivay, by 1940, was larger than Yanque. Chivay's growth accelerated as Yanque declined. By 1961, Chivay, geographically more conveniently situated where the road from Arequipa enters the Colca valley, was about half again as large as Yanque, and the disparity had widened by 1972. Whatever the internal population growth taking place within Yanque in recent times, it appears to have been siphoned off via emigration, to more active economic centers such as Chivay, or perhaps more important, Arequipa. The explosive urban growth of that Peruvian city since 1940 has been fed by the escape of not only Yanqueños in search of an elusive better life, but also other villagers of Arequipa's hinterland.[17]

The population history of Yanque may not represent the experience of all South Andean communities in Peru in the eighteenth century, but the results are at least suggestive of parallel developments elsewhere. Epidemics were not restricted to one locale. If disease struck Yanque in 1700, then it is highly likely that the same epidemic afflicted a much wider area. Similar patterns of mortality were shared by neighboring Indian communities. The movement of deaths followed weather and agricultural cycles. The demographic experience of Yanque reflects that of nearby native settlements in other ways. Droughts, earthquakes and other major disasters had a concurrent effect over a broad section of the south Peruvian Andes. Further, Indians in the southern section of Peru migrated to the colonial urban administrative center of Arequipa in the centuries following the foundation of the city. Yanque may also provide a good example of the social structure of south Peruvian Indian villages. The moiety was a distinctive characteristic of Yanque's organization. The strength and persistence of moiety endogamy is a feature which was probably shared by many Indian communities in the region. Further, the ayllu was an important part of the social organization of Yanque, but was in process of decay and atrophy in the eighteenth century. Yanque provides a clear glimpse of the demographic experience of the south Peruvian Andes during the period from 1685 to 1800. But the view is incomplete. Future research in other parish registers will assist in developing a truly comprehensive vision of the historical demography of the region.

NOTES

1. Several general works on parish research in Latin America are available. See Nicolas Sánchez-Albornoz, "Les registres paroissiaux en Amérique Latine. Quelques considerations sur leur exploitation pour la démographie historique," Revue Suisse d'Histoire 17 (1967), pp. 60-71; and Claude Morin, "Los libros parroquiales como fuente para la história demográfica y social novohispana," Historia Mexicana 21 (1972), pp. 389-418.

2. Thomas Calvo, "Démographie historique d'une paroisse Mexicaine: Acatzingo (1606-1810)," Cahiers des Ameriques Latines, 6 (1972), pp. 7-41; Claude Morin, Santa Inés Zacatelco (1646-1812) (Mexico City: Departamento de Investigaciones Históricas, INAH, 1973); Elsa Malvido, "Factores de despoblación y de reposición de la población de Cholula (1641-1810)," Historia Mexicana, 23 (1973), pp. 52-110; David A. Brading and Cecilia Wu, "Population Growth and Crisis: León, 1720-1860," Journal of Latin American Studies, 5 (1973), pp. 1-36; Michael M. Swann, "The Spatial Dimensions of a Social Process: Marriage and Mobility in Late Colonial Northern Mexico," in David J. Robinson (ed.), Social Fabric and Spatial Structure in Colonial Latin America (Syracuse University: Dellplain Latin American Studies, 1979), pp. 117-180; and the studies of David J. Robinson, Linda Greenow, and John K. Chance in this volume.

3. Günter Vollmer, "Bevölkerungspolitik und Bevölkerungsstruktur im Vizekönigreich Peru zu Ende der Kolonialzeit, 1741-1821," (Ph.D. dissertation, University of Köln, 1965); George Kubler, The Indian Caste of Peru, 1795-1940, Smithsonian Institution, Institute of Social Anthropology, No. 14 (Washington, 1952); David G. Browning and David J. Robinson, "The Origin and Comparability of Peruvian Population Data: 1776-1815," Jahrbuch für Geschichte von Staat, Vol. 14 (1979), pp. 199-222.

4. Pablo Macera, Tierra y población en el Perú, siglos xviii-xix (4 vols., Lima: Seminario de Historia Rural Andina, 1972); Claude Mazet, "Récherches Historiques sur le Pérou: la Population de Lima aux XVIe-XVIIe siècles: parroquia San Sebastián (1562-1689)" (M.A. thesis, University of Nice, 1975); and the same author's "Population et société à Lima aux XVIe et XVIIe siècles," Cahiers des Amériques Latines 13/14 (1976), pp. 51-102.

5. Katherine Coleman, "Provincial Urban Problems: Trujillo, Peru, 1600-1784," in Robinson, Social Fabric, pp. 369-408.

6. Magnus Mörner, Perfil de la sociedad rural del Cuzco a fines de la colonia (Lima: Universidad del Pacífico, 1978).

7. Nicolas P. Cushner, "Slave Mortality and Reproduction on Jesuit Haciendas in Colonial Peru," Hispanic American Historical Review, 55 (1975), pp. 177-199.

8. Noble David Cook, "La población de la parroquia de Yanahuara, 1738-47. Un modelo para el estudio de las parroquias coloniales peruanas," in Franklin Pease (ed.), Collaguas I (Lima: Universidad Católica, 1977), pp. 13-34; and the same author's "Recent Research Trends in Peruvian Historical Demography," Latin American Population History Newsletter, 1 (1978), pp. 3-9.

9. The Colca valley, well photographed by air in the famous Johnson expedition of the National Geographic Society presents one

of the most spectacular series of irrigated terraces of the south Peruvian Andes. In spite of this glimpse of the area almost a half century ago, the region has stimulated little scholarly investigation from the outside world. See George R. Johnson, Peru from the Air (American Geographical Society, Special Publication No. 12, 1930); Philip Ainsworth Means, Fall of the Inca Empire and the Spanish Rule in Peru, 1530-1780 (New York, 1932); and Handbook of South American Indians, Vol. 2, Plates 4 and 85. See also Máximo Neira Avendano, "Los Collaguas," (Ph.D. dissertation, University of Arequipa, 1961).

10. Francisco Xavier Echeverría, "Memoria de la Santa Iglesia de Arequipa," in Victor M. Barriga (ed.), Memorias para la historia de Arequipa (Arequipa, 1952), 4, pp. 80-104.

11. In spite of incomplete data, much useful information can be taken from the parish registers for social history. Peter Laslett presents a good argument for attempting the task in E. A. Wrigley (ed.), An Introduction to English Historical Demography from the Sixteenth to the Nineteenth Century (New York: Basic Books, 1966), pp. 1-13.

12. Henry F. Dobyns, "Andean Epidemic History to 1720," Bulletin of the History of Medicine, 37 (1963), pp. 493-515; and Juan B. Lastres, Historia de la medicina Peruana (Lima: San Marcos, 1951), 2, pp. 174-180, 299-303.

13. See N. David Cook, "La población indígena en el Perú colonial," Anuario de Investigaciones Históricas, 8 (1965), pp. 73-110.

14. For generalizations on migration from the Collaguas to Yanahuara see N. David Cook, "La población de la parroquia de Yanahuara, 1738-47," in Collaguas I, pp. 13-34.

15. Lastres, Historia de la medicina, 3, pp. 20-34.

16. The 1876, 1940, 1961 and 1972 census results have been published by the Peruvian government. See the appropriate returns for Caylloma, Yanque and Chivay in these volumes.

17. I was brought into close contact with the present-day residents of the Colca valley in 1974, through Dr. Franklin Pease, then director of the Museo Nacional de la Historia in Lima. The Museum had in its archive a nearly complete visita of the urinsaya half of the repartimiento of Yanque Collaguas, which was prepared by colonial officials in 1591. This census provides an excellent panorama of the late sixteenth century Indian world of the middle and upper Colca valley. A group of Dr. Pease's students at the Universidad Pontifícia Católica del Perú transcribed the document and prepared studies based on the rich data it contains. Through the support of the Peruvian Office of the Ford Foundation, Dr. Pease, a group of students, professors of the Universidad Nacional de San Agustín of Arequipa, and myself, were able to conduct preliminary field research in the valley in October of 1974. For an outline of the project see N. David Cook and Franklin Pease, G.Y., "New Research Possibilities in Los Collaguas, Peru," Latin American Research Review, 10 (1975), pp. 201-202. Father Pablo Hagan and Sister Antonia Kayser of the parish of Yanque provided, both times my wife and I were in the village, support and hospitality without which the research would have been difficult if not impossible. My thanks also to Dean Robert FitzGeral of the University of Bridgeport who assisted with University travel funds in 1979.

Index

Achies, 230
Age, 17, 19, 29, 33, 203, 227, 259
Altiplano, 36
Alto Perú, 25, 35
Ameca, 127, 133, 138, 144
Analysis
  catchment, 3
  diachronic, 158
  ecological, 7
Antequera, 93, 114
Arequipa, 244, 248, 257, 262, 267, 268
Artisans, 111
Ausentes, 51, 54, 55
Ayllus, 27, 29, 33, 248, 268

Bacalar, 158
Bajío, 130
Birth control, 233
Bogotá, 55, 79
Bolaños, 133
Buenos Aires, 25, 32, 267

Caciques, 33, 54, 57, 201, 227
Cajamarca, 5
Cakchiquel, 177
California, 138, 218
Calkiní, 160, 165
Campeche, 154
Carangas, 25
Castas, 93, 102
Caste, 18
Catarrh, 231
Caylloma, 268
Census, 2, 5, 6, 11, 14, 19, 25, 36, 62, 79, 93, 189, 202

Chapala, 124, 142, 144
Chayanta, 25, 34, 36
Chiapas, 196
Chibcha, 4, 5, 45, 81
Chichas, 25
Chikindzonot, 160
Childbirth, 259
Chivay, 247, 263, 268
Choluteca, 223
Chucuito, 38
Chuquisaca, 35
Cities, 2, 6, 15
Ciudad Vieja, 175
Clans, 2
Class, 2, 5, 6, 7, 29, 203
  consciousness, 111
Classification, 83
Climatic controls, 3
Cochabamba, 25, 34, 36, 37
Coito, 263
Colca River 244
  valley, 268
Collaguas, 4, 244
Comayagua, 220, 221, 232
Community, 48, 52, 53, 79, 150, 169, 202, 233, 257, 260, 262
Compadrazgo, 111, 149
Compostela, 127, 133, 142, 144
Conkal, 152, 160, 165
Conquest, 2, 17, 53, 184, 198, 199, 202, 218, 228, 230
Consensual unions, 18
Coporaque, 262
Crop failures, 80
Croup, 261
Cuchumatán highlands, 195

Cuzco, 28, 35, 36, 244, 248, 260, 267

Diets, 3, 232
Diffusion, 4
Diptheria, 206
Diseases, 2, 3, 4
Dysentery, amoebic, 230

Ebtún, 165
Ecology, 3, 45, 93
Ecosystems, 3
Eighteenth century, 65, 114, 150, 154, 195, 196, 203, 210, 243, 268
Ekmul, 160
El Salvador, 218
Emigration, 52, 53, 54, 60
Encomienda, 12, 55, 149, 151, 195
Endogamy, 140, 145, 264
Epidemics, 40, 80. 140, 181, 182, 189, 199, 201, 211, 230, 254, 257, 260, 268
Epidemiology, 2, 3, 80
Ethnic, 2, 5, 6, 7, 15, 93
Euan, 160
Exogamy, 129, 138, 140, 154, 168, 264
 spatial, 130

Facing block, 94, 111
Family, 2, 6, 14, 16, 169
 nuclear, 6, 52
 size, 40
Fertility, 42, 82
Foodstuffs, 82
Forasteros, 27, 28, 33, 34, 38, 54, 60, 168
Francisco de Toledo, 25
Frontier, 151, 152, 167

Geobiographies, 6
Geographical space, 96
Gracias a Dios, 220
Guadalajara, 5, 121, 129, 133, 145
Guanajuato, 130, 140
Guatemala, 175, 184, 207, 218, 230

Halachó, 160
Hay fever, 231

Hinterlands, 2
Honduras, 3, 178, 217
Hookworm, 230
Households, 6, 14, 15, 53, 220, 227, 231
Houselists, 14, 15, 17
Huehuetenango, 196
Hunger, 80

Ica, 267
Images, 2, 11
Index of dissimilarity, 97
Indigo, 232
Infanticide, 234
Influenza, 206, 260, 267
Interaction, 6
Izamal, 165

Japan, 80

Kin, 5
Kinship, 52, 111, 149

Labor, 13, 45, 47, 52, 53, 60, 181, 224
 forced, 81, 179
Lake Quinizilapa 175, 187
Lake Titicaca, 244, 262
Lambayeque, 267
Land tenure, 81
La Paz, 25, 35, 38
Larecaja, 25
Lari, 247, 262
Life expectancy, 42
Lima, 28, 32, 35, 38, 114, 243, 261, 264, 266
Linear block, 94

Mainas, 260
Malaria, 231
Malnutrition, 233
Maní, 160
Manila, 138
Manzanas, 94
Marriage, 17, 18, 82, 119, 250, 254, 262, 265
 field, 138, 140
 migration, 120, 144, 145
Matlazahuatl, 202
Matrilineal, 52
Measles, 80, 206, 260, 261
Mérida, 151, 152, 154, 165
Mexico City, 138

Michoacán, 140
Migrants, 2, 5, 154, 263, 264
Migration, 5, 7, 140
  paths, 167
Mines, 81, 232
Mingas, 27
Mita, 25, 34, 37
Mobility, 2, 15, 140
Mobility transition, 5
Monogamy, 53
Mortality, 210, 254, 258
  infant, 253

Naborías, 227
Naco, 220, 229
Natural resources, 12-13
Neighborhoods, 2, 15
New Granada, 62
Nicaragua, 217, 219
Nueva Galicia, 119, 130
Nutrition, 82

Oaxaca, 93
Obrajes, 233
Occupational groups, 93
Olancho, 223, 229
Omasuyu, 25
Originario, 27, 28, 37, 119, 142
Oruro, 38

Pacajes, 25
Paratyphoid, 230
Paria, 25, 34
Parish, 5, 12
  books, 14, 18, 33
  boundaries, 121, 144
  records, 53, 80
  registers, 4, 13, 19, 20, 42, 151, 160, 189, 243, 248
Parral, 130
Patrias chicas, 5
Patrilocal, 52
Peasants, 2, 5, 93
Perceptions, 2, 19
Peste, 257
Peto, 160
Piura, 267
Plague, 202, 230
  pneumonic, 231, 260
  pulmonary, 199
Polygyny, 53
Porco, 25

Potosí, 25, 27, 28, 34, 35, 36, 263

Quiché, 196
Quito, 25, 32

Race, 17
Ranchos, 121
Repartimiento, 52, 168
Requinteros, 60
Reservados, 48, 55, 57
Resettlement, 82
Residential patterns, 93
Romadizo, 231

Sabana de Bogotá, 4
San Blas, 138, 144
San José de Analco, 142
San Luis Potosí, 130
San Miguel Acatán, 211
San Miguel Dueñas, 175, 187
Santa Fe, 47, 80
Segregation, 93, 94
  index, 102
Servant, 16, 221, 231, 234
Seventeenth century, 49, 60, 64, 210, 218, 227, 265
Sex ratio, 42, 233, 252
Sicasica, 25
Silao, 140
Simulation, 4
Sixteenth century, 2, 13, 48, 52, 175, 179, 184, 202, 217, 221, 248
Slaves, 12, 14, 16, 178, 179, 181, 184, 187, 218, 219, 228, 264
  trade, 235
Smallpox, 80, 199, 206, 207, 210, 230, 260, 266
Social
  distance, 96
  interaction, 119
  organization, 13
  stratification, 96
  structure, 11
Socioeconomic Groups, 96
Soloma, 210
Sotuta, 152, 160
Spain, 138
Staples, 82
Subsistence, 2

Taloa, 230
Tarija, 25
Taxation, 168
Taxes, 82
Tecax, 160
Tegucigalpa, 234
Tekax, 152
Tepic, 120, 124, 127, 144
Tequila, 124, 129, 133, 140, 144
Terrazgos, 179
Territoriality, 52
Tisco, 247, 262
Tixkokob, 152, 160
Tlaquepaque, 129, 142
Tlaxcala, 199
Tonalá, 142
Tostón, 224
Totonicapán, 196, 198, 201
Traders, 111
Transients, 5, 14
Tributary, 32, 36, 40, 45, 47, 51, 62, 65, 83, 184, 187
Tribute, 5, 48, 49, 60, 151, 182, 202, 221, 224, 227, 267
  lists, 4
Trujillo, 220, 227, 228, 244
Tucumán, 25, 38
Tunja, 48
Tuti, 244
Typhoid, 230
Typhus, 206, 207, 210, 231, 260, 267
  epidemic, 211

Umán, 152, 160
Underregistration, 40, 252
Urban
  network, 6, 15
  space, 15
  system, 6

Valladolid, 133, 152
Vilcashuaman, 32
Visitas, 49, 55, 222, 259

Yamparaes, 25
Yanaconas, 27, 34
Yanahuara, 244
Yanque, 4, 244
Yellow fever, 231
Yucatán, 149

Yungas, 36, 37

Zacatecas, 140
Zapopan, 129, 142, 144